The I-Series

Microsoft®
Windows® XP

Complete

The I-Series

Microsoft® Windows® XP

Complete

Stephen Haag
University of Denver

James T. Perry
University of San Diego

Barrie Sosinsky

Efren Estevez

 Irwin

Boston   Burr Ridge, IL   Dubuque, IA   Madison, WI   New York   San Francisco   St. Louis
Bangkok   Bogotá   Caracas   Kuala Lumpur   Lisbon   London   Madrid   Mexico City
Milan   Montreal   New Delhi   Santiago   Seoul   Singapore   Sydney   Taipei   Toronto

Irwin

The I-Series: Microsoft Windows XP, Complete

Published by McGraw-Hill/Irwin, an imprint of The McGraw-Hill Companies, Inc. 1221 Avenue of the Americas, New York, NY 10020. Copyright © 2002 by The McGraw-Hill Companies, Inc. All rights reserved. No part of this publication may be reproduced or distributed in any form or by any means, or stored in a database or retrieval system, without the prior written consent of The McGraw-Hill Companies, Inc., including, but not limited to, in any network or other electronic storage or transmission, or broadcast for distance learning.

Some ancillaries, including electronic and print components, may not be available to customers outside the United States.

This book is printed on acid-free paper.

1 2 3 4 5 6 7 8 9 0 WEB/WEB 0 9 8 7 6 5 4 3 2

ISBN 0-07-284399-3

Publisher: *George Werthman*
Sponsoring editor: *Dan Silverburg*
Developmental editor: *Melissa Forte*
Manager, marketing and sales: *Paul Murphy*
Media producer: *Greg Bates*
Project manager: *Mary Conzachi*
Production supervisor: *Rose Hepburn*
Senior designer: *Jennifer McQueen and Mary Christianson*
Senior supplement producer: *Rose M. Range*
Cover design: *Asylum Studios*
Interior design: *Asylum Studios*
Typeface: *10/12 New Aster*
Compositor: *GAC Indianapolis*
Printer: *Webcrafters, Inc.*

Library of Congress Cataloging-in Publication Data

Microsoft Windows XP : complete/Stephen Haag [et al.]
      p.   cm.—(The I-series)
   ISBN 0–07–284399–3 (alk. paper)
   1. Microsoft Windows (Computer file) 2. Operating systems (Computers) I. Haag,
Stephen.   II. Series.
QA76.76.063 M5241322549 2003
005.4'469—dc21   2002035060

http://www.mhhe.com

INFORMATION TECHNOLOGY AT MCGRAW-HILL/IRWIN

At McGraw-Hill Higher Education, we publish instructional materials targeted at the higher education market. In an effort to expand the tools of higher learning, we publish texts, lab manuals, study guides, testing materials, software, and multimedia products.

At McGraw-Hill/Irwin (a division of McGraw-Hill Higher Education), we realize that technology has created and will continue to create new mediums for professors and students to use in managing resources and communicating information to one another. We strive to provide the most flexible and complete teaching and learning tools available as well as offer solutions to the changing world of teaching and learning.

McGraw-Hill/Irwin is dedicated to providing the tools for today's instructors and students to successfully navigate the world of Information Technology.

- **SEMINAR SERIES**—McGraw-Hill/Irwin's Technology Connection seminar series offered across the country every year demonstrates the latest technology products and encourages collaboration among teaching professionals.

- **MCGRAW-HILL/OSBORNE**—This division of The McGraw-Hill Companies is known for its best-selling Internet titles, *Internet & Web Yellow Pages* and the *Internet Complete Reference*. For more information, visit Osborne at www.osborne.com.

- **DIGITAL SOLUTIONS**—McGraw-Hill/Irwin is committed to publishing digital solutions. Taking your course online doesn't have to be a solitary adventure, nor does it have to be a difficult one. We offer several solutions that will allow you to enjoy all the benefits of having your course material online.

- **PACKAGING OPTIONS**—For more information about our discount options, contact your McGraw-Hill/Irwin sales representative at 1-800-338-3987 or visit our Web site at www.mhhe.com/it.

THE I-SERIES PAGE

By using the I-Series, students will be able to learn and master applications skills by being actively engaged—by *doing*. The "I" in I-Series demonstrates Insightful tasks that will not only Inform students, but also Involve them while learning the applications.

How will The I-Series accomplish this for you?

Through relevant, real-world chapter opening cases.

Through tasks throughout each chapter that incorporate steps and tips for easy reference.

Through alternative methods and styles of learning to keep the student involved.

Through rich, end-of-chapter materials that support what the student has learned.

I-Series titles include:

- Microsoft Office XP, Volume I
- Microsoft Office XP, Volume I Expanded
- Microsoft Office XP, Volume II
- Microsoft Word 2002 (Brief, Introductory, Complete Versions) 12 Chapters
- Microsoft Excel 2002 (Brief, Introductory, Complete Versions) 12 Chapters
- Microsoft Access 2002 (Brief, Introductory, Complete Versions) 12 Chapters
- Microsoft PowerPoint 2002 (Brief, Introductory Versions) 8 Chapters
- Microsoft Windows 2000 (Brief, Introductory, Complete Versions) 12 Chapters
- Microsoft Windows XP and Bonus Books to come!

To accompany the series:
The I-Series Computing Concepts text (Introductory, Complete Versions)

For additional resources, visit the I-Series Online Learning Center at www.mhhe.com/i-series/

GOALS/PHILOSOPHY

The I-Series applications textbooks strongly emphasize that students learn and master applications skills by being actively engaged—by *doing*. We made the decision that teaching how to accomplish tasks is not enough for complete understanding and mastery. Students must understand the importance of each of the tasks that lead to a finished product at the end of each chapter.

Approach

The I-Series chapters are subdivided into sessions that contain related groups of tasks with active, hands-on components. The session tasks containing numbered steps collectively result in a completed project at the end of each session. Prior to introducing numbered steps that show how to accomplish a particular task, we discuss why the steps are important. We discuss the role that the collective steps play in the overall plan for creating or modifying a document or object, answering students' often-heard questions, "Why are we doing these steps? Why are these steps important?" Without an explanation of why an activity is important and what it accomplishes, students can easily find themselves following the steps but not registering the big picture of what the steps accomplish and why they are executing them.

I-Series Applications for 2002

The I-Series offers three levels of instruction. Each level builds upon knowledge from the previous level. With the exception of the running project that is the last exercise of every chapter, chapter cases and end-of-chapter exercises are independent from one chapter to the next, with the exception of Access. The three levels available are

Brief   Covers the basics of the Microsoft application and contains Chapters 1 through 4. The Brief textbooks are typically 200 pages long.

Introductory   Includes chapters in the Brief textbook plus Chapters 5 through 8. Introductory textbooks typically are 400 pages long and prepare students for the Microsoft Office User Specialist (MOUS) Core Exam.

Complete   Includes the Introductory textbook plus Chapters 9 through 12. The four additional chapters cover advanced level content and are typically 600 pages long. Complete textbooks prepare students for the Microsoft Office User Specialist (MOUS) Expert Exam. The Microsoft Office User Specialist program is recognized around the world as the standard for demonstrating proficiency using Microsoft Office applications.

In addition, there are two compilation volumes available.

Office I   Includes introductory chapters on Windows and Computing Concepts followed by Chapters 1 through 4 (Brief textbook) of Word, Excel, Access, and PowerPoint. In addition, material from the companion Computing Concepts book is integrated into the first few chapters to provide students an understanding of the relationship between Microsoft Office applications and computer information systems.

Office II   Includes introductory chapters on Windows and Computing Concepts followed by Chapters 5 through 8 from each of the Introductory-level textbooks including Word, Excel, Access, and PowerPoint. In addition, material from the companion Computing Concepts book is integrated into the introductory chapters to provide students a deeper understanding of the relationship between Microsoft Office applications and computer information systems. An introduction to Visual Basic for Applications (VBA) completes the Office II textbook.

Approved Microsoft Courseware

Use of the Microsoft Office User Specialist Approved Courseware logo on this product signifies that it has been independently reviewed and approved to comply with the following standards: Acceptable coverage of all content related to the Microsoft Office Exams entitled Microsoft Access 2002, Microsoft Excel 2002, Microsoft PowerPoint 2002, and Microsoft Word 2002, and sufficient performance-based exercises that relate closely to all required content, based on sampling of the textbooks. For further information on Microsoft's MOUS certification program, please visit Microsoft's Web site at www.microsoft.com.

STEPHEN HAAG

Stephen Haag is a professor and Chair of Information Technology and Electronic Commerce and the Director of Technology in the University of Denver's Daniels College of Business. Stephen holds a B.B.A. and an M.B.A. from West Texas State University and a Ph.D. from the University of Texas at Arlington. Stephen has published numerous articles appearing in such journals as *Communications of the ACM*, *The International Journal of Systems Science*, *Applied Economics*, *Managerial and Decision Economics*, *Socio-Economic Planning Sciences*, and the *Australian Journal of Management*.

Stephen is also the author of 13 other books including *Interactions: Teaching English as a Second Language* (with his mother and father), *Case Studies in Information Technology*, *Information Technology: Tomorrow's Advantage Today* (with Peter Keen), and *Excelling in Finance*. Stephen is also the lead author of the accompanying *I-Series: Computing Concepts* text, released in both an Introductory and Complete version. Stephen lives with his wife, Pam, and their four sons, Indiana, Darian, Trevor, and Elvis, in Highlands Ranch, Colorado.

JAMES PERRY

James Perry is a professor of Management Information Systems at the University of San Diego's School of Business. Jim is an active instructor who teaches both undergraduate and graduate courses. He holds a B.S. in mathematics from Purdue University and a Ph.D. in computer science from The Pennsylvania State University. He has published several journal and conference papers. He is the co-author of 56 textbooks and trade books such as *Using Access with Accounting Systems*, *Building Accounting Systems*, *Understanding Oracle*, *The Internet*, and *Electronic Commerce*. His books have been translated into Dutch, French, and Chinese. Jim worked as a computer security consultant to various private and governmental organizations including the Jet Propulsion Laboratory. He was a consultant on the Strategic Defense Initiative ("Star Wars") project and served as a member of the computer security oversight committee.

MERRILL WELLS

The caption next to **Merrill Wells'** eighth grade yearbook picture noted that her career goal was to teach college and write books. She completed an M.B.A. at Indiana University and began a career as a programmer. After several years of progressive positions in business and industry, she returned to academia, spending 10 years as a computer technology faculty member at Red Rocks Community College and then becoming an information technology professor at the University of Denver, Daniels College of Business. She completed her first published book in 1993 and began presenting at educational seminars in 1997. Other publications include *An Introduction to Computers*, *Introduction to Visual Basic*, and *Programming Logic and Design*.

BARRIE SOSINSKY

Barrie Sosinsky is an analyst and consultant who follows the server, storage, and network operating system markets. His company, the Sosinsky Group (www.sosinsky-group.com), publishes an industry newsletter called the *Sosinsky Report* that covers news and trends for information technology professionals. He is the author of more than 25 books and 600 articles that have appeared in numerous industry trade publications. His previous books include *Mastering Solaris for Sybex* and *Teach Yourself Windows 2000 Server in 24 Hours* by Sams.

EFREN ESTEVEZ

Efren Estevez received his Bachelor's degree from SUNY Albany in 1980. In addition to being an author, he has owned and managed a commodities brokerage and import/export business for over 10 years. Efren has worked as a programmer and network administrator in the medical field and food industry and holds advanced Microsoft certification. He has been a contributing author to national and international industry publications, as well as developing database systems for several companies in the beverage industry that involved customizing existing programs for individual application. Efren lives with his wife, Jo Ann, his daughter, Chelsea, and his son, Ian, on Long Island in New York.

Each textbook features the following:

Did You Know   Each chapter has six or seven interesting facts—both about high tech and other topics.

Sessions   Each chapter is divided into two or three sessions.

Chapter Outline   Provides students with a quick map of the major headings in the chapter.

Chapter and MOUS Objectives   At the beginning of each chapter is a list of 5 to 10 action-oriented objectives. Any chapter objectives that are also MOUS objectives indicate the MOUS objective number also.

Chapter Opening Case   Each chapter begins with a case. Cases describe a mixture of fictitious and real people and companies and the needs of the people and companies. Throughout the chapter, the student gains the skills and knowledge to solve the problem stated in the case.

Introduction   The chapter introduction establishes the overview of the chapter's activities in the context of the case problem.

Another Way and Another Word   Another Way is a highlighted feature providing a bulleted list of steps to accomplish a task, or best practices—that is, a better or faster way to accomplish a task such as pasting a format onto an Excel cell. Another Word, another highlighted box, briefly explains more about a topic or highlights a potential pitfall.

Step-by-Step Instructions   Numbered step-by-step instructions for all hands-on activities appear in a distinctive color. Keyboard characters and menu selections appear in a **special format** to emphasize what the user should press or type. Steps make clear to the student the exact sequence of keystrokes and mouse clicks needed to complete a task such as formatting a Word paragraph.

Tips   Tips appear within a numbered sequence of steps and warn the student of possible missteps or provide alternatives to the step that precedes the tip.

Task Reference and Task Reference Round-Up   Task References appear throughout the textbook. Set in a distinctive design, each Task Reference contains a bulleted list of steps showing a generic way to accomplish activities that are especially important or significant. A Task Reference Round-Up at the end of each chapter summarizes a chapter's Task References.

MOUS Objectives Summary   A list of MOUS objectives covered in a chapter appears in the chapter objectives and the chapter summary.

Making the Grade   Short answer questions appear at the end of each chapter's sessions. They test a student's grasp of each session's contents, and Making the Grade answers appear at the end of each book so students can check their answers.

Rich End-of-Chapter Materials   End-of-chapter materials incorporating a three-level approach reinforce learning and help students take ownership of the chapter. Level One, review of terminology, contains a fun crossword puzzle that enforces review of a chapter's key terms. Level Two, review of concepts, contains fill-in-the blank questions, review questions, and a Jeopardy-style create-a-question exercise. Level Three is Hands-on Projects.

Hands-on Projects   Extensive hands-on projects engage the student in a problem-solving exercise from start to finish. There are six clearly labeled categories that each contain one or two questions. Categories are Practice, Challenge!, On the Web, E-Business, Around the World, and a Running Project that carries throughout all the chapters.

We understand that, in today's teaching environment, offering a textbook alone is not sufficient to meet the needs of the many instructors who use our books. To teach effectively, instructors must have a full complement of supplemental resources to assist them in every facet of teaching, from preparing for class to conducting a lecture to assessing students' comprehension. The **I-Series** offers a complete supplements package and Web site that is briefly described below.

INSTRUCTOR'S RESOURCE KIT

The Instructor's Resource Kit is a CD-ROM containing the Instructor's Manual in both MS Word and .pdf formats, PowerPoint Slides with Presentation Software, Brownstone test-generating software, and accompanying test item files in both MS Word and .pdf formats for each chapter. The CD also contains figure files from the text, student data files, and solutions files. The features of each of the three main components of the Instructor's Resource Kit are highlighted below.

Instructor's Manual Featuring:

- Chapter learning objectives per chapter

- Chapter outline with teaching tips

- Annotated Solutions Diagram to provide Troubleshooting Tips, Tricks, and Traps

- Lecture Notes, illustrating key concepts and ideas

- Annotated Syllabus, depicting a time table and schedule for covering chapter content

- Additional end-of-chapter projects

- Answers to all Making the Grade and end-of-chapter questions

PowerPoint Presentation

The PowerPoint presentation is designed to provide instructors with comprehensive lecture and teaching resources that will include

- Chapter learning objectives followed by source content that illustrates key terms and key facts per chapter

- FAQ (frequently asked questions) to show key concepts throughout the chapter; also, lecture notes, to illustrate these key concepts and ideas

- End-of-chapter exercises and activities per chapter, as taken from the end-of-chapter materials in the text

- Speaker's Notes, to be incorporated throughout the slides per chapter

- Figures/screen shots, to be incorporated throughout the slides per chapter

PowerPoint includes presentation software for instructors to design their own presentation for their course.

Test Bank

The I-Series Test Bank, using Diploma Network Testing Software by Brownstone, contains over 3,000 questions (both objective and interactive) categorized by topic, page reference to the text, and difficulty level of learning. Each question is assigned a learning category:

- Level 1: Key Terms and Facts

- Level 2: Key Concepts

- Level 3: Application and Problem-Solving

The types of questions consist of 40 percent Identifying/Interactive Lab Questions, 20 percent Multiple Choice, 20 percent True/False, and 20 percent Fill-in/Short Answer Questions.

ONLINE LEARNING CENTER/ WEB SITE

The Online Learning Center that accompanies the I-Series is accessible through our Information Technology Supersite at http://www.mhhe.com/catalogs/irwin/it/. This site provides additional review and learning tools developed using the same three-level approach found in the text and supplements. To locate the I-Series OLC/Web site directly, go to www.mhhe.com/i-series. The site is divided into three key areas:

- **Information Center** Contains core information about the text, the authors, and a guide to our additional features and benefits of the series, including the supplements.

- **Instructor Center** Offers instructional materials, downloads, additional activities and answers to additional projects, answers to chapter troubleshooting exercises, answers to chapter preparation/post exercises posed to students, relevant links for professors, and more.

- **Student Center** Contains chapter objectives and outlines, self-quizzes, chapter troubleshooting exercises, chapter preparation/post exercises, additional projects, simulations, student data files and solutions files, Web links, and more.

RESOURCES FOR STUDENTS

Interactive Companion CD This student CD-ROM can be packaged with this text. It is designed for use in class, in the lab, or at home by students and professors and combines video, interactive exercises, and animation to cover the most difficult and popular topics in Computing Concepts. By combining video, interactive exercises, animation, additional content, and actual "lab" tutorials, we expand the reach and scope of the textbook.

SimNet XPert SimNet XPert is a simulated assessment and learning tool. It allows students to study MS Office XP skills and computer concepts, and professors to test and evaluate students' proficiency within MS Office XP applications and concepts. Students can practice and study their skills at home or in the school lab using SimNet XPert, which does not require the purchase of Office XP software. SimNet XPert will contain new features and enhancements for Office XP, including:

NEW! **Live Assessments! SimNet *XPert*** now includes live-in-the-application assessments! One for each skill set for Core MOUS objectives in Word 2002, Excel 2002, Access 2002, and PowerPoint 2002 (total of 29 Live-in-the-Application Assessments). Multiple tasks are required to complete each live assessment (about 100 tasks covered).

NEW! **Computer Concepts Coverage! SimNet *XPert*** now includes coverage of computer concepts in both the Learning and the Assessment sides.

NEW! **Practice or Pretest Questions! SimNet *XPert*** has a separate pool of 600 questions for practice tests or pretests.

NEW! **Comprehensive Exercises! SimNet *XPert*** offers comprehensive exercises for each application. These exercises require the student to use multiple skills to solve one exercise in the simulated environment.

ENHANCED! **More Assessment Questions! SimNet *XPert*** includes over 1,400 assessment questions.

ENHANCED! **Simulated Interface!** The simulated environment in **SimNet *XPert*** has been substantially deepened to more realistically simulate the real applications. Now students are not graded incorrect just because they chose the wrong sub-menu or dialog box. The student is not graded until he or she does something that immediately invokes an action.

DIGITAL SOLUTIONS FOR INSTRUCTORS AND STUDENTS

PageOut PageOut is our Course Web Site Development Center that offers a syllabus page, URL, McGraw-Hill Online Learning Center content, online exercises and quizzes, gradebook, discussion board, and an area for student Web pages. For more information, visit the PageOut Web site at www.pageout.net.

Online Courses Available OLCs are your perfect solutions for Internet-based content. Simply put, these Centers are "digital cartridges" that contain a book's pedagogy and supplements. As students read the book, they can go online and take self-grading quizzes or work through interactive exercises.

Online Learning Centers can be delivered through any of these platforms:

McGraw-Hill Learning Architecture (TopClass)

Blackboard.com

College.com (formerly Real Education)

WebCT (a product of Universal Learning Technology)

Did You Know?

A unique presentation of text and graphics introduce interesting and little-known facts.

did you
know?

the *Penny is the only coin currently minted in the United States with a profile that faces to the right. All other U.S. coins feature profiles that face to the left.*

the *world's largest wind generator is on the island of Oahu, Hawaii. The windmill has two blades 400 feet long on the top of a tower, twenty stories high.*

the *only house in England that the Queen may not enter is the House of Commons, because she is not a commoner. She is also the only person in England who does not need a license plate on her vehicle.*

former *U.S. Vice President Al Gore and Oscar-winning actor Tommy Lee Jones were roommates at Harvard.*

Chapter Objectives

* Plan and document a workbook
* Create formulas containing cell references and mathematical operators (MOUS Ex2002-5-1)
* Write functions including Sum, Average, Max, and Min (MOUS Ex2002-5-2)
* Use Excel's AutoSum feature to automatically write Sum functions
* Learn several ways to copy a formula from one cell to many other cells
* Differentiate between absolute, mixed, and relative cell reference (MOUS Ex2002-5-1)
* Adjust column widths (MOUS Ex2002-3-2)
* Set a print area (MOUS Ex2002-3-7)
* Move text, values, and formulas (MOUS Ex2002-1-1)
* Insert and delete rows and columns (MOUS Ex2002-3-2)
* Format cells (MOUS Ex2002-3-1)
* Create cell comments (MOUS Ex2002-7-3)

CHAPTER

2

two

Planning and Creating a Worksheet

Chapter Objectives

Each chapter begins with a list of competencies covered in the chapter.

Task Reference

Provides steps to accomplish an especially important task.

task reference

Changing Relative References to Absolute or Mixed References

* Double-click the cell containing the formula that you want to edit or click the cell and then press **F2**
* Move the insertion point, a vertical bar, to the left of the cell reference you want to alter
* Press function key **F4** repeatedly until the absolute or mixed reference you want appears
* Press **Enter** to complete the cell edit procedure

Making the Grade

Short-answer questions appear at the end of each session and answers appear at the end of the book.

SESSION 2.1 | *making the grade*

1. Explain how AutoSum works and what it does.
2. Suppose you select cell A14 and type D5+F5. What is stored in cell A14: text, a value, or a formula?
3. You can drag the _____, which is a small black square in the lower-right corner of the active cell, to copy the cell's contents.
4. Evaluation of a formula such as =D4+D5*D6 is governed by order of precedence. Explain what that means in general and then indicate the order in which Excel calculates the preceding expression.
5. Suppose Excel did not provide an AVERAGE function. Show an alternative way to compute the average of cell range A1:B25 using the other Excel statistical functions.

Copying a formula from one cell to many cells:

1. Click cell **G4** to make it the active cell. The cell's formula, =F4/B4, appears in the formula bar

2. Click **Edit** on the menu bar and then click **Copy** to copy the cell's contents to the Clipboard. Notice that a dashed line encloses the cell whose contents are on the Clipboard

tip: *You can press **Ctrl+C** instead of using the Copy command. Those of you who keep your hands on the keyboard may favor this keyboard shortcut.*

3. Click and drag cells **G5** through **G8** to select them. They are the target range into which you will paste the cell G4's contents

4. Click **Edit** on the menu bar and then click **Paste.** Excel copies the Clipboard's contents into each of the cells in the selected range and then adjusts each cell's formula to correspond to its new location. Notice that the Paste Options Smart Tag appears below and to the right of cell G8 (see Figure 2.16). The Paste Options Smart Tag provides several formatting and copying options in its list. You can access the options by clicking the Smart Tag list arrow

FIGURE 2.16
Copied formulas' results

	A	B	C	D	E	F	G	H
1	Aluminum Can Recycling Contest							
2								
3	City	Population	Jan	Feb	Mar	Total	Per Capita	
4	Arcata	15855	10505	24556	12567	47628	3.003974	
5	Los Gatos	28951	24567	21777	26719	73063	2.523678	
6	Pasadena	142547						
7	San Diego	2801561						
8	Sunnyvale	1689908						
9	Total		437					
10	Minimum		1					
11	Average		875					
12	Maximum		271					
13								
14								

tip: *You can press Ctrl+ ... paste the Clipboard's conte...*

5. Press **Escape** to cl... line from the sourc... and view the formu...

Step-by-Step Instruction

Numbered steps guide you through the exact sequence of keystrokes to accomplish the task.

Tips

Tips appear within steps and either indicate possible missteps or provide alternatives to a step.

---

hands-on projects

LEVEL THREE

practice

...' Work Hours
...r Wexler's Tool and
...age a group of five
...r group has a differ-
...record on a weekly
...ch employee works,
..., and percentage of
...at each employee's
...ing the information
...icient way to record
...Alan Gin, the com-
...r, wants you to pre-
...report your group's
...ages. You create a
...nd wages.

...**Wages.xls** and

...on sheet and then
...ove to that work-

...all the employees'

...ve row 1: Click cell
..., and release the
...e Menu bar and

...he range and type

...click cell **C1**, type
...**Wages**, click cell

12. Click cell **E3** and type the formula that represents the employee's percentage of the total wages: **=D3/D$8*100**
13. Copy the formula in cell E3 to the cell range **E4:E7**
14. Select cell range **A1:E8**, click **Format**, click **AutoFormat**, select the **Simple** format, and click **OK**
15. Select cell range **E3:E7** and click the **Decrease Decimal** button enough times to reduce the displayed percentages to two decimal places
16. Click cell **A10** and type your first and last names
17. Set the left, right, top, and bottom margins to two inches
18. Either execute **Print** or execute **Save As,** according to your instructor's direction

2. Creating an Invoice

As office manager of Randy's Foreign Cars, one of your duties is to produce and mail invoices to customers who have arranged to pay for their automobile repairs up to 30 days after mechanics perform the work. Randy's invoices include parts, sales tax on parts, and labor charges. State law stipulates that customers do not pay sales tax on the labor charges. Only parts are subject to state sales tax. State sales tax is 6 percent. Create and print an invoice whose details appear below.

Screen Shots

Screen shots show you what to expect at critical points.

End-of-Chapter Hands-on Projects

A rich variety of projects introduced by a case lets you put into practice what you have learned. Categories include Practice, Challenge, On the Web, E-Business, Around the World, and a running case project.

---

*another*word

. . . about Smart Tags

Microsoft Office Smart Tags are a set of buttons that are shared across the Office applications. The buttons appear when needed, such as when Excel detects you may have made an error in an Excel formula, and gives the user appropriate options to change the given action or error.

Another Way/ Another Word

Another Way highlights an alternative way to accomplish a task; Another Word explains more about a topic.

---

reference roundup

Task	Location	Preferred Method
Writing formulas	EX 2.9	• Select a cell, type **5**, type the formula, press **Enter**
Modifying an AutoSum cell range by pointing	EX 2.11	• Press an arrow key repeatedly to select leftmost or topmost cell in range, press and hold **Shift**, select cell range with arrow keys, release **Shift**, press **Enter**
Writing a function using the Paste Function button	EX 2.17	• Select a cell, click **Paste Function**, click a function category, click a function name, click **OK**, complete the Formula Palette dialog box, click **OK**
Copying and pasting a cell or range of cells	EX 2.21	• Select source cell(s), click **Edit**, click **Copy**, select target cell(s), click **Edit**, click **Paste**
Copying cell contents using a cell's fill handle	EX 2.23	• Select source cell(s), drag the fill handle to the source(s) range, release the mouse button

Task Reference RoundUp

Provides a quick reference and summary of a chapter's task references.

acknowledgments

The authors want to acknowledge the work and support of the seasoned professionals at McGraw-Hill. Thank you to George Werthman, publisher, for his strong leadership and a management style that fosters innovation and creativity. Thank you to Dan Silverburg, sponsoring editor, who is an experienced editor and recent recruit to the I-Series. Dan quickly absorbed a month's worth of information in days and guided the authors through the sometimes-difficult publishing maze. Our special thanks go to Melissa Forte, developmental editor, who served, unofficially, as a cheerleader for the authors. The hub of our editorial "wheel," Melissa shouldered more than her share of work in the many months from prelaunch boot camp to bound book date. We are grateful to Gina Huck, developmental editor, for her dedication to this project. From the project's inception, Gina has guided us and kept us on track. Sarah Wood, developmental editor, paid attention to all the details that required her special care.

Thank you to Valerie Bolch, a University of San Diego graduate student, who did a wonderful job of creating some of the end-of-chapter exercises and tech editing the Excel manuscript. Ron Tariga helped categorize and display several Office XP toolbar buttons. Thank you to Stirling Perry, who took screen shots of all of the Office XP toolbar buttons and organized them into logical groups. Wendi Whitmore, who provided screen shots of Office 2000 toolbars, prior to the release of Office XP. Many thanks to Linda Dillon, who provided creative input and feedback for the PowerPoint end-of-chapter materials. Also, the labor of Carolla McCammack in tech editing many of the Access chapters has been invaluable.

Special thanks also go to Janice Manweiller for her very important contributions to the Windows texts and thanks to Mali Jones for her excellent technical editing of the majority of texts in this series.

We all wish to thank all of our schools for providing support, including time off to dedicate to writing: University of San Diego, University of Denver, and the College of Southern Idaho.

If you would like to contact us about any of the books in the I-Series, we would enjoy hearing from you. We welcome comments and suggestions that we might incorporate into future editions of the books. You can e-mail book-related messages to us at i-series@mcgraw-hill.com. For the latest information about the I-Series textbooks and related resources, please visit our Web site at www.mhhe.com/i-series.

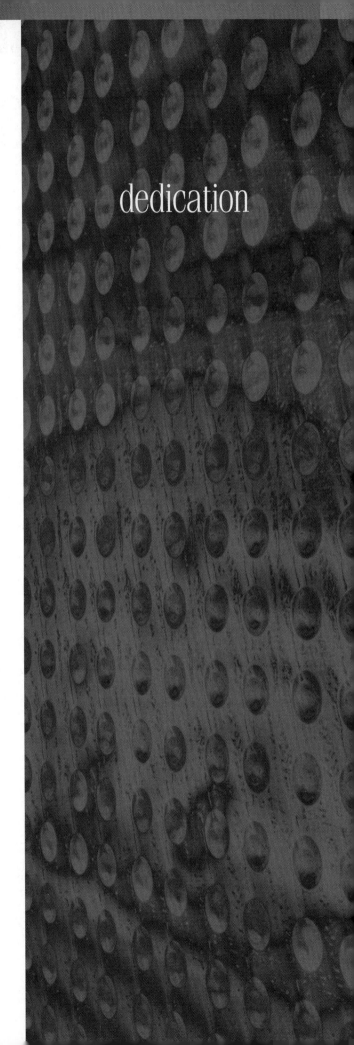

TO the memory of my grandmother, Margaret Lesser.

B.S.

FOR Jo Ann, Chelsea, and Ian and all the times I was writing instead of having fun with you.

E.E.

dedication

brief contents

xvi

table of contents

CHAPTER 3

3

CUSTOMIZING YOUR WORK ENVIRONMENT WINXP 3.1

12

Chapter Objectives

- Start and log on to Windows XP

- Become familiar with the Windows XP Start Menu

- Select and move objects using the mouse

- Explore common features of the Windows interface

- Shut down Windows XP

- Create and save a file

- Print a file

- Close and open a file

- Use the Help and Support center

CHAPTER

1

one

Windows XP
Professional
Basics

E-logic Systems Inc., Eugene, Oregon

A new software consulting company called E-logic Systems Inc. opened in Eugene. The company ran an ad for 30 new employees. The ad read "Computer training helpful, but willing to train. Excellent opportunity for the right people."

Ellen Kirkpatrick read the ad with interest and decided to fill out an application. While she had very little exposure to computers, she was tired of working as an office assistant. She had always wanted to learn about technology but had few opportunities since leaving college. It would be a good experience to learn more about computers and the Internet.

After her interview, Ellen was offered a position in the Human Resources office as an administrative assistant to the director of Human Resources. She would receive training in the use of the computers. Later that morning, she was shown to her workstation and given a training manual for her new computer.

Ellen was told that the computers at E-logic Systems use the Windows XP operating system. To start, she would at least have to know what the Windows XP screens looked like, how to use the mouse, and how to get more information. Ellen opened her Windows XP manual and got started learning the basics of the operating system.

INTRODUCTION

This chapter covers the basics of the Windows XP Professional operating system. You'll learn what Windows XP looks like and how to use your mouse. You'll also learn the basics of working with a file. You'll learn how to properly shut down the operating system. Finally, you'll find out how to get help if you run into trouble.

What is Windows XP? If you're new to computers or to Windows, then the Windows XP Professional operating system, like any **operating system,** controls the basic functions of a personal Desktop computer or a laptop computer. It controls all of the equipment connected to your computer, including the mouse, printers, a **modem** for connecting to the Internet, and disk drives for floppy disks or CDs. Within the computer, the operating system runs all the applications you use to create **files** such as documents, spreadsheets, or pictures, and controls the storage space where these files are kept.

If you've used Windows NT or Windows 2000 in the past, then Windows XP will look somewhat familiar to you. There have, however, been a few changes.

First of all, the system requirements for Windows XP are different and slightly higher than those of either Windows 2000 or Windows NT.

Operating System	Processor	RAM	Hard Drive Space
Windows NT Workstation	Pentium	16–32 MB	110 MB
Windows 2000 Professional	Pentium/133 MHz	64 MB	650 MB
Windows XP Professional	Pentium II/233 MHz	128 MB	1.5 GB

Next we'll look at some items that are new to Windows XP. If any of these terms are new to you, don't worry about it. They will be explained in more detail later in the book.

The most obvious difference between XP and the earlier versions of Windows operating systems is the way it looks. The *Graphic User Interface,* or GUI (pronounced goo-ey), is the on-screen graphics, buttons, and controls. It has been radically changed from the previous Windows GUI design that existed. While some of the interface elements of older versions of Windows remain—such as the Desktop, Start menu, and the taskbar—the look and feel are different. Keep in mind that if you prefer the "classic" Windows view, you can revert to it at any time.

One of the first things that users will notice is that the Start menu is different from the older GUI. The Start menu now displays as two columns as shown in Figure 1.2. The right column is closer to the traditional Start menu; the lower left column automatically displays your most recently used programs. Additionally, the user's name appears as a bar across the top of the entire Start menu, while the Log Off and Turn Off Computer buttons appear at the bottom. This entire view can be customized as will be seen later in the chapter.

FIGURE 1.1

Comparing Windows system requirements

FIGURE 1.2

The redesigned Start menu displays in two columns

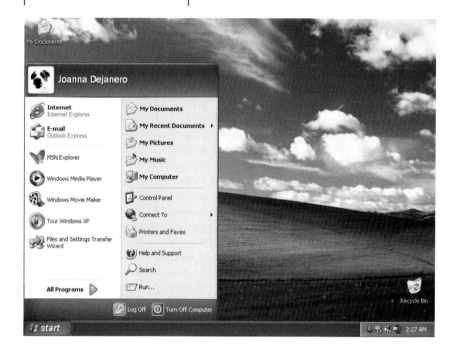

Previous versions of Windows provided Help files, but XP comes with a new application called *Help and Support Center.* Help and Support Center works not only with the files that come with XP but also with Microsoft's online Knowledge Database and other vendors' online sources to provide more information to your queries.

Online Assisted Support allows you to submit information about your system in an e-mail to Microsoft so that a technician can assist you more rapidly because he or she has the information about your system right at hand.

With *Remote Assistance,* you can invite a knowledgeable friend or other qualified person to view your screen and even manipulate it via a secure connection between your two computers. This is invaluable if you are having a problem doing something that the other person knows how to do.

The *Remote Desktop Connection* allows you to remotely access your computer from another computer. This provides access to your data and applications even when you're not at your desk. Once connected, you can manipulate files and folders as if you were actually at your computer.

Windows Update. Previous versions of Windows provided opportunities to update. However, this feature in XP is proactive, running periodically and offering to download and install the latest updates for you.

Files and Settings Transfer Wizard. A related feature is the Files and Settings Transfer Wizard, a new feature that allows you to transfer files and settings from one computer to another or to another part of your computer if you have more than one operating system installed.

User Switching. Like previous versions of Windows, XP allows multiple users to use the same machine while keeping each person's files separate so that they cannot be seen or used by someone else (unless you have shared them). Under older versions of Windows, however, the first user had to close everything he or she was working on and log off before the second user could begin to use the machine. XP allows several users to remain logged on at the same time, with their applications running in the background. Only one user can be the active user that is actually working on the computer at a time, but with XP you can switch users quickly without stopping everything.

.NET. The idea behind Microsoft's .NET initiative is that it creates a personalized Internet experience for the user, remembering preferences and delivering predetermined data regardless of where you are or what kind of device you are using to access the Internet. .Net Passport serves as the central repository for this information about you to permit universal, distributed access. You provide your information once to Passport and from whatever location and anywhere you go on the Internet, you are recognized. This provides an easy way, for example, of buying items from multiple vendors of goods and services without have to log in and provide a credit card number each time. Or it may allow you to access proprietary information about your organization's sales, inventory, or customer database from any computer. Instead of having to sign in each time you go to a different location and enter a password, Passport stores your user name, password, address, domain name, credit card information, and so forth, so that you don't have to reenter it each time. You log in once to Passport and all other logins happen automatically.

While this makes using the Web more convenient and powerful, there is a trade-off in terms of privacy that many users have a problem with. The more information provided to Passport, the more useful, but also the more potentially invasive it becomes. Your personal information could be compromised and widely known without your permission. For these reasons, Passport remains controversial and it remains to be seen how it will play out in the marketplace.

As with previous versions of Windows, XP contains an *Internet Connection Sharing* feature that allows you to use one connection for multiple computers that are networked. This is particularly useful if you access the Internet through a broadband connection such as a cable modem or DSL line. Also, a new Internet Connection Firewall provides better security for that shared Internet Connection.

In addition, XP introduces a new version of Internet Explorer (version 6). Most of the improvements in this area have to do with multimedia: images, music, and videos can all be saved more easily. Digital photos can be resized directly, and many types of files can be opened by Internet Explorer rather than having to download some new piece of software to access them. Some of the most touted new features of XP (at least by Microsoft in its advertising) are the multimedia enhancements. Many improvements in this area are featured, including a new version of Windows Media Player (version 8)—which now acts as a video, DVD, and CD player—an Internet radio receiver, and a jukebox for playing digital-audio files. This version of media player even provides built-in CD burning capabilities.

Further, XP has several improvements for capturing and handling images from scanners, cameras, and video cameras. The new Scanner and Camera Wizard perform most of these duties, but some of the older features also help. The My Pictures folder now allows you to do some basic image handling, Image Preview lets you display an image, and the Paint tool permits the opening and saving of other images in addition to bitmap (BMP) files, such as JPEG, GIF, and TIFF files.

SESSION 1.1 STARTING WITH WINDOWS

In this session, you will learn about the most basic elements of the Windows XP Professional operating system.

WINDOWS XP

You'll learn about the Desktop and the objects on it. You'll practice using the mouse to work with the items on the Desktop. You'll work with common elements of Windows XP Professional. Finally, you'll learn how to shut down Windows XP properly.

STARTING AND LOGGING ON AND OFF TO WINDOWS

Windows XP starts automatically when you turn on your computer. To start using Windows, log on at the Welcome screen that appears. This screen displays a list of users who have accounts set up on the computer. By default, all you need to do is click your *user name.* This name identifies you to the computer and the network. If an administrator has set up your system to require a *password,* you'll need to enter that as well. A password is a secret code or word to protect access to your system.

FIGURE 1.3

Click your user name to log on to Windows XP

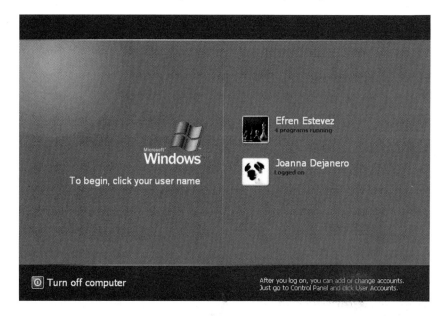

If your computer is connected to a domain, the operating system opens with the Windows XP Log On screen. You must enter your user name and password to identify yourself to the system before you can begin using Windows XP.

To log off, you click the Start button, and then click the Log Off button. When you log off, Windows closes all the applications and files you have open and displays the Log Off dialog box.

The Log Off Windows dialog box also contains a button named Switch User. When you switch users, Windows keeps your files open and applications open (as opposed to closing them when you log off) and reverts to the Welcome screen so that another user can log on.

task reference

Starting Windows XP

- Turn on the computer
- Click your user name
- Type your password and press **Enter**

Starting Windows XP:

You are assigned to help Ellen get started and an obvious first place to start is to show her how to start her machine. Ellen already knows how to do this from reading the manual, and you ask her to show you how she does it. She knows how to turn on her machine but cannot start Windows because her user name is not displayed. You log on to Windows and create a user account for her and tell her to try again. This time she gets on without difficulty.

1. Turn on your computer

2. After Windows finishes loading, the Welcome screen appears

3. Click your user name

4. If Windows is set up to require a password, type your password in the password text box

5. Press **Enter** or click the button that looks like a green arrow

---

THE WINDOWS DESKTOP

The Windows XP *Desktop* displays when you first log on to Windows XP Professional. It is the starting point for all your activities.

If you're new to Windows, think of the Desktop as a virtual Desktop, with an open space you can use to work, plus drawers and compartments you can use to store files and information.

The Desktop is made up of the following basic elements:

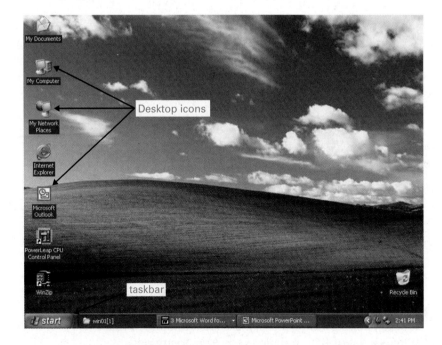

FIGURE 1.4

The Windows XP Professional Desktop

- *Icons.* An *icon* on the Desktop may represent a file, a folder, or an application. When you first use Windows XP, there are only a few icons on the Desktop, but you'll learn in later chapters how to create your own icons for easy access to your information.

- *Taskbar.* The ***taskbar*** is the bar across the bottom of the Desktop. It may also be moved to other edges of the screen or can be hidden until you need it. It performs several functions. The Start menu, discussed in more detail later, provides access to your programs and files. The taskbar can include icons representing programs available on your computer. The taskbar also shows you what programs, folders, and files are currently open on your Desktop.

USING THE MOUSE

The ***mouse*** is the most common way to interact with your computer and with Windows XP. You've already had to use the mouse when logging on to the operating system, when you clicked your user name to log on to Windows XP. While the mouse is the most common device, there are other pointing devices that can perform this function. Your PC or laptop may have a trackball, a touchpad, or a joystick. While these objects operate slightly differently, the basic function is the same.

You use the mouse to select, open, and move objects on the screen. The mouse is represented on the screen by different symbols, depending on what the mouse is pointing to. On the Desktop, the mouse is usually in the form of an arrow. The arrow or other symbol indicates the location of the mouse and tells you what object will be affected when you perform an action using the mouse.

FIGURE 1.5

The various mouse pointers

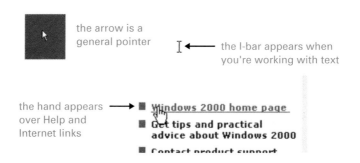

the arrow is a general pointer

the I-bar appears when you're working with text

the hand appears over Help and Internet links

A mouse may have several buttons. The left and right buttons are the most commonly used. With these buttons, you can perform the following actions:

- *Click.* To ***click*** is to press the left mouse button once while the pointer is over an object. Clicking an object will make that the active, or selected, object.

- *Right-click.* To ***right-click*** is to press the right mouse button once while the pointer is over an object. Right-clicking an object displays a context menu of options related to the current object.

- *Double-click.* To ***double-click*** is to quickly press the left mouse button twice in succession while the pointer is over an object. Double-clicking an object displays the contents of that object, such as a list of files, a dialog box, or a document.

- *Drag.* To ***drag*** is to press the left mouse button and hold it down as you move the mouse. Dragging is used to either move objects or select text. When the object is in the proper location or all of the text is selected, you release the mouse button.

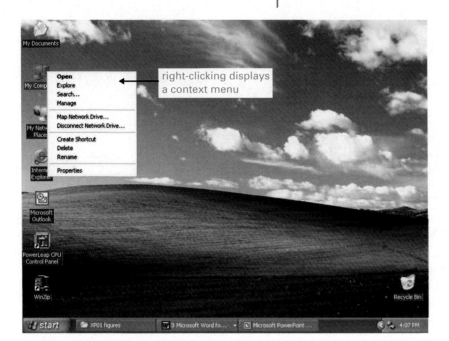

FIGURE 1.6a

The My Computer context menu
displayed by right-clicking

task reference

Using the Mouse

- To select an object, move the mouse over the object, then click with the left mouse button

- To display a context menu related to an object, move the mouse over the object, then click with the right mouse button

- To open an object, move the mouse over the object, then double-click with the left mouse button

- To move an object to another part of the screen, move the mouse over the object. Click the left mouse button and hold it down, then move the mouse in the direction you want to move the object. Release the mouse button when the object is in the correct place

Practicing with the mouse:

Since it's obvious that Ellen is eager to learn, once she is logged on, you show her some basic things to do with the mouse. Ellen says it looks easy enough, and you leave her on her own to practice her skills.

1. Click the **My Computer** icon on the Desktop. Note that the icon is shaded to indicate that it is selected

2. Click the **Desktop** to deselect My Computer

3. Right-click the **My Computer** icon to display a context menu of options. Release the mouse button to hide the menu again

WINDOWS XP

4. Double-click the **My Computer** icon to display a window containing the list of drives on your computer

5. Click the close ⌧ button at the top right corner to close the window again

6. Click the **My Computer** icon, then hold the mouse button down and move the mouse to the right. The icon moves as you move the mouse. Release the mouse button to place the icon in the new location on the Desktop

COMMON ICONS

Later in this book you will learn about how to place your own icons on the Desktop. When it is first installed, Windows XP displays only the Recycle Bin icon and the taskbar on your Desktop. However, there are several folders and icons that are in the Start menu (in older versions of Windows they were on the Desktop), and you should know what they are.

FIGURE 1.6b

Common Windows icons and folders in the Start menu

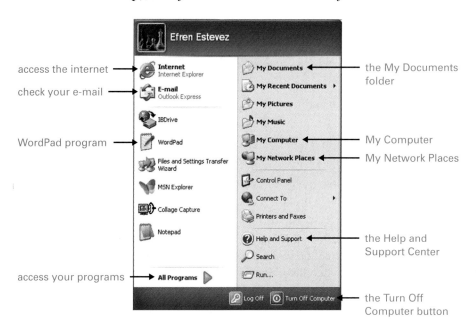

My Documents

The My Documents folder is the default location where Windows XP stores the documents you create when you use an application program. You'll learn later in the book how to create and navigate to your own set of folders.

My Computer

The My Computer icon displays all the drives on your computer. You use My Computer as a starting point for navigating through your computer. Each drive is represented by a letter of the alphabet (Figure 1.7). The most commonly used drives are:

- The **hard drive,** the storage space that comes with your computer. The hard drive is usually letter C. Your hard drive may be split into multiple hard drives, with the first C, the second D, and so on.

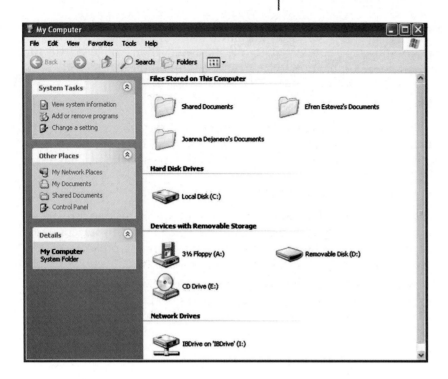

FIGURE 1.7
My Computer contains your
computer's drives

- The *floppy disk drive,* used for 3½″ floppy diskettes. The floppy
  drive is most often assigned the letter A.
- A CD-ROM or DVD drive, used for CDs.

My Network Places

If your computer is linked to a network, then the My Network Places icon
lists those network connections (Figure 1.8). You use My Network Places
to navigate to information on a network.

FIGURE 1.8
My Network Places lists the
networks you're connected to

Recycle Bin

When you delete a file from the hard drive, it is placed in the Recycle Bin.
Once a file is in the Recycle Bin, you can then either delete the file permanently or retrieve the file if you've deleted it by mistake.

Internet Explorer

If your computer is connected to the Internet, then you can use the Internet Explorer application to view information on the World Wide Web.

Taskbar

The taskbar starts off locked across the bottom of the screen, but it can be moved along one side or across the top of the screen. It can also be hidden until called up. If you're new to Windows and don't see the taskbar, click near the bottom of the screen to display it.

The taskbar is made up of the following elements:

- *Start menu.* The **Start menu,** at the far left of the taskbar, provides access to the programs, folders, and files installed on your computer. It also provides access to functions for changing preferences concerning how your computer looks and behaves.

- *Toolbars.* By default, the toolbars are hidden. You can display any or none of these toolbars simply by right-clicking an empty area of the taskbar and pointing your mouse over Toolbars from the context menu that appears. This will display a submenu that lists the available toolbars. There are four toolbars available; most users find at least the first two especially useful.

  1. *Quick Launch toolbar.* Next to the Start menu, the **Quick Launch bar** contains shortcuts for (from left to right) Internet Explorer, the Desktop, and Windows Media Player. You click these icons to launch the programs or display the Desktop.

  2. *Desktop toolbar.* This toolbar contains shortcuts to all the icons on your Desktop, certain items in the Start menu, and to Internet Explorer. If only the >> button is displayed, click it to display these items.

  3. *Address toolbar.* This toolbar displays an address text box to type a site's location. You click the Go button to open an Internet Explorer window for the selected site.

  4. *Links toolbar.* This toolbar displays your customized links from Internet Explorer.

- *Buttons for currently active windows.* When you open a window, it becomes a button on the taskbar. When we talk about windows and how they work, you'll find out how to use these buttons.

- *Notification area.* As the computer runs, some programs such as sound and virus control run at all times. These constantly running programs may provide information or alerts that are represented as icons on the far right of the taskbar.

- *Time.* The time is the last item on the right of the taskbar. This is the time the computer uses to determine when files have been created and changed.

FIGURE 1.9

Objects on the taskbar

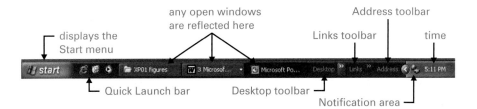

COMMON WINDOWS FEATURES

One of the features of Windows is that it brings a common interface to everything you do. No matter what program you're using or where you're navigating, you'll always see the same types of objects. Whenever you use a new program, you will at least be familiar with its building blocks. These building blocks include:

- Windows
- Dialog boxes
- Menus
- Toolbars

Windows

Since the operating system is named "Windows," you can guess that the window is the most basic element of the Windows XP operating system.

A *window* displays a program or document. When you double-click an icon on the Desktop, you display a window. Windows allows you to display multiple windows at the same time and move back and forth among them. All windows have the same features.

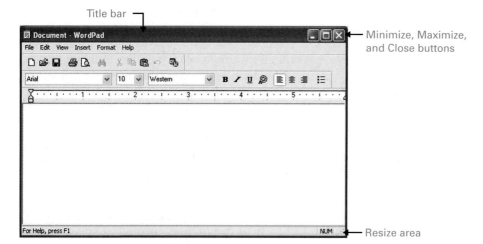

Title bar

Minimize, Maximize, and Close buttons

Resize area

FIGURE 1.10

Elements of a window

- *Title bar.* The **Title bar** tells you what's in the window. It may be the name of a directory or the title of a document. You can also click the Title bar to select a window and use the Title bar to move the window to another place on the screen. The Title bar also tells you whether the window is *active,* whether this is the current window that will be affected by your actions. If you have multiple windows open, then the active window is the one with the darker colored Title bar. If you click on another window, that becomes the active window.

- *Minimize button.* The **Minimize button,** the first button located at the far right of the Title bar, allows you to minimize a window if you're not going to work on it for a little while. When you minimize the window, it becomes a button on the taskbar. You click the button to display the window again.

- *Maximize button.* The **Maximize button,** the middle button located at the far right of the title bar, makes the window take up the entire screen.

- *Restore down button.* If the window takes up the entire screen, then the button in the middle becomes the **Restore Down button,** which restores the window to the size it was before you clicked the maximize button.

- *Close button.* The **Close button** is at the far right of every window. Click the Close button to close the window entirely. The window disappears and the button is removed from the taskbar. The computer discards the information you were working with unless you save it.

- *Resize area.* Along with making a window the size of the screen, and minimizing it to the taskbar, you can also simply make the window larger or smaller. The **Resize area,** at the bottom right corner of the window, allows you to resize the window. To resize the window, click and drag the Resize area.

Dialog Boxes

When a program requires additional information in order to complete a task, a dialog box often appears. **Dialog boxes** allow you to enter information.

Dialog boxes have some features similar to a window. They have a Title bar to identify them and a Close button to close them. You can also move a dialog box similar to the way you would a window. Unlike windows, however, you cannot resize a dialog box.

In a dialog box, you use the fields and tools to set the information and then click a button (usually labeled OK) at the bottom of the dialog box to close the dialog box and put the information you specified into effect. Alternately, you can leave everything as is and click Cancel to close the dialog box.

Dialog boxes use different types of fields, tools, and buttons for you to enter or change information. Not every type of field appears on every dialog box. Some of the most common elements are:

- *Text box.* An area where you type the requested information.

- *Drop-down list box.* A text box that displays the selected item and a down arrow button. Click the down arrow button to display a drop-down list of items and then click the item you want to select.

- *Check box.* A check box allows you to indicate whether you accept or reject an option. Click the check box once to fill it in with a check. Click it again to clear it.

- *Radio button.* A radio button is round (like the knob on a radio) and used to select one option among a few mutually exclusive options. You click the radio button to select the option next to it.

- *Button.* You use buttons to perform actions on the information in the dialog box. The buttons are usually at the bottom of the dialog box. Click the button to perform the function listed on the command. For example, click the OK button to indicate that the information is correct and you want it to go into effect. Click the Cancel button to cancel the information.

- *Tab.* Sometimes a dialog box contains too many fields to be displayed together. In that case, the fields are divided into groups, and each group is put on a tab. A tab resembles the tab on a file folder and performs a similar function. You click a tab to display the fields contained on it.

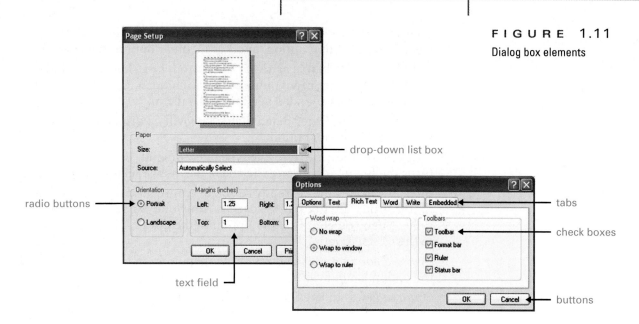

Menus

A *menu* is basically a list of options. A menu option may display a dialog box, change a setting, or perform an action.

There are two kinds of menus. Most windows have a menu bar near the top. The *menu bar* contains several menus, each represented by a label on the bar. You click a menu label to display the menu it represents.

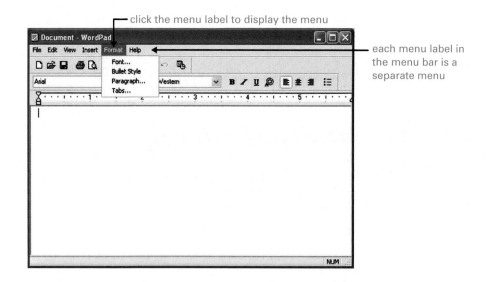

Context menus display when you right-click an object. A *context menu* contains the functions you can perform on the object you right-clicked. For example, if you right-click a document, one of the options in the context menu might be to print that document.

All menus operate in the same way. Once you open a menu, you move the mouse down the menu until the correct command is selected. A colored highlight bar appears over the selected command. Click the selected command to put it into effect.

There are different types of menu options, indicated by symbols in the menu.

- *Right arrow.* A right arrow next to a menu option indicates that when you select that option, another menu of options displays.
- *Double arrow.* A double arrow at the bottom of a short menu indicates that there are more options that are hidden. Click the double arrow to see the expanded version of the menu.
- *Ellipsis (. . .).* Indicates that a dialog box will be displayed when you select the menu option.
- *Check mark.* Indicates a toggle type of command. If selected, it turns the feature on or off. The check means the feature is on.
- *Bullet.* Indicates the currently selected feature, and that the options in that group are mutually exclusive. Only one can be selected at a time. When you click another option in the group, the bullet moves to the selected option.
- *Dimmed command.* If the text of the menu option looks gray, then the option is not available and you cannot select it.
- *Shortcut key.* Indicated by text such as Ctrl+C after the menu option. A **shortcut key** is a key or combination of keys you can use to execute a command without using the menu. For example, Ctrl+C after a Copy option indicates that if you press the Ctrl key on your keyboard, and then hold it down while pressing the C key, a selected object will be copied.

Windows XP also allows you to personalize your menus. Once you become comfortable with using Windows XP settings, you can explore these options to make menus work for you.

Toolbars

Most windows, as well as the taskbar, include a graphical toolbar. The **toolbar** contains buttons you can use to quickly perform functions without having to search through a menu.

FIGURE 1.13

Toolbars provide quick access to functions

toolbar buttons provide shortcuts to functions

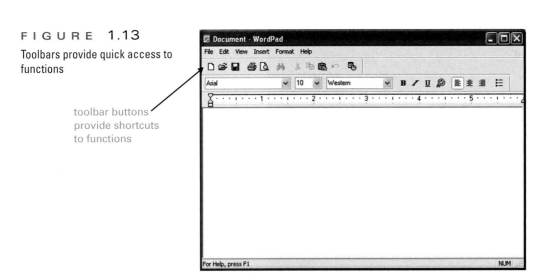

If you're not sure what a toolbar button will do if you click it, then just move the mouse pointer over it. A small box called a **ToolTip** displays, indicating the function of the button. The ToolTip disappears automatically after giving you a few seconds to read it.

task reference

Working with Windows

- To move a window, click and drag the Title bar
- To resize a window, click and drag the Resize area at the bottom right
- To minimize a window to the taskbar, click the Minimize button
- To make a window full screen, click the Maximize button. Click the Restore Down button to restore the original size
- To close a window and any program running in it, click **Close**

Working with Dialog Boxes

- Fill in the fields in the dialog box
- Click **OK** to close the dialog box and implement your changes
- Click **Cancel** to close the dialog box without implementing your changes

Working with Menus

- On a menu bar, click a menu label to open the menu
- To display a context menu, right-click an object
- To select a menu option, move the mouse over the menu option, and then click it

Working with Toolbars

- To display a ToolTip for a Toolbar button, move the mouse over the button
- To select a Toolbar button, click it

Practicing with windows:

Returning to see how Ellen is coming along, she shows you that she has the basic mouse movements down. You proceed to show her how to work with some of the basic elements—windows, dialog boxes, menus, and toolbars—and give her some exercises to do on her own.

1. Double-click the **My Computer** icon
2. Click and drag the Resize area of the My Computer window to make it larger
3. Click the Maximize button to make the window full screen
4. Click the Restore Down button to restore the window's size
5. Click the Minimize button to minimize the window. The window is now a button on the taskbar
6. Click the Taskbar button to restore the window
7. Click **Close**

WINDOWS XP

Practicing with menus:

1. Double-click the **My Computer** icon
2. Click **View** to display the View menu
3. In the View menu, click **Details.** Note how the bullet moved to the Details option
4. Click the **View** menu again
5. In the View menu, click **Arrange Icons by.** Note that a submenu displays
6. In the submenu, click **Name**
7. Click the Close button to close the My Computer window

Practicing with toolbars:

1. Move the mouse to the taskbar bar, next to the Start menu
2. Hold the mouse over each icon in turn. The ToolTip for each icon displays as the mouse passes over it

SHUTTING DOWN

When you're finished working, you must use the Windows XP Turn Off Computer button to properly shut down the system. The Turn Off Computer button is in the Start menu.

When you select Turn Off Computer from the Start menu, the Turn Off Computer dialog box displays. Three buttons are displayed. The Turn Off button closes Windows XP and prepares your computer to be shut down. The Stand By button shuts down the monitor and other devices but keeps you logged on to the operating system. This option is used to save power if you need to step away for a while. The Restart button closes Windows XP and restarts the computer. Some commands require you to restart the computer for the instructions to take effect. Restarting is also something you will want to do if the computer freezes.

task reference

Turning Off Windows XP

- Click the **Start** button
- In the Start menu, click **Turn Off Computer**
- In the Turn Off Computer dialog box, select the type of shutdown

Turning off Windows XP:

Ellen's basic training session is over, so the last thing you show her is how to properly turn off her computer. You go through the steps without actually shutting off the machine and then ask Ellen to perform a shut down procedure on her own.

1. Click the **Start** button on the taskbar

2. In the Start menu, click **Turn Off Computer**

3. In the Turn Off Computer dialog box, click the **Turn Off** button

---

making *the grade*   SESSION 1.1

1. When you log on to Windows XP, you use your _____ and _____ to identify yourself.

2. By default Windows stores the files you create in the _____ folder.

3. You _____ the mouse to display a context menu.

4. To display a window as a full screen you click the _____ button on the Title bar.

5. The _____ option in the Turn Off Computer dialog box closes Windows XP and restarts the computer.

SESSION 1.2 RUNNING PROGRAMS

Most of the work you perform in Windows XP involves running applications or programs. Technically, a ***program*** is a set of instructions to the computer. An ***application*** is a computer program designed for a specific purpose; for example, you use WordPad, which comes with Windows XP, to create a text file. In practice, these two words are often used interchangeably.

Windows XP is designed so that all of the applications that run on it have the same look and feel: in other words, they use the same types of windows, menus, dialog boxes, and toolbars. Once you use one Windows application, you'll be able to find the most basic functions in any other application.

You most often use applications to create and work with files such as documents. You can save these files to your computer and send files to the printer.

In this session, you'll use the WordPad application to create, save, and print a simple text file. You'll also learn how to open and close files both from within an application and from the Desktop. WordPad is a mini word-processing application that comes with Windows XP. Although you'll likely use a full-blown word-processing program such as Word or Word-Perfect for your documents, the principles you'll learn with WordPad apply just as well, and since it's included with XP, every user of this operating system will have access to it.

WINDOWS XP

LAUNCHING PROGRAMS

The Programs option of the Start menu provides access to all of the programs installed on your computer. Starting a program is known as launching it.

To start a program, click the Start button, and then click All Programs. A list of programs and program groups displays (Figure 1.14). Groups that have an arrow next to them can be clicked to display a submenu. Clicking an application starts that application.

FIGURE 1.14

The Programs menu

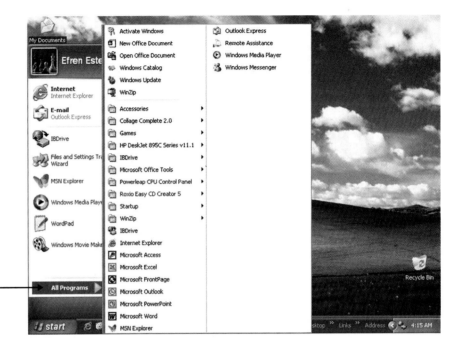

the Programs menu lists the programs on your computer

---

task reference

Launching Programs from the Start Menu

- Click the **Start** button

- In the Start menu, click **All Programs**

- Navigate through the programs and program groups in the menu until you get to the program you want

- Click the program name to start the application

Launching WordPad:

Ellen realizes that in order to be productive, she will have to learn how to run the programs on her computer. From her reading, she has an idea of how to do this, and while waiting for her next training session, she decides to give it a try. She turns on her computer, logs on, and tries to start an application.

1. Click the **Start** button

2. In the Start menu, click **All Programs**

3. In the Programs menu, click **Accessories**

4. In the Accessories **menu,** click **WordPad.** The WordPad window displays on the Desktop

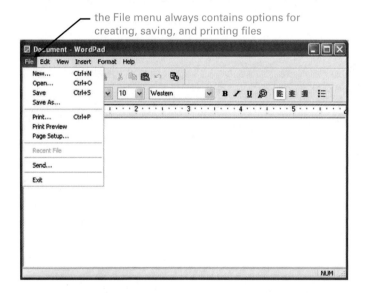

FIGURE 1.15

The WordPad window

CREATING AND SAVING FILES

Once a program is launched, you use the File menu, always at the far left of the menu bar, to create and save a file (Figure 1.16).

the File menu always contains options for creating, saving, and printing files

FIGURE 1.16

The WordPad File menu

In the File menu, the *New* option creates a new instance of the type of file generated by the application. For WordPad, the *New* option creates a blank text document.

Once you've finished working on the file, the *Save* option in the File menu allows you to **save** a copy of the finished document to your computer. When you save a file, you must give the file a name. Filenames can be up to 255 characters long and can include spaces. By default, Windows XP assumes you want to store the file in the My Documents folder.

You may also want to create a copy of a file and start to work with that copy. To do this, you use the **Save As** option. Selecting Save As allows you to save the same file to a new location or with a new name. You then continue working on that new file.

---

task reference

Creating and Saving Files

- To create a new file using an application, click **New** in the application's File menu
- To save the file to the computer, click **Save** in the File menu, then specify the file's name and location
- To save a copy of the file with a new name or location, click **Save As** in the File menu, then specify a new name or location for the file

---

FIGURE 1.17

A new WordPad file

Creating a WordPad file:

When you arrive for the day's training session, you realize that Ellen is already familiarizing herself with WordPad, so you decide to use this program to teach her some basic things that apply not only to this program but to all Windows programs.

1. In the WordPad File menu, click **New**
2. In the dialog box that displays, click the **OK** button to accept the default settings and display a blank text file
3. In the new file, type your name, then press **Enter** on the keyboard to go to the next line
4. Type today's date

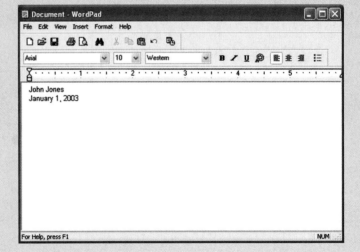

Saving the file:

1. In the File menu, click **Save.** The Save dialog box opens
2. In the Filename field, type **My WordPad File**
3. Click the **OK** button. The file is saved into the My Documents folder, and the title of the window changes to reflect the file's name

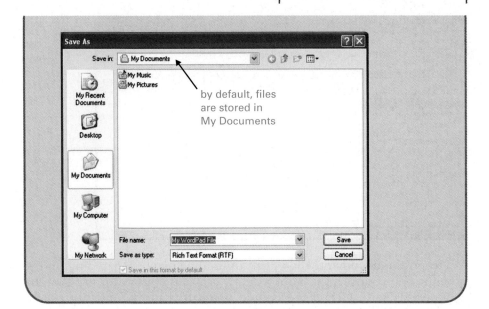

FIGURE 1.18
Saving a WordPad file

Saving a copy of the file:

1. In the document, press **Enter** to add a new line
2. Type **A third line of text**
3. In the File menu, click **Save As.** The Save As dialog box opens
4. In the Filename field, type **My Second WordPad File**
5. In the Save in drop-down list at the top of the dialog box, select Desktop from the list that appears when you click the down arrow
6. Click the **OK** button. The new file is saved onto the Desktop, and the title of the window changes again to reflect the new filename

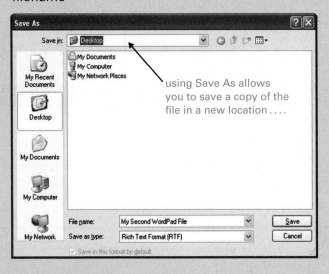

FIGURE 1.19
Using Save As creates a copy
of a file

PRINTING FILES

Most computers have a printer attached to them, either directly or as part of a network. The Print option, located in the File menu, allows you to *print* the file to create a paper version of the document (Figure 1.20).

FIGURE 1.20

The Print option is in the File menu

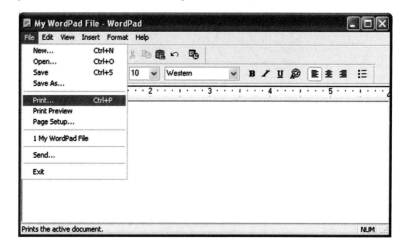

To print a document, click Print in the File menu. Depending on the program and your file, the Print window provides options for printing the document (Figure 1.21). For example, you can print multiple copies of a document or print only a portion of a document.

FIGURE 1.21

The Print dialog box

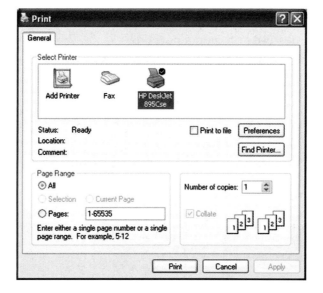

reference

Printing a File

- In the File menu, click **Print**

- In the print dialog box, set any options for printing, such as printing multiple copies or printing only a portion of the file

- Click the **OK** button to send the file to the printer

Printing a WordPad File:

Ellen is rightly quite proud of her achievement so far and wants to print out a copy of a new document she created in WordPad to remind herself of some techniques she has learned. She asks you to show her how to print a hard copy of her document, and you proceed to do so.

1. In the WordPad File menu, click **Print**

2. On the General tab of the print dialog box, change number of copies to **2**

3. Click the **Print** button to send the document to the printer. The printer should produce two copies of the document

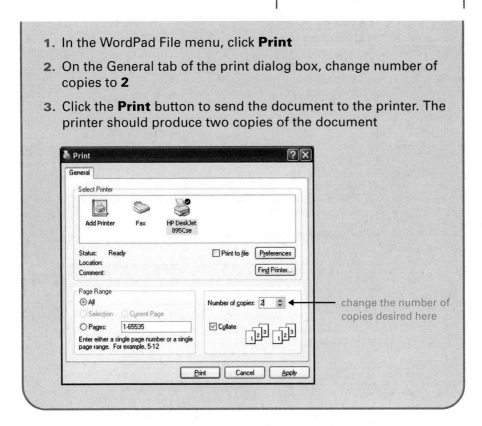

FIGURE 1.22
Printing the WordPad file

change the number of copies desired here

CLOSING AND OPENING FILES

To close both a file and the application, click the Close button at the top right of the application window. You can also close a file while keeping the application open. To do this, select the Close option from the File menu. The file is closed, but the application remains open so that you can create or open another file.

You also have a couple of options for opening a file. If the file's application is open, then select Open from the File menu. You use the browser window to navigate to the file's location. If the file is displayed in a folder or on your Desktop, you can double-click the file to open it.

FIGURE 1.23
The Open a file dialog box

WINDOWS XP

task reference

Closing and Opening Files

- To close a file and the application, click the Close button at the top right of the window

- To close a file without closing the application, select **Close** from the **File** menu

- To open a file from within the application, select **Open** from the **File** menu. Use the dialog box to find and open the file

- To open a file directly from a folder or the Desktop window, double-click the icon representing the file

---

Closing and opening a file in an application:

Now that Ellen has the hang of some basics, you want her to get out of WordPad so that you can show her another program. Before you do, you show her the proper way to close and open a file.

1. In the File menu, click **Close.** The WordPad window contains a blank document

2. In the File menu, click **Open.** The Open file dialog box opens to the My Documents folder, containing the two files you created earlier

3. In the list of files, click **My WordPad Document**

4. Click the **Open** button to open the file in WordPad

Closing the application and opening a file from the Desktop:

1. Click the **Close** ⊠ button at the top right of the WordPad window. Both the file and the application are closed

2. Double-click the **My Documents** icon on the Desktop. The two files you created will be listed in the window that displays

3. Double-click **My WordPad Document** to open the file in WordPad

---

INSTALLING AND REMOVING PROGRAMS

Despite the fact that Windows XP comes with many types of programs built into it—such as basic word processing (WordPad) and graphics (Paint), e-mail (Outlook), and an Internet Browser (Internet Explorer)—you will certainly want to add other programs. Installing new programs is done by using yet another type of program built into Windows XP known as an ***applet.*** Applets are mini-programs of limited function that are bundled together as part of Windows. You use the Add or Remove Programs applet in the Control Panel folder to install a new program. Please note that XP only allows a user with administrative rights to install and remove programs.

---

task reference

Installing a Program

- Click **Start,** then **Control Panel**

- Click **Add or Remove Programs**

- Click the **Add New Programs** button

- Click the **CD or Floppy** button. Insert the CD or other disk if you have not already done so

- Click the **Next** button

- Click the **Finish** button

---

anotherway

It is just as easy to install a program by running its setup routine, which will automatically launch as soon as you insert the CD, DVD, or other media that the program comes on. If it does not launch automatically after inserting the program's disk, double-click the program's folder and open the setup file inside. Windows will begin installing the program.

Installing a program using Add or Remove Programs

Since Ellen learned WordPad quickly, you want to show her Microsoft Word, which is a more full-featured word-processing program. To do so, this program must first be installed on Ellen's machine, and you take this opportunity to show her how to install a program so that next time, she can do it on her own.

1. Click **Start,** then **Control Panel.** The Control Panel window opens

2. Click **Add or Remove Programs.** The Add or Remove Programs window opens

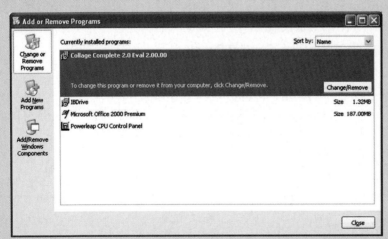

FIGURE   1.24

The Add or Remove Programs window

3. Click the **Add New Programs** button

4. Click the **CD or Floppy** button to the right of the screen, even if you are installing from a network or hard drive. The Add Programs Wizard window opens

5. If the program you wish to install is on a CD or other removable media, make sure the disk is inserted if you have not already done so

6. Click the **Next** button. Windows XP searches for the program's setup file and displays it in the Run Installation Program dialog box

tip: If Windows can't find the file, or if Windows displays the wrong program's file, click the **Browse** button to navigate to the program's folder and manually select the program's setup file and click **Open**

7. Click **Finish.** XP begins the program's setup routine

Using the same Add or Remove Programs utility, you can remove a program. It is a good idea to periodically eliminate programs that you don't use as they take up space and can clutter your Start menu's Programs list.

task **reference**

Removing a Program

- Click **Start,** then **Control Panel**
- Click **Add or Remove Programs**
- Click the **Change or Remove Programs** button
- In the list under *Currently installed programs*, click the name of the program you want to remove
- Click **Remove**
- Click **OK**

Removing a program using Add or Remove Programs:

When Ellen was installing the new program, she noticed a list of other programs on her computer that she didn't know. She asks you about them, and you realize that one or two of them are old programs that Ellen will never need to use. Accordingly, you decide this is a good time to show her how to remove unwanted programs.

1. Click **Start,** then **Control Panel.** The Control Panel window opens

2. Click **Add or Remove Programs.** The Add or Remove Programs window opens

3. Click the **Change or Remove Programs** button

4. In the list under *Currently installed programs*, click the name of the program you want to remove. Information displays about the program: its size, how often you use the program (Frequently, Occasionally, or Rarely), and the date you last used it

   tip: *If you are searching to get rid of any programs you rarely use, use the* **Sort by** *drop-down list in the upper right corner of the window to sort by either Frequency of Use or Date Last Used*

5. Click the **Remove** button. XP checks to see if any user is currently logged on to the computer in case they are working with this program. If so, XP displays a warning dialog box since the program may not uninstall completely if it is running

6. Depending on the program you are uninstalling, you will get either a dialog box that asks you if you are sure you want to delete the program or a dialog box that allows you to uninstall all or only part of the program. Choose the desired uninstall options, then click **OK**

---

making the grade

1. A program written for a specific purpose is called an

   _____.

2. The Programs menu is located in the _____.

3. In most applications, the _____ menu provides access to the create, save, and print functions.

4. Save stores the current file, while Save As creates a _____ of the file.

5. To remove a program, click the Start menu, then click the

   _____.

SESSION 1.3 GETTING HELP

The Windows XP *Help and Support Center* allows you to find and display information on how to use the components of Windows XP. If you have a question about how something works, or want instructions on performing a specific task, the Help and Support Center is the place to start.

In this session, you'll learn about the new feature in XP, the Help and Support Center. You'll learn how to browse Help topics, and you'll use the search function to find a specific word or phrase. You'll also learn how to use Favorites and how to print out Help topics. Finally, you'll also look at another new XP feature, Remote Assistance.

ELEMENTS OF THE HELP AND SUPPORT CENTER

The Help and Support Center displays from the Start menu. The Help and Support Center home page has a toolbar across the top, as shown in Figure 1.26.

F I G U R E   1.26

The Help and Support Center home page

the Search text box

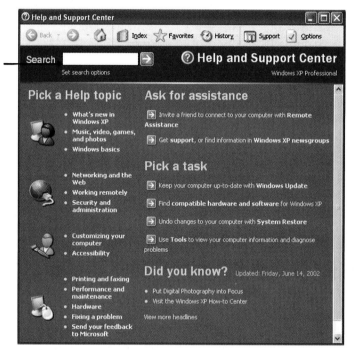

Notice that the interface looks like a Web page. Among the most powerful new features of XP Help are its links to online knowledge databases from Microsoft and affiliated companies. The Help and Support Center home page has two columns. The one on the left, titled Pick a Help Topic, allows you to browse through some general topics that may be of interest. The right pane of the Help and Support Center window displays additional methods for getting to the information you need. Ask for Assistance lists links to Remote Assistance, Support, and Windows XP Newsgroups. Pick a Task provides links to general tasks that may be related to the information you seek. The Did You Know? section is regularly updated and includes tips on topics of general interest.

Click a topic to display more information. The topic selected is displayed in the right pane. The content pane at the right contains the actual information for a single help topic.

The toolbar across the top contains buttons that allow you to work with the Help and Support Center window.

- The Back and Forward buttons display the previous and next topics that you displayed. When you first display the Help window, these buttons are disabled.

- The Home button returns you to the home page of the Help and Support Center.
- The Index button allows you to browse for Help topics in the Index.
- The Favorites button allows you to reference topics you look at often.
- The History button allows you to jump throughout the various pages of your search quickly.
- The Options button displays a menu of options for customizing the interface.

task reference

Displaying the Help and Support Center Window

- To display the Help and Support Center window, click the **Start** button, then click **Help and Support**

Displaying the Help and Support Center window:

Since Ellen has some time to learn the computer on her own, she asks you how she can get more information when you are not available to teach her. The easiest way, you explain, is to use the Help and Support Center. When Ellen asks what that is, you show her how to access it and how to search for what she needs.

1. Click the **Start** button
2. In the Start menu, click **Help and Support** Center

USING SEARCH IN THE HELP AND SUPPORT CENTER

If you don't see the information you're looking for, the Search text box in the upper left corner of the screen allows you to search for specific words and phrases in order to find the information you need. Type a word or phrase related to your topic in the Search text box, then press Enter or click Start Searching button.

The Search Results appear in the left pane. To display one of the topics listed, click the topic. The topic contents display on the right, in the content pane. The word or words you used for the search are highlighted in the topic, as shown in Figure 1.27.

task reference

Using the Help and Support Center Search

- In the *Search* text box of the Help and Support Center, type the keyword or words to search for, then press **Enter**

- To display a topic, click the topic

FIGURE 1.27

The Search Result pane of the Help and Support Center

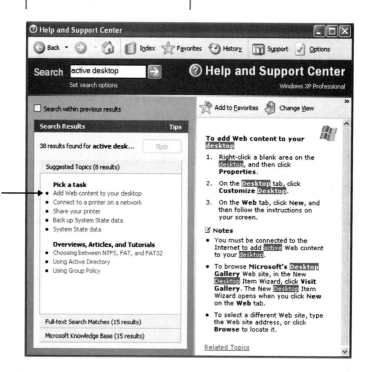

clicking a result in the left pane displays the relevant information in the right pane

---

Finding information using Search in the Help and Support Center:

1. In the *Search* text box of the Help and Support Center, type **arranging windows**

2. Press **Enter.** The Search Results window appears

3. Click **Arrange all open windows** in the Search results pane on the left. The information related to this topic is displayed on the right. Note that the words "arrange" and "windows" are highlighted in the topic to indicate you used these words for the search

---

At the head of the Search Results column is a line of text that indicates the total number of results found for your search. These results are divided into three main sections: Suggested Topics, Full-Text Search Matches, and Microsoft Knowledge Base. Suggested Topics indicate that a keyword in your search terms matches a keyword in the displayed topics. Full-Text Search Matches are topics that have your search term in the body of their text. Microsoft Knowledge Base results provide extra and more detailed information about your search terms. Display a category by clicking its heading, then click a search result within the category to display the information in the right pane of the window.

A toolbar appears over the right column containing four buttons: Add to Favorites, Change View, Print, and Locate in Contents. Once you've found the information you are

*another*word

The Microsoft Knowledge Base contains a huge amount of information and is one of the main tools that Microsoft support personnel use to answer technical questions. It contains answers to questions that users have asked, from very basic to very advanced. Each answer is identified by an Article ID number, which begins with a Q followed by a six-digit number (Q123456, for example) and is labeled with a title to indicate the topic covered.

seeking, click the Change View button at the top of the right column to hide any extraneous information to your subject. To print the current topic, click the Print button, then click the Print button in the Print dialog box that appears.

SETTING SEARCH OPTIONS IN THE HELP AND SUPPORT CENTER

If the search process returns information that is not relevant, you can use the Set Search Options to clarify what you're looking for.

---

task *reference*

Using the Set Search Options

- Click **Start,** then click **Help and Support**

- Click the **Options** button on the navigation bar

- In the Options list in the left pane, click the check box next to *Set Search Options.* Enter the desired options on the right pane and click the arrow next to the *Search* text box

---

Using the Set Search Options:

1. Click **Start,** then click **Help and Support**

2. Click the **Options** button on the navigation bar. The Options window appears

3. In the Options list in the left pane, click the check box next to *Set Search Options.* The Set Search Options window appears, as shown in Figure 1.28

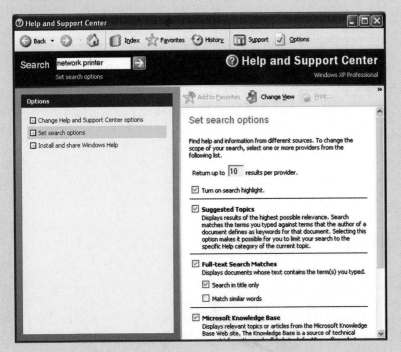

FIGURE 1.28

The Set Search Options window

4. In the Return up to xx results per provider text box, type **10.**

5. Under the Full-Text Search Matches, click the check box next to Search in the Title only

6. Click the arrow button next to the *Search* text box

If you're still unsuccessful, click the Support button on the toolbar at the top of the screen to connect to resources on the Internet. Throughout your search, additional links will be displayed that you can click to pursue further subtopics. To search for a different topic, click the icon on the toolbar that looks like a house to return to the Home page.

WORKING WITH FAVORITES IN THE HELP AND SUPPORT CENTER

The top of the right pane is the Add to Favorites button. This command is convenient if you need to look up the same information often. Also, perhaps you want to keep a certain series of instructions for performing some action readily available, for yourself or other users. The Favorites button allows you to save a personal list of Help topics so you can get to them easily. You can delete a topic whenever you need to.

F I G U R E   1.29

The Add to Favorites and Favorites buttons of the Help and Support Center window

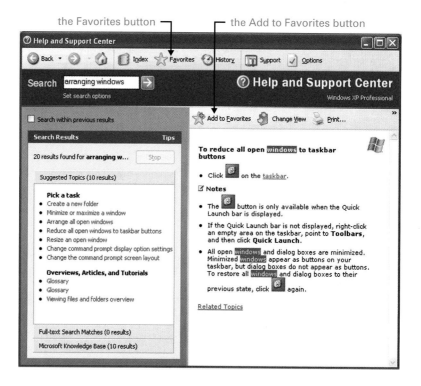

To save a topic to your Favorites, the topic must be displayed in the content pane. Click the Add to Favorites button to add the current topic to the list of favorites. To display a favorite topic, you click the topic in the list, then click the Display button. To remove a favorite, you click the topic, then click the Remove button.

---

task reference

Using Favorites in the Help and Support Center

- Click the **Favorites** button on the toolbar to display the Favorites pane

- To add the current topic to the list of favorites, click the **Add to Favorites** button

- To rename a favorite topic, click the topic, then click **Rename**

- To delete a favorite topic from the list, click the topic, then click **Remove**

Working with Favorites:

Ellen has found several topics that she wants to go back to in the Help and Support center, so she has written them down on a piece of paper. During her next training session, you notice this and show her there is an easier way to do this by using Favorites.

1. While the arranging windows topic is still displayed, click the **Add to Favorites** button to add the topic to the favorites list. A dialog box appears indicating that the item has been added to your Favorites list

2. Type **Remote Assistance** in the Search text and press **Enter** to display this topic

3. Click **Remote Assistance** in the Search results pane on the left. The information about this topic appears on the right pane

4. Click the **Add to Favorites** button again

5. Click the **Favorites** button on the toolbar at the top of the page to display your Favorites list

---

USING REMOTE ASSISTANCE

An excellent new feature of Windows XP is Remote Assistance. As the name implies, Remote Assistance allows you to request and receive help from a knowledgeable user such as a network administrator, a colleague, or a friend. Your assistant must also be running Windows XP. You send an invitation using e-mail or Windows Messenger, and once the other user responds, you accept her help.

Your assistant can see your screen, and if you give her permission to do so, she can take control of your computer. This can be enormously helpful if you're having a problem, but be choosy about whom you give this permission to. Although you will see what she is doing and can take back control at any time, it only takes a moment to wreck havoc if the person is more helpful than informed, or more malicious than you think. Make sure you know who your assistant is. Protect your Remote Assistance connection with a password known only to your assistant.

task reference

Working with Remote Assistance

- Display System Properties dialog box by clicking the System link of the Performance and Maintenance window of the Control Panel
- Click the **Remote** tab
- Click the **Advanced** button
- Click **OK,** then **OK** again

Working with Remote Assistance:

Ellen discovers a feature called Remote Assistance that allows her to get help from her trainer, even when he is not physically present. She reads through the information she has found about it in the Help and Support Center and decides to try it.

1. Click **Start,** then click **Control Panel**

2. Click **Performance and Maintenance** from the Pick a Category list on the right

3. Click **System** from the Control Panel icon on the right of the Performance and Maintenance window. The System Properties dialog box appears (Figure 1.30)

FIGURE 1.30

The System Properties dialog box

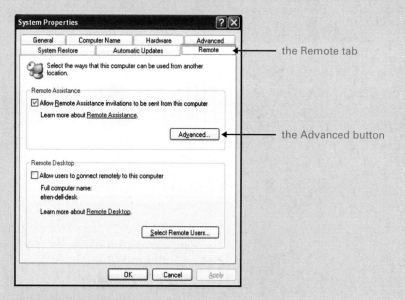

the Remote tab

the Advanced button

4. Click the **Remote** tab. In the Remote Assistance area, make sure the check box next to *Allow Remote Assistance invitations to be sent from this computer* is selected

5. Click the **Advanced** button. The Remote Assistance Settings dialog box opens

6. Make sure the check box next to *Allow this computer to be controlled remotely* is selected

7. In the Invitations area, use the drop-down list to shorten the maximum time invitations remain open to **10 days**

8. Click **OK.** The Remote Assistance Settings dialog box closes, and you are returned to the System Properties dialog box

9. Click **OK.** The System Properties dialog box closes

---

task **reference**

Sending a Remote Assistance Invitation Using E-Mail

- Click **Start/All Programs/Remote Assistance**

- Click **Invite someone to help you**

- Type your assistant's e-mail address in the *Type an e-mail address* text box and click **Invite this person**

- In the text box under *Message,* enter a description of the problem and click **Continue**

- Specify a time limit for the response from the recipient and a password and click the **Send Invitation** button

---

Sending a Remote Assistance invitation using e-mail:

Now that Ellen has enabled Remote Assistance on her computer, she wants to notify her trainer. She follows the instructions she finds in the Help and Support Center.

1. Click **Start/All Programs/Remote Assistance.** The Help and Support Center window opens with the Remote Assistance topic displayed

2. Click **Invite someone to help you.** The Pick how you want to contact your assistant window pane opens, as shown in Figure 1.31

3. Type your assistant's e-mail address in the *Type an e-mail address* text box and click **Invite this person.** The Provide contact information pane opens

4. In the text box under *Message*, enter a description of the problem

5. Click **Continue.** The Set the invitation to expire pane opens

6. Using the two drop-down lists, specify **4 hours** as a time limit for the recipient to respond to your invitation

7. If it is not already checked, click the check box next to *Require the recipient to use a password*, then type a password in the *Type password* and *Confirm password* text boxes

F I G U R E   1.31

Pick how you want to contact
your assistant is displayed in the
right pane of the Remote
Assistance window

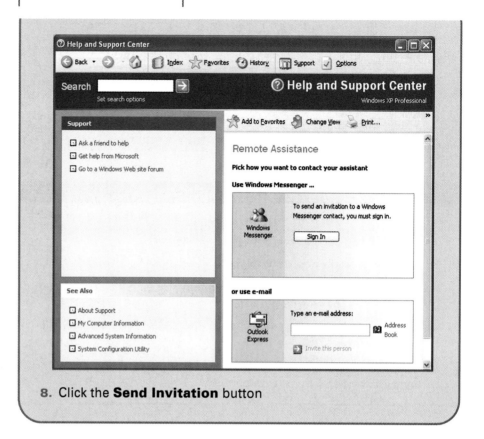

8. Click the **Send Invitation** button

---

task reference

Receiving Remote Assistance

- Click the **Yes** button to begin the Remote Assistance session

- To chat with your assistant type a message in the *Message Entry* text
  box and click the **Send** button

- Give your assistant control of your computer in the Remote
  Assistance—Web Page Dialog dialog box by clicking the **Yes** button to
  accept

- Click the **Disconnect** button to end the session

Receiving Remote Assistance:

*Ellen's trainer responds, indicating that he's delighted that Ellen has taught
herself how to ask for Remote Assistance, since this will also make his job
much easier. He indicates that he'd be happy to help her. Now Ellen has to
figure out how to receive the Remote Assistance.*

1. When your assistant accepts your invitation, the Remote
   Assistance dialog box will appear. Click the **Yes** button to
   begin the session

2. When the Remote Assistance window with the chat pane and control buttons opens, type a message in the *Message Entry* text box and click the **Send** button

3. If your assistant requests control of your computer, the Remote Assistance—Web Page Dialog dialog box opens. Click **Yes** to accept

tip: *To regain sole control over your computer, press the **Esc** key at any time*

4. Click the **Disconnect** button to end the session

---

making *the grade*   **SESSION 1.3**

1. To display the Help and Support Center click _____.

2. In the Help and Support Center, the _____ button allows you to reference topics you look at often.

3. The _____ text box in the upper left corner of the Help and Support Center window allows you to search for specific words and phrases.

4. In order to Set Search Options in the Help and Support Center, click the _____ button on the navigation bar.

5. You get to the Remote Assistance dialog box by clicking _____.

SESSION 1.4 SUMMARY

The Windows XP operating system controls all of the functions of your computer and the equipment connected to it. The operating system starts whenever you turn your computer on. If your computer is connected to a network, you may need to type a user name and password in order to get into the system.

The initial Windows Desktop has the taskbar at the bottom and the Recycle Bin, which contains files you have deleted. The taskbar includes the Start menu. In the Start menu are several common icons. My Computer lists the drives on your computer, and My Network Places indicates any network connections. My Documents is the default place for storing your files. Your Desktop may contain other icons for opening files and applications.

You use your mouse to interact with these elements: click once to select, double-click to open, and right-click to display a pop-up menu of options. You can also use the mouse to drag an item to another part of the screen.

Windows XP also runs applications. All Windows applications have a similar look and feel, making it easy to learn new applications. From Windows XP, you can create files such as text documents and save them to your computer. You can also open a file that has already been created and print a file using a printer.

If you have questions or run into a problem, you can use Windows XP's Help and Support Center to get more information. The Help and Support Center includes menus and buttons to help you navigate through the information. You can also search for a specific word or phrase and save a personal list of topics you refer to often. The Help and Support Center also provides access to a list of Web pages with even more information.

When you're finished working for the day, you use the Windows XP Turn Off Computer feature to correctly shut down the operating system.

task reference roundup

Task	Page #	Preferred Method
Starting Windows XP	WINXP 1.6	• Turn on the computer
		• Click your user name
		• Type your password and press **Enter**
Using the mouse	WINXP 1.9	• To select an object, move the mouse over the object, then click with the left mouse button
		• To display a context menu related to an object, move the mouse over the object, then click with the right mouse button
		• To open an object, move the mouse over the object, then double-click with the left mouse button
		• To move an item to another part of the screen, move the mouse over the object. Click the left mouse button and hold it down, then move the mouse in the direction you want to move the object. Release the mouse button when the object is in the correct place
Working with windows	WINXP 1.17	• To move a window, click and drag the Title bar
		• To resize a window, click and drag the Resize area at the bottom right
		• To minimize a window to the taskbar, click the Minimize button
		• To make a window full screen, click the Maximize button. Click the Restore Down button to restore the original size
		• To close a window and any program running in it, click **Close**
Working with dialog boxes	WINXP 1.17	• Fill in the fields in the dialog box
		• Click **OK** to close the dialog box and implement your changes
		• Click **Cancel** to close the dialog box without implementing your changes
Working with menus	WINXP 1.17	• On a menu bar, click a menu label to open the menu
		• To display a context menu, right-click an object
		• To select a menu option, move the mouse over the menu option, then click it
Working with toolbars	WINXP 1.17	• To display a ToolTip for a Toolbar button, move the mouse over the button
		• To select a Toolbar button, click it

task reference roundup

Task	Page #	Preferred Method
Turning off Windows XP	WINXP 1.18	• Click the **Start** button
		• In the Start menu, click **Turn Off Computer**
		• In the Turn Off Computer dialog box, select the type of shutdown
Launching programs from the Start menu	WINXP 1.20	• Click the **Start** button
		• In the Start menu, click **All Programs**
		• Navigate through the program groups until you get to the program you want
		• Click the program name to start the application
Creating and saving files	WINXP 1.22	• To create a new file using an application, click **New** in the application's File menu
		• To save the file to the computer, click **Save** in the File menu, then specify the file's name and location
		• To save a copy of the file with a new name or location, click **Save As** in the File menu, then specify a new name or location for the file
Printing a file	WINXP 1.24	• In the File menu, click **Print**
		• In the print dialog box, set any options for printing, such as printing multiple copies or printing only a portion of the file
		• Click **OK** to send the file to the printer
Closing and opening files	WINXP 1.26	• To close a file and the application, click the Close button at the top right of the window
		• To close a file without closing the application, select **Close** from the File menu
		• To open a file from within the application, select **Open** from the **File** menu. Use the dialog box to find and open the file
		• To open a file directly from a Desktop window, double-click the icon representing the file
Installing a program	WINXP 1.27	• Click **Start,** then **Control Panel**
		• Click **Add or Remove Programs**
		• Click the **Add New Programs** button
		• Click the **CD or Floppy** button. Insert the CD or other disk if you have not already done so
		• Click the **Next** button
		• Click the **Finish** button
Removing a program	WINXP 1.28	• Click **Start,** then **Control Panel**
		• Click **Add or Remove Programs**
		• Click the **Change or Remove Programs** button

task reference roundup

Task	Page #	Preferred Method
		• In the list under *currently installed programs*, click the name of the program you want to remove
		• Click **Remove**
		• Click **OK**
Displaying the Help and Support Center window	WINXP 1.31	• To display the Help and Support Center window, click the **Start** button, then click **Help and Support**
Using the Help and Support Center search	WINXP 1.31	• In the *Search* text box of the Help and Support Center, type the keyword or words to search for, then press **Enter**
		• To display a topic, click the topic
Using the Set Search options	WINXP 1.33	• Click **Start**, then click **Help and Support**
		• Click the **Options** button on the navigation bar
		• In the Options list in the left pane, click the check box next to *Set Search Options*
		• Enter the desired options on the right pane and click the arrow next to the *Search* text box
Using Favorites in the Help and Support Center	WINXP 1.35	• Click the **Favorites** button on the toolbar to display the Favorites pane
		• To add the current topic to the list of favorites, click the **Add to Favorites** button
		• To rename a favorite topic, click the topic, then click **Rename**
		• To delete a favorite topic from the list, click the topic, then click **Remove**
Working with Remote Assistance	WINXP 1.36	• Display System Properties dialog box by clicking the System link of the Performance and Maintenance window of the Control Panel
		• Click the **Remote** tab
		• Click the **Advanced** button
		• Click **OK**, then **OK** again
Sending a Remote Assistance invitation using e-mail	WINXP 1.37	• Click **Start/All Programs/Remote Assistance**
		• Click **Invite someone to help you**
		• Type your assistant's e-mail address in the *Type an e-mail address* text box and click **Invite this person**
		• In the text box under *Message*, enter a description of the problem and click **Continue**
		• Specify a time limit for the response from the recipient and a password and click the **Send Invitation** button

task reference roundup

Task	Page #	Preferred Method
Receiving Remote Assistance	WINXP 1.38	• Click the **Yes** button to begin the Remote Assistance session
		• To chat with your assistant type a message in the *Message Entry* text box and click the **Send** button
		• Give your assistant control of your computer in the Remote Assistance—Web Page Dialog dialog box by clicking the **Yes** button to accept
		• Click the **Disconnect** button to end the session

review of
terminology

CROSSWORD PUZZLE

Across

1. What Windows XP Professional is
5. To click the mouse twice in rapid succession
7. Displays when you right-click an object
10. Allows you to enter information
11. The main building block of Windows XP Professional
12. To make a window full screen
13. Contains the Start menu

Down

2. A computer program created for a specific purpose
3. Small picture representing an object
4. File menu option that creates a copy of a file
5. The Windows work area
6. Pointing tool for interacting with the computer
8. Connects your computer to the Internet
9. Used to move a window

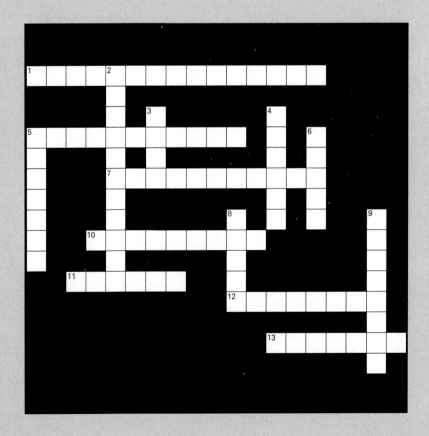

FILL-IN

1. The _____ button in the Help and Support Center allows you to reference topics you need to look up often.

2. The _____ allows you to change the size of a window by clicking and dragging.

3. The _____ indicates which programs and files are open.

4. Use the _____ menu option to store a file to the computer.

CREATE THE QUESTION

For each of the following answers, create an appropriate, short question:

ANSWER	QUESTION
1. This piece of equipment connects your computer to the Internet	_____
2. This File menu option creates a copy of a file	_____
3. This Desktop object contains your deleted files	_____
4. This menu lists the applications on your computer	_____
5. It allows you to find out what other systems your computer is connected to	_____

SHORT ANSWER

1. How do you move a window on the Desktop?

2. What letter usually represents your computer's hard drive?

3. What does ". . ." after a menu option mean?

4. What is the correct method for restarting your computer?

5. Which menu in a Windows application contains the Print option?

1. Using the Quick Launch Button on the Taskbar

Randy Green is a production assistant at Sterling Video Productions using Windows XP as his operating system. Randy often has many windows open on his Desktop, checking and editing videotape digitally. He likes to keep shortcuts to the programs he uses all the time on his Desktop. His problem, however, is that he frequently has to minimize each window he has open, one by one, to get back to the Desktop in order to double-click the program's icon to launch it. He explains to you how this inconveniences him, and you tell him that you think you have a solution.

1. Right-click an empty area of the taskbar. A context menu opens
2. Click **Properties** from the context menu. The taskbar and Start Menu Properties dialog box open, as shown in Figure 1.32
3. In the Taskbar tab, click the check box next to *Show Quick Launch*
4. Click **OK.** The Quick Launch toolbar now appears immediately to the right of the Start button on the taskbar
5. On the Quick Launch toolbar, click the middle icon, the **Show Desktop** icon. No matter what is open on your screen, the Show Desktop icon takes you to the Desktop

6. Open several overlapping windows of any type on your Desktop; it doesn't matter what they are
7. Leaving all the windows open, click the **Show Desktop** icon on the taskbar. All the windows are minimized, and you are returned to a clean Desktop
8. Click the **Show Desktop** icon again. All the windows you had open are displayed just the way they were previously

2. Checking for Windows XP Requirements on Your Computer

Arthur Kane runs the network for Remington Associates, an information technology service firm. One of his duties is to upgrade computers to new versions of the Windows operating system and to assess whether any computer requires an upgrade to operate properly. As part of Remington's asset management program, Kane must collect information on each computer, what the computer's name is, how fast a microprocessor it has, how much memory, disk space, and other vital details. This information is written down and later collected in a spreadsheet for analysis and for accounting purposes like asset depreciation.

1. Open the **Start** menu and move your mouse over **My Computer** until it is highlighted, then right-click it. A context menu appears
2. Select **Properties.** The System properties dialog box opens
3. Starting on the **General** tab, write down the following pieces of information:

- **What version of the Windows operating system is this computer running?**
- **What kind of processor do you have?**
- **How much RAM do you have?**

FIGURE 1.32

Use the Taskbar and Start Menu Properties dialog box to display the Quick Launch toolbar on the taskbar

the Taskbar tab

click this check box to show the Quick Launch toolbar

the Show Desktop icon on the Quick Launch toolbar

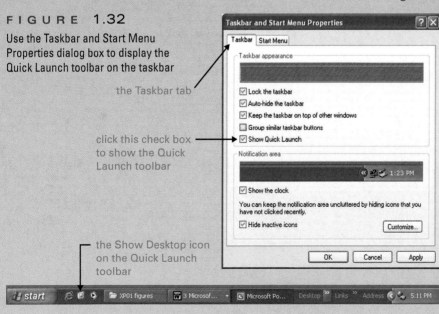

4. Click the **Computer Name** tab and write down the following pieces of information:

   - **What is the name of your computer?**

   - **What workgroup or domain does this computer belong to?**

5. Close the System properties dialog box

6. Click **Start,** then **My Computer**

7. Click the **Local Disk C:** icon

8. Select **File,** then the **Properties** command to view the Properties dialog box for the Local Disk C:

9. In the **General** tab, write down the following information:

   - **How much free space is left in your hard drive?**

10. Click the **Close** button of the Properties dialog box for the Local Disk C:

11. Click the **Close** button of the My Computer window

12. From the information you have gathered, determine how much more than the minimum requirements for Windows XP Professional presented earlier in this chapter (Figure 1.1) this system contains

hands-on
projects

challenge

1. Using the View Menu to Arrange a Window

Elena Stallings manages an electronics and computer store in a busy downtown location. She has just received a shipment of monitors with excellent picture quality, and she wants to show them off in her storefront window. All of the monitors are connected to computers running Windows XP as the operating system. She asks you to display beautiful pictures in each of the monitors that are in her store's window.

1. Click **Start,** then **My Pictures**
2. Double-click the **Sample Pictures** folder. Four small pictures are displayed
3. Right-click on **Sunset;** a context menu appears
4. Click **Open with** and select **Paint** from the submenu. The Sunset picture appears in a window of the Paint application
5. Click **View** on the menu bar, then click **View Bitmap.** The Sunset picture takes up the entire screen of your monitor, as shown in Figure 1.33. To return to Normal view, click anywhere within the picture, then close Paint and the Sample Picture folder without saving your changes

FIGURE 1.33

The Sunset picture from the Sample Pictures folder viewed as a bitmap takes up your entire monitor screen

on the web

1. Using Help to Fix a Frozen Mouse

Bill Trevor, head of Human Resources at Remington, came to Arthur Kane with a problem: his pointer is frozen on his screen. He has tried to reboot his computer, but to no avail; the problem won't go away. He's asked Arthur to figure out just what is wrong with his mouse.

Arthur knows that there are many sources of help available to solve problems like these. First, Arthur goes to the Windows Help Center by selecting the **Help and Support** command from the **Start** menu. Click the **Search** text box, then type the word **mouse.** Scroll the list of topics until you come to the troubleshooting topic and select

it. The troubleshooter is a Wizard that will guide you through fixing specific hardware problems.

If this doesn't help, the next thing to do is click the **Support** button in the toolbar at the top of the screen. Click *Get help from Microsoft* option on the left pane of the window that opens. This action will open your Web browser and direct you to the Microsoft Web site. Enter **mouse pointer in Windows XP doesn't work** into the *search* box, then press the **Enter** key. The search results list resources on the Microsoft Web site, articles in the Knowledge Base database, and even MSDN (Microsoft Developer Network) articles to help you.

e-business

1. Arranging Multiple Windows on a Desktop

Larry Frost works for Wonder Widget Co., a manufacturer of parts for chemical plants. His boss has assigned Larry a project that involves research. It seems that Wonder Widget's competitors are realizing big savings in purchasing by managing their suppliers through a private Internet portal. Larry's boss doesn't know what a private portal is, but he wants Larry to find out all he can and prepare a report for tomorrow's executive meeting.

Larry realizes that the quickest way for him to find the information he needs to prepare his report is to check the Internet. He wants to check several Web sites and compare the different data from each one. In order to do this, he wants to have multiple Web pages open on his Desktop at the same time so he can easily go back and forth between them.

1. Click **Start,** then **Internet Explorer** to access the Internet

2. Type the following Internet address into the Address bar of your Internet Explorer window: ***www.infoworld.com.*** Then press **Enter.** The Info World home page opens

3. Click the File menu and select **New.** Click **Window** from the submenu. Another window opens with the same page displayed

4. In the address bar of this new window, type ***www.techweb.com,*** then press **Enter**

5. Arrange the window with the Tech Web page so that it is in front, slightly below and to the left of the Info World page so that the Title bars of both pages are visible, as in Figure 1.34. *Hint:* Drag the windows to the position you want by clicking and dragging the Title bar with your mouse.

6. Repeat steps 3 to 5 again, arranging the windows as before, for the following addresses:

   www.wired.com
   www.pcmagazine.com

   Your final result should resemble Figure 1.34. Practice switching between pages by clicking the Title bars to make the selected page active

FIGURE 1.34

The properly arranged Internet Explorer windows

around the world

1. Preparing an Itinerary in WordPad

An executive from Remington Enterprises is visiting Finland, Estonia, and Latvia for meetings with potential clients. You are in charge of preparing an itinerary for him, including lists of cities, hotels, meetings, and the like. Click **Start, Programs, Accessories,** and **WordPad** to open the WordPad application, which is a basic word-processing program that comes with Windows XP. Type the following itinerary:

> **March 17—Arrive Helsinki, Finland 9:30 a.m. local time**
>
> - **Check in the Ambassador Hotel**
> - **Meeting at 2:00 p.m.**
>
> **March 18—Leave Helsinki 10:30 a.m., arrive Tallinn, Estonia at 12:00 p.m.**
>
> - **Check in the Novotel Hotel**
> - **Meeting at 3:30 p.m.**
>
> **March 19—Leave Tallinn 8:45 a.m., arrive Riga, Latvia 9:15 a.m.**
>
> - **Check in Metropol Hotel**
> - **Lunch meeting at 12:30 p.m.**
>
> **March 20—Leave Riga 10:30 a.m. for return flight home**

Click **Save** and name the document **Itinerary** and print it out.

WINDOWS XP

did you know?

SETI, *the Search for Extraterrestrial Intelligence organization, reached a milestone in the spring of 2002 by having spent 1 million years of computer time searching for a sign that something other than us is out there. SETI accomplished this in only three "real" years thanks to millions of people who allowed their computers to be used when idle to combine their computing power in the search.*

mexico *is the eleventh ranked country in the world as a tourist destination, with sales to the United States alone reaching almost 1 billion dollars a year.*

according *to a poll, while 90 percent of patients want to exchange e-mail with their doctors, only 15 percent of doctors do so.*

a *cat walking across a computer keyboard can enter random data and commands, which may damage files or the computer itself, but a new shareware program can distinguish "cat typing" from "human typing" within two paw steps and emit a sound that irritates the cat so that it gets off the keyboard.*

mosquitoes *are attracted to humans by the carbon dioxide we exhale when we breathe. Therefore, if you don't want to attract mosquitoes, don't breathe.*

Chapter Objectives

- Learn to navigate the file system
- Move, copy, and delete files
- Learn about WordPad and Notepad, two applications for creating text files
- Set paragraph margins and alignment
- Create bulleted lists
- Change the size, style, and typeface of text

CHAPTER

2

two

Word
Processing and
Basic File
Management

The Printed Word

Stacey Keith is a freshman at the local college. For the summer break she took a position as receptionist and office manager at The Printed Word, a typing service used by authors to save them from having to do their own typing. Computers had long ago replaced the typewriters, and the "typists," now called "word processors," submitted their work as word-processing files on floppy disks. These files were copied to a computer at the main office, where they were sent out for printing. After a certain amount of time, the files were removed from the system.

As the receptionist, Stacey would be responsible for typing all the memos and other correspondence for the firm. The company used a specific format for its documents—always the same font and margins, with the company name across the top of the page. Stacey's first task was to write a letter to a client using the WordPad application. The letter contained a list of the documents they would be working on for that client.

Stacey also was responsible for keeping track of the files submitted by the word processors. She needed to set up a system of folders on her computer to organize the files and copy the files from floppy disks to these folders. She'd need to move files among folders and delete files when they became obsolete.

F I G U R E   2.1
Stacey's memo

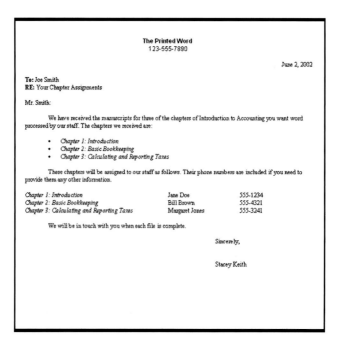

INTRODUCTION

Creating documents and managing files are two of the most common tasks performed using a computer.

Windows XP Professional comes with WordPad and Notepad, two programs for creating text files. You can use WordPad to create basic documents with some degree of formatting. Notepad only creates plain text files.

You store your files on your computer using Windows XP's hierarchical system of folders. You can move and copy files among folders and delete files you no longer need.

You can also store your files on floppy disks. The disks must be correctly formatted so you can copy files onto them.

This chapter explores the basics of using a word processor to create a file, including formatting text and changing fonts. It also provides an introduction to managing files and working with floppy disks.

SESSION 2.1 MANAGING FILES AND FOLDERS

The Windows XP Professional environment makes it easy to organize your work.

Managing your files in Windows XP is exactly like working in an office and filing your papers in manila folders. You can create new folders, move information among folders, and discard information when you no longer need it.

NAVIGATING THE DIRECTORY STRUCTURE

You can use My Computer or Windows Explorer for viewing and managing folders and files.

Using My Computer

My Computer is one of the icons on your Start menu. Click My Computer to display a list of drives.

Double-click a drive to display the files and folders in that drive. Double-click a folder to display the folders and files it contains. Double-click a file to open that file using an appropriate application.

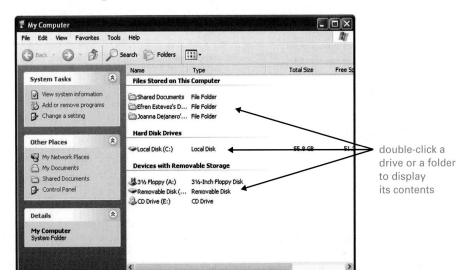

FIGURE 2.2

Navigating in My Computer

double-click a drive or a folder to display its contents

task **reference**

Navigating with My Computer

- In the Start menu, click **My Computer** to display the drives on your computer
- Double-click a drive to display the folders in that drive
- Double-click a folder to display the contents of that folder
- Double-click a file to open the file

USING WINDOWS EXPLORER

Like a map, Windows Explorer shows you the location of every file and folder on your computer. Windows Explorer also helps you understand the relationship between files, folders, and drives. It does this by organizing and displaying the contents of your computer or local network graphically in a hierarchical structure, known as a tree structure.

*another*word

The Windows key, also called the "Winkey" (pronounced "win-key," not wink-key), is a potentially valuable shortcut to use for many commands. Many keyboards have one of them on either side of the space bar. Pressing the Winkey opens the Start menu, and pressing it again closes it. As described in the text, pressing the **Winkey + E** opens Windows Explorer. **Winkey + D** displays the Desktop. Another useful command is **Winkey + M,** which minimizes all the windows you have open, while **Winkey + Shift + M** maximizes all your windows again.

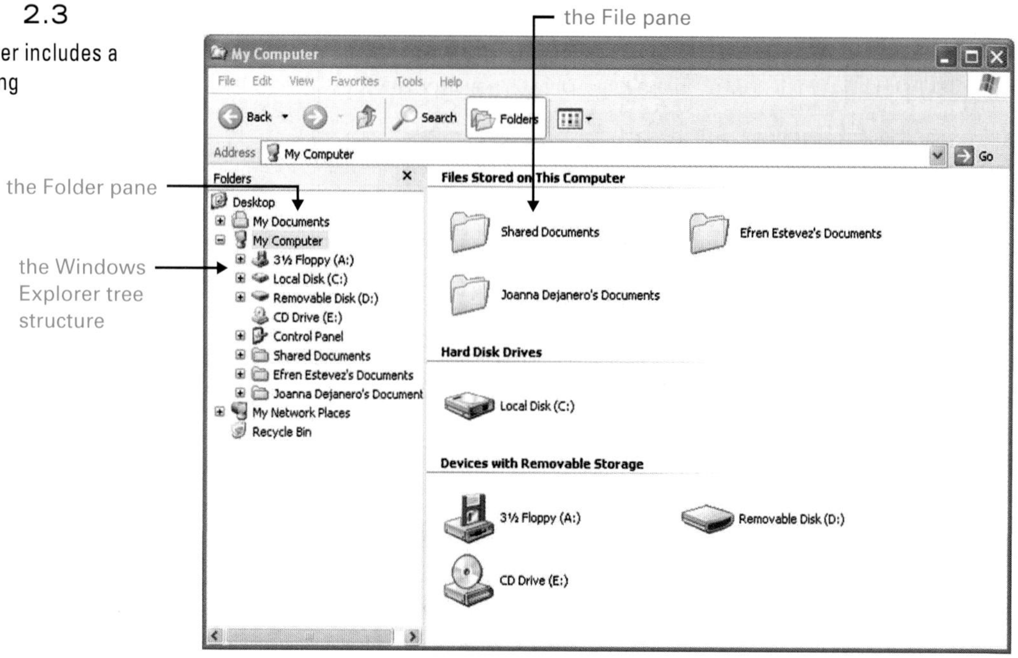

Windows Explorer adds a tree structure to the left of the window. Explorer's left pane is called the Folder pane, and it contains a hierarchical listing of files and folders. Explorer's right pane is called the File pane, and it displays the files and folders inside the selected drives or folders.

To display Windows Explorer, hold down the Windows key (the key with the Windows logo on your keyboard, usually located next to the Alt or Ctrl keys) and press E.

Alternately, you can also right-click a drive or folder, then click Explore in the context menu.

FIGURE 2.3

Windows Explorer includes a tree for navigating

the File pane

the Folder pane

the Windows Explorer tree structure

The top level of the hierarchy lists the drives from My Computer. Click a plus sign to display in the tree the folders contained in a drive or folder. Click a minus sign to hide the folders contained in that drive or folder.

If a folder only contains files, it does not display a plus or minus sign. Only drives and folders display in the tree.

Click a folder in the tree to display its contents in the right pane. The right pane works exactly like My Computer.

---

task reference

Displaying and Navigating with Windows Explorer

- To display the Explorer, right-click **My Computer,** then click **Explore** in the context menu

- Click a plus (+) sign to display in the tree the folders contained in the drive or folder

- Click a minus (−) sign to hide the folders contained in the drive or folder

- Click a drive or folder to display its contents in the right pane

---

FIGURE 2.4

Navigating in Windows Explorer

click a + sign to display the next level of folders

click a folder to display its contents in the right pane

click a − sign to hide the next level of folders

Practicing with navigating My Computer and Windows Explorer:

Stacey had a few minutes and she decided to use the time to familiarize herself with the way The Printed Word had its files and folders set up. She used the Start menu to go eXPloring.

1. Click the **Start** menu, then click **My Computer**
2. Double-click your **C** drive to display the folders and files on your computer

---

WINDOWS XP

3. Double-click the **Program Files** folder

4. Double-click the **Windows NT** folder

5. Double-click the **Accessories** folder

6. Close all the windows

7. Right-click **My Computer** in the Start menu

8. In the context menu, click **Explore**

9. Click the + sign next to the C drive

10. Click the + sign next to the **Program Folders** file

11. Click the + sign next to the **Windows NT** folder

12. Click the **Accessories** folder. The right pane now contains the same folders as the last window you displayed using My Computer

ABOUT CONTEXT MENUS

Every object you use in Windows XP displays a context menu when you right-click it. For the purpose of this discussion, the term "object" includes everything on the Desktop or within Windows Explorer.

Every context menu for a file or a folder contains several sections (separated by a line in the menu), and each section has a different purpose. The sections and options that display depend on the properties of the object.

F I G U R E   2.5

Any object, folder, file, or icon displays a context menu when right-clicked

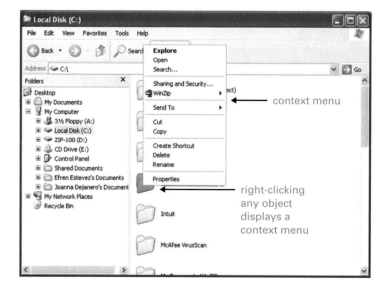

Actions

The first section of the context menu tells you what kinds of actions you can perform with the object. The default action—normally Open—appears in boldface. Sometimes a Print action appears. If you right-click a folder icon (as opposed to a file icon), you'll normally see an Explore and a Search listed along with Open.

If you have WinZip (a very useful utility that compresses and decompresses your files) installed, the menu will offer three options: zipping the file, quick zipping the file based on a suggested zip filename, and finally zipping the file and e-mailing it. All of these actions are very useful. If you don't have WinZip, you can download it from www.zdnet.com.

Another option you may see in the context menu is Open With . . ., which allows you to choose which program to use to open the file.

Send to

This entry in the context menu allows you to send the folder to another location, whether it's another folder or drive. Windows XP lists your floppy disk, the Desktop (to create a shortcut), Mail Recipient, My Documents, and any Removable drives you may have installed as destinations.

Editing

This section of the context menu contains entries for Cut, Copy, and Paste. You can copy an object and then paste copies as needed into other areas.

Note that these are actually copies of the object, not a shortcut. If you cut an object, Windows doesn't remove the icon from the display. It grays out the icon and waits until you paste the object somewhere else before removing it permanently. This prevents you from accidentally erasing objects. Cutting a new object before pasting the first one leaves the first object intact. Windows XP waits to remove the first file until you find a new location for it.

Network

This section usually contains a single entry: Sharing. Note that some objects support sharing and others don't. Chapter 8 will discuss networking and sharing.

Manipulation

This section usually contains three entries. The Create Shortcut option enables you to place a link to a file or folder someplace else on your computer (usually the Desktop). The Delete option sends the file to the Recycle Bin. The Rename option allows you to change the name of the object.

Compression and Decompression

These two entries are only visible if you have an NTFS formatted drive. One enables you to compress the file; the other enables you to decompress it.

Properties

This entry displays a dialog box that enables you to view and configure the properties of that particular object. This is a quick and easy way to reconfigure any one of a number of different options, even run Maintenance tools if you open a disk's properties. It is worth your time to investigate the Properties dialog box of your objects.

Other Options

In addition to the options described above, some objects have specialized context menu entries. The Recycle Bin, for example, has an option to empty it. The Desktop has a New option you can use to create new files.

CHANGING HOW FOLDERS DISPLAY

Up to now you've used the Windows XP default settings for displaying files and folders. Windows XP provides other options for how files and folders are represented on the screen; it also allows you to sort files so they're in the order you need.

Using Different Views

Windows XP Professional has "views" for displaying files and folders. Each view represents the information slightly differently.

- *Tiles.* A large icon labeled with its name represents each file or folder. You can drag the icons to different areas of the window. This view is best for folders with few files or folders.

FIGURE 2.6

Tiles view displays large folder icons

change Folder views using the View menu

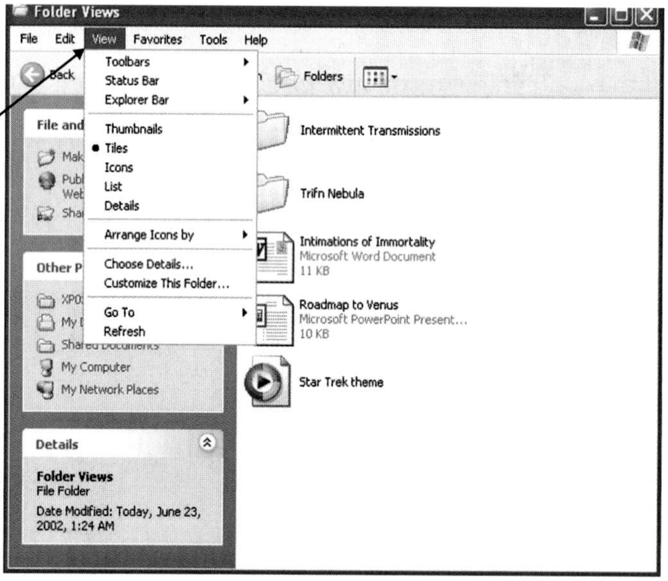

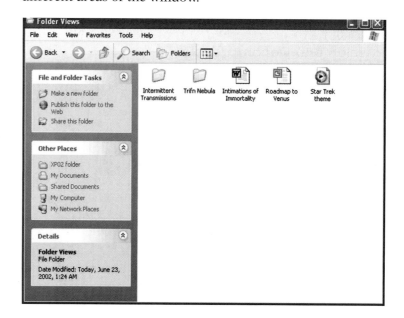

- *Icons.* Represents each object with a smaller icon, with the name underneath. As in the Tiles view, you can move the objects to different areas of the window.

FIGURE 2.7

Icons view displays smaller icons than Tiles view

- *List.* Like Small Icons, a small icon represents each object with the name to the right. However, you cannot move the icons in the window. The list of objects wraps to additional columns.

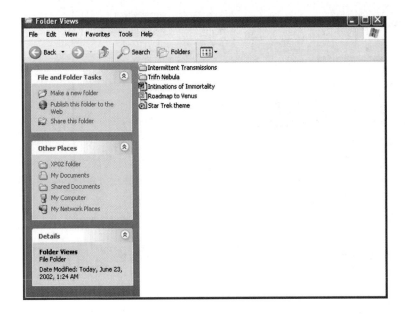

FIGURE 2.8
List view

- *Details.* The Details view is a table listing the files and folders in the first column. Additional columns contain each object's size, type of file, and the date the object was last changed.

FIGURE 2.9
Details view

- *Thumbnails.* If a folder contains graphic files, the Thumbnails view displays small versions of each picture, with the name underneath it.
- *Filmstrip.* Pictures folders have a Filmstrip view allowing you to scroll through multiple images using the buttons in the middle of the screen.

Windows XP provides multiple methods for changing the view. The easiest method is to use the View button on the window's toolbar.

F I G U R E   2.10

Thumbnails view is good for displaying graphic files

F I G U R E   2.11

Pictures folders have a Filmstrip view allowing you to scroll through multiple images

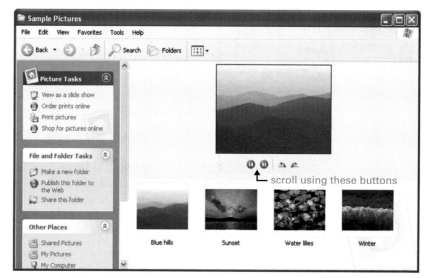

scroll using these buttons

---

*another*way

. . . to Change Views

You can also use the View menu or the folder window's context menu to change the view. In the **View** menu, click the view you want to use

Or

Right-click the folder's window. In the context menu, click **View.** In the **View** submenu, click the view you want to use

---

task reference

Changing the Folder View

- On the menu bar, click the **View** button

- In the list of views, click the view you want to use

Sorting Files and Folders

By default, Windows XP sorts objects by name. If a folder contains both folders and files, the folders are sorted by name first, and then the files are sorted.

You may, however, want to sort information differently. You might want to group your WordPad files together or see which file you last updated.

Windows XP allows you to sort files by the following:

- *Name.* The default. Alphabetizes the files and folders.

- *Type.* Groups the folders and files by type. Within each type, alphabetizes the objects.
- *Size.* Sorts the files by size.
- *Date.* Sorts the files by the date they were last updated.

The Arrange Icons option in the View menu or the context menu allows you to sort the objects.

---

task reference

Sorting Files and Folders

- Click the **View** menu, and click **Arrange Icons,** *or* right-click the window, then click **Arrange Icons** in the context menu

- In the Arrange Icons submenu, click the method to sort the objects

- To reverse the sort order, sort the window again by the same method

---

anotherway

. . . to Sort Objects

Using the Details view makes it very easy to sort files:

Just click the heading of the column you want to sort by. Click a second time to reverse the order of the sort

---

Practicing viewing and sorting files:

1. Open the Accessories folder **(Start/All Programs/ Accessories)**

2. Click the **View** button on the toolbar, then click **Icons** in the menu

3. Use the View button again to change the view to **Details**

4. Click the **Type** column heading. Note how the files are grouped by their file extensions

5. Click the **Name** column heading

6. Click the **Name** column heading again. The files are sorted in reverse order

---

CREATING FOLDERS

Once you begin creating your own files, you'll want to create folders in which to store them. You can create folders in a drive or in another folder.

To create a folder in the current drive or folder, you can use the File menu or the window's context menu. You're prompted for a name for the folder when you create it.

---

task reference

Creating a Folder

- Click the **File** menu, and click **New,** *or* right-click the window, then click **New** in the context menu

- Click the **New** submenu, then click **Folder**

- Type the name of the new folder, then press **Enter**

WINDOWS XP

FIGURE 2.12

New folders

> ### *Creating folders to organize documents:*
>
> *When Stacey first arrived, she needed to organize the current files they had received from the word processors. Stacey decided she should set up individual folders for each word processor—one for Jane Dorman, one for Bill Brown, and one for Mary Jones.*
>
> 1. Open **My Documents**
> 2. Right-click an empty space in the right side of the window
> 3. In the context menu, click **New,** then click **Folder**
> 4. In the folder label, type **Dorman,** then press **Enter**
> 5. Create another folder named **Brown**
> 6. Create a third folder named **Jones**

RENAMING FILES AND FOLDERS

You may sometimes want to change the name of a file or folder. Windows XP provides a quick way to rename a file or folder.

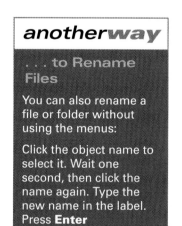

task reference

Renaming a File or Folder

- Right-click the file or folder
- In the context menu, click **Rename.** The Rename option is also in the File menu
- Type the new name in the object label
- Press **Enter**

Renaming a folder:

After creating her new folders, Stacey realized that she should add the first name to Bill Brown's folder, since Gwen Brown would be starting work in a couple of weeks.

1. Click the **Brown** folder

2. Click the folder again

3. In the text label, type **Bill Brown**

tip: *If you're renaming a file (not a folder), make sure not to type over the file extension (.doc, .txt, etc.). This may make the file unreadable*

4. Press **Enter**

FILE NAMING CONVENTIONS

File naming conventions are naming rules for files. These rules are not the same on all operating systems. Windows XP supports long filenames that can consist of up to 256 characters, including spaces.

However, you probably shouldn't create filenames with 256 characters. Most programs cannot interpret extremely long filenames. Long filenames also can be cumbersome to view in their entirety. Unless you enlarge the Name column, only a certain number of characters at the beginning of a filename are displayed.

It's worth it to spend a little time coming up with short, yet descriptive as possible, filenames. Too short and you won't know what the file is. Too descriptive and you'll end up with a cumbersome name to work with. Don't think that software designers don't spend a lot of time, trial, and error making sure the default names assigned to files and folders in their programs are clear, concise, and descriptive. Additionally, filenames cannot contain the following characters: \ / : * ? " < > |

If you use the classic Windows view, you can rename an object by slowly (wait between clicks) double-clicking the filename. Then just type the new name underneath the icon. From any view, you can rename a file or folder by right-clicking it and then clicking Rename in the context menu. You do not need to open the file or folder to rename it. The name of system folders such as Documents and Settings, Winnt, or System32 cannot be changed because they are required for Windows to run properly.

MOVING AND COPYING FILES AND FOLDERS

Moving and copying are two common functions you need to perform while managing files. When you *move* an object, you physically remove it from one location and place it in another. When you *copy* an object, you make a copy of an object and place the copy in another location. The original object remains in place.

Windows XP provides multiple methods for moving and copying files and folders.

Selecting Objects to Move or Copy

You can copy and move more than one object at a time.

To select a group of objects that are next to each other, click the first object, and then press the Shift key as you click the last object.

To select individual objects one at a time, click the first object, and then hold down the Ctrl key as you click each additional object.

To select all the objects in a folder, click the Edit menu, and then click Select All.

F I G U R E   2.13

Selecting objects to move or copy

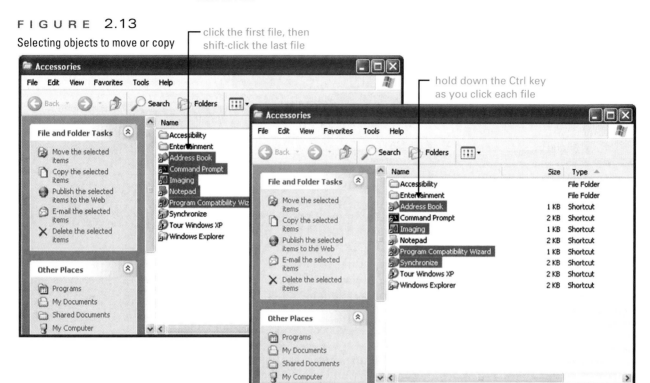

task reference

Selecting Files and Folders to Move or Copy

- To select a range of objects, click the first object, then press the **Shift** key as you click the last object

- To select individual objects, click the first object, then hold down the **Ctrl** key as you click each additional object

- To select all of the objects in a folder, click the **Edit** menu, then click **Select All**

Copying or Moving by Dragging

One way to move or copy objects is to drag them to the new location.

In My Computer, you can drag objects to folders within the current folder or to the window for another folder. You can drop the object in the window of a folder or drag the object over the destination folder. The destination folder is highlighted when the object is over it.

In Windows Explorer, you can drag objects to the folders in the tree structure.

Windows XP has rules for determining whether an object is copied or moved when you drag it. If you drag an object to a folder on the same drive, Windows assumes you want to move it to that location. To create a copy instead, press the Alt key as you drag the file.

If you drag an object to a different drive, such as a floppy disk or a network, Windows assumes you want to copy it. To move the object instead, press the Shift key as you drag the file.

If a plus sign (+) appears next to the objects as you drag them, then they are being copied.

---

task reference

Copying and Moving Objects by Dragging

- Select the objects to move or copy

- Drag the objects until they are in the new location. Hold down the **Alt** key to make sure the files are copied, or the **Shift** key to make sure the files are moved

- Release the mouse button to copy or move the files to the new location

---

Using Cut/Copy and Paste to Copy and Move Files

Another way to move and copy files is to use the Cut and Copy options in the Edit menu.

The Copy option makes a copy of the selected objects and places it on the Clipboard. The selected objects remain in their original location.

The Cut option deletes the selected objects and places them on the Clipboard.

Once you have the objects on the Clipboard, navigate to the new location, and then use the Edit menu's Paste option to paste the objects from the Clipboard to the new location.

If you paste a copied object in the same location, the words "Copy of" are placed in front of the pasted object's name.

Even after you paste the objects, they remain on the Clipboard until you cut or copy another object. You can paste cut or copied objects into multiple locations.

---

task reference

Copying and Pasting Objects

- Select the objects to copy

- Click the **Edit** menu, then click **Copy**

- Open the location where you want to copy the objects

- Click the **Edit** menu, then click **Paste**

Cutting and Pasting Objects

- Select the objects you want to move

- Click the **Edit** menu, then click **Cut**

- Open the location where you want to move the objects

- Click the **Edit** menu, then click **Paste**

Moving and copying files:

Stacey needed to copy each word processor's files into their respective folders. The name of each file included the name of the word processor. In your data files for this chapter, locate the XP02copymove-data folder. Inside this folder are the files you need for this exercise.

1. Click **Bell Chapter Three_Brown**

2. As you hold down the **Ctrl** key, click **Jackson Article_Brown,** then click **Kelman White Paper_Brown**

3. Drag the selected files to the **Bill Brown** folder

4. When the **Bill Brown** folder is highlighted, release the mouse button. The files are copied to the **Bill Brown** folder

5. Use the same technique to move **Bell Chapter Two_Dorman, Bell Chapter Four_Dorman,** and **McDougal Proposal_Dorman** to the **Dorman** folder

6. Click **Bell Chapter One_Jones**

7. Press the **Shift** key, then click **Young Proposal_Jones.** All three remaining files are selected

8. Drag the files to the **Jones** folder

DELETING FILES AND FOLDERS

Once files become outdated or obsolete, you'll want to delete them from the computer.

To delete folders or files, select the objects you want to delete, and then select Delete from the File menu. You can also use the Delete key on the keyboard.

When you delete a file from your computer, it is initially placed in the Recycle Bin, where it stays until you empty the bin. You can remove a file from the Recycle Bin before it is permanently deleted.

Once you're sure you don't want the file, you can empty the Recycle Bin to delete the file permanently.

The Recycle Bin only works with files that are on your computer. When you delete files from a floppy disk or the network, they are deleted permanently.

*another*way

. . . to Delete Objects

Instead of selecting **Delete** from the File menu, you can press the **Delete** key to delete selected objects

task reference

Deleting Files and Folders

- Select the objects to delete
- Click the **File** menu, then click **Delete**

Retrieving Deleted Objects from the Recycle Bin

- Double-click the **Recycle Bin**
- Drag the object from the **Recycle Bin** to the Desktop or a folder on your computer

task reference

Emptying the Recycle Bin

- Right-click the **Recycle Bin**
- In the context menu, click **Empty Recycle Bin**

Deleting a file:

Stacey's boss called to let her know that the Young proposal file had to be deleted from the system. Mr. Young had his finished file and wanted to make sure it was removed from The Printed Word's computer.

1. Double-click the **Jones** folder
2. Click **Young Proposal_Jones**
3. Click the **File** menu, then click **Delete**
4. Double-click the **Recycle Bin.** The Recycle Bin now contains the deleted file

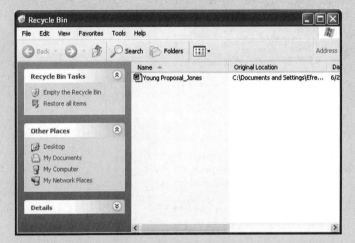

FIGURE 2.14

Recycle Bin with a deleted file

5. Click the **File** menu, then click **Empty Recycle Bin**
6. Click **Yes** to confirm you want to permanently delete the file

making the grade

SESSION 2.1

1. The difference between My Computer and Windows Explorer is that Windows Explorer adds a _____ on the left pane of the window.

2. To make sure files are copied and not moved, hold down the _____ key as you drag the files.

3. The _____ view is mostly used for graphics.

4. Hold down the _____ key when selecting individual files that are not next to each other.

5. You permanently remove deleted files by _____ the Recycle Bin.

SESSION 2.2 FINDING FILES ON YOUR COMPUTER

FINDING RECENTLY USED FILES

Windows XP makes managing your frequently used files easy. It does this by keeping track of the last files you opened or saved. Windows displays the names of these files in a submenu of My Recent Documents in the Start menu. In this way, you can quickly locate and open any of these recently worked on files to review or make changes to them.

When you select a file from the list in the Start menu, the program that created the file is launched and it opens the selected file. This is obviously faster than having to search through multiple layers of hierarchical folders and files to get where you want to be, then opening the particular file. The list displays an icon next to each filename associated with the program that created it, as shown in Figure 2.15, making finding the one you're looking for easier.

FIGURE 2.15

The My Recent Documents submenu in the Start menu

task reference

Opening Recently Used Files

- Click **Start,** then **My Recent Documents**

- Click the file you want to open

Opening recently used files:

1. Click **Start**

2. Click **My Recent Documents.** The list of recently used files opens

3. Click the file you want to open; the program is launched automatically and the selected file opens

You can clear this list of recently used files at any time. Clearing the list is useful when the list becomes full of files that you no longer need regular access to, for example, after you finish a project you've been working on. Clearing the list of recently used files does not delete the files from their original location.

---

task reference

Clearing the My Recent Documents List

- Right-click the **Start** button, then click **Properties**
- In the **Start Menu** tab, click **Customize . . .**
- Click the **Advanced** tab
- Click the **Clear List** button

Clearing the My Recent Documents list:

1. Right-click the **Start** button. A context menu opens

2. Click **Properties.** The Taskbar and Start Menu Properties dialog box opens

FIGURE 2.16

The Taskbar and Start Menu Properties dialog box

3. Click the **Start Menu** tab

4. Click the **Customize...** button. The Customize Start Menu dialog box opens

5. Click the **Clear List** button

6. Click **OK** to close that dialog box, then click **OK** again to close the Taskbar and Start Menu Properties dialog box. If you display the My Recent Documents list, you'll see that it is now empty

WINDOWS XP

FIGURE 2.17

The Customize Start Menu dialog box

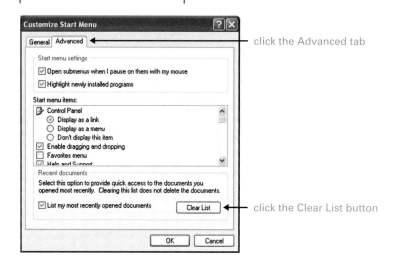

click the Advanced tab

click the Clear List button

SEARCHING FOR DOCUMENTS

If the file you want to work with is not on the list of recently used files, you have to search for it. Finding documents can be difficult, particularly if you are working on a hard disk with hundreds of megabytes of data.

Fortunately, Windows has a very powerful search feature named Search Companion. You can search your computer's hard drive or the Internet, or you can search for people and other computers you want to access. You can locate a file by its name, extension, modification date, size, or other criteria such as author. You can even find a file that contains specific text, even if you don't know the file's name. The Search Companion tool also allows you to look for a file even if you are not exactly sure what the name of the file is. You can also open documents directly from the Search Results dialog box using its associated application.

FIGURE 2.18

The Search Companion window

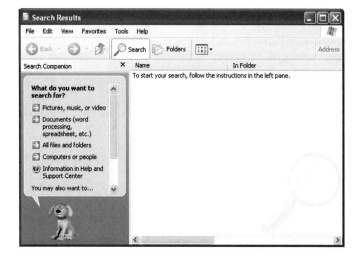

anotherword

. . . on Search Locations

If you think you know the folder where the file is located, you can specify it as part of the search. In the Look in drop-down list, click **Browse.** In the dialog box that displays, click the folder in which to search, then click **OK.**

Searching for a File by Name

The most basic search is to search for a file by name.

reference

Finding a File by Name

- In the Start menu, click **Search**
- In the Search menu, click **All Files and Folders**
- In the All or part of the filename field, type the name of the file you are looking for
- In the Look in drop-down list, select the drive to search in
- Click the **Search** button

Finding a file by name:

1. Click **Start**

2. Click **Search.** The Search Companion window opens

3. Click **All Files and Folders**

4. In the All or part of the filename field, type **setup**

tip: *Instead of typing the entire name of a file, just type the first few letters. Unless the beginning of the filename happens to be a very common one among your files, the list of files found will be short and include the document you are looking for*

5. In the Look in drop-down list, select your hard drive

6. Click the **Search** button. The Search Results window displays the name, location, and other information about all the files whose names contain the word "setup." The contents of the left pane of the window remain visible, while the results of your searches display in the right pane.

7. Double-click the name of the file you are searching for to open it

---

This is the most basic search. There are several more advanced forms of searching, which will be discussed next, but all require you to follow the same steps described above, only the various search options you use on the left pane of the Search Companion window are different.

OTHER SEARCH OPTIONS

Searching for Text within a File

A very useful function of the Search Companion is its ability to locate files that contain a particular word or phrase. This is handy because you can find a file that contains specific text, even if you don't know the file's name.

For example, say you wrote a letter to your mother but can't remember what you called it, but you do remember that you mentioned your pet fish

F I G U R E 2.19

The results of a Search window

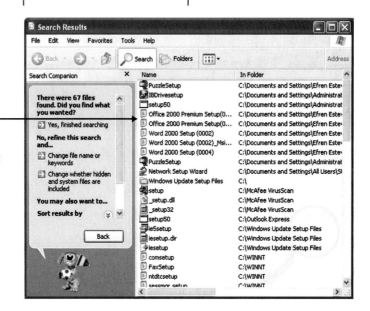

the Search Companion displays all the files and folders found with the word Setup in the title in the right pane of the window

anotherword

. . . on Performing Text Searches

When using a text search, be sure to pick a word or phrase that is unique to that file, rather than common words or phrases, to avoid an unmanageably long list of search results

Sharkey in the text of the letter; you can search for a file that contains the word "Sharkey." Just type "Sharkey" or the unique word or phrase you believe will distinguish the file you seek from all the others in the Containing text field.

A ***text search*** takes longer for Windows to do than other types of searches, since what it is doing is checking the content of every file in the computer, not just the name of the file. This means Windows has a lot more ground to cover.

task reference

Performing a Text Search

- In the Start menu, click **Search**
- In the Search menu, click **All Files and Folders**
- In the *A word or a phrase in the file* field, type the word or phrase you are searching for
- Click the **Search** button

Performing a text search:

1. Click **Start**
2. Click **Search**
3. Click **All Files and Folders**
4. In the *Look in* field, type **C:\WINNT\system;** this narrows the search to a particular folder and all the contents of the selected folder display

5. In the *A word or a phrase in the file* field, type **windows set-up;** this will search for a file in the selected folder that contains the text "windows setup"

6. Click the **Search** button. The search results display in the right pane of the window

7. Close the Search Companion window

You can get access to additional search options by clicking the search options in the lower left pane of the window. Click the link for each option you want to use for the search, then select the criteria for that option by clicking the appropriate radio button.

The additional search options include

- *When was it modified?* This option allows you to find a file by its date.
- *What size is it?* Allows you to search for a file based on its size.
- *More advanced options.* Allows you to search hidden files (files the operating system needs to use and which you normally don't need to change) and to perform a case sensitive search. Case sensitive searches are for filenames that are an exact match in terms of upper and lowercase letters; for example, in a case sensitive search, a search for "Cat" would not find "cat."

Stopping and Clearing Searches

To stop a search at any time, click the Stop button located in the left pane of the Search Companion window. To start a new search, click the Start a new search link at the bottom of the left pane to clear the search criteria you entered and begin a new search.

reference

Stopping a Search

- In the left pane of the Search window, click **Stop**

Clearing the Search Fields

- At the bottom of the left pane of the Search window, click **Start a new search**

SAVING A SEARCH

If you regularly perform the same search, you can save this information so you don't repeatedly have to input the same parameters. The Search Companion utility allows you to save the criteria statements that you have already developed.

After defining the criteria in the Search Results window, you select the Save Search option from the File menu. The saved search criteria are placed in the My Documents folder by default and are represented by a Search icon.

task reference

Saving a Search

- In the Search window, run the search you want to save
- In the File menu, click **Save Search**
- Make any changes for the filename and location, then click **Save**

FIGURE 2.20

The Save Search dialog box

Saving a search:

1. Click **Start**
2. Click **Search**
3. Click **All Files and Folders**
4. In the *All or part of the filename* text box, type **My Pictures**
5. Click the **Search** button
6. In the File menu, click **Save Search.** The Save Search dialog box opens

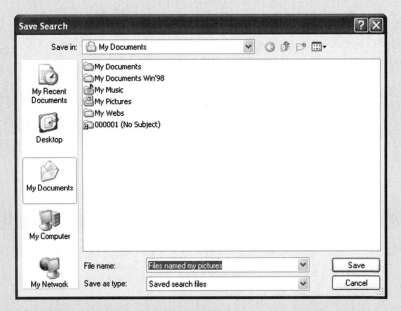

7. Click the **Save** button. Windows saves the search as Files named my pictures in the My Documents folder
8. Close the **Search Results** window
9. Double-click **My Documents** on the Desktop
10. Double-click **Files named my pictures.** The Search Results windows opens and displays the saved search
11. Close the **My Documents** window

SEARCHING USING WILDCARD CHARACTERS

Now you know how to locate individual files, but what if you need to locate a group of files to rename, copy, or move them? Or what if you cannot remember a file's exact name or folder location? Fortunately, this is not a problem as the Search Companion utility allows you to find files using what are called *wildcard characters.*

Wildcard characters are the question mark (?) and the asterisk (*). These characters can help you focus your search by locating specific files, or groups of files, on a disk. The question mark replaces any single character in a filename, while the asterisk can represent several or all the characters in a filename or extension.

For example, if you replace unknown characters in a filename with a question mark when you perform the query WIN???.EXE, matching files that display would include WINZIP.EXE and WINFIX.EXE. When you use an asterisk, it represents zero or more characters in the designated position to represent entire names or extensions. Thus, the query *.DOC will bring up all the files with the .DOC extension.

---

task reference

Using Wildcard Characters to Search

- To represent an individual character in a search field, type **?**

- To represent an unknown number of characters in a search field, type *****

Using wildcard characters to search:

One of The Printed Word's staff comes to Stacey with a problem. He has put all the files related to a particularly difficult project in the account file of the customer. He wants to access that file because he has another project for a different customer that almost exactly duplicates it.

Unfortunately, he can't remember the exact name of the original customer. Stacey shows the staff member that he can substitute an asterisk for the unknown account name and Windows will find any files or folders that match the name.

1. In the Start menu, click **Search**

2. In the Search Results window, click **All files and folders**

3. In the *All or part of a filename* field, type **c???????.exe**

4. Click the **Search** button. After a few moments, the right pane displays the results of your search

5. Click the **Change file name or keywords** link. A new text box opens

6. Type ***.exe**

7. Click **Search.** All the files with the .exe filename extension display

making the grade

1. _____ are a set of rules for naming files.

2. A type of search for when you remember a word or words used in a file is a _____ search.

3. If you are curious about what files are taking up the most room on your hard drive, do a search by file _____.

4. Use _____ in the search criteria if you want to find all the files with the .exe filename extension.

5. If you frequently need to do the same search, you should _____ it.

SESSION 2.3 USING WORDPAD

You will find that a good percentage of the work you do on the computer is with a word-processing program.

For working with text, Windows XP Professional comes with WordPad. WordPad is a basic *word processor.*

This session discusses WordPad and shows you how to use this program to create and format documents.

THE WORDPAD INTERFACE

Starting WordPad

Like all programs, WordPad is available from your All Programs menu, in the Accessories submenu.

task reference

Starting the WordPad Application

- Click the **Start** button

- In the Start menu, click **All Programs**

- In the Programs menu, click **Accessories**

- In the Accessories submenu, click **WordPad**

Opening the WordPad application:

1. Click the **Start** button

2. In the Start menu, click **All Programs**

3. In the All Programs menu, click **Accessories**

4. In the Accessories submenu, click **WordPad.** The WordPad window opens, with a new blank document displayed

The WordPad window has the same elements as all windows.

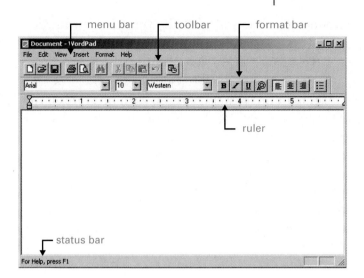

FIGURE 2.21
The WordPad window

WordPad Menus

The WordPad menu bar provides access to options for creating, formatting, and printing your documents.

FIGURE 2.22
The WordPad menu bar

- *File.* Provides options for creating, saving, and printing your file.
- *Edit.* Provides access to basic editing functions, such as cutting, copying, and pasting text, plus a find option to search for or replace a word or phrase.
- *View.* Allows you to turn window elements on or off.
- *Insert.* Allows you to insert the date and time, or another object. Inserting objects is discussed later in the book.
- *Format.* Provides options for changing the format of paragraphs and text.
- *Help.* Provides access to WordPad's Help window.

WordPad Toolbar

The WordPad toolbar provides easy shortcuts to some of the functions in the menus.

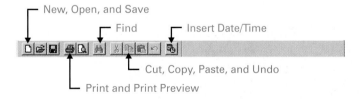

FIGURE 2.23
The WordPad toolbar

- *New.* Creates a new blank document.
- *Open.* Displays a window to allow you to find and open a file that's already been created.
- *Save.* Saves the work you have created. The first time you save the file, you must give it a name and location.

- *Print.* Sends your document to your default printer to be printed.
- *Print Preview.* Shows you what your document will look like when it's printed.
- *Find.* Allows you to find a word or words in a document.
- *Cut.* Cuts a highlighted word or phrase in the document. It is temporarily placed on a virtual ***clipboard*** and can be pasted somewhere else in the document.
- *Copy.* Creates a copy of a highlighted word or phrase and places it on the Clipboard.
- *Paste.* Pastes the last cut or copied text into the document.
- ***Undo.*** Undoes your last move.
- *Insert Date/Time.* Allows you to insert the current date and/or time in the document.

Format Bar

The format bar below the toolbar also provides a quick way to perform functions from the menu. It allows you to quickly change the format of your text.

FIGURE 2.24

The WordPad format bar

It allows you to select a font size and type, and to highlight your text with bold, italic, underline, and color.

You can use bullets, change the text to left justified, centered, or right justified, simply by clicking the button that depicts the format you want.

Ruler

The ruler allows you to modify paragraph indents and tab stops.

FIGURE 2.25

The WordPad ruler

Status Bar

The status bar at the bottom of the WordPad window displays status messages from WordPad on the left. On the right are indicators that show whether the Caps Lock and Num Lock keys are depressed.

FIGURE 2.26

The WordPad status bar

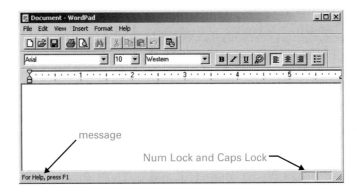

Turning Window Elements On and Off

You can turn the toolbar, format bar, ruler, and status bar on and off, either to see more of your document or because you don't prefer to use those tools.

The View menu allows you to quickly turn these elements on and off.

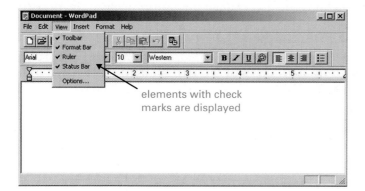

elements with check marks are displayed

FIGURE 2.27

The View menu

In the View menu, each element that is displayed has a check mark in front of it. When you select an element from the menu, the check mark is removed and the element disappears.

Select the element again, and the check mark and element are restored.

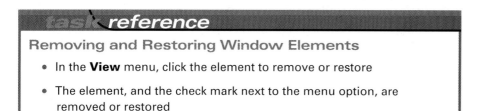

task **reference**

Removing and Restoring Window Elements

- In the **View** menu, click the element to remove or restore

- The element, and the check mark next to the menu option, are removed or restored

Removing and restoring the toolbar:

1. In the **View** menu, click **Toolbar.** The toolbar is removed from the screen

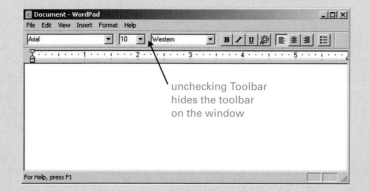

unchecking Toolbar hides the toolbar on the window

FIGURE 2.28

The WordPad window without the toolbar

2. In the View menu, click **Toolbar** again. The toolbar is restored

FORMATTING PARAGRAPHS

Setting a Unit of Measurement

For the purposes of the exercises in this chapter, you will always be using inches, the default unit of measurement.

However, if necessary, you can change the unit of measurement used on the ruler.

---

task **reference**

Changing the Unit of Measurement

- In the View menu, click **Options**
- In the Options dialog box, click the **Options** tab
- Click the radio button next to the unit of measurement you want to use
- Click **OK**

F I G U R E 2.29

Setting the unit of measurement

click a radio button to select a unit of measurement

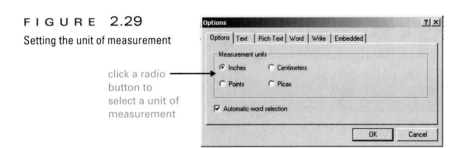

Practicing changing the unit of measurement:

1. In the View menu, click **Options**
2. Click the **Options** tab
3. Click the **Centimeters** radio button
4. Click **OK.** Notice that the ruler has changed to display centimeters instead of inches

F I G U R E 2.30

Ruler displaying centimeters

the ruler adjusts to reflect a different unit of measurement

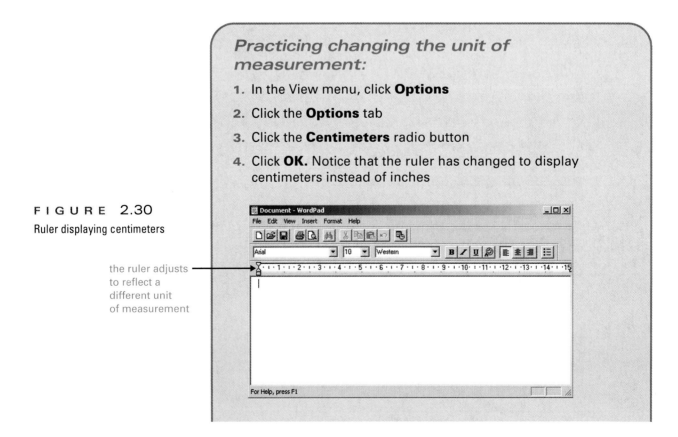

5. Display the **Options** dialog box again

6. Set the unit of measurement back to **Inches**

7. Click **OK**

Setting the Overall Document Margins

Your document needs to be aligned on the paper. You do this by setting *margins* for the document—the space around the edges of each page.

The Page Setup option of the File menu displays a dialog box to allow you to set the document's margins.

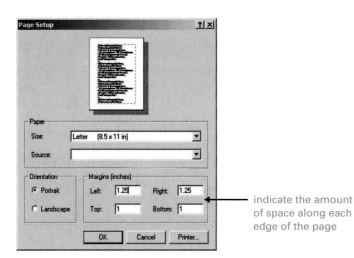

indicate the amount of space along each edge of the page

F I G U R E 2.31

The Page Setup dialog box

---

task reference

Setting a Document's Margins

- In the File menu, click **Page Setup**

- In the Margins area, type the amount of space to use for each edge of the document

- Click **OK**

Setting your document's margins:

The Printed Word's standards included a 1-inch margin around each page of the document. Stacey's first step in creating her memo was to make sure the margins were correct.

1. In the File menu, click **Page Setup**

2. In the Page Setup dialog box, make sure the **Left, Right, Top,** and **Bottom** fields all read 1″

3. Click **OK**

Typing and Creating Paragraphs

To begin creating a WordPad document, you just click the text area and begin typing. The most important divisions of the text are paragraphs.

In WordPad, every time you press the Enter key, you create a new paragraph. Even single letters, lines, or words have paragraph status if you press Enter after typing them. If you press Enter on a blank line, WordPad will consider that a paragraph, although an empty one. You can use blank paragraphs to separate paragraphs with space so they're easier to read.

---

task **reference**

Typing Paragraphs

- Click in the text area, then begin typing

- Press the **Enter** key whenever you want to start a new paragraph

- Use blank paragraphs to create additional space between paragraphs

---

Typing your document text:

Stacey knew the entire text of the memo she had to compose. She started by typing in all of the text. She'd add the formatting later. For the purposes of this exercise, you'll be copying the text of the memo from an existing file.

1. Find the file **XP02memo-data**

2. Open the file

3. In the Edit menu, click **Select All.** The entire memo is highlighted

4. In the Edit menu, click **Copy**

5. Create a new file in WordPad

6. In the Edit menu, click **Paste**

7. Save the new file into the **My Documents** folder as **JoeSmithMemo**

Aligning Paragraphs

While the margin indicates the space around each page, *alignment* refers to where the text in a paragraph sits within the margins.

- *Left justified.* The default standard. Used for most text. Causes the text to be placed flush with the left margin and ragged along the right margin.
- *Center justified.* Centers every line of the paragraph.
- *Right justified.* Causes the text to be placed flush against the right margin and ragged on the left.

Full justification, meaning even margins on the left and right, is not supported by WordPad. More sophisticated word-processing applications do support it. Full justification is often used for newspapers or column type documents.

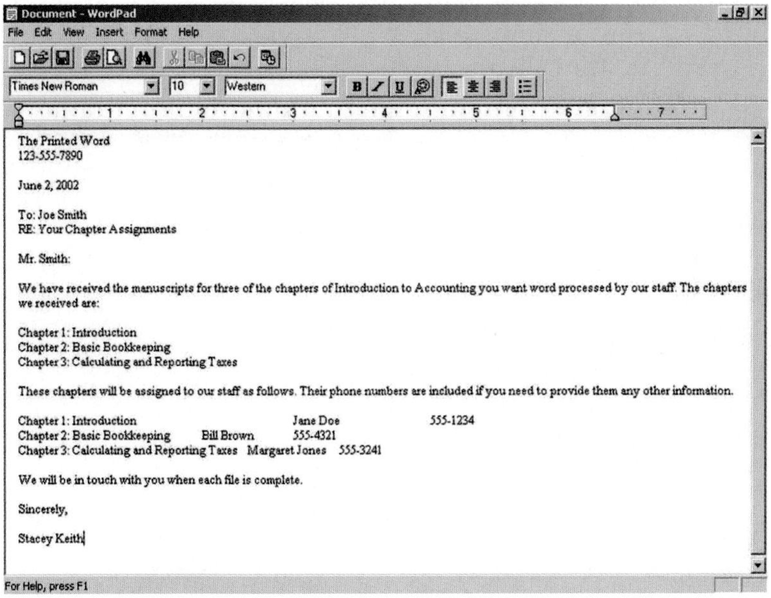

FIGURE 2.32
Memo text without formatting

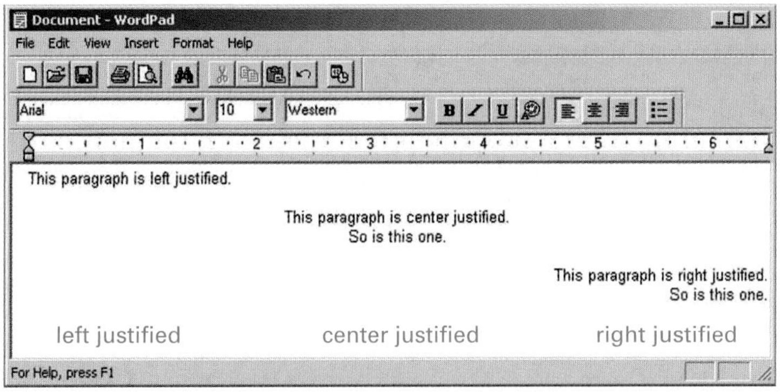

FIGURE 2.33
Paragraphs and alignment

The format bar includes buttons for viewing and setting a paragraph's alignment. To view a paragraph's alignment setting, click the paragraph. The alignment buttons indicate the current setting. You can tell because the button will look like it has been depressed.

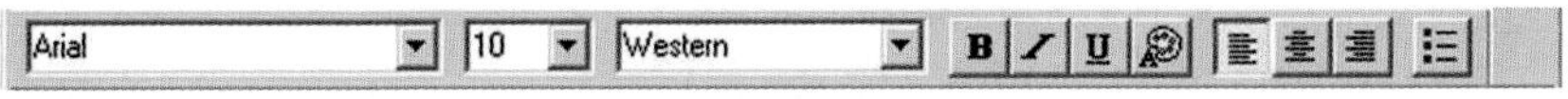

FIGURE 2.34
The alignment buttons on the format bar

task reference

Changing a Paragraph's Alignment

- Move the insertion point to the paragraph
- Click the toolbar icon representing the alignment you want

  or

- In the Format menu, click **Paragraph,** *or* right-click the paragraph, then click **Paragraph** in the context menu
- In the Alignment drop-down list, click the alignment to use
- Click **OK**

Aligning paragraphs:

Now that all of the text was in place, Stacey knew she had to change the alignment of some of the paragraphs. The company name and phone number had to be centered, and the date aligned to the right.

1. Click in the first paragraph. Hold down the mouse button and drag down until the company name and phone number are highlighted

2. In the Format menu, click **Paragraph**

3. From the Alignment drop-down list, select **Center**

4. Click **OK**

5. Click the paragraph containing the date

6. Click the right align button on the format bar

7. Click **Save**

FIGURE 2.35

Memo with new alignments

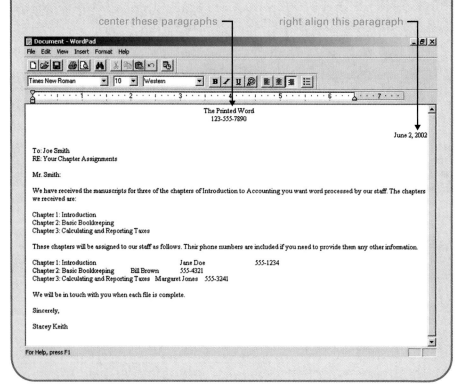

Setting Paragraph Indents

While the margins indicate the overall position of the text on each page, ***indents*** determine how far the edges of a paragraph are from the margins. Indents fall into three categories:

- *Left.* How far in from the left margin a paragraph is placed.
- *Right.* How far in from the right margin a paragraph is placed.
- *First Line.* How far in or out from the left indent the first line of the paragraph is placed. If the first line starts to the left of the rest of the paragraph, it's referred to as an ***outdent.***

You set indents using either the Paragraph dialog box or the ruler. On the ruler, you use the icons on the left and right to adjust the indents.

click and drag to adjust the first line indent

| · · · · · | · · · · 1 · · · · | · · · · 2 · · · · | · · · · 3 · · · · | · · · · 4 · · · · | · · · · 5 · · · · | · · · · |

click and drag to adjust the left indent

F I G U R E   2.36

Adjusting indents on the ruler

task reference

Adjusting Indents Using the Paragraph Dialog Box

- Place the insertion point in the paragraph or select several paragraphs

- In the Format menu, click **Paragraph,** or right-click the paragraph, then click **Paragraph** in the context menu

- Type the indents you want

- Click **OK**

Adjusting Indents Using the Ruler

- Place the insertion point in the paragraph you want to change or select several paragraphs whose setting you want to change

- To adjust the left indent, click the **block** at the bottom of the left margin and drag it to the right

- To adjust the right indent, click the **triangle** at the right margin and drag it to the right

- To adjust the first line indent, click the **top triangle** at the right margin and drag it to the right or left

---

Adjusting paragraph indents:

Stacey's document required different indents for some of the paragraphs. The first line of each paragraph had to be indented .5 inches, and the signature had to be indented 4 inches from the left.

1. Click the first paragraph in the memo ("We have received the manuscripts . . .")

2. In the Format menu, click **Paragraph**

3. In the First Line Indent field, type **.5**

tip: *If you type only a number, the indent will be in inches. If you're using another unit of measurement, you need to specify it in the indent fields. Type* ***cm*** *after the number for centimeters,* ***pt*** *for typesetter's points, or* ***pi*** *for typesetter's picas*

4. Click **OK**

5. Repeat for the other two body paragraphs ("These chapters will be assigned . . ." and "We will be in touch . . .")

6. Select the signature block

WINDOWS XP

7. Click the **square** at the bottom of the left marker on the ruler

8. Drag the marker to the **4**-inch mark, then release the mouse button

9. Click **Save**

FIGURE 2.37

Memo with indents

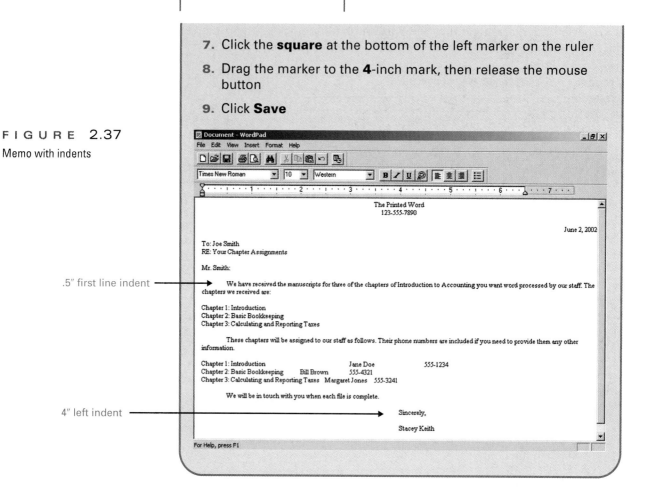

.5″ first line indent ⎯⎯⎯⎯⎯⎯

4″ left indent ⎯⎯⎯⎯

Using Bullets

It is common practice to set off items in a list using ***bullets.*** Bullets make it easier to pick out each item in the list. Bullets are usually bold circular dots but may also be other symbols offset to the left of a paragraph.

FIGURE 2.38

A bulleted list

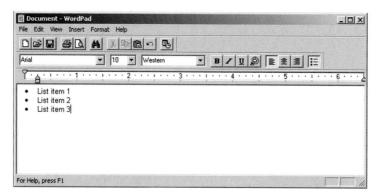

You add bullets to a paragraph by either using the Format menu's Bullet Style option or clicking the bullet icon on the toolbar. Click the icon or select the option again to remove the bullets.

When you add bullets to a paragraph, the bullet is placed at the original left indent of the paragraph, while the rest of the paragraph is shifted to the right in a block fashion. You can change these positions by adjusting the paragraph's indents.

task reference

Adding Bullets to a Paragraph

- Place the cursor in the paragraph to be bulleted or select a group of paragraphs
- In the Format menu, click **Bullet Style,** *or* right-click the paragraph, then click **Bullet Style** in the context menu, *or* click the bullet icon on the toolbar

Creating a bulleted list:

Part of the memo Stacey was creating included a list of chapters. She wanted to add bullets to the list to make it stand out.

1. Select the paragraphs listing the chapters
2. Click the bullet button on the toolbar. You now need to adjust the indents to make the list fit the other paragraphs
3. In the Format menu, click **Paragraph**
4. In the Left field, type **.75**
5. In the First Line field, type **–.25**
6. Click **OK.** The bulleted list is now lined up with the other paragraphs
7. Click **Save**

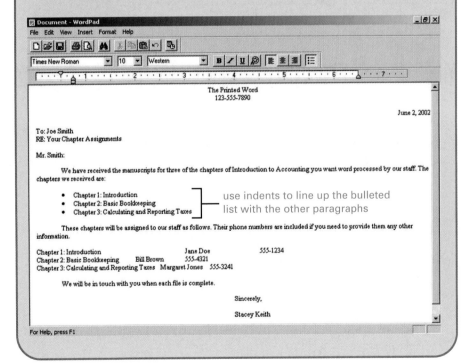

FIGURE 2.39
Memo with bulleted list

Working with Tabs

You might sometimes want to create columns similar to a table within a document. While more advanced word processors will include a table function, in WordPad you use tabs to do this.

You can set up custom **tab stops** in any WordPad document. A tab stop is a place the cursor moves to when you press the Tab key. Default tab stops are already set up in half-inch increments across the page. When you set a tab manually, the default tab stops to the left of it are eliminated.

You create, change, and delete tab stops using either the Tabs dialog box or the ruler.

FIGURE 2.40

The Tabs dialog box

list of custom tab stops

creates a tab stop

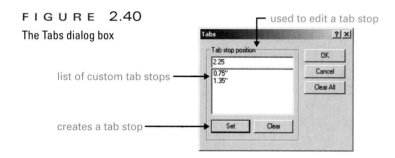

An "L" on the ruler represents any tabs you set manually. If you click the ruler, a new tab is added at that spot. Clicking and dragging the marker moves the tab. If you click and drag the marker off the ruler, the tab is removed.

FIGURE 2.41

Representing tabs on the ruler

custom tabs are represented by an "L"

---

task reference

Adjusting Tab Stops Using the Tabs Dialog Box

- Select the paragraph or paragraphs you want to use the tabs
- In the Format menu, click **Tabs,** or right-click the paragraphs, then click **Tabs** in the context menu
- To create a new tab, type the position in the box, then click **Set**
- To remove a tab, click the tab in the list, then click **Clear**
- When you're finished adjusting the tabs, click **OK**

Adjusting Tabs Using the Ruler

- Select the paragraph or paragraphs you want to use the tab settings
- To create a new tab, click the ruler at the spot you want the new tab
- To move a tab, click the marker and drag it to the new location on the ruler
- To remove a tab, click the marker and drag it off the ruler

Adding tabs to paragraphs:

Part of the memo included a small table with chapter titles, employee names, and phone numbers. Stacey needed to add tabs to the paragraphs so the columns would line up properly.

1. Select the paragraphs listing the chapters and their assigned typists

2. On the ruler, click the **3**-inch mark

3. On the ruler, click the **4½**-inch mark

4. Click **Save**

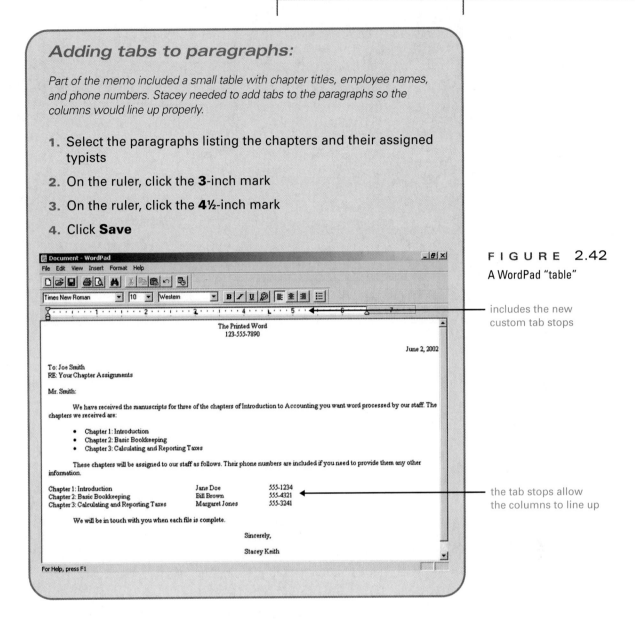

F I G U R E   2.42

A WordPad "table"

includes the new custom tab stops

the tab stops allow the columns to line up

CHANGING THE APPEARANCE OF TEXT

Within each paragraph, you can change the appearance of a single word or the entire paragraph by adjusting:

- The typeface. A typeface is the type of lettering used. Chapter 5 discusses typefaces in more detail.
- The type size.
- The type style (bold, italic, underline).
- The text color.

WordPad's Font dialog box, available from the Format menu, allows you to set all these elements.

However, the easiest way to adjust fonts is to use the format bar. Just select the text you want to change; then use the drop-down lists and icons on the format bar to set individual aspects of the text.

F I G U R E   2.43

Font dialog box

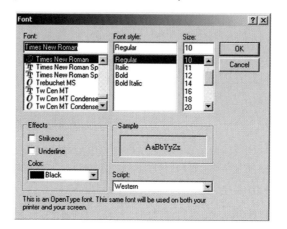

task reference

Changing the Appearance of Text Using the Font Dialog Box

- In the Format menu, click **Font**
- In the Font list, click the typeface you want to use
- In the Font style list, click the type style to indicate whether the text is bold or italic
- In the Size list, click the size of the text
- Under Effects, click the **Underlined** check box to add or remove underlining
- In the Color drop-down list, click the color to use for the text
- Click **OK**

Using the Format Bar to Change Text's Appearance

- Select the text
- Select a typeface from the drop-down list
- Select the type size from the drop-down list
- Click the **B** button to make the text bold
- Click the **I** button to make the text italicized
- Click the **U** button to underline the text
- Click the palette button to display a list of possible text colors, then click a color to select it

Changing the appearance of text:

Stacey knew that she had to change some of the typefaces and styles to fit The Printed Word's style for memos.

A. The company name needed to be **Arial 12 point bold**
B. The company number **Arial 10 point regular**
C. "**To**" and "**RE**" had to be in bold
D. The chapter names had to be italicized

1. Select the company name and number

2. In the typeface drop-down list, click **Arial**

3. Select the company name

4. In the size drop-down list, click **12,** then click the **B** button

5. Select "**To:,**" then click the **B** button

6. Select "**RE:,**" then click the **B** button

7. Select "**Chapter 1: Introduction,**" then click the **I** button. Repeat with the remaining chapter names

8. Click **Save**

Stacey's memo was now complete.

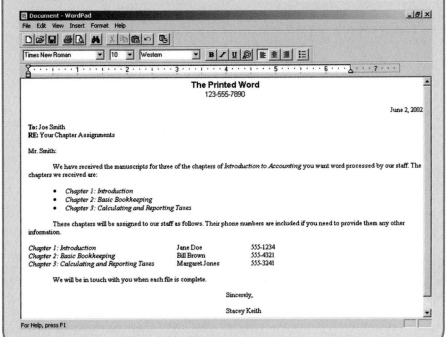

FIGURE 2.44

The final memo

making the grade

1. The _____ menu allows you to display or remove the toolbar.

2. The _____ bar allows you to select a typeface.

3. Default tab stops are set up in _____ increments across the page.

4. If the first line starts to the left of the rest of the paragraph, it's referred to as an _____.

5. The _____ allows you to set tab stops and indents.

SESSION 2.4 USING NOTEPAD

Notepad, a simple *text editor*, allows little in the way of formatting but is useful for keeping notes and writing source code or scripts in plain text. Unlike in WordPad, where you were able to format your text, you can only use Notepad to edit plain text.

Notepad does have some advantages. It takes up much less memory and starts up quicker. You can keep it open all the time, so you can make notes on it whenever you need to. Notepad can provide a convenient place to jot notes or open documents stored as text files. So if the format of the text isn't an issue, feel free to use Notepad.

While older versions of Notepad could not open files that exceeded about 50K in size, Notepad for Windows XP can open files of any size.

F I G U R E 2.45

A Notepad file

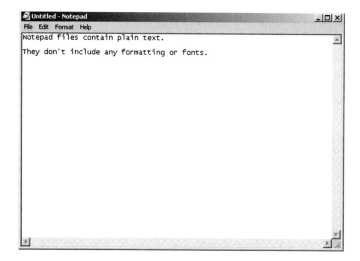

Plain text files are not much to look at. For example, you can only use one font for the entire file. Their basic advantage is that they provide a medium for exchanging text between programs and even between different types of computers. Every system has a different way to create and display text files. Plain text files are the medium for most of the e-mail messages that fly back and forth on the Internet and other information services.

Source code for computer programs is also stored as text files. You may at some point have to edit system configuration files, which qualify as programs. You would use Notepad to edit them.

The plain text files Notepad creates are ***ASCII*** files. ASCII is a basic set of 256 characters (letters, numbers, and punctuation). Windows XP also supports a text called ***Unicode,*** a type of character set that stores twice the information of the common character sets we usually use. This extra storage space is for languages that have more than 256 characters. If you create a file in Notepad and save it, you will have the option to save it in Unicode format. Some programs, however, expect their files to be in ASCII text and will not understand Unicode.

If you use Notepad to open a nonplain text document, the document will open but will not look right. All the extra code used for layouts and fonts display as gibberish.

If you open a nontext file in Notepad, *do not make any changes* to it and *do not save the file.* If you do, you may not be able to use the file, even in the program that originally created it.

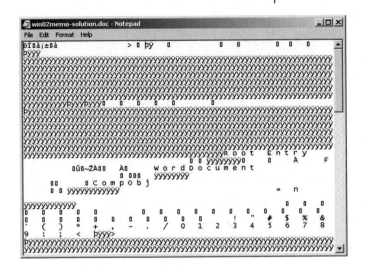

FIGURE 2.46

A nonplain text file opened in Notepad

CREATING NOTEPAD FILES

Starting the Notepad Application

Notepad, like WordPad, is available from the Accessories submenu of the Programs menu.

---

task reference

Starting the Notepad Application

- In the Start menu, click **All Programs**
- In the All Programs menu, click **Accessories**
- In the Accessories submenu, click **Notepad**

Starting Notepad:

Stacey knew she had to go to the office supply store later that day. She decided to quickly type a shopping list in Notepad.

1. Click **Start**
2. In the Start menu, click **Programs**
3. In the Programs menu, click **Accessories**
4. In the Accessories submenu, click **Notepad**

Working with Notepad Text

Notepad has no toolbars or status bars. This reflects Notepad's lack of layout and formatting options.

To enter text in Notepad, just start typing. Text created in Notepad generally looks like text you type on a typewriter.

WINDOWS XP

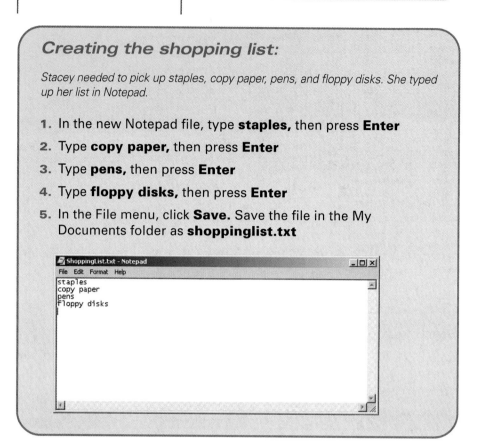

FIGURE 2.47

A Notepad shopping list

In WordPad, when you reached the right margin, the line wrapped automatically. In Notepad, as you reach the end of the window, Notepad just keeps going.

To get the text to wrap to the confines of the displayed window, go to the Format menu and click Wrap. The text automatically wraps to another line when it gets to the right side of the window. This process is called *word wrap*ping.

FIGURE 2.48

Text with and without word wrapping

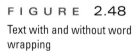

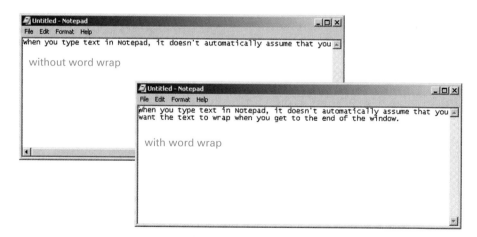

task reference

Wrapping Text in Notepad

- In the Format menu, click **Wrap**

PRINTING NOTEPAD FILES

When you print a Notepad file, Notepad allows you to set up headers and footers. A **_header_** prints on the top of every page. A **_footer_** prints at the bottom of every page.

You set up the headers and footers using the Page Setup dialog box, available from the File menu.

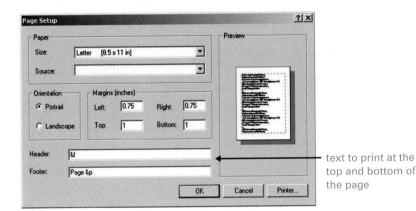

text to print at the top and bottom of the page

FIGURE   2.49

The Notepad Page Setup dialog box

The headers and footers can include text, plus Notepad allows you to enter symbols to represent specific pieces of information.

- _&f._ Notepad prints the name of the file, or "Untitled" if you print the file before you save it.
- _&d._ Notepad prints the current date.
- _&t._ Notepad prints the current time.
- _&p._ Notepad prints the page number.
- _&&._ Notepad prints an ampersand.
- _&l._ Notepad left aligns the header or footer.
- _&c._ Notepad centers the header or footer.
- _&r._ Notepad right aligns the header or footer.

You can also combine the text and symbols. For example, if you want the page number to be preceded by the word "Page," you would type "Page &p" in the Footer field.

Once you set up the headers and footers, they appear on the document every time you print it.

---

task reference

Setting Up Notepad Headers and Footers

- In the File menu, click **Page Setup**
- In the Header field, type the information to print at the top of every page
- In the Footer field, type the information to print at the bottom of every page
- Click **OK**

Printing the shopping list:

Before she printed her list, Stacey wanted to put "Shopping List" in the header and the date in the footer.

1. In the File menu, click **Page Setup**
2. In the Header field, type **Shopping List**
3. In the Footer field, type **&d**
4. Click **OK**
5. In the File menu, click **Print.** The page should print with the header and footer you specified

F I G U R E 2.50

The printed shopping list

```
                          Shopping List
staples
copy paper
pens
floppy disks




                      Tuesday, June 18, 2002
```

SESSION 2.4

making **the grade**

1. The symbol &d puts the _____ in a header or footer.
2. The ASCII character set contains _____ characters.
3. Notepad is considered a _____.
4. The _____ feature keeps text within the window.

SESSION 2.5 SUMMARY

In this chapter you learned that Windows XP Professional includes tools for managing your files and disks. You learned to use My Computer, which lets you look at one folder or resource at a time, and Windows Explorer, which provides a separate tree structure for viewing many resources at once. You learned how to change the view to determine what information displays about the contents of each folder.

You learned how to create folders to manage your files and how to move and copy files among those folders. You also learned how to delete files and how to retrieve deleted information using the Recycle Bin.

You learned to use the WordPad word-processing program. You created a WordPad document, using WordPad's formatting tools to change the margins, alignment, indents, and text formatting.

You also learned how to use the Notepad text editor to create and print plain text files.

task reference roundup

Task	Page #	Preferred Method
Navigating with My Computer	WINXP 2.4	• In the Start menu, click **My Computer** to display the drives on your computer
		• Double-click a drive to display the folders in that drive
		• Double-click a folder to display the contents of that folder
		• Double-click a file to open the file
Displaying and navigating with Windows Explorer	WINXP 2.5	• To display the Explorer, right-click **My Computer**, then click **Explore** in the context menu
		• Click a plus sign (+) to display in the tree the folders contained in the drive or folder
		• Click a minus sign (−) to hide the folders contained in the drive or folder
		• Click a drive or folder to display its contents in the right pane
Changing the folder view	WINXP 2.10	• On the menu bar, click the **View** button
		• In the list of views, click the view you want to use
Sorting files and folders	WINXP 2.11	• In the **View** menu, click **Arrange Icons**, *or* right-click the window, then click **Arrange Icons** in the context menu
		• In the Arrange Icons submenu, click the method to sort the objects
		• To reverse the sort order, sort the window again by the same method
Creating a folder	WINXP 2.11	• In the **File** menu, click **New**, *or* right-click the window, then click **New** in the context menu
		• In the New submenu, click **Folder**
		• Type the name of the new folder, then press **Enter**
Renaming a file or folder	WINXP 2.12	• Right-click the file or folder
		• In the context menu, click **Rename**. The Rename option is also in the File menu.
		• Type the new name in the object label
		• Press **Enter**

task reference roundup

Task	Page #	Preferred Method
Selecting files and folders to move or copy	WINXP 2.14	• To select a range of objects, click the first object, then press the **Shift** key as you click the last object
		• To select individual objects, click the first object, then hold down the **Ctrl** key as you click each additional object
		• To select all of the objects in a folder, click the **Edit** menu, then click **Select All**
Copying and moving objects by dragging	WINXP 2.15	• Select the objects to move or copy
		• Drag the objects until they are in the new location. Hold down the **Alt** key to make sure the files are copied, or the **Shift** key to make sure the files are moved.
		• Release the mouse button to copy or move the files to the new location
Copying and pasting objects	WINXP 2.15	• Select the objects to copy
		• In the **Edit** menu, click **Copy**
		• Open the location where you want to copy the objects
		• In the **Edit** menu, click **Paste**
Cutting and pasting objects	WINXP 2.15	• Select the objects you want to move
		• In the **Edit** menu, click **Cut**
		• Open the location where you want to move the objects
		• In the **Edit** menu, click **Paste**
Deleting files and folders	WINXP 2.16	• Select the objects to delete
		• In the **File** menu, then click **Delete**
Retrieving deleted objects from the Recycle Bin	WINXP 2.16	• Double-click the **Recycle Bin**
		• Drag the object from the **Recycle Bin** to the Desktop or a folder on your computer
Emptying the Recycle Bin	WINXP 2.17	• Right-click the **Recycle Bin**
		• In the context menu, click **Empty Recycle Bin**
Opening recently used files	WINXP 2.18	• Click **Start**, then **My Recent Documents**
		• Click the file you want to open
Clearing the My Recent Documents list	WINXP 2.19	• Right-click the **Start** button, then click **Properties**
		• In the **Start Menu tab**, click **Customize . . .**

task reference roundup

Task	Page #	Preferred Method
		• Click the **Advanced** tab
		• Click the **Clear List** button
Finding a file by name	WINXP 2.21	• In the Start menu, click **Search**
		• In the Search menu, click **All Files and Folders**
		• In the All or part of the filename field, type the name of the file you are looking for
		• In the Look in drop-down list, select the drive to search in
		• Click the **Search** button
Performing a text search	WINXP 2.22	• In the Start menu, click **Search**
		• In the Search menu, click **All Files and Folders**
		• In the *A word or a phrase in the file* field, type the word or phrase you are searching for
		• Click the **Search** button
Stopping a search	WINXP 2.23	• In the left pane of the Search window, click **Stop**
Clearing the Search fields	WINXP 2.23	• At the bottom of the left pane of the Search window, click **Start a new search**
Saving a search	WINXP 2.24	• In the Search window, run the search you want to save
		• In the File menu, click **Save Search**
		• Make any changes for the filename and location, then click **Save**
Using wildcard characters to search	WINXP 2.25	• To represent an individual character in a search field, type **?**
		• To represent an unknown number of characters in a search field, type *****
Starting the WordPad application	WINXP 2.26	• Click the **Start** button
		• In the Start menu, click **All Programs**
		• In the Programs menu, click **Accessories**
		• In the Accessories submenu, click **WordPad**
Removing and restoring window elements	WINXP 2.29	• In the **View** menu, click the element to remove or restore
		• The element, and the check mark next to the menu option, are removed or restored
Changing the unit of measurement	WINXP 2.30	• In the View menu, click **Options**
		• In the Options dialog box, click the **Options** tab
		• Click the radio button next to the unit of measurement you want to use
		• Click **OK**

task reference roundup

Task	Page #	Preferred Method
Setting a document's margins	WINXP 2.31	• In the File menu, click **Page Setup**
		• In the Margins area, type the amount of space to use for each edge of the document
		• Click **OK**
Typing paragraphs	WINXP 2.32	• Click in the text area, then begin typing
		• Press the **Enter** key whenever you want to start a new paragraph
		• Use blank paragraphs to create additional space between paragraphs
Changing a paragraph's alignment	WINXP 2.33	• Move the insertion point to the paragraph
		• Click the toolbar icon representing the alignment you want
		or
		• In the Format menu, click **Paragraph,** *or* right-click the paragraph, then click **Paragraph** in the context menu
		• In the Alignment drop-down list, click the alignment to use
		• Click **OK**
Adjusting indents using the Paragraph dialog box	WINXP 2.35	• Place the insertion point in the paragraph or select several paragraphs
		• In the Format menu, click **Paragraph,** or right-click the paragraph, then click **Paragraph** in the context menu
		• Type the indents you want
		• Click **OK**
Adjusting indents using the ruler	WINXP 2.35	• Place the insertion point in the paragraph you want to change or select several paragraphs whose setting you want to change
		• To adjust the left indent, click the **block** at the bottom of the left margin and drag it to the right
		• To adjust the right indent, click the **triangle** at the right margin and drag it to the right
		• To adjust the first line indent, click the **top triangle** at the right margin and drag it to the right or left
Adding bullets to a paragraph	WINXP 2.37	• Place the cursor in the paragraph to be bulleted or select a group of paragraphs
		• In the Format menu, click **Bullet Style,** *or* right-click the paragraph, then click **Bullet Style** in the context menu *or* click the bullet icon on the toolbar
Adjusting tab stops using the Tabs dialog box	WINXP 2.38	• Select the paragraph or paragraphs you want to use the tabs
		• In the Format menu, click **Tabs,** or right-click the paragraphs, then click **Tabs** in the context menu

task reference roundup

Task	Page #	Preferred Method
		• To create a new tab, type the position in the box, then click **Set**
		• To remove a tab, click the tab in the list, then click **Clear**
		• When you're finished adjusting the tabs, click **OK**
Adjusting tabs using the ruler	WINXP 2.38	• Select the paragraph or paragraphs you want to use the tab settings
		• To create a new tab, click the ruler at the spot you want the new tab
		• To move a tab, click the marker and drag it to the new location on the ruler
		• To remove a tab, click the marker and drag it off the ruler
Changing the appearance of text using the Font dialog box	WINXP 2.40	• In the Format menu, click **Font**
		• In the Font list, click the typeface you want to use
		• In the Font style list, click the type style to indicate whether the text is bold or italic
		• In the Size list, click the size of the text
		• Under Effects, click the **Underlined** check box to add or remove underlining
		• In the Color drop-down list, click the color to use for the text
		• Click **OK**
Using the format bar to change text's appearance	WINXP 2.40	• Select the text
		• Select a typeface from the drop-down list
		• Select the type size from the drop-down list
		• Click the **B** button to make the text bold
		• Click the **I** button to make the text italicized
		• Click the **U** button to underline the text
		• Click the palette button to display a list of possible text colors, then click a color to select it
Starting the Notepad application	WINXP 2.43	• In the Start menu, click **Programs**
		• In the Programs menu, click **Accessories**
		• In the Accessories submenu, click **Notepad**
Wrapping text in Notepad	WINXP 2.44	• In the Format menu, click **Wrap**

task reference roundup

Task	Page #	Preferred Method
Setting up Notepad headers and footers	WINXP 2.45	• In the File menu, click **Page Setup**
		• In the Header field, type the information to print at the top of every page
		• In the Footer field, type the information to print at the bottom of every page
		• Click **OK**

CROSSWORD PUZZLE

Across

5. Tool for changing the appearance of text in WordPad
7. The _____ view contains multiple columns of information
9. To regulate, you can use My Computer or Windows _____
10. What Notepad is

Down

1. Cut or copied text and objects go here
2. The main building block of a text document
3. Allows you to line up columns of text in WordPad
4. Indicates how a paragraph is positioned within the margins
6. Where deleted files are placed
8. Prints along the bottom of every page

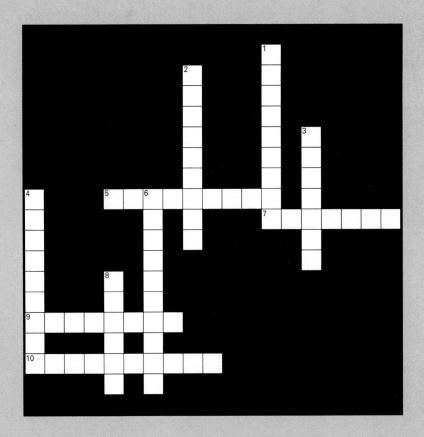

FILL-IN

1. Only drives and _____ display in the Windows Explorer tree.

2. The _____ option retrieves information from the Clipboard.

3. To quickly create a tab stop, click the _____.

4. A _____ can transport small files.

5. The _____ option cancels your last action.

CREATE THE QUESTION

For each answer, create a short question:

ANSWER	QUESTION
1. The distance from the left margin to a paragraph	_____
2. Used to select a range of adjacent files	_____
3. The basic set of 256 characters	_____
4. The default view for a window	_____
5. Alignment used in newspaper columns; not available in WordPad	_____

SHORT ANSWER

1. How do you add bullets to a paragraph in a WordPad document?

2. What symbol represents the page number in a Notepad header or footer?

3. Where in the Start menu are the WordPad and Notepad applications?

4. What view allows you to easily sort files and folders?

5. If you drag a file from your computer to a floppy disk, is it copied or moved?

1. Setting Up a Folder System

Darren Fusco is a friend of yours with a grandmother who wants to dictate her memoirs into a permanent record. Someone has told her this can be done on the computer, and she gets so excited that she runs out and buys a computer specifically for this purpose.

Darren brings you along when he visits his grandmother. You see that the store got her the right hardware and software for the job. She bought a laptop and will be speaking into a microphone while her words are recorded with voice recognition software. Windows XP is the installed operating system. Darren's grandmother eXPlains that the local store was very helpful and showed her how to work some basics and told her to come back if she has any questions.

You know that voice recognition software in general is far from infallible and explain to Darren that he will probably have to spend some time with his grandmother going over the transcriptions, making sure that mistakes are corrected. He says that's OK with him.

Darren's grandmother tells you she wants to keep track of her reminiscences by the decade. You help her set up the folders in My Documents so that they are categorized this way.

1. In the My Documents folder, create three new folders and name them **The 20's, The 30's,** and **The 40's**
2. Create a fourth folder and name it **Memoirs**
3. Move the three decade folders into **Memoirs**
4. Open **Memoirs**
5. Make a copy of **The 20's**
6. Rename the copy to **The 50's**

At the end of this project, the Memoirs folder window should look like the one in Figure 2.51.

FIGURE 2.51

The final view of the Memoirs folder project

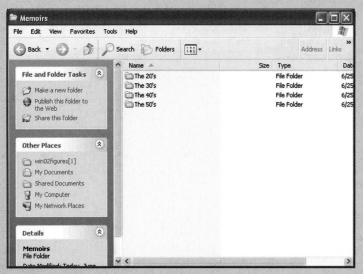

WINDOWS XP

challenge

1. Reformatting a Document

Your company, Universal Telecommunications Corp., has been thinking about upgrading its operating system to Windows XP. Colleagues send you articles all the time. You've just received an article that looks interesting, but it is all scrambled. You want to fix this article so you can pass it along to your network administrator. Open your data file named **Windows Deployment.**

The different sections of this document are out of sequence. The last paragraph should be the first, and the title should be on top. Make these changes by selecting the objects (the last paragraph and the title) and dragging them with your mouse to where they belong. Practice dragging; do *not* use copy and paste to complete this task.

Insert the current Date and Time, and type **From the desk of <your name>** at the bottom. Format these additions in **10**-point **Verdana** font. The final document should look like the one in Figure 2.52. Print the document.

FIGURE 2.52

The final draft of the Windows Deployment document

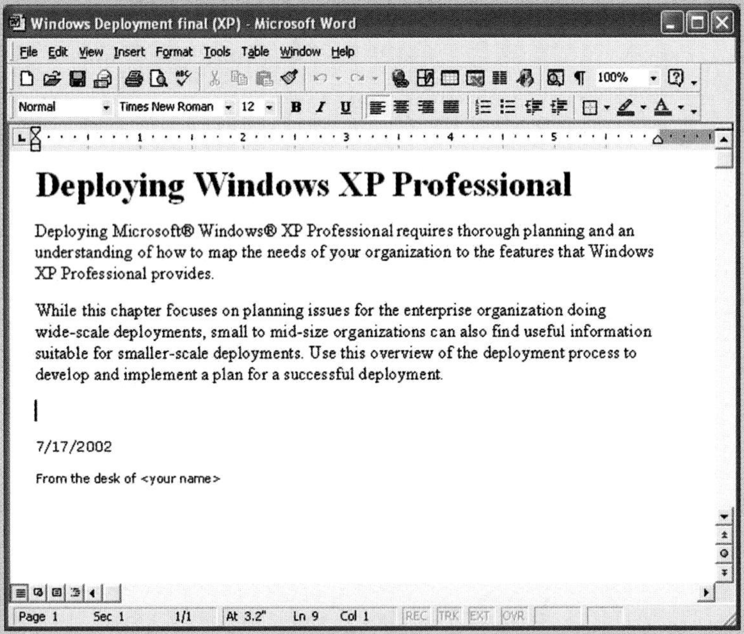

1. Creating an Outline of the Windows XP Professional Web Page

Sarah Fuller performs billing work for Gigantic Insurance Company. Her entire department has just been migrated to Windows XP from Windows NT. She wants to learn more about her new operating system and visits Microsoft's home page to get more information. Her supervisor walks by while she is online and becomes interested in what she is doing. Her supervisor asks her to write a short outline if she finds anything interesting, as he is trying to learn more about Windows XP himself.

Visit www.microsoft.com/windowsXP/pro/default.asp and choose an article about Windows XP that looks interesting. Open WordPad and write a short outline: a couple of sentences to introduce the topic and then a bulleted list of four or five items you learned from the article. Give your outline a title, using **Arial** and **bold.** Type your name on the outline and save it as **My W2K Outline.** Print it.

FIGURE 2.53

The Windows XP Professional Web page

e-business

1. Formatting a Document for E-Centric Inc.

Frank Dominik is a vice president of Business Development for E-Centric Inc., a leading player in the e-commerce industry. He is in the process of writing a white paper he will present at a conference on the Business-to-Business (B2B) Marketplace. The topic of his white paper is the bottom-line practicality of implementing e-business solutions for a variety of industries. Special Internet-based software provides better control over traditional ways of doing standard business activities such as buying, selling, distribution, and production. The use of this technology will result in substantial cost savings to those businesses that make the investment in time and technology now. He wants to make the white paper available for distribution, so formatting issues are important. Frank approaches you to ask your help in cleaning up the document.

Open the data file named **B2B Marketplace,** which contains the first two paragraphs of the white paper. Locate the title "the Value Driven Marketplace" and select it. In the Format menu, change the font to **Arial** and the point size to **18.** Capitalize the "t" in "the."

Notice that instead of quotation marks, footnote markings are displayed on lines 2 and 3 in the words "industry[1]s," "it[1]s," and "[3]virtual.[2]" Change these footnotes to quotation marks. Insert a blank space between the paragraphs.

Finally, replace the author of the paper's name with your name. The finished project should look like Figure 2.54. Save your changes, rename the document **My White Paper,** and print a copy of the document.

FIGURE 2.54

The correctly formatted B2B Marketplace white paper

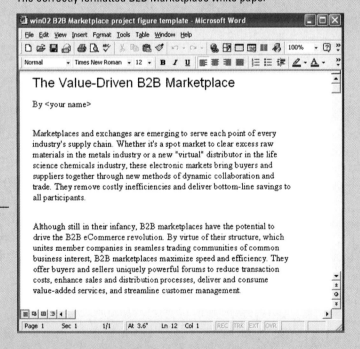

1. Organizing and Renaming Folders

The Burlington Archaeological Society is planning a trip to China. During the trip, members will be meeting with Chinese archaeologists who will be taking them to archaeological sites throughout China.

The trip will take place over six weeks, and members hope to visit over 20 different sites. China is an area rich in archaeological treasures. There are many dinosaur fossils scattered throughout the Northwest, several important sites for early Homo sapiens in the South and East, and multiple sites with 5,000 years of Chinese artifacts scattered throughout.

As the start of the trip is a few months away and the itinerary is a busy one, the members want to create an overview, organized by region, of the different sites and the important things to see in each.

One of the members has begun this project by creating a set of folders named after each of the Chinese provinces that are part of the itinerary. Meanwhile the members have decided that this directory should be reorganized by region, and new folders for each of the provinces should be created in each, which in turn can be cross-referenced to the original list. You have just taken on this job as part of your effort to get ready for the trip.

Since Chinese place names are difficult for Westerners to spell, rather than retyping the name of each province, you have decided to cut and paste the folder names. This is also critical because these folders need to cross-reference to the original set of folders, and one little difference will throw the relationship off.

Find the folder in your data files called **China folder** and open it. Inside this folder you will see 10 additional folders, one for each of the Chinese province names. Create three new folders called **North, East,** and **South.** Within each of these three folders, you need to create additional folders that correspond to the 10 names for each of the provinces. Name them by copying and pasting the original Chinese name to the new folder. Create the new folders for the first three names of provinces in the North folder. Create new folders for the next three province names in the East folder. Create new folders for the last four province names in the South Folder. Keep all these new folders in the China folder, so that at the end of the project it contains three new folders named North, East, and South, with the appropriate province name in each. Do *not* simply move the existing province folders into these three new folders to achieve this result; practice creating new folders and copying and pasting their file names from the existing ones.

almost 100 planets outside of our own solar system have been discovered to date, with the smallest one being 40 times the size of the Earth.

missionaries to Hawaii designed the Polynesian alphabet that has only 12 characters and is still in use today.

IBM is in the process of building the world's fastest computer for the U.S. weather forecasting agency; the computer is expected to be able to do more than 100 trillion calculations per second when completed in the year 2009.

the word "cantaloupe" means singing wolves, and the fruit is so named because of a town in Italy named Cantaloupe that produced the well-known melons and (originally) had many howling wolves.

a new Web service called DelayedMail.com promises to store an e-mail for future transmission in its server for up to 97 years so that it can be sent at a predetermined time in the future to a recipient regardless of what happens to the sender, for example from an elderly person to one of their grandchildren when they reach a certain age.

CHAPTER

3

Chapter Objectives

- Customize the taskbar's toolbars
- Change the appearance of your Desktop
- Set up a screen saver
- Learn to create an active desktop
- Practice switching to Windows Classic view
- Adjust the settings for your mouse
- Adjust the sounds assigned to different actions
- Adjust settings to reflect different user abilities
- Create and remove Desktop shortcuts

three

Customizing
Your Work
Environment

Too Limited Corporation

Dan Casaubon was recently promoted to assistant buyer for the Too Limited Corporation, a clothing, footwear, and accessory company with 12 retail stores in the Southwest.

Dan's new position required him to carry and use a laptop computer. He was issued a laptop with the Windows XP Professional operating system installed on it.

The first thing Dan wanted to do was to personalize his laptop to create his own work environment.

He wanted to make some of the applications he used accessible from the taskbar, so he could open them with a single click. He also needed to check the date and time to make sure they were accurate.

Dan thought the default Windows colors were boring and wanted to change the color scheme to something that was a little more interesting. A graphical background on the screen would make the environment friendlier as well. He'd also see what resolution would work the best on the laptop's screen.

Dan also wanted to have fun with some of the sounds associated with clicking the mouse and opening windows.

Finally, Dan wanted to have easy access to his files and to the applications he used the most. Desktop shortcuts and the taskbar would be the best tools to put everything within easy reach.

INTRODUCTION

While the Windows XP default colors and settings work well for most people, Windows XP includes several functions to make your Desktop and computer look and function exactly right for you.

You can customize the taskbar with new icons and toolbars, and you can use the Display Properties dialog box to change the color scheme to create your own personal Desktop environment.

The way folders display can be customized so that, for example, all the folders related to one project look the same.

You can also make adjustments to components such as the mouse and keyboard to compensate for differing abilities, and you can add sounds to your setup to indicate different actions.

Finally, Desktop shortcuts provide a quick way to get to your most commonly used applications and files.

SESSION 3.1 CUSTOMIZING THE TASKBAR

Windows XP allows you to customize the taskbar and the Desktop. You can add and remove icons and toolbars from the taskbar, and you can use the Display Properties dialog box to change the color scheme, screen saver, and screen resolution.

ADDING ICONS TO THE QUICK LAUNCH BAR

As mentioned in Chapter 1, one of the elements that can be displayed on the taskbar is the Quick Launch bar. The Quick Launch bar contains buttons, each of which represents an application. You click a button to start that program. By default, it consists of Windows Media Player, Internet Explorer, and ***Show Desktop.*** Show Desktop minimizes all open windows, to save you the trouble of minimizing them one at a time.

the Quick Launch bar

FIGURE 3.1

The Quick Launch bar

You can also add programs or files to the Quick Launch bar for easy access. You find the object on the computer and then drag it onto the bar.

---

task reference

Adding an Icon to the Quick Launch Bar

- Use My Computer or Windows Explorer to navigate to the object
- Drag the object to the Quick Launch bar

---

*another*way

. . . to Add an Icon to the Quick Launch Bar

If the object you want to add is already on the Desktop, just drag the icon to the Quick Launch bar.

Adding a program to the Quick Launch bar:

Dan knew he'd need the calculator quite a bit when he was on his travels. He decided to add the Calculator tool to the Quick Launch bar for easier access. In order to do the following exercise, make sure the Quick Launch bar is displayed on your taskbar (right-click an empty area of the taskbar, click Toolbars, and then click Quick Launch).

1. Click the **Start** button
2. Move your mouse over **All Programs,** then over **Accessories**
3. In the Accessories menu, click and drag the **Calculator** icon to the Quick Launch toolbar

the Calculator is now part of the Quick Launch bar

FIGURE 3.2

Quick Launch bar with Calculator icon

REMOVING AND RESTORING TOOLBARS

The Quick Launch bar is just one of the toolbars you can display on the taskbar.

- The *Address* toolbar allows you to type an Internet Web address and get access to the Internet without first having to open Internet Explorer. We'll discuss the Internet and Internet Explorer in Chapter 7.
- The *Links* toolbar starts you off with Microsoft's links. These links contain Microsoft's Internet official Web site, as well as tips on customizing your Links bar. You can drag your favorite links to the Links toolbar.
- The *Desktop* toolbar contains all the icons on your Desktop.

FIGURE 3.3

Address, Links, and Desktop toolbars

double arrow indicates there are additional hidden icons

You can easily display and remove these toolbars using the taskbar's context menu. In the context menu, each toolbar that is displayed has a check mark next to it.

task reference

Removing and Restoring Toolbars

- Right-click a blank area of the toolbar
- In the context menu, click **Toolbar**
- In the Toolbar submenu, click the toolbar you wish to add or remove

> **Removing and restoring the Quick Launch bar:**
>
> 1. Right-click an empty area of the taskbar
>
> 2. In the context menu, click **Toolbar**
>
> 3. In the Toolbar submenu, click **Quick Launch**

MOVING TOOLBARS ON THE SCREEN

Like the taskbar itself, you can drag individual toolbars to other areas of the Desktop.

You can attach a toolbar to one edge of the screen or have it display anywhere on the Desktop.

FIGURE 3.4

Toolbars can be moved around the Desktop

First the taskbar must be unlocked by right-clicking it and selecting Unlock the Taskbar. Once the taskbar is unlocked, move a toolbar by clicking the toolbar, then dragging it to its new location.

task reference

Moving Toolbars on the Screen

- Make sure the taskbar is unlocked by right-clicking it and selecting **Unlock the Taskbar**

- Click the toolbar

- Drag the toolbar onto the Desktop, then release the mouse button

- To attach the toolbar to an edge of the screen, drag it toward that edge until the toolbar snaps into place

> ### Practicing moving a toolbar:
>
> 1. Click the **Quick Launch** bar
> 2. Drag it to the left edge of the screen until it snaps into place
> 3. Continue dragging to the upper edge of the screen until the toolbar snaps into place
> 4. Continue dragging to the right edge of the screen until the toolbar snaps into place
> 5. Drag the toolbar to the center of the Desktop
> 6. Return the Quick Launch bar to the taskbar

CREATING A TOOLBAR

You can also turn any folder into a toolbar. Each file or folder in that folder then becomes a button on the toolbar.

---

task reference

Creating a Taskbar Toolbar

- Right-click an empty area of the taskbar
- In the context menu, click **Toolbars** then **New Toolbar...**
- Use the navigation tree to select a folder
- Click **OK**

> ### Creating a taskbar toolbar from My Documents:
>
> 1. Right-click an empty area of the taskbar
> 2. In the context menu, click **Toolbars**
> 3. In the **Toolbars** submenu, click **New Toolbar...**
> 4. Click **My Documents**
> 5. Click **OK.** The My Documents folder is now a toolbar

CHANGING THE DATE AND TIME

You can also use the taskbar to set the date and time for your computer. This date and time determines the time displayed when files are created and saved; it is also used when you insert dates and times in documents. To display the Date/Time dialog box from the taskbar, double-click the time displayed on the taskbar.

On the Date & Time tab, you use the drop-down lists and the calendar to set the date. You can then set the time by clicking on either the hour, minute, second, AM, or PM. Then, click the up or down arrows to adjust the time. You use the Time Zone tab to change the time zone.

F I G U R E   3.5

Adjusting the date and time

use the Time Zone tab to select the time zone

select a month

select a year

select a day

adjust the time

task reference

Adjusting the Date and Time

- Double-click the time displayed on the taskbar

- On the Date & Time tab, use the drop-down lists and calendar to select the month, year, and day

- Use the up and down arrows to adjust the time

- On the Time Zone tab, select a time zone

- Click **OK**

anotherway

. . . to Display the Date/Time Dialog Box

The Control Panel also provides access to the Date/Time dialog box. In the Start menu, click **Control Panel**. In the Control Panel, double-click the **Date/Time** icon

making the grade

SESSION 3.1

1. To display the Quick Launch bar, right-click the _____ and select Toolbars, and then Quick Launch.

2. You can turn any _____ into a toolbar.

3. To display the Date/Time dialog box from the taskbar, double-click the _____ displayed on the taskbar.

4. You can unlock the taskbar by _____ it and selecting Unlock the Taskbar.

SESSION 3.2 CUSTOMIZING THE DESKTOP

You use the Display Properties dialog box to customize the appearance of your Desktop. You can add wallpapers and patterns to the background, set up a new color scheme, and activate a screen saver. You can display this dialog box directly from the Desktop.

task reference

Displaying the Display Properties Dialog Box

- Right-click the Desktop

- In the context menu, click **Properties**

anotherway

. . . to Display the Display Properties Dialog Box

The Control Panel also provides access to the Display Properties dialog box:

In the Start menu, click **Control Panel**

In the Control Panel, double-click the **Display** icon

WINDOWS XP

FIGURE 3.6

The Display Properties dialog box

> ### Displaying the Display Properties dialog box:
>
> *Dan was ready to customize his Desktop. He started by displaying the Display Properties dialog box.*
>
> 1. Right-click an empty area of the Desktop
> 2. In the context menu, click **Properties**

CHANGING YOUR WALLPAPER AND BACKGROUND

The Background tab of the Display Properties dialog box contains options for adding wallpaper to the background of your Desktop. In Windows, *wallpaper* is a bitmapped picture that displays in the background of a window.

You can select a type of wallpaper provided by Windows XP or browse for a picture you'd like to see on your Desktop. You can use any picture—a photo of a friend or a copy of your favorite painting. To be used as wallpaper, the file must end with a .jpg, .bmp, .dib, .gif, or .htm extension. You can have the picture displayed in the center of the screen, *tile*d (repeated over and over, like tiles on a floor) to fill the screen, or stretched to take up the entire screen.

task reference

Selecting Wallpaper

- To select an existing wallpaper, click the wallpaper in the list

- To select a picture from your computer, click **Browse,** then navigate to and select the file

- In the *Display* drop-down list, click **Center** to center the picture on the screen, **Tile** to repeat the picture to fill up the screen, or **Stretch** to stretch the picture to fit the screen

- Click **Apply** or **OK**

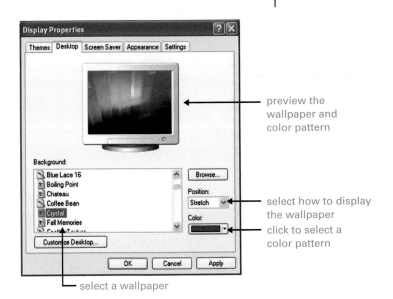

preview the
wallpaper and
color pattern

select how to display
the wallpaper

click to select a
color pattern

select a wallpaper

The Color button allows you to fill any background not taken up by the
wallpaper with a color pattern.

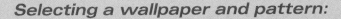

Selecting a wallpaper and pattern:

*Dan knew he didn't want a plain Desktop. He decided to have a picture in the
center of the screen.*

1. In the list of wallpapers, click **Red moon desert**
2. In the *Display* drop-down list, click **Stretch**
3. In the *Color* drop-down list, click the black color box
4. Click **Apply**

tip: *On the Display Properties dialog box, click **Apply** to apply the changes
without closing the dialog box; or click **OK** to apply the changes and close the
dialog box*

CUSTOMIZING DESKTOP APPEARANCE AND SCHEMES

The Appearance tab allows you to customize virtually every aspect of the windows you use in Windows XP Professional.

FIGURE 3.9

Appearance tab

preview area

used to select an entire scheme

these options are enabled or disabled depending on the selected element

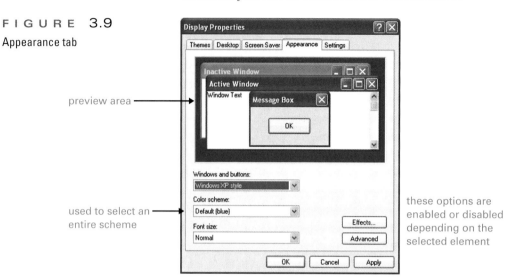

The Appearance tab includes two sample windows and a sample message box. These provide a preview of any changes you make before you put them into effect. These three items should cover just about all the changes you can make.

On the Appearance tab, you can select a scheme and change individual properties. A ***scheme*** is a collection of colors and fonts that give the screen a certain look and feel. When you first use Windows XP Professional, the default scheme is called Windows XP style.

After you select a scheme, you can also change individual elements to make the screen more appealing. For example, you may like the colors used by a scheme, but not the fonts the scheme uses in the menus. When you change the default value for a scheme element, the scheme is no longer officially selected. Selecting the scheme again reverts all the settings to the default for that scheme.

task reference

Selecting a Scheme

- Open the Appearance tab of the Display Properties dialog box
- In the *Color Scheme* drop-down list, click the scheme to use
- In the *Font size* and the *Windows and buttons* drop-down lists, click an option
- Click **Apply** or **OK**

Selecting and customizing a scheme:

Dan definitely didn't want to stick with the Windows default colors. His favorite color was silver, so he decided to select a scheme that used those colors and use a similar color for the background.

1. Click the **Appearance** tab

2. In the *Color Scheme* drop-down list, click **Silver.** The sample windows change to reflect the new scheme

3. Click **Apply**

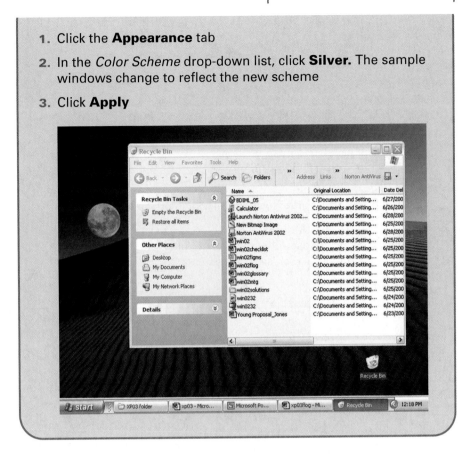

FIGURE 3.10

The new color scheme

SETTING UP A SCREEN SAVER

The Screen Saver tab of the Display Properties dialog box allows you to set up a screen saver. A *screen saver* displays an image or animated sequence after a defined period of inactivity on your computer.

The Screen Saver tab includes a sample monitor to preview the screen saver options.

The Settings button allows you to make adjustments that are applicable to the screen saver you choose. Many of these settings have to do with the speed and the size of the screen saver objects, as well as others.

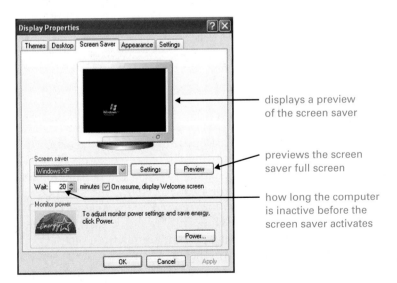

displays a preview
of the screen saver

previews the screen
saver full screen

how long the computer
is inactive before the
screen saver activates

FIGURE 3.11

The Screen Saver tab

The Preview button allows you to see the screen saver full screen for a couple of seconds, and the Wait selection dictates how long your computer will be idle before the screen saver activates.

---

task reference

Setting Up a Screen Saver

- In the Screen Saver drop-down list, click the screen saver to use

- Click the **Settings** button to view and set any settings for the screen saver

- Click the **Preview** button to see a full screen preview of the screen saver

- In the Wait field, adjust the number of minutes for the computer to be inactive before the screen saver activates

- Click **Apply**

Activating a screen saver:

Dan knew he wanted to use a screen saver after the computer was inactive for 7 minutes. He decided to have the words "Dan's Computer" display and move across the screen.

1. Click the **Screen Saver** tab

2. In the *Screen Saver* drop-down list, click **3D Text**

3. Click the **Settings** button. The 3D Text Settings dialog box opens

4. In the *Custom Text* text box, type **Dan's Computer**

5. Click **OK**

6. In the Wait field, adjust the time to **7** minutes

7. Click **Preview**

8. Click **Apply**

CHANGING YOUR MONITOR'S COLOR AND RESOLUTION

The Settings tab is a more advanced area of your display properties and should be approached with caution. Depending on your system, the Settings tab may look slightly different from what you see here.

You use the Colors quality drop-down list to select the number of colors the monitor displays. The more colors that display, the sharper the image. The number of colors becomes more important if you start working with graphics or other multimedia. Some software, especially computer games, may also require that you select a specific number of colors.

The screen resolution settings control the apparent "size" of the screen. The ***resolution*** of the monitor is measured in pixels per inch and indicates

FIGURE 3.12
Color and resolution settings

the number of pixels horizontally and vertically. So if the resolution is 640x480, the screen is 640 pixels wide by 480 pixels high. The monitor itself does not change size, so if you increase the resolution, the objects on the screen become smaller. The larger your monitor, the higher the resolution you can use.

task reference

Adjusting Monitor Settings

- In the *Colors quality* drop-down list, click the number of colors
- Under *Screen resolution*, slide the bar to the left or right to increase or decrease the resolution
- Click **OK**

Practicing with monitor settings:

1. Click the **Settings** tab
2. Drag the *Screen resolution* slider to the left or right. Notice how the image at the top of the tab changes as you select different resolutions
3. In the *Color quality* drop-down list, select different numbers of colors. Notice how the color bar changes to reflect how many colors are available

CREATING AN ACTIVE DESKTOP

An *Active Desktop* enables Web pages to be turned into Desktop items that are updated automatically. A Web site that regularly updates such information—such as the weather, stock market listings, or a news summary—can be displayed on your Desktop, so you can monitor the desired information.

When you enable the Active Desktop feature, Windows automatically displays your current home page on the Desktop. Your Desktop at periodic intervals will reflect any changes that occur on the Web site. Making a Web page into an Active Desktop actually integrates that Web page into your Desktop as if you had a window open to it on Internet Explorer.

---

task reference

Creating an Active Desktop

- Right-click a blank area of the Desktop
- In the context menu, click **Properties**
- Click the **Desktop** tab and click the **Customize Desktop...** button
- Click the **Web** tab, then Click **New...**
- On the New Active Desktop Item dialog box, in the Location field, select a Web page to make your Active Desktop
- Click **Yes** and **OK** to confirm your selection

Creating an Active Desktop:

Since part of Dan's job involves purchasing, he travels quite a bit. Because of this, he often is checking the weather in other parts of the country. Besides not wanting to be stuck somewhere in bad weather conditions, he also wants to know what to pack. To avoid having to log onto the same Web site often, he creates an Active Desktop that he can check for the current weather conditions anywhere in the United States.

1. Right-click a blank area of the Desktop
2. In the context menu, click **Properties**
3. In the Display Properties dialog box, click the **Desktop** tab. The Desktop Items dialog box opens
4. Click the **Web** tab
5. Click **New . . . .** The New Desktop Item dialog box opens
6. Click the **Visit Gallery** button to go to Microsoft's Active Desktop Gallery Web site. Internet Explorer launches and opens the Active Desktop Gallery page
7. Scroll down the page until you find the Weather Map from MSNBC and then click that item
8. Click the **Add to Active Desktop** button next to the weather map. A dialog box opens asking if you want to add an Active Desktop item to your Desktop
9. Click **Yes** to add the item to your Desktop; the next dialog box that opens asks you to confirm that you have chosen the weather map to add to your Active Desktop
10. Click **OK** to confirm your selection. Your Desktop now displays the weather map

---

anotherway

. . . to Add an Active Desktop Item

You can make a Web page your Active Desktop by dragging onto your Desktop the URL's *e* icon from the Internet Explorer Address bar while holding down the right mouse button. A context menu will appear; choose **Create Active Desktop Item(s) Here.** Enter the appropriate responses when prompted by the Wizard to finish creating your Active Desktop.

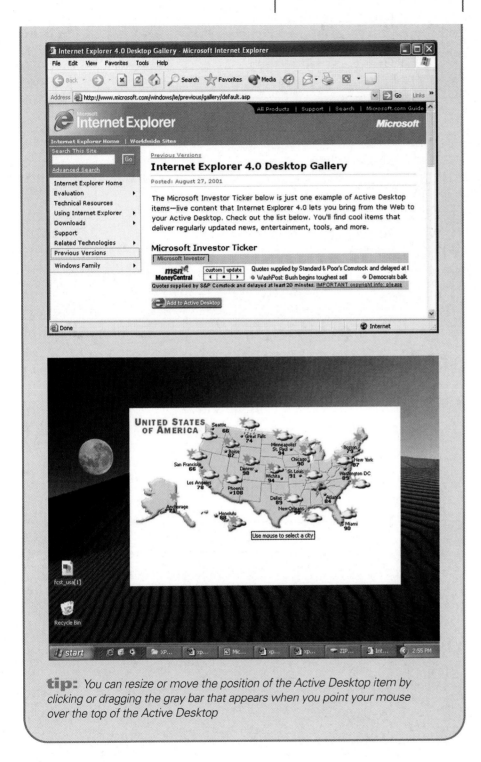

FIGURE 3.13

The Microsoft Active Desktop
Gallery Web page

FIGURE 3.14

Active Desktop with the weather
map from the Microsoft Gallery
displayed

tip: *You can resize or move the position of the Active Desktop item by clicking or dragging the gray bar that appears when you point your mouse over the top of the Active Desktop*

SWITCHING TO WINDOWS CLASSIC VIEW

If you have worked with previous versions of Windows, you will be familiar with what Microsoft calls the Windows "Classic" view, which is what Windows looked liked before the XP version came along. Some people prefer to work with this plain interface rather than the more graphic intensive interface of XP. If so, XP has an easy way to switch to this view, using the Display Properties dialog box in the Control Panel we've been working with in this chapter.

WINDOWS XP

FIGURE 3.15

The Windows Classic view

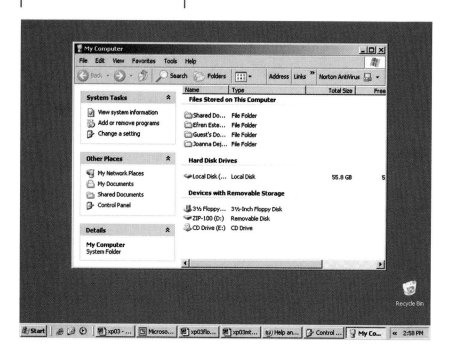

reference

Switching to Windows Classic View

- Click **Start,** then **Control Panel**
- Double-click **Display**
- In the Themes tab, under *Theme*, click **Windows Classic**
- Click **OK**

Switching to Windows Classic view:

After a while, Dan found it was easier to work with fewer graphics on his Desktop and he decided to use the Classic Windows view.

1. Click **Start,** then **Control Panel**
2. Double-click **Display.** The Display Properties dialog box opens
3. In the Themes tab, under *Theme*, click **Windows Classic**
4. Click **OK**

anotherword

After you select Windows Classic, you can change individual Windows elements, such as window borders, icons, and menus. Click the **Appearance** tab, and then click **Advanced** to make your changes.

Since there are many computers both at home and in the workplace using the Windows Classic view, you should be comfortable working in this format. Accordingly, many figures in the following chapters will be displayed in Classic view. Note, however, that regardless of the view, either XP or Windows Classic, the steps to perform any action are *identical.*

making the grade

1. A _____ is a collection of colors and fonts you can use on your Desktop.

2. A _____ displays an image or animated sequence after a defined period of inactivity on your computer.

3. To open the Display Properties dialog box, right-click the _____.

4. A picture displayed on the background of your Desktop is called _____.

5. The screen _____ settings control the apparent size of your screen.

SESSION 3.3 CUSTOMIZING HOW YOU INTERACT WITH THE COMPUTER

Windows XP allows you to set up your mouse and keyboard to work for you. You can make adjustments for left-handedness and to help you if you press buttons and keys too quickly or too slowly. Windows XP also provides a selection of sounds you can use to notify you when you perform certain actions or when certain events occur. If sound is a problem, Windows XP also includes options for replacing sounds with visual cues.

These options are all available from the Control Panel, a comprehensive set of tools for tasks such as setting up hardware, adding or removing software, and making adjustments to settings. We've already talked about the Date/Time and Display functions, which are part of the Control Panel.

FIGURE 3.16

The Control Panel

*another*way

. . . to Open the
Control Panel

In the Start Menu, click
My Computer

Click the **Control Panel**
link on the left pane of
the window in the
middle box under
Other Places

---

task **reference**

Displaying the Control Panel

- In the Start menu, click **Control Panel**

CUSTOMIZING THE MOUSE

You use the mouse just about every time you use your computer. Windows XP Professional allows you to customize the way your mouse pointer looks and performs.

If you're left-handed, you can set up the mouse so it's easier to use with your left hand. You can adjust how you open files using the mouse.

You can also change the pointers that display on the screen.

From the Control panel, double-click the Mouse icon to open the Mouse Properties dialog box.

---

task **reference**

Opening the Mouse Properties Dialog Box

- From the Control Panel, double-click the **Mouse** icon

Configuring the Mouse Buttons

The Buttons tab of the Mouse Properties dialog box controls how the buttons on your mouse behave. It consists of three sections:

- Button configuration
- Double-click speed
- ClickLock

F I G U R E   3.17

The Buttons tab of Mouse
Properties

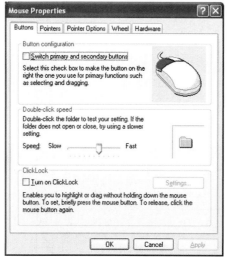

The *Button configuration* section allows you to switch the functions of the mouse's right and left buttons. If you are left-handed and would like to use your left hand to control the mouse, click the check box labeled *Switch primary and secondary buttons*. This in effect makes your mouse buttons function in a mirror image of the right-handed functions, with the index finger of your left hand on the right button and the middle finger on the left button.

The *Double-click speed* section has a slide selector for adjusting your double-click speed. The double-click speed indicates the span of time within which two clicks are considered a double-click. If you are not a particularly fast double-clicker, you can change your double-click speed to a slower setting. The Test area allows you to test the new speed. Double-click the folder in the Test area to see how well the new speed works for you.

The *ClickLock* section allows you to highlight or drag without holding down the mouse button. Click the check box in this section labeled *Turn on ClickLock*. Once this is done, you activate ClickLock by pressing briefly the mouse button as if you were starting to drag it. To release, click the mouse button again.

---

task reference

Configuring Your Mouse Buttons

- In the Mouse Properties dialog box, click the **Buttons** tab

- Under *Button Configuration*, click the **Switch primary and secondary** check box to switch the mouse buttons to the left-handed configuration

- Under Double-click speed, use the slider bar to increase or decrease the space between clicks for a double-click

- Under *ClickLock,* click the **Turn on ClickLock** check box to enable you to highlight or drag without having to hold down the mouse

- Click **Apply** or **OK**

Changing the Mouse Pointers

The Pointers tab allows you to customize the look of your mouse pointers.

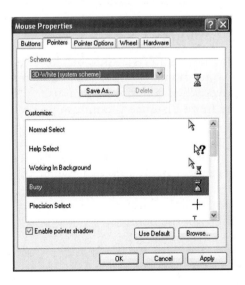

FIGURE 3.18
The Pointers tab in Mouse Properties

Windows provides pointer schemes for the mouse, similar in concept to the schemes provided for the Desktop. In the case of the mouse, each scheme is a collection of pointers to represent different states of the mouse (when it's over a link, when the system is busy, etc.).

When you select a scheme from the Scheme drop-down list, the Customize box displays the pointers in that scheme.

You can also customize individual pointers within a scheme. Click the pointer, and then click the Browse button to find another pointer to use. Click Use Default to return the pointer to the default setting.

---

task *reference*

Changing Mouse Pointers

- In the Mouse Properties dialog box, click the **Pointers** tab
- In the *Scheme* drop-down list, click a scheme
- To change an individual pointer within a scheme, click the pointer, then click **Browse** to begin searching for another pointer
- To return a pointer to its default value, click the pointer, and then click **Use Default**
- Click **Apply** or **OK**

Changing mouse pointers:

1. Click the **Pointers** tab
2. In the Schemes drop-down list, click **3-D Bronze (System Scheme)**
3. Click **Apply**
4. Try moving the mouse on the screen. You'll see the new pointer
5. In the Schemes drop-down list, click **None**
6. Click **Apply**

Adjusting the Mouse's Pointer Options

The first section in the Pointer Options tab contains a slide bar for controlling the speed and acceleration of your mouse pointer. This indicates how fast and far the mouse pointer moves when you move the mouse. The higher the speed and acceleration, the more distance the mouse pointer will cover as you move the mouse.

The next section in the Pointer Options tab includes a Snap to default check box. If this box is checked, the mouse pointer automatically moves to the default button (the button you're most likely to select) when you open a dialog box.

Lastly, the Pointer Options tab has a Visibility area that gives you the ability to increase or decrease the visibility of the pointer.

---

task *reference*

Customizing the Mouse Speed

- In the Mouse Properties dialog box, click the **Pointer Options** tab
- Use the Speed slide bar to adjust the mouse speed
- Select a mouse acceleration
- Click **Apply** or **OK**

The Pointer Options tab in Mouse
Properties

Customizing mouse speed:

1. Click the **Pointer Options** tab

2. Move the **Speed** slide bar to **Fast**

3. Click **Apply**

4. Move the mouse pointer around the screen. Notice now that very small movements of the mouse will cause the mouse pointer to move very quickly

5. Change the speed and acceleration settings back to their original state

6. Click **Apply**

SETTING SOUNDS

Windows XP Professional allows you to customize the sounds that play when you perform certain actions or when certain events occur. For example, you can have a sound play whenever you click an object or whenever you close a program. When the software "plays" a sound, it is executing a sound file, typically a .wav file. Your computer must have a sound card and speakers installed for you to use the sound capabilities.

You set your sounds from the Sounds and Audio Devices Properties dialog box, which you display by double-clicking on the Sounds and Audio Devices icon in the Control Panel.

task reference

Displaying the Sounds and Audio Devices Properties Dialog Box

- In the Control Panel, double-click the **Sounds and Audio Devices** icon

The Volume tab also allows you to adjust the volume control of your devices and speakers.

WINDOWS XP

The Sounds tab lists Sound schemes. Like the Desktop and the mouse, sounds also have schemes, collections of related sounds. The Schemes drop-down list contains the list of available sound schemes. To choose a scheme, select it from the Schemes drop-down list. You can also customize the sound for program events.

ACCESSIBILITY OPTIONS

Computer users are of all ages and abilities. Windows XP Professional offers features to customize keyboard, mouse, and display settings to better cope with special needs. Many of these features may also make using the computer easier for average users.

You can access these features by double-clicking the Accessibility Options icon of the Control Panel.

---

task **reference**

Displaying the Accessibility Options Dialog Box

- In the Control Panel, double-click the **Accessibility Options** icon

---

Making Adjustments to the Keyboard

The Keyboard tab allows you to make adjustments to how the keyboard functions. It provides access to three main tools:

FIGURE 3.20

The Keyboard tab in Accessibility Options

- *StickyKeys.* Some functions require that you press multiple keys simultaneously. This can be difficult for some users. **StickyKeys** helps alleviate this problem. When this option is checked, symbols of the Shift, Ctrl, Alt, and Windows logo keys are placed in the taskbar. Users can press these keys one at a time and have the same effect as pressing them simultaneously. When each key is pressed, its taskbar symbol is shaded. The keys remain pressed until the action is complete. For example, in many applications you can save a file by pressing the Ctrl and S keys simultaneously. With StickyKeys turned on, you would press Ctrl, and then press S.
- *FilterKeys.* This option is for users who frequently press the same key repeatedly when they only meant to press it once. When the

FilterKeys option is turned on, you can substantially reduce the amount of repeated keystrokes or briefly held keystrokes. Click the Settings button to display a dialog box in which you can adjust the repeat rate for brief keystrokes and repeated keystrokes.

- *ToggleKeys*. If the *ToggleKeys* option is checked, a tone or a sound plays whenever you press the Caps Lock, Num Lock, and Scroll Lock keys. The tone is different depending on whether you are turning these keys on or off.

---

reference

Setting Keyboard Accessibility Options

- Click the **Keyboard** tab in the Accessibility Options dialog box

- Check **Use StickyKeys** to be able to press the Ctrl, Alt, Shift, and Windows logo keys separately instead of simultaneously

- Check **Use FilterKeys** to be able to prevent unintended repeat characters

- Check **Use ToggleKeys** to hear a sound every time you press the Num Lock, Caps Lock, and Scroll Lock keys

- For each option, click the **Settings** button to customize the option

---

Practicing with keyboard Accessibility Options:

1. In the Accessibility Options dialog box, click the **Keyboard** tab

2. Check the **Use StickyKeys** check box

3. Check the **Use ToggleKeys** check box

4. Click **Apply**

5. Press the **Ctrl** key. Note that the Ctrl symbol on the taskbar is highlighted

6. Press the **Alt** key

7. Press the **Delete** key. A window displays and the key symbols are no longer highlighted

8. Click **Cancel** to close the window

9. Press the **Num Lock** key. You should hear a tone when you pressed the key

10. Press the **Num Lock** key again. Did you hear a different tone?

11. Uncheck the special keyboard settings, and then click **Apply**

Replacing Sounds with Visual Cues

The Sound tab offers a couple of choices for those who need a visual signal to warn them that a sound has played.

FIGURE 3.21

The Sound tab in Accessibility
Options

- *SoundSentry.* If the **SoundSentry** option is turned on, the system
  flashes a visual warning every time one of the system sounds plays.
  These are the sounds you assigned to events using the Sounds and
  Multimedia Properties dialog box. Click the Settings button to
  choose where you want the flash to occur—the caption bar of the
  active window, the entire active window, or the Desktop.
- *ShowSounds.* The **ShowSounds** option is used to provide visual
  cues for sounds played by other programs. Activating ShowSounds
  displays the information in a visual format.

---

task reference

Replacing Sounds with Visual Cues

- Click the **Sound** tab on the Accessibility Options dialog box

- Check **Use SoundSentry** to display a visual warning whenever a
  system sound plays

- Click **Settings** to determine where the warning displays

- Check **Use ShowSounds** to display a visual cue whenever a program
  plays a warning sound

Changing to a High Contrast Display

The Display tab offers options and settings to alter the color for reading.

These options allow users with impaired vision to see text more legibly
by increasing the contrast between the text and its background.

To use one of these other settings, click the Use High Contrast check
box, then click the Settings button. You can then select one of these special
color schemes.

FIGURE 3.22
High Contrast color scheme

---

reference

Changing to a High Contrast Display

- Click the **Display** tab on the Accessibility Options dialog box
- Check the **Use High Contrast** check box
- Click the **Settings** button to display the list of available high contrast color schemes
- Select a scheme, then click **OK**

Replacing the Mouse with the Keyboard

The Mouse tab allows you to turn on the *MouseKeys* option, so you can use the numeric keypad at the right of your keyboard to control the mouse pointer. This option is useful for those who have difficulty using the mouse or simply prefer not to use the mouse. Once this option is set, you use the keys as follows to work the "mouse."

- *Move the mouse pointer.* Press the 1, 2, 3, 4, 6, 7, 8, or 9 keys. The relative position of the key on the keypad indicates the direction the mouse pointer moves.
- *Left-click.* Press the forward slash (/) key, and then the 5 key.
- *Right-click.* Press the minus (−) key, and then the 5 key.
- *Double-click.* Press the + key.
- *Drag.* Press the 0 key, and then move the mouse to the target location. Press the Del key.

Click the Settings button to display a dialog box for adjusting the speed of your mouse keys, just like you adjusted the mouse speed in the Mouse Properties dialog box.

F I G U R E 3.23

MouseKeys equivalents

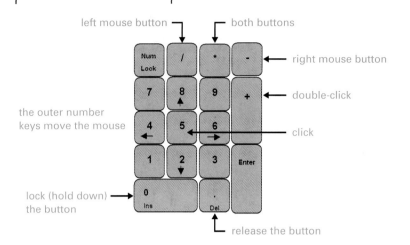

reference

Replacing the Mouse with the Keyboard

- Click the **Mouse** tab on the **Accessibility Options** dialog box
- Check the **Use MouseKeys** check box
- Click the **Settings** button to display a dialog box for adjusting the mouse speed
- Click **Apply** or **OK**

Using MouseKeys

- To move the mouse pointer, press the **1, 2, 3, 4, 6, 7, 8,** or **9** key
- To click with the left mouse button, press the forward slash (/) key, and then the **5** key
- To right-click, press the minus (−) key, then the **5** key
- To double-click, press the plus (+) key
- To drag, press the **0** key, and then move the mouse to the target location. Press the **Del** key

General Tab

The General tab gives you four options for administering Accessibility Options.

- *Automatic reset.* Allows you to have accessibility features turn off automatically after a preset amount of time of up to 30 minutes.
- *Notification.* Provides options to display a visual message whenever an accessibility feature is turned on, and to make a sound when an accessibility feature is turned on or off.

The next two options are for advanced users or administrators, but we will explain them briefly here.

- *SerialKeys.* Allows the computer to accommodate a peripheral input device that plugs into a serial port. The Settings button allows you to point the device to the correct port.
- *Administrative Options* (Administrators only). Allows the Accessibility Options to be in place when users log on. Also allows the options to apply by default to all new users.

FIGURE 3.24

The General tab in Accessibility
Options

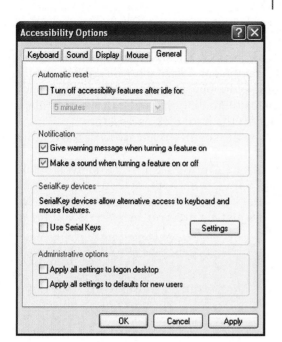

---

task reference

Administering Accessibility Options

- Click the **General** tab on the **Accessibility Options** dialog box

- To turn off the options after a certain amount of time, check the **Automatic reset** check box, then click a time in the drop-down list

- To display a warning when an accessibility feature is turned on, check the **Give warning message when turning a feature on** check box

- To play a sound when an accessibility feature is turned on or off, check the **Make a sound when turning a feature on or off** check box

- If you're an Administrator, to apply the current accessibility options at the log on screen, check the **Apply all settings to logon Desktop** check box

- If you're an Administrator, to apply the current accessibility options as the default for all new users, check the **Apply all settings to defaults for new users** check box

---

making the grade   SESSION 3.3

1. If you set the mouse to open objects with a single click, you select an object by _____.

2. The options for setting sounds, mouse properties, and accessibility options are found in the _____.

3. The _____ function saves users from having to press certain "command" keys simultaneously.

4. With MouseKeys, you use the _____ key on the keypad to move the mouse diagonally up and to the right.

5. The _____ option replaces system sounds with visual cues, while the _____ option replaces sounds made by programs.

WINDOWS XP

SESSION 3.4 USING SHORTCUTS

Windows XP Professional allows you to create *shortcuts.* A shortcut is a link, or pointer, to a program, folder, file, or device that you use frequently.

Shortcuts save you the trouble of looking through folders and files for the appropriate item. You can place them directly on the Desktop or place a group of shortcuts in any folder on the hard disk or Desktop.

You can recognize a shortcut by the small, curved arrow at the bottom left corner of the icon.

Once you create shortcuts, you can move, organize, and even delete them. Because a shortcut is only a link to an item, deleting the shortcut won't affect the original item. By the same token, deleting the original item does not delete the shortcut. You'll just get an error message if you try to use it.

CREATING A SHORTCUT

Windows allows multiple methods for creating a shortcut. You can right-click an object and then drag it to the Desktop. You can copy an object and paste a shortcut on the Desktop. You can also create a new shortcut on the Desktop and then assign an object to it.

---

task reference

Creating a Shortcut

- Right-click an object
- Hold down the right mouse button as you drag the object to the Desktop
- Release the mouse button
- In the context menu, click **Create Shortcut(s) Here**

  or

- Right-click an object
- In the context menu, click **Copy**
- Right-click the Desktop
- In the context menu, click **Paste Shortcut**

  or

- Right-click the Desktop
- In the context menu, click **Create Shortcut**
- In the field, type the path to the object, *or* click **Browse** to find the object
- Click **Next**
- Type a name for the shortcut
- Click **Finish**

---

anotherway

. . . to Create a Shortcut

You can also create shortcuts by right-clicking an object and then clicking Create Shortcut in the context menu

The shortcut is placed in the same folder as the object. You can then move the shortcut to its proper location

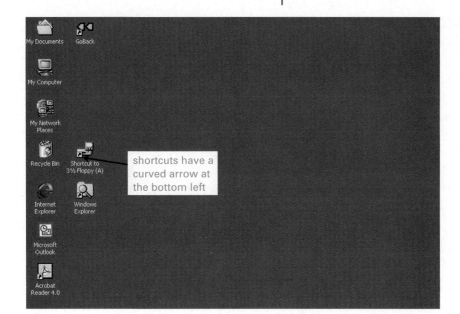

Creating a shortcut on the Desktop:

Dan found that it was natural for him to go to the Desktop when he needed to run a program. He wanted to put the Calculator program right on his Desktop rather than only on the taskbar.

1. In the Start menu, click **All Programs**

2. In the All Programs menu, click **Accessories**

3. In the Accessories submenu, click **System Tools**

4. Right-click **Calculator,** then hold down the right mouse button and drag Calculator from the System Tools menu onto the Desktop

5. Release the right mouse button

6. When the shortcut menu appears, click **Create Shortcut(s) here.** A shortcut icon to the Calculator displays on the Desktop

7. To use the Calculator, double-click the shortcut

FINDING OUT INFORMATION ABOUT SHORTCUTS

After you create a shortcut, you can use its context menu to find out what the shortcut points to.

In the shortcut's context menu, click Properties. The dialog box that displays includes a field listing the source of the shortcut. This information can be useful if you're trying to troubleshoot a shortcut that won't work.

FIGURE 3.26

Shortcut properties

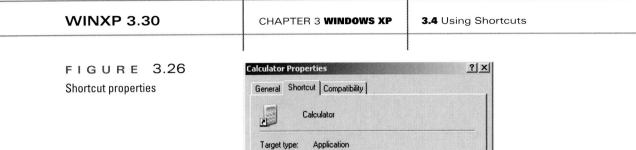

location of the
original item

RENAMING SHORTCUTS

A shortcut behaves like any other Windows object. You rename a shortcut the same way you would any file or folder.

reference

Renaming a Shortcut

- Right-click the shortcut

- In the context menu, click **Rename**

- Type the new name in the shortcut label

- Press **Enter**

ARRANGING SHORTCUTS AND ICONS ON THE DESKTOP

You can arrange shortcuts and other icons on the Desktop by simply clicking them and dragging them to the position you choose. The default arrangement of icons on the Desktop is in a top to bottom column down the left side of the Desktop. When you add a new shortcut, it displays at the bottom of the column.

You can also use the Desktop's context menu to arrange icons on the Desktop. The Line Up Icons option arranges your icons in neat rows and columns.

The Arrange Icons option displays a submenu of methods for arranging the icon. These are the same options you used to sort objects in windows.

- *Name.* The icons are arranged alphabetically on the Desktop.
- *Size.* The icons are arranged from smallest to largest. The shortcut icons are arranged by the size of the number of bytes needed to store the icon on the disk, not the size of the file, folder, or program the shortcut points to.

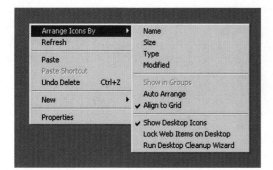

FIGURE 3.27
The Arrange Icons submenu

- *Type.* The icons are arranged so that all the folders are grouped together. The programs are also grouped together, as are the short-cuts. Within each group, they are sorted alphabetically.
- *Modified.* The icons are arranged from the oldest to the newest, with the date indicating when the shortcut was created, not when the file or folder was created.
- *Auto Arrange.* Turns on the Auto Arrange feature, which aligns the icons to an imaginary grid from the top left to the bottom right of the Desktop. If Auto Arrange is turned on, you cannot move the icons. To turn off Auto Arrange, toggle the option to the off position.

---

task **reference**

Arranging Desktop Icons

- Right-click the Desktop
- Click **Line Up Icons** to line up the icons in columns and rows
- In the Arrange Icons submenu, click **Name** to sort the objects by name
- In the Arrange Icons submenu, click **Type** to sort the objects by type
- In the Arrange Icons submenu, click **Size** to sort the objects by size
- In the Arrange Icons submenu, click **Modified** to sort the objects by the date they were created
- In the Arrange Icons submenu, click **Auto Arrange** to turn on or off the Auto Arrange feature, which locks the objects in columns at the left of the Desktop

---

Arranging icons on the Desktop:

1. Right-click a blank spot on the Desktop
2. In the context menu, click **Arrange Icons By**
3. In the Arrange Icons submenu, click **Name.** The shortcut icons are arranged in alphabetical order on the left side of the screen
4. In the Arrange icons submenu, click **Auto Arrange.** The icons are arranged according to an invisible grid of rows and columns on the Desktop and will not allow movement

WINDOWS XP

5. Select **Auto Arrange** again. This toggles the option off and you can once again move the icons around the Desktop

tip: *If, when you move a Desktop icon, it refuses to stay where you put it, it means that Auto Arrange is turned on*

If your Desktop becomes cluttered with shortcuts, you can create a folder and place the shortcuts in the folder.

DELETING SHORTCUTS

Deleting a shortcut works exactly like deleting any other file or folder. Like other objects, deleted shortcuts are sent to the Recycle Bin until you delete them permanently.

Remember that deleting a shortcut does not delete the original object.

task reference

Deleting Shortcuts

- Click the shortcut to delete

- Press the **Delete** key

SESSION 3.4   *making the grade*

1. The _____ option prevents you from moving Desktop objects.

2. A shortcut is a _____ to a file, folder, or program.

3. To arrange Desktop objects alphabetically, select _____ from the Arrange Icons submenu.

4. Does deleting a shortcut to a file delete the file itself?

SESSION 3.5 SUMMARY

In this chapter you learned how to customize the Windows environment to suit your own needs and preferences.

You learned how to work with the Quick Launch bar and other taskbar toolbars. You learned how to change the appearance of your Desktop with different wallpapers and screen savers. You learned about using different screen resolutions to change the size of your work area. You also learned what an Active Desktop is and how to create it.

This chapter also explained how to customize some of the other areas of your work environment. You learned how to make adjustments to your mouse and how to set up sounds to reflect different actions and events. You saw how to use Accessibility Options to customize computers for different types of users.

Finally, you learned how to create and manage shortcuts to programs, folders, and files.

task reference roundup

Task	Page #	Preferred Method
Adding an icon to the Quick Launch bar	WINXP 3.3	• Use My Computer or Windows Explorer to navigate to the object
		• Drag the object to the Quick Launch bar
Removing and restoring toolbars	WINXP 3.4	• Right-click a blank area of the toolbar
		• In the context menu, click **Toolbar**
		• In the Toolbar submenu, click the toolbar you wish to add or remove
Moving toolbars on the screen	WINXP 3.5	• Make sure the taskbar is unlocked by right-clicking it and selecting **Unlock the Taskbar**
		• Click the toolbar
		• Drag the toolbar onto the Desktop, then release the mouse button
		• To attach the toolbar to an edge of the screen, drag it toward that edge until the toolbar snaps into place
Creating a taskbar toolbar	WINXP 3.6	• Right-click an empty area of the taskbar
		• In the context menu, click **Toolbars,** then **New Toolbar...**
		• Use the navigation tree to select a folder
		• Click **OK**
Adjusting the date and time	WINXP 3.7	• Double-click the time displayed on the taskbar
		• On the Date & Time tab, use the drop-down lists and calendar to select the month, year, and day
		• Use the up and down arrows to adjust the time
		• On the Time Zone tab, select a time zone
		• Click **OK**
Displaying the Display Properties dialog box	WINXP 3.7	• Right-click the Desktop
		• In the context menu, click **Properties**
Selecting wallpaper	WINXP 3.8	• To select an existing wallpaper, click the wallpaper in the list
		• To select a picture from your computer, click **Browse,** then navigate to and select the file
		• In the *Display* drop-down list, click **Center** to center the picture on the screen, **Tile** to repeat the picture to fill up the screen, or **Stretch** to stretch the picture to fit the screen
		• Click **Apply** or **OK**
Selecting a scheme	WINXP 3.10	• Open the Appearance tab of the Display Properties dialog box
		• In the *Color Scheme* drop-down list, click the scheme to use

WINDOWS XP

task reference roundup

Task	Page #	Preferred Method
		• In the *Font size* and the *Windows and buttons* drop-down lists, click an option
		• Click **Apply** or **OK**
Setting up a screen saver	WINXP 3.12	• In the Screen Saver drop-down list, click the screen saver to use
		• Click the **Settings** button to view and set any settings for the screen saver
		• Click the **Preview** button to see a full screen preview of the screen saver
		• In the Wait field, adjust the number of minutes for the computer to be inactive before the screen saver activates
		• Click **Apply**
Adjusting monitor settings	WINXP 3.13	• In the *Colors quality* drop-down list, click the number of colors
		• Under *Screen resolution*, slide the bar to the left or right to increase or decrease the resolution
		• Click **OK**
Creating an Active Desktop	WINXP 3.14	• Right-click a blank area of the Desktop
		• In the context menu, click **Properties**
		• Click the **Desktop** tab and click the **Customize Desktop ...** button
		• Click the **Web** tab, then click **New...**
		• On the New Active Desktop Item dialog box, in the Location field, select a Web page to make your Active Desktop
		• Click **Yes** and **OK** to confirm your selection
Switching to Windows Classic View	WINXP 3.16	• Click **Start,** then **Control Panel**
		• Double-click **Display**
		• In the Themes tab, under *Theme*, click **Windows Classic**
		• Click **OK**
Displaying the Control Panel	WINXP 3.18	• In the Start menu, click **Control Panel**
Opening the Mouse Properties dialog box	WINXP 3.18	• From the Control Panel, double-click the **Mouse** icon
Configuring your mouse buttons	WINXP 3.19	• In the Mouse Properties dialog box, click the **Buttons** tab
		• Under *Button Configuration,* click the **Switch primary and secondary** check box to switch the mouse buttons to the left-handed configuration
		• Under Double-click speed, use the slider bar to increase or decrease the space between clicks for a double-click

task reference roundup

Task	Page #	Preferred Method
		• Under *ClickLock,* click the **Turn on ClickLock** check box to enable you to highlight or drag without having to hold down the mouse
		• Click **Apply** or **OK**
Changing mouse pointers	WINXP 3.20	• In the **Mouse Properties** dialog box, click the **Pointers** tab
		• In the *Scheme* drop-down list, click a scheme
		• To change an individual pointer within a scheme, click the pointer, then click **Browse** to begin searching for another pointer
		• To return a pointer to its default value, click the pointer, then click **Use Default**
		• Click **Apply** or **OK**
Customizing the mouse speed	WINXP 3.20	• In the Mouse Properties dialog box, click the **Pointer Options** tab
		• Use the Speed slide to adjust the mouse speed
		• Select a mouse acceleration
		• Click **Apply** or **OK**
Displaying the Sounds and Audio Devices Properties dialog box	WINXP 3.21	• In the Control Panel, double-click the **Sounds and Audio Devices** icon
Displaying the Accessibility Options dialog box	WINXP 3.22	• In the Control Panel, double-click the **Accessibility Options** icon
Setting Keyboard Accessibility Options	WINXP 3.23	• Click the **Keyboard** tab on the Accessibility Options dialog box
		• Check **Use StickyKeys** to be able to press the Ctrl, Alt, Shift, and Windows logo keys separately instead of simultaneously
		• Check **Use FilterKeys** to be able to prevent unintended repeat characters
		• Check **Use ToggleKeys** to hear a sound every time you press the Num Lock, Caps Lock, and Scroll Lock keys
		• For each option, click the **Settings** button to customize the option
Replacing sounds with visual cues	WINXP 3.24	• Click the **Sound** tab on the Accessibility Options dialog box
		• Check **Use SoundSentry** to display a visual warning whenever a system sound plays
		• Click **Settings** to determine where the warning displays
		• Check **Use ShowSounds** to display a visual cue whenever a program plays a warning sound
Changing to a High Contrast display	WINXP 3.25	• Click the **Display** tab on the Accessibility Options dialog box

WINDOWS XP

task reference roundup

Task	Page #	Preferred Method
		• Check the **Use High Contrast** check box
		• Click the **Settings** button to display the list of available high contrast color schemes
		• Select a scheme, then click **OK**
Replacing the mouse with the keyboard	WINXP 3.26	• Click the **Mouse** tab on the Accessibility Options dialog box
		• Check the **Use MouseKeys** check box
		• Click the **Settings** button to display a dialog box for adjusting the mouse speed
		• Click **Apply** or **OK**
Using MouseKeys	WINXP 3.26	• To move the mouse pointer, press the **1, 2, 3, 4, 6, 7, 8,** or **9** key
		• To click with the left mouse button, press the **/** key, then the **5** key
		• To right click, press the minus (−) key, then the **5** key
		• To double-click, press the plus (+) key
		• To drag, press the **0** key, then move the mouse to the target location. Press the **Del** key
Administering Accessibility Options	WINXP 3.27	• Click the **General** tab on the **Accessibility Options** dialog box
		• To turn off the options after a certain amount of time, check the **Automatic reset** check box, then click a time in the drop-down list
		• To display a warning when an accessibility feature is turned on, check the **Give warning message when turning a feature on** check box
		• To play a sound when an accessibility feature is turned on or off, check the **Make a sound when turning a feature on or off** check box
		• If you're an Administrator, to apply the current accessibility options at the log on screen, check the **Apply all settings to logon Desktop** check box
		• If you're an Administrator, to apply the current accessibility options as the default for all new users, check the **Apply all settings to defaults for new users** check box
Creating a shortcut	WINXP 3.28	• Right-click an object
		• Hold down the right mouse button as you drag the object to the Desktop
		• Release the mouse button
		• In the context menu, click **Create Shortcut(s) Here**
		or
		• Right-click the object
		• In the context menu, click **Copy**
		• Right-click the Desktop

task reference roundup

Task	Page #	Preferred Method
		• In the context menu, click **Paste Shortcut**
		or
		• Right-click the Desktop
		• In the context menu, click **Create Shortcut**
		• In the field, type the path to the object, *or* click **Browse** to find the object
		• Click **Next**
		• Type a name for the shortcut
		• Click **Finish**
Renaming a shortcut	WINXP 3.30	• Right-click the shortcut
		• In the context menu, click **Rename**
		• Type the new name in the shortcut label
		• Press **Enter**
Arranging Desktop icons	WINXP 3.31	• Right-click the Desktop
		• Click **Line Up Icons** to line up the icons in columns and rows
		• In the Arrange Icons submenu, click **Name** to sort the objects by name
		• In the Arrange Icons submenu, click **Type** to sort the objects by type
		• In the Arrange Icons submenu, click **Size** to sort the objects by size
		• In the Arrange Icons submenu, click **Modified** to sort the objects by the date they were created
		• In the Arrange Icons submenu, click **Auto Arrange** to turn on or off the Auto Arrange feature, which locks the objects in columns at the left of the Desktop
Deleting shortcuts	WINXP 3.32	• Click the shortcut to delete
		• Press the **Delete** key

CROSSWORD PUZZLE

Across

1. Saves having to press certain keys simultaneously
2. An image on the background of the Desktop
5. Replaces the mouse with the keypad
8. A link to a program, file, or folder
9. Enhances system sounds with a visual cue
10. Locks Desktop icons in place
12. A collection of related properties
13. The number of pixels per inch on the screen
14. The _____ Options are used to compensate for differing abilities

Down

1. Enhances program sounds with visual cues
3. Using a Web page as your desktop is called an _____ desktop
4. Sounds a tone when the Caps Lock key is pressed
7. Before you can move the Taskbar around the Desktop, you must first _____ it
8. Arranges icons in neat rows and columns
11. To repeat an image to fill the Desktop

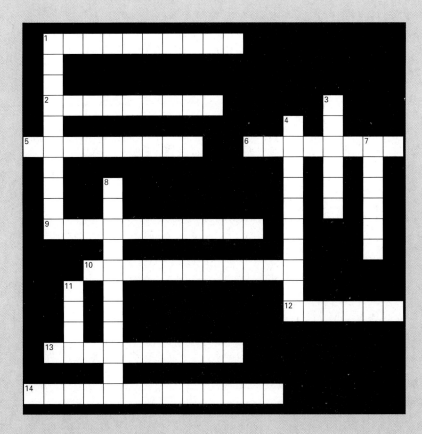

FILL IN

1. The _____ on the taskbar contains icons representing applications.

2. The _____ dialog box allows left-handed people to switch the mouse buttons.

3. The _____ repeats a wallpaper image to fill the Desktop.

4. Windows XP and Windows Classic are two examples of _____.

CREATE THE QUESTION

For each answer, create a short question:

ANSWER	QUESTION
1. A link to a file, folder, or program	_____
2. Prevents users from accidentally typing a character multiple times	_____
3. A collection of related properties for the Desktop, sounds, or mouse pointers	_____
4. Where you find the Accessibility Options	_____

SHORT ANSWER

1. What feature can make text more visible to the visually impaired?

2. Which key produces a double-click when MouseKeys is enabled?

3. What file extension is used by the sound files you assign to system events?

4. How do you make Desktop icons appear smaller and the screen area larger?

practice

1. Changing the Computer Settings for Visually and Hearing Impaired Users

Rosemary Sullivan works at the local assisted-living Senior Care Center. The center has just bought a new computer for the residents to use and installed it in the common lounge where the residents gather to talk, watch TV, and play games.

Because many of the residents have hearing or visual impairments, Rosemary asks you to help her change the settings on the computer so it will be easier for them to use.

1. Navigate to **Accessibility Options** in the **Control Panel** and open it
2. Click the **Keyboard** tab and select the *Show extra keyboard help in programs* check box near the bottom of the dialog box
3. Click the **Sound** tab and select the *Use ShowSounds* check box
4. Click the **Display** tab and select the *Use High Contrast* check box
5. Click **OK**

challenge

1. Using a Wallpaper and a Screen Saver on the Desktop

Alejandro Vaughn Studios specializes in elegant wedding photography and videotaping. Since the studio keeps archives of its work on computers that clients can click through to examine, the owner wants you to create a more appropriate Desktop environment than the default.

Select **Chateau** wallpaper for the Desktop. Try tiling and stretching it to fill the screen.

Next, set up the **3D Text** screen saver to display after 2 minutes. Type the company name, **Alejandro Vaughn Studios,** to display as a screen saver.

1. Creating a Project Folder of Shortcuts on the Taskbar

Jerry Sunshine works as a currency trader for the Fidelity Traders Corp. His company buys and sells currencies from different countries around the world. It is vital to his job to stay on top of fluctuating international exchange rates.

He does this by regularly checking a Web page that posts up-to-the-minute changes on world currencies rates. He also uses the Calculator and the Notepad in the Windows Accessories menu. Since he often needs to make quick decisions, he asks you if there is a quick way to access all these different tools without having to plod through the various menus and submenus.

Create a folder of shortcuts to the Calculator and Notepad applications, which includes a shortcut to a Web page that provides currency exchange information: www.oanda.com. Make the folder into a toolbar on the taskbar.

e-business

1. Adding a Shortcut to the Links Bar

Ron Brown runs an import/export business dealing in high-tech parts for medical research companies. Ron has frequent visitors, both customers and suppliers, visiting his office from all over the world. As a result, he spends two or three nights a week eating out with his business associates.

Since he is bored with taking his associates to the same places every time, Ron has asked you to find new restaurants that would be appropriate for him to have business meetings. You know Ron places as much value on a quiet ambience and fast service as anything else, so you need to find out about the restaurants in advance.

After some searching, you find that the Web site www.zagat.com provides you with all the information you need. Since you're always checking this site, you want to be able to get to it quickly.

Launch your Web browser and go to www.zagat.com. Locate the Web page's icon, which looks like a little blue "e" on a page next to the Web site's address in the Address bar. Drag this icon directly to the taskbar. Position your mouse over this new icon and right-click it. Select **Properties** from the context menu that appears. Click the **Shortcut** tab, then click the **Change Icon . . .** button. Make a selection from one of the various different icons in order to differentiate this icon from that of the others on your Desktop.

FIGURE 3.28

The Zagat's Web page

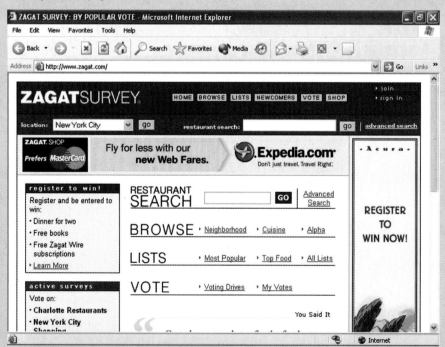

1. Customizing a Desktop Display

California Concentrators produces grape juice concentrate made from California grapes. There are several types, or varietals, of grapes it produces, some of which are used for wine production. Grape juice concentrate when reconstituted and fermented turns from concentrated juice to wine. The most popular grape varietals for wine production are Chardonnay, Riesling, Sauvignon Blanc, Cabernet Sauvignon, and Merlot.

Canada in particular is a big outlet for these varietal grape juice concentrates. The Canadian government places very stiff duty rates on bottled wine imported from outside the country. As a result, many Canadian wineries bottle their own wine to avoid these high tariffs. The problem is that Canada does not produce enough wine-grade grapes to meet the demand. In order to increase production, Canadian wineries buy grape concen-trate from other countries that have lots of grapes. Then they blend, ferment, and bottle the grape concentrate in Canada, thus avoiding the excessive duty rates.

Diane Capa works for California Concentrators, which has just completed a large contract with a Canadian winery for shipments extending over a year. Diane must make sure the deliveries correspond to the shipping schedule.

Diane asks you to help her redesign her Desktop. She wants to have her taskbar appear on the left side of her screen. The redesigned Desktop should appear similar to Figure 3.30.

Diane is also left-handed and asks you to reverse the mouse options to make them suitable for her. Change the mouse options to the opposite orientation, and then change them back to the original settings. (*Hint:* Do this in the Control Panel.)

FIGURE 3.29

Desktop with the taskbar displayed on the left of the screen

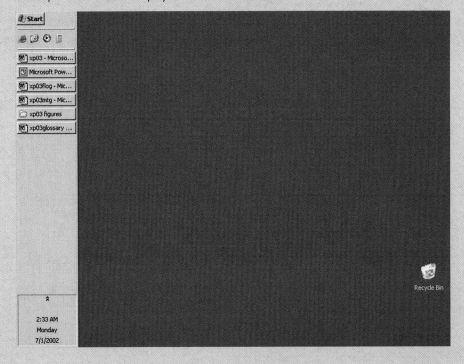

did you know?

two *inventors in California have developed a voice mail system that detects the degree of anger of the caller. This system is meant to direct impatient or furious callers to customer service representatives specially trained to handle annoyed customers.*

in *the search for the tiniest computer circuitry possible, researchers at Lucent Technologies have built a transistor in which the layer that switches currents on and off is only one molecule thick.*

the *Grand Duchy of Luxembourg, a tiny country (smaller than Rhode Island) in Europe, has the highest per capita income in the world, currently more than $48,000.*

a *computer known as "Deep Blue" (developed by a team of graduate students at Carnegie Mellon University) beat World Grand Champion Gary Kasparov at Chess on May 11, 1997, an accomplishment many, including Mr. Kasparov, said would never happen. All previous attempts by a computer, including Deep Blue's predecessor "Deep Thought," to beat a chess master at that level had failed.*

Chapter Objectives

- Learn about how Windows XP uses storage, about different types of storage disks, and how to format a hard drive

- Learn about some basic disk problems and use the maintenance tools provided by Windows XP Professional such as Disk Cleanup, Check Disk, and Disk Defragmenter to analyze, correct, and prevent disk errors

- Learn how to schedule tasks to run automatically on your computer

- Learn how to back up your hard drive, some strategies for backing up, and how to restore your backup in case of a disk failure

Children's Care Center (CCC), Syosset, New York

Kate is a sophomore in a local college in Glen Cove, New York, studying computers. She lives with her parents and wants to get some work experience to put on her résumé when she looks for a full-time job after she graduates. She also would not mind having a little more spending money.

Kate mentions to one of her neighbors, Mary Ann Nola, what she's looking for. Mrs. Nola works as an office manager in a busy medical office named Children's Care Center. There are six pediatricians in the office. All the billing, insurance, scheduling of appointments, payroll, and patient database, in fact everything having to do with the medical office, is done on five linked computers running Windows XP. Mrs. Nola says that although the computer systems seem to be working fine, she's worried that one day there will be a crash of the system and all the vital information will be lost. Obviously, this would be disastrous for the office, not to mention the enormous downtime and hassles this will create. Mrs. Nola says that she always plans to back up the computers but just never seems to get to it in the course of a normal workweek. She needs somebody to come in once a week for a few hours to do the routine backup that the system requires. Kate likes the idea, and though she explains that she is not an expert, she is willing to give it a go.

She starts coming in on Saturdays in the late afternoon after the office is closed for the week and backs up the systems onto a Zip drive that the office has purchased especially for this purpose. As she does this, she discovers there are many other basic steps she can take to make sure the computers are working smoothly.

SESSION 4.1 WORKING WITH REMOVABLE MEDIA

One of the most basic benefits of using computers is greater accessibility of information. But how you store information is as important as what you store. If the information from your computer is not accessible, it is as if it wasn't there.

BASIC STORAGE

In an office, information is recorded on pieces of paper with writing on it, which is in turn kept in folders, which are in turn kept in storage cabinets. Computers write and keep track of information electronically with "storage cabinets" called *disks.* The pieces of paper with information on them equate to *files,* which can be documents, pictures, audio tracks, programs, and so forth.

There are various kinds of disks. Inside your computer there is a hard disk. This is probably your main storage receptacle. In addition, common disks on a computer are portable disks of various kinds—floppy disks, CDs, Zip disks, Tape drives, DVDs, and the like. All these track and archive your information and are known as *removable media,* because they can be used on multiple different computers (as opposed to your hard drive, which is fixed inside the computer).

Open Windows Explorer (Windows + E) and click the plus sign next to My Computer. Notice in the left pane of the window how many different volumes there are on each disk in your computer: hard drives, floppy disks, CDs, and any other disks. (See Figure 4.1.) Despite the different media, the computer displays each volume the same way, as a window with folders and files hierarchically arranged.

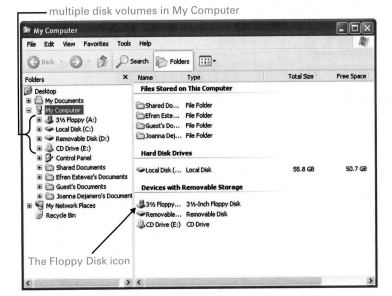

multiple disk volumes in My Computer

The Floppy Disk icon

F I G U R E 4.1

The My Computer window of Windows Explorer

FLOPPY DISKS

Floppy disks allow you to transport and store small files. Your floppy disk drive is usually letter A under My Computer. In general, it works like any other drive. You can create folders on it, move and copy files to and from it, and delete files from it. Since floppy disks are a common removable disk on many computers, we will learn how to work with them. But the techniques shown here can work (with minor variations) on other removable media.

Floppy disks are so called because not too long ago, they were made of thin plastic that wiggled when shaken. Nowadays, a hard plastic outer shell is the norm. But the cute name has stuck. Floppies come in two different capacities. Double-density disks hold 720 kilobytes (KB) of information. High-density disks can hold twice as much, or 1.44 megabytes (MB). Again, in the early days of personal computing, this amount of room was adequate for most storage situations. Today, it is pitifully little. Some computers are no longer even made with floppy drives.

However, floppies remain useful for many tasks, such as providing copies of small files to another user who is not connected to you via a network.

FORMATTING A FLOPPY DISK

The way information is structured on a disk is called its *format.* Formatting sets up the space on the disk so it is able to store files from the Windows operating system. Any disk, whether it is a floppy disk or a hard drive, must be formatted before information can be stored on it. However, formatting removes all the information on a disk. If the disk you plan to format is blank (like a brand new floppy disk you just purchased), then this is not a problem. However, if the disk you are formatting has been used before (like an old hard drive), make sure there isn't any data on it that you wish to keep. Many disks are already formatted when you buy them, but you may run into a disk that hasn't been formatted, or you may want to reformat a disk to clear all the information on it.

---

task reference

Formatting a Floppy Disk

- Insert a floppy disk and click **Start,** then click **My Computer**
- Click the floppy drive icon
- Click **File,** then click **Format...**
- Specify options, such as the size and name of the disk
- Click **Start,** then click **OK**

Formatting a floppy disk:

Kate realizes that in addition to the larger capacity Zip disks, it would be useful for CCC to have some floppies to back up some critical files right away rather than waiting for the weekly backups that she will be performing on Saturdays. Accordingly, she purchases a box of floppy disks to keep available for the administrative staff and formats them so that they are ready for use.

1. Insert the floppy disk you plan to format into the floppy drive of your computer

2. Click **Start,** then **My Computer.** This will open the My Computer window

3. Click the floppy drive icon (usually labeled **A:**)

4. Click **File**

5. Click **Format**.... The Format dialog box appears

6. Click the *Capacity* drop-down list to select the size of the disk

7. Click the *File system* drop-down list to select **FAT32**

8. Click the *Volume label* text box and type a friendly name for the disk that describes its contents or function

9. Click **Start** to begin formatting. An alert message appears, warning you that formatting will erase all the information on the disk

10. Click **OK** to continue. When formatting is complete, a dialog box will appear to advise this

11. Click **OK** to close the dialog box

tip: *If you are having problems formatting a disk, it may be damaged. To avoid damaging your disks, keep them away from moisture, heat, and magnets (many telephones have magnets in the handset, so it's a good idea to keep floppies away from phones).*

COPYING ONE FLOPPY DISK TO ANOTHER

Windows XP also provides a convenient way for you to copy the contents of one floppy disk to another without having to copy all of the files onto the computer.

task reference

Copying One Floppy Disk to Another

- Insert the disk you want to copy

- In My Computer, click the floppy disk drive icon

- In the File menu, click **Copy Disk**

- Indicate the disk you want to copy from and the disk you want to copy to, then click **Start**

- When prompted, remove the first disk and replace it with the disk you're copying to

making the grade   SESSION 4.1

1. Can you create folders on a floppy disk?

2. When you _____ a floppy disk, all information on it is cleared.

3. The _____ option allows you to copy an entire floppy disk.

4. Tape drives, CDs, and floppy disks are all examples of _____ media.

SESSION 4.2 WORKING WITH HARD DRIVES

CONVERTING A DRIVE TO AN NTFS FILE SYSTEM

Formatting your hard drive involves installing a *file system* to keep track of data stored on the disk. Windows XP Professional is designed to use the NTFS file system. FAT32, which is an upgrade of the old FAT file system, is also a very common file system you will see. FAT stands for File Allocation Table and is the part of Windows that keeps track of where data is stored on disk.

Let's examine the advantages of NTFS over FAT first. NTFS has better file security, stability, and disk compression than FAT. FAT slows down considerably as a hard drive gets larger. If your hard drive is bigger than 5 gigabytes, FAT is not an option. In addition, FAT is susceptible to greater file fragmentation, further slowing down performance. Most importantly, a disk formatted in FAT is very insecure. NTFS offers much more sophisticated security.

The newer version of FAT is FAT32, which provides support for larger partitions and uses space on those partitions more efficiently than previously. FAT32 also supports longer filenames. FAT32, however, does not give you as much flexibility as NTFS.

Accordingly, a computer running Windows XP Professional and using the FAT or FAT32 file system is a candidate for file system conversion. Keep in mind that this is a one-way trip, however. Once you convert a volume to NTFS, you can't go back to FAT. Make sure you have no reason to go back before you convert a drive. If you are not sure, it is a good idea to do some research before deciding. You might want to consider partitioning your hard drive and only converting a part of it to NTFS.

*another*word

. . . on Converting to NTFS

Do *not* think, however, that because you are running Windows XP, you must convert all your disks to NTFS right away. In certain circumstances the older FAT file system can be a better performer, such as if your hard drive is smaller than 2 gigabytes. NTFS is overkill with small volumes. After NTFS's security and other overhead is taken into account, there is very little space left over in a small volume for actual data. Plus FAT is a simpler system, which lends itself to being faster on small volumes. Another reason the older FAT file system is popular is that multiple operating systems other than Windows XP can access data from a FAT volume. Any of the following operating systems can be installed on one computer and have no trouble with a FAT volume: MS-DOS, OS/2, Linux, Windows 3.x, Windows 95/98/NT/2000

*task*reference

Converting a Drive to NTFS

- Click **Start, All Programs, Accessories,** and **Command Prompt**
- Type **convert,** and then press the spacebar
- Type the letter of the drive you wish to convert followed by a colon (**:**), and then press the spacebar
- Type **/fs:ntfs,** and then press the **Enter** key
- Type **Y** (for Yes)
- Type **exit,** and then press the **Enter** key

Converting a drive to NTFS:

1. Click **Start**
2. Click **All Programs**

3. Click **Accessories**

4. Click **Command Prompt.** The Command Prompt window appears

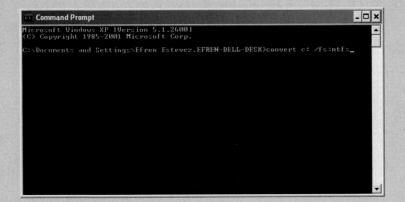

FIGURE 4.2

The Command Prompt window with NTFS instructions

5. Type **convert,** and then press the spacebar

6. Type the letter of the drive you wish to convert followed by a colon (**:**), and then press the spacebar

7. Type **/fs:ntfs** and then press the **Enter** key. Windows returns information about the type of file system in use and will ask if you would like to schedule the conversion the next time the system restarts

8. Type **Y** (for Yes). Windows confirms your instructions

9. Type **exit,** and then press the **Enter** key to close the Command Prompt window. The next time the computer starts, Windows executes the conversion automatically

PARTITIONS

A *partition* is a section of a hard drive that acts like a separate disk or volume. When you partition a hard drive, a part of it is reserved for a specific purpose. For example, if you have the room on your hard drive, partitioning can give you the ability to use different operating systems depending on your needs. This is known as a *dual-boot* configuration. This is useful if you have programs that can only run on older operating systems. Another reason you may want to partition a hard drive is in order to use one partition to store programs and the other to store data. This makes backing up easier as you only have the data section of the hard drive to worry about.

A hard drive can have one large partition or be divided into up to four smaller partitions. Each partition is given a separate letter to identify it. An unpartitioned hard drive will typically just have the letter C: After partitioning, drives C:, D:, E:, and F: could be on the same physical disk, but they would act like four separate drives to the operating system and user. A tool called Disk Management displays the partition(s) on the hard drive and the amount of unallocated, or free, space available for additional partitions.

task reference

Using Disk Management to View Drive Information

- Click **Start,** then **Control Panel**
- Double-click the **Administrative Tools** icon
- Double-click the **Computer Management** icon
- Click **Disk Management**

Using Disk Management to view drive information:

1. Click **Start**
2. Click **Control Panel.** The Control Panel window opens
3. Double-click on the **Administrative Tools** icon. The Administrative Tools window opens
4. Double-click **Computer Management.** The Computer Management window opens
5. Click **Disk Management.** The right pane of the window displays information about your hard drive and the partition(s) on it

FIGURE 4.3

The Disk Management view in the Computer Management

click Disk Management to view drive information

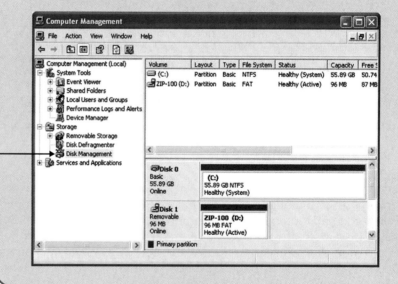

Note that the main part of your hard drive is named the primary partition. The ***primary partition*** is the first division of a hard disk drive. The primary partition is often the only one on the disk, and in this case it occupies the entire disk volume. When creating a new partition, you can create either a primary partition or an extended partition. An ***extended partition*** can contain multiple drives, called logical drives. Note that if there are multiple partitions, the primary partition is the one that holds the operating system. If you have more than one operating system on your hard drive, they must be stored on a primary partition. A hard drive can contain up to four primary partitions. If you want to create more than four sections, create an extended partition, which can be further subdivided into logical drives.

Note: If you add a new hard drive to your computer, you must partition it first before it can store information.

---

task reference

Creating a New Partition

- Navigate to the Disk Management area of the Computer Management window **(Start, Control Panel, Administrative Tools, Computer Management, Disk Management)**

- Right-click the unallocated space of a basic disk you wish to partition, then click **New Partition**

- In the New Partition Wizard, click **Next,** click **Primary Partition** or **Extended Partition,** and follow the instructions on your screen

---

Creating a new partition:

Kate gets feedback from Mrs. Nola that once a year, when it's time to mail out holiday cards to all the patients, the CCC staff would like to use an old bulk mailing program. The problem is that this particular program doesn't run on Windows XP, only Windows 95. Kate decides to take one computer that is not used for any essential tasks and partition the hard drive. This will allow for a dual-boot configuration that will enable both Windows XP and Windows 95 to be run on the same computer, which in turn will allow the office staff to use the desired mailing program that only works with the older operating system. Since operating systems should only be installed on a primary partition, this is the type of partition she will create.

1. Go to the Disk Management area of the Computer Management window **(Start, Control Panel, Administrative Tools, Computer Management, Disk Management)**

2. Right-click the unallocated space you wish to partition. A context menu appears

3. Click **New Partition.** The New Partition Wizard opens

4. Click **Next.** The Select Partition Type screen appears

tip: *Windows XP Professional supports a maximum of four primary partitions in a hard drive, or three primary partitions and one extended partition.*

5. Click the radio button next to *Primary partition*, then click **Next.** The Specify Partition Size screen appears

6. In the *Partition Size in MB* spin box, double-click the number and type the amount of disk space you want to use to create the partition, then click **Next**

tip: *This window will give you information about the minimum and maximum amount of space available on your hard drive.*

7. The Completing the New Partition Wizard screen appears. Click **Finish** to close the Wizard and create the partition. You are returned to the Computer Management window, which graphically displays the new partition

*another*word

. . . on Using Multiple Operating Systems

If you have more than one operating system installed, your computer at startup will prompt you to choose which one to use to start the computer. If no selection is made, the default operating system will be used. You can change which operating system is considered the default

task reference

Changing the Default Operating System

- Click **Start,** then click **Control Panel**
- Double-click **System**
- Click the **Advanced** tab
- In the *Startup and Recovery* area, click **Settings**
- Select the desired operating system and then click **OK**
- Click **OK**

Changing the default operating system:

After Kate partitions the hard drive on the designated computer that will have a dual-boot configuration, she wants to make Windows XP the default operating system on that computer, since it will likely only need to boot the older OS a few times near the end of the calendar year.

1. Click **Start**
2. Click **Control Panel.** The Control Panel window opens
3. Double-click **System.** The System Properties dialog box opens
4. Click the **Advanced** tab
5. In the *Startup and Recovery* area, click **Settings.** The Startup and Recovery dialog box opens with the default operating system highlighted
6. In the drop-down list, select the **Microsoft Windows XP Professional** operating system
7. Click **OK**
8. Click **OK** to close the System Properties dialog box

VOLUMES

A hard drive may be broken up into different logical sections, called **volumes,** with a different file system on each one.

Note: In addition to being a logical storage unit, the term volume can also indicate a physical storage unit, such as a hard disk, floppy disk, disk cartridge, CD-ROM disk, or reel of tape.

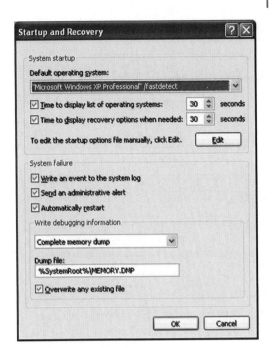

FIGURE 4.4
The Startup and Recovery dialog box

To create a logical drive within an extended partition, follow the steps outlined above to open the Disk Management section of the Computer Management window. Right-click an area of unallocated space, and then click Create Logical Drive. The New Partition Wizard opens, allowing you to create the logical drive in an extended partition.

making the grade

SESSION 4.2

1. The file format designed for use by Windows XP Professional is _____.

2. The _____ is the first division of a hard disk drive.

3. A hard drive can be broken up into multiple _____ to allow for logical use of storage space.

4. _____ prepares a disk to accept data.

SESSION 4.3 DIAGNOSING DISK PROBLEMS

DISK CLEANUP

Most people end up using this utility when they try to download something or install a new program. A dialog box appears telling them that there is not enough empty space on their hard drive. Ideally, you want to manage what's on your computer better than that. A good habit to get into is regularly cleaning your disk drives. Programs often create temporary files for one purpose and then do not delete them later. These junk files can clutter your hard drive, taking up unnecessary space. The Disk Cleanup tool finds and removes these files. This process frees up disk space.

task **reference**

Running Disk Cleanup

- Click **Start, All Programs, Accessories, System Tools, Disk Cleanup**
- Click **OK,** then click **Yes**
- Click **OK**

Running Disk Cleanup:

Kate decides that by getting rid of unneeded files, folders, and programs that take up room and are never used, she will maximize the operations of all the computers in the office. This process will also reduce the time needed to make backups. Accordingly, she begins to systematically go through all the computers in the office and run Disk Cleanup.

1. Click **Start, All Programs, Accessories, System Tools, Disk Cleanup.** Windows automatically checks your hard drive for files that are candidates for deletion. When complete, the Disk Cleanup dialog box opens listing some potential files to delete. It also advises you of the total amount of space you will gain if you delete these files

FIGURE 4.5

The Disk Cleanup dialog box

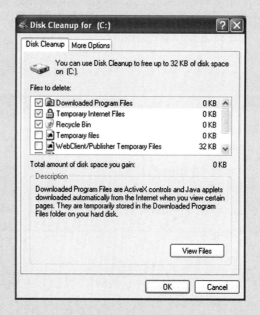

2. Remove the check from the check box for any files you do not want discarded

tip: *To see what is in these files before deleting, highlight the files you want to examine and then click **View Details***

3. Click **OK** when you are ready to go ahead with the cleaning

4. Click **Yes** to confirm that you want to delete these files. Disk Cleanup removes the files

*another*way

. . . to Clean Up a Disk

Click **Start,** then **My Computer**

Right-click the **Local Disk (C:)**

Select **Properties** from the context menu. The Local Disk (C:) Properties dialog box opens

In the *General tab*, click the **Disk Cleanup** button

Unused files are not the only culprits that waste disk space. Often there are programs installed on the computer that you never use, or games you haven't played in years, that take up lots of room. The More Options tab in the Disk Cleanup window allows you to get rid of windows components and installed programs that you do not use.

---

task reference

Removing Windows Components and Installed Programs

- Click **Start, All Programs, Accessories, System Tools, Disk Cleanup**
- Click the **More Options** tab
- Click **Clean Up . . .,** then select the components you want to remove

---

Removing windows components and installed programs:

1. From the Disk Cleanup for Local Disk (C:) dialog box, which you opened in the previous exercise, click the **More Options** tab

FIGURE 4.6

The More Options tab of the Disk Cleanup dialog box

2. In the top section labeled *Windows Components*, click **Clean Up . . .** This launches the Windows Components Wizard

3. Select the components you want to remove and click **Next.** The system will remove components based on your instructions

tip: *If you don't know what a particular component does, click the component you want to know more about, and then click the Details . . . button. Windows opens a dialog box with a description of that particular component*

*another*way

. . . to Remove Windows Components

There is a more direct way to add or remove windows components if you are not already in the Disk Cleanup dialog box:

Click **Start,** then **Control Panel**

Double-click **Add/Remove Programs**

Click **Add/Remove Windows Components**

Select the components to remove

FIGURE 4.7

The Windows Components
Wizard launched from the More
Options tab of the Disk Cleanup
dialog box

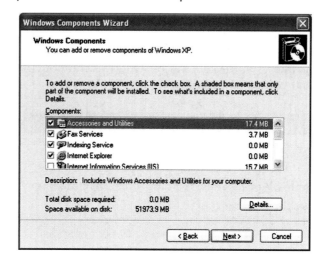

DISK DIRECTORIES AND FOLDERS

A *directory* is a simulated file folder on disk. In fact, another name for a
directory is a folder, and these two names are often used interchangeably in
the Windows world. Think of walking into the lobby of a large office building in a city. A building directory will list all the companies that have offices
in the building and where in the building they are located (for example,
ABC Company, 3rd Floor, Suite # 305). In the
same way, computers provide you with a
directory to what's on your computer.

Applications, documents, pictures, music
—in fact everything that is on your computer
is organized into files and folders. These files
and folders are listed in your computer's directory. On a Windows computer this directory is
displayed via Windows Explorer.

Use Windows Explorer to view disk directories. Play around by clicking on the plus
sign in front of the C drive to view its subdi-
rectory. Keep going down through the differ-
ent layers, and then go back up the layers by clicking on the minus sign to
collapse the subdirectories.

anotherword

. . . on Directories and Files

Directories or folders use the visual analogy of
compartments, but this is an illusion. In reality, the
files created are scattered all over your hard disk
(more about disk defragmentation later in this
chapter). For organizational purposes, Windows
takes all these scattered bits of data and presents
your folders and files in a clear, logical manner

Types of Errors and Problems That Can Occur on a Disk

From time to time, the data collected on your computer can become corrupted. Your hard drive can lose pieces of files. (File system errors include
problems such as lost file fragments, which are pieces of data no longer
associated with a file.) Programs can start acting bizarrely. For no apparent reason, graphics will change or gibberish will appear instead of
English. The computer will suddenly stop letting you do something you
routinely perform.

Unfortunately, these bugs are something that affects all computers to
one degree or another. These types of problems can often be fixed by something as simple as restarting your computer. However, Windows XP
Professional provides you with a tool, called Check Disk, for fixing many of
these minor problems.

task reference

Running Check Disk

- Click **Start,** then click **My Computer**
- Right-click the **Local Disk (C:)** drive
- In the context menu, click **Properties**
- Click the **Tools** tab
- Click the **Check Now . . .** button
- Click the two check boxes to accept both options
- Click **OK,** then click **OK** again

Running Check Disk:

Kate receives a note on her desk when she comes in on Saturday telling her that one computer in the office is behaving strangely. The first thing she does is run Check Disk on the computer of concern.

1. Click **Start,** then click **My Computer**

2. Right-click the **Local Disk (C:)** drive

3. In the context menu, click **Properties.** This opens the Local Disk (C:) drive Properties dialog box

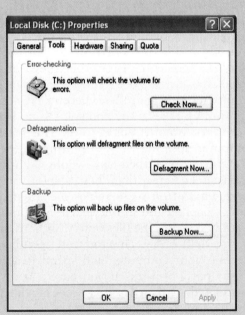

FIGURE 4.8
The Tools tab of the Local Disk (C:) Properties dialog box

4. Click the **Tools** tab

5. Click the **Check Now . . .** button. The Check Disk window opens

6. You have two options at this point: **Automatically fix file system errors** and **Scan for and attempt recovery of bad sectors.** Click the two check boxes to accept both options

FIGURE 4.9

The Check Disk dialog box

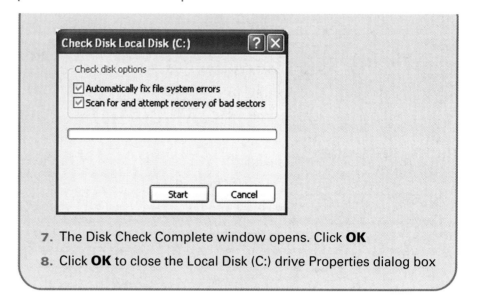

FIGURE 4.9

The Check Disk dialog box

7. The Disk Check Complete window opens. Click **OK**

8. Click **OK** to close the Local Disk (C:) drive Properties dialog box

Run Check Disk about once a month, but more often if you notice strange things happening. It usually will not take long to do its work, so you can do this task anytime.

DISK DEFRAGMENTATION

Think of a storage closet. Imagine this closet belongs to somebody who's always in a hurry. Each time they put something down wherever there is empty space (usually just inside the closet door). After a while, they run out of empty space. In addition, things are likely all over the place. Say this very busy person is a skier. The ski boots are shoved all the way in the back, while the ski poles are right inside the door. And the skis are—well you get the idea. It's not a very efficient setup. Every time they want to go skiing, they have to dig around all over the place to find what's needed.

In the same way, your computer puts your files wherever it finds empty space on your hard drive. It often takes a file and splits it up between different areas of your hard drive—fragmenting it to fit. This process is invisible to a user. Your computer does the work of putting all the fragments together so that you can work with them as a whole. What will be apparent over time is that things take longer than they used to.

The process of **_disk defragmentation_** reassembles the fragments so that all the pieces that belong together are in one place, nice and neat. Actually, the Defragmenter utility rewrites the files onto your hard drive in the right order. This reduces the amount of time your computer will spend locating all the parts of a file. If you have a badly fragmented hard drive, this process will noticeably improve its performance.

Defragmentation reorganizes the disk by putting files into contiguous order. Because the operating system stores new data in whatever free space is available, data files become spread out across the disk if they are updated often.

It is a good idea to defragment your hard drive about once every two or three months. This will not create more free space on your

anotherword

The task of regular disk defragmentation has its critics. The argument goes that with hard drives today being so fast, disk defragmentation does not provide a noticeable improvement in performance. Additionally, defragmentation is a potentially risky process as it involves touching every piece of data on your hard drive. Regardless of your point of view, the topic of disk defragmentation has its merits as a teaching tool for understanding that data are written to a disk noncontiguously

hard drive, but it will make it easier and quicker for your computer to find and access your files.

Note: You do not defragment other drives such as floppy drives, CDs, or other removable drives.

---

task reference

Using the Disk Defragmenter

- Click **Start, All Programs, Accessories, System Tools, Disk Defragmenter**
- Click the drive you want to defragment and click the **Analyze** button
- Click **Defragment**
- Click **Close**

Using the Disk Defragmenter:

After running Check Disk on the computer she has been told is behaving strangely in order to diagnose the problem, Kate performs a disk defragmentation on the same computer in order to make sure it is operating as efficiently as possible.

1. Click **Start**

2. Click **All Programs**

3. Click **Accessories**

4. Click **System Tools**

5. Click **Disk Defragmenter**

6. The Disk Defragmenter window appears and displays the available drives on your computer. Click the drive you want to defragment

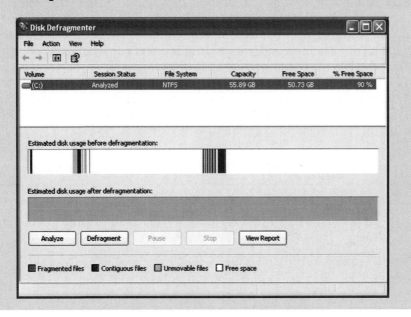

FIGURE 4.10

The Disk Defragmenter window

*another*way

. . . to Defragment Your Hard Drive

You can also defragment your hard drive this way:

Open **My Computer** and right-click drive **Local Disk (C:).** In the context menu, click **Properties.** Click the **Tools** tab. Click **Defragment Now . . .**

7. Click the **Analyze** button on the bottom of the window. After a few moments, a dialog box named Analysis Complete appears. It lets you know whether the volume you have selected needs defragmenting. A bar graph provides a representation of the status of the volume in different colored stripes. The legend at the bottom of the window details what each colored section describes in terms of Fragmented Files, Free Space, and so forth

8. Click **Defragment.** The lower bar graph indicates the progress of the defragmentation. When the process is completed, another dialog box appears

9. Click **Close** to close the dialog box. You can also click the **View Report** button in the Disk Defragmenter window to view details of the process

10. Click the window's **Close** button to close the Disk Defragmenter window

tip: *Disk defragmentation can take a long time, especially if you have not defragmented the disk recently. Consequently, this is not a good activity to schedule in the middle of the day, when you need to get the computer back to finish other work. Although you can select the **Pause** option in the middle of defragmentation in order to attend to something else, this slows the process. It is generally better to schedule this event at the end of a workday, or before a long break, so that the utility can do its thing undisturbed. Ideally, disk defragmentation is a process you schedule to take place automatically during the computer's downtime with the Scheduled Tasks utility (see the section below)*

SCHEDULING MAINTENANCE

The good news is that you do not have to wallpaper your monitor with yellow sticky notes to remind yourself to do all these basic maintenance tasks. The Scheduled Tasks tool can automatically execute routine chores like disk cleanup or disk defragmentation at predefined intervals. You can set specific days (such as every week or every month) and times (such as during lunch time or after hours) when the computer will run these utilities all by itself. You'll want to slot these activities to occur when you are not likely to be using the computer for anything else so that you don't get interrupted. You want to schedule the maintenance and forget about it.

In addition to scheduling routine maintenance, Scheduled Tasks is useful to run other programs. For example, it can launch Outlook Express every time you start the computer to check for new e-mail.

task reference

Using Scheduled Tasks

- Click **Start, All Programs, Accessories, System Tools, Scheduled Tasks**

- Double-click **Add Scheduled Task,** then click **Next**

- Click the program you want to schedule, then click **Next**

*tas**k* *reference*

- Click one of the radio buttons to select when to perform this task, then click **Next**

- Click the appropriate box and type the Start time and frequency for the task, then click **Next**

- Type your password, and then type it again in the **Confirm Password** field; then click **Next**

- Click **Finish**

Using Scheduled Tasks:

After having attended to some of the basics, Kate feels she has a pretty good handle on what needs to be done to keep things in order with the computers. Now she begins to change her focus to automating as many of the routine maintenance tasks as possible so that things will be maintained in good order without a lot of extra effort. She begins to add as many maintenance tasks as possible to the Scheduled Tasks.

1. Click **Start, All Programs, Accessories, System Tools, Scheduled Tasks.** The Scheduled Tasks window opens

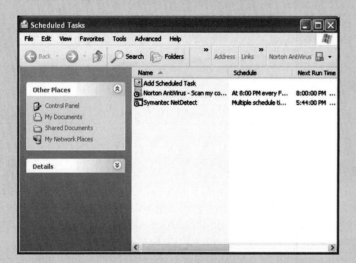

FIGURE 4.11
The Scheduled Tasks window

2. Double-click **Add Scheduled Task.** This launches a Wizard

3. Click **Next**

4. Click the program you want to schedule. If you do not see the program you want, click **Browse**

5. Click **Next**

6. Type a descriptive name for the task; otherwise Windows will provide a default name

7. Click one of the radio buttons to select when to perform this task, then click **Next**

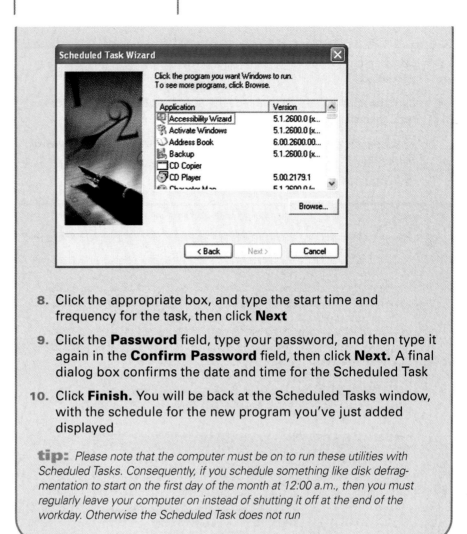

8. Click the appropriate box, and type the start time and frequency for the task, then click **Next**

9. Click the **Password** field, type your password, and then type it again in the **Confirm Password** field, then click **Next.** A final dialog box confirms the date and time for the Scheduled Task

10. Click **Finish.** You will be back at the Scheduled Tasks window, with the schedule for the new program you've just added displayed

tip: *Please note that the computer must be on to run these utilities with Scheduled Tasks. Consequently, if you schedule something like disk defragmentation to start on the first day of the month at 12:00 a.m., then you must regularly leave your computer on instead of shutting it off at the end of the workday. Otherwise the Scheduled Task does not run*

Stopping a Scheduled Task

Despite your best efforts, a scheduled task may start to run when you are in the middle of something you do not want to stop. In this situation, follow the steps above to open the Scheduled Tasks window. Right-click the task you want to stop, and then select End Task.

If you want to *temporarily* stop scheduled tasks from running at all, go to the Scheduled Tasks window and click the Advanced menu and choose Pause Task Scheduler.

When you are ready for the scheduled task to begin again, click the Advanced menu and choose Continue Task Scheduler.

Modifying a Scheduled Task

You may find that a scheduled task does not run the way you thought it would. Or that a time you originally thought would be convenient is actually not. Change the settings for a task by opening the Scheduled Tasks window as shown above. Right-click the icon for the task you wish to modify, and choose Properties. From the dialog box that appears, click the appropriate tab (Task, Schedule, or Settings) to modify the task. When you are finished, click Apply and then OK.

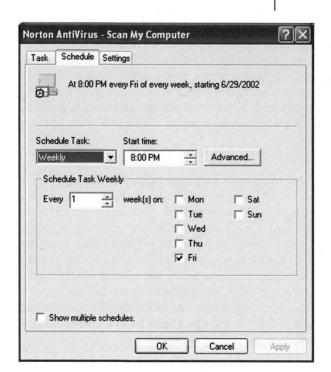

FIGURE   4.13
Modifying the schedule for a task in Schedule Task

Note: You may need to log on as an Administrator to be able to change these or other settings for a particular task.

Deleting a Scheduled Task

To delete a scheduled task entirely, navigate to the Scheduled Tasks window, locate the icon for the task you want to delete, and right-click it. Choose Delete from the shortcut menu. Click Yes to confirm the deletion.

After deletion, the icon for the task is removed from the Scheduled Tasks window.

---

making the grade   SESSION 4.3

1. A Wizard that automatically runs a program at specific times is the _____ Wizard.

2. To delete programs and components you no longer use to free up hard disk space, go to the _____ and use Add/ Remove Programs.

3. Relocating all the data on a disk so that it fits together more efficiently refers to _____.

4. The path you navigate to get to the Task Scheduler is _____.

5. The utility program _____ searches a storage disk for errors.

SESSION 4.4 BACKUP AND RECOVERY

BACKING UP DISK DATA

Windows XP Professional provides an essential utility called Backup that allows you to copy the data on your hard drive onto another storage device for safekeeping. This process prevents data loss and damage caused by disk failures, power outages, accidental erasure, viruses, or malicious individuals. It is a useful tool that's important to learn. Backup is located in the System Tools folder in the Accessories menu. Backup allows you to specify what information you want backed up and also where you want the copied data stored. You can choose to back up all the information on your hard drive or only the specific items you select.

STRATEGIES FOR BACKING UP FILES

A backup plan, regularly and religiously implemented, is a nonnegotiable requirement in any serious individual or collective endeavor. Most hard drives should be backed up at least once a week. However, critical data should be backed up daily or even more frequently. The question to ask is how much would losing your latest data cost to replace. This must be weighed in comparison with the amount of time needed to perform your backup and restoring the lost files. In some cases, the cost of losing even a small amount of data may be very high. In addition to weekly backups, it is wise to make quick copies of critical data on removable disks as needed. In addition, to protect against fire, flood, and theft, keep a complete second backup of your data off your primary premises.

---

task reference

Using the Backup Tool

- Click **Start, All Programs, Accessories, System Tools, Backup**

- Click the **Backup Wizard** button, then click **Next**

- Click the appropriate radio button to select what you want to back up, then click **Next**

- Click the check box beside each item you want to back up, then click **Next**

- Select the drive where you want to store your backup file and type a name for the backup file

- Click **Open,** then click **Next**

- Click **Finish**

Using the Backup tool:

Kate is now ready to focus on the main purpose for which she was hired: to perform regular backups of the office data. In the relatively short time she has been at CCC, she has come to the conclusion that one of the most critical files in the office is the main database of patient records.

She decides to begin by making a complete backup of the primary computer that houses these records. Once that is complete, she will move on to other data until she is confident that in the event of a hard disk failure, she will be able to get the office up and running in a relatively short time.

She labels the backup disks carefully and puts them in a safe place. Further, she makes a complete second backup, which she gives to Mrs. Nola to take home. That way, even if there is a catastrophic event in the office, there will be a complete copy of all the files in a secure off-premise location.

1. Click **Start, All Programs, Accessories, System Tools, Backup.** The Backup and Recovery Tools window opens.

tip: *The first time Backup is launched, the Backup or Restore Wizard is automatically launched. The main screen has a check box, which controls whether the Wizard is always launched whenever Backup is selected. If the Wizard is not automatically launched, click the program button next to the Backup Wizard to launch it.*

FIGURE 4.14

The Welcome screen of the Backup or Restore Wizard

2. Click **Next**

3. Click the appropriate radio button to select what you want to back up. For this exercise, select **Back up files and settings,** then click **Next.** The What to Back up screen opens

4. Click the radio button beside the item(s) you want to back up, then click **Next.** The next screen asks you to choose a place to save the backup and what to name it

5. Use the drop-down list to select a place to save the backup and type **My Backup** in the text box that asks you to name the backup. After completing these steps, click **Next**

6. You get a confirmation from the Wizard of the settings you have chosen. To start the backup, click **Finish.** The Backup Progress dialog box opens and advises you when the process is complete

7. Click the **Close** button to close the dialog box

8. Click the window's **Close** button to close the Backup window

Windows XP Professional allows you to run backups of files or drives you choose automatically at certain scheduled times. This process ensures that your backups get done regularly without fail.

F I G U R E   4.15

Completing the Backup Wizard window displaying the Advanced button

Using the Advanced backup options:

1. Click the **Advanced** button in the Completing Backup Wizard window

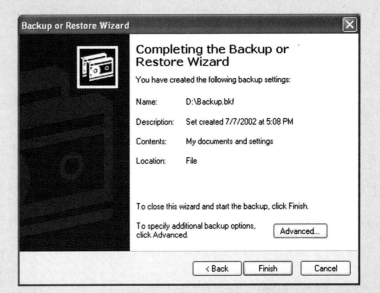

2. Select the type of backup operation to perform. A Normal backup is what you should perform the first time you back up a set of files. Copy backup backs up selected files, but does not mark them as backed up. Incremental or Differential backup backs up any data that has changed since the last time a backup was performed. A Daily backup backs up whatever data has been added or changed that day. For the purpose of this exercise, select **Normal** backup, then click **Next**

3. Click the check box next to *Verify data after backup* and click **Next**

4. Click the appropriate radio button to indicate what to do if the archive media already contains backups. If you are replacing the data, click the check box to allow only the owner and Administrator access to the backup data. Click **Next**

5. The When to Back Up window opens. Click the appropriate radio button to select whether to Back up Now or Later. For the purpose of this exercise, select the radio button next to *Later*

6. Click the *Job name* text box, and type a name for the backup job

7. Click the **Set Schedule** button. The Schedule Job dialog box opens

8. From the **Schedule Task** drop-down list, select how often you want the backup to run

9. From the **Start Time** spin box, select when you want the backup to begin, then click **OK.** You are returned to the When to Back Up dialog box

F I G U R E　4.16

The Schedule Job dialog box in
the Backup Wizard

10. Click **Next,** which opens the Set Account Information dialog box

11. If you agree with the user name for the account Windows has chosen, go to the next step; otherwise, type in a new account name

12. Type a password in the *Password* text box, then type in the same password again in the *Confirm Password* text box, and click **OK**

13. The Completing Backup Wizard window opens, which confirms the settings you have chosen. If all is the way you want it, click **Finish.** The Backup tool will run the job at the scheduled time

RESTORING BACKUP FILES

The above sections dealt with taking the steps to prepare for loss of data. Once a disk failure occurs, the focus changes from preventing to fixing the problem. If you have taken care to make regular backups, you have the tools to get up and running again. ***Restoring*** is the opposite of backing up. It takes the files on your backup and copies them back onto the hard drive. Any files that are lost, damaged, or accidentally deleted can be replaced in this way. If necessary, the entire hard drive can be restored, but make sure it is working properly before you do so by running Check Disk (see Session 4.2).

From the Backup and Recovery Tools window, you start the Restore Wizard. You will also need to insert the portable medium that stores your data backup. If your data is stored on more than one disk or cartridge, you need to begin the process by inserting the first disk you made. Files must be restored in the order they were originally backed up.

task reference

Running the Restore Wizard

- Click **Start, All Programs, Accessories, System Tools, Backup,** then click **Next**

- Click the radio button next to *Restore files and settings* and click **Next**

- Click the check box next to any drive, folder, or file that you want to restore and then click **Next**

- Click **Finish**

- Locate the file you want to use, then click **OK**

- Click **Close,** then click the close button to close the Backup window

---

FIGURE 4.17

The What to Restore dialog box

Running the Restore Wizard:

1. Click **Start, All Programs, Accessories, System Tools, Backup,** then click **Next**

2. Click the radio button next to *Restore files and settings* and click **Next.** The What to Restore window opens

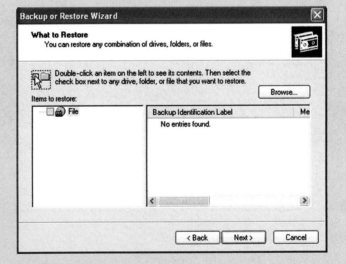

3. In the left pane of the window, click the check box next to any drive, folder, or file that you want to restore. Navigate through the folders by clicking the plus (+) sign next to the items. When finished, click **Next**

4. Confirm the settings you have chosen and then click **Finish.** The Enter Backup File Name dialog box opens

5. The Restore from backup file area shows the name and location of the last backup file created. To select a different backup file, click **Browse**

6. Once you have located the file you want to use, click **OK**

7. The Restore Progress dialog box opens, indicating the status of the restore operation. A message will appear in the upper left corner confirming the restore is complete. If you wish to create a report, click the **Report** button

8. Click **Close** to close the dialog box

9. Click the **close** button to close the Backup window

making the grade

1. The Backup and Recovery Tools window is located in the _____ folder.

2. Backups of important data should be done at least once a _____.

3. The opposite of backing up is _____.

4. A type of backup that only copies files that have changed since your last backup is called a(n) _____ backup.

SESSION 4.5 SUMMARY

In this chapter you learned how Windows uses storage, keeping track of information electronically on disks. You studied the differences between types of storage disks, and the pros and cons of each type. You learned how to format your hard drive.

You studied some basic maintenance steps for the Windows XP Professional operating system. You practiced two different ways of running disk cleanup. You studied disk directories and folders, what they are, and how they work. You learned about the types of errors and problems that can occur on a disk and practiced running a check for errors by using Check Disk. The concept of disk defragmentation was introduced, and you practiced using the Disk Defragmenter tool step by step. In addition, the very important tool Scheduled Tasks (which allows you to automate the disk maintenance tasks you just learned) was introduced and practiced. You were shown how to stop, modify, and delete a scheduled task.

Finally, you learned the importance of having a regular backup schedule and sticking to it. You practiced backing up your hard drive, and how to restore it in the event of a failure using the Restore Wizard.

task reference roundup

Task	Page #	Preferred Method
Formatting a floppy disk	WINXP 4.4	• Insert the floppy disk and click **Start,** then click **My Computer**
		• Click the floppy drive icon
		• Click **File,** then click **Format**
		• Specify options, such as the size and name of the disk
		• Click **Start,** then click **OK**
Copying one floppy disk to another	WINXP 4.5	• Insert the disk you want to copy
		• In My Computer, click the floppy disk drive icon
		• In the File menu, click **Copy Disk**
		• Indicate the disk you want to copy from and the disk you want to copy to, then click **Start**
		• When prompted, remove the first disk and replace it with the disk you're copying to
Converting a drive to NTFS	WINXP 4.6	• Click **Start, All Programs, Accessories, Command Prompt**
		• Type **convert,** and then press the spacebar
		• Type the letter of the drive you wish to convert followed by a colon (:), and then press the spacebar
		• Type **/fs:ntfs,** and then press **Enter**
		• Type **Y** (for Yes)
		• Type **exit** and then press the **Enter** key
Using Disk Management to view drive information	WINXP 4.8	• Click **Start,** then click **Control Panel**
		• Double-click the **Administrative Tools** icon
		• Double-click the **Computer Management** icon
		• Click **Disk Management**
Creating a new partition	WINXP 4.9	• Navigate to the Disk Management area of the Computer Management window (**Start, Control Panel, Administrative Tools, Computer Management, Disk Management**)
		• Right-click the unallocated space of a basic disk you wish to partition, then click **New Partition**
		• In the New Partition Wizard, click **Next,** click **Primary partition** or **Extended Partition,** and follow the instructions on your screen
Changing the default operating system	WINXP 4.10	• Click **Start,** then click **Control Panel**
		• Double-click **System**
		• Click the **Advanced** tab

task reference roundup

Task	Page #	Preferred Method
		• In the *Startup and Recovery* area, click **Settings**
		• Select the desired operating system and then click **OK**
		• Click **OK**
Running Disk Cleanup	WINXP 4.12	• Click **Start, All Programs, Accessories, System Tools, Disk Cleanup**
		• Click **OK,** then click **Yes**
		• Click **OK**
Removing Windows components and installed programs	WINXP 4.13	• Click **Start, All Programs, Accessories, System Tools, Disk Cleanup**
		• Click the **More Options** tab
		• Click **Clean Up . . .,** then select the components you want to remove
Running Check Disk	WINXP 4.15	• Click **Start,** then click **My Computer**
		• Right-click the **Local Disk (C:)** drive
		• In the context menu, click **Properties**
		• Click the **Tools** tab
		• Click the **Check Now . . .** button
		• Click the two check boxes to accept both options
		• Click **OK,** then click **OK** again
Using the Disk Defragmenter	WINXP 4.17	• Click **Start, All Programs, Accessories, System Tools, Disk Defragmenter**
		• Click the drive you want to defragment and click the **Analyze** button
		• Click **Defragment**
		• Click **Close**
Using Scheduled Tasks	WINXP 4.18	• Click **Start, All Programs, Accessories, System Tools, Scheduled Tasks**
		• Double-click **Add Scheduled Task,** then click **Next**
		• Click the program you want to schedule, then click **Next**
		• Click one of the radio buttons to select when to perform this task, then click **Next**
		• Click the appropriate box and type the Start time and frequency for the task, then click **Next**
		• Type your password, and then type it again in the **Confirm Password** field; then click **Next**
		• Click **Finish**
Using the Backup tool	WINXP 4.22	• Click **Start, All Programs, Accessories, System Tools, Backup**
		• Click the **Backup Wizard** button, then click **Next**

WINDOWS XP

task reference roundup

Task	Page #	Preferred Method
		• Click the appropriate radio button to select what you want to back up, then click **Next**
		• Click the check box beside each item you want to back up, and then click **Next**
		• Select the drive where you want to store your backup file and type a name for the backup file
		• Click **Open,** then click **Next**
		• Click **Finish**
Running the Restore Wizard	WINXP 4.26	• Click **Start, All Programs, Accessories, System Tools, Backup,** then click **Next**
		• Click the radio button next to *Restore files and settings* and click **Next**
		• Click the check box next to any drive, folder, or file that you want to restore and then click **Next**
		• Click **Finish**
		• Locate the file you want to use, then click **OK**
		• Click **Close,** then click the close button to close the Backup window

CROSSWORD PUZZLE

Across

1. A storage device
4. The first division of a hard drive is the _____ partition
6. The processs of placing data contiguously on your hard drive
9. Three-letter abbreviation at the end of a filename to indicate the file type
11. A storage device for transferring and copying small files
12. A configuration where more than one operating system is installed
13. A system tool to run if your computer is behaving oddly

Down

1. Lists of files and folders arranged in a logical and hierarchical order
2. A way of formatting files on the computer
3. On a hard drive, the amount of storage space
5. A tool that automatically executes routine maintenance
7. The file system designed to be used with Windows XP
9. Different logical sections of a hard drive, also another name for disks
10. Recovering and replacing a lost resource

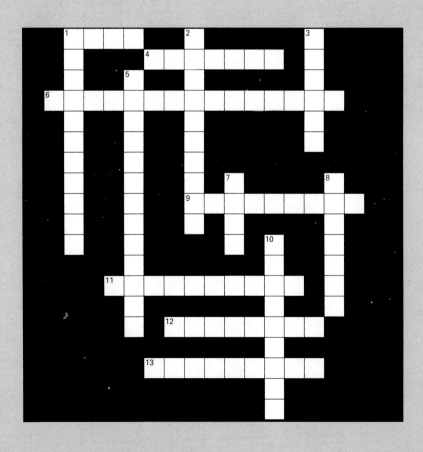

FILL-IN

1. Having the ability to use more than one operating system on your computer is called a _____ configuration.
2. A tool you run to quickly make some room on your hard drive is called _____.
3. A _____ disk is good for getting a small file to another computer that's not connected to yours.
4. The operating system on your computer is stored on a disk called the _____.
5. A System tool used to automatically run programs at predefined times is the _____ utility.

CREATE THE QUESTION

For each of the following answers, create an appropriate, short question:

ANSWER	QUESTION
1. A System tool used to automatically run programs at predefined times	_____
2. A tool you run to quickly make some room on your hard drive	_____
3. If you don't run this tool often, don't cry if you lose all the data on your hard drive	_____
4. If your hard drive does go down, run this tool to replace the lost files	_____
5. Putting all the bytes in order so that the processor can access them quicker is the goal of this System tool	_____
6. The operating system on your computer is stored on one of these disks	_____
7. Good for getting a small file to another computer that's not connected to yours	_____
8. Just in case you can't get Windows started, this is a good disk to have already made and handy	_____
9. Make sure this disk has a lot of storage space, as all your important files have to go on it	_____
10. Good for passing around a demonstration of your latest graphics work to someone who might want to employ you	_____

TRUE OR FALSE

1. If you install more than one operating system on your computer, the computer will automatically boot up the first operating system installed.
2. If your hard drive does go down, run the Backup and Recovery tool to replace the lost files.
3. Putting all the bytes in order so that there is more room on your hard drive is the goal of the Disk Defragmenter.
4. A floppy disk is good for passing around a demonstration of your latest graphics work to someone who might want to employ you.
5. Check Disk is a utility that takes a while to do its work, so schedule it for when the computer will not be otherwise occupied for a couple of hours.

1. Running Check Disk and Disk Cleanup

Pro Entertainment Inc. is an award-winning video, film, and audio productions company specializing in the production of television programming, motion pictures, television and radio commercials, musical scores, jingles and videos, corporate presentations and commercials, instructional videos, and media of all types.

Pro Entertainment has more than 80 years of experience; it has produced major motion pictures, national television specials and series, award-winning commercials, and corporate presentations of every type and length.

They have contacted you because recently their computers have been acting strangely and they are concerned that something is wrong. When you arrive at their offices, you notice that they are using the Windows XP OS. After making sure that they have a current backup of all their important files, the first thing you do is run Check Disk and Disk Cleanup.

1. Run Check Disk by opening **My Computer**
2. Right-click the **Local Disk (C:)** drive, and choose **Properties** from the context menu
3. Click the **Tools** tab and click the **Check Now . . .** button
4. Click **OK,** then click **OK** again. Now run Disk Cleanup
5. Navigate to the Disk Cleanup tool **(Start/All Programs/Accessories/System Tools/Disk Cleanup)**
6. Select the drive to clean up, and then select the files to delete
7. Click **OK,** and then click **Yes**
8. Click **OK** to finish

2. Converting a Drive to NTFS for Lady Jane's Table Etiquette Parties

Jane Trelawny runs Lady Jane's Table Etiquette Parties, which teaches table manners to boys and girls, ages 5 to 12, in the form of birthday parties. Jane has a storefront that she has redecorated to look like an elegant Victorian salon. The children learn how to set a traditional table, table manners, and even how to make and accept an invitation to dance. They come dressed in their finest outfits and must address each other as "Master" and "Miss" throughout the party. Since this is like

a visit to a foreign country for most children, they have great fun and the parents are very impressed with what they learn.

Jane's great idea for children's birthday parties has resulted in her becoming very busy. She now also runs advanced sessions for those children who have "graduated" from one of her parties. She has a staff of three, and besides doing the parties, they are constantly doing promotional mailings to names on their mailing list in the form of newsletters and discount postcards to previous customers.

There are three computers that Jane just recently bought running Windows XP. All the computers have 20-GB hard drives as Jane wants to make sure she has plenty of room to grow. She also wants to make sure her computers are as stable as possible and are not likely to crash. Further, she plans to do a lot more work in the future on her Web site and therefore wants to make sure her information is as secure as possible.

You are brought in as a computer consultant. Jane asks if anything else is needed. Everything is new and just installed. Considering the updated version of all the software and the lack of legacy applications, you can't think of any reason she shouldn't convert all her hard drives to NTFS. You explain that Windows XP ideally runs on this file system. The advantages over the older, and currently installed, FAT32 file system include greater stability, which Jane is interested in. And the large size of the hard drives makes it more likely that NTFS will work better. She has no legacy software that she needs to run. Her computers are new and installed with the most current versions of the programs she needs. Finally, she has no legacy operating systems or programs that she needs to run.

This exercise requires access to a hard drive that's available for NTFS conversion.

1. Navigate to **Start, All Programs, Accessories,** and **Command Prompt**
2. Type **convert,** and then press the spacebar
3. Type the letter of the drive you wish to convert followed by a colon (**:**), and then press the spacebar
4. Type **/fs:ntfs,** and then press the **Enter** key
5. Type **Y** (for Yes)

challenge

1. Formatting a Floppy Disk

Jennifer Stallings does medical transcriptions from her home for 10 to 15 doctors' offices in her area. Mostly she types letters and reports from a portable dictation machine into which the doctor has dictated what he wants typed. She visits each office on a regular basis, picks up the doctor's dictation machine, goes home, performs the transcriptions, and returns to the doctor's office with her work printed out.

Jennifer is very good at what she does, but even so, sometimes a letter has to be retyped because a medical term was not used correctly or the doctor's voice was garbled and the dictation didn't correspond to what he wanted typed. Rather than visiting the office to pick up the typing again, she came up with a better system. In addition to the typed pages, Jennifer also saves all the documents for each office onto a floppy disk, which she leaves with the office manager. If anything needs to be changed, it can be done quickly right in the office and she doesn't have to return.

Help Jennifer by formatting a floppy disk for her. You will need an unformatted floppy for this exercise. Format the disk so it is ready to accept information, and name it **Doctor One.**

1. Launching Internet Explorer Automatically upon Login

Martin Siegel has just been relocated by his company, Advanced Mineral Resources, to a new office. He finds that all the computers in this new office have Windows XP Professional installed. Since Martin has never worked with this operating system before, he wants to increase his knowledge of Windows XP. He visits the Microsoft Web site and discovers that there are many training tools available online.

Since Martin has some free time this week, he decides that every morning he will go online and spend one hour at *www.microsoft.com* exploring the links and seeing what he can learn. He tells you his plan. You inform Martin that Windows XP can be set up to automatically launch Internet Explorer as soon as Martin logs onto it. Use the Scheduled Tasks tool to set this up for Martin. In the Scheduled Tasks Wizard, select **Internet Explorer** as the application to launch when the user logs on. Use your own user name and password. Click the check box to access the **Advanced** Properties. In the **Settings** tab, indicate that the computer should stop the task if it takes more than one hour to perform. Rename the task **Daily Training.** Your Scheduled Tasks window should have an entry for Daily Training that looks like the one in Figure 4.18.

F I G U R E 4.18

The Scheduled Tasks window with a new entry

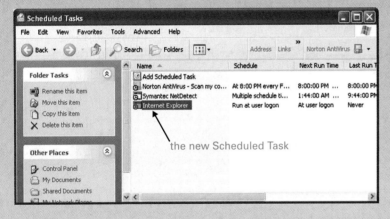

e-business

1. Scheduling Disk Defragmenter to Run Automatically

Red Hot Music is an online seller of early New Orleans jazz recordings by Louis Armstrong, Sidney Bechet, Freddie Keppard, and Joe Oliver. Red Hot Music is a labor of love of the two owners, Walt and Don, who process orders and respond to customer inquiries on nights and weekends. They both work out of Walt's garage, which they have converted into a small office and warehouse for their company. Their online storefront features a list of available recordings and audio samples of each selection, along with all the pricing, ordering, and shipping information. Artist biographies and general articles about the music of this period are also on the site.

After two and a half years of business, Red Hot Music has developed a strong cult following worldwide. Since Walt and Don both have day jobs, they don't have a lot of extra time to do anything outside of dealing with customers.

You are a customer of Red Hot Music and after having discovered that it is based in the town where you live, you usually stop by on Saturdays to pick up your orders. During one of these visits, Don mentions that although they don't have the income to pay for someone's salary, they could use some help with the two computers they use. In particular, their computers seem to be getting slower and slower. What happens is that many contacts share audio files of rare recordings with Red Hot Music. These are downloaded from the Web site and copied onto CDs for archive purposes. However, even after being deleted to create more room on the hard drive, over the years the computers' performance has suffered. Since you've studied Windows XP, and this is the operating system that Red Hot Music uses, you tell Don that a likely reason is disk defragmentation. Over time the result will be a deterioration of performance. A solution would be to run Disk Defragmenter regularly. Don explains that neither he nor Walt is familiar with computers other than the tasks they do often and, in any case, they don't have the time to get to this kind of project. Rather than try to convince him of how easy it is to schedule tasks, you offer to come in one day and set up Disk Defragmenter to run on the first Monday of every month at 9 a.m., when it is unlikely that the computers will be used.

1. Creating a Backup

Florida Sunshine Juice Co. imports frozen concentrated orange juice from Brazil and Mexico. This manufacturer then blends these concentrates with Florida orange concentrate to produce their final product.

Their major suppliers in Brazil and Mexico have been supplying them with the same quality orange juice concentrate for many years. Due to new USDA requirements that become effective as of January 1, 2003, Florida Sunshine Juice needs to change their specifications for the first time in many years. The next time Florida Sunshine contracts for the crop of orange concentrate, all the purchased product must conform to the new specs. Since these contracts are formalized well in advance, it is urgent that all suppliers are given as much time as possible to review the specifications and make any necessary adjustments. Accordingly, they have put together a packet that identifies what the new requirements are and sent the packet out via International air courier service. The suppliers have 30 days to study the specs and respond with any comments or questions. Florida Sunshine plans to also call each and every Quality Control and Production manager for the suppliers in Brazil and Mexico after the 30-day period to discuss their reactions. In addition, preshipment samples must be produced by the manufacturers overseas and sent for prior approval by Florida Sunshine labs.

All the information for this project is kept in one folder called New Specifications. You have been assigned to oversee this project and ensure that the transition goes smoothly. One of the first things you realize is that if the information in the folder is lost, it will create an enormous disruption, possibly leading to the new specifications not being implemented on a timely basis. This would have disastrous consequences for both the company and your career. As a result you want to immediately make a backup of this critical folder and make sure it can be restored properly.

Create a new folder on your Desktop called **New Specifications.** Use the Backup tool to create a backup of it on a floppy disk.

did you know?

a new game called geocaching involves hiding a box of small, unique items (called the "cache") somewhere in the woods, a park, a beach, or other public place and then posting the cache's coordinates on a Web site. Enthusiasts then try to find the cache using a GPS (Global Positioning System) device, which leads them to within 30 feet of the cache's location. If you find the cache, you can take any one of the items but must replace it with something else. This geocaching game is increasingly popular, with more than 18,000 caches presently out in 122 countries.

most drugs come from plants; for instance, aspirin is an ancient remedy originally found in willow bark.

an industrial design student in England has created a toaster built with a microprocessor connected via telephone to a Web server that imprints the surface of the toasting bread with a picture of that day's weather forecast: a sun, a cloud, or raindrops. Cereal eaters will presumably have to wait for the next generation of machine before being meteorologically correct.

Chapter Objectives

- Learn several ways of printing files: from within the application that created it, without opening an application, and from your Desktop by creating a printer shortcut
- Understand how to cancel or pause a print job
- Know what the print queue and spooling are and how they relate to executing print jobs
- Understand the difference between a local printer and a network printer
- Learn how to install a local printer using the Add Printer Wizard
- Understand how to connect to a network printer
- Learn how to configure your printer using Printer Preferences and Printer Properties
- Know what fonts are and why they are important in terms of your printed documents
- Learn different types of fonts and when to use them
- Know font attributes and font types
- Understand how to install and delete fonts
- Learn how to troubleshoot some common problems that occur with fonts when printing

Dimos Importing Co.

Peter Dimos works for his father, who owns Dimos Importing Co., a small importer of specialty food items from Greece. The business is located in Toronto and has been in operation for over 50 years. Dimos Importing's main item is olive oil, which it imports and warehouses locally for distributors to pick up. His dad wants Peter to take over the business from him eventually, but for right now, Peter, who's a recent college graduate, is responsible for some basic administration duties and computer support.

As he spends some time at his father's company, Peter finds that the computers in the administration office are not managed in an efficient way. Four computers are used primarily for the billing of customers, tracking inventory, paying vendors, and printing payroll checks. A certain amount of general office correspondence is also done from these machines, such as faxes and letters. All of this work is done with an accounting program and a word-processing program.

Insisting that there is a better way to do the jobs at hand, Peter convinces his father to upgrade the operating system for the computers in the administration office. Peter also gets approval to purchase a new printer to replace an ancient one that's barely functional. His father gives him a budget and tells Peter he has to be responsible for setting the printer up, connecting it to the computers, and learning everything that needs to be known about it. If any of the office staff have to be trained or have questions about the new systems, Peter is the one who needs to take care of it.

Peter upgrades the computers at Dimos Importing to Windows XP. He installs new versions of the programs the Dimos administration people are used to working with. He researches printers and finds an inexpensive laser printer that is more than adequate for the job. After the new printer is delivered, Peter goes about setting it up and installing it to only his computer. He spends some time getting familiar with the new system before even beginning the process of changing over the old system. Once Peter gets comfortable, he sets about the task of showing the administration staff the basics.

INTRODUCTION

Printing documents is one of the most basic functions you'll perform with your computer. Windows XP's Plug and Play technology allows you to easily connect a new printer. A printer can be connected directly to your computer, or you can use a network printer shared by multiple users.

Once installed, you can use the Printers tool to set a variety of printing preferences. You can monitor the progress of a print job, and pause or cancel it.

You use different typefaces and fonts to make a document more readable or to change the appearance of a document. Windows XP comes with a wide selection of fonts, plus you can install new fonts.

SESSION 5.1 PRINTING BASICS

Very early in your progress with computers you will need to produce a paper copy of something you've done. For many tasks (though fewer now with the prevalence of e-mail and the Internet), the printed copy *is* the product of the task. It is extraordinarily frustrating to be working under a deadline and be done with inputting into the computer only to have the project stuck in the printing process. Thus, understanding and becoming thoroughly familiar with the printing process is a key to productivity.

PRINTING FILES

There are several ways of printing a file. Probably the most common method is from within the application that created it.

---

task reference

Printing a File from within an Application

- In the File menu, click **Print**
- Click **OK**

Printing a file from within an application:

Peter creates a fax letterhead in WordPad. He wants to print a hard copy to pass around the office to get the staff's comments and suggestions. In the process of doing so, Peter realizes he can demonstrate the process of printing to the staff at the same time and accomplish some basic training.

1. Open the file to be printed in the program used to create it

2. Click **File** on the menu bar

3. Click **Print.** The Printer dialog box opens, as shown in Figure 5.1

4. Click **OK.** The file prints

FIGURE 5.1

The Printer dialog box

indicate the number of copies desired here

set page range here

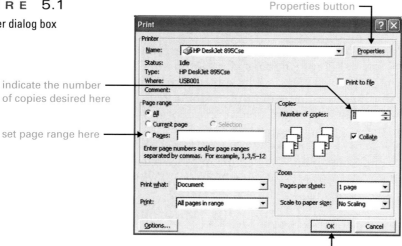

press OK when ready to print

You can also print a file without having the program open that created it. This is useful if you want to quickly print a file from My Documents or Windows Explorer.

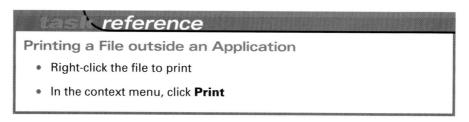

Printing a File outside an Application

- Right-click the file to print

- In the context menu, click **Print**

Printing a file outside an application:

1. Select the file you want to print

2. Right-click the file. A context menu opens, as shown in Figure 5.2

FIGURE 5.2

Right-clicking a file displays a context menu with the Print option

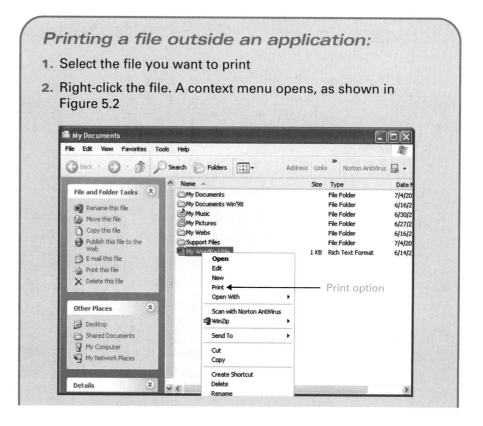

3. Click **Print.** Windows automatically starts the application that created the file until the file is printed and then closes the application; a printer icon appears on the taskbar next to the clock while the printing is in progress

Yet another way of printing a file is to drag the file you want to print to the printer's icon in the Printer folder. This means, however, that you have to dig through the various folder hierarchies in My Computer. There's an easier way to do this, and it involves creating a shortcut to a printer on your Desktop.

---

task **reference**

Creating a Printer Shortcut

- In the Start menu, click **Printers and Faxes**

- In the Printers window, right-click the printer

- In the context menu, click **Create Shortcut**

- Click **Yes** to allow Windows to create a shortcut on the Desktop

---

Creating a printer shortcut:

Peter wants to configure the office operating system to be as efficient as possible. He studies how the users' Desktop should be set up to make their jobs easier. Since everyone will be sharing the same printer, and printing is a common task in the office, why not create a printer shortcut right on the Desktop? This way all the staff has to do when they want to print is drag the file over to the printer icon.

1. In the Start menu, click **Printers and Faxes.** The Printers and Faxes window opens

2. Use the right mouse button to drag a printer to the Desktop, and then release the mouse button. A context menu opens

3. Click **Create Shortcut(s) Here.** An icon for the printer displays; now you can print by dragging files to this printer's shortcut icon.

CANCELING PRINT JOBS

Unfortunately, it is not unusual to send a file to be printed and realize in the process that you made a mistake and need to make a correction before the file prints. When you send a file to be printed, it gets sent to the ***Print queue.*** The Print queue (pronounced Q, like the letter) is disk space that forms a waiting line for output designated for a printer until the printer can receive it. If several print jobs are sent to the printer at once, the Print queue lines up the jobs in an orderly fashion. It's like waiting in a line to be

FIGURE 5.3

Using the right mouse button to drag a printer icon onto the Desktop opens a context menu, which allows you to create a printer shortcut in that area of the Desktop

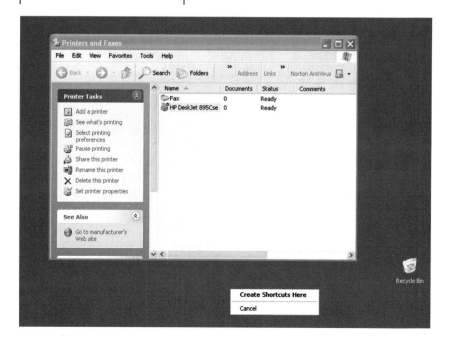

served at a delicatessen: first come, first served. Canceling a print job takes you out of the Print queue and avoids tying up the printer unnecessarily and wasting paper.

---

task reference

Canceling a Printing Job

- In the Start menu, click **Printers and Faxes**
- In the Printers and Faxes window, double-click the printer you are using
- Click the name of the file you want to cancel
- In the Document menu, click **Cancel**

Canceling a printing job:

1. In the Start menu, click **Printers and Faxes**
2. In the Printers window, double-click the printer you are using; a window opens, displaying the status of each print job
3. Click the file you no longer want to print
4. In the Document menu, click **Cancel;** the file is removed from the Print queue

---

Even if the file has started to print, you can cancel the operation. However, sometimes this is more trouble than it is worth, as the printer may have problems with the next print job. Keep in mind also that if your printer is very fast and your document very short (and there is no one else in the print queue ahead of you), you may not be able to completely abort the operation.

PAUSING PRINTING

You may discover that the printer needs some attention before it can correctly print all the jobs sent to it. It may be out of toner or paper, or you may have to clear a paper jam. In these situations, the Pause Printing command is useful.

---

task **reference**

Using Pause Printing

- In the Start menu, click **Printers and Faxes**
- In the Printers and Faxes window, double-click the printer you want to pause
- In the Printer menu, click **Pause Printing**

Using Pause Printing:

1. In the Start menu, click **Printers and Faxes**

2. Double-click the printer to pause; a window opens displaying the status of the print job(s)

3. In the Printer menu, click **Pause Printing.** The Title bar of the window displays the word "Paused" to indicate that the print job(s) are paused

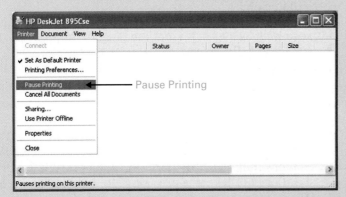

4. When you are ready for the printer to begin printing again, click **Pause Printing** again in the Printer menu. This directs the printer to resume printing again

FIGURE 5.4

The Pause Printing command in the Printer menu

anotherway

. . . to Pause Printing

In the **Printers and Faxes** window, select a printer. In the left pane of the window, under **Printer Tasks,** click **Pause Printing.**

---

making **the grade**

1. The _____ is disk space that holds output designated for the printer until the printer can receive it.

2. By creating a _____ to a printer on your Desktop, you can print by dragging the file you want to print over the printer's icon.

3. If you discover that you have to clear a paper jam, you use the _____ command to temporarily halt printing and give you time to attend to the printer.

4. Click _____ on the menu bar to print the document you currently have open.

5. While the printing is in progress, a printer icon appears on the _____.

SESSION 5.2 PRINTER SETUP

INSTALLING PRINTERS

Before you can start to use a printer, it must be installed on your computer so that it is recognized and a usable connection established. Printers can be installed on Windows XP in several different ways. You can install a *local printer* on your computer. A local printer is a printer attached directly to your computer. This is contrasted to a *network printer,* which you access through a network and is typically shared by multiple users, often within one department or area of an office.

When you send a command to print a file, the printer must be able to understand the commands your computer is using. A *print driver* is software that allows your computer to communicate with a printer. The print driver translates the commands from your computer into a format that your printer can understand. Print driver software typically comes on a floppy disk or a CD with a printer when you buy it, and it must be installed before you can use the printer.

Additionally, Windows XP comes with many of these standard print drivers (and other common device drivers) already built in. Support for *Plug and Play* printer devices makes installing a local printer very easy. Plug and Play is a set of specifications that allows a computer to automatically detect and configure a device and install the appropriate drivers. If your printer is recognized as a Plug and Play printer by Windows, the print drivers needed to allow the printer and your computer to communicate are available from within Windows itself. Simply attach the printer to the computer with the appropriate cable and Windows XP automatically starts the Add Printer Wizard. Usually, printers that use USB ports are Plug and Play, whereas printers that use serial or parallel ports are not Plug and Play and require that you manually open the Add Printer Wizard to install them.

The following exercise walks you through the Add Printer Wizard, including how to get to the Wizard if it doesn't launch automatically. Make sure the printer you want to install is connected via cable to your computer before beginning these exercises.

***another*word**

. . . on Installing Printers

You must be logged onto your computer or network as an administrator in order to install a printer.

---

task reference

Opening the Add Printer Wizard

- In the Start menu, click **Printers and Faxes**

- In the left pane of the Printers and Faxes window, click the **Add a Printer** link

Installing a local printer—opening the Add Printer Wizard:

When Peter first received the new printer, he had to install it on his computer before he could use it. He connected the cable between the printer and the computer and plugged the printer in. The next thing to be done was install the printer software on the computer. Since his computer salesperson told him Windows would not recognize this printer as Plug and Play, Peter knew what to do. In order to install the printer software, he would use the Wizard called Add Printer.

1. In the Start menu, click **Printers and Faxes.** The Printers and Faxes window opens

2. In the left pane of the Printers and Faxes window, click the **Add a Printer** link (Figure 5.5). The Add Printer Wizard opens, as shown in Figure 5.6. Note that the welcome window indicates you do not need to use the Add Printer Wizard if you have a Plug and Play printer.

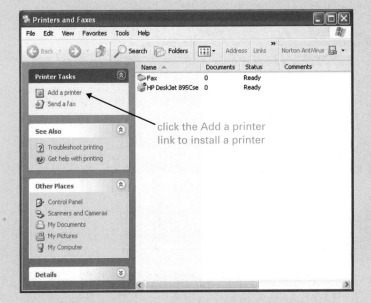

FIGURE 5.5

Adding a new printer in the Printers and Faxes window

FIGURE 5.6

The Add Printer Wizard welcome window

---

task reference

Using the Add Printer Wizard to Install a Local Printer

- From the Add Printer Wizard welcome window, click **Next**
- Click **Local Printer,** then click **Next**
- Click the port you want to use, then click **Next**
- Select the manufacturer and model of the printer, then click **Next**
- Select a name for the printer, then click **Next**
- Decide if you want this printer to be your default printer, then click **Next**
- Click that you don't want to share this printer, then click **Next**

Using the Add Printer Wizard to install a local printer:

1. From the Add Printer Wizard welcome window, click **Next.** The Local Printer dialog box opens, as shown in Figure 5.7

FIGURE 5.7

The Local Printer dialog box of the Add Print Wizard

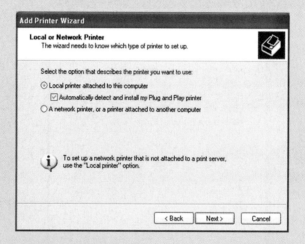

2. Click the radio button next to *Local printer attached to this computer*

3. Click the check box next to *Automatically detect and install my Plug and Play printer,* then click **Next.** The Select a Printer Port dialog box opens, as seen in Figure 5.8

4. Select the port you want your printer to use from the drop-down list next to *Use the following port,* then click **Next.** The Select Printer Manufacturer and Model dialog box opens

5. If your printer is not Plug and Play, you must specify the make and model. In the left pane of the window, click the name of the manufacturer. In the right pane of the window, click the model name. If the name of your printer does not appear on the list, proceed with the next step. If the name of your printer is on the list, skip to Step 7

6. Insert the Installation Disk that came with the printer into the drive (if your printer does not appear on the list and did not

come with an Installation Disk, try selecting a similar model from the same manufacturer on the list). Click the **Have Disk** button and press the **Enter** key

7. Click **Next.** The Name Your Printer dialog box opens, as shown in Figure 5.10. Windows displays a suggested name for the printer. If you want to name it differently, highlight the suggested name and type in the new name

F I G U R E   5.8

The Select a Printer Port dialog box of the Add Print Wizard

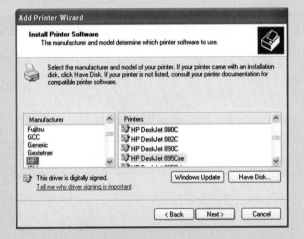

F I G U R E   5.9

The Manufacturer and Model dialog box of the Add Print Wizard

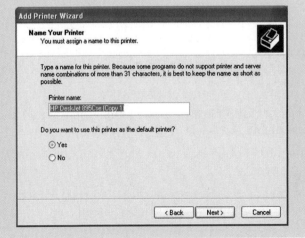

F I G U R E   5.10

The Name Your Printer dialog box of the Add Print Wizard

WINDOWS XP

8. Click an appropriate radio button if you wish to make this printer your default printer; this means that all print jobs will be automatically sent to this printer, then click **Next**

9. Click on the appropriate radio button to indicate that you do not want to share this printer with users on a network (see the next section for connecting to a network printer), then click **Next**

10. Click **Yes** to indicate that you want to print a test page, then click **Next.** The Wizard indicates that you have successfully completed the Add Printer Wizard

11. Click **Finish.** In the dialog box, click **OK** if the test page printed. You will be returned to the Printers and Faxes window and will see a new icon for the printer you just installed

---

*another*word

. . . on Adding a Printer

If you made the new printer the default printer, a check mark appears on its icon.

If you have access to several printers, make the one you use most often the default printer. There is a direct way of doing this rather than going through the Add Printer Wizard as shown above.

---

task reference

Designating a Default Printer

- In the Start menu, click **Printers and Faxes**

- Right-click the printer you want to set as the default printer

- In the context menu, click **Set as Default Printer**

Designating a default printer:

Thinking more about the best way to organize everyone's computer, Peter realizes that he will want to connect other printers in the Dimos warehouse to the computers in the administration office so that a document, such as an inventory report, can be printed anywhere in the building. However, most of the print jobs generated in the administration office will generally be printed on the new administration office printer. This being the case, it will save time if the office printer is designated as the default. If no other destination is specified, print jobs will automatically be sent to that printer.

1. In the Start menu, click **Printers and Faxes.** The Printers and Faxes window opens

2. Right-click the printer you want to set as the default printer. A context menu opens

3. In the context menu, click **Set as Default Printer.** A check mark will appear over the selected printer's icon

CONNECTING TO A NETWORK PRINTER

If every computer user in an organization had his or her own printer attached to his or her personal computer, this would result in a lot of inefficiencies. Many of these printers would sit around unused a good part of the day. Instead, organizations typically connect a few printers to a network so that everyone in an area or department can share them. Usually network printers are set up in some central space so that all the users can access them easily. Even if an office has as few as two or three people in it, setting up one shared printer is a best practice to conserve resources.

task reference

Using the Add Printer Wizard to Connect to a Network Printer

- In the Start menu, click **Printers and Faxes**
- In the left pane of the Printers and Faxes window, click the **Add a Printer** link
- Click the radio button next to *Network Printer*
- Type the name of the printer you wish to connect to, or Browse to find it

Using the Add Printer Wizard to connect to a network printer:

Now Peter has to connect the other computers in the administration office to the printer. He creates a network connection so that everyone in the administration offices can share the printer. On each computer he uses the Add Printer Wizard to set up a network printer.

1. In the Start menu, click **Printers and Faxes**
2. In the left pane of the Printers and Faxes window, click the **Add a Printer** link. The Add Printer Wizard opens. Click **Next**
3. Click the radio button next to *A network printer, or a printer attached to another computer*, then click **Next.** The Specify a Printer window opens
4. If you don't know the name of the printer you wish to connect to, click **Next** to browse the network for the printer. The Browse for Printer dialog box opens.

tip: *If you do know the name of the printer, click the radio button next to* Connect to this printer *or* Connect to a printer on the Internet *and type the name in the text box next to* Name, *and then click **Next***

5. In the *Shared printers* area, click the printer to connect to, then click **Next**
6. Click either the **Yes** or **No** radio button to indicate whether you want to make this printer your default printer, then click **Next**
7. A window opens indicating that you have successfully completed the Wizard. Click **Finish.** The Printers window displays an icon for the printer you just connected to

WINDOWS XP

F I G U R E   5.11

The Browse for Printer dialog
box

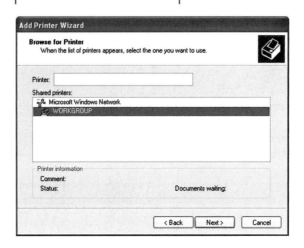

You can connect to multiple network printers, though some may be off-limits for one reason or another. You also may need to install a particular protocol or network service to access certain printers. If you want to delete a network printer, go to the Printers and Faxes window and right-click the printer, then select Delete from the context menu.

SHARING A PRINTER

You can share a printer connected to your computer with other users on a network. This process is demonstrated in the next exercise. Keep in mind, however, that both your computer and your printer must be turned on in order for others to share your printer.

---

task reference

Sharing Your Printer

- In the Start menu, click **Printers and Faxes**
- Click the icon for the printer you wish to share
- In the File menu, click **Sharing . . .**
- In the Sharing tab, click the *Share this printer* radio button, then type a friendly name so that others can easily identify the printer. Click **OK** when done

---

Sharing your printer with others:

Since everyone in the administration office has equal rights to the printer, Peter wants to enable sharing on all computers. After establishing the network connection to the printer, each computer is configured to allow access to the printer.

1. In the Start menu, click **Printers and Faxes**

2. Click the icon for the printer you wish to share

3. In the File menu, click **Sharing . . .** The Printer Properties dialog box opens

4. In the Sharing tab, click the *Share this printer* radio button

5. Type a friendly name in the text box next to *Share name* so that others can easily identify the printer, as shown in Figure 5.12

6. Click **OK.** In the Printers window, an upturned hand displays under the shared printer's icon to indicate that it is available for others to use

---

making the grade   **SESSION 5.2**

1. A _____ is a printer attached directly to your computer.

2. A _____ is accessed through a network and is typically shared by multiple users, often within one department or area of an office.

3. If you need to connect to a network printer for the first time, you do so by using the _____ Wizard.

4. The printer you use most often should be your _____ printer.

5. _____ is a set of specifications that allows a computer to automatically detect and configure a device and install the appropriate drivers.

6. A _____ is software that allows your computer to communicate with a printer.

SESSION 5.3 PRINTER CONFIGURATION

PRINTING PREFERENCES

Configuring your printer's settings can help you reduce mistakes and improve your efficiency. You configure a printer by using the Printing Preferences. The Printing Preferences determine how a printer will print your files.

If you've used Windows 98 or Windows NT, then you know Printing Preferences as Document Defaults.

Basic options available for modification are as follows:

- *Orientation.* Specifies how the document is positioned on the page. Portrait orients the print vertically, whereas Landscape orients the print horizontally
- *Page Order.* Specifies the order in which your pages will be printed. Front to Back prints the document so that Page 1 is on the top of the stack, whereas Back to Front prints Page 1 on the bottom of the stack
- *Pages Per Sheet.* Specifies how many pages of your document to print on one piece of paper: 1 prints one page on a sheet of paper, whereas 2 prints two pages side by side on one sheet of paper
- *Paper Source.* Specifies where the paper is located in the printer such as the upper or the lower tray if you have a printer with different paper trays for different size papers, for example; usually, it is best to leave this option as Automatically Select, since this will automatically select the paper tray that supports the paper size you have selected
- *Media.* Selects the type of print media you want to use, for example, plain paper, photo paper, transparency, and so forth

Depending on the printer, different advanced options are available. Some advanced options are the following:

- *Quality Settings.* Specifies the quality level of the printer output; the better the quality, the slower the printing. Use Best for the final copy of a finished document, Normal for a good standard quality, and Draft for quickly printing a rough draft; use Custom to override the predefined quality combinations associated with the Best, Normal, and Draft quality settings
- *Color.* Specifies whether to print in color or Black and White

Again depending on the individual printer you are working on, clicking the Advanced button in the Printing Preferences will give you more options, including the following:

- *Paper Size.* Allows you to select a different size of paper to print on
- *Copy Count.* Allows you to change the number of copies you want to print
- *Print Quality.* Specifies to a greater degree of detail the print quality you want to use than the generic Best, Normal, and Draft. Print quality depends on the **resolution** of your printer, which is the number of dots printed per inch on a page. Sharper, more detailed images have a higher resolution, whereas lower resolution prints quickly

---

task reference

Changing the Printing Preferences

- In the Start menu, click **Printers and Faxes**
- Click the printer whose preferences you want to change
- In the File menu, click **Printing Preferences**
- Click the **Layout** or **Paper/Quality** tab
- Click the appropriate button to change Orientation, Page Order, Pages Per Sheet, Paper Source, Media, Quality Settings, or Color

Changing the Printing Preferences:

Peter notices that it is not necessary for most print jobs to print in Normal quality. The draft quality is adequate; it is also faster and uses less ink than Normal. But Normal quality is the default setting in Windows. He wants to change this.

1. In the Start menu, click **Printers and Faxes**

2. Click the printer whose preferences you want to change

3. In the File menu, click **Printing Preferences . . .** The Printing Preferences dialog box opens, as shown in Figure 5.13

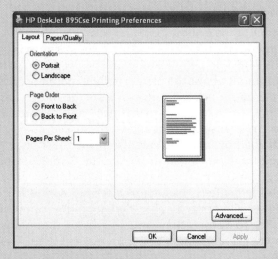

FIGURE 5.13

The Printing Preferences dialog box

4. Click the appropriate radio button to change the Orientation; note that the graphic in the right pane of the window changes each time you make a change to show what your printed page will look like

5. Click the appropriate radio button to change the Page Order

6. From the Pages Per Sheet drop-down list, select the number of pages that will be printed on a sheet of paper

7. Click the **Paper/Quality** tab, shown in Figure 5.14

FIGURE 5.14

The Paper/Quality tab in Printing Preferences

WINDOWS XP

8. From the Paper Source drop-down list, select where the paper you want to use is coming from

9. Click the appropriate radio button to indicate the desired print quality (this option may not be available on all printers)

10. Click the appropriate radio button to indicate whether you want to print in black and white or color (this option may not be available on all printers)

PRINTER PROPERTIES

The Printer Properties dialog box allows greater control over a printer's performance. This becomes particularly important if your printer is part of a network and shared by multiple people. You can specify the location of the printer and add a comment about the printer to help people determine if they want to use the printer. If needed, you can view the model and features of the printer, such as the maximum print speed and maximum resolution. You can access the Printing Preferences (discussed above) from the Printer Properties dialog box, and you can also print a test page.

Another aspect of printing you can control from the Printer Properties dialog box is *spooling.* When you print a document, Windows sends small bits of it at a time out to the printer so as not to interfere with other tasks you are doing in Windows. This process is called spooling. Spooling returns use of the computer to you so that you can perform another task while the printer prints your documents.

---

task reference

Changing the Printer Properties

- In the Start menu, click **Printers and Faxes**

- Click the printer whose properties you want to change

- In the File menu, click **Properties**

- In the Properties dialog box, click the **Advanced** tab

- Click the appropriate button to change Availability times, Priority, Spooling, and to print a Separator Page between print jobs

---

Changing the Printer Properties:

First thing Monday morning, one staff member has the job of printing out an updated inventory report and distributing it around Dimos Importing. The problem is that these inventory reports take some time to print. Sometimes other staff people have already started sending their jobs to the printer and the inventory report printing gets delayed. In order to avoid this situation, Peter makes the office administration printer unavailable for the first hour Monday morning on every computer except the one used to prepare the inventory report. This way the report no longer gets delayed.

1. In the Start menu, click **Printers and Faxes**

2. Click the printer whose properties you want to change

3. In the file menu, click **Properties.** The Properties dialog box opens, as shown in Figure 5.15

F I G U R E 5.15
The General tab of the Printer Properties dialog box

4. Click the **Advanced** tab, as shown in Figure 5.16. This tab provides you with several options to manage your printer in a shared networking environment where other users have access to your printer

F I G U R E 5.16
The Advanced tab of the Printer Properties dialog box

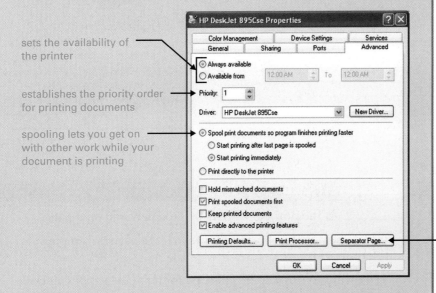

sets the availability of the printer

establishes the priority order for printing documents

spooling lets you get on with other work while your document is printing

the Separator Page button

5. Click the radio button next to *Available from* and click the up and down arrows in the spin box to adjust the *Available from* and *To* times you want to allow the printer to be available

6. In the *Priority* spin box, click the up or down arrows to adjust the printing priority for your documents

tip: *To make sure your documents will always jump to the front of the printing queue, enter the* **99,** *which is the highest priority setting*

7. Click the radio button next to *Spool print documents so program finishes printing faster* to take advantage of spooling, which allows you to work on another task on your computer while printing

8. Click the radio button next to *Start printing immediately*

9. Click the **Separator Page** button. The Separator Page dialog box opens, as shown in Figure 5.17. This option is useful if many people print documents from the same printer as it inserts a separator page between each printed document. The separator page also displays the date and time the document was printed and the name of the person who sent the document to the printer

FIGURE 5.17

The Separator Page dialog box

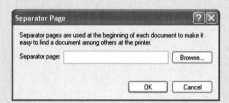

10. In the Separator Page field, type the name and location of the separator page you want to use, then click **OK**

11. Click **OK** to close the Printer Properties dialog box

tip: *If you find yourself often having to change your standard printer properties and preferences for a particular type of job you print frequently, there is a way to make your life easier. Install another copy of your regular printer. Specify the particular settings for your job in the Printer's Properties. Rename this new printer icon in the Printers and Faxes window with the name of the print job you do on it, such as "Sales Projections." Whenever you want to print your Sales Projections with their special printing settings, use the Sales Projections printer.*

SESSION 5.3 | *making* **the grade**

1. _____ is the number of dots printed per inch on a page.

2. Plain paper, photo paper, and transparencies are examples of different print _____.

3. If you want to print a test page, go to the _____ dialog box.

4. Orientation, Page Order, and Pages Per Sheet can all be changed by going to the _____ dialog box.

5. _____ returns use of the computer to you so that you can perform another task while the printer prints your files.

SESSION 5.4 WORKING WITH FONTS

FONT OVERVIEW

A *font* is a style of type, a set of letter characters designed in a specific way. There are thousands of different fonts, all of which determine the way text looks both on the computer screen and on the printed page.

> ### *another*word
>
> The terms "typeface" and "font" are used interchangeably, but technically speaking, typeface refers to the primary design, while font refers to the particular implementation and variation of the typeface.

The way letters are formed influences the impression written words have on the reader. Think of fonts as like the clothes a person wears; the same person wearing different clothes can make a completely different impression. In the same way, fonts can make print look reliable, serious, and all-business or zany, fun, and creative. Figure 5.18 shows an example of the same set of words written in two different fonts.

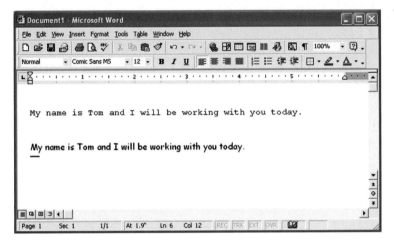

FIGURE 5.18

Examples of different font styles

Each of these statements, although they use the same words, provides a different impression of who Tom is and what kind of work you will be doing with him. The first font, Courier, makes a pretty dry impression, while the second, Comic Sans, creates a more warm and fuzzy feeling. Thus by using fonts attentively, your printed documents can have their desired effect in a stronger way.

USING FONTS

Typically, you change the font by highlighting the text you want to change and going to Format on the menu bar and using the Font command. This may vary, however, depending on the program you are using. In Microsoft Word, a popular word-processing program, there is also a View that displays the Formatting toolbar. The Formatting toolbar includes a drop-down list displaying the font you are currently working with. Clicking the drop-down arrow displays your available fonts. The font name is displayed in the actual font itself so that you have an idea what text will look like when printed in that particular font.

There are a number of fonts that are included with Windows XP; some of the more common and their uses include

- *Arial.* Good font for heading and titles
- *Courier.* A very plain, easy-to-read typing font. Courier is a monospaced font, which means that each character takes up the same space as all the other characters

- *Times.* An easy-to-read font that is professional looking and good for a body of text
- *Wingdings.* As the name implies, a fun font that is composed of little pictures instead of letters. Wingdings are useful to spice up your documents with graphics to make a point, but use them sparingly

Some other common fonts and their uses include

- *Helvetica.* This font is good for international correspondence: no ornamentation, no emotion, just a clear presentation of information. Helvetica font has been around since the 1950s and is still one of the most popular sans serif fonts (more about serif and sans serif fonts below in Font Types)
- *Old English.* This font has regal initial capitals and a legible lower-case; it is ideal for certificates, diplomas, or any application that should have the look of stateliness and authority
- *Palatino.* A font designed for maximum readability, it was designed in Europe as a typeface that remained legible even on the inferior paper of the post–World War II period

Font Attributes

Fonts have attributes such as bold, italics, and underline, which can be formatted within a document. Some fonts are listed as if they were different fonts when really they are the same font with different attributes. In these font variations, you will see the original font name followed by "Old Style," "New," "Bold," "Italic," or "Bold Italic."

Another obvious font attribute is size. Font size is measured in ***points,*** of which there are 72 to an inch. The higher the point number, the bigger the font. A good point size for text readability is 10 or 12. Headlines and titles are often bigger.

Font Types

Several different types of fonts exist in the Font Folder of Windows XP. TrueType fonts appear on the screen exactly as they will print (hence the name). They can be stretched or shrunk to any size.

OpenType fonts are an improvement upon the basic TrueType font. An OpenType font produces characters from mathematical formulas. The advantage of this is that if you change the size of an OpenType font, the letters will look the same. An OpenType font, like a TrueType font, will print on the page exactly the same as it looks on your computer screen.

Vector and raster font is an older type of font used by old Windows applications. It is also known as screen font or fixed font. It looks good in a few sizes (for instance, as shown by the font's name, Courier 10, Courier 12, or Courier 15 indicate that the Courier font looks good only at 10, 12, and 15 points). The raster type of font is designed with a specific size and resolution and cannot be scaled or rotated.

PostScript fonts are designed for use with PostScript printers. These fonts are located in special folders with their own utility for font management. Whether you download PostScript (Type 1) fonts from the Internet or have a CD full of typefaces, in order to use them in your word processor or other programs you must install them using Adobe Type Manager. The primary type of PostScript font is Type 1 font. Type 3 is a type of PostScript font used to create complex designs.

Besides differences in type, another difference between fonts is whether there are small lines to finish off a main stroke at the tops and bottoms of any straight lines. These fonts are called *serif* fonts, and they make reading easier. Times is an example of a serif font. A *sans serif* font, on the other hand, lacks these embellishments. These fonts are best for headlines and titles because they are not as easy to read in text. Arial is an example of a sans serif font. Note the examples of serif and sans serif fonts in Figure 5.19.

FIGURE 5.19

Examples of serif and sans serif fonts

Previewing a Font

If you want to see what a particular font looks like and get more information about it, there is an easy way to do it.

---

task reference

Previewing a Font

- In the Start menu, click **Control Panel**
- Double-click the **Fonts** folder
- Double-click the font you wish to preview

Previewing a font:

1. In the Start menu, click **Control Panel**
2. Double-click the **Fonts** folder
3. In the Fonts window, double-click the font you wish to preview. A window opens providing details and multiple samples of the font in different sizes (Figure 5.20)

tip: *If you use fonts a lot, print the preview window on a sheet of paper for each font. It is much easier to flip through pages of fonts than having to open and close each font icon in the Fonts window repeatedly to see what it looks like.*

FIGURE 5.20

The Font preview window

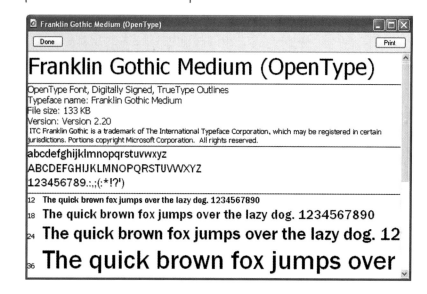

Character Map

Previewing the font by double-clicking its icon allows you to get a sense of what it looks like. If, however, you want to see the entire repertoire of the font, all its letters and symbols, you use the Character Map tool. In fact, to use a font like Wingdings that is composed of little pictures instead of letters, you must use the Character Map tool to see what you are doing.

---

task reference

Using the Character Map

- Click **Start, All Programs, Accessories, System Tools, Character Map**
- From the Fonts drop-down list, select a font
- Double-click the desired character(s)
- Click **Copy**
- Open the document you want to copy into
- In the Edit menu, click **Paste**

Using the Character Map:

1. Click **Start, All Programs, Accessories, System Tools, Character Map** (Figure 5.21)

2. In the *Font* drop-down list, click **Wingdings**

3. Click and hold the mouse button on a character that looks interesting; the character you've selected is magnified

4. Double-click a character; the character then appears in the text box labeled *Characters to copy*. You can double-click more characters to add to this text box if you wish

5. Click **Copy;** the characters you've selected are copied into the Windows clipboard

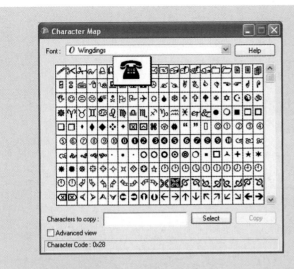

FIGURE 5.21
The Character Map dialog box

6. Click **Close**

7. Open the document you want to copy the characters into

8. In the Edit menu, click **Paste** to paste the characters into the document

INSTALLING AND DELETING FONTS

Besides the fonts that come with Windows XP, there are thousands of additional fonts available. You can obtain new fonts (often for free) from CDs, floppy disks, your network, or the Internet. As many fonts as you wish can be installed, but keep in mind that every font takes up storage space. New fonts can be installed by using a special command in the Fonts window, as shown in the next steps.

task reference

Installing New Fonts

- In the Start menu, click **Control Panel**
- Double-click the **Fonts** folder
- In the File menu, click **Install New Font . . .**
- Navigate to the folder with the fonts you wish to install
- Click the font(s) you want to add
- Click **OK**

Installing New Fonts:

Along with the printer software, in the box along with the new printer came a CD of extra fonts. Peter wants to liven up the office correspondence used to announce specials to the distributors. Accordingly, he goes about using the new CD to add some new fonts to try out. After he picks out a few, he installs these fonts on his computer.

1. In the Start menu, click **Control Panel**

2. Double-click the **Fonts** folder

3. In the File menu, click **Install New Font . . .** (Figure 5.22)

FIGURE 5.22

The Add Fonts dialog box

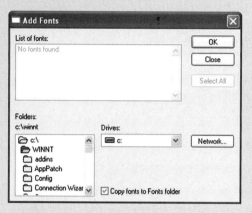

4. In the *Drives* drop-down list, select the drive containing the fonts you want to add

5. Double-click the folder containing the fonts

6. In the *List of Fonts*, click the font(s) you want to add. Click the **Select All** button if you want to install all the fonts shown

7. Click **OK.** Windows installs the selected fonts into your computer

tip: *When obtaining new fonts, make sure you get the Windows version of the fonts. Some fonts are designed for only certain types of operating systems, such as Macintosh*

*another*way

. . . to Add a Font

Drag and drop a new font icon from the source window into the Fonts window

You can remove the fonts you do not need by deleting them. This is a good practice to avoid excessive clutter, especially if you've gone through a period of extended font collecting. Be careful, however, as some fonts are required by Windows or other programs. Fonts shown with a red A in the Fonts window are required by Windows and should not be deleted. If you want to get back a font that you've deleted, open the Recycle Bin and right-click on the font. Select Restore from the menu that appears.

*task*reference

Deleting Fonts

• In the Start menu, click **Control Panel**

• Double-click the **Fonts** folder

• Right-click the font you want to delete

• Click **Delete**

• Click **Yes** at the Alert message

Deleting fonts:

After completing the distributor special with two new fonts, Peter realizes he got a little carried away and installed several fonts that didn't meet his needs. As a result, his list of fonts has gotten too large and cluttered. He wants to clean up the list by getting rid of some fonts he knows he'll never use.

1. In the Start menu, click **Control Panel**
2. Double-click the **Fonts** folder
3. Right-click the font you want to delete
4. In the dialog box that displays, click **Delete.** An Alert dialog box displays (Figure 5.23)

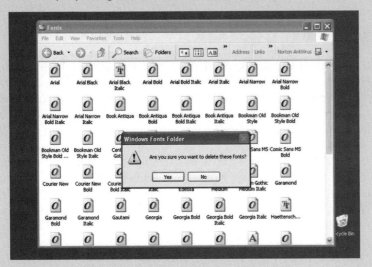

F I G U R E   5.23

The Delete Fonts Alert message

5. Click **Yes.** The font is moved to the Recycle Bin

TROUBLESHOOTING FONTS

Font problems usually become apparent when you print a document. Typically reinstalling the font you are having a problem with will solve your problems. Figure 5.24 shows some common problems and possible solutions.

F I G U R E   5.24

Troubleshooting fonts

Problem	Troubleshooting Steps
Font does not print as expected	Reinstall the font
Font is distorted or illegible	Try a different font size or a different font
	Copy and paste the text into another document and see if it prints correctly
	Reinstall the font
Printing is slow	Try printing the document from a different computer
	Reinstall the font
Fonts are clipped	Check that you are not sending documents that cover a larger area than the printer is capable of printing to

making the grade

1. A _____ is a set of letter characters designed in a specific way.

2. An easy-to-read font that is professional looking and good for a body of text is _____.

3. Bold, italics, and underline are examples of font _____, which can be formatted within a document.

4. Font size is measured in _____.

5. Fonts with small lines to finish off a main stroke at the tops and bottoms of any straight lines are called _____ fonts, and they make reading easier.

SESSION 5.5 SUMMARY

In this chapter you learned several ways of printing files: from within the application that created it, without opening an application, and from your Desktop by creating a printer shortcut. You learned how to print files and how to cancel or pause a print job. In this context, you also learned about what the print queue and spooling are and what they have to do with the process of executing a print job.

You studied the difference between a local printer and a network printer and how to install a local printer using the Add Printer Wizard. In this context, you learned what Plug and Play is and you learned what a print driver is. You learned how to connect to a network printer. You practiced making the printer you use the most your default printer. You learned how to configure your printer using Printer Preferences and Printer Properties.

You learned what fonts are and why they are important in terms of your printed documents. You studied the differences in types of fonts and when to use them, along with what font attributes and font types are. You learned how to install and delete fonts. Finally, you were shown some common problems that occur with fonts when printing and how to troubleshoot them.

task reference roundup

Task	Page #	Preferred Method
Printing a file from within an application	WINXP 5.3	• In the File menu, click **Print**
		• Click **OK**
Printing a file outside an application	WINXP 5.4	• Right-click the file to print
		• In the context menu, click **Print**
Creating a printer shortcut	WINXP 5.5	• In the Start menu, click **Printers and Faxes**
		• In the Printers window, right-click the printer
		• In the context menu, click **Create Shortcut**
		• Click **Yes** to allow Windows to create a shortcut on the Desktop

task reference roundup

Task	Page #	Preferred Method
Canceling a printing job	WINXP 5.6	• In the Start menu, click **Printers and Faxes**
		• In the Printers and Faxes window, double-click the printer you are using
		• Click the name of the file you want to cancel
		• In the Document menu, click **Cancel**
Using Pause Printing	WINXP 5.7	• In the Start menu, click **Printers and Faxes**
		• In the Printers and Faxes window, double-click the printer you want to pause
		• In the Printer menu, click **Pause Printing**
Opening the Add Printer Wizard	WINXP 5.8	• In the Start menu, click **Printers and Faxes**
		• In the left pane of the Printers and Faxes window, click the **Add a Printer** link
Using the Add Printer Wizard to install a local printer	WINXP 5.10	• From the Add Printer Wizard welcome window, click **Next**
		• Click **Local Printer**, then click **Next**
		• Click the port you want to use, then click **Next**
		• Select the manufacturer and model of the printer, then click **Next**
		• Select a name for the printer, then click **Next**
		• Decide if you want this printer to be your default printer, then click **Next**
		• Click that you don't want to share this printer, then click **Next**
Designating a default printer	WINXP 5.12	• In the Start menu, click **Printers and Faxes**
		• Right-click the printer you want to set as the default printer
		• In the context menu, click **Set as Default Printer**
Using the Add Printer Wizard to connect to a network printer	WINXP 5.13	• In the Start menu, click **Printers and Faxes**
		• In the left pane of the Printers and Faxes window, click the **Add a Printer** link
		• Click the radio button next to *Network Printer*
		• Type the name of the printer you wish to connect to, or Browse to find it
Sharing your printer	WINXP 5.14	• In the Start menu, click **Printers and Faxes**
		• Click the icon for the printer you wish to share
		• In the File menu, click **Sharing . . .**
		• In the Sharing tab, click the *Share this printer* radio button, then type a friendly name so that others can easily identify the printer. Click **OK** when done

WINDOWS XP

task reference roundup

Task	Page #	Preferred Method
Changing the Printing Preferences	WINXP 5.16	• In the Start menu, click **Printers and Faxes**
		• Click the printer whose preferences you want to change
		• In the File menu, click **Printing Preferences**
		• Click the **Layout** or **Paper/Quality** tab
		• Click the appropriate button to change Orientation, Page Order, Pages Per Sheet, Paper Source, Media, Quality Settings, or Color
Changing the Printer Properties	WINXP 5.18	• In the Start menu, click **Printers and Faxes**
		• Click the printer whose properties you want to change
		• In the File menu, click **Properties**
		• In the Properties dialog box, click the **Advanced** tab
		• Click the appropriate button to change Availability times, Priority, Spooling, and to print a Separator Page between print jobs
Previewing a font	WINXP 5.23	• In the Start menu, click **Control Panel**
		• Double-click the **Fonts** folder
		• Double-click the font you wish to preview
Using the Character Map	WINXP 5.24	• Click **Start, All Programs, Accessories, System Tools, Character Map**
		• From the Fonts drop-down list, select a font
		• Double-click the desired character(s)
		• Click **Copy**
		• Open the document you want to copy into
		• In the Edit menu, click **Paste**
Installing New Fonts	WINXP 5.25	• In the Start menu, click **Control Panel**
		• Double-click the **Fonts** folder
		• In the File menu, click **Install New Font . . .**
		• Navigate to the folder with the fonts you wish to install
		• Click the font(s) you want to add
		• Click **OK**
Deleting fonts	WINXP 5.26	• In the Start menu, click **Control Panel**
		• Double-click the **Fonts** folder
		• Right-click the font you want to delete
		• Click **Delete**
		• Click **Yes** at the Alert message

review of terminology

CROSSWORD PUZZLE

Across

1. The waiting line for printer output
3. Bold, italic, and underline are all examples of font _____
6. A font type that is an improvement on the original TrueType
7. Used to refer to a printer connected directly to your computer
9. A font made up of little pictures rather than letters
11. A type of font that has small lines to finish off the strokes of the letter

Down

1. Allows a computer to automatically detect and configure a device
2. A font with no lines finishing off the strokes
4. The number of dots per inch on a page
5. Lets you do something else while your print job is being executed
8. Software that allows a computer to communicate with a printer
10. The printer you use most often should be your _____ printer

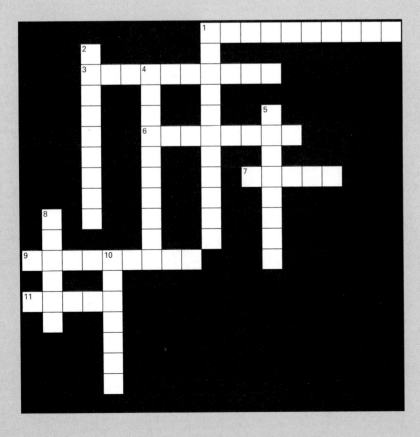

TRUE OR FALSE

1. If you designate a default printer, its icon will appear underlined in the Printers window.

2. Arial is a good font for use in a body of text.

3. Landscape orientation prints horizontally.

4. You use the Printer Properties dialog box to install a new printer.

5. The print queue is the line of people that forms in front of a printer on a busy day.

CREATE THE QUESTION

For each of the following answers, create an appropriate, short question.

ANSWER	QUESTION
1. A printer that is connected directly to your computer	_____
2. The printer your computer automatically prints to unless instructed otherwise	_____
3. If you don't have this printer software installed, your printer will not be able to understand the commands your computer gives it	_____
4. A printer that you have designated as available for others on a network to use	_____
5. An Advanced Option in the Printer Properties dialog box that inserts a sheet of paper between print jobs	_____
6. This Advanced Option allows you to change the resolution of a printed document	_____
7. Selecting this tab in the Printer Properties dialog box takes you to an option that allows you to make a printer available only during certain hours	_____
8. The way font size is measured	_____
9. This type of font was designed to appear on a computer screen exactly the way it will print	_____
10. A non-Windows program you must use in order to install PostScript fonts	_____

1. Using Fonts to Enhance a Document

Impact Public Relations specializes in promoting new businesses in the local community. The major avenue for this type of promotion is via press releases that Impact distributes to all the local newspapers, community groups, libraries, and meeting places. Each press release is allowed to have only a brief statement indicating that a new business is opening; the name, address, and phone number of the new business; and a short, one-sentence description of what the new business does. Working within these constraints, you are brought in to produce these press releases and give each one a bit of flair. You immediately realize that the easiest way to have the desired effect is to use different fonts for different types of businesses.

Open the data disk and locate the following files: **xp05robertson, xp05arthouse,** and **xp05natinsurance.** Each of these data files contains a different company's press release as prepared by Impact Public Relations. Experiment using different font styles that you think most accurately reflect the type of business you are promoting. Use only one font style per press release. Note that these files are created in WordPad, which is a small word-processing program included with Windows XP. WordPad has several types of fonts to choose from. If you have access to a full-blown word-processing program, such as Microsoft Word, use that instead of WordPad, as you will have many more options in terms of font selection.

2. Connecting to a Network Printer

Gina Petrillo does computer graphic design for a toy packaging company, Hillsdale Marketing Inc. Gina does all the design work from home, only occasionally going into Hillsdale's office to meet with clients or discuss future projects. Gina prepares the artwork, layout, and design, then e-mails her clients the initial proofs to get their feedback. As the projects progress, however, the clients want to see how the projects will look on paper. At these times, when the clients come into Hillsdale's office for a preview, Gina needs to access a special printer in the office to print out her work. Gina asks you to connect her home computer to this special printer in Hillsdale's office so that she can print directly to it, without having to go into the office.

1. Open the **Printers and Faxes** window, and double-click the **Add Printer** link to launch the Add Printer Wizard
2. Use this Wizard to add a network printer named **Hillsdale Special Printer.** Do not make this printer the default printer

challenge!

1. Designating a Default Printer and Creating a Shortcut for It on the Desktop

Reliable Equipment Leasing Corporation leases heavy machinery such as excavators, cranes, and steamrollers to contractors on a short-term basis, usually six months to two years. Reliable has a customer base of several hundred accounts that periodically return for new leases. The Accounting Department bills these accounts on a monthly basis. Chip Clemens runs the department and is looking for ways to improve the efficiency of the billing cycle, as the company finances are his primary responsibility. Since many hundreds of invoices are sent out monthly, three office administrators are used at the end of the month to get the bills out in a timely manner. Chip notices that each time the invoices are to be printed, the staff has to dig through various layers of folders to get to the desired printer. Further, a few bills have to be stamped before going out and these are printed on an Accounting Department office printer, while the majority of the others are printed on a printer directly in the mail room to be immediately stuffed into envelopes and mailed. Thus, the staff person has to make a decision about which printer to use.

You are brought in to try and streamline this process. Since the majority of the time the printer used is the one in the mail room, you explain that designating this printer as the default will save the trouble of having to select each time which printer to use. Further, placing the most frequently used printer right on the users' Desktop will save the time of having to dig through the computer files to find the correct one. Over the course of thousands of invoices printed over many months, these small changes will make a big difference in office efficiency. You spell out your ideas to Chip, and he gives you the go-ahead.

For this exercise, either use an existing printer on your computer or install a new one and rename it (temporarily) **Mail Room Printer.** Designate it as the default printer and create a shortcut on the Desktop for it.

2. Printing to a Remote Printer

Rosie Max works for a Flavor House as a "professional nose." That is what she calls herself. What she does all day is blend different flavors and aromas, experimenting to find the right combination that will give her clients the flavor, the scent, and the "mouth feel" that they want. Her clients are food companies that use Rosie's company, Robex Associates, for imparting a particular flavor to their products.

Robex has 47 employees, all connected by a networked computer system. The lab people frequently correspond with clients to ask questions, prepare product analyses, and comment on projects that they are working on. Rosie wants to take advantage of this ongoing stream of communication to flaunt the company's new laboratory equipment, which she has bought at great expense and is very proud of. She prepares a small brochure that she wants stuffed into all the envelopes that go to clients. Since the lab people are constantly sending hard copies of their correspondence to the customers anyway, Rosie decides this is a perfect opportunity to inform the clients of Robex's equipment upgrades. Rosie tells her lab people to use the printer in the administration office instead of the one in the lab so that the administration staff can stuff the correspondence with the equipment brochures.

Rosie asks you to help her. You explain that first the lab people need to make sure they have access to the administration printer. Once this is done, they need to set it up as their default printer, so that they don't have to worry about remembering to send print jobs to that printer. Use the Add Printer Wizard to add a new network printer called **Administration.** Make it your default printer.

1. Installing New Fonts on Your Computer

Camden Pro Press is a printer that does the printing jobs for a variety of different businesses. In the 15 years of Camden's history, however, it has developed a niche with advertising companies in the Camden area. These advertising companies often work under tight deadlines, and Camden is known for its fast turnaround on jobs. In addition, Camden has developed an additional service of providing the layout and design for ads directly from ideas brought to them by their clients. As the advertisers have sought to differentiate their ideas from a crowded field, they have sought more interesting and exotic design elements. As a result, some of the standard fonts that have been used for years have become less preferable than new and different ones. Your job is to find interesting fonts on the Web and download them so that they can be incorporated into future projects.

Using your favorite search engine, find sites on the Internet that offer free fonts for downloading. Download and install at least three fonts that are not presently on your computer. Print a preview page for each new font.

e-business

1. Pausing and Canceling a Print Job

Alan Kendall works for all-points-express.com, a delivery service that specializes in fast deliveries to remote parts of the United States. Alan's job is to promote the ability of all-points-express.com to beat out other competitors in terms of price, speed, and service to locations outside of major metropolitan areas.

Alan will be attending a major trade show in the next few days at which all-points-express.com will have an exhibit booth. All the materials for the trade show have already been shipped to the convention center. You work with Alan and bring to his attention an article in a trade paper. It details the results of an independent marketing evaluation showing that all-points-express.com was ranked higher than any other major carrier in several categories. Alan wants to print several hundred copies of this article and bring it with him when he goes to the trade show. Open the data files and find the file named **All Points article.** Set your printer to print **10** copies in **Draft** mode and begin printing. **Pause printing** (using the **Printer and Faxes** file) by right-clicking your printer and selecting **Pause** from the context menu, and then restart it. After the printing begins again, **Cancel** the print job in the **Printers** window by double-clicking the printer you are using and clicking the name of the file you want to cancel.

around the world

1. Using the Character Map and Changing the Printer Properties

Laura Vasconcelos is a Spanish teacher at the New Bridge Elementary School. She needs to print a study guide for her students listing the capitals of Spanish-speaking Central American countries.

Type the following list into a new WordPad document and use the Character Map **(Start, All Programs, Accessories, System Tools, Character Map)** to type foreign punctuation for the letters é, ó, and á.

Country	Capital
Costa Rica	San José
Honduras	Tegucigalpa
Panamá	Ciudad de Panamá
Nicaragua	Managua
El Salvador	San Salvador
Guatemala	Guatemala
México	Ciudad de México

Save the document and name it **Central American Capitals.** Print three copies of this document, changing the printer properties to make this document the first priority and printing a separator page between each copy.

unicode *is a character encoding system for computers that enables almost all the alphabets of the world to be represented. Up to 65,536 possible characters can be represented in Unicode, and of that number, about 39,000 have been assigned to date—21,000 for Chinese characters alone.*

the *World Wide Web was started in 1989 by Tim Berners-Lee at the CERN physics laboratory in Switzerland. The original goal was to develop a system for researchers around the world to share and exchange ideas.*

the *biggest company in the world, in terms of market value, is Microsoft at $300 billion.*

a *new computer keyboard called Prodikeys comes attached with a 37-key piano keyboard that simulates the sound of different musical instruments, presumably enabling you to jam with your coworkers when the mood strikes.*

Chapter Objectives

- Learn about attaching and managing devices
- Use the Paint application to create bitmap graphics
- Create screen captures
- Play sound files from audio CDs using the CD Player
- Play sound or video files using the Windows Media Player
- Play DVDs using the DVD Player

CHAPTER

6

six

Multimedia

Ronstock Multimedia, Baton Rouge, Louisiana

Ronstock Multimedia provides audio and visual services to corporations. Many talented and creative people who are well versed in audio and visual applications work on the staff. Ronstock does many different types of work. It does in-house logo design, both graphic and audio. The audio logo is the little piece of sound that is played when the company logo flashes on a screen, as you often see at the beginning of a movie.

Ronstock also does Web graphic design, working with clients to design their Web pages. All the visuals for various types of Web sites are created in-house according to what the individual client wants, but what Ronstock specializes in are advanced designs for technology companies that want to make a strong impact on their sites. These types of clients want to demonstrate their leading edge aspect by creating state-of-the art visuals.

Jason Pollack is a new hire at Ronstock Multimedia. One of the first things he notices is that all the computers at Ronstock run Windows XP as their operating system. Although much of the advanced work is done on specialized software, Jason knows he can do some basic work just with the tools that come as part of Windows XP Professional.

INTRODUCTION

While most of your work may be done with a word processor, Windows XP also has features to handle multimedia—graphics, sound, and video. This chapter covers the basics of creating graphics and playing sound and video files from within Windows XP. This chapter also discusses how to attach equipment such as printers and scanners to your computer.

Windows comes with an application called Paint that you can use to create your own colorful images. You can also use Paint to capture images off your computer screen.

Windows also provides tools for playing sound and video files. The CD Player allows you to play your audio CDs from your computer's CD-ROM drive. You use Windows Media Player to play both sound and video files from your computer or the Internet. And if your computer includes a DVD drive, you can watch movies on your monitor with the DVD Player.

SESSION 6.1 CONNECTING DEVICES TO YOUR COMPUTER

> ### *another*word
>
> Multimedia applications have very large requirements for power and memory, much more so than word processing, spreadsheets, e-mail, and the like. If you are going to be doing any serious work in multimedia, you'll need a fast, powerful computer with lots of memory.

In the previous chapter, you learned about the Windows Plug and Play feature and about some of the basics of managing devices. A printer is one example of a device.

A ***device*** is any piece of equipment that is attached to your computer. That includes some of the basic elements such as a monitor, keyboard, and mouse, plus other equipment such as your printer, speakers, DVD Player, or a scanner.

Each device in turn requires a ***driver,*** the software that controls the device. Windows XP includes drivers for several commonly installed pieces of equipment, plus the equipment itself should come with a disk containing the driver.

INSTALLING A PLUG AND PLAY DEVICE

In earlier versions of Windows, attaching a new piece of equipment could be a complicated task. You had to manually check and make sure that none of the devices were stepping on each other's toes—trying to use the same computer resources.

If the device supports Plug and Play, then the process is very simple. You just attach the device to the computer. Windows XP automatically determines what resources the device requires and whether Windows XP already has the required drivers. If not, it prompts you for the disk.

> ### task reference
>
> **Installing a Plug and Play Device**
>
> - Connect the device to the computer
> - If prompted, insert the disk containing the device driver

INSTALLING A NON–PLUG AND PLAY DEVICE

While most of today's devices are designed to be Plug and Play, you may occasionally have to install equipment without the Plug and Play option.

Once you connect the device to the computer, the Add Hardware Wizard takes you through the steps of setting it up. The Add Hardware Wizard is accessed through the Control Panel.

---

task reference

Installing a Non–Plug and Play Device

- Connect the device to your computer

- Click **Start,** then click **Control Panel**

- Double-click **Add Hardware**

- Click **Next** at the Welcome screen of the Add Hardware Wizard

- Click the radio button next to *Yes, I have already connected the hardware,* then click **Next**

- The Wizard displays a list of already installed hardware (Figure 6.1). Click **Add a new hardware device** at the very end of the list, then click **Next**

- Click the radio button next to *Install the hardware that I manually select from a list (Advanced),* then click **Next**

- In the *Common hardware types* list box (Figure 6.2), select the type of hardware you're installing and click **Next**

- If you allow Windows to detect the new device, click **Next.** If you select not to have Windows detect the device, click the check box next to *Don't detect my device; I will select it from a list,* then click **Next**

- Select the brand name and model of the device, *or* click **Have Disk** if it isn't listed

- Click **Next,** then follow the remaining instructions for installing the device

---

*another*way

. . . to Install Non–Plug and Play Devices

For printers, modems, scanners, cameras, and game controllers, the Control Panel has specific icons for installing them. Double-click the icon, then follow the instructions.

FIGURE 6.1

Indicating to add a new device

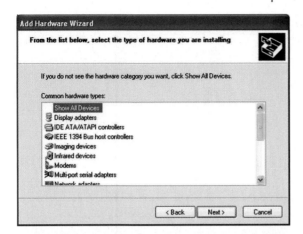

FIGURE 6.2
Selecting the type of device

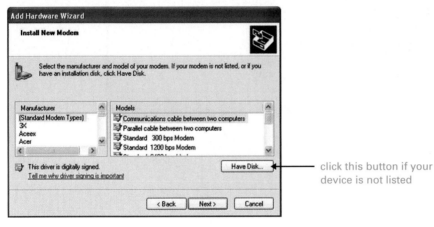

FIGURE 6.3
Selecting the brand and model
of device

click this button if your
device is not listed

MANAGING DEVICES

The Device Manager allows you to see the status of all the devices attached to your computer. It's available from the System Properties in the Control Panel.

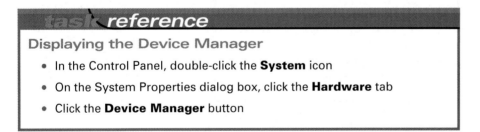

Displaying the Device Manager

- In the Control Panel, double-click the **System** icon
- On the System Properties dialog box, click the **Hardware** tab
- Click the **Device Manager** button

The Device Manager displays a tree structure listing types of devices and the devices installed for each type, as shown in Figure 6.4.

If one of the devices has a problem, it will have a yellow exclamation point or red x next to it.

For each device, you can display its properties. Double-click the device to display the Properties dialog for the device (Figure 6.5). If a device has a problem, the General tab of the Properties dialog box includes the system's best guess at the problem. If Windows thinks it knows how to fix the problem—for example, if the driver is missing—click the button below that description to take that action. If Windows can't figure out the problem, the button reads Troubleshooter and will lead you to various resources that can help you determine and fix the problem.

FIGURE 6.4

The Device Manager

tree of device types
and the devices for
each type

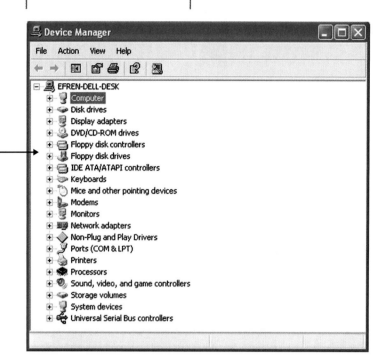

FIGURE 6.5

A device Properties dialog box

task reference

Troubleshooting Devices

- If a device has a problem, a yellow exclamation point or red x is next to the device name

- Double-click the device to display its Properties dialog box

- If Windows has a possible solution, click the button below the problem description to begin that course of action

- If Windows cannot determine the problem, click the **Troubleshooter** button to begin additional research on the problem

making *the grade*

1. What do you call the software used to control a device?

2. The _____ displays the status of all your devices.

3. To install a non–Plug and Play device, use the _____ Wizard from the Control Panel.

4. Is your mouse a device?

SESSION 6.2 VIEWING AND CREATING GRAPHICS

Included in Windows XP are several tools to handle still images. The My Pictures folder is the default location for images and includes some basic image manipulation tools. Image Preview allows you to preview an image. Paint is an image handling application in addition to a drawing application.

Many documents and Web pages use graphics to enhance their content. In this session, you'll learn about different types of graphics and how to use the Paint application to create and manipulate your own images.

TYPES OF GRAPHICS AND GRAPHIC FILES

Object versus Bitmapped Graphics

Graphics you create on the computer fall into two categories:

- *Object (vector) graphics.* These graphics are generally line drawings, flowcharts, and diagrams. In an object graphic, you can individually select, move, and otherwise edit each element of the graphic. You create these graphics using what are called drawing programs, or drawing tools within other programs

- *Bitmapped graphics.* A bitmapped graphic is like a painting. When you paint a picture, once you put down a brush stroke, you can't move or erase it

Types of Bitmapped Files

There are several types of bitmapped graphic files. While the same picture may look the same in each type, there are differences. Some file types are better used for photographs or for pictures. Some file types create larger or smaller files. And some file types are designed specifically for use on the Internet.

Figure 6.6 shows the most common graphic file types you'll see when using Windows XP.

STARTING THE PAINT APPLICATION

Windows XP comes with Paint, a basic program for creating and editing bitmap, JPEG, GIF, and TIFF files. The Paint application, like Notepad and WordPad, is available from the Accessories submenu of the All Programs menu.

FIGURE 6.6

Comparing graphic file types

Bitmap (.bmp)	Bitmap files provide a high level of color and detail; they aren't used on the Internet, and the file sizes are much larger than the next two.
JPEG (.jpg)	JPEGs are specifically used for photographs, especially on the Internet; they are *compressed,* which reduces the file size by adjusting the colors. JPEG files tend to be small in comparison to bitmaps.
GIF (.gif)	GIFs are also compressed files and, therefore, are also small in size; they are used on the Internet for graphics that aren't photographs such as logos.
PNG (.png)	A newer format, similar to GIF; PNG is unlicensed and can be freely used for storing graphics and photos on the Web.
TIFF (.tif)	TIFs are widely supported in different platforms (PCs and Macs) and are often large in size. These files are not used on the Internet but are used for archiving master copies of images.

task reference

Starting the Paint Application

- In the Start menu, click **All Programs**

- In the All Programs menu, click **Accessories**

- In the Accessories submenu, click **Paint**

Starting the Paint application:

Jason was sent a series of images via e-mail that he needed to manipulate. In the accompanying e-mail, a coworker told him a client was looking for a particular effect and he wanted Jason to look at the graphics and come up with some ideas.

1. In the Start menu, click **Programs**

2. In the Programs menu, click **Accessories**

3. In the Accessories submenu, click **Paint.** The Paint application opens with a blank picture displayed

4. Maximize the window to give yourself more working space

ELEMENTS OF THE PAINT INTERFACE

The interface of the Paint application includes the following elements:

- *Toolbox.* The toolbox is made up of eight rows of buttons. The top three rows are used to select a part of and manipulate your picture. The bottom five rows are used to add objects to your picture. When you click a tool, the area below the tool is filled in with any options for that tool, such as the width of a line

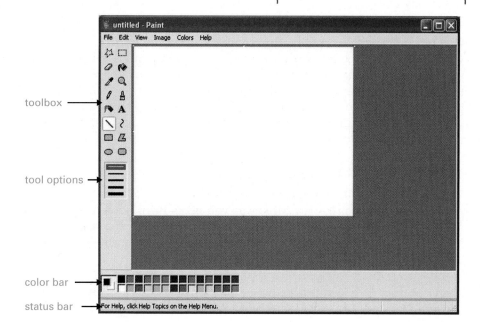

FIGURE 6.7

Elements of the Paint interface

- *Color bar.* The color bar displays the current foreground and background colors, and allows you to select those colors
- *Status bar.* The status bar contains three fields: The first field displays messages; the next field contains, in pixels, the exact position of the mouse within the image, calculated from the top-left corner; the third field contains the width and height of the image
- *Text bar.* The text bar first displays when you add text to your picture. It allows you to select the font used in your text object

You use the View menu to hide and restore these elements.

---

task reference

Removing and Restoring Paint Toolbars

- In the View menu, click the element to remove or restore

ABOUT THE UNDO COMMAND

The Undo command can be a valuable ally, especially when you're first learning a program such as Paint. The Undo option is in the Edit menu. It allows you to undo up to the last three actions. So if you draw a line and don't like the result, just click Undo. If you change your mind about the Undo, click Repeat.

---

task reference

Using Undo and Repeat

- To undo the last action, in the Edit menu, click **Undo** *or* press **Ctrl+Z**

- To restore the action, click **Repeat** *or* press **Ctrl+Y**

CREATING SCREEN CAPTURES

One type of graphic you may want to use is a ***screen capture,*** an image of your computer screen. Screen captures can come in handy if you're trying to explain exactly how to perform a task, or if you want a copy of an error message that displayed to use when you call Customer Service.

Windows XP Professional allows you to use the Print Screen button on your keyboard to grab the current screen. You can paste the captured screen into a text document or create a new graphic file from it.

CAPTURING AND PASTING THE SCREEN

To capture the entire screen, press the Print Screen key. To capture only the active window, press the Alt key as you press Print Screen. The screen or window is copied to the Clipboard. You can paste the image into a WordPad file or into Paint. If you paste the screen capture into Paint, you can save the file as a .bmp image to use in other files.

---

task **reference**

Creating a Screen Capture

- To capture the entire screen, press the **Print Screen** key
- To capture only the active window, press **Alt+Print Screen**
- Paste the capture into a word-processing or graphic file

Practicing creating screen captures:

Jason produced some preliminary designs on his Desktop to show his supervisor. Since the file sizes were rather large, he wanted to take a screen shot of some of the designs.

1. Right-click your Desktop and select **Properties**

2. In the Desktop tab, select **Autumn** from the *Background* drop-down list, then click **OK**

3. Press **Print Screen**

4. Open **Paint** from the Accessories folder of All Programs

5. In the Edit menu, click **Paste.** The screen capture is pasted into the document (Figure 6.8)

6. Minimize the **Paint** window, then open the **My Computer** window

7. Press **Alt+Print Screen**

8. Maximize the **Paint** window, and paste the screen capture again. Only the **My Computer** window has been captured

9. Close Paint without saving the new file

FIGURE 6.8
Screen capture of entire screen

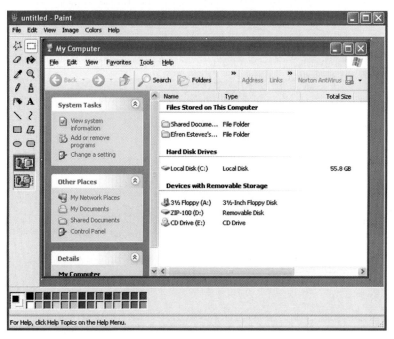

FIGURE 6.9
Screen capture of active window

making *the grade*

1. The _____ tool draws a straight line.

2. How do you capture only the active window?

3. The _____ key captures the screen.

4. When you capture the screen, where is the image placed?

SESSION 6.3 PLAYING SOUNDS AND VIDEO

The computer has evolved into a powerful tool for handling sound and video; besides the entertainment value, businesses use this technology to market and promote their products and services. The Web itself is a multimedia showcase as more businesses find ways to connect to suppliers and customers via digital sound and images. More advanced applications, like multicasting or videoconferencing, are also used but are beyond the scope of this book.

CHANGING THE SOUND VOLUME

All types of different sounds play on your computer. When you first log on, there is the Windows welcome sound. Depending on what actions you take, there are various types of alerts associated with different system events. You can increase or decrease the volume, or mute and turn on these sounds at any time.

You can adjust the sound volume in two ways. One way involves changing the volume for all the devices on your computer. This volume is called the system sound volume. Any sound that plays on your computer will be heard at this volume. The other way allows you to change the volume for individual devices, for example, if you want the CD player volume to be louder (or softer) than the system volume.

---

task reference

Changing the System Sound Volume

- Click **Start, Control Panel, Sounds, Speech, and Audio Devices**
- Click the **Adjust the system volume** link
- Click the **Volume** tab
- Drag the slider to the *Low* or *High* volume marks to decrease or increase the sound volume
- Click the **Mute** check box to turn off the sound
- Click the **Mute** check box to turn the sound back on
- Click the **Place volume icon in the taskbar** check box to display the speaker icon on your taskbar
- Click **OK**

When playing audio or video on your computer, you may want to adjust the volume level for these particular devices without changing your overall system sound volume. You can change the sound level for all the devices at once or for each particular device individually.

---

task reference

Changing the sound volume for individual devices

- Click **Start, All Programs, Accessories, Entertainment, Volume Control**
- Drag the volume slider for a device up or down to increase or decrease the volume

- Drag the balance slider left or right to adjust the sound balance for a device

- To turn off the sound, click the **Mute** check box

- To turn on the sound, click the **Mute** check box again

- Click **Options,** then **Properties** to specify which devices appear in the window

- Click the **Playback** or **Recording** radio button to list the devices in either category

- Click the check box next to the desired device to have it appear in the volume control window

ASSIGNING SOUNDS TO WINDOWS EVENTS

Windows XP has certain sounds associated with certain events that occur in the course of typical computing, for example, when it displays an Alert dialog box. These occurrences are known as program events. You can associate different sounds with these program events by using the Properties dialog box of Sounds and Audio Devices in the Control Panel.

These sounds can be customized to create your own, or your own organization's, personalized sound scheme. Sound files can be downloaded for free and purchased on the Internet.

task reference

Assigning Sounds to Events

- Click **Start,** then click **Control Panel**

- Double-click **Sounds and Audio Devices**

- In the Sounds tab, use the drop-down list under *Sound Scheme* to select the desired scheme

- In the list under *Program Events*, select the event for which to change the associated sound

- Change the sound associated with the program event by selecting the desired sound from the *Sounds* drop-down list

Assigning sounds to events:

Jason found that many of the tasks he had to perform required him to work with audio material. As a result, the sounds Windows makes when certain events occurred interfered with his work. He wanted to change the default settings for these audio cues.

1. Click **Start,** then click **Control Panel.** The Control Panel window opens

2. Double-click **Sounds and Audio Devices.** The Sounds and Audio Devices Properties dialog box opens

WINDOWS XP

3. In the Sounds tab, use the drop-down list under *Sound Scheme* to select **Utopia Sound Scheme.** All the Program events listed with a speaker icon next to them will now play a sound when the event occurs

tip: *Click **No** when the dialog box appears asking if you want to save the previous scheme*

4. Click the **Play** button to hear the sound (shown in Figure 6.10)

FIGURE 6.10

The Sounds tab of the Sounds and Audio Devices Properties dialog box

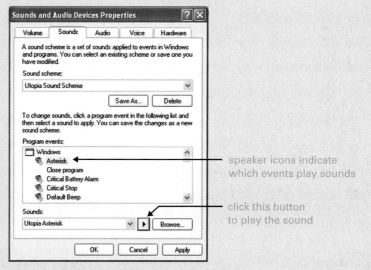

speaker icons indicate which events play sounds

click this button to play the sound

5. Use the drop-down list next to *Sounds* to select the following sounds; click the **Play** button after each one: **Windows XP Ding, Windows XP Exclamation, Utopia Asterisk**

6. In the list under *Program Events*, select **Asterisk** and click the **Play** button. The sound is the same as the last one you heard

7. Change the sound associated with the program event *Asterisk* by selecting **Windows XP Ding** from the *Sounds* drop-down list

8. Click the **Play** button. The sound associated with the program event *Asterisk* is now associated with Windows XP Ding, instead of Utopia Asterisk, as it was before

9. To keep your changes, click **OK.** To revert to your original Sounds settings, click **Cancel**

USING SOUND RECORDER

You can also create your own sound files. A utility that comes with Windows XP named Sound Recorder allows you to record and edit sounds from any sound device, such as a microphone, MIDI keyboard, or CD Player. These sounds can be used to enhance a presentation, emphasize important points in a meeting, and professionalize company gatherings. The right music during a technical presentation can relax attendees and keep them interested.

Sound Recorder is a basic sound acquisition and editing tool. Far more sophisticated programs are available.

task reference

Using Sound Recorder

- Click **Start, All Programs, Accessories, Entertainment, Sound Recorder**
- Click the **Start** button to start recording
- Click the **Stop** button to stop recording
- Click the **Play** button to play the recording

Using sound recorder:

1. Click **Start, All Programs, Accessories, Entertainment, Sound Recorder.** The Sound Recorder window opens, as shown in Figure 6.11

FIGURE 6.11

The Sound Recorder window

2. Insert an audio CD into your computer
3. Click the **Start** button to start recording (Figure 6.11)
4. Click the **Stop** button to stop recording
5. Click the **Play** button to play the recording

Sound Recorder also lets you insert another sound file into an existing recording. This is useful, for example, if you wanted to play your organization's sound logo in addition to the narrator's voice when the logo appears in a presentation.

task reference

Inserting a Sound File over an Existing Recording

- Open Sound Recorder to an existing recording
- Drag the slider to where you want to insert the new sound file
- Click **Edit,** the click **Insert File . . .**
- Click the sound file you want to insert, then click **Open** to add the sound to the existing recording

Inserting a sound file over an existing recording:

As part of the presentation, the client wants the logo sound to be heard every time their company logo appears on the screen. Jason knows he can use Sound Recorder to drop in additional sounds into preexisting recordings.

1. Open Sound Recorder to an existing recording

2. Drag the slider to where you want to insert the new sound file

3. Click **Edit,** then click **Insert File . . .** The Insert File dialog box opens

4. Click the sound file you want to insert, then click **Open** to add the sound to the existing recording

*another*word

. . . on Sound Files

Only sound files that are in Wave format can work in Sound Recorder, so if you import sound files from the Internet, for example, they must be in this format.

PLAYING AUDIO CDs

The CD Player software that comes bundled with XP allows you to listen to audio CDs from your computer.

Starting the CD Player

If you put a CD in your CD drive, CD Player starts automatically. If you need to open the CD Player, it's one of Windows Entertainment accessories.

task reference

Starting CD Player

- In the Start menu, click **All Programs**

- In the All Programs menu, click **Accessories**

- In the Accessories submenu, click **Entertainment**

- In the Entertainment submenu, click **CD Player**

The CD Player Interface

The CD Player interface looks and functions like a CD player on a stereo. You can adjust volume, skip backward and forward, and select different modes for listening (Figure 6.12).

FIGURE 6.12

The CD Player interface

if the album is in your database, displays the album, track title, and artist

changes to Tiny View

allows you to set CD Player preferences

Mode button

Options for the CD Player Interface

You don't have to use the CD Player's full interface. You can use a smaller version of the interface, called Tiny View, or run the CD Player from your taskbar.

    To switch to Tiny View, click the button next to the close button on the Title bar (Figure 6.13).

Returns to the full CD Player interface

FIGURE 6.13

Tiny View

    To use the taskbar, click the Options button, then on Player Options tab, check Show Control on Taskbar. Click the taskbar icon to play the CD, and right-click to display a context menu with more options (Figure 6.14).

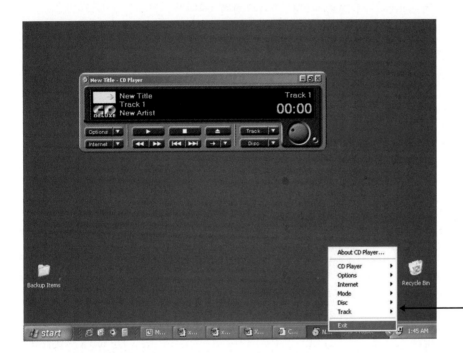

right-click the icon to
display a context menu

FIGURE 6.14

The CD Player taskbar icon

---

task reference

Changing to Tiny View

- Click the button next to the **Close** button

Using the Taskbar Icon

- Click the **Options** button
- In the Preferences dialog box, click the **Player Options** tab
- Check the **Show Control on Taskbar** check box
- Click **OK**
- To run CD Player, click the icon
- To display a context menu of options, right-click the icon

Selecting a Playback Mode

CD Player provides the following modes for playing the CD:

- *Standard.* Plays all of the tracks once in the default order
- *Random.* Plays all of the tracks once in random order
- *Repeat Track.* Plays the current track over and over
- *Repeat All.* Plays the entire CD over and over
- *Preview.* Plays the first five seconds of each track; click the play button to play the entire track

To change the mode, click the mode button, then select the mode from the drop-down list.

---

task reference

Changing CD Player's Playback Mode

- Click the **Mode** button
- In the drop-down list, click **Mode**
- When in Preview mode, click the **Play** button to play the entire track

---

About CD Playlists

CD Player's **Playlist** function allows the track information to display as the CD plays. It also allows you to control the default track order and content for each CD.

When you first insert a CD, CD Player offers to download the track information from the Internet. If it's able to find the information, it adds the CD track information to the album database, a collection of track information. If it's unable to find the track information, you can create the Playlist manually.

Once the Playlist is in the database, you can manipulate to change the track order, remove tracks, and repeat tracks.

The Playlist tab is on the Preferences dialog box. It includes a tree structure listing the CD currently in the drive and the CDs with information in the album database.

---

task reference

Displaying the Playlist Tab

- Click the **Options** button
- In the Preferences dialog box, click the **Playlist** tab (Figure 6.15)

Creating a Playlist

You can only create a Playlist for a CD that's in the drive. In the Playlist tab, click the CD that's in the drive, then click Create Playlist. On the CD Playlist Editor dialog box, enter the artist and title, then type the title of each track (Figure 6.16).

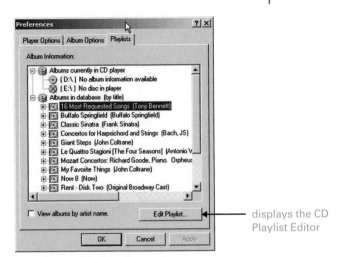

F I G U R E 6.15
The Playlist tab

displays the CD
Playlist Editor

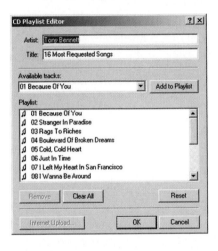

F I G U R E 6.16
CD Playlist Editor

task reference

Creating a Playlist

- On the Playlist tab, click the CD that's in the CD drive
- Click **Create Playlist**
- In the Artist field, type the name of the artist
- In the Title field, type the title of the CD
- For each track in the *Playlist* list, type the track's name
- Click **OK**

Editing a Playlist

Once the Playlist is in the album database, you can edit it to reflect your own preferences. You can change the default order of the tracks. If you really dislike a track, you can remove it so that CD Player never plays it. If you really like a track, you can arrange to have it show up more than once in the Playlist.

WINDOWS XP

> ### task reference
>
> **Editing a Playlist**
>
> - On the Playlist tab, click the CD for which you want to edit the Playlist
> - Click **Edit Playlist**
> - To move a track, click it and drag it up or down in the list
> - To remove a track, click it, then click **Remove**
> - To add another instance of the track, select the track from the **Available Tracks** drop-down list, then click **Add to Playlist**
> - Click **OK**

USING WINDOWS MEDIA PLAYER

The most common interface for video on your computer is Windows Media Player. With XP, Microsoft has bundled a completely new version, version 8, of Media Player that greatly improves upon previous versions. Media Player allows you to play sound and video files from your computer or the Internet. If you double-click one of these files, Media Player opens automatically to play the file. Media Player is located in Accessories, under the Entertainment submenu. If you have the Quick Launch toolbar displayed on your taskbar, it can also be accessed this way.

FIGURE 6.17

The Windows Media Player icon on the Quick Launch toolbar of the taskbar

the Windows Media Player icon

> ### task reference
>
> **Starting Windows Media Player**
>
> - In the Start menu, click **All Programs**
> - In the All Programs menu, click **Accessories**
> - In the Accessories submenu, click **Entertainment**
> - In the Entertainment submenu, click **Windows Media Player**

Types of Sound and Video Files

For sound files, you'll most often see the following file types:

- *Wave (.wav) files.* These are used for all of the system sounds. A .wav file reproduces sound faithfully and can be used for music and for speech
- *MIDI (.mid) files.* MIDI files are digital reproductions of sounds. A MIDI, while smaller in size than a .wav file, generally sounds artificial
- *MP3 (.mp3) files.* MP3 is a fairly recent sound file format designed to make sound files available via the Internet

For video files, you'll most often see the following file types: .avi, .mpg, and .mov. Media Player can also let you hear or see continuous sound or video on the Web, such as a live concert or sporting event. These files are known as *streaming media* files.

The Media Player Interface

The Windows Media Player interface includes the elements shown in Figure 6.18.

F I G U R E   6.18
The Windows Media Player interface

You can play and repeat a clip using Media Player. *Clip* is the term Media Player uses to refer to the sound and video files it plays. If you double-click a sound or video file, Media Player begins playing it automatically.

You can also open the file from within Media Player, then click the play button to play it. You can use the controls to go backward and forward in the clip, or drag the seek bar to a specific point in the clip (Figure 6.19). You can also set an option to repeat the clip a specific number of times or indefinitely.

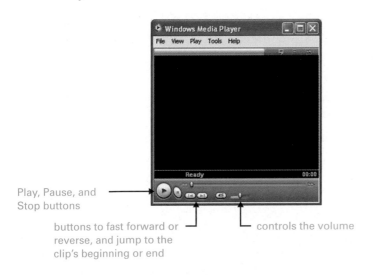

Play, Pause, and Stop buttons

buttons to fast forward or reverse, and jump to the clip's beginning or end

controls the volume

F I G U R E   6.19
Using the control buttons and seek bar

WINDOWS XP

task reference

Playing and Controlling a Clip

- Click the **Play** button to resume playing the clip
- Use the control buttons to pause, stop, and jump to the beginning or end of the clip
- Use the seek bar to go to a specific point in the clip

Repeating a Clip

- In the View menu, click **Options**
- Click the **Playback** tab
- To repeat the clip a specific number of times, type the number
- To repeat the clip continuously, click **Repeat Forever**
- Click **OK**

PLAYING DVDs ON YOUR COMPUTER

If your computer includes a DVD drive, then you can use the DVD Player to play your DVDs. When you insert a DVD in the drive, DVD Player starts automatically. Like CD Player and Media Player, DVD Player is an Entertainment accessory.

task reference

Starting DVD Player

- In the Start menu, click **All Programs**
- In the All Programs menu, click **Accessories**
- In the Accessories submenu, click **Entertainment**
- In the Entertainment submenu, click **DVD Player**

The DVD Player interface provides controls similar to the ones you use on the DVD player that's connected to your television set.

SESSION 6.3   making the grade

1. The _____ indicates the default order in which to play a CD's tracks.

2. Windows Media Player's _____ allows you to move to a specific point in a clip.

3. What type of sound file is used for Windows system sounds?

4. DVD Player requires what device?

SESSION 6.4 SUMMARY

This chapter has provided an overview of how you attach and manage devices, the equipment connected to your computer. You learned that Plug and Play technology makes installing new equipment fairly easy. You were introduced to the Device Manager, which lists the status of all the devices and can help you troubleshoot problems.

You also learned about different types of graphic files used by Windows and how to use Paint, a Windows XP accessory, to create and manipulate bitmap files.

You learned how to capture images of your computer screen to save as graphic files or to paste into a text file such as a WordPad file.

Finally, you were introduced to Windows XP's built-in tools for playing sound and video files. CD Player allows you to play your audio CDs from a CD drive and to customize the default order of the tracks. Windows Media Player is used to play audio and video files on your computer or from the Internet. If you have a DVD drive, you can use DVD Player to watch movies on your computer screen.

task reference roundup

Task	Page #	Preferred Method
Installing a Plug and Play device	WINXP 6.3	• Connect the device to the computer
		• If prompted, insert the disk containing the device driver
Installing a non-Plug and Play device	WINXP 6.4	• Connect the device to your computer
		• Click **Start**, then click **Control Panel**
		• Double-click **Add Hardware**
		• Click **Next** at the Welcome screen of the Add Hardware Wizard
		• Click the radio button next to *Yes, I have already connected the hardware,* then click **Next**
		• The Wizard displays a list of already installed hardware. Click **Add a new hardware device** at the very end of the list, then click **Next**
		• Click the radio button next to *Install the hardware that I manually select from a list (Advanced),* then click **Next**
		• In the *Common hardware types* list box, select the type of hardware you're installing and click **Next**
		• If you allow Windows to detect the new device, click **Next**. If you select not to have Windows detect the device, click the check box next to *Don't detect my device; I will select it from a list,* then click **Next**
		• Select the brand name and model of the device, *or* click **Have Disk** if it isn't listed
		• Click **Next**, then follow the remaining instructions for installing the device

task reference roundup

Task	Page #	Preferred Method
Displaying the Device Manager	WINXP 6.5	• In the Control Panel, double-click the **System** icon
		• On the System Properties dialog box, click the **Hardware** tab
		• Click the **Device Manager** button
Troubleshooting devices	WINXP 6.6	• If a device has a problem, a yellow exclamation point or red x is next to the device name
		• Double-click the device to display its Properties dialog box
		• If Windows has a possible solution, click the button below the problem description to begin that course of action
		• If Windows cannot determine the problem, click the **Troubleshooter** button to begin additional research on the problem
Starting the Paint application	WINXP 6.8	• In the Start menu, click **All Programs**
		• In the All Programs menu, click **Accessories**
		• In the Accessories submenu, click **Paint**
Removing and restoring Paint toolbars	WINXP 6.9	• In the View menu, click the element to remove or restore
Using Undo and Repeat	WINXP 6.9	• To undo the last action, in the Edit menu, click **Undo** *or* press **Ctrl+Z**
		• To restore the action, click **Repeat** or press **Ctrl+Y**
Creating a screen capture	WINXP 6.10	• To capture the entire screen, press the **Print Screen** key
		• To capture only the active window, press **Alt+Print Screen**
		• Paste the capture into a word-processing or graphic file
Changing the System Sound Volume	WINXP 6.12	• Click **Start, Control Panel, Sounds, Speech, and Audio Devices**
		• Click the **Adjust the system volume** link
		• Click the **Volume** tab
		• Drag the slider to the *Low* or *High* volume marks to decrease or increase the sound volume
		• Click the **Mute** check box to turn off the sound
		• Click the **Mute** check box to turn the sound back on
		• Click the **Place volume icon in the taskbar** check box to display the speaker icon on your taskbar
		• Click **OK**
Changing the sound volume for individual devices	WINXP 6.12	• Click **Start, All Programs, Accessories, Entertainment, Volume Control**

task reference roundup

Task	Page #	Preferred Method
		• Drag the volume slider for a device up or down to increase or decrease the volume
		• Drag the balance slider left or right to adjust the sound balance for a device
		• To turn off the sound, click the **Mute** check box
		• To turn on the sound, click the **Mute** check box again
		• Click **Options,** then **Properties** to specify which devices appear in the window
		• Click the **Playback** or **Recording** radio button to list the devices in either category
		• Click the check box next to the desired device to have it appear in the volume control window
Assigning sounds to events	WINXP 6.13	• Click **Start,** then click **Control Panel**
		• Double-click **Sounds and Audio Devices**
		• In the Sounds tab, use the drop-down list under *Sound Scheme* to select the desired scheme
		• In the list under *Program Events*, select the event for which to change the associated sound
		• Change the sound associated with the program event by selecting the desired sound from the *Sounds* drop-down list
Using Sound Recorder	WINXP 6.15	• Click **Start, All Programs, Accessories, Entertainment, Sound Recorder**
		• Click the **Start** button to start recording
		• Click the **Stop** button to stop recording
		• Click the **Play** button to play the recording
Inserting a sound file over an existing recording	WINXP 6.15	• Open Sound Recorder to an existing recording
		• Drag the slider to where you want to insert the new sound file
		• Click **Edit,** then click **Insert File . . .**
		• Click the sound file you want to insert, then click **Open** to add the sound to the existing recording
Starting CD Player	WINXP 6.16	• In the Start menu, click **All Programs**
		• In the All Programs menu, click **Accessories**
		• In the Accessories submenu, click **Entertainment**
		• In the Entertainment submenu, click **CD Player**
Changing to Tiny View	WINXP 6.17	• Click the button next to the **Close** button
Using the Taskbar icon	WINXP 6.17	• Click the **Options** button

WINDOWS XP

task reference roundup

Task	Page #	Preferred Method
		• In the Preferences dialog box, click the **Player Options** tab
		• Check the **Show Control on Taskbar** check box
		• Click **OK**
		• To run CD Player, click the icon
		• To display a context menu of options, right-click the icon
Changing CD Player's playback mode	WINXP 6.18	• Click the **Mode** button
		• In the drop-down list, click the **Mode**
		• When in Preview mode, click the **Play** button to play the entire track
Displaying the Playlist tab	WINXP 6.18	• Click the **Options** button
		• On the Preferences dialog box, click the **Playlist** tab
Creating a Playlist	WINXP 6.19	• On the Playlist tab, click the CD that's in the CD drive
		• Click **Create Playlist**
		• In the Artist field, type the name of the artist
		• In the Title field, type the title of the CD
		• For each track in the Playlist list, type the track's name
		• Click **OK**
Editing a Playlist	WINXP 6.20	• On the Playlist tab, click the CD for which you want to edit the Playlist
		• Click **Edit Playlist**
		• To move a track, click it and drag it up or down in the list
		• To remove a track, click it, then click **Remove**
		• To add another instance of the track, select the track from the **Available Tracks** drop-down list, then click **Add to Playlist**
		• Click **OK**
Starting Windows Media Player	WINXP 6.20	• In the Start menu, click **All Programs**
		• In the All Programs menu, click **Accessories**
		• In the Accessories submenu, click **Entertainment**
		• In the Entertainment submenu, click **Windows Media Player**
Playing and controlling a clip	WINXP 6.22	• Click the **Play** button to resume playing the clip
		• Use the control buttons to pause, stop, and jump to the beginning or end of the clip
		• Use the seek bar to go to a specific point in the clip

task reference roundup

Task	Page #	Preferred Method
Repeating a clip	WINXP 6.22	• In the View menu, click **Options**
		• Click the **Playback** tab
		• To repeat the clip a specific number of times, type the number
		• To repeat the clip continuously, click **Repeat Forever**
		• Click **OK**
Starting DVD Player	WINXP 6.22	• In the Start menu, click **All Programs**
		• In the All Program menu, click **Accessories**
		• In the Accessories submenu, click **Entertainment**
		• In the Entertainment submenu, click **DVD Player**

CROSSWORD PUZZLE

Across

3. A graphic representing the current contents of your computer screen
4. A utility that allows you to record and edit sounds from any sound device
9. Windows Media Player plays sound and _____ files
10. Contains the order of a CD's tracks
11. Holding down this key while pressing Print Screen captures only the active window
12. A graphic file used for photographs, especially on the Internet
13. Reduced in file size by adjusting the colors
14. A smaller instance of the CD Player interface

Down

1. Continuous sound or video on the Web, such as a live concert or sporting event, which can be heard or viewed using Windows Media Player
2. Any piece of equipment attached to your computer
5. An _____ graphic has individually selectable elements
6. The software that controls a device
7. The Windows accessory for creating and viewing bitmaps
8. Another word for a sound or video file

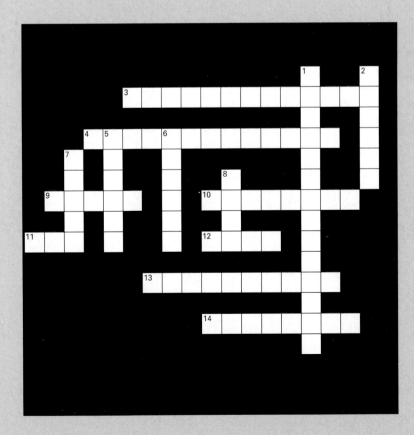

FILL-IN

1. Use the _____ to record a sound over an existing one.

2. The _____ menu contains options for manipulating an image selection.

3. If your device is not _____, use the Add Hardware Wizard to install it.

4. On the Internet, _____ and _____ are the two most common types of graphics.

5. _____ plays both sound and video files.

CREATE THE QUESTION

For each answer, create a short question:

ANSWER	QUESTION
1. The software that controls a device	_____
2. To distort a graphic by pulling on its opposite edges	_____
3. The keyboard shortcut for capturing an individual window	_____
4. The tracks on a CD and the default order for playing them	_____
5. An artificial-sounding audio file format	_____

SHORT ANSWER

1. Where do you find the current status of both your mouse and your monitor?

2. What is the difference between an object graphic and a bitmapped graphic?

3. How do you keep lines straight or draw a square instead of a rectangle?

4. What CD Player mode plays five-second samples of each track?

1. Changing Your Desktop's Look and Feel

Styx Enterprises requires that all of their computers have a certain look and feel, in keeping with the rather dark nature of their namesake. One of Randy Jones's tasks is to alter each Desktop and to recommend to the MIS director changes that would be attractive. To do this, he must open the Desktop Control Panel and alter some of the settings there, and then he will take a screen shot of his favorite modifications to put in his report.

A screen shot is a picture of your screen. Windows has a built-in screen shot utility. You press the **Print Screen** key (**Prt Scr**) at the top right of your keyboard to take a picture of the entire screen, or press the **Alt** key and the **Prt Scr** key together to take a screen shot of your current active window. The picture is copied to the Clipboard, and you can paste it into any Windows application to view.

1. To open Paint, click **Start,** click **Run,** and then type **mspaint** and press the **Enter** key
2. Minimize Paint by clicking on the **Minimize** button at the top right-hand corner of the Title bar
3. Right-click on the Desktop and select the **Properties** command
4. On the Desktop tab, scroll the *Background* list box, then select the background you like the best. Click **Apply**
5. Press the **Alt+Prt Scr** keystroke, then click on the **Paint** button in the taskbar
6. Select the **Paste** command on the Edit menu, or press the **Ctrl+V** keystroke to copy the contents of the Clipboard into Paint, as shown in Figure 6.20
7. Select the **Print** command from the File menu, or press **Ctrl+P** to print to a printer (use a color printer if possible)
8. Type the name of the background picture on your printout

2. Creating a Map

Jane's expecting relatives to visit this weekend. She's already sent them written directions but would like for them to have a map to help them locate her house.

Use Paint to reproduce the map shown in Figure 6.21.

1. Draw the intersecting streets, Maple Avenue and Main Street, first. In Paint, select the **Line** tool from the toolbox. When the lines of varying thickness appear below the toolbox, choose a thinner one for Maple Avenue and a thicker one for Main Street. Use the **Shift** key to create straight lines

Hint: If you make a mistake, remember the eraser tool and the Undo (**Ctrl+Z**) command!

2. Draw the curve for Sycamore Street next. Select the **Curve** tool and click a point about halfway up Maple Avenue as the starting point, then drag the line up and to the right. About midway on this new line, click and drag down to create the curve

FIGURE 6.20

Microsoft Paint is a convenient utility in which to view and print screen shots

3. Use the shape tools to create the landmarks. Select the **Rectangle** tool first, and click the middle of the three options underneath the toolbox for an outline with a fill color. Click the **olive green** color box. Right-click to the left of the vertical Maple Avenue line and drag to the right and down to create a rectangle for the McDonald's. Now click the **bright red** color box and repeat the process just above the first rectangle to create the fire station. Select the **dark brown** color box and hold down the **Shift** key to create a square shape for Jane's house

4. To create the traffic light, select the **Line** tool and select a thicker line, then select the **Rectangle** tool again. Click the **black** color box and create the outline for the traffic light

5. Select the **Ellipse** tool, and while holding down the **Shift** key, draw a red circle inside the outline of the traffic light. Repeat this process with yellow and green. Select the **blue** color box and draw an oval shape for the pond

6. To draw the church, start by selecting the **Rectangle** tool, the option to fill the shape with no outline, and the dark purple color box. Draw a square for the lower half of the church. To draw the church steeple, select the **Polygon** tool and the brown color box. Click a corner to begin and drag the mouse to draw a side. Click to end the side. When you finish the polygon, double-click

7. Finally, you want to label each of the landmarks. Select the text tool and the option to not use a background. Click and drag the text object until it is the right size and in the proper location. Type the text for each of the landmarks

in **Comic San MS** font, **bold,** and **9**-point size. Remember that you cannot edit text after it is added to the picture, so make sure your labels are correct before going on to the next one. Leave the Maple Avenue label for last

8. Type the text for **Maple Avenue** horizontally as you did the others. In order to get this label to be displayed vertically the way it is in the picture, click the **Select** box and click and drag a box around the Maple Avenue label to select it. In the Image menu, choose **Flip/Rotate . . .** Click the radio button next to *Rotate by angle* and select **270°.** The Maple Avenue label now appears correctly

9. Print out the map you've created

FIGURE 6.21

Street map to Jane's house

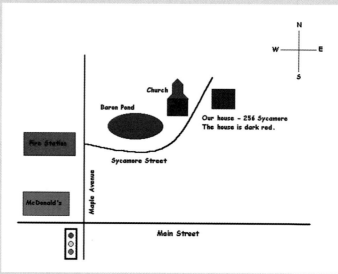

1. Creating and Manipulating a CD Playlist

Pick one of your favorite audio CDs and insert it into the drive. Make sure it's not a CD that's already in your album database.

When CD Player offers to download a Playlist, select **No.** Use the CD Playlist Editor to add all of the album's tracks in the current order to the Playlist. Use the Preview mode to make sure all of the tracks are present and in the correct order.

Change the order of the Playlist, then use Preview mode again to make sure the change is in effect.

Remove two tracks from the Playlist, then use Preview mode once again to make sure the tracks you removed do not play.

2. Creating Screen Captures

Jim needs to teach a coworker how to use the Paint application. He's created a WordPad file that describes how to use the Edit Colors dialog box. To accompany his instructions, he needs two screen captures—the entire Paint window and the Edit Colors dialog box.

Capture these two screens and paste each of them into a WordPad file. Show the Paint window as it displays on the Windows Desktop. For the Edit Colors dialog box, show only the dialog box itself and not the rest of the Paint window.

1. Open **Paint** and **WordPad** (Start/All Programs/Accessories/)
2. In Paint, press the **Print Screen** key
3. In WordPad, press **Ctrl+V** to paste. The screen captured Paint window appears
4. **Save** the document in **My Pictures** and name it **Paint window**
5. Return to Paint. In the **Colors** menu, select **Edit Colors . . .** The Edit Colors dialog box opens
6. Press **Alt+Print Screen**
7. Return to WordPad and press **Ctrl+V.** The Edit Colors dialog box appears. This image should look like the one in Figure 6.22
8. Save the document in **My Pictures** and name it **Edit Colors**

FIGURE 6.22

A screen capture of the Edit Colors dialog box only pasted in WordPad.

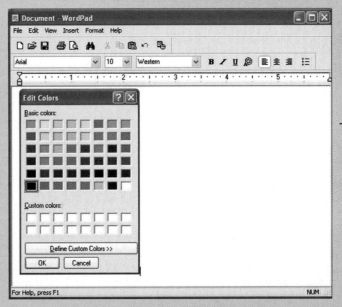

on the web

1. Downloading a Playlist

Joan Park is a program director at WLMN, a non-commercial public radio station that specializes in classical music and news. One of her job responsibilities is to oversee the compilation of Playlists for the music portions of the programming. Potential Playlists are submitted by the disc jockeys to her for review and approval.

Joan also coordinates news features and interviews with what gets played on the air. As a result, she frequently needs to make sure the music that is played corresponds to an artist's latest work. She gives you a stack of music CDs to verify.

Insert an audio CD into your CD drive, one that you haven't played before. When prompted, allow CD Player to search the Internet for the Playlist to your CD. When the Playlist is downloaded, check the downloaded results against your actual CD. Is the Playlist correct? Are all of the tracks listed with the correct titles?

e-business

1. Checking Your Modem

Simon Chester sells rare porcelain on the Internet. His Web site displays pictures and descriptions of his offerings. Customers enter their credit card numbers online, and he ships orders all over the world. Access to the Web site requires a modem, but Simon has just discovered that his modem is not working. He needs to buy a new one to replace it. Simon was happy with the way everything was working and wants to buy a modem that is, if not exactly the same, as close as possible to what he had.

Use the Device Manager to display the properties of the modem installed in your computer. Jot down the following information on a piece of paper. Who manufactured your modem? What speed is it? What is the current status of your modem?

Use any search engine and look up **modems for sale** or go to a Web site you know of that sells modems. Try to find the same exact modem as the one in your computer. If it is not available, find one by the same manufacturer that is close to it.

around the world

1. Assigning a Downloaded Sound Clip to an Event

Sarah Myers was a French major in school and has gotten a job at the French Institute as an office administrator. She wants to incorporate some French sounds into the sound scheme of her computer.

Browse the Internet and visit www.personal.cmich.edu/~franc1m/ref.htm. Click number 17 "Sound Clips of National Anthems." Download the French national anthem to the Desktop of your computer.

Assign this sound clip in the **Sounds and Audio Devices** dialog box located in the **Control Panel.** In the **Sounds** tab, select **Close program** from the Program event list. Use the Browse button to select the sound file of the French national anthem you just downloaded. Click OK to assign this sound clip. When you close a program, you should hear the clip played.

did you know?

the *true father of the recording industry is not Thomas Edison, but less well known Emile Berliner, who invented the microphone, the flat recording disk, and the gramophone player.*

an *eWine book, a wireless computer the size of a book, is making an appearance in some restaurants to provide help to diners wishing to pick wine to go with dinner. The e-book provides a description of the wine, profiles of the wineries, and recommendations of wines to accompany selected dishes at the restaurant.*

according *to the latest estimates, our planet loses 3 or 4 species an hour, 80 species a day, and 30,000 species a year, the highest rate of extinction in 65 million years.*

the *Wikipedia, created in January 2001 by a philosophy Ph.D. named Larry Singer, is "a collaborative project to build a complete encyclopedia from scratch." Located at* www.wikipedia.com *, anyone can write or edit an article on anything, the goal being to reach a target of 100,000 entries. One visitor might begin an article, and someone else at another time is free to add to or edit it. The Wikipedia attracts more than 1,000 new entries per month on areas from astronomy and astrophysics to visual arts and design.*

Chapter Objectives

- Learn how to set up a connection to the Internet
- Launch Internet Explorer
- Customize the Internet Explorer interface
- Display and navigate within Web sites
- Find previously visited Web pages
- Create and manage a collection of favorite Web pages
- Use Outlook Express to receive and send e-mail
- Use the Address Book to maintain a list of contacts

Henry's Nursery, Manassas, Virginia

Henry Fremont has been running a small nursery business for the last several years. He grows and sells houseplants and flowers, and each spring he helps his customers get their gardens started. Henry is also a member of several garden and flower associations and attends some national gardening events each year.

Henry just got a new computer running Windows XP. He originally bought it to keep his records and type orders, but he's heard a lot about e-mail and the Internet and thinks that he might be able to use these tools to help with his business and other activities.

He could find and order his supplies much quicker over the Internet, instead of mailing in order forms or waiting on hold on the phone. He knew that several seed and supply companies had Web sites where one could buy their products.

Some of his gardening associations had Web sites, and major events such as the Philadelphia Flower Show provided detailed information on their Web sites. He wouldn't have to wait for the announcement to show up in the mail.

Henry also planned to visit Longwood Gardens, a botanical garden in Pennsylvania. From what he'd heard, he'd be able to get directions and find out all about the place on the Internet. That would be a lot better than calling for information and waiting for them to send a brochure. He could also make travel plans and reservations without picking up the phone.

With e-mail, Henry could stay in touch with colleagues and friends, many of whom had been nagging him to "get on the Net." No more busy signals, answering machines, or postage stamps.

The first thing Henry would have to do is to set up the Internet connection. Then he could start exploring the world of the Web.

INTRODUCTION

Over the last several years, the Internet has changed how people do just about everything—get news, do banking, shop, travel, and communicate. The Internet has also changed the way the world does business. The advent of networks means that the different branches of a company, whether across town or across the world, can rapidly communicate and share resources. Organizations can globally distribute promotional materials about products or services simply by posting it to their Web site.

Windows XP includes tools for establishing and using an Internet connection.

Internet Explorer allows you to find and display information from Web sites around the world or just next door. With Outlook Express, you can keep in touch with family, friends, and colleagues.

SESSION 7.1 CONNECTING TO THE INTERNET

Using the Internet requires an Internet connection—a modem plus an account with an Internet Service Provider. Once that connection is set up, you can launch Internet Explorer and customize it to fit your needs.

ABOUT THE INTERNET AND THE WEB

The *Internet* is a network—a group of connected computers. Nowadays the terms Internet and World Wide Web are used interchangeably, but the *World Wide Web* is actually a subset of the Internet, although most Internet users deal almost exclusively with the World Wide Web. The Web is a collection of servers and files. The files are created using a language called *HTML*—Hypertext Markup Language. This markup language specifies the content, formatting, graphics, and navigation for the file, called a *Web page.* Web pages are grouped into *Web sites,* a group of connected and related Web pages.

Web pages are viewed using an application called a *browser,* Internet Explorer being one example. The browser processes the HTML files to generate the display and manage your navigation (Figure 7.1).

Over the years, Web content and functionality have become more robust and complex. There are applications for playing games and checking your bank balance. You can hold online meetings and view live video.

SETTING UP AN INTERNET CONNECTION

Internet Connection Prerequisites

Before you can do anything on the Internet, you need to have an Internet connection, an official entryway to the Internet.

Your computer must have a modem installed and connected to a phone or cable line. A *dial-up* modem allows your computer to connect to the Internet via a telephone line. Dial-up connections are relatively inexpensive, although they tend to be slow.

You can achieve a faster connection using a cable or DSL modem. A DSL line is a special kind of telephone line you have installed to connect to your computer. A cable modem uses a cable television line to transmit data from the Internet.

F I G U R E   7.1

HTML file and displayed Web page

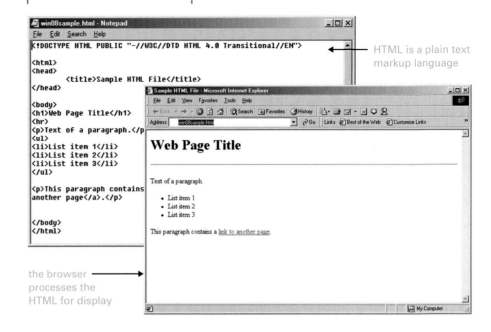

HTML is a plain text markup language

the browser processes the HTML for display

With the modem and line in place, you also need an ***Internet Service Provider (ISP).*** An ISP provides e-mail service and access to the Internet via one of their Internet servers. America Online is an example of one of the more popular ISPs. If you use a cable modem, then your cable company is also your ISP.

Using the Internet Connection Wizard to Set Up an Account

For dial-up accounts, if you don't yet have an ISP, you can quickly sign up for an account using the New Connection Wizard. The Wizard finds out what options are available to you, then connects you to the ISP of your choice. The New Connection Wizard is another Windows XP accessory, available from the Communications submenu.

***another*way**

. . . to Get to the New Connection Wizard

You can also get to the New Connection Wizard from the Network Connections folder. In the **Start** menu, click **Control Panel,** then double-click **Network Connections.** Click the **Create a new connection** link on the left pane of the window under *Network tasks*. The New Connection Wizard opens.

task reference

Starting the New Connection Wizard

- In the Start menu, click **All Programs**
- In the All Programs menu, click **Accessories**
- In the Accessories submenu, click **Communications**
- In the Communications submenu, click **New Connection Wizard**

LAUNCHING INTERNET EXPLORER

Starting the Internet Explorer Application

Internet Explorer is your Start menu. To start Internet Explorer, double-click the icon. If you have a dial-up account, Internet Explorer prompts you to use that to connect to the Internet. Once the connection is established, Internet Explorer opens to your home page. The ***home page*** is the first page that opens whenever you launch Internet Explorer. Most of the time the home page is related to your ISP.

FIGURE 7.2
New Connection Wizard

task **reference**

Starting Internet Explorer

- Click **Start,** then double-click the **Internet Explorer** icon

- If prompted, click **Connect** to connect to the Internet

Starting Internet Explorer:

With his Internet account in place, Henry was ready to begin using the Internet.

1. In the Start menu, double-click the **Internet Explorer** icon

2. If prompted, click **Connect** to establish the connection; Internet Explorer opens to your home page

Elements of the Internet Explorer Interface

Internet Explorer includes the following interface elements, as shown in Figure 7.3. As with other applications, you use the View menu to hide or display these elements.

- *Address bar.* Contains the address of the page that's displayed; the **address,** also referred to as the **URL (Uniform Resource Locator),** is the full path to the page
- *Standard buttons.* Provide options for navigating backward and forward, stopping and refreshing a page, and displaying Explorer bar tools
- *Links bar.* Provides quick access to a list of Web pages
- *Status bar.* Provides information about the current status of the current page and your Internet connection
- *Explorer bar.* Displays when you activate the Search, Favorites, or History function

We'll talk more about these elements and how to use them in Sessions 7.2 and 7.3.

FIGURE 7.3

Elements of the Internet Explorer interface

Standard buttons

Address bar

Explorer bar can contain Search, Favorites, or History

status bar

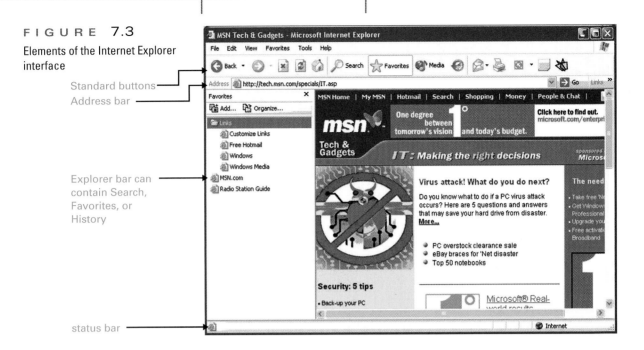

CUSTOMIZING INTERNET EXPLORER

Customizing Security

Security is an important consideration when exploring the Internet. With so large a network accessible to so many people, it's not surprising that unscrupulous people will try to take advantage. If you shop over the Internet, you need to be careful about how you use your credit card. You should also be careful about giving out personal information and about copying programs from the Internet to your computer.

Internet Explorer allows you to set security options to help keep your information and your computer secure. You set security from the Security tab of the Internet Options dialog box.

---

task **reference**

Displaying the Security Tab

- In the Tools menu of Internet Explorer, click **Internet Options**

- In the Internet Options dialog box, click the **Security** tab

---

At the top of the tab are Internet Explorer's four security zones, as shown in Figure 7.4.

- *Internet.* Used for all Internet sites that you haven't designated as Trusted or Restricted

- *Local intranet.* Used for all intranet sites; an ***intranet*** uses Internet technology but is internal to an organization. Many companies use an intranet to share information

- *Trusted.* Used for sites you have added to the trusted list, sites that you are absolutely sure pose no risk to your computer. Generally, the Trusted zone is less stringent with security than the other zones

- *Restricted.* Used for sites you have added to the Restricted list; these sites use the most stringent security

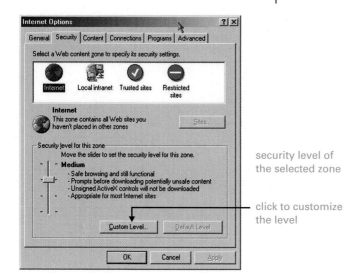

FIGURE 7.4
Internet Explorer security zones

security level of
the selected zone

click to customize
the level

---

task reference

Adding Sites to Security Zones

- In the Security tab, click the zone to which you want to add a site

- Click **Sites**

- Click the **Advanced . . .** button

- In the top field, type the address of the site

- Click **Add**

- Click **OK**

Each security zone is assigned a security level, indicated at the bottom of the tab.

anotherword

. . . on Security Zones
The right section of the status bar lists the security zone for the current page.

- High
- Medium
- Medium-Low
- Low

To set the security level for a zone, first click the zone, then use the slider to select a security level. As the slider moves to each level, a description of the level displays next to the slider.

---

task reference

Setting a Security Level

- In the Security tab, click the zone for which to set the level

- Click the slider bar, then drag it to one of the four security levels

- Click **Apply** or **OK**

You can also customize the security level for a zone. Click the Custom Level button to display the Security Settings dialog box, as shown in

Figure 7.5. The Security Settings box contains sets of radio buttons used to adjust different areas of your Internet security. Click the radio buttons to adjust the settings as needed.

F I G U R E   7.5

Security Settings dialog box

use radio buttons
and check boxes
to adjust settings

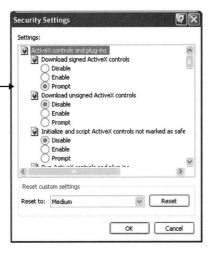

---

task reference

Customizing a Security Level

- In the Security tab, click the zone for which to customize the security level

- Click the **Custom Level** button

- In the Settings box, click the appropriate radio buttons to set the security options

- To reset the values to one of the default levels, use the **Reset to** drop-down list to select the level, then click **Reset**

- Click **OK**

---

*another*word

. . . on Cookies

A ***cookie*** is a small piece of information about you that Web sites save to your computer. It allows them to do things like greet you by name the next time you visit or suggest products based on previous purchases.

If you find this intrusive or a cause for concern, then in the Internet Options dialog box, under the Privacy tab, change the settings for cookies. You can disable them entirely or ask Internet Explorer to prompt you by displaying a message whenever someone tries to save a cookie on your machine.

Customizing Fonts and Colors

Most pages now have their colors and fonts specified by the Web designer, but you can specify colors and fonts to be used when they're not already specified, and you can override the page's settings if you need to. For example, if you need to have larger text because of poor eyesight, you can have the text always display in the same size, font, and color.

The font and color settings are available from the General tab of the Internet Options dialog box, as shown in Figure 7.6.

To set the colors used by the browser, click the Colors button. In the Colors dialog box, you can select:

- The color of the text
- The color of the page background
- The color of a link you have clicked

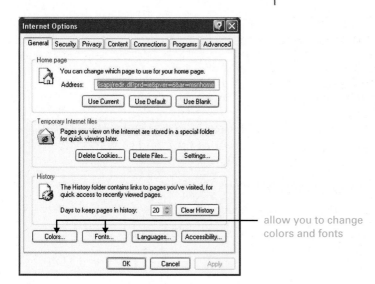

allow you to change
colors and fonts

- The color of a link you haven't clicked
- The color of a link when you position the mouse over it, but you haven't clicked it

To set a color, click the color button to display the Color dialog box.

color of text if not
specified by the page

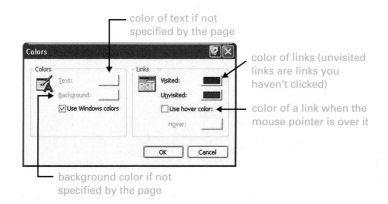

color of links (unvisited
links are links you
haven't clicked)

color of a link when the
mouse pointer is over it

background color if not
specified by the page

reference

Setting Web Page Colors

- In the Internet Options dialog box, click the **General** tab

- In the General tab, click the **Colors** button

- To be able to select custom colors for the text and background, uncheck the **Use Windows colors** check box

- To be able to select a color for when the mouse pointer is over a link, check the **Use hover color** check box

- To change the color of an option, click the color button

- In the Color dialog box, select the color to use, then click **OK**

- When you've finished selecting colors, click **OK** in the Colors dialog box

- In the Internet Options dialog box, click **OK** or **Apply**

Setting Web page colors:

After looking at a few Web sites, Henry decided he preferred a lighter background with dark text. He also decided to adjust the link colors to make sure he knew which pages he had already visited.

1. In your data files, double-click the file **xp07sample.html.** This file has no specifications for color or font, and so will reflect your new settings

2. In the Tools menu, click **Internet Options**

3. In the General tab, click **Colors**

4. In the Color dialog box, uncheck **Use Windows colors**

5. Click the **Text** color button

6. Select black, then click **OK**

7. Click the **Background** color button

8. Create or select a beige color, then click **OK**

9. Click the **Visited** color button

10. Select a dark red, then click **OK**

11. Click the **Unvisited** color button

12. Select a dark blue, then click **OK**

13. Click **OK** to close the **Colors** box. The Web page reflects the new colors, as shown in Figure 7.8

FIGURE 7.8

Page with new colors

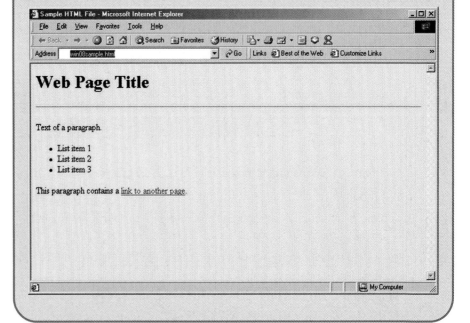

To set the fonts used by Web pages, click the Fonts button on the General tab. In the Fonts dialog box, you can set two fonts: one for regular text and one for what is called plain text, as shown in Figure 7.9. Plain text is like the text you type in a Notepad file.

F I G U R E   7.9
Fonts dialog box

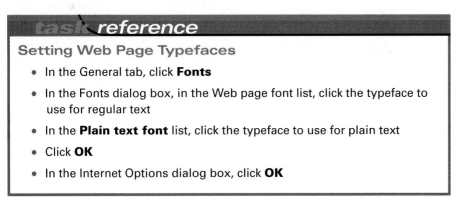

Setting Web Page Typefaces

- In the General tab, click **Fonts**
- In the Fonts dialog box, in the Web page font list, click the typeface to use for regular text
- In the **Plain text font** list, click the typeface to use for plain text
- Click **OK**
- In the Internet Options dialog box, click **OK**

The Font dialog box only allows you to change the typeface. To change the size of the text, you use the Text Size submenu of the View menu. The Text Size submenu provides five relative sizes: Largest, Larger, Medium, Smaller, and Smallest, as shown in Figure 7.10.

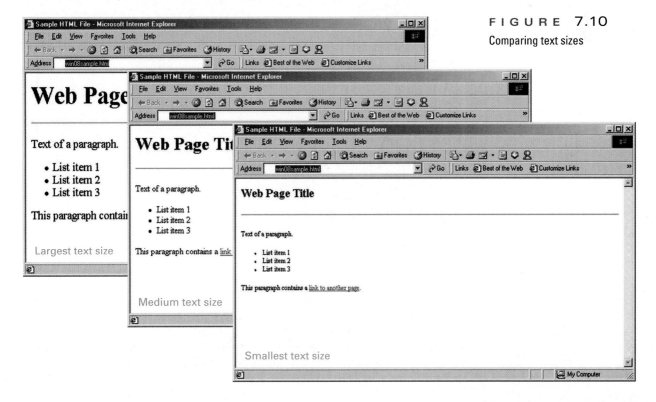

F I G U R E   7.10
Comparing text sizes

WINDOWS XP

---

reference

Customizing the Size of Text

- In the View menu, click **Text Size**

- In the Text Size submenu, click the size to use

Setting Web page fonts:

Henry also decided to set default fonts so that he could control how this aspect of Web pages displayed on his computer.

1. In the Tools menu, click **Internet Options**

2. In the General tab, click **Fonts**

3. In the *Web page font* list, click **Verdana**

4. In the *Plain text font* list, click **Lucida Console**

5. Click **OK**

6. Click **OK** to close the Internet Options dialog box and apply the new settings

7. In the View menu, click **Text Size**

8. In the Text Size submenu, click **Smaller.** The Web page reflects the new font settings, as shown in Figure 7.11

FIGURE 7.11

Page with new fonts

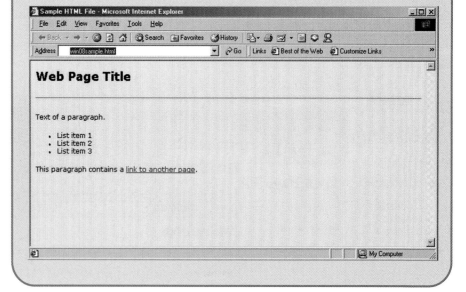

You will only see your font and color settings if the Web page doesn't specifically request a font or color. You can, however, override the Web page's fonts and colors.

In the General tab, click the Accessibility button. In the Accessibility dialog box, shown in Figure 7.12, use the Formatting check boxes to indicate whether the browser should ignore any of the Web pages fonts and colors in favor of your own selections.

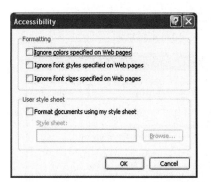

FIGURE 7.12
Accessibility dialog box

task reference

Overriding Web Page Fonts and Colors

- In the General tab, click the **Accessibility** button

- In the Accessibility dialog box, under Formatting, check and uncheck boxes to indicate which settings to override

- Click **OK**

- In the Internet Options dialog box, click **OK** or **Apply**

About Other Settings

The Internet Options dialog box provides access to several other options.

The *Content* tab, shown in Figure 7.13, allows you to control the types of pages that users can navigate to.

The *Connections* tab, shown in Figure 7.14, provides access to the Internet Connection Wizard and allows you to make adjustments to the settings used to connect your computer to the Internet.

The *Programs* tab, shown in Figure 7.15, allows you to assign different applications to open files and to perform different functions while you're on the Internet.

FIGURE 7.13

Internet Options—Content tab

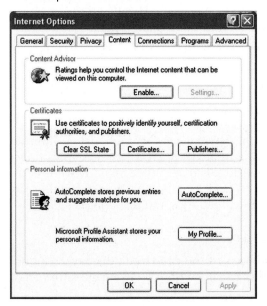

FIGURE 7.14

Internet Options—Connections tab

WINDOWS XP

FIGURE 7.15

Internet Options—Programs tab

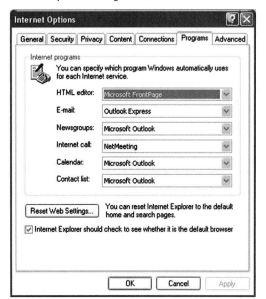

FIGURE 7.16

Internet Options—Advanced tab

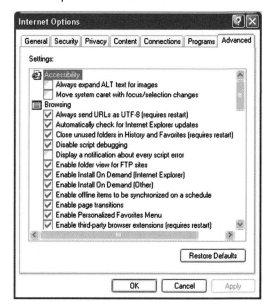

The *Advanced* tab, as shown in Figure 7.16, contains an assortment of advanced settings that don't fit into the other categories. You use the radio buttons and check boxes to make adjustments to these settings.

SESSION 7.1

making the grade

1. An _____ provides you with an account for gaining access to the Internet.

2. Which Internet Options tab allows you to control access to Web pages?

3. The first page that displays when you launch Internet Explorer is called the _____.

4. Use the _____ button on the General tab to make sure Internet Explorer always uses your colors and fonts.

SESSION 7.2 NAVIGATING AND SEARCHING IN INTERNET EXPLORER

This session covers the basics of navigating the Web using Internet Explorer. The browser opens with a home page. You can click links to get where you want to go or use the Address bar to type an address directly. The Search function allows you to find exactly what you're looking for. From the Internet, you can also download files and print pages.

USING THE ADDRESS BAR

The Address bar contains the address of the page that's displayed (Figure 7.17). You can also use the Address bar to go directly to a page or to return to a previous entry.

F I G U R E   7.17

Using the Address bar

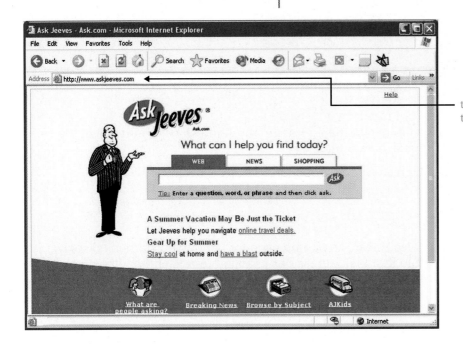

type the address,
then press Enter

Addresses are made up of the protocol, the domain name, plus the specific page path within the domain:

- **Protocol.** The method used to transmit the data for that page. On the Web, it is usually **http (Hypertext Transfer Protocol);** in an address, the protocol is followed by ://

- **Domain name.** The name of the Web site. Most domain names begin with www, indicating a Web site. The domain name ends with .com (www.yahoo.com) or some other suffix to indicate the type of site. com indicates a general commercial site. Sites for educational institutions such as universities end in .edu (www.harvard.edu), sites for nonprofit organizations end in .org (www.redcross.org), and government sites end in .gov (www.whitehouse.gov). Sites from other countries use a code representing that country (www.louvre.fr)

- *Page path.* The domain name is followed by a / and the path to the specific page. A Web site can be made up of a complex hierarchy of folders and files

To use the Address bar to go to a Web site, type the address, then press the Enter key or click the Go button at the right of the Address bar.

If you only specify the domain (www.xxx.com), the site opens up to the page designated by the designer as the site's home or starting page.

anotherway

. . . to Type an Address

If you don't have the Address bar displayed, then in the **File** menu, click **Open**. A dialog box displays in which you can type the address. Click **OK** to close the dialog box and open the page.

task reference

Using the Address Bar to Navigate

- Double-click the Address bar to select the current address
- Type the address you want to go to
- Press **Enter**, or click the **Go** button next to the bar

Entering an address:

Henry first wanted to see what he could find out about Longwood Gardens. He'd heard that a lot of Internet addresses were just www.<name>.com, so he'd try that first.

1. Double-click the address in the Address bar so that all of the text is highlighted

2. Type *www.longwoodgardens.com*

tip: *You can usually leave out the http:// part of the address, as most computers fill it in automatically*

3. Press **Enter.** The home page for Longwood Gardens displays; note that the address has changed to reflect the full path to the page

If you look closely, you'll see that the Address bar is actually a drop-down list. The Address bar maintains a list of the entries you've typed into it. You can use the drop-down list to select and display a previous entry.

NAVIGATING WITH PAGE LINKS

About Links

Once you're in a Web site, you usually use links to navigate. A ***link*** is a phrase or image you can click to navigate to another page. A link usually takes the form of underlined text. As mentioned in the previous session, you can customize the colors that represent links. Depending on how the site is designed, it may be difficult to pick out what is selectable. One way to know whether you're over a link is to move the mouse pointer over it. The pointer changes to a pointing hand whenever it's over a link, as shown in Figure 7.18.

FIGURE 7.18

Links

the mouse cursor becomes a pointing hand when over a link

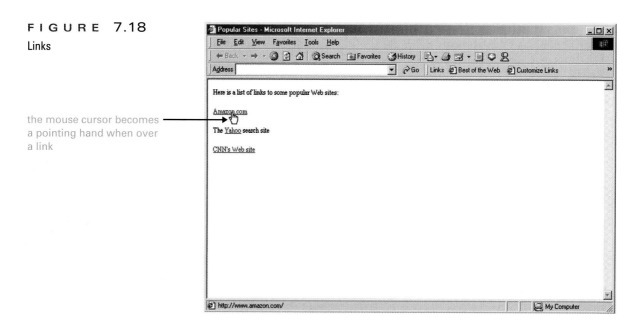

When you click a link, Internet Explorer uses the information for the link to perform an action or to display another page.

About Frames

One strategy page designers use to help you navigate within a Web site is to use frames. A *frame* is a container for a Web page. When a site uses frames, each Web page is actually made up of separate individual Web pages. In the most common use, one frame contains the table of contents for the site. When you click a link in one frame, the other frame is filled in with the destination page for the link (Figure 7.19)

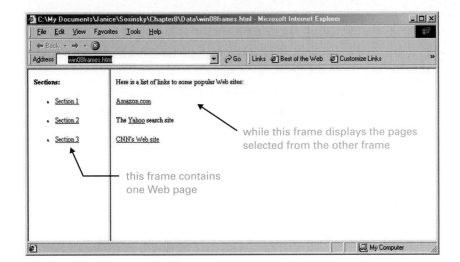

while this frame displays the pages selected from the other frame

this frame contains one Web page

FIGURE 7.19

Frames

Downloading Files

To *download* is to copy a file from the Internet to your computer. A link can lead to another page, or it can allow you to download another type of file such as a word-processing file or video clip.

When you click a link to another file, Internet Explorer displays a message asking whether you want to simply open the file or save it to your computer. It also checks whether your computer has the proper tools installed to open that file (Figure 7.20).

FIGURE 7.20

Download message

USING THE BACK, FORWARD, AND HOME BUTTONS

On the Standard Buttons toolbar, the Back and Forward buttons allow you to quickly go to previous and next pages you've displayed. The Home button takes you directly to your home page.

anotherway

. . . to Go Back, Forward, and Home

The Go To submenu of the View menu also allows you to go back, forward, and home. In the Go To submenu, click **Back** to go back, **Forward** to go forward, or **Home Page** to go to your home page. Below these options is a list of previous pages you can also navigate to.

- ⬛ Click the Back button to display the previous page. When you move the mouse pointer over the Back button, you see that it's a drop-down list of the last few pages you visited; select a page from the drop-down list to navigate to that page
- ⬛ If you've used the Back button to return to previous pages, click the Forward button to go forward to the next page. Like the Back button, the Forward button also contains a drop-down list of the next few pages you can use to navigate
- ⬛ Click the Home button to display your home page

task reference

Using the Back, Forward, and Home Buttons

- To return to the previous page, click the **Back** button; you can also select a page from the Back drop-down list
- To return to the next page after using the **Back** button, click the **Forward** button; you can also select a page from the Forward drop-down list
- To return to your home page, click the **Home** button

Navigating in Web sites:

Now that he'd found the Longwood Gardens Web site, Henry decided to see what he could find out about it.

1. On the Longwood Gardens home page, click one of the links
2. From the page that displays, click the **Back** button. You return to the previous page that was displayed, the Longwood Gardens home page
3. Click the **Forward** button. You return to the page you had navigated to using the link
4. Click the **Home** button to return to your home page

anotherword

. . . on Your Home Page

Any page can be your home page. In the General tab of the Internet Options dialog box, check the **Use current** check box to make the displayed page your home page, or type the address of the page you want to use.

USING THE STOP AND REFRESH BUTTONS

The Stop and Refresh buttons control the loading of a page.

- ⬛ Click the Stop button to stop loading the page. You'll most often do this if a page is taking too long or if you realize it's not the page you were looking for

-  Click the Refresh button to reload the current page. You might do this if the page didn't load correctly or if you think the content might have changed since it was first loaded

---

task reference

Using the Stop and Refresh Buttons

- To stop loading a page, click the **Stop** button

- To reload the current page, click the **Refresh** button

---

anotherway

. . . to Stop and Refresh a Page

The View menu also includes **Stop** and **Refresh** options to stop loading a page and to reload the current page.

SEARCHING

You may not always know the exact site or page you're looking for. Internet Explorer provides a search tool for finding information on the Internet. The Internet also has sites you can use to conduct searches.

Displaying the Search Tool

To display Internet Explorer's Search tool in the Explorer bar, click [Search] (Figure 7.21).

specify search criteria...

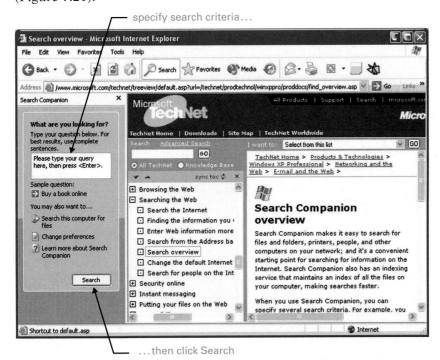

...then click Search

FIGURE 7.21

Internet Explorer with Search tool

---

task reference

Displaying Internet Explorer's Search Tool

- On the Standard Buttons toolbar, click the **Search** button

---

Conducting a Search

The search tool allows you to search in various different ways:

- *Find a Web page.* The most common type of search; allows you to type a word or phrase to find a Web page

- *Find a person's address.* Allows you to search for a mailing address or e-mail address for a person
- *Find a business.* Allows you to search for an address for a business
- *Previous searches.* Allows you to select from previous searches
- *Find a map.* Generates a map of a location and directions to that location
- *Look up a word.* Allows you to look up information in an online encyclopedia, dictionary, or thesaurus
- *Find a picture.* Allows you to search for pictures on the Internet

To use the Search tool, in the field provided, type the information to use in the search, then click the Search button. The Search tool runs the search and displays the results.

---

task reference

Using the Search Tool

- In the Standard Buttons toolbar, click the **Search** button
- In the fields that display, type or select the information to use in the search
- Click the **Search** button

Searching for a Web page:

Henry wasn't sure of the Internet address for the next Philadelphia Flower Show, one of the biggest gardening events of the year. He'd have to do a search to find it.

1. Click **Search**
2. In the search field, type **Philadelphia Flower Show**
3. Click **Search**
4. In the search results, click the links until you find the one for the upcoming show

---

PRINTING PAGES

Internet Explorer also allows you to print Web pages. To print the current Web page, click [Print] on the toolbar or select Print from the File menu.

If you select the Print menu option, the Print dialog box includes an Options tab to allow you to specify exactly how to print the page (Figure 7.22). For pages with frames, you can print only a selected frame (good if you want the content and not the table of contents), the exact layout, or each frame in turn. You can print all of the pages that have links on the page or print a list of the links.

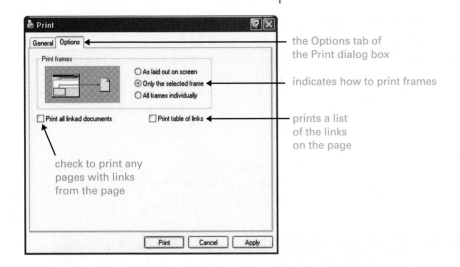

FIGURE 7.22
Options for printing a Web page

the Options tab of
the Print dialog box

indicates how to print frames

prints a list
of the links
on the page

check to print any
pages with links
from the page

---

task reference

Printing a Web Page

- Click the **Print** button

  or

- In the File menu, click **Print**

- Click the **Options** tab

- Under *Print frames,* click a radio button to indicate how to print them

- Check **Print all linked documents** to also print any pages that have links on this page

- Check **Print table of links** to also print a list of links on this page

- Click **Print**

Printing a Web page:

1. Open the file **xp07frames.html**

2. In the File menu, click **Print**

3. Click the **Options** tab

4. Click the **As laid out on screen** radio button

5. Click **Print.** The printout should replicate what you see on the screen

6. Click somewhere in the bottom right frame

7. In the File menu, click **Print**

8. In the Options tab, click the **Only the selected frame** radio button

9. Check **Print table of links**

10. Click **Print.** Only the material in the selected frame prints, along with a table listing the links on that page

USING LINKS, HISTORY, AND FAVORITES

If you often visit the same pages over and over again, you'll want an easier way to get to them than just typing the address all the time. The Links and Favorites functions allow you to have sets of frequently visited pages easily accessible, while the History function allows you to return to pages you've visited up to three weeks ago.

Using Links

The Links toolbar provides quick access to a short list of pages. By default the Links list contains pages sponsored by Microsoft, but you can customize this list with your own pages (Figure 7.23).

FIGURE 7.23

The Links toolbar contains a list of pages

You can add a link to the list either from the Address bar or from a link on a Web page. From the Address bar, click the icon in front of the address and drag it to the Links bar. On a Web page, click a link and drag it to the Links bar.

To change the order of the links, click a link and drag it to a new place on the bar. To remove a link, right-click it, then select Delete from the context menu.

task reference

Using the Links Toolbar

- To add a link from the Address bar, click the icon next to the address in the Address bar, then drag it to the **Links** toolbar

- To add a link from a Web page, click a link, then drag it to the **Links** toolbar

- To rearrange links on the toolbar, click a link, then drag it to its new spot on the toolbar

- To remove a link, right-click it, then click **Delete** in the context menu

USING HISTORY

The History tool allows you to return to pages you displayed up to a specified number of days ago. To display the History tool, click [Print] on the Standard Buttons toolbar (Figure 7.24).

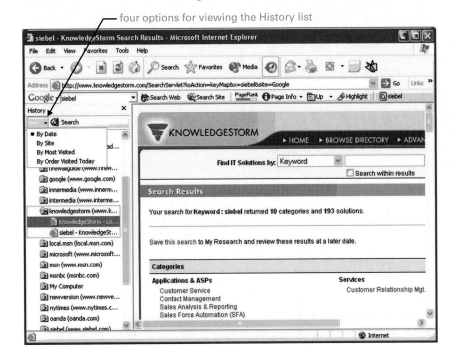

four options for viewing the History list

FIGURE 7.24

The History tool

History Views

The History tool has four views. You can use the View option on the History tool to switch among them.

- *By Date.* Displays four categories: Three Weeks Ago, Two Weeks Ago, Last Week, and Today. Click a category to display a list of sites visited in that time period
- *By Site.* Displays an alphabetical list of sites you visited in the last three weeks
- *By Most Visited.* Lists the sites you've visited the most
- *By Order Visited Today.* Lists the sites you've visited today in the order you visited them

Customizing the History Tool

The General tab of the Internet Options dialog box includes options for customizing and clearing the History tool (Figure 7.25). You adjust the number of days Internet Explorer saves history information or clear the current list.

---

task reference

Using the History Tool

- To display the History tool, click the **History** button
- To change the view, click **View,** then click an option in the menu
- To display a page from the History, click it

F I G U R E   7.25

Customizing the History tool

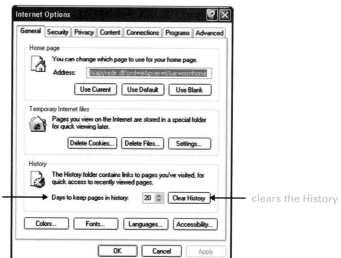

used to indicate how far back to save History information

clears the History

---

reference

Customizing the History Tool

- In the Tools menu, click **Internet Options**
- Click the **General** tab
- Under History, in the *Days to keep pages in history* field, set the number of days to keep History information
- Click **Clear History** to clear the History
- Click **OK**

Practicing with the History tool:

1. On the Standard Buttons bar, click **History**

2. In the History View list, click **By Site.** The sites you've visited are listed in alphabetical order

3. In the History View list, click **By Order Visited Today.** The sites you've visited are listed in the order you visited them

4. In the Tools menu, click **Internet Options**

5. On the General tab, click **Clear History.** The History tool is cleared

---

About the Cache

When you visit a Web page, Internet Explorer stores it in the *cache* (pronounced "cash"). If you visit the page again while you're online, or if you try to display a page when not connected to the Internet, Internet Explorer uses the copy in the cache.

The Temporary Internet Files section of the Internet Options dialog box allows you to determine how often Internet Explorer should check for new pages and how much space to use for the cache. You can also delete the cache.

USING FAVORITES

Internet Explorer's Favorites function allows you to save and organize a larger collection of pages so that you can get to them easily. There are two ways to work with Favorites:

- Using the Favorites menu
- Using the Favorites tool in the Explorer bar

The Favorites menu contains options for adding and organizing favorites, followed by the list of your current Favorites (Figure 7.26).

To display the Favorites tool in the Explorer bar, click ▣ (Figure 7.27).

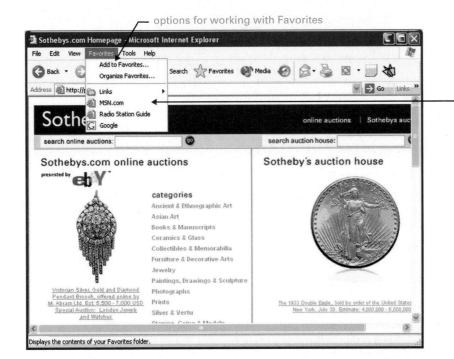

F I G U R E 7.26

Favorites menu

F I G U R E 7.27

Favorites tool in the Explorer bar

Favorites can be organized into a hierarchy of folders, just like the folders on your computer. Internet Explorer usually comes with a default set of folders, but you can create your own folders as well when adding or organizing your Favorites.

Adding Favorites

You can add the current page to Favorites from the Favorites menu, the Favorites tool, or the page's context menu. When you add a page to Favorites, Internet Explorer prompts you for a name and where to place the Favorite in the Favorites hierarchy (Figure 7.28).

FIGURE 7.28

Add Favorite dialog box

name of the favorite →

← click to choose a folder in which to place the new Favorite

anotherway

. . . to Add a Favorite

You can also add a page from the History tool to Favorites. Right-click a page in History, then in the context menu click **Add to Favorites.**

task reference

Adding the Current Page to Favorites

- In the Favorites menu, click **Add to Favorites** or click **Add** on the Favorites tool or right-click the page, then click **Add to Favorites** in the context menu
- In the *Add Favorite* dialog box, in the *Name* field, edit the Favorite's name as needed
- If the Create in folder list is not displayed, click **Create in**
- To create a new folder, click the folder in which to create the new folder, then click **New Folder.** Type the folder name, then click **OK**
- To select a folder in which to place the new Favorite, click that folder
- Click **OK**

Adding Favorites:

Henry was excited about the prospect of being able to save Web pages to Favorites. He wanted to be able to check out information from the Massachusetts and Pennsylvania Horticultural Societies, have the Longwood Gardens site accessible, and be able to get to the sites for Burpee and Ortho, two of his suppliers.

1. In the *Standard Buttons* bar, click **Favorites.** The Favorites tool displays in the Explorer bar
2. Display the Longwood Gardens site (**www.longwoodgardens.com**)
3. In the Favorites tool, click **Add**
4. In the Add Favorite dialog box, click **OK**
5. Go to **www.ortho.com**
6. In the Favorites menu, click **Add to Favorites**

7. In the Add Favorite dialog box, click **OK**

8. Go to **www.pennsylvaniahorticulturalsociety.org**

9. Right-click the page, then click **Add to Favorites** in the context menu

10. In the Add Favorite dialog box, click **OK**

11. Go to the following addresses and add them to your favorites: **www.masshort.org** and **www.burpee.com**

Organizing Favorites

A simple way to change how Favorites are organized is to click the Favorite and drag it to a new location in either the Favorites menu or the Favorites tool. You can also use the Organize Favorites dialog box. To display the Organize Favorites dialog box, click Organize Favorites in the Favorites menu or click Organize on the Favorites tool (Figure 7.29). From the Organize Favorites dialog box, you can rearrange items, create folders, rename items, and delete items.

adds a folder to the bottom of the list

allows you to rename the selected folder or Favorite

F I G U R E   7.29
Organize Favorites dialog box

prompts you to select a folder in which to place the selected folder or Favorite

information about the selected folder or Favorite

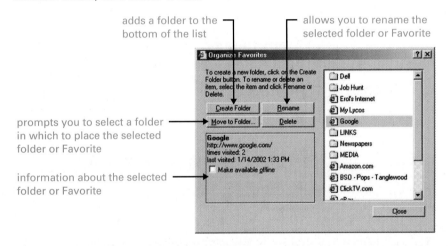

---

task reference

Using the Organize Favorites Dialog Box

- To display the dialog box, in the Favorites menu, click **Organize Favorites** *or* click **Organize** on the Favorites tool

- To display the contents of a folder, click the folder

- To move a page or folder, click and drag it to the new location

- To create a new folder, click **Create Folder.** Type the name, then press **Enter**

- To rename a folder or Favorite, click it, then click **Rename.** Type the new name, then press **Enter**

- To move a Favorite or folder to another folder, click **Move To Folder.** In the tree of folders that displays, click the folder you want, then click **OK**

- To delete a Favorite or folder, click it, then click **Delete**

- Click **Close**

---

anotherway

. . . to Delete and Rename Favorites

In the Favorites menu and Favorites tool, the context menu includes options for renaming and deleting Favorites. Right-click the Favorite or folder, then click **Rename** or **Delete** in the context menu.

WINDOWS XP

Organizing Favorites:

Henry realized that if he continued to add Favorites, he'd soon have a hard time finding a specific one in the list. He decided to organize the favorites he had so far into three folders: Gardens, Suppliers, and Clubs.

1. In the Favorites menu, click **Organize**

2. Click **Create Folder**

tip: *When you click a page or folder, information about it displays at the left.*

3. In the label for the new folder, type **Gardens**

4. Press **Enter**

5. Use the same technique to create a Suppliers folder and a **Clubs** folder

6. Drag the Favorites for the **Burpee** and **Ortho** sites to the **Suppliers** folder

7. Click the **Longwood Gardens** Favorite

8. Click **Move To Folder**

9. In the tree, click the **Gardens** folder, then click **OK**

10. Move the remaining two Favorites to the **Clubs** folder

11. Click **Close**

SESSION 7.2   *making the grade*

1. To return to a previous Web page, use the _____ button.

2. www.jcpenney.com is an example of a _____.

3. In an Internet address, the suffix of a college's Web site is _____.

4. To change which Search services Internet Explorer uses, click _____ on the Search tool.

5. A Web page made up of multiple individual pages uses _____.

6. The _____ toolbar contains a short list of pages.

7. Where do you go to clear the History?

8. _____ can be organized into folders.

9. You can add the current page to Favorites, or you can add Favorites from _____.

10. In an address, a .org suffix indicates a _____ organization.

SESSION 7.3 USING OUTLOOK EXPRESS

E-mail is a vital way to communicate with coworkers, customers, suppliers —anyone who is on the Internet. You can send them notes at any time without worrying about voice mail or hold time. This session goes over the basics of using Outlook Express, Windows XP's default tool for receiving and composing e-mail. You can also use the Newsgroups function to participate in online discussions concerning a wide variety of topics.

LAUNCHING AND SETTING UP OUTLOOK EXPRESS

Starting Outlook Express

Outlook Express is usually one of the default items in the Start menu. To start Outlook Express, click the icon.

Setting Up a Mail Account

Before you can send and receive e-mail, Outlook Express must know the servers used to send and receive e-mail. When you set up your Internet account, your ISP may automatically configure the e-mail as well, but you may have to enter the information manually.

---

task reference

Setting Up an E-Mail Account

- In the Tools menu, click **Accounts**
- On the Mail tab of the Internet Accounts dialog box, click **Add**
- In the pop-up list, click **Mail**
- Use the Internet Connection Wizard to enter the information supplied by your ISP

click to add a new account to the list

list of e-mail accounts

FIGURE 7.30
Internet Accounts dialog box

Elements of the Outlook Express Interface

The Outlook Express interface is made up of the following elements, as shown in Figure 7.31:

- *Folders list.* A tree structure of e-mail and newsgroup folders
- *Message list.* A list of messages in the selected folder
- *Preview pane.* The content of the selected message from the message list
- *Contacts.* A list of the names in your Address Book

FIGURE 7.31

Elements of the Outlook Express interface

Folders list ──

mail list for the selected folder ──

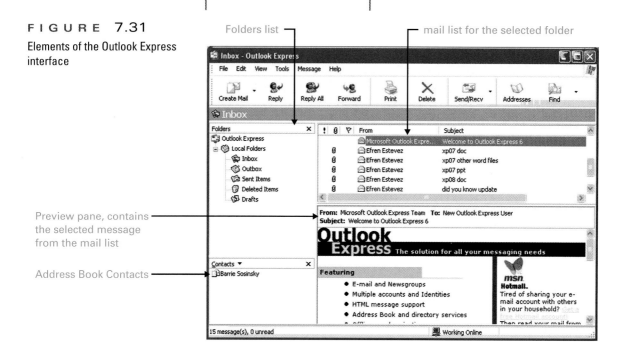

Preview pane, contains the selected message from the mail list ──

Address Book Contacts ──

You can display or remove these elements using the Layout option of the View menu. The Window Layout Properties dialog box (Figure 7.32) contains check boxes representing each element. Check the box if you want the element to display, or clear the box to remove the element.

FIGURE 7.32

Window Layout Properties dialog box

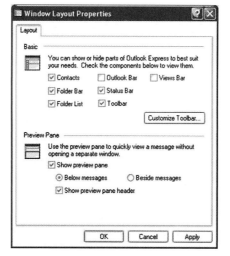

anotherword

. . . on Hiding Components

You can close the Contacts list and Folder List using the close buttons at the top right of these elements. You can use their context menus of the Outlook bar and toolbar to hide them.

task reference

Displaying or Removing Outlook Express Interface Elements

- In the View menu, click **Layout**

- In the Window Layout Properties dialog box, click an element's check box to either remove or display the element

- Click **OK**

RECEIVING E-MAIL

Downloading Messages

E-mail is stored on a mail server (either your organization's mail server or your ISP's mail server) until you download it to your machine. To check your e-mail server for new messages, click the Send/Recv button on the toolbar. Any new messages are added to the list in the Inbox folder.

You can also set up a schedule for checking the e-mail server while you're connected to the Internet. In the Tools menu, click Options. In the General tab, under Send/Receive Messages, type a number of minutes to indicate how often Outlook Express should check for new messages. You can also have Outlook Express check for messages when it is launched and have a sound play when new messages arrive (Figure 7.33).

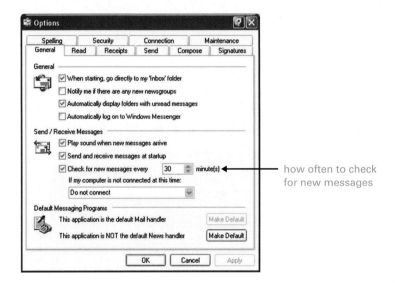

how often to check for new messages

FIGURE 7.33

Setting a schedule to check for new messages

---

task reference

Downloading Messages

- Click the **Send/Recv** button

Setting Options for Check for Messages

- In the Tools menu, click **Options**

- In the General tab, under Send/Receive Messages, click the **Check for new messages** check box

- In the field, type the number of minutes to indicate how often to check for new messages

- To check for new messages when you start Outlook Express, check the **Send and receive messages at startup** check box

- To play a sound when a new message arrives, check the **Play sound when new messages arrive** check box

- Click **OK**

Setting up a message download schedule:

Henry decided that he would have Outlook Express check his e-mail server when it first launched and every 15 minutes after that.

1. In the Tools menu, click **Options**

2. In the General tab, check the **Check for new messages** check box

3. In the field next to the check box, type **15**

4. Check the **Send and receive messages at startup** check box

5. Click **OK**

Managing Mail Lists

The Inbox is one mail list (Figure 7.34). Like all mail lists, the Inbox is made up of multiple columns that can include information such as the sender, the message title, and whether the message has an attachment. You can control the width of each column and also which columns display.

F I G U R E   7.34

Inbox

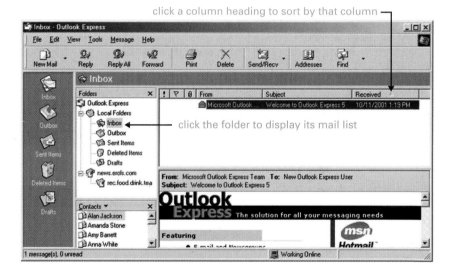

Hiding and displaying mail list columns

F I G U R E   7.35

Hiding and displaying mail list columns

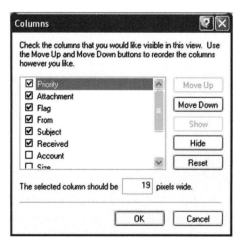

To change the width of a column, click the border between columns and drag it to the right or left. To change the order of the columns, click a column heading, then drag it to the right or left. To change which columns display, right-click the column headings, then click Columns in the context menu. You can then check and uncheck columns.

To sort the mail list, click the column heading of the column you want to sort by. Click again to reverse the sort order.

Managing a Mail List

- To change the width of a column, click a column border and drag it to the left or right

- To change the order of the columns, click a column heading, then drag it to its new location

- To hide or display columns, right-click the column headings, then click **Columns.** Check and uncheck columns, then click **OK**

- To sort the mail list, click the column heading

Reorganizing a mail list:

For his incoming messages, Henry only wanted to see when they arrived, the sender, and the subject line.

1. Click **Inbox**

2. Right-click the column heading in the Inbox mail list

3. In the context menu, click **Columns**

4. Uncheck all of the boxes except **From, Sender,** and **Received**

5. Click **OK**

6. Click the **Received** column, then drag it in front of the **From** column

Reading a Message and Its Attachments

If you have the Preview pane displayed, you can read the message by scrolling through the Preview pane. You can also double-click a message in the mail list to open a window containing the message itself.

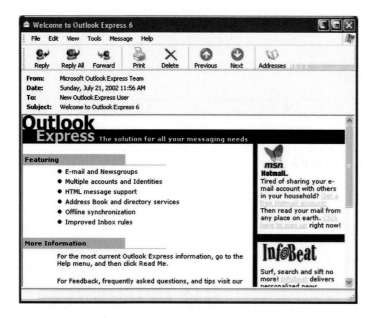

FIGURE 7.36
Message window

Messages may also have **attachments,** which are other files included with the message. On the Preview pane, attachments are represented by a paperclip in the top corner. On a message window, attachments are listed below the subject line.

When you select an attachment, Outlook Express attempts to open it using the assigned application for that type of file.

---

task reference

Reading Messages and Attachments

- To open a message window, double-click the message in the list

- To open an attachment from the Preview pane, click the paperclip, then click the attachment

- To open an attachment from the message window, double-click the attachment

---

Replying to and Forwarding Messages

To send a reply to the message, click either the Reply or Reply All button. Reply sends your reply only to the person who sent it. Reply All sends your reply to anyone who received the original message. A new message window opens with the current message displayed. You can then type your response before sending it.

To send a message to someone else who didn't receive it, click the Forward button. A new message window opens with the message and any attachments listed. You specify the recipient, then add any notes before sending the message.

*another*way

. . . to Handle Messages

Each message also has a context menu with options including Reply and Forward. To display the context menu, right-click the message in the mail list.

---

task reference

Replying to and Forwarding Messages

- To send a response only to the person who sent the message, click **Reply**

- To send your response to everyone who received the message, click **Reply All**

- To send the message to someone else who didn't receive it, click **Forward**

Storing and Deleting Messages

Once you've read a new message, you probably don't want to keep it in your Inbox forever. Outlook Express allows you to set up folders for storing and organizing your e-mail messages.

To create an e-mail folder, right-click the Folder List, then click New Folder in the context menu. Type the name of the new folder, then select the folder in which to place it. As with your Favorites, you can create entire hierarchies of mail folders.

task reference

Creating a Mail Folder

- Right-click the **Folder List**
- In the context menu, click **New Folder**
- In the Create Folder dialog box, type the name of the new folder in the *Folder Name* field
- In the folder tree, click the folder in which to place the new folder
- Click **OK**

anotherway

. . . to Create a New Folder

If you don't have the Folder List displayed, you can also create a folder from the File menu. In the File menu, click **Folder**, then click **New**. To then add the folder to the Outlook Bar, right click the **Outlook Bar,** then click **New Outlook Bar Shortcut.** Select the folder, then click **OK**.

Creating mail folders:

Henry knew he'd need to set up a good system of mail folders if he wanted to be able to keep track of his e-mail. He decided to create one folder for e-mail from suppliers, one for his gardening clubs, and another for personal messages. He'd put all of these folders in another folder called Storage.

1. Right-click the **Folder List**
2. In the context menu, click **New Folder**
3. In the Folder Name field, type **Storage**
4. In the folder tree, click **Local Folders**

tip: *Create the first level of new folders under Local Folders.*

5. Click **OK**
6. Right-click the **Folder List,** then click **New Folder**
7. In the Folder Name field, type **Suppliers**
8. In the folder tree, click the **Storage** folder
9. Click **OK**
10. Create two more folders, **Clubs** and **Personal,** in the **Storage** folder

To move a message to one of these folders, click the message in the mail list and drag it to the folder. You can also use the context menu to move and copy messages. To delete a message, either click the Delete button or drag the message to the Deleted Items folder.

task reference

Moving, Copying, and Deleting Messages

- To move a message to another folder, click the message in the mail list, then drag it to the folder
- To copy a message, hold down the **Ctrl** key as you drag it to another folder
- To delete a message, click the **Delete** button or drag the message to the **Deleted Items** folder

As you can see by the icon, Deleted Items acts as a Recycle Bin for your deleted messages. Deleted messages remain in the Deleted Items folder until you delete them from that folder.

These messages can pile up, so if you don't want to save deleted messages at all, you can arrange for Outlook Express to empty the Deleted Items folder whenever you close Outlook Express.

---

task reference

Arranging to Empty Deleted Items Automatically

- In the Tools menu, click **Options**
- Click the **Maintenance** tab
- Check the **Empty messages from 'Deleted Items' on exit** check box
- Click **OK**

About Message Rules

You can arrange for Outlook Express to handle some messages automatically based on criteria you specify. For example, you may want to sort incoming messages by placing messages from certain senders in certain folders, or automatically delete messages from senders you don't want to hear from.

In the Tools menu, the Message Rules submenu provides options for setting up criteria to handle incoming messages and block messages from senders.

SENDING E-MAIL

To create a new message, click the New Mail on the toolbar. The New Message window displays (Figure 7.37) to allow you to create and send a message.

FIGURE 7.37

New Message window

message recipients

message title

Formatting bar for rich text messages

type message text here

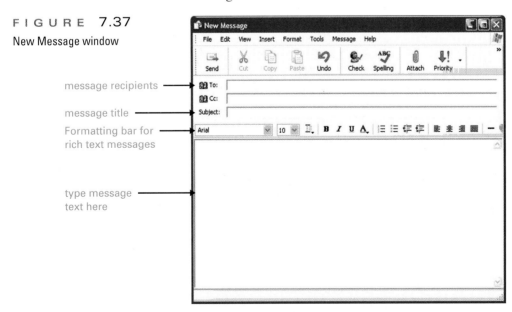

The New Message window also displays when you reply to or forward a message. If you're replying to a message, then the recipients and subject are already filled in. If you're forwarding a message, then the subject is filled in.

Addressing a Message

The fields at the top of the New Message window are used to address the message and tell recipients what the message is about. You can type e-mail addresses manually, or click the field label to display the Address Book and select recipients from there (Figure 7.38).

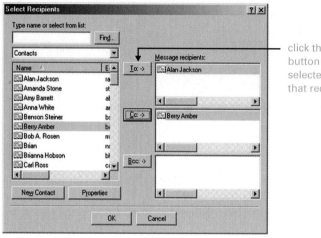

click the appropriate button to move the selected contact to that recipient list

FIGURE 7.38

Selecting recipients from the Address Book

The To field contains the e-mail addresses of the message's main recipients.

The Cc: field contains the e-mail addresses of additional recipients. As with paper memos, you Cc: a person who might be interested in the information but is not being addressed directly.

The Bcc: field (blind cc) allows you to send a copy of the message to someone without the other recipients knowing about it.

In the Subject field, type the subject of the e-mail. This is what displays in your recipients' Inboxes.

Formatting a Message

After addressing the message, you begin typing the text of the message. For e-mail messages, you have two choices of format—rich text and plain text.

Rich text is like a WordPad file and allows you to incorporate different fonts, formatting, and colors. Plain text is like a Notepad file. It uses a single, monospaced font and does not allow any formatting other than line returns (Figure 7.39).

Not all e-mail programs can display rich text. If you know your recipient only receives plain text messages, then you might want to create the message in plain text. To switch between formats, in the Format menu, click the format.

Adding Attachments to Messages

You use the attachment function to attach a file to your message. To add an attachment, click the Attach button on the toolbar. Navigate to the file, then click Attach. You can also open a folder on your Desktop, then drag a file from the folder to the New Message window.

FIGURE 7.39

Plain text and rich text messages

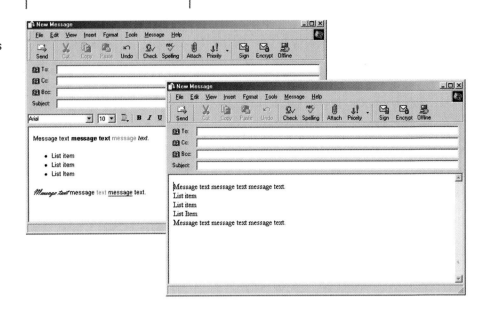

Sending Messages

To send the message, click the Send button. The message is placed in the Outbox folder until it has been sent, at which point it is placed in the Sent Items folder. Items remain in the Sent Items folder until you delete them.

---

task reference

Creating and Sending a Message

- Click **New** on the Outlook Express toolbar

- In the To:, Cc:, and Bcc: fields, specify the e-mail addresses of the message's main recipients

- In the Subject field, type the subject of the message

- In the message text box, type the text of the message

- To change the text format of the message, in the Format menu, click **Rich Text** or **Plain Text**

- To attach a file to the message, click the **Attach** button, then navigate to the file and click **Attach,** *or* drag a file from a Desktop folder to the New Message window

- To send the message, click the **Send** button

---

*another*word

. . . on Creating Messages

If you're unable to complete a message at once, you can save the message to the Drafts folder. Just click Save in the File menu. You can then open the message from the Drafts folder and finish it at a later time.

SETTING UP AN ADDRESS BOOK

The Address Book allows you to set up a list of people and their contact information. You can organize your contacts into groups.

Although you can display the Address Book from within Outlook Express, the Address Book is also a stand-alone Windows accessory.

You can use the View menu to change how the Address Book displays.

displays the properties of the
selected contact or group

allows you to
create a contact
or group

Displaying the Address Book

- From Outlook Express, click the **Addresses** button on the toolbar

  or

- In the Start menu, click **All Programs**

- In the All Programs menu, click **Accessories**

- In the Accessories submenu, click **Address Book**

Creating a Contact

To add a contact, click the New button, then click Contact in the drop-down list. You can also select New Contact from the File menu.

The information about a contact is divided into the following tabs:

- *Name.* The person's name and e-mail addresses
- *Home.* The person's home address and telephone, plus the address of his or her personal Web site if he or she has one
- *Business.* The person's business address and telephone, plus the address of his or her business Web site if he or she has one
- *Personal.* Information about the person's spouse, children, gender, birthday, and anniversary
- *Other.* Additional free text notes about the person, plus the groups in which he or she is a member
- *NetMeeting.* Information about how the person can participate in online conferences using Internet Explorer's NetMeeting tool
- *Digital IDs.* Information about online security certificates relating to this person

Fill out the information you want, then click OK to create the contact.

F I G U R E   7.41

Contact Properties dialog box

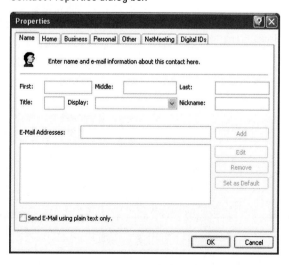

WINDOWS XP

<hr>

task reference

Creating an Address Book Contact

- Click the **New** button

- In the pop-up list, click **New Contact**

- In the Properties dialog box, type the information about the contact. You must at least specify a name

- Click **OK**

<hr>

Practicing creating contacts:

To practice creating contacts, add the members of your family to your Address Book.

1. Click the **New** button

2. In the pop-up list, click **New Contact**

3. On the Name tab, type the person's first and last names

4. On the Home, Business, and Personal tabs, type any other information you have about the person

5. Click **OK**

Creating a Group

A group is a collection of related contacts. For example, you might frequently need to send e-mail to the members of your department. By creating a group with those contacts, you can address the e-mail to the group instead of each contact individually, ensuring that you never miss anyone when creating those messages. A single contact may be a member of multiple groups.

To create a group, click the New button in the Address Book, then click New Group.

FIGURE 7.42

Group Properties dialog box

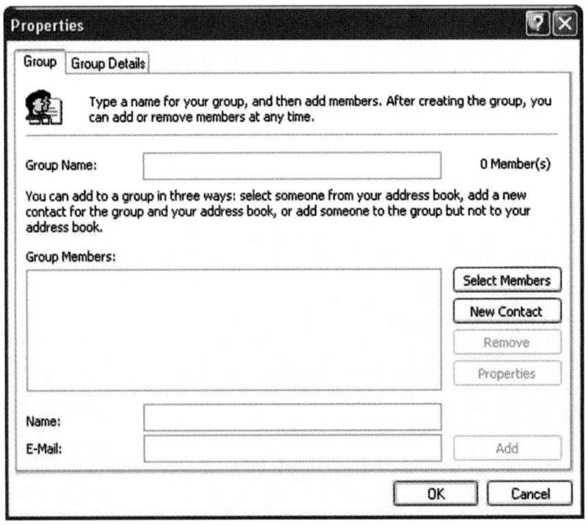

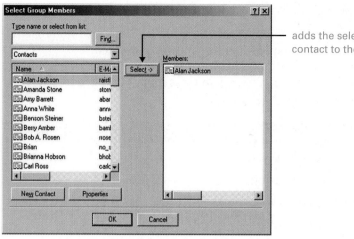

FIGURE 7.43

Select Group Members dialog box

adds the selected
contact to the group

On the Group tab, you give the group a name, then click Select Members to display a dialog box from which to select the group's members.

The Group Details tab allows you to specify address, telephone, and Web page information about the group.

---

task reference

Creating an Address Book Group

- Click the **New** button
- In the pop-up menu, click **New Group**
- In the Group Name field, type the name of the group
- Click **Select Members**
- In the Select Group Members dialog box, select the contacts for the group, then click **OK**
- Click **OK** to create the new group

Creating a group:

Now that you've added contacts to your Address Book, you can create groups to organize them.

1. Click the **New** button
2. In the pop-up list, click **New Group**
3. In the *Group Name* field, type **My Group**
4. Click **Select Members**
5. In the list of contacts, select one of your new contacts
6. Click **Select**
7. Add two more contacts to the list
8. Click **OK**
9. Click **OK** again to create the new group

Editing and Deleting Contacts and Groups

To edit a group or contact, double-click it in the list. You can then use the Properties dialog box to change the information as needed.

To delete a group or contact, click the group or contact, then click the Delete button. Note that when you delete a group, you do not delete the contacts that were assigned to the group.

---

task reference

Editing a Contact or Group

- Double-click the contact or group
- In the Properties dialog box, edit the information
- Click **OK**

Deleting a Contact or Group

- Click the contact or group
- Click the **Delete** button

USING NEWSGROUPS

A *newsgroup* is an Internet forum for conducting online conversations about a specific topic. The conversation takes the form of individual e-mail messages sent to the newsgroup.

Each newsgroup has a name that reflects the type and topic of the discussion. The first part of the name is the general category, followed by a "." and other words to specify the topic. For example, talk. environment is a discussion about the environment, and sci.space.history is a scientific discussion about the history of space exploration.

To use newsgroups, you must first set up an account with a news server. You can then follow and participate in the discussions on that server.

Creating a News Account

Creating a News account is similar to creating an e-mail account. In the Tools menu, click Accounts. In the News tab, click Add, then select News. Use the Wizard to enter the information about the news server.

---

task reference

Creating a News Account

- In the Tools menu, click **Accounts**
- In the Accounts dialog box, click **News**
- Click **Add**
- In the pop-up list, click **News**
- Use the Wizard to enter the information about the news server

---

Subscribing to a Newsgroup

Once you set up a news account, the newsgroup server is listed as a folder in the Folders list. To get to the list of newsgroups on the server, click the server, then select Newsgroups from the Tools menu.

FIGURE 7.44

Newsgroup Subscriptions dialog box

list of newsgroups in the selected server

list of news servers with which you have accounts

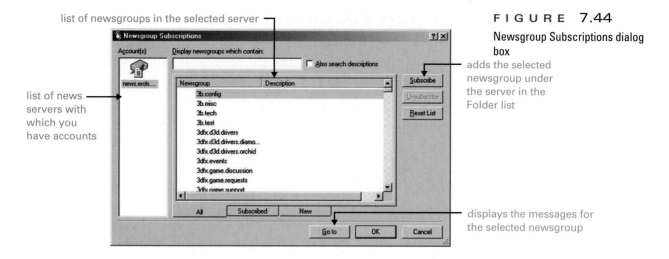

adds the selected newsgroup under the server in the Folder list

displays the messages for the selected newsgroup

You may only be interested in one or two of the discussions on the news server. While you can always display the messages for any of the discussions, when you subscribe to a newsgroup, that newsgroup is added as a folder under the news server.

task reference

Subscribing to a Newsgroup

- In the Folders List, click the news server

- In the Tools menu, click **Newsgroups**

- In the Newsgroup Subscriptions dialog box, click **All** to list the newsgroups on that server

- To subscribe to a newsgroup, double-click it

Viewing and Participating in a Newsgroup Discussion

Once you've displayed a newsgroup's messages, it works pretty much like any other mail list. You can read messages, reply to specific messages, create new messages, and set up rules for handling the newsgroup messages.

anotherword

. . . on Viewing Newsgroup Messages

You don't have to subscribe to a newsgroup in order to view its messages. To view messages for a newsgroup from the Newsgroup Subscriptions dialog box, click the newsgroup, then click Go to.

making the grade
SESSION 7.3

1. The _____ folder contains the messages you've created, but haven't sent.

2. A _____ is an online discussion of a topic.

3. The _____ contains a list of people and their contact information.

4. How do you display the list of newsgroups on a news server?

5. What function allows you to control how incoming messages are handled?

WINDOWS XP

SESSION 7.4 SUMMARY

This chapter has provided an introduction to the Internet.

You learned how to use the Internet Connection Wizard to set up an Internet account and how to connect to the Internet using Internet Explorer. Within Internet Explorer, you learned how to navigate to and within Web sites. You used the Search tool to find information and also learned how to save frequently visited pages to Favorites. You learned how to use the History tool to return to previous pages.

This chapter also introduced Outlook Express, Windows' default tool for sending and receiving e-mail. You learned how to set up an account, download and manage incoming mail, and create new e-mail messages.

The Address Book allows you to create and manage a complete list of contacts. You can store detailed information about a contact and organize the contacts into groups.

Finally, this chapter introduced Outlook Express's tools for managing newsgroups, or online discussions. You found out how to set up a news account, how to subscribe to a newsgroup on a news server, and how to view the messages in a newsgroup discussion.

task reference roundup

Task	Page #	Preferred Method
Starting the New Connection Wizard	WINXP 7.4	• In the Start menu, click **All Programs**
		• In the All Programs menu, click **Accessories**
		• In the Accessories submenu, click **Communications**
		• In the Communications submenu, click **New Connection Wizard**
Starting Internet Explorer	WINXP 7.5	• Click **Start**, then double-click the **Internet Explorer** icon
		• If prompted, click **Connect** to connect to the Internet
Displaying the Security tab	WINXP 7.6	• In the Tools menu of Internet Explorer, click **Internet Options**
		• In the Internet Options dialog box, click the **Security** tab
Adding sites to security zones	WINXP 7.7	• In the Security tab, click the zone to which you want to add a site
		• Click **Sites**
		• Click the **Advanced . . .** button
		• In the top field, type the address of the site
		• Click **Add**
		• Click **OK**
Setting a security level	WINXP 7.7	• In the Security tab, click the zone for which to set the level
		• Click the slider bar, then drag it to one of the four security levels
		• Click **Apply** or **OK**

task reference roundup

Task	Page #	Preferred Method
Customizing a security level	WINXP 7.8	• In the Security tab, click the zone for which to customize the security level
		• Click the **Custom Level** button
		• In the Settings box, click the appropriate radio buttons to set the security options
		• To reset the values to one of the default levels, use the **Reset to** drop-down list to select the level, then click **Reset**
		• Click **OK**
Setting Web page colors	WINXP 7.9	• In the Internet Options dialog box, click the **General** tab
		• In the General tab, click the **Colors** button
		• To be able to select custom colors for the text and background, uncheck the **Use Windows colors** check box
		• To be able to select a color for when the mouse pointer is over a link, check the **Use hover color** check box
		• To change the color of an option, click the color button
		• In the Color dialog box, select the color to use, then click **OK**
		• When you've finished selecting colors, click **OK** in the Colors dialog box
		• In the Internet Options dialog box, click **OK** or **Apply**
Setting Web page typefaces	WINXP 7.11	• In the General tab, click **Fonts**
		• In the Fonts dialog box, in the Web page font list, click the typeface to use for regular text
		• In the Plain text font list, click the typeface to use for plain text
		• Click **OK**
		• In the Internet Options dialog box, click **OK**
Customizing the size of text	WINXP 7.12	• In the View menu, click **Text Size**
		• In the Text Size submenu, click the size to use
Overriding Web page fonts and colors	WINXP 7.13	• In the General tab, click the **Accessibility** button
		• In the Accessibility dialog box, under Formatting, check and uncheck boxes to indicate which settings to override
		• Click **OK**
		• In the Internet Options dialog box, click **OK** or **Apply**
Using the Address bar to navigate	WINXP 7.15	• Double-click the Address bar to select the current address
		• Type the address you want to go to
		• Press **Enter,** or click the **Go** button next to the bar

task reference roundup

Task	Page #	Preferred Method
Using the Back, Forward, and Home buttons	WINXP 7.18	• To return to the previous page, click the **Back** button. You can also select a page from the Back drop-down list
		• To return to the next page after using the **Back** button, click the **Forward** button. You can also select a page from the Forward drop-down list
		• To return to your home page, click the **Home** button
Using the Stop and Refresh buttons	WINXP 7.19	• To stop loading a page, click the **Stop** button
		• To reload the current page, click the **Refresh** button
Displaying Internet Explorer's Search tool	WINXP 7.19	• On the Standard Buttons toolbar, click the **Search** button
Using the Search tool	WINXP 7.20	• In the Standard Buttons toolbar, click the **Search** button
		• In the fields that display, type or select the information to use in the search
		• Click the **Search** button
Printing a Web page	WINXP 7.21	• Click the **Print** button
		or
		• In the File menu, click **Print**
		• Click the **Options** tab
		• Under *Print frames,* click a radio button to indicate how to print them
		• Check **Print all linked documents** to also print any pages that have links on this page
		• Check **Print table of links** to also print a list of links on this page
		• Click **Print**
Using the Links toolbar	WINXP 7.22	• To add a link from the Address bar, click the icon next to the address in the Address bar, then drag it to the **Links** toolbar
		• To add a link from a Web page, click a link, then drag it to the **Links** toolbar
		• To rearrange links on the toolbar, click a link, then drag it to its new spot on the toolbar
		• To remove a link, right click it, then click **Delete** in the context menu
Using the History tool	WINXP 7.23	• To display the History tool, click the **History** button
		• To change the view, click **View,** then click an option in the menu
		• To display a page from the History, click it
Customizing the History tool	WINXP 7.24	• In the Tools menu, click **Internet Options**
		• Click the **General** tab

task reference roundup

Task	Page #	Preferred Method
		• Under History, in the *Days to keep pages in history* field, set the number of days to keep History information
		• Click **Clear History** to clear the History
		• Click **OK**
Adding the current page to Favorites	WINXP 7.26	• In the Favorites menu, click **Add to Favorites** *or* click **Add** on the Favorites tool *or* right-click the page, then click **Add to Favorites** in the context menu
		• In the *Add Favorite* dialog box, in the *Name* field, edit the Favorite's name as needed
		• If the Create in folder list is not displayed, click **Create in**
		• To create a new folder, click the folder in which to create the new folder, then click **New Folder.** Type the folder name, then click **OK**
		• To select a folder in which to place the new Favorite, click that folder
		• Click **OK**
Using the Organize Favorites dialog box	WINXP 7.27	• To display the dialog box, in the Favorites menu, click **Organize Favorites** *or* click **Organize** on the Favorites tool
		• To display the contents of a folder, click the folder
		• To move a page or folder, click and drag it to the new location
		• To create a new folder, click **Create Folder.** Type the name, then press **Enter**
		• To rename a folder or Favorite, click it, then click **Rename.** Type the new name, then press **Enter**
		• To move a Favorite or folder to another folder, click **Move To Folder.** In the tree of folders that displays, click the folder you want, then click **OK**
		• To delete a Favorite or folder, click it, then click **Delete**
		• Click **Close**
Setting up an e-mail account	WINXP 7.29	• In the Tools menu, click **Accounts**
		• In the Mail tab of the Internet Accounts dialog box, click **Add**
		• In the pop-up list, click **Mail**
		• Use the Internet Connection Wizard to enter the information supplied by your ISP
Displaying or removing Outlook Express interface elements	WINXP 7.30	• In the View menu, click **Layout**
		• In the Window Layout Properties dialog box, click an element's check box to either remove or display the element
		• Click **OK**

WINDOWS XP

task reference roundup

Task	Page #	Preferred Method
Downloading messages	WINXP 7.31	• Click the **Send/Recv** button
Setting options for Check for Messages	WINXP 7.31	• In the Tools menu, click **Options**
		• In the General tab, under Send/Receive Messages, click the **Check for new messages** check box
		• In the field, type the number of minutes to indicate how often to check for new messages
		• To check for new messages when you start Outlook Express, check the **Send and receive messages at startup** check box
		• To play a sound when a new message arrives, check the **Play sound when new messages arrive** check box
		• Click **OK**
Managing a mail list	WINXP 7.33	• To change the width of a column, click a column border and drag it to the left or right
		• To change the order of the columns, click a column heading, then drag it to its new location
		• To hide or display columns, right-click the column headings, then click **Columns.** Check and uncheck columns, then click **OK**
		• To sort the mail list, click the column heading
Reading messages and attachments	WINXP 7.34	• To open a message window, double-click the message in the list
		• To open an attachment from the Preview pane, click the paperclip, then click the attachment
		• To open an attachment from the message window, double-click the attachment
Replying to and forwarding messages	WINXP 7.34	• To send a response only to the person who sent the message, click **Reply**
		• To send your response to everyone who received the message, click **Reply All**
		• To send the message to someone else who didn't receive it, click **Forward**
Creating a mail folder	WINXP 7.35	• Right-click the **Folder List**
		• In the context menu, click **New Folder**
		• In the Create Folder dialog box, type the name of the new folder in the *Folder Name* field
		• In the folder tree, click the folder in which to place the new folder
		• Click **OK**
Moving, copying, and deleting messages	WINXP 7.35	• To move a message to another folder, click the message in the mail list, then drag it to the folder

task reference roundup

Task	Page #	Preferred Method
		• To copy a message, hold down the **Ctrl** key as you drag it to another folder
		• To delete a message, click the **Delete** button or drag the message to the **Deleted Items** folder
Arranging to empty deleted items automatically	WINXP 7.36	• In the Tools menu, click **Options**
		• Click the **Maintenance** tab
		• Check the **Empty messages from 'Deleted Items' on exit** check box
		• Click **OK**
Creating and sending a message	WINXP 7.38	• Click **New** on the Outlook Express toolbar
		• In the To:, Cc:, and Bcc: fields, specify the e-mail addresses of the message's main recipients
		• In the Subject field, type the subject of the message
		• In the message text box, type the text of the message
		• To change the text format of the message, in the Format menu, click **Rich Text** or **Plain Text**
		• To attach a file to the message, click the **Attach** button, then navigate to the file and click **Attach**, *or* drag a file from a Desktop folder to the New Message window
		• To send the message, click the **Send** button
Displaying the Address Book	WINXP 7.39	• From Outlook Express, click the **Addresses** button on the toolbar
		or
		• In the Start menu, click **All Programs**
		• In the All Programs menu, click **Accessories**
		• In the Accessories submenu, click **Address Book**
Creating an Address Book contact	WINXP 7.40	• Click the **New** button
		• In the pop-up list, click **New Contact**
		• In the Properties dialog box, type the information about the contact. You must at least specify a name
		• Click **OK**
Creating an Address Book group	WINXP 7.41	• Click the **New** button
		• In the pop-up menu, click **New Group**
		• In the Group Name field, type the name of the group
		• Click **Select Members**

WINDOWS XP

task reference roundup

Task	Page #	Preferred Method
		• In the Select Group Members dialog box, select the contacts for the group, then click **OK**
		• Click **OK** to create the new group
Editing a contact or group	WINXP 7.42	• Double-click the contact or group
		• In the Properties dialog box, edit the information
		• Click **OK**
Deleting a contact or group	WINXP 7.42	• Click the contact or group
		• Click the **Delete** button
Creating a News account	WINXP 7.42	• In the Tools menu, click **Accounts**
		• In the Accounts dialog box, click **News**
		• Click **Add**
		• In the pop-up list, click **News**
		• Use the Wizard to enter the information about the news server
Subscribing to a newsgroup	WINXP 7.43	• In the Folders List, click the news server
		• In the Tools menu, click **Newsgroups**
		• In the Newsgroup Subscriptions dialog box, click **All** to list the newsgroups on that server
		• To subscribe to a newsgroup, double-click it

CROSSWORD PUZZLE

Across

2. An online discussion of a topic
3. To copy information from the internet to your computer
4. A network of micro computers and networks spanning the globe
6. A freqently visited Web page you save
9. A collection of related Web pages
10. A person in your address book
13. Containers for Web pages
14. Allows you to review which Web sites you've visited
15. A small piece of informaiton saved to your computer

Down

1. The name of a Web location. Includes a three-character suffix
5. The first page that displays when users open Internet Explorer
7. The full path to a Web page
8. Application that processes and displays Web pages
11. Temporary storage area on a computer where visited Web sites are stored
12. Default location of incoming e-mail messages

FILL-IN

1. The _____ dialog box allows you to configure Internet Explorer's security options.

2. A _____ is a small piece of information copied to your computer.

3. The _____ is a tool for setting up or editing an Internet account.

4. The _____ folder contains messages you haven't yet sent.

5. Use the _____ button to send a message you received to someone who hasn't seen it.

CREATE THE QUESTION

For each answer, create a short question:

ANSWER	QUESTION
1. Stores the pages you have visited; used by Internet Explorer for quicker displays	_____
2. The full path to a Web page	_____
3. Temporary location of outgoing messages	_____
4. Where newsgroups are located	_____
5. The domain name suffix for colleges and universities	_____

SHORT ANSWER

1. What Internet Explorer tool would allow you to see what pages you visited last week?

2. In what security zone would you place a site that you weren't sure of?

3. How do you get back to your home page?

4. Which folder is the default location of new messages?

5. What search option would allow you to get directions to a friend's house?

1. Setting Up Mail Folders—Overtime Sporting Goods

Overtime Sporting Goods receives and processes e-mail orders for team uniforms and equipment for some of the local high schools. They also order the trophies for the local bowling league.

For Eastern High School, they provide equipment for the football team, the baseball team, and the softball team. For Washington High School, they provide equipment for field hockey and basketball.

Overtime needs to set up e-mail folders to manage the flow of incoming mail.

In the Outlook Express Folder List, create three folders—one for the bowling league and one for each high school.

Make sure that Outlook Express is open in order to do the following exercise.

1. Right-click the **Folder List**
2. In the context menu, click **New Folder**
3. In the Create Folder dialog box, next to the *Folder Name* field, type the name of the new folder, **Bowling League**
4. In the folder tree, click the **Local folder** as the place in which to place the new folder
5. Click **OK**
6. Repeat steps 1 through 5 to create new folders for **Eastern High School** and **Washington High School;** within the high school folders, create folders for each of the sports for which Overtime handles their equipment
7. Within the Eastern High School folder, repeat the above steps to create a folder for **Football, Baseball,** and **Softball**
8. Within the Washington High School folder, repeat the above steps to create a folder for **Hockey** and **Basketball**

2. Creating and Organizing Address Book Contacts—PrintWell Printing

The Address Book can be a convenient way to organize information about the people you keep in touch with by e-mail, phone, or regular mail.

PrintWell printing has two graphics people (Henry and Maura) and two editors (Ellen and Steve). They also use Quick Office Supplies, with Jim Barnes as their contact person.

The current contact list, named **xp07practice contacts-data.txt,** which you'll find in your data files, includes everyone's name, e-mail address, and phone number. Next to the names are the person's birthday and a contact name. Most of the contacts are spouses, except for Ellen's, which is her daughter. The Graphics Department and the supplier also have fax numbers.

Use the Address Book to enter the contact information from the file. In Outlook Express, click the **Tools** menu, then **Address Book . . .** to open the Address Book.

1. Click the **New** button
2. In the pop-up list, click **New Contact . . .**
3. In the Properties dialog box, type the information about the first contact
4. Click **OK**
5. Repeat steps 1 through 4 for each of the other contacts

When you're done, create a **Graphics** group containing the two graphics people and an Editors group for the two editors. Create an **Employees** group containing both of the other groups.

6. Click the **New** button
7. In the pop-up list, click **New Group . . .**
8. In the Properties dialog box, type the name of the first group, **Graphics**
9. Click the **Select Members** button to add the names you added to the Address Book in the earlier steps of this exercise
10. In the Select Group members dialog box, click the names of the two graphics people: Henry and Maura
11. Click the **Select** button
12. Click **OK**
13. Repeat steps 6 though 12 to create the **Editors** and **Employees** groups and add the members of those groups

challenge!

1. Subscribing to Newsgroups

You work for a steel manufacturer, American Steel Producers, as an executive assistant to the head of the company. Your boss has asked you to join a newsgroup and provide him with all the relevant news about proposed steel tariff changes. Newsgroups are one way to participate in online discussions about almost any topic. Newsgroups are maintained on news servers.

Use Internet Explorer to search for a newsgroup about a favorite topic or hobby. Your Internet Service Provider may also provide access to a news server containing a broad range of newsgroups. Remember that to use Outlook Express, you need the name of the news server that houses the newsgroup.

Use Outlook Express to set up the account with the news server. Display the list of newsgroups in the server. Download the messages for one of the newsgroups without subscribing to it. Subscribe to one of the newsgroups. Use the Folder List to display the messages in that newsgroup.

2. Downloading an Application

Rodney Jones was born in England and moved to the United States when he was in his teens. Every once in a while he gets a craving for some food from his homeland, and he goes online to find recipes. Today he is looking for a recipe for Black Pudding. He finds a recipe and downloads it, but to his dismay, his computer can't display it because the recipe is in PDF format. He asks you for help.

You tell him that Adobe Acrobat Reader is a program that allows you to view PDFs (Portable Document Files), a format commonly used to share printable files. A PDF is a snapshot of a document.

Acrobat Reader is available free on the Internet from the Adobe Acrobat Web site. Find the Web site and the area on the site for downloading files. Download and install the latest version of Adobe Acrobat Reader for Windows.

1. Getting Your Daily News

The Internet has become a primary source of news and information. News agencies can distribute new information very quickly, and readers can get new information without having to wait for the next newspaper or turn on a television set.

Both print and television media have made the move to the Web. You can read your local newspaper online or get news from your favorite national television news organization.

See if you can find the home page of today's *New York Times*. Can you find today's weather forecast for the New York area? What's today's headline for arts and entertainment? What are the books in the most recent book review?

Now try finding the *Los Angeles Times*. What's the headline for today's local news? Can you find the classified ads? Does the site tell you how to get a regular subscription?

Now try television news. Try finding CNN's Web site. What's today's science and technology headline? What are the headlines for the Asia-Pacific region? CNN also has a feature that allows you to sign up to receive news summaries in your e-mail. Find the page that allows you to sign up for one of these summaries.

ABC News also has a Web site. Can you find the local news for Denver, Colorado? What are the features on today's Good Morning America?

Finally, see if you can find Internet sites for your local newspapers and television stations. Is your hometown newspaper on the Net?

LEVEL THREE

e-business

1. Shopping for Books

The Internet has revolutionized the way people "go shopping." No matter what the product, you probably can find a Web site that sells it and arrange to have it delivered to your doorstep. There are sites that allow you to order groceries and sites for some of your favorite department stores. The Internet also makes comparison-shopping easier. You can find a product on multiple sites and quickly compare prices and shipping costs.

One popular product that is sold online is books. Several bookstore chains have accompanying Internet sites, and there are also Internet-only sites for finding and buying your favorite book.

Amazon is the most famous Internet retailer of books. The Barnes & Noble bookstore chain has an accompanying Web site, as does Borders. Doubleday Books also sells books on a Web site as well as in its retail stores.

Find each of these Internet sites. As you display each site, save it into a Favorites folder called **Bookstores.**

On each site, look for a paperback edition of Charles Dickens' *A Tale of Two Cities.* Do all of the sites have this book in stock? Which site offers the best price for the book? Which site charges the most for shipping?

Now do a search on each site for books about how to use Internet Explorer. Which site has the most books? Are any of the books on all of the sites?

Search for other sites that sell books online. Are there sites that sell used books?

1. Museum Hopping

The Internet also allows people to virtually travel the globe. You can instantly (or as fast as your modem will allow) drop by museums and monuments across the country or around the globe. Several of the world's greatest museums have Internet sites that allow you to find out about their exhibits, check out visiting hours and admissions, and take virtual tours.

On the Internet, find the site for the Louvre museum in Paris, France. What are the current exhibits? What is the price of admission?

Next, go to the home page of the British Museum in London, England. Can you find floor plans for the museum? What are the museum's visiting hours? What are the permanent exhibits?

Find the home page of the Metropolitan Museum of Art in New York City. What are the current exhibits? How do you join the museum? Can you find a link to the Met's branch museum? What is that museum called?

Finally, go to the National Gallery of Art in Washington, D.C. Can you find its floor plans? What are its current exhibits? Can you find the upcoming events? How about the gift shop?

After exploring these sites, use your History tool to add the home pages for these sites to a Favorites folder called **Museums.**

Chapter Objectives

- Learn about the different types of networks
- Learn how to log on and log off your network
- Consider the various hardware devices and software settings required to connect to a network
- Be introduced to the TCP/IP (Transmission Control Protocol/Internet Protocol), the address space of the Internet
- Set up dial-up networking on your system
- Learn how to map drives; and to share drives, folders, files, and printers
- Locate computers on your network
- Learn about domains and the role of the Active Directory
- Explore My Network Places and learn how to use the Add Network Place Wizard
- Learn what protocols are, why they are important to networking, and how to install a protocol

CHAPTER

8

eight

Network
Services

David Chin works for Geo Technologies as a manufacturer's sales representative. Geo Technologies has its headquarters in Taiwan, where it manufactures network devices such as print servers, hubs, and switches. Geo Technologies has a Sales and Marketing office in San Diego where David works.

David has a conference coming up in a few days in Las Vegas at which he will introduce some new products to existing customers. This is the most important once-a-year show that Geo attends in the United States. Several technical representatives come from Taiwan especially for this convention. An exhibit booth is rented at the conference, and David spends most of his time meeting with clients at Geo's booth. Many customers use the conference to contract for their annual needs.

Most of the inventory Geo sells in the United States is kept overseas in Taiwan, where the warehousing costs are lower. The products are then shipped to the United States on order. In the San Diego Sales office, David connects to the home office in Taiwan via a WAN. He gets all his inventory information, upcoming product designs, and pricing information directly from the home office over the network. Maintaining this connection throughout the upcoming conference is vital. David spends some time before leaving for Las Vegas preparing his laptop computer, which he will be bringing to the show, to make sure all the network connections are correctly set up.

SESSION 8.1 NETWORKING BASICS

For many, networking *is* computing. That is, the primary reason to get on a computer is to network. Much of what is associated with computers today —e-mail, the Internet, instant messaging, chat rooms, sharing music and pictures, and so forth—is based on networking. Nowadays, a computer without networking capabilities of some kind seems fairly useless. But this was not always the case.

Networking is one of the most fundamental and, at the same time, potentially one of the most advanced topics to study in Windows XP Professional. A book several times the size of this one could easily be written (and has been written) only about networking. Needless to say, the aim of this chapter is not to provide much more than the basics.

A *network* is a group of computers (two or more) that are linked together to allow them to exchange information and share resources. Today virtually anyone who uses a computer has access to some sort of network. Even if the computer is the only one in a home or office, it can access the largest network in the world, the Internet, which connects millions of computers. Such a computer is still known as a *stand-alone computer,* which means that it is not permanently connected to a network of some kind, even if it can access the Internet. However, whether you realize it or not, when you double-click your Web browser's icon on a stand-alone computer, you are connecting to a network.

The need for networks became apparent relatively early in the computer's history as a result of different users needing to share information. Before networking became as prevalent as it is today, the common way of sharing information was simply to copy the file onto a floppy disk and give the floppy to the person you wanted to share the file with. This basic way of sharing information became known by the cute name of "sneakernet," because you walked (in your sneakers presumably) the floppy disk over to another computer in order to get the information from one place to another. Obviously this was a time-consuming way of doing things. You were also limited by the size of the disk, which prevented you from copying large files. The advent of networks eliminated the need for sneakernet. A particular file or document or picture could be shared without moving from your computer. In addition, you weren't limited by the disk size when sending a file; large files that took up more room than the disk could hold could be sent in the same way. Further, not only could you share information, but you could also share network resources, like a printer, scanner, or other device with other users. A *resource* is any device that can be used by the members of the network. By sharing resources, several people could use the same printer. This was an economical solution, as you didn't need to buy a separate printer to connect to each computer. And if everyone shared an Internet connection, you did not have to buy a separate modem for each user or pay a fee for each user connection.

As networks became widespread, another benefit of networking became apparent. This was the ability to manage multiple computers and users from a central location. If the Graphics Department was the only department allowed to use the fancy new laser printer, you could block all nongraphics computers from sending print jobs to that printer. This centralization had a further advantage in that all the important data could be secured and managed much more easily. Access to the information about the brand new, top-secret design for a product could be limited to only those employees who needed to know. When that hot new product got launched, all the information about it could be input into one central location and shared by everyone. Additionally, if someone was having a problem with a particular program or computer, a network administrator could see what the problem was and troubleshoot it without having to be physically present at the problem computer. A **network administrator** is someone in an organization who has the job of making sure the organization's network functions the way it is supposed to.

A further benefit of networks is the ability to have people access information from wherever they are. In this way the user is not tied to a particular computer in the office or the building. If a particular computer is down and cannot access a central database, you can access the relevant information from another computer. A user can even access information from another company office in a different city, or while they are traveling on the road, or if they are working from home.

Hopefully, for all the reasons mentioned above having to do with improved communication, economic advantages, and improved management and security, you can see why networking is such an important concept in computers.

LOGGING ON AND OFF

When Windows is started, you can either log on to your own computer or log on to a network (assuming you are connected to one). At the Welcome to Windows screen, hold down the Ctrl and Alt keys while pressing the Delete key. The Log on to Windows screen opens and prompts you to enter your User Name and Password. If you are connected to a network, this screen also gives you the option to log on to a domain on a network in the drop-down list next to *Log on to*. A domain is a group of computers on a network that are grouped together. (You will learn more about domains in Session 8.4.) The user name and password you enter identify you and the type of access you have been given to the network. Logging on as a user provides more restrictive access and will not allow you to perform certain tasks. Logging on as an administrator (if you have been given permission to do so) allows you to perform any task.

Note: It is a good idea to be logged on as an administrator, if possible, so that you can perform many of the exercises in this (and other) chapters.

When Windows is shutting down, it gives you the option to log off the network. This option saves your personal settings, closes any programs that are still open, and logs you off the network. If others besides yourself use the same computer, logging off allows another person to log on to the network without having to restart the computer.

NETWORK HARDWARE

The physical media is the equipment that constitutes and supports a network. This equipment provides the link between your computer and other resources on the network. Since this book is about software—Windows XP Professional, a very powerful operating system, but software nonetheless—a question may arise as to why talk about hardware. The fact is that software and hardware connections are an integral part of getting your computer ready for information exchange. Most of the rest of this chapter will discuss making the necessary software connections for networking, but first, let's look at the physical media underlying the software.

Modem

A *modem* is a device that allows computers to exchange information via a telephone line. Modem is short for modulator-demodulator, and it converts digital pulses to audio frequencies and back again to allow transmission over analog phone circuits. The term "modem" also refers to faster cable or DSL modems or to ISDN terminal adapters, though these devices are all digital and technically not modems. A modem connects your computer to a telephone line via an RJ-11 jack, which is the standard connection to plug a telephone into the wall. Most people recognize the sounds modems make as a set of high-pitched squeals, both sending and receiving them in order to negotiate a connection, a process called "handshaking."

Network Interface Card (NIC)

A *network interface card,* also known by the acronym NIC and sometimes called a network adapter, is a circuit board that is installed inside a computer. It controls the exchange of data between a computer and the network.

The NIC port (which is on the edge of the network card) is for plugging in a network cable and is located at the back of your computer. Like many other devices, many network cards are Plug and Play compatible, so Windows XP will detect the network cards when they are newly installed. Also, like other hardware, network cards have device drivers, which allow them to communicate with the computer they are installed in.

The transmission method used by the network adapters determines the architecture of the network. *Network architecture* refers to the method of transferring information on a network. All the devices on a network must use the same network architecture to transmit and access information. The most common forms of network architecture are Ethernet and Token Ring. Ethernet is particularly common because it is economical and easy to set up. Each type requires a different NIC card to support the connection.

anotherword

The term "network architecture" can also refer to the design of a network, which includes the hardware, software, information transfer methods, and protocols used.

Transmission Medium

Transmission medium is simply something that allows computers and other devices to exchange information. It is basically a fancy way of describing cabling, though it includes technologies such as radio or infrared waves that are used on wireless networks. Cables—such as twisted pair, coaxial, or fiber optic—connect network adapters to adapters on other computers or to other network equipment, such as hubs, routers, or switches. With computers it is possible to use the phone lines and even your power lines as your network wiring. But most networks are built using dedicated Ethernet cables, called CAT5 or Category 5 coaxial cable.

Hub

A *hub* is a central connecting device in a network that joins all the computers and other devices together. Along with a modem, network cards, and cables, hubs are the most common feature of almost every network. Although hubs are often inexpensive and perform relatively simple functions, in recent years higher-end models have become very intelligent and powerful, capable of incorporating the functions of routers and switches, and even hosting operating systems and CPUs, turning the hub into a network file server. Hubs are rated for the speeds that they support, and many are auto sensing, supporting both 10 Mbps (Megabits per second) and 100 Mbps speeds—also known as 10BaseT and 100BaseT Ethernet.

Switch

A *switch* is similar to a hub but provides more intelligent though limited routing capabilities. Depending upon your setup, you may need what is called a crossover cable in order to successfully connect a device like a computer to a switch.

You can use a switch to connect to either another switch or a separate hub or computer, whereas you can only connect a hub to another hub using the two uplink ports found on most hubs. Thus a switch is a very valuable device for growing a network, allowing you to perform what is known as "fan out" of devices.

Router

A *router* is a device that forwards data from one network to another. Routers are actually very specialized computers that direct data in the most efficient and quickest way throughout even the largest network. As networks grow, routers are used to segment parts of the network in order to balance traffic and to filter it for security purposes and policy management. Routers are also used at the edge of the network to connect remote offices.

Bridge

A *bridge* is a device that connects two networks together. It can do this even if the networks are of dissimilar types, such as Ethernet and Token Ring. A bridge is also inserted into a network to segment it and keep traffic contained within the segments to improve performance.

TYPES OF NETWORKS

Although there are many types of networks in use today, there are two major ones, namely, a local area network (LAN) and a wide area network (WAN). A *local area network (LAN)* connects a group of users in the same physical location (such as in one building) so that they can share information and resources, like printers and Internet connections, with each other. LANs are the most common type of network.

A *wide area network (WAN)* connects people in the same company or organization but in different physical locations. Several different networks are connected even though they may be in different cities or even in different countries. These wide area networks can be large and very expensive to build and maintain. With a WAN, the need to share resources is not the major consideration; instead, the need to share information is the major objective. A WAN allows members to share files, databases, and e-mail. A WAN owned and managed by one organization or company is sometimes called an *enterprise network.* The Internet is a prime example of a WAN.

Other networking types you may encounter are MANs or metropolitan area networks, which are used for distances that are accommodated by fiber optic cabling (about 25 miles), and SANs for storage area networking. SANs use a special type of cabling called fibre channel cable and special fibre channel hubs to provide a separate network upon which computer/storage network traffic may be routed.

1. A _____ is a group of computers linked together for the purpose of sharing information and resources.

2. A computer that is not permanently connected to a network is a _____ computer.

3. A _____ is a circuit board that controls the exchange of data between a computer and the network.

4. A network that connects a group of users in the same physical location so that they can share information and resources with each other is called a _____.

5. A _____ is a device that connects two networks together.

SESSION 8.2 NETWORK CONFIGURATION

Having established the physical requirements of networking, the next step is to configure the software. As a Windows XP user, you will primarily be interested in establishing and optimizing a connection to a network. This session walks you through the basic steps necessary for this and also continues to explore the concept of different types of networking.

NETWORK SETUP WIZARD

Windows XP has a new Wizard that makes setting up a Peer-to-Peer network much easier than it used to be. The Network Setup Wizard (Figure 8.1) automatically configures each computer on your network. One thing to be aware of, however, is that all the computers on your network must be running Windows 98 or later versions as their operating system. Machines with Windows 95 or Windows NT must be manually configured.

Note that in order to create a Client/Server network, you need to have a server operating system, such as Windows 2000 Server; the Network Setup Wizard does not support this.

F I G U R E 8.1

The Network Setup Wizard Welcome window

> ## task reference
>
> ### Using the Network Setup Wizard
>
> - Click **Start, All Programs, Accessories, Communications, Network Setup Wizard**
> - At the Welcome window, click **Next**
> - In the Before You Continue window, review the checklist for creating a network, then click **Next**
> - Select the statement that best describes your network, then click **Next**
> - Follow the on-screen prompts

DIAL-UP NETWORKING

Connecting to a network using a telephone line, rather than simply a cable, is known as ***dial-up networking.*** A dial-up network can be accessed remotely via modem. This form of networking is useful when you are home or on the road and need to access a computer somewhere else. This is the most common way for people to connect to a network, but it is also a relatively slow method. Broadband methods such as cable and DSL are gradually displacing telephone lines because of their superior speed. The current speed limitation of modems is on the order of 56 Kbps, but it is possible with Windows to couple two modem connections together in a session to simulate the speed of an ISDN modem.

When you are connected to the desired computer, you can work with the files on that computer as if the files were actually stored on your own computer. This connection can then be used to access, for example, the office database or inventory information, so that you can have up-to-date information for that important presentation while traveling. It can also be used to stay on top of your e-mail when away from your main computer. All you need to connect in this way is a regular telephone line and a modem. You also need permission from the other computer to access it, and the destination computer needs to be configured to allow for this type of connection.

Most people connect to the Internet through an ISP (Internet Service Provider) such as America Online, MSN (Microsoft Network), Earthlink/ Mindspring, AT&T Worldnet, or CompuServe. When you log on, you are logging on to that system's computers (servers) and being authenticated for their use. In effect, you have joined your ISP's network.

Windows dial-up networking is the part of the Windows XP operating system that allows you to make a new connection using a phone line. Each connection you create supports a particular location and set of settings, although you can only use one connection per modem at a time. Let's take a look at how to set up dial-up networking using the New Connection Wizard.

> ## another word
>
> The computer you want to connect to has to be powered on; otherwise, you will not be able to connect to it.

task reference

Making a New Connection

- Click **Start** and then click **Control Panel**
- Double-click **Network Connections**
- Click the **Create a new connection** link
- Choose the type of connection, enter the phone number, and choose the availability you want for this connection, then click **Finish**

Making a new connection:

David Chin has just checked into his hotel room at the conference. As he unpacks his bag, he realizes that he needs an updated inventory from the manufacturer in Taiwan in case a customer wants to place an order in a hurry. He takes out his laptop and modem. Using a cable with an RJ-11 jack, he plugs his computer into the data socket next to where the phone line is plugged into the wall (or on the phone itself). The next thing he has to do is create a connection.

1. Click **Start,** then click **Control Panel.** The Control Panel window opens

2. Double-click **Network Connections.** The Network Connections window opens

3. Click the **Create a new connection** link in the left pane of the window. The New Connection Wizard opens (Figure 8.2)

FIGURE 8.2

The Welcome window of the New Connection Wizard

4. Click **Next.** The Network Connection Type window opens

5. Click the **Connect to the network at my workplace** radio button, then click **Next**

tip: *If you have more than one dial-up connection, you will be prompted to choose which one you want to use. Click the desired device, and then click **Next***

6. Click the **Dial-up connection** radio button, then click **Next**

7. Type **My Organization** in the text box that appears in the Connection Name window, then click **Next**

8. Type the telephone number of the computer you wish to connect to in the *Phone Number* field, then click **Next**

9. The New Connection Wizard summarizes the information you have entered; click **Finish** to create the connection

What happens if the computer you connect to now has a new phone number? Or what if you want to have Windows dial another number if the first number is unavailable? Suppose you want to prevent other people with whom you share your computer from using a particular dial-up connection? By default Windows redials the connecting phone number three times if it is unsuccessful in its first attempt; what do you do if you want Windows to keep trying until a connection is established? Or suppose you want to create a waiting period in between redial attempts? You can change these settings, along with several others, in the Properties dialog box of the dial-up connection you've created. In addition, you can set it up so that your computer automatically redials the connecting phone number if you get disconnected. Also, you can designate the amount of time that Windows will wait while your computer is idle before disconnecting. This way if you forget to disconnect or get caught up in something else, your computer doesn't stay connected for a long time while it is idle.

---

task reference

Changing the Dial Out Settings

- From the Network Connections window, click the connection whose settings you want to change, click **File,** then click **Properties**
- Click the **General** tab to enter a new phone number or change an existing one
- Click the **Alternates** button, then click the **Add** button to type an alternate phone number to dial in case the first number fails to connect
- Click the **Options** tab to require a name and password, to change the number of redial attempts, to change the amount of time between redial attempts, to change the amount of idle time before automatically disconnecting, or to have Windows automatically redial if the line gets disconnected

---

Changing the dial out settings:

David Chin realizes that since the last time he used his laptop, his office in San Diego has added a few new lines to connect in the event the main remote connection line is busy. He sets about entering these alternate phone numbers into his computer so that if the first number does not get through, other numbers will automatically be dialed by Windows.

1. Click **Start,** then click **Control Panel.** The Control Panel window opens

2. Double-click **Network Connections.** The Network Connections window opens

3. Click the icon for the dial-up connection for which you want to change the settings, then click **File** and **Properties.** The Properties dialog box opens

4. Click the **General** tab. Double-click the field box under *Phone number* and type the new phone number you wish to substitute

5. Click the **Alternates** button. The Alternate Phone Numbers dialog box opens

6. Click the **Add** button. The Add Alternate Phone Number dialog box opens (Figure 8.3). Type an alternate phone number (**212-555-5678** for the purpose of this exercise) to dial in case the connection cannot be established with the first number

FIGURE 8.3
The Add Alternate Phone Number dialog box

7. Click the **Options** tab (Figure 8.4). Clicking the check box next to *Prompt for name and password, certificate, etc.,* requires the user to enter this information before the connection is established

8. Double-click the field next to *Redial Attempts*, and type **50** for the number of times you want Windows to keep redialing until a connection is made

tip: *It is a good idea to set this option to a high number, such as 50 or more, in order to increase the chances of having the connection made*

9. Click the drop-down list next to *Time between redial attempts* and select **30 seconds**

10. Click the drop-down list next to *Idle time before hanging up* and select **1 hour**

11. Click the check box next to *Redial if line is dropped* to have Windows automatically attempt to reestablish the connection if it becomes disconnected

12. Click **OK** to confirm the changes

anotherway

You can also duplicate a connection file, rename that duplicate file, and change the phone number in the Properties dialog box to create additional connections to your ISP's other POPs (or point of presence), which are connecting phone lines.

WINDOWS XP

FIGURE 8.4

The Options tab of the Dial-up
Connection Properties dialog box

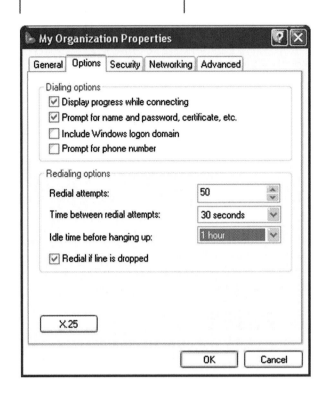

Another option you have with Windows dial-up networking is to create an incoming connection so that you can access the information on your computer in the office from another location, such as from home or while traveling. If you want to be able to get at your computer in this way, you have to create a network connection so that Windows knows what to do with the attempt to connect when it comes in. Keep in mind that by enabling a connection to your computer, you can also access anything that's on the network your computer is attached to. If there is a central database back at the office that contains data you need, you can connect to it if you have established an incoming connection on your computer.

Note: This incoming connection does not by itself give you access to everything on your computer. Before using the connection to dial up, you must share the resources on your computer that you wish to access, such as folders or devices. For more information about sharing folders, see Session 8.3, Sharing Resources.

This incoming connection has other benefits besides the obvious one of greater accessibility of information. For instance, in certain circumstances it is desirable to have the option of being able to use the printers in another location rather than the ones you have at hand, especially if you are away from the location where you regularly work. Just as you would if you were sitting at your computer in the office sending a job to the printer, so you can print documents that you send from a remote location.

Part of the process of setting up an incoming connection involves selecting the devices that you want your computer to use to accept this connection. For example, if you use a broadband cable modem for connection to the Internet, having a regular modem that attaches to a telephone jack in the wall will give you more flexibility when you want to connect from a remote location. In this case, in the process of using the New Connection Wizard (which is how you create an incoming connection) you will be prompted to select which modem installed on your computer to use to accept incoming connections.

task reference

Setting Up an Incoming Connection

- From the Network Connections window, double-click **Create a new connection**

- Click the *Set up an advanced connection* radio button, then Click **Next**

- Click the radio button next to *Accept incoming connections,* then click **Next**

- Click the check box next to the connection device you want other computers to use to connect to your computer, then click **Next**

- Click the radio button next to *Do not allow virtual private connections,* then click **Next**

- Click the check box next to each user you want to allow to connect to your computer, then click **Next**

- Click the check box next to each networking component you want to use for incoming connections, then click **Next**

- Click **Finish**

Setting up an incoming connection:

Before he leaves for the conference, David Chin prepares his computer in the office so that he can connect to it from the road. In order to do this he will need to set up what's called an incoming connection. An incoming connection will allow David to access information on his office computer from another computer in a remote location. After sharing the relevant folders, David calls his office to make sure the computer is left on all the time so that he can access it whenever he needs to, day or night. He wants to print out the orders on a printer back at his office as he gets them, so a sales assistant can begin processing the orders with the manufacturer overseas right away, rather than having to wait until he returns with the original contracts.

1. Click **Start** and then click **Control Panel.** The Control Panel window opens

2. Double-click **Network Connections.** The Network Connections window opens

3. Click **Create a new connection**

4. The New Connection Wizard opens. Click **Next**

5. The Network Connection Type window opens. Click the *Set up an advanced connection* radio button, then click **Next**

6. The Advanced Connection Options window opens (Figure 8.5). Click the *Accept incoming connections* radio button, then click **Next**

7. The Devices for Incoming Connections window opens. Click the check box next to the device you want other computers to use to connect to your computer, then click **Next**

F I G U R E   8.5

The Advanced Connection
Options window

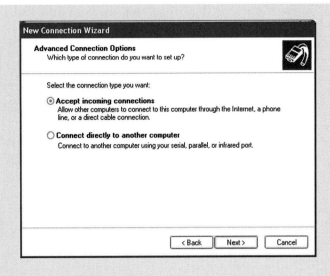

8. The Incoming Virtual Private Connection window opens. Click the *Do not allow virtual private connections* radio button, then click **Next**

9. The User Permissions window opens. Click the check box next to each user you want to allow to connect to your computer, then click **Next**

10. The Networking Software window opens (Figure 8.6). Click the check box next to each networking component you want to use for incoming connections, then click **Next**

tip: *At the very least, you want to enable two protocols: Internet Protocol (TCP/IP) and File and Printer Sharing for Microsoft Networks. For more information about protocols, see Session 8.4.*

F I G U R E   8.6

The Networking Software
window in the Network
Connection Wizard

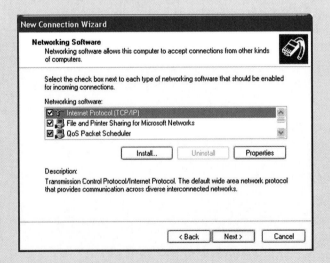

11. The Completing the New Connection window opens. The name this connection will have is displayed. Click **Finish.** An icon for the newly created Incoming Connection appears in the Network Connections window

PEER-TO-PEER AND CLIENT/SERVER NETWORKING

The fundamental difference between a Peer-to-Peer network and a Client/Server network is expressed very well by their names. A ***Peer-to-Peer network*** is simply two or more computers linked together, sharing resources such as a printer, scanner, or Internet connection, and storing files and programs on their own hard drives. Assuming the owner has shared his or her folders, everyone can access the information on anyone else's computer. It is, as the name implies, a network among equals.

Windows XP Professional has an artificial limit of 10 connected computers that may share files or share an Internet connection. To connect to more network computers, you need to use a network operating system like Windows NT or Windows XP Server where the limit set is the power of the hardware itself.

A Client/Server network, on the other hand, involves a centralized form of networking. In a ***Client/Server network,*** at least one computer is designated as a ***server,*** which means that it is a central computer in the network. The other computers come to this server for a variety of purposes, for example, to access information. A file server is a computer that serves as a central repository of files that are available to other computers on the network, which are known as ***clients.*** A client is a machine that's requesting something from another computer; a server responds to the request with the desired data or service.

Note: A computer is either a client or a server depending on its function. For example, a computer storing a central database that other computers come to access is operating as a server. But this same computer with the database, when attempting to print a document, may have to go to another computer, which acts as a print server; in this capacity it is acting as a client.

Peer-to-Peer networking is the easiest and most inexpensive way to network your computers. As soon as you have more than one computer in a working environment, it becomes an asset to be able to share information and resources, for all the reasons discussed in the beginning of this session about the benefits of networking. For the price of the network adapter cards, some cabling, and (in most cases) an inexpensive hub, your organization can take advantage of sharing devices, files, and folders, and an Internet connection. Even in a relatively low-tech environment, such as a home with two computers that are not connected to any outside network except the Internet, the benefits of creating a Peer-to-Peer network are obvious. It is a very good solution for those on a limited networking budget who need to connect two to ten computers together.

A Client/Server network is more expensive and complicated to set up and manage, but for medium to large networks, the benefits are considerable. For instance, say you work in an organization with 300 to 500 computers where everyone uses one particular program to send e-mail. Suppose there is an important update to this program, which you want everyone to immediately use. In a Peer-to-Peer network, each individual user (or the poor, overworked network administrator) would have to install this update on each computer. Think of how time-consuming that is. Now imagine that you have a Client/Server network. The required e-mail update could be distributed to everyone on the network for installation at one time. It would be even easier if the e-mail program were installed on a mail server; the program in this case would just need to be updated on the server and nowhere else. From the time the mail server was updated, any computer accessing the e-mail program would be using the updated version.

Another benefit scenario involves security. Client/Server networks are inherently more secure than a Peer-to-Peer network. By putting critical data on a central file server, you can easily control who has access and who doesn't. And if situations change and someone who does not have access now needs it, or vice versa, these changes in access permissions can be easily adjusted from one location. Different users can be grouped together by department and security permissions set for the entire group rather than for each individual user.

This last point alludes to another benefit, which is increased ease in managing users and groups. For example, suppose the Sales Department has three new hires who need to access the network. Assuming the hardware is in place, adding the new users to the Sales workgroup is a matter of a few keystrokes on a server. For the same reason, if your organization buys new computers to accommodate these new Sales hires, you can even install Windows XP Professional on all the computers directly from a server rather than having to go to each machine and manually install the operating system.

Additionally, if all the critical data are stored on one computer, which everyone accesses, it is much easier to make sure a current backup is kept. The alternative in a Peer-to-Peer network is that every user has to be responsible for making a backup of their own hard drive. By diluting the responsibility for this all-important task, it also makes the backup much less likely to get done consistently.

These are only a few of the benefits of a Client/Server network; there are many more. This does not mean that if you have a network, you are better off making it a Client/Server model than a Peer-to-Peer. The pros of Client/Server networking must be weighed against the cons (greater expense and more difficult to manage). Many network environments work perfectly well as Peer-to-Peer.

DISTRIBUTED NETWORKING AND WEB SERVICES

Many large networks cannot rely on either Peer-to-Peer or Client/Server networks because either their transaction load is highly variable or their connection is not reliable (as is the case often with Internet connections). Thus enterprise class networks often use what is called an n-Tier network with different servers in different layers performing different tasks. For example, in a 3-tier network you have backend servers, a set of middleware servers, and the computers (clients) that people work on. When you purchase something online, that transaction may go to a middleware or messaging server, which stores the transaction for you until the server that processes the transaction is available to do so. Thus the network has better fault tolerance and more efficient processing.

As the Internet develops and many companies and people are directly connected to it, companies like IBM, Microsoft, and Oracle are creating what have come to be called Web services. A Web service can provide an authentication function, can store your profile to be used by your travel agency or store, and can offer a computing function like an accounting engine, among others. Web services are in their infancy, and the full extent of their development is yet to be determined.

making *the grade*

1. The current speed limitations of the average modem are _____ Kbps.

2. To create a new connection, use the _____ Wizard.

3. After you share the resources on your computer, you still must establish an _____ in order to use them from a remote location.

4. Two or more computers sharing resources equally is known as a _____ network.

5. _____ involves connecting to a network using a telephone line, rather than simply a cable.

SESSION 8.3 SHARING RESOURCES

SHARING FOLDERS AND PRINTERS

Sharing data and resources is the main reason to install a network. Windows XP has a user-friendly interface that allows you to share just about anything on your network. You should not share casually, however; spending some time considering your sharing options is time well spent.

When a folder is shared, users can access the folder and all the files and subfolders inside. The default when you share a folder is Full Control to the Everyone group. This means that other users on the network have access to everything within the folder that you share and are able to use the shared items just as if the files and folders were on their own computers. Depending on how you assign them to other users, however, you can allow three different sets of permissions: only reading, reading and changing, or full control over the file. Some files need to be accessed and changed by others; other files do not. You may not want to allow others to change that critical report that you've worked so hard to prepare. What happens if someone accidentally alters it or, worse, deletes it? You do have a backup, don't you? In this situation, a wiser choice would be to allow others to read your report only. Sometimes the best solution is to create separate groups with different permissions. Perhaps creating a group called Management that has read and change permissions while keeping all other users in a separate group as read only would solve the problem. The point is to think before just blindly sharing your important files.

*another*word

One of the major advantages of the NTFS file system (see Chapter 4) that is designed for Windows XP is that, unlike the older FAT file system, you can set permissions at the file level in addition to the folder level. This means, for instance, that you can choose to make a shared folder accessible to everyone with read and change permission, *except* one file in the shared folder that is read only. File level permissions can be accessed in the Security tab of the shared file's Properties dialog box. Be careful, however: file level permissions can complicate things considerably. If possible, use the folder level permissions instead.

If you wish to give the folder that you share a different name from the one that it has on your computer, you can create a share name without affecting the original name you see when you view it on your local machine. You can also provide more information to someone who wants to share a folder by adding a comment. This comment option may be useful to help others identify what is in the shared folder. A brief indication of who the folder belongs to and what's in it is helpful to someone browsing through the network.

You also have the option of indicating the number of people who can share your folder at one time. The limit Windows establishes is 10 users at a time, but this may not be realistic as each additional user slows your computer. You can also decide, of course, to discontinue sharing your data altogether by stopping the folder share.

---

task reference

Sharing a Folder

- Click the folder you wish to share. Click **File,** then click **Sharing and Security . . .** The Properties dialog box opens

- In the Sharing tab, click the *Share this folder on the network* check box. If you wish to give the folder a Share name, do so in this dialog box

- To allow others to modify data in the folder, click the *Allow network users to change my files* check box

- Click **OK**

Sharing a folder:

The first thing David did before leaving for the conference was to make sure that all the important folders that he may need to access while on the road are shared. He spent a few minutes carefully choosing which folders to make available, including reviewing all the sharing options and making sure they are set properly.

1. Click the folder you wish to share

2. Click **File,** then click **Sharing and Security . . .** The Properties dialog box opens (Figure 8.7)

3. In the Sharing tab, click the **Share this folder** *on the network* check box

4. If you wish to change the name of the folder to give it a different share name, double-click on the name in the *Share name* text box and type in the new name

5. To allow others to modify data in the folder, click the **Allow network users to change my files** check box

6. Click **OK.** An upturned hand appears under the folder to indicate it is shared

tip: *To stop sharing a folder, simply open the Properties dialog box and click the Share this folder on the network check box to deselect it.*

---

another way

. . . to Share a Folder

Click the folder you wish to share, and then click the **Share this folder** link in the left pane of the Windows Explorer window. This will open the folder's Properties dialog box with the Sharing tab opened. Click the **Share this folder** *on the network* check box, then click **OK.**

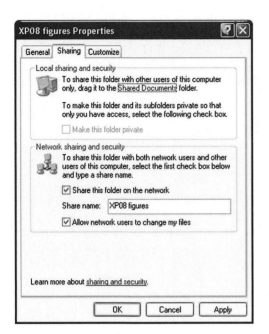

The Sharing tab of the Properties dialog box

Sharing a Printer

Besides sharing information, one of the main reasons to set up a network is to share resources, such as expensive external peripherals. The most commonly shared resource is a printer. You can share your local printer with others, and if someone else has shared their printer, then you can print to that printer just as if it were local to your computer.

task reference

Sharing a Printer

- Click **Start,** then click **Printers and Faxes**

- In the Printers window, click the icon for the printer you wish to share

- In the **File** menu, click **Sharing . . .**

- Click the **Share this printer** radio button, then type a friendly name so that others can easily identify the printer

- Click **OK**

Sharing a printer with others:

David calls his office to make sure the computer is left on all the time so that he can access it whenever he needs to, day or night. He wants to print out the orders on a printer back at his office as he gets them, so a sales assistant can begin processing the orders with the manufacturer overseas right away, rather than having to wait until he returns with the original contracts. He asks someone at the office to share the printer in the Sales Administration Department.

1. Click **Start,** then click **Printers and Faxes**

2. In the Printers and Faxes window, click the icon for the printer you wish to share

3. Click **File,** then click **Sharing.** The Printer Properties dialog box opens (Figure 8.8)

FIGURE 8.8

The Sharing tab in Printer Properties

4. Click the **Share this printer** radio button

5. Type a friendly name so that users will be able to identify it

6. Click **OK.** In the Printers window, an upturned hand displays under the shared printer's icon to indicate that it is available for others to use

task reference

Connecting to a Shared Printer

- Click **Start,** then click **Printers and Faxes**

- Click the **Add Printer** link

- Click the **A network printer, or a printer attached to another computer** radio button

- Type the name of the printer you wish to connect to, or browse to find it

Connecting to a shared printer:

Having gotten word that the printer in the Sales Administration office is now shared, David wants to connect to it from his laptop. He proceeds to set up the software on his laptop to enable this function.

1. Click **Start,** then click **Printers and Faxes**

2. In the left pane of the Printers and Faxes window, click the **Add Printer** link. The Add Printer Wizard launches (Figure 8.9)

FIGURE 8.9

The Add Printer Wizard

3. In the Add Printer Wizard, click **Next**

4. Click the **A network printer, or a printer attached to another computer** radio button, then click **Next.** The Specify a Printer window opens (Figure 8.10)

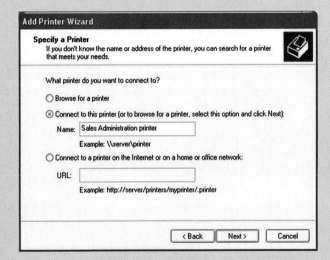

FIGURE 8.10

The Specify a Printer dialog box

5. If you know the name of the printer you wish to connect to, click the **Connect to this printer** radio button, type the name in the *Name* text box, and then click **Next.** If not, click **Browse for a printer** radio button and click **Next** to browse the network for the printer. The Browse for a Printer dialog box opens

6. In the *Shared Printers* area, click the printer to connect to, then click **Next**

7. Click either the **Yes** or **No** radio button to indicate whether you want to make this printer your default printer

8. Click **Next.** A window opens indicating that you have successfully completed the wizard

9. Click **Finish.** The Printers window displays an icon for the printer you just connected to

WINDOWS XP

DRIVE MAPPING

Sometimes you frequently need to access information on another computer in the network. Having to access the needed information often requires you to spend time hunting for the drive or folder through multiple layers of the network hierarchy. If this is the case, it can save lots of time to map the drive. *Mapping* a network drive allows you to access the needed drive as if it were on your computer. The process of mapping makes the folder or drive appear as an icon in My Computer just as if the drive itself was inside your computer. Windows will assign a single letter on your local machine to indicate the location on the network of the mapped drive. Once this is done, the entire process of connecting to and finding the mapped drive is transparent to the user.

---

task reference

Mapping a Network Drive

- Right-click the folder on the network you want to map and click **Map Network Drive**

- Select the drive letter you wish to use and click **Finish**

Mapping a network drive:

David Chin realizes he will need to access the inventory database back at the office several times each day of the conference in order to provide his customers with the latest data on product availability. He doesn't want to have to plow through multiple layers of folders on the network each time he needs to update his information. This would be especially embarrassing if he was sitting with a customer at a meeting, drumming his fingers while he searched for the necessary information. He decides to map the folder with the relevant information to his computer.

1. Navigate to the folder you want to map on the network. Right-click the folder to open the context menu

2. Click **Map Network Drive.** The Map Network Drive dialog box opens

3. A suggested letter for this drive is displayed. Click the drop-down list to select **H**

tip: *It is a good idea not to use the first available drive letter as any other actual physical drives you install will replace the letter for the mapped network drive. Most physical drives will use the letters D or E, but to give yourself room to expand, start with H as your first mapped drive letter.*

4. Click the check box next to *Reconnect at logon* to have the mapped drive appear every time you start Windows

5. Click **Finish.** A window opens, displaying the contents of the network drive you just mapped. In the My Computer window, the mapped drive is displayed by an icon of a disk with a cable attached. Double-clicking the icon accesses the drive

EXPLORING MY NETWORK PLACES

To view the network, you use the tool called My Network Places that is located in the Start menu (Figure 8.11). My Network Places can also be accessed from Windows Explorer.

Using My Network Places is just like using Windows Explorer. Each item that is listed in the My Network Places window displays an icon to differentiate between computers and folders. You select a listed machine to see the drives and folders contained within. From there, you navigate through the directory hierarchy to find the file you need. My Network Places only shows the resources that are available for access; if you're looking for a folder and can't find it, you may not have permission to access it.

Keep in mind, however, that the icons for the shared drives and folders you see in My Network Places are not the "real" files. Even though the process of mapping makes accessing a shared folder on another computer transparent to the user, you can delete a shared folder from My Network Places without deleting the actual folder itself.

If you have worked with a shared folder on the network before, the shared folder is displayed in the My Network Places window. This helps you to access the shared folder quickly the next time you use My Network Places. Note, however, that printers do not show up here, even if you've worked with them before. If you've used a network printer before, the printer appears in the Printers and Faxes window (Start/Printers and Faxes). You can, however, right-click a printer in the Printers window and drag it to another location like your Desktop. When you create the shortcut to that printer, you will be able to drag and drop documents you wish to print on that printer by dragging them onto that icon.

My Network Places also lets you access files in different operating systems, but you must tell Windows which platform you want to access. In addition to other Microsoft Windows operating systems, you can also work with folders created in Novell's Netware or Apple's Macintosh operating system, or files found on a network attached storage device like a Snap!Server or Maxtor MaxAttach, for example.

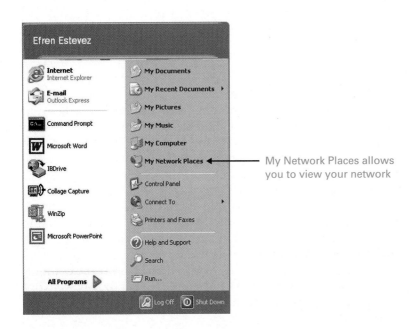

My Network Places allows you to view your network

FIGURE 8.11

My Network Places in the Start menu

WINDOWS XP

---

task reference

Browsing in My Network Places

- Click **Start,** then click **My Network Places**
- Double-click **Entire Network**
- Click the hyperlink *entire contents*
- Double-click the type of operating system, the domain, and the computer you want to access
- Double-click the files or folders to open them

Browsing in My Network Places:

1. Click **Start,** then click **My Network Places.** The My Network Places window opens
2. Double-click **Entire Network** to view all the resources available to you on the network
3. Click the hyperlink *entire contents* in the *You may also view the entire contents of the network* statement. The available types of network operating systems appear
4. Double-click the type of operating system you want to access. The domains available on your network appear
5. Double-click the domain containing the computers you want to access. All the available computers in the domain appear
6. Double-click the computer containing the resources you want to access. The available resources appear. You can work with these resources now as if they were on your computer
7. Double-click the files or folders to open them

ADDING A NETWORK PLACE

Once the connections between computers are established, the Add Network Place Wizard displays a list of shared folders and printers. From there, you simply select the resource you want to access. The Add Network Place Wizard also allows you to change the name of the resource you've selected. Changing the name of the resource on your local machine does not change the name of the resource on the network. After completing the Wizard, the resource you've added is displayed in the My Network Places window. If you selected a folder, a window opens where the contents of the folder are displayed. This makes it easy to get started quickly. All the files and folders operate as if they were on your local computer.

When you finish accessing resources, you can disconnect the computers. The next time you attempt to access the shared folder, the My Network Places window automatically displays the resources accessed during the previous sessions.

reference

Adding a New Network Place

- Click **Start,** then click **My Network Places**

- Click the **Add a network place** link

- Click **Choose another network location**

- Type \\ followed by the name of the computer you want to access, then type \ (for example, **computer**)

- Click **Next,** then click **Finish**

Adding a new network place:

1. Click **Start,** then click **My Network Places.** The My Network Places window opens

2. Click the **Add a network place link.** The Add Network Place Wizard opens (Figure 8.12)

FIGURE 8.12

The Add Network Place Wizard

3. Click **Next,** then click **Choose another network location**

4. Type \\ followed by the name of the computer you want to access; then type \ (for example, **\\host computer**). The resources you can access on the desired computer are listed

5. Click the resource you wish to access

6. Click **Next.** The Wizard suggests a name for the Network Place, which you can change by clicking the text box and typing a new name

7. Click **Finish.** The resource you chose appears in the My Network Places window. If a folder was selected, the contents of the folder are displayed. You can now work with these items as if they were on your local machine

SEARCHING FOR A COMPUTER

Windows XP has a very powerful search function. You can look for a computer on the network in the same way you search for a file or folder on your own local machine. This search function is especially useful if you are operating in a large network environment that includes many resources. Note, however, that if this is the case, it may take awhile for Windows to find the desired machine. If you think you may need to access this network computer again, it would be a good idea to add it to your Network Places with the Add Network Places Wizard (see Figure 8.12).

After the search is finished, the search results display all the computers found that matched your criteria, along with the location of each computer. Once found, the computer may be browsed to see what folders and other resources are available on that machine. Not everything may be visible, however, because either you don't have permission to access the item or the computer is disconnected from the network. You may also need to enter a name and password to view resources.

One of the important new features that the Windows 2000 Server Active Directory adds to network computing (see the section Active Directory that follows later in this chapter) is a searchable database of network resources or "objects." When Active Directory is running on your network, it is possible to search for things like different types of computers or printers, types of people, locations, asset tags—anything that is stored in the Active Directory.

---

task reference

Searching for a Computer

- Open **My Network Places**
- Click **Search**
- Type the name of the computer you want to find
- Click the **Search** button
- Double-click the found computer name in the Search Results—Computers pane to view the folders and other resources available on the selected machine

---

Searching for a computer:

1. Open **My Network Places.** The My Network Places window opens

2. Click **Search.** The Search for Computers area opens in the left pane of the My Network Places window (Figure 8.13)

3. Type the name of the computer you want to find in the text box under *Computer Name*

tip: *Use the asterisk (*) and the question mark (?) as wildcard characters to help you search. An asterisk represents multiple unknown characters, while the question mark indicates one unknown character. For example, searching for a network computer named "File*" would bring up a result of FileServer. Searching for a computer named "FileServer?" would bring up a result of FileServer1.*

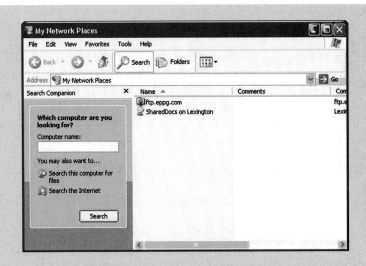

FIGURE 8.13

The Search for Computers pane of the My Network Places window

4. Click the **Search** button to begin searching. When the search is complete, the Search Results—Computers pane on the right of the window displays all the computers found that matched the entered criteria

5. Double-click the found computer name in the Search Results—Computers pane to view the folders and other resources available on the selected machine. The resources shared by the computer appear and can be used as if you just found them on your local machine

*another*way

. . . to Search for a Computer on Your Network

Click **Start,** then click **Search.** Click the link named **Computers or people** in the Search companion in the left pane. Click the **A computer on the network** link. Then proceed with searching as described above.

making *the grade*

SESSION 8.3

1. When doing a search for a computer on the network, an asterisk represents _____ unknown characters, while the question mark indicates _____ unknown character.

2. _____ a network drive allows you to access the needed drive as if it were on your computer.

3. With the _____ you can make a shared folder accessible to everyone with read and change permission, *except* one file in the shared folder that is read only.

4. If you think you may need to access this network computer again, it would be a good idea to add it to your Network Places with the _____ Wizard.

SESSION 8.4 WORKGROUPS, DOMAINS, AND PROTOCOLS

WORKGROUPS AND DOMAINS

A *workgroup* is a logical grouping of network resources without any one computer given overall network administration responsibilities. A workgroup allows a small number of users, usually 10 or less, to share each other's resources. Workgroups are used as logical units on a network to provide organized access to resources.

Although the term "workgroup" is applied to any group of computers that are connected, a workgroup can be set up as a unit of a larger network that is more regulated. This allows the members of the workgroup who work on common projects to share resources among each other while the other parts of the network operate in a more secure environment. An example of this might be the Art Department of a large organization that operates as an independent workgroup within the larger network that includes other network entities such as Legal or Accounting, which are administered by a central server.

A ***domain*** is a logical grouping of computers that share network resources with one or more computers, called domain controllers, which act as administrators for the entire domain. A domain controller stores and manages the SAM or security access manager database, which controls log-on, access to system resources and applications, and many other things. From a user's standpoint the SAM stores three essential pieces of information: the user's account name and associated password, and the computer or system's machine account. This information is stored as a set of unique SIDs, or system identification numbers, and encrypted or scrambled to prevent unauthorized access to the information.

The major difference between a workgroup and a domain is the level of security and the fact that security is maintained in a central location. The same security policy provides a consistent way for a user to access resources on a network. A user needs to remember only one domain user name and password to log in from any computer in the domain.

A server that holds the security information for a domain is called the ***primary domain controller (PDC).*** Since domain services are central to Windows networking, domains support the creation of ***backup domain controllers (BDCs)*** that contain a nearly up-to-date replicated version of the SAM. BDCs are helpful to provide fault tolerance if your PDC becomes unavailable, to load balance (spread out) security requests between servers, and to improve performance by distributing domain servers about the enterprise. Although there can only be one PDC, there can be many BDCs. In fact, many companies create a BDC in their home office and ship it to a remote office when the connection between the two offices is slow. That greatly lessens the time it takes to synchronize the two servers, and only updates are transmitted.

A server that provides network services without handling the security information is called a ***member server.*** Windows XP Professional cannot act as a domain controller; you need Windows XP Server operating system to do this. Most of the time member servers are configured to run network applications such as e-mail, databases, multimedia streaming, file and print, or data caching applications. Those servers are often referred to as application servers: with database server, messaging server, and so forth, specifying the type. While smaller organizations often put network applications on domain controllers, larger organizations keep their domain controllers separate to improve both performance and security.

Microsoft sells a package called Microsoft Small Business Server, or SBS, which bundles a domain server, the Exchange messaging server, the IIS Web server, the SQL Server database, Internet Security, and Acceleration Server (ISA—a firewall and caching server) into a single package. IBM, Novell, and others sell similar all-in-one packages. However, although this product is economical, limitations are built into SBS that limit the number of connected systems, block the use of BDCs, and so on. Products of this type are complex and are meant to be installed by trained vendors, often called VARs or value added resellers.

You can change the workgroup or domain your computer belongs to. This involves changing the identity of your computer on the network. You must be logged on as an administrator to change the identity of any computer. The identity of a computer includes its name and the domain or workgroup it belongs to. Every computer on a network must have a unique name. The name can contain letters, numbers, and hyphens, but not spaces. The name also cannot contain any of the following characters: " < > * ? = + \ | . , ; : A name is automatically entered when Windows is installed on a computer; however, it is a good idea to enter a descriptive name that will easily identify your computer to others on the network. With the exception of the primary domain controller, you can change the name of any system on the network quickly and without penalty. To change the name of your PDC requires that you demote the PDC to a member server or a BDC using a program called DCPROMO.

Joining a workgroup is easier than joining a domain, for obvious reasons given the greater security of a domain. To join a domain, you must enter the name and password of an account that has permission to add a computer to the domain. Additionally, once you join the domain, a user account needs to be set up on the domain's server. A user account will allow you to access the resources on the domain you are joining. For these reasons, joining a domain will probably involve the assistance and coordination of your organization's network administrator.

---

task reference

Changing the Identity of a Computer on a Network

- Click **Start,** then click **Control Panel**

- Double-click **System,** then click the **Computer Name** tab

- Click the **Change** button

- Indicate whether you want to join a domain or a workgroup, and indicate the name of the domain or workgroup you want to join

- If you chose to join a domain, type the name and password of an account with permission to join the domain. Click **OK**

- Click **OK** through the next four dialog boxes; then click **Yes** to reboot

---

Changing the identity of a computer on a network:

1. Click **Start,** then click **Control Panel.** The Control Panel window opens

2. Double-click **System.** The System Properties dialog box opens

3. Click the **Computer Name** tab (Figure 8.14). Your computer name and the workgroup or domain it belongs to are displayed

4. Click the **Change** button to change your computer's identity. The Computer Name Changes dialog box opens (Figure 8.15)

5. Type a new name in the text field under *Computer name*

FIGURE 8.14

The Computer Name tab in System Properties

FIGURE 8.15

The Computer Name Changes dialog box in the Computer Name tab of System Properties

6. Click the radio button next to either *Domain* or *Workgroup* to indicate you want to join

7. Click the appropriate text field and type the name of the domain or workgroup you want to join

8. Click **OK.** If you chose to join a workgroup, skip to step number 13. If you chose to join a domain, the Domain Username and Password dialog box opens

9. Type the name and password of an account with permission to join the domain in the appropriate text field next to *Name* and *Password*

10. Click **OK.** The Network Identification Welcome dialog box opens

11. Click **OK.** Another dialog box opens, indicating that you must reboot the computer for the changes to take effect

12. Click **OK.** You are returned to the Computer Name tab of the System Properties dialog box, where the new name and domain or workgroup are displayed

13. Click **OK.** The System Settings Change dialog box will open, asking if you want to reboot your computer

14. Click **Yes** to reboot

ACTIVE DIRECTORY

The Active Directory is a major topic in terms of Windows 2000 Server. Entire books have been written about it. Most of the information, however, is relevant to the Windows 2000 Server operating system and network administration, which is an area outside the scope of this book. As a user on a network, you should understand in general terms what the Active Directory is and what it does. This can be explained simply and in relatively straightforward terms.

The *Active Directory* is a hierarchical, object-based directory service whose primary purpose is the efficient management of users, groups, and network resources. The analogy for a directory service is a telephone book. When you want to find someone's phone number, you search through a list of names in a telephone directory. The Active Directory is the same concept expanded exponentially. It can do the searching for you, allows you to add or delete entries, and keeps itself updated automatically. Instead of just names, addresses, and phone numbers, it contains objects like users, groups, servers, printers, computers, and security policies.

The Active Directory replicates directory information to make it available to users throughout the network and to prevent the loss of data due to failures. It partitions the directory information into logical areas to make resources easy to manage and find. It also enforces the security policies defined by the network administrator. The Active Directory stores information such as user names, passwords, and permissions. A user account is an object in the directory, and the user's name and password are attributes of that user.

When you fill out a system dialog box, chances are that that information is stored in the Active Directory. And since Active Directory is extensible, applications can rely on, modify, and add to entries made in the Active Directory, even defining new fields to store different types of data. Applications have to be programmed to use the Active Directory, so versions of applications released prior to Windows 2000 aren't likely to have this feature.

One of the main advantages of the Active Directory is that you can search by an object's attributes. For example, if an administrator specifies that a particular printer is capable of double-sided printing, a user can search the network for all the printers that have this attribute.

PROTOCOLS

A *protocol* is analogous to a language, or a set of rules, that determines how computers communicate with each other. Imagine a meeting at the United Nations where representatives of different countries from around the world are attending. Suppose that these representatives only know their own native language. How are they going to communicate? How is anything going to get done? Now suppose they come up with an entirely new language to talk to each other. In the same way, in a computer network, different types of computers, often running different operating systems, must communicate with each other in order to get anything done. Accordingly, all computers and other devices on a network must use the same protocol before they can work together.

A network protocol determines how information transfers from one computer to another in a network. Many network protocols are designed specifically for use with one type of network, and the type of network determines the type of protocol you must have installed. For instance, the protocol needed to connect to a Novell network is IPX/SPX; the protocol to connect to an Apple network is AppleTalk (though TCP/IP is also used). Certain Windows environments, especially small networks, use NetBEUI (pronounced net-BOO-ey) protocol. When you install Windows, several network protocols are automatically installed if your computer has a network interface card (NIC).

TCP/IP

One of the earliest problems to be overcome in the history of networking was how to get different types of computers to be able to talk to each other. This was done by creating the ***Transmission Control Protocol/Internet Protocol (TCP/IP).*** The fact that TCP/IP was developed in 1969 and is still the common language of the Internet today indicates what geniuses the people who developed it were. TCP/IP is actually not just one protocol but a suite of protocols. TCP/IP allows computers with even totally different architectures to talk to one another. The TCP portion tells the computers how to talk to each other, and the IP portion acts as the "packaging" used to ship messages from one computer to another. Two computers establish communication with TCP and then exchange data within the package of IP.

A network can use several different protocols at the same time for specific tasks. For example, IPX/SPX may be used to send jobs to a network printer, while TCP/IP may be used to connect to the Internet. Although Windows includes the most popular protocols, you may need to install a protocol when you connect to a different type of network.

---

task **reference**

Installing a Network Protocol

- Click **Start,** then click **Control Panel**
- Double-click **Network Connections**
- Click the icon for the connection for which you want to add a protocol; click **File,** then **Properties**
- Click **Install**
- Click **Protocol,** then the **Add** button
- Click the protocol you want to install, then click **OK**

Installing a network protocol:

1. Click **Start,** then click **Control Panel.** The Control Panel window opens

2. Double-click **Network Connections.** The Connections window opens

3. Click the icon for the connection for which you want to add a protocol

4. Click **File,** then click **Properties.** The Local Area Connection Properties dialog box opens (Figure 8.16). The list under *This connection uses the following items* shows the protocols and other components installed on your computer

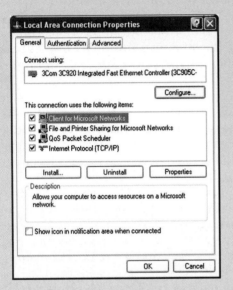

F I G U R E 8.16

The Local Area Connection Properties dialog box

5. Click the **Install** button. The Select Network Component Type dialog box opens

6. Click **Protocol**

7. Click the **Add** button. The Select Network Protocol dialog box opens (Figure 8.17)

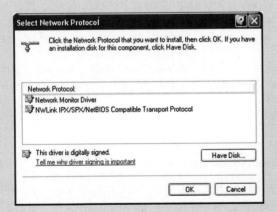

F I G U R E 8.17

The Select Network Protocol dialog box

8. Click the protocol you want to install

9. Click **OK.** The Local Area Connection Properties dialog box opens and lists the protocol you just installed

10. Click **Close**

DHCP, DNS, and WINS

Although these three protocols run on servers rather than Windows XP Professional, it is important for your overall understanding of networking to know what each of these programs does.

Every computer on a network must have a unique *IP (Internet Protocol) address.* Just like the address of a house or building, an IP address identifies where a computer is located on the network. IP addresses are written as four sets of numbers separated by periods, for example, 192.171.64.2. In the old days, network administrators simply wrote down the number assigned to a computer. But computers are moved or taken out of service, and users sometimes just make up a new address if they can't get onto the network with their regular one. All these events could cause conflicts within the network if the administrator didn't find out about it and correct the IP address in time. *DHCP (Dynamic Host Configuration Protocol)* automatically assigns IP addresses to client computers logging onto a network. This address is valid as long as the computer stays logged on to the network and goes back into the pool of available addresses once the computer logs off. The major advantage of this system is to reduce the amount of administration needed to manually assign and keep track of an address assigned to a client, and to allow networks to use a small number of static addresses (or even one static address) to service all of their network computers. DHCP is often used to assign a temporary IP address to a computer that is dialing into an ISP for an Internet session, for example.

DNS (Domain Name System) software converts descriptive host names to IP addresses, something that used to be maintained manually in a text table. The DNS server maintains a database of domain names (host names) and their corresponding IP addresses. For example, if the address www.microsoft.com were presented to a DNS server, it would convert this easy-to-remember name to the actual IP address 204.0.8.51 of the corresponding server. The benefits of this system are obvious, especially if one considers it in the light of the Internet, with millions of addresses. Imagine if you could just dial someone's name, j-o-h-n-d-o-e, into your telephone rather than having to remember their phone number. Wouldn't this be easier? This is what DNS does for IP addresses. The Internet itself has as its central feature a set of large DNS databases or root servers that maintain the friendly name to IP address mapping for the different extensions such as .com, .gov, .org, .mil, .edu, and so forth, with one set of servers for each root.

In a Windows-only network with clients using older operating systems such as Windows 95 or Windows NT, *WINS (Windows Internet Name Service)* provides name-to-IP address resolution. As such it is the counterpart to DNS, although use of WINS is being slowly phased out, particularly on larger networks.

Determining Your Network Settings

At some point you may need to check to see whether your network settings are correct to determine why you are experiencing a certain network behavior. Each NIC card has its own set of network settings, which include, among other things, protocols that have been "binded" to that card, IP addresses, the IP address of the system used to connect to the Internet (the gateway), what the DNS or WINs server's address is, and whether the card's address is static (set with a discrete value) or dynamic (served up as a "leased" address using the DHCP service). The place you find all of this information is the Properties dialog box of each network interface.

Your IP address either is set dynamically (automatically) using DHCP or is a static address in the address range used for your network and, more specifically, the part of the network or subnet that your computer is entered. The subnet mask is used to divide a network address space into different zones. The default gateway is the address of the server that functions as your connection to the Internet. Finally, you can opt to either obtain name-to-IP translations from a DNS server that is named automatically or enter addresses of DNS servers that you know are reliably available. Many people use their ISP's DNS servers for this purpose, but large networks often use their own DNS servers internal to the network. It's possible to use any DNS server that is publicly available, so often people use their university's DNS server.

---

task reference

Determining Your Network Interface Settings

- Click **Start,** then click **Control Panel**
- Double-click **Network Connections**
- Click **Local Area Connection,** and then click **File,** then **Properties**
- Double-click **Internet Protocol** (TCP/IP)
- Click the radio button next to *Obtain an IP address automatically* to have the IP address set by a DHCP server
- Click the radio button next to *Use the following IP address* and enter an address in the text boxes below
- Click the radio button next to *Obtain DNS Server address automatically* to get your network servers to provide the DNS server address
- Alternately, click the radio button next to *Use the following DNS server address,* and enter the address in the text boxes below; then click **OK**

---

making the grade

SESSION 8.4

1. A server that holds the security information for a domain is called a _____.

2. Every computer on a network must have a _____ name.

3. A server that provides network services without handling the security information is called a _____.

4. The _____ is a hierarchical, object-based directory service whose primary purpose is the efficient management of users, groups, and network resources.

5. A _____ is a logical grouping of network resources without any one computer given overall network administration responsibilities.

SESSION 8.5 SUMMARY

In this chapter you learned some of the basics of networking, including the benefits of networking computers even if there are only a few computers working together. You learned about the hardware of networking, such things as modems, network cards, transmission media, hubs, and routers. You learned about different types of networking—dial-up networking, Peer-to-Peer networking, and Client/Server networking—as well as the situations when to use one or the other. You learned how to establish a connection to another computer and how to allow others to share resources on your own computer.

You also learned about sharing folders and files with others on your network and how to create permissions for sharing. You learned how to share a printer and how to connect to a network printer. You studied what mapping is and how to map a drive. You explored My Network Places and learned how to use the Add Network Place Wizard.

Finally, you looked at the differences between workgroups and domains, and how to join them. You also learned the basics of what the Active Directory is and what it does. Finally, you learned what protocols are, why they are important to networking, and how to install a protocol.

task reference roundup

Task	Page #	Preferred Method
Using the Network Setup Wizard	WINXP 8.8	• Click **Start, All Programs, Accessories, Communications, Network Setup Wizard**
		• At the Welcome window, click **Next**
		• In the Before You Continue window, review the checklist for creating a network, then click **Next**
		• Select the statement that best describes your network, then click **Next**
		• Follow the on-screen prompts
Making a new connection	WINXP 8.9	• Click **Start,** then click **Control Panel**
		• Double-click **Network Connections**
		• Click the **Create a new connection** link
		• Choose the type of connection, enter the phone number, and choose the availability you want for this connection, then click **Finish**
Changing the dial out settings	WINXP 8.10	• From the Network Connections window, click the connection whose settings you want to change, click **File,** then click **Properties**
		• Click the **General** tab to enter a new phone number or change an existing one
		• Click the **Alternates** button, then click the **Add** button to type an alternate phone number to dial in case the first number fails to connect
		• Click the **Options** tab to require a name and password, to change the number of redial attempts, to change the amount of time between redial attempts, to change the amount of idle time before automatically disconnecting, or to have Windows automatically redial if the line gets disconnected
Setting up an incoming connection	WINXP 8.13	• From the Network Connections window, double-click **Create a new connection**
		• Click the *Set up an advanced connection* radio button, then Click **Next**

task reference roundup

Task	Page #	Preferred Method
		• Click the radio button next to *Accept incoming connections,* then click **Next**
		• Click the check box next to the connection device you want other computers to use to connect to your computer, then click **Next**
		• Click the radio button next to *Do not allow virtual private connections,* then click **Next**
		• Click the check box next to each user you want to allow to connect to your computer, then click **Next**
		• Click the check box next to each networking component you want to use for incoming connections, then click **Next**
		• Click **Finish**
Sharing a folder	WINXP 8.18	• Click the folder you wish to share. Click **File,** then click **Sharing and Security . . .** The Properties dialog box opens
		• In the Sharing tab, click the *Share this folder on the network* check box. If you wish to give the folder a Share name, do so in this dialog box
		• To allow others to modify data in the folder, click the *Allow network users to change my files* check box
		• Click **OK**
Sharing a printer	WINXP 8.19	• Click **Start,** then click **Printers and Faxes**
		• In the Printers window, click the icon for the printer you wish to share
		• In the **File** menu, click **Sharing . . .**
		• Click the **Share this printer** radio button, then type a friendly name so that others can easily identify the printer
		• Click **OK**
Connecting to a shared printer	WINXP 8.20	• Click **Start,** then click **Printers and Faxes**
		• Click the **Add Printer** link
		• Click the **A network printer, or a printer attached to another computer** radio button
		• Type the name of the printer you wish to connect to, or browse to find it
Mapping a network drive	WINXP 8.22	• Right-click the folder on the network you want to map and click **Map Network Drive**
		• Select the drive letter you wish to use and click **Finish**
Browsing in My Network Places	WINXP 8.24	• Click **Start,** then click **My Network Places**
		• Double-click **Entire Network**
		• Click the hyperlink *entire contents*
		• Double-click the type of operating system, the domain, and the computer you want to access

task reference roundup

Task	Page #	Preferred Method
		• Double-click the files or folders to open them
Adding a new network place	WINXP 8.25	• Click **Start**, then click **My Network Places**
		• Click the **Add a network place** link
		• Click **Choose another network location**
		• Type \\ followed by the name of the computer you want to access, then type \ (for example, **computer**)
		• Click **Next**, then click **Finish**
Searching for a computer	WINXP 8.26	• Open **My Network Places**
		• Click **Search**
		• Type the name of the computer you want to find
		• Click the **Search** button
		• Double-click the found computer name in the Search Results—Computers pane to view the folders and other resources available on the selected machine
Changing the identity of a computer on a network	WINXP 8.29	• Click **Start**, then click **Control Panel**
		• Double-click **System**, then click the **Computer Name** tab
		• Click the **Change** button
		• Indicate whether you want to join a domain or a workgroup, and indicate the name of the domain or workgroup you want to join
		• If you chose to join a domain, type the name and password of an account with permission to join the domain. Click **OK**
		• Click **OK** through the next four dialog boxes; then click **Yes** to reboot
Installing a network protocol	WINXP 8.32	• Click **Start**, then click **Control Panel**
		• Double-click **Network Connections**
		• Click the icon for the connection for which you want to add a protocol; click **File**, then click **Properties**
		• Click **Install**
		• Click **Protocol**, then the **Add** button
		• Click the protocol you want to install, then click **OK**
Determining your network interface settings	WINXP 8.35	• Click **Start**, then click **Control Panel**
		• Double-click **Network Connections**
		• Click **Local Area Connection**, and then click **File**, then **Properties**

task reference roundup

Task	Page #	Preferred Method
		• Double-click **Internet Protocol** (TCP/IP)
		• Click the radio button next to *Obtain an IP address automatically* to have the IP address set by a DHCP server
		• Click the radio button next to *Use the following IP address* and enter an address in the text boxes below
		• Click the radio button next to *Obtain DNS Server address automatically* to get your network servers to provide the DNS server address
		• Alternately, click the radio button next to *Use the following DNS server address,* and enter the address in the text boxes below; then click **OK**

review of terminology

CROSSWORD PUZZLE

Across

3. Any device that can be used by the members of the network
4. A network that connects people in the same company or organization but in different physical locations
8. A device that forwards data from one network to another
10. A type of network with two or more computers linked together to share resources
11. Software that converts descriptive host names to IP addresses
13. A server that provides network services without handling the security information
14. A computer that responds to the request from a client with the desired data or service
18. A server that holds the security information for a domain
20. A central connecting device in a network that joins all the computers and other devices together
21. A circuit board that controls the exchange of data between a computer and the network

22. A protocol that allows computers with totally different architectures to talk to one another; it is also the common language of the Internet

Down

1. Something that allows computers and other devices to exchange information, cables are an example
2. A device that connects two networks together
5. A hierarchical directory service whose primary purpose is the efficient management of users, groups, and network resources
6. A logical grouping of computers that share network resources without any one computer being given overall network administration responsibilities
7. Written as four sets of numbers separated by periods (for example, 192.171.64.2) and which identify where a computer is located on the network
9. A centralized form of networking where at least one computer is designated as a server
12. A language, or a set of rules, that determines how computers communicate with each other
15. A network which connects a group of users in the same physical location
16. A process that makes the folder or drive appear as an icon in My Computer just as if the drive itself was inside your computer
17. A machine that requests something from a server
19. Automatically assigns IP addresses to client computers logging onto a network

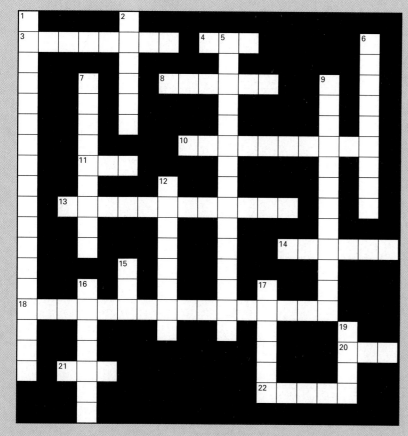

FILL-IN

1. A _____ is a logical grouping of computers that share network resources with one or more computers acting as administrators for the entire domain.

2. The computer name Jack+Jill-computer was not accepted by the system; using the same descriptive information, rewrite it so it does get accepted. _____

3. The _____ stores information such as user names, passwords, and permissions.

4. A _____ is analogous to a language, or a set of rules, that determines how computers communicate with each other.

5. _____ automatically assigns IP addresses to client computers logging onto a network.

CREATE THE QUESTION

For each answer, create a short question:

ANSWER	QUESTION
1. Besides a password, this is the only thing a user needs to remember to log in to a domain from any computer in the domain	_____
2. This database contains objects like users, groups, servers, printers, computers, and security policies	_____
3. This protocol allows computers with even totally different architectures to talk to one another	_____
4. These are written as four sets of numbers separated by periods, for example, 192.171.64.2	_____
5. In a Windows-only network with clients using older operating systems such as Windows 95 or Windows NT, *this service* provides name-to-IP address resolution	_____

TRUE OR FALSE

1. A workgroup allows for a small number of users, usually 20 or less.

2. The major difference between a workgroup and a domain is the level of security.

3. Windows XP Professional cannot act as a domain controller; you need Windows XP Server operating system to do this.

4. Joining a domain will probably involve the assistance and coordination of your organization's account manager.

5. A DHCP assigned address is valid forever.

practice

1. Sharing Resources for Different Departments

Unique Art Publishing prints coffee table art books. For the most part, these books are distributed to specialty bookshops in limited quantities as the books are made from expensive materials and priced accordingly. Three or four times a year they come out with a new title, so several books are always in the production stage. Often members of the production team need to go to museums, galleries, or private collectors' houses to photograph pieces of art for the upcoming books. At the same time, the members of the layout and design team are working on putting the copy on a page with the photograph. These design people would like to show the photographers outside the office what the finished page is going to look like so that if pictures need to be taken again or from a different angle for the best effect, they can do so while they are on location.

You are asked to share the files with the proposed layout, so that they can be accessed via dial-up networking.

Share the My Pictures folder in your own computer. Give it a new share name. Add the comment "Proposed layout for new book" in the Properties dialog box, and set the maximum number of users to five.

1. Click the **My Pictures** folder to share
2. Click **File,** then click **Sharing and Security.** The Properties dialog box opens
3. Click the *Share this folder on the network* radio button
4. Type a new share name of **Unique Art Publishing Pictures**
5. Click the **Allow network users to change my files** radio button. The final result should look like Figure 8.18

2. Changing the Dial Out Settings

Acme Pickle Corporation, one of the world's largest manufacturers of pickles, has just been acquired by Terrance Holdings, an investment company. Terrance Holdings plans to keep Acme's manufacturing facilities intact but wants to integrate Acme's existing computer network into their own to achieve greater control and information sharing.

You are brought in to oversee the transition of one of Acme's small satellite plants to connect to the new network. The first thing you realize has to be done is to change the dial out settings on the computers. The main phone number (714-555-1234) for Terrance Holdings will have to be substituted for the old one at Acme. Additionally, Terrance Holdings has an alternate number (714-555-6789) that has to be added. Terrance Holdings also has a network policy, which requires everyone who connects to their network to log in using their user name and password. Finally, due to a lot of traffic on the phone lines to Terrance Holdings, you want to set the number of redial attempts to 100.

Use an existing *dial-up* connection and input the information above as if to change the dial out settings, but click **Cancel** at the end of the steps so you do not alter the existing connection.

1. From the Network Connections window, click a dial-up connection to change the settings by clicking **File,** then click **Properties**

FIGURE 8.18

The My Pictures Properties dialog box

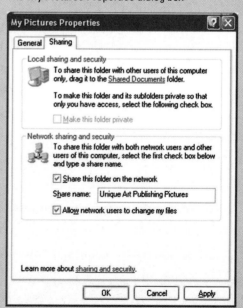

2. Click the **General** tab to enter the new phone number for Terrance Holdings, **714-555-1234**

3. Click the **Alternates** button, then click the **Add** button to type **714-555-6789** as the alternate phone number to dial in case the first number fails to connect

4. Click **OK,** then **OK** again to return to the **General** tab

5. Click the **Options** tab, and click the check box next to *Prompt for name and password, certificate, etc.* to require a name and password

6. Double-click the text box next to *Redial attempts*, and type **100** to change the number of redial attempts

1. Sharing a Printer

Sam Madison, who works in the Design Department of Lockhart Toys, has a colleague named Troy on another floor with a problem. Troy is doing a sales presentation to a potential client that has never given its business to Lockhart Toys before. They are considering it now because they have a new product that requires special equipment, which Lockhart has. Troy is making his presentation at the end of the week, and the potential client has just called and indicated that they would like to see a mock-up of the design for their new toy at the meeting. If Troy can come up with a convincing sample, they would feel more comfortable about using Lockhart Toys for this project. Troy has gotten an in-house artist to prepare a 3-D graphic according to the client's specifications. But Troy needs Sam to do him a favor. The graphic is not printing out right on the printers available upstairs. Troy wants to use a special printer in the Design Department that is normally off-limits to everyone on the network. Can Sam get him onto the special printer so that he can use it to print the graphic for the sales presentation?

Sam asks you to help him share the printer. Using any printer connected to your computer, change its settings to enable sharing and share it with the title "Special Design Printer."

At the end of the exercise, click **Cancel** to return the printer settings to what they were before you started this exercise.

1. Mapping a Network Drive

The Great Barrington Museum of American Art is developing a Web site of their collection of American paintings. Ruth Larkin is in charge of the project. In addition to posting the museum's paintings, she is providing images of other works not in the Great Barrington collection in order to present a comparison of the artist's oeuvre. She finds that she is frequently downloading images and information from a Web site named www.askart.com, such as the one in Figure 8.19.

She downloads these images into a network folder on the Great Barrington network. Since Ruth has to access it frequently, though, she wants to avoid spending time hunting for the network drive through multiple layers of the network hierarchy. She asks you to help her map the drive.

For this exercise, you will need to have access to a computer on a network. Pick any folder on the network, and use the context menu to map it. Right-click the folder you want to map, and click **Map Network Drive.** Select the drive letter you wish to use. Normally you click **Finish,** but for this exercise click **Cancel** to keep the current settings on the computer.

FIGURE 8.19

A Web page from *askart.com*

e-business

1. Adding a New Network Place

Thomson Auto Parts has contracts with the Big Three automakers in Detroit to supply parts for new cars. Rick Miles of Thomson has been informed by one of their big customers that they are implementing supply chain management software that allows them to collaborate much more closely with suppliers. Thomson has been given six months to be fully integrated with this new e-procurement system.

The first thing Rick knows he has to do is establish a regular connection to the customer's network. In order to perform this exercise, you will need access to a computer connected to a network.

1. Open **My Network Places**
2. Click **Add a network place**
3. Type \\ followed by the name of the computer you want to access, then type \ (for example, **\\host computer**)
4. Click **Next,** then click **Finish**

around the world

1. Installing a Network Protocol

Bicycle Planet imports specialty bicycles of all kinds from Manchester, England, Parma in Italy, and Marseille, France. These special bikes are custom ordered for bicycle enthusiasts in the United States.

Nick Virgilio is in charge of communicating with the bicycle manufacturers, as well as reviewing the various styles, models, and specifications. Since Bicycle Planet has been dealing with these manufacturers since the mid-1980s, the relationship between them is very close. In fact, Bicycle Planet is in the process of setting up a network connection with these manufacturers. Nick will use this connection in order to access information about new models or changes in existing design.

Although Bicycle Planet uses Windows XP as their operating system, the manufacturers in Europe all use older versions of the Windows operating system. Nick asks you if this will present any problems. You tell him that it shouldn't, but since you know that older versions of Windows use NetBEUI protocol, you tell him it's a good idea to install it on the Bicycle Planet system to make sure the computers are speaking the same language.

1. Click **Start,** then click **Control Panel**
2. Double-click **Network Connections**
3. Click the icon for the connection for which you want to add a protocol, click **File,** then **Properties**
4. Click **Install**
5. Click **Protocol,** then the **Add** button. The Select Network Protocol dialog box opens as in Figure 8.20
6. Click the **NetBEUI protocol** to install, then click **OK**

FIGURE 8.20

The Select Network Protocol dialog box

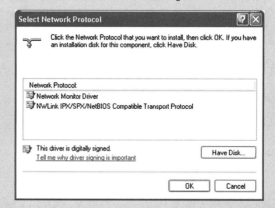

did you know?

moore's law, the computer axiom made in 1965 by Gordon Moore, the cofounder of Intel, predicted that the number of transistors on a chip would double every 18 months. Because the price of each chip stays roughly the same, the cost falls exponentially every time the power doubles. This means that as computers become more powerful, the cost of computing becomes cheaper. Moore forecast that this trend would continue through 1975; in fact the semiconductor industry now predicts this trend will continue at least until 2015.

until the 1900s, anyone could be a doctor. Doctors had no qualifications other than how successful they were treating their patients, many of whom died in the process.

for those people who have trouble remembering their passwords, a new alternative has been developed using pictures instead of text. A password is created by clicking in various parts of a complex picture, for example, an anatomical drawing. The locations chosen are then converted into a number that represents the password. By clicking in the same locations in the same order the next time, the users identify themselves to the computer.

Chapter Objectives

- Learn security considerations dealing with having too much security versus too little
- Understand what security is and why it is important to any organization
- Learn the importance of security planning and some strategies of how to prepare a plan
- Learn what some of the potential security threats are and a profile of how an actual attack takes place
- Learn about the Windows XP security model and the improvements that have been made over previous versions of Windows
- Study passwords, what they accomplish, and what the best practices are to manage them
- Learn what a user is and why this designation is so important to security in Windows
- Learn about groups and the different types of groups
- Study permissions and how they interact with one another
- Learn about the three major types of authentication used in Windows: key encryption, Kerberos, and certificates
- Learn what a firewall is and what the functions and features are

Secure Server Services, Madison, Wisconsin

Secure Server Services is a consulting company that offers its services to clients throughout the Madison area. It specializes in improving network security in all types of different industries. When a client requests intervention, Secure Server Services will send one of its representatives on site to meet with management and the IT staff (if any) to discuss what their security needs and goals are, and what can be done to meet these goals.

Kiri Ellison from Secure Server Services has been assigned to visit a long-distance telephone service provider in Madison. Once the initial meeting takes place, she returns to her office and prepares a detailed analysis of the current security scenario, the steps that can be taken, employee training that must take place, and the time frame for implementation. These steps are provided in different price tiers, depending on the amount of work the client wants done.

The long-distance provider has agreed to a series of basic security measures to get started and has asked that Kiri begin the process right away. She arrives the following Monday morning and begins.

SESSION 9.1 SECURITY OVERVIEW

GENERAL SECURITY CONSIDERATIONS AND ISSUES

The topic of security is inherently related to networking: if you were all alone in the universe at your computer, you wouldn't have to worry about anyone accessing your data without your permission. Because of this, many terms introduced in Chapter 8, Network Services, will be used in this chapter. Make sure you understand the basics of networking before plunging into security.

Although this is a book about Windows XP Professional, this operating system rarely is the only one in a network. While a small workgroup with only Windows XP Professional machines in a Peer-to-Peer arrangement is certainly possible, this is not usually the case. If the network is any kind of size, or if security is a concern, you may have a version of Windows 2000 Server, the big brother of Windows Professional, in Client/Server arrangement on the network. As a result, the Windows 2000 Server operating system, in addition to Windows XP Professional, has to be included in our discussion of security since, if you're interested in maximizing security at your organization, a Client/Server structure is preferred. In the real world, this issue is even broader as you often have Unix, IBM, Novell, Apple, and older versions of Windows operating systems—such as 3.x, 95, 98, or NT—on your network. However, these other platforms *are* outside the scope of this book

Interrelated with the discussion of Windows 2000 Server is network administration. Windows 2000 Server is an operating system run by network administrators. It is much more powerful and complex than the Windows XP Professional operating system we have been studying. As a result, topics relating to Windows Server have to be discussed from the vantage point of someone who is in charge of at least a piece of the network. Because of this, topics will be discussed from the point of view that you are responsible in some way for network security. This does not mean that you will be qualified as a network administrator after getting done with this section; the brief overview provided here is only enough to give you as a user in a network an idea of some of the concepts involved. Being responsible for managing a network requires far more knowledge and experience. But between the two extremes of a clueless user and a top-level administrator, there is a middle ground that is worth investigating. Perhaps you will draw an assignment to handle some security details for your local workgroup. Maybe you will find yourself assigned to manage a print server that has a few printers attached. Or maybe you will just be the one who knows the most about computers in a small organization that doesn't have the budget or need to hire a network administrator. By learning more about security not only will you be taking steps toward protecting your data, but you will also be making yourself a more valuable member of your organization. This is not only good for those you work for, but good for you as well, because sooner or later a knowledge of security issues leads to more opportunities for advancement and increasing income. Computer security is one of the fastest expanding fields of work in the early twenty-first century.

Security (in terms of computers) can be defined as the protection of data against unauthorized access. Computer security, and especially network security, is a vast topic unto itself. Even tiny networks with just four or five nodes require some kind of security if they are to avoid catastrophic loss. Yet security is a double-edged sword: too much and you limit users' flexibility in a restrictive environment of passwords and policies. This leads to low worker morale, inhibits creative interaction, and hinders productivity. On the other hand, too little security and data can be lost, damaged, or get into the wrong hands. It can result in lost revenue, loss of an organization's reputation, and possibly (if you are the one responsible for security) the loss of your job. A network administrator must strike a balance. Realistically you will never have a system that guarantees complete security. And adding some flexibility to your network inevitably creates an opening that can be taken advantage of by someone with the right knowledge and determination. Contrary to popular belief, would-be hackers do not need an enormous amount of technical prowess; anyone with a lot of time on their hands and enough motivation can find a way to compromise a network's security or at least create some havoc. Further, although precautions can be taken to prevent unauthorized access, it is very difficult to determine if a valid user is deliberately doing something malicious. Someone may have valid access to a particular file for data entry, but little is going to stop them from entering phony data if they want to. When all is said and done, effective security is always a balancing act and involves not just imposing rules on users but rather knowing their needs and wants. Understanding this, it is very useful to get input from users to come up with a security plan that works. Keep in mind, though, that users will often complain that they need more access (whether they really do or not), but they will never complain that they have *too much* access.

SECURITY PLANNING

To achieve network security, you need a plan. There are several reasons to spend the time needed to work out a plan (a written one). For one, without a plan you will not know what your security goals are or what you need to do to achieve them. What parts of your network are absolutely vital to have secured? How much access does management need to all areas of the network? Who are the people you will trust with greater access? What types of security breaches are unique to your industry?

Most networks have security problems of one kind or another from time to time. Whenever an employee leaves, there is a potential hole in your security system. If someone takes on added responsibilities and you need to increase their permissions on the network, there's a chance you may give them too much access. Suppose a group manager, who legitimately needs administrative control for his group, accidentally gives someone rights to a sensitive folder, like the one containing everyone's salary figures? Or suppose a manager is away from the office for a few days and leaves a senior subordinate to hold down the fort in his or her absence? You might need to give that person temporary access to certain network areas that are not normally required. A way to detect these types of situations is by comparing the current network state with the original security plan you drew up. This ability to see what has changed can tip you off to potential problem areas.

Another benefit to a written security plan, signed off by top management, falls into the category of personnel management. Unless you write down the agreed upon rules according to which the network is secured, someone could claim that you as a network administrator are biased to certain users or groups of users. If the security plan is clearly written and specific, you can use it to back up your reasons for certain policy decisions.

Write a security plan by breaking down the overall network into smaller sections. This process will divide your organization into various security areas. Breaking down the plan into smaller pieces reduces the complexity of making your organization secure. There are several ways to break down a security design for an entire company. One way is by department; users who work together tend to have the same needs in terms of network access. Another method is by seniority within the company. All managers at a certain level tend to have similar needs. Keep an eye out for special users who wear multiple hats within the organization and therefore may need access to more than one area. Another way to break down a security design is by people who work on the same project. These may include members from several different departments. You can assign the same person to more than one security group. Yet another breakdown is by the types of applications or equipment a group of users need. Once you create these groups, try as much as possible to avoid making exceptions. Exceptions open the door to complexity and confusion, which in turn can result in security breaches.

POTENTIAL SECURITY PROBLEMS

Many security problems arise from security breakdowns due to changes in an organization. As mentioned before, common things like employees being hired or fired, promotions, temporary changes in responsibilities, as well as confusion resulting from mergers of different branches or other organizations, can all lead to security gaps. However, understanding a little bit about how network security is breached from the outside can give you the scope of the problem and the reason for concern when it comes to security. This is far from a manual on the subject; the aim is simply to alert you to what's involved so that you can be forewarned and take practical countermeasures.

The first step someone takes who wants to break into a network is to find out as much as possible about the target organization. This is equivalent to a burglar "casing the joint" before attempting a robbery. You want to find the unlocked doors and windows, the routine comings and goings of the target, the number of people who are inside, and when the place is empty. You want to see if any neighbors keep an eye out or if the entranceways are watched. A huge amount of data is available to the general public through the Internet, and this is usually the first place a hacker will look. An organization would do well to examine what they post on the Web from a potential hacker's viewpoint and consider what would be lost if some of this sensitive information were removed.

The next step is to identify the domain names and discover the associated networks related to the target organization. Domain names are the Internet equivalent to your organization's name, as in "mycompany.com." Again, there are several databases on the Internet that can be searched for different domains associated with one organization. This not only provides some clue of how big a company is (how many departments, locations, or

anotherword

The term "hacker" has become notorious to describe a person who breaks into a computer system without authorization in order to do damage (destroy files, steal credit card numbers, plant viruses, etc.). Originally, however, a hacker was someone who wrote detailed programming code in the sense that the person was sitting there "hacking away" at a large, boring chore. The original term for someone who commits the illegal act of breaking into a computer system without invitation is a "cracker," meaning someone who has some hacking skill but is using it to "crack into" a network, and in that sense being a criminal hacker. Because a cracker uses low-level hacker skills to do cracking, the terms cracker and hacker became synonymous. Sadly, today the term hacker is more commonly used to describe the malicious individual rather than the honest, hard-working professional who performs skilled computer work.

branches) but also provides choices in terms of where to attempt to break in. A small remote branch domain may be less secure than the company's main office domain, for example. Along with a domain name, other information also will likely provide a contact name and e-mail address, which might be useful to someone who wanted to impersonate a network administrator. (A good defense against this is to provide, if possible, a fictitious name as the public contact, which will alert network users that someone is trying to pretend to be someone else.)

Another sought after piece of information is the name of a server that manages the database of names mapped to IP addresses within an organization. This server is known as a **DNS server.** Because this is an important database that needs to be updated constantly, a process called zone transfer takes place between two or more DNS servers so that there is redundancy of information in case of failure and to provide better service to larger networks. The problem arises if a would-be intruder is able to intercept one of these zone transfers and thereby acquire a complete and up-to-date road map of an organization's internal network. This provides potential access paths to penetrate the network. In other words, going back to our burglar analogy, this is equivalent to having a blueprint of the premises you want to rob. The way to reduce the chances of this happening is to restrict zone transfers to authorized servers only.

The next step is to determine which of the potential access paths will let the hacker into the network. In our burglar scenario, this is the same as rattling a few doors and peering into the windows to see what's inside. It is accomplished by scanning the network and IP addresses obtained earlier to see if they go somewhere interesting and if access is permitted down these paths. This scanning process can be detected and blocked if preventive countermeasures are taken.

The next step for the attacker is to attempt to zero in on an exposed network resource or valid account. Once a valid user name or share is found, it is usually just a matter of time before the correct password or some other weakness in the system can be guessed by the potential intruder. These loopholes are usually easy to fix but also hard to find out about in a timely fashion.

At this point, the attacker is finally ready to do the theft or mischief that is the goal of all the previous activity. Some of the possible activities are as follows:

- *Unauthorized access for the purpose of obtaining information.* Depending on the information obtained, this can be embarrassing to extremely harmful to your organization. Obviously, plans for a merger with another company or secret designs for a new product would have a devastating impact if uncovered and provided to competitors

- *Modification attacks.* These include any type of change to existing information on your network such as inserting false data, deleting existing data, or changing existing data

- *Denial of service.* These are attacks that deny the use of a target organization's resources to legitimate users of the system. Often these types of attacks are carried out by flooding a Web site with so much dummy traffic that the site is taken out of commission temporarily

- *Cyber-graffiti.* Just as in the case of someone who is angry at a particular organization (or just malicious) coming along and spray-painting graffiti on the window of that organization's storefront, hackers can put embarrassing or offensive messages on your organization's Web site. Although this can be regarded as a prank and is easily fixed, the cause for concern is that someone was able to penetrate your security enough to do it

THE WINDOWS XP SECURITY MODEL

The Windows XP security model is based on *user level security,* which means that the access to a file, printer, or other network resource is based on the user name. User level permissions are stored in a central server and managed by the network administrator. This provides greater protection than share level security, which is the security model for older versions of Windows, because users are identified individually or within a group. With share level security, if you have the password for the share, you can access the data or resource without further authentication. A share is a folder or printer that has been shared for use over a network.

PASSWORDS

A *password* is a secret word or code used as a security measure against unauthorized access to data and resources. Along with your user name, your password is your key to the door of your computer or network. As such, choosing a password should not be taken lightly. Windows XP accepts passwords up to 14 characters long. Passwords are case sensitive, which means you must pay attention to using uppercase or lowercase letters when creating a password. If, for example, **Windows** is your password, you won't be able to log on with **WINDOWS** or **windows.**

To give you an idea of the level of increased security with Windows XP over earlier Windows operating systems, at the logon screen that appears when you first start your computer, Windows 95/98 provided the option of simply hitting the Esc key to bypass the entire logon system! This means that anyone could get access to your computer. With Windows XP, you are forced to enter a valid user name and password to access the computer. The following are some general guidelines for passwords:

- Your password should be at least seven or eight characters long (the longer the stronger, the shorter the weaker) and contain a mix of uppercase and lowercase letters, symbols, and numbers: for example, SKIPpy!321 or ?ObfuS098
- Don't use obvious passwords like your name, birthday, and definitely not your social security number. The ideal password is easy for you to remember, but hard for others to guess. A good way of doing this is to take a phrase that's easy to remember like "Peas are good for you" and substitute numbers and abbreviations (like people do on license plates) to create a password of PsRgood4u!
- Lock the user out after three failed login attempts. Do not permit unlimited tries, as this will eventually lead to an attacker figuring out your password
- Change your password regularly; the longer you use the same password, the more likely it will be compromised
- Change your password if someone else has assigned it to you
- Always log off before leaving your computer unattended
- Don't tell others what your password is
- Commit your password to memory; it's not much good if you follow all the above steps and leave a yellow sticky on your monitor with the password information on it. It's like locking the door of your house and leaving the keys in the lock

WINDOWS XP

If you forget your password to log on to the network, someone with administrative rights must log on and set up a new password for you. Change it immediately to a different password.

You can change the password you use to log on to your computer or network at any time in the Windows Security dialog box.

---

task reference

Changing Your Password

- Press and hold the **Ctrl** and **Alt** keys as you press the **Delete** key

- Click **Change Password**

- Type your old password and your new password

- Click **OK** then **OK** again

Changing your password:

Walking through the office, Kiri Ellison notices an area supervisor with a yellow sticky attached to his computer monitor. On it are written his password and his group administrator's password. She briefly discusses the importance of password security and suggests that he change the current passwords right away. The area supervisor agrees and gets to work.

1. On your keyboard, press and hold the **Ctrl** and **Alt** keys as you press the **Delete** key. All other open windows are closed and the Windows Security window opens

2. Click **Change Password.** The Change Password dialog box opens

3. Type your old password in the text box next to *Old Password*

4. Type your new password in the text box next to *New Password,* then in the text box next to Co*nfirm New Password*

5. Click **OK.** A dialog box opens, confirming your change of password

6. Click **OK**

7. Click **Cancel** to close the Windows Security dialog box

If you have local computer access permission, after you log on, your password and user name are checked by Windows against a local security account database called the Security Accounts Manager (SAM). If you have access to a domain, your password and user name are checked against a database stored in the Active Directory.

Another difference in Windows XP versus earlier operating systems such as Windows NT is that Windows XP uses the Kerberos security system (more about this later). Kerberos is an Internet security protocol. As a result, passwords are encrypted before being sent across the network. This adds another layer of security.

Most of the objects in Windows XP have security information attached in the form of an *Access Control Entry (ACE)*. Each ACE has a list of users allowed to access the object and what their rights and abilities are. The ACE also includes what group the user belongs to. A collection of ACEs is called an *Access Control List (ACL)*.

---

making *the grade*

1. A password should be at least _____ characters long and contain a mix of uppercase and lowercase letters, symbols, and _____.

2. _____ is an operating system run by network administrators that is more powerful and complex than the Windows XP Professional operating system.

3. The name of a server that knows the database of names mapped to IP addresses within an organization is known as a _____ server.

4. Attacks that deny the use of a target organization's resources to legitimate users of the system and are carried out by flooding a Web site with so much dummy traffic that the site is taken out of commission temporarily are called _____ attacks.

5. The Windows XP security model is based on _____, which means that the access to a file, printer, or other network resource is based on the user name.

SESSION 9.2 USERS AND GROUPS

USERS

A *user* is any individual who interacts with the computer. Before a user can log on to Windows XP, he or she needs an account. User accounts indicate the abilities and rights that the user has. One of the first things you need to be able to do if you are in charge of a workgroup or its security is to add a new user. This is also useful if you share your computer with others because by creating a new user account, each person can have their own personalized settings and private data. This system of user accounts means that unless you give someone else who uses your computer permission, they cannot access your files.

Until you add groups to Windows XP (for more information on these different groups and what they can do, see Figure 9.5 in the next section entitled Groups), there are only two user account types: Computer Administrator and Limited. There is also a Guest account that can be set up if someone needs to temporarily use your computer, but this is deactivated by default.

Before you add new users, make sure you understand what their job function is and what type of access they will need. It is not advisable to make someone a Computer Administrator if they are new or if they do not have your trust as they can create problems if they don't know what they are doing or if they have a malicious intent. For someone new, it is wiser to select the Limited user option, as they will be able to operate the computer and save documents but can't install programs or make other potentially damaging changes.

Figure 9.1 illustrates the different rights of the Computer Administrator and Limited user accounts.

FIGURE 9.1

User account rights

Rights	Computer Administrator	Limited
Install programs and hardware	Yes	No
Make systemwide changes	Yes	No
Access and read all nonprivate files	Yes	No
Create and delete user accounts	Yes	No
Change other people's accounts	Yes	No
Change your own account name or type	Yes	No
Change your own user picture	Yes	Yes
Create, change, or remove your own password	Yes	Yes

*another*word

You must be logged on as a Computer Administrator to create and delete user accounts.

When creating a new user account, you are asked to provide a user name and password. Windows will store any special settings for the new user, and when the user logs on, their own settings will be displayed.

task reference

Adding a New User

- Navigate to the **Control Panel** and double-click **User Accounts**

- Click the **Create a new account** link

- Type a name for the new user and click **Next**

- Choose an account type for the new user, then click **Create Account**

- Click **Change an Account,** click the new user you just created, then click **Create Password**

- Type a password twice, then click **Create Password**

Adding a new user:

Kiri has just been informed by management that several new technicians will be coming next week from a branch office to get some specialized training. While they are in town, they will need to access the corporate network in order to oversee some projects they are in the middle of back at the branch. Since Kiri has often explained to management that these kinds of personnel adjustments often lead to security holes in the network infrastructure, they have asked that she manage the temporary assignment of these individuals to computers in the home office. Kiri realizes that she will have to create new user accounts for these technicians that have a limited amount of rights and data access.

1. Click **Start.**

2. Click **Control Panel.** The Control Panel window opens

3. Double-click **User Accounts.** The User Accounts dialog box opens as shown in Figure 9.2

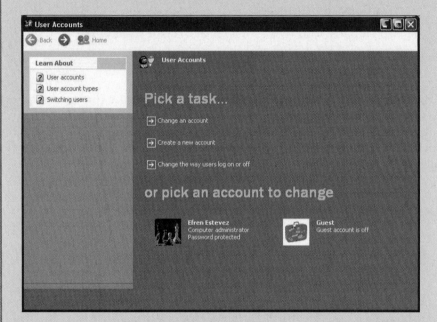

F I G U R E 9.2

The User Accounts dialog box

4. Click the **Create a new account** link

5. Type a user name in the text box, then click Next. The Pick an account type dialog box opens (Figure 9.3)

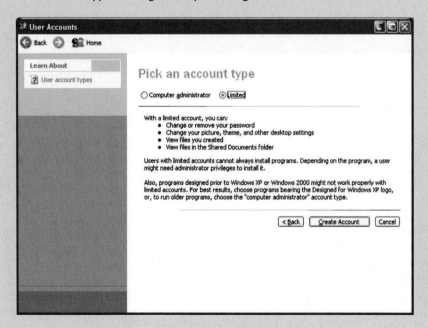

F I G U R E 9.3

The Pick an account type dialog box

*another*way

You can also add new users in the Local Users and Groups folders in **Control Panel/Administrative Tools/Computer Management.** Double-click the **Users** folder, then right-click in an empty area in the right pane and choose **New User . . .** The New User dialog box opens.

tip: *A user name can be a maximum of 20 characters long and is not case sensitive*

6. Choose an account type for the new user, then click **Create Account.** The new account is created and displayed in the User Accounts dialog box

7. Click **Change an Account,** and click the new user you just created

8. Click **Create Password**

9. Type a password twice, then click **Create Password**

Once a user account is established, you can modify the user's properties in the Local Users and Groups folder (Control Panel/Administrative Tools/Computer Management/Local Users and Groups/Users). By right-clicking the name of the user and choosing Properties, you will be taken to the User Properties dialog box (Figure 9.4). Note that in the General tab you have several options, which are relevant to look at.

FIGURE 9.4

The User Properties dialog box

The first check box is *User must change password at next logon.* Clicking this check box is particularly useful if you have just set up a new user account and want to make sure the person makes up their own password the next time they log on. The next check box is if you want to prevent the user from changing their password. This is not a good idea since, as discussed above, regular password change is a best practice for security. The next check box will ensure that the user's password will never expire. Again, this may be fine in a situation where security is not a concern, such as a home office, but it is a good idea to regularly change a password. The next check box is an important one to know about if you need to eliminate a user's account from the system, say, if the user just left the organization and you want to quickly disable their account. The last option is the Account is locked out option. This option is unavailable; Windows activates it if a person attempts to log on and exceeds the limit of password attempts.

The next tab in the User Properties dialog box is the Member of tab. The purpose of this tab is simple: if you want to add a user to a group, click Add and select a group. A more detailed discussion about groups is in the next section. You are better off knowing more about groups before adding users to any of them.

The last tab in the User Properties dialog box is the Profile tab. A *user profile* is the user's personal preferences for his or her computer including such things as how the Desktop is displayed, network connections, printer settings, and so forth. There are three types of user profiles:

- *Local user profile.* The most common profile, it is created the first time a user logs on. It is stored in the hard drive of the user's (local) computer

- *Roaming user profile.* This profile is saved on a network server and is available on any computer within the network. It is particularly useful if you "roam" about a building and need to use whatever computer is at hand. Your settings remain the same anywhere you log on. Only a network administrator can create this profile

- *Mandatory user profile.* This type of user profile is useful if a network administrator wants to enforce a particular type of setting systemwide. Like the roaming user profile, anywhere you log on will result in the same settings, but the difference is that the network administrator will determine the settings

Switching Users

If you share your computer with other users, once you have created a new user on your computer, you will need to be able to switch from one user to another. This is accomplished by logging off the first user and logging on the other.

---

task reference

Switching from the Current User to Another

- Click **Start,** then **Log Off**

- Click **Switch User**

- Select the user name from the Welcome screen

Switching from the current user to another:

One of the secretaries stops Kiri and explains to her that she shares her computer with a part-time administrative assistant. With the new user accounts that have been assigned, the assistant has been given a more restrictive user profile than the secretary. The secretary is confused as to how this will work, as they both share the same computer. Kiri explains that multiple users with completely different rights can use the same machine without difficulty, and she shows the secretary how to do this.

1. Click **Start,** then **Log Off.** The Log Off Windows screen opens

> **tip:** *When you log off, your session remains active, with the programs and files you were using staying open*

2. Click **Switch User**

3. Windows displays the Welcome screen, from which the new user can select their name in order to log on

*another*word

Switching users has some drawbacks. If the new user shuts down the computer after they're through, you will lose any work you haven't saved. For this reason, it is a good idea to save any work before you log off.

Additionally, leaving multiple user sessions open consumes memory and processing power, which will slow down the computer.

GROUPS

A *group* is a collection of user accounts. Groups can be given permission to access files, rights to activities on different computers, and special abilities on the network. Groups are defined by what they do. By using groups, a network administrator can create collections of user accounts that have the same rights.

The following table provides a breakdown of the default Windows XP Professional groups; you can also create custom groups.

FIGURE 9.5

Default Windows XP groups

Groups	Rights and Abilities
Administrators	This is the top-level group, which has total access and can do anything
Backup Operators	This group has the special rights associated with performing backups; although an Administrator often performs this task, the rights of this group allow someone in a standard user group to be delegated the task of managing backups
Guests	A group for temporary or infrequent users with limited access and abilities, for instance, someone who connects via a computer outside your network to use shared folders
Network Configuration Operators	This group can modify network configuration and dial-up settings, but not individual users' settings, like an Administrator
Power Users	A group for those who have above average understanding of their computer and the network. Users should not be put in this group casually, as they have access to processes that can cause problems if they don't know what they are doing
Remote Desktop Users	This group has the right to log on from a remote location
Replicators	A special category of the standard user group, which allows members to perform file and folder replication
Users	The lowest level and most limited group; it is also probably going to contain the greatest number of people in your organization. This group will allow a person to perform their duties, but not make any changes to the system
Help Services Group	This is a collection of users for the Help and Support Center

You can define custom groups if you need to assign a combination of rights from the above default groups, for example, a Power Users group that needs some Administrator rights.

---

task reference

Adding New Groups

- Navigate to the Computer Management window **(Start, Control Panel, Administrative Tools, Computer Management)**

- Click the plus sign next to *Local Groups and Users,* then right-click **Groups**

- Click **New Group . . .** from the context menu

- Type a Group name and description, then click **Add**

- Click the users to add, then click the **Add** button. Click **OK** when done

- Click the **Create** button, then click **Close**

Adding new groups:

1. Click **Start, Control Panel, Administrative Tools, Computer Management**

2. Click the plus sign next to *Local Groups and Users*

3. Right-click **Groups** and click **New Group . . .** from the context menu. The New Group dialog box opens as shown in Figure 9.6

4. Type a group name in the *Group name* text box

5. Type a description in the *Description* field

tip: *For future reference, provide a brief summary of the special access this new group provides in the Description field*

6. Click the **Add** button. The Select Users dialog box opens as shown in Figure 9.7

FIGURE 9.6
The New Group dialog box

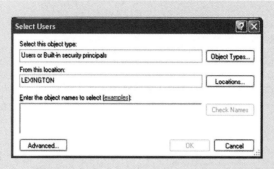

7. Click the users you wish to add to this new group you are creating, then click the **Add** button

tip: *The list of users displayed is from the local machine. If you wish to add users from another computer on the network, click the* **Locations** *button*

8. When you are done adding users, click the **OK** button. You are returned to the New Group dialog box

9. Click the **Create** button, then click **Close**

10. To see the newly created group in the Computer Management dialog box, press **F5** to refresh the list of groups

You will want to customize this group's rights by adding rights to the new group. This will be covered in the next section, called Permissions.

If you need to remove a group (or a user), that is accomplished in the Computer Management window, as demonstrated in the next series of steps. Consider carefully before you do this. Removing a group or a user is permanent. It is usually better to disable an account than to delete it outright. For example, if someone leaves your organization, the first instinct is to delete that user's account. However, it is often the case that someone else is hired to take the place of the person who left. In such a situation, if you delete the old user account, you have to make a new one and go about the process of assigning the rights to it again. If you simply disabled the account, you could rename it and give it to the new user without any further intervention (assuming the new hire has the same responsibilities as the employee who left).

---

task reference

Deleting a User or Group

- Navigate to the Computer Management window **(Start, Control Panel, Administrative Tools, Computer Management)**

- Click the plus sign next to *Local Groups and Users,* then click **Groups**

- Right-click the group you want to delete

- Click **Delete** from the context menu

> ### Deleting a user or group:
>
> 1. Click **Start, Control Panel, Administrative Tools, Computer Management**
>
> 2. Click the plus sign next to *Local Groups and Users*
>
> 3. Click **Groups** (or **Users** if you want to delete a user)
>   The group list will appear in the right pane of the window
>
> 4. Right-click the group you wish to delete. The context menu opens
>
> 5. Click **Delete.** A dialog box like the one in Figure 9.8 opens asking you to confirm if you really want to delete this account, emphasizing the point that the change is permanent
>
>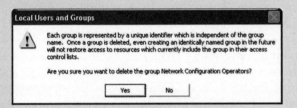
>
> 6. Click **Yes**

F I G U R E 9.8

The Confirmation of User or Group deletion dialog box

PERMISSIONS

The whole point of discussing users and groups is to assign the users and groups permissions to access shares, folders, and files. A **permission** is a rule associated with an object that determines which users or groups have access and rights to that object. For the most part, greater access permissions will do everything lower access permissions will do, and then some.

Windows XP provides for a broad range of capability in the area of granting permissions. Note, however, that file level security is only available on NTFS formatted drives.

Shared Folder Permissions

As discussed before, sharing a folder containing data that users need access to is one of the major benefits of a network. Creating shared folder *permissions* prevents unauthorized access to the data in a shared folder. With shared folder permissions, a greater flexibility exists for granting access to legitimate users by dividing users into groups, thereby allowing some groups to access some aspects of the data in the shared file but not other groups. For example, group A could be given read only permission while group B could be given permission to both read and write data.

Permissions come with an increasing level of complexity, with shared folder permissions being the simplest. There are far fewer permission options available at the share level than at the file level. Shared folder permissions are applied to a folder and affect all the files and subfolders beneath the folder. Because shared folder permissions offer fewer options than file level permissions, they are inherently less secure. File permissions allow you a far greater degree of granularity. "Granularity" is a computer term meaning specificity or preciseness. More granularity indicates more flexibility in customizing a system, because there are more, smaller increments (granules) from which to choose. With this granularity, however, comes additional complexity. It can be time-consuming to apply permissions at the file level, and troubleshooting can be difficult. For this reason, it is a good idea to use file permissions sparingly; too many file permissions can lead to an administrative nightmare. Try to use shared folder permissions instead of file permissions if at all possible.

Additionally, the file system installed affects what your options are. One of the major benefits of the NTFS file system over File Access Table (FAT) is the ability to create file level permissions. If a share is created on a FAT partition, you will not be able to use file permissions. On FAT partitions, folder permissions are the only way to secure a folder.

When you create a share, the default permission is Full Control to the Everyone group. This is a supergroup that includes all groups, including any new ones you may create. Since this allows anyone access to the file, in most cases you will want to modify this for each share.

Keep in mind that share level permissions only operate across a network. Someone without a share level permission of any kind could access a share if it can be accessed from a local machine that contains the file. Since the local machine in this case is operating as a file server, direct access through the local machine is not considered "shared," so it will allow access without referring to the share level permissions.

Three sets of permissions that can be set at the shared folder level are outlined in Figure 9.9. These permissions—Read, Change, and Full Control—can individually be "Allowed" or "Denied."

There are two scenarios in which a user will be denied access to a shared folder. First, if the user does not have user level permissions (that is, he or she is not personally assigned access) and they don't belong to a group that has access permission to the share, access will be denied. The second scenario is when the user has been denied, either as an individual user or as a member of a group that has been denied access. Deny permission always overrides access permission.

FIGURE 9.9

Shared folder permissions

Shared Folder Permission	Description
Read	Permits the user to read information in a shared folder and also to display subfolder names and to view filenames and attributes
Change	Permits writing of data into a shared folder, including creating new files and folders, appending data (to the end of a file, but not changing any existing data within the file), and changing file attributes
Full Control	Permits changing of the folder's permissions and taking ownership of a folder; by default the Everyone group has Full Control to a new share

task reference

Changing Permissions for a Shared Folder

- Click to select the folder you wish to change permissions for; then click **File,** then **Sharing and Security . . .**
- Click the **Permissions** button
- Click one of the listings under *Group or user names* to view their permissions and click in a check box to change the permission type to allow or deny
- To add a user or group, click the **Add** button
- Click the name of the user or group you want to allow access to, then click **Add**
- Click **OK**

Changing permissions for a shared folder:

1. Click to select the folder you wish to change permissions for
2. Click **File**
3. Click **Sharing and Security . . .** The Properties dialog box opens
4. Click the **Permissions** button. The Permissions dialog box opens
5. The list under *Group or user names* indicates each user or group that can access this folder. Click one of the listings to view their permissions
6. The list under *Permissions* displays the permission types available and whether these permissions are allowed or denied. Click in a check box to change the permission type to allow or deny
7. To add a user or group, click the **Add** button. The Select Users or Groups dialog box opens. The list under *Select this object type* indicates the users or groups you can grant access to
8. In the *Enter the object names to select box*, enter the name of the user, group, or computer you want to allow access to, then click **OK**
9. You are returned to the Permissions dialog box with the user, group, or computer you selected listed in the *Group or User Names* list
10. Click **OK** to confirm your changes

NTFS Permissions

The next level of permissions, NTFS permissions, adds another layer of complexity. Remember these permissions are only available on an NTFS formatted drive. If you right-click a file on an NTFS drive and then select

Properties, one of the tabs is labeled Security. This tab will allow you to set NTFS permissions, but this tab will not appear if you are working in a FAT drive.

As compared to shared folder permissions, NTFS file permissions are used to control access to *files*. The five different types of NTFS permissions are outlined and described in Figure 9.10. As always, the higher access permissions encompass the lower, more restrictive permissions. For example, the Modify permission in Figure 9.10 includes the Read, Write, and Execute permissions, in addition to the Modify permissions.

NTFS *folder* permissions (as opposed to NTFS file permissions) allow access to a folder and the files and subfolders within that folder. These permissions are outlined and described in Figure 9.11. Note that the major distinction between NTFS file permissions and NTFS folder permissions is the List Folder Contents in the NTFS folder permissions. This specific

FIGURE 9.10

NTFS file permissions

NTFS File Permission	Description
Read	Permits reading of the file and viewing of its attributes, ownership, and permissions
Write	Permits overwriting of the file, changing attributes, viewing its ownership, and viewing the permissions
Read & Execute	Permits running and executing the application that created the file
Modify	Permits modification and deletion of a file
Full Control	Permits changing the permission set and taking ownership of the file

FIGURE 9.11

NTFS folder permissions

NTFS Folder Permission	Description
Read	Permits reading files, folders, and subfolders of the parent folder and viewing folder's attributes, ownership, and permissions
Write	Permits creating new files and folders within the parent folder, as well as changing the folder's attributes and viewing the folder's ownership and permissions
List Folder Contents	Permits viewing the files and subfolders within the parent folder
Read & Execute	Permits navigation through all the files and subfolders and grants the ability to run programs in the folder
Modify	Permits modification and deletion of the folder
Full Control	Permits changing the permissions and taking ownership of the folder

folder permission is used to prevent browsing through a particular folder's directory of files and subfolders. A user with List Folder Contents permission must know the specific filename and location in a folder he or she has access to; the user cannot search for the desired file through the folder's directory tree structure.

NTFS file permissions override NTFS folder permissions. A user with access to a file because of NTFS file permissions can access that file even though he or she may not have access to the parent folder of that file. As stated above, however, this user could not access said file through the folder (this would require List Folder Contents permission).

By default, when NTFS permissions are assigned to a parent folder, all the same permissions are applied to the subfolders and files of that parent folder. This process is called *inheritance.* Subfolders and files inherit NTFS permissions from their parent folder. Any new folders created within that parent folder also inherit the parent's NTFS permissions.

Special Access Permissions

Special access permissions provide a further level of granularity and complexity beyond NTFS permissions. Figure 9.12 lists the special access permissions. The standard NTFS file and folder permissions outlined in Figures 9.10 and 9.11 are actually composed of several of these special access permissions.

As you may have guessed, this issue of permissions can get quite complicated. For example, what happens if there are conflicting permissions? Suppose a user is a member of two different groups with different access privileges to the same data? Which set of permissions takes precedence? The answer is that a denied permission will override an allowed permission. If the same user is a member of one group that is allowed access to a file and another group that is denied access to the same file, then the user who is a member of both groups would not gain access. This arrangement makes sense, in that the default is to the more conservative option.

The term given to this concept is *effective permissions.* The effective permissions for users are what they actually have access to, according to the rules that govern overlapping permissions. This becomes particularly important in a large network, where a user will commonly both have individual permissions at the user level and be a member of a group that also has permissions. Keep in mind what was stated above: the deny permission will always override the allow permission.

---

making the grade   SESSION 9.2

1. A _____ is any individual who interacts with the computer.

2. Before a user can log on to Windows XP, he or she needs a
_____.

3. A _____ is a collection of user accounts.

4. Subfolders and files _____ NTFS permissions from their parent folder.

5. NTFS _____ permissions override NTFS _____ permissions.

FIGURE 9.12

Special access permissions

Special Access Permissions	Description
Traverse Folder/Execute File	Permits browsing through a folder's subfolders and files, and grants the ability to run programs in the folder
List Folder/Read Data	Permits viewing of subfolders and filenames in the parent folder; also permits the viewing of data within these same files
Read Attributes	Permits viewing of the standard NTFS attributes of a file or folder
Read Extended Attributes	Permits viewing of the extended NTFS attributes of a file or folder, which are defined by programs and may vary
Create Files/Write Data	Permits the creation of new files within the parent folder; also permits modification and overwriting of existing data in a file
Create Folders/Append Data	Permits the creation of new folders within the parent folder; also permits addition of data to the end of the files, but not making changes to any existing data within a file
Write Attributes	Permits the changing of attributes of a file or folder
Write Extended Attributes	Permits the changing of extended attributes of a file or folder, which are defined by programs and may vary
Delete Subfolders and Files	Permits the deletion of files and subfolders with a parent folder, even if the Delete special access permission has not been granted
Delete	Permits the deletion of files and subfolders with a parent folder
Read Permissions	Permits reading of standard NTFS permissions of a file or folder
Change Permissions	Permits changing of standard NTFS permissions of a file or folder
Take Ownership	Permits taking ownership of a file or folder. The owner of a file or folder can change its permissions regardless of any other permission
Synchronize	Permits different threads to wait on the handle for the file or the folder and synchronize with another thread. Applies only to multithreaded, multiprocessing programs

SESSION 9.3 NETWORK SECURITY

The Windows XP network security system relies upon security services, which are added to the operating system as additional layers of security beyond that provided by user accounts. Only after a user has been authenticated should they be granted access to resources. This authentication is achieved by the use of various authentication protocols.

AUTHENTICATION METHODS

Previous discussions involved the assignment of access rights and privileges to users and groups, as well as methods for managing passwords. Securing a WAN network involves an additional level of security concerns because many communications in a WAN environment routinely travel across public space outside of the common internal network of an organization. Thus, **authentication,** or verifying the identity of a user and verifying message integrity, which is the protection of a transmitted message from accidental or malicious modification, becomes critical. Windows XP supports several types of authentication using methods such as public key encryption, Kerberos authentication, and certificates. There are other methods supported by Windows XP, some used for backward compatibility with older versions of Windows, but these are the three we will look at here.

Key Encryption

Private key encryption requires that both sides of a communication have the same key. In order to decrypt the sender's message, you must provide a secret code that proves you have authorized access. The critical security concern in this type of system is protecting the key. This is the most widely used and fastest type of encryption; however, it presents a problem. When the two parties exchange their agreed upon key, they are vulnerable to someone eavesdropping and detecting the key. Let's take a simple example from outside the world of computers. A general is meeting with his officers the night before a battle in his tent. He tells his officers he wants regular reports from the battlefield. In order to make sure communications are secure, the agreed upon key is "Robin Hood." Any officer reporting back from the battlefield must use "Robin Hood" to prove his identity. The problem is that unknown to the general or his men, a spy outside the general's tent has overheard this key. Now the entire operation is vulnerable. This is the problem with private key encryption.

Public key encryption, on the other hand, requires two keys; one key is used to encrypt the data and the other is used to decrypt. This system of key pairs offers much stronger security than private key. The way it works is that one key is a public key and made available freely, while the other key is kept secret. In order for authentication to occur, both keys must be used together. If you have only one of the keys, communication cannot take place. The user sending the message looks up the recipient's public key and uses it to encrypt his message. The recipient uses his own secret private key to decrypt the message. There is never the need to transmit the private keys to anyone in order to have a message decrypted, and so the private keys are not in transit and are not vulnerable.

This is necessary in any type of network because otherwise there is no way of proving identity. Any user can log on to any computer in the system. The IP address of the computer you log on to does not prove you are who you say you are. A technique used by hackers called IP spoofing impersonates an authorized IP address in order to access resources.

Additionally, consider a situation within a network in which a server does not authenticate itself to another server before relaying data. Someone impersonating an authorized server could acquire an enormous amount of confidential information, not only about resources and data but also about how the entire network infrastructure is set up. The consequences would be dramatic. So it can be seen that in a network environment, both the server and the user must be able to prove their identities.

Certificates

This system of key pairs requires a further level of authentication. A key must be proven to be both valid *and* that it belongs to a particular user or organization. This is accomplished by setting up an entity called a **Certificate Authority (CA),** which issues certificates. A **certificate** is a digital document that verifies that the public key contained in the certificate actually belongs to the entity named in the certificate. A Certificate Authority keeps track (in the Active Directory) of both the public key and a list of the certificates that have been issued.

This system requires that at least one trusted Certificate Authority has been configured. Windows XP supports various certificates, including CA certificates generated by commercial certifying authorities. Although this idea of certificates in not unique to Windows, this operating system differs from most operating systems in that it provides a centralized management and operating system support for the concept.

Kerberos Authentication

Now that key pairs and certificates have provided user identification to other entities on the network, there has to be a method to allow that user to gain access to authorized resources.

Windows XP uses a method for authentication based on the Kerberos version 5 protocol. **Kerberos** is a security system developed at MIT that authenticates users. It does not provide authorization to specific resources, however. Instead, it establishes identity at logon, and this in turn is used throughout the session. Kerberos accomplishes this by creating a session ticket. In Windows XP, when you request access to a network resource you are authorized to access, the ticket Kerberos creates for your session (which contains encrypted data) is passed along to the access control list for that resource. Any Windows XP system supports the Kerberos protocol, and its operation is handled transparently by the operating system. There are no settings for a network administrator to attend to. Computers running an operating system other than XP or Windows 2000 can't use Kerberos for authentication or encryption.

FIREWALLS

The term "firewall" is actually a bit of a misnomer, since what a firewall does in real life is to prevent fires from spreading from one area to another in a building. In computer terms, a **firewall** is anything (be it hardware or software) that inspects traffic between an internal network and the outside world; its function is to block some network traffic and allow other traffic through. Perhaps a better analogy would be a telephone screener, like a secretary, who accepts all the incoming calls for an organization and lets the authorized calls through while blocking the nonauthorized calls. But imagine also that this is a very advanced type of phone screener, so much so that it can block outgoing calls to certain destinations that are off-limits. It also keeps meticulous records of everything it does. This gives you a better sense of what a firewall can do.

Before we continue our discussion of firewalls, let's look at some networking terms, as they will be important in our discussion of firewalls.

Packets are blocks of data. You can think of them as a 100-page report you send via regular mail at the post office. The report, which in this case represents the data, is sent inside an envelope or, rather, multiple envelopes, since you can't get 100 pages inside an envelope (let's pretend). So you have to break the 100-page report into 10 envelopes of 10 pages each. On each envelope is written the From (source) and To (destination) addresses. Also on the envelope might be delivery instructions: first class mail, book rate, confirm delivery, and the like. Since you are sending multiple envelopes, you also have to include some information (such as "Number 3 of 10") written on the outside indicating the order of these different envelopes when the 100-page report broken down into 10 different envelopes, or packets, is put back together on the receiving end. This analogy works the same way in a network. A network packet contains information about the recipient and the sender, special options, what order the related blocks of data belong in on the receiving end, and, finally, the actual data to be delivered.

This information about packets is important because of how a firewall treats these incoming and outgoing blocks of data. These blocks of data are subject to inspection by the firewall in order to determine which ones conform to a list of rules and which ones don't. The firewall checks a list of rules, called packet filters. If the packet conforms with the rules, it is sent on without modification. If not, a packet is discarded and blocked from entry into the network. This process is called packet filtering.

Not only does a firewall block undesirable incoming and outgoing packets based on the information associated with it, but, it remembers that a response is due. When a firewall receives an outgoing packet, it notes that a response will likely be coming back. This feature is called "stateful" packet filtering, as opposed to "stateless," which did not remember a packet's "state." If an unexpected packet arrives at the firewall saying that it is in response to an outgoing packet, the firewall can block the impostor packet.

But advanced firewall features do even more than just packet filtering. An advanced firewall is capable of application proxy. While packet filtering merely allows a packet entry that conforms to the rules, an application proxy re-creates an allowed packet. An actual new packet is built and sent from the firewall. This provides a further layer of security than packet filtering because even a packet that meets with your guidelines can still contain undesirable material, such as a virus. By replacing the packet with a new one created by the application proxy function of a firewall, you ensure that this doesn't happen.

Another important networking term concerning firewalls is "IP addressing." An IP address is the address of a computer attached to a network. IP addresses are unique on the Internet; theoretically at least, no two computers own the same IP address. Going back to our post office analogy, that would be like two people sharing the same address (again, let's pretend that's not possible even though it happens in the real world that two or more people live at the same address). An IP address is represented by four sets of numbers separated by periods. Further, every IP address is composed of two parts: some of the numbers represent the address of the network and some of the numbers represent the address of the host. (A ***host*** indicates any device connected via an IP address to a network.) The reason IP addressing is important in terms of firewalls is not only because certain IP addresses can be blocked from network entry but also because of Network Address Translation (NAT).

With NAT, the world outside your network sees only one IP address outside of the firewall. This has obvious advantages in terms of security and keeping confidential IP addresses within your organization confidential. But in addition, while NAT displays a public address for all the world to see, it also frees your internal network to use any private IP address. NAT was originally designed to provide additional *internal* IP addresses to networks so that there would not be a shortage of IP addresses with the growing popularity of the Internet. With NAT, all computers on the internal network use a private range of IP addresses. When they make a connection with the outside world, the NAT computer replaces the private IP address listed as source IP address with its own public IP address. The destination computer on the Internet thinks the original sender is the public IP address and responds back to this IP address. The NAT computer receives a response for the public IP address and replaces the destination IP address with the original address to go full circle on the internal network.

Finally, another important term from the standpoint of firewalls is *port.* A port is a number assigned to an application (it can also mean a point of connection to your computer, but it is the former definition that we are talking about here). It indicates the application both outside the network and inside the network that needs to communicate in order to deliver the data in a packet. The port number indicates where a packet has come from and where it wants to go. Again, this is important because a firewall can be configured to block or allow certain packets based on their port numbers.

anotherword

Keep in mind that separating the Internet from your internal network traffic is the default behavior of most firewalls. Since what you *want* to be able to do is access the Internet, probably the first thing you will do after installing a firewall is change the defaults and allow selected traffic through.

See Figure 9.13 for the most common functions of firewalls.

FIGURE 9.13

Firewall functions

Function	Description
Blockage of incoming traffic based on where it came from (source) or where it's going (destination)	This is the most common usage for a firewall, namely, to block unwanted traffic coming from outside your organization
Blockage of outgoing traffic based on source or destination	Firewalls also screen your internal network traffic from visiting unwanted Web sites. This is a more advanced feature of some firewalls
Blockage of incoming traffic based on its content	Advanced firewalls can screen traffic for viruses, for example
Block or allow access to internal resources	Firewalls can be configured to prevent or permit access to individual resources inside your network
Allow remote access connections to your network	Some firewalls make it easy for people working outside of an office—either on the road or from home—to access their organization's internal network
Feedback on traffic and firewall activities	A reporting mechanism that logs firewall activity, used, for example, to see who tried to enter your network or access resources that are off-limits

Windows Firewall Services

The latest versions of Windows have included many aspects of security as part of the operating system, including firewalls. The question then is whether it is necessary to get a separate firewall product if you have Windows running on the machines that connect to the Internet. Given the discussion we've just had about what a firewall can do, let's take a look at what the firewall features of Windows XP are.

- *Packet filtering.* Windows XP can be programmed to allow or block incoming or outgoing traffic based on port, source, and destination address
- *Network Address Translation (NAT).* Windows XP Professional contains a simplified version of NAT called Internet Connection Sharing (ICS). Windows 2000 Server contains an implementation of NAT as a part of Routing and Remote Access Service
- *Encrypted tunneling to permit remote access connections to your network.* Windows XP can create a Virtual Private Network (VPN) connection using L2TP technology. IPSec can also be used to authenticate or encrypt data packets traveling between two Windows XP computers connected to the Internet without using a VPN connection

Some of the shortcomings of Windows with regards to advanced firewall features are:

- Windows XP cannot take advantage of application proxies
- Windows XP can report events in the Event logs, but this is not the same as the reporting mechanisms built into firewalls

Thus, the answer to the question about whether to use only the Windows operating system as a firewall is dependent on your security needs. Most companies will want to use a dedicated firewall product to protect their connection to the Internet.

With this in mind, let's take a look at the Internet Connection Firewall (ICF) included as part of XP. ICF is a stateful firewall that keeps a table of all communications that have originated from the ICF computer. All inbound traffic from the Internet is compared against the entries in the table. Inbound Internet traffic is only allowed to reach the computers in your network when there is a matching entry in the table that shows that the communication exchange began from within your computer or private network.

another word

Do not enable Internet Connection Firewall (ICF) on any connection that does not directly connect to the Internet as it will interfere with communications with other computers on the network. For example, if you have a small office or home office network and each computer connects through a hub or gateway to the Internet, ICF should not be enabled.

task reference

Enabling the Internet Connection Firewall

- Click **Start, Connect To, Show All Connections**
- Right-click the icon for your Internet connection and click **Properties**
- In the **Advanced** tab, click the check box in the ICF area
- Click **OK**

WINDOWS XP

FIGURE 9.14

Enabling Internet Connection Firewall

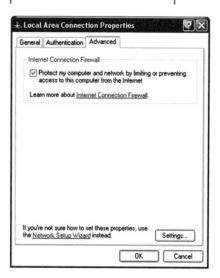

SESSION 9.3   *making the grade*

1. In a key pair, a _____ key is transmitted to others and a _____ key is closely held.

2. A certificate is a digital document that verifies that the _____ contained in the certificate actually belongs to the entity named in the certificate.

3. The entity that authenticates that a key is both valid and belongs to a particular individual or enterprise is called a _____.

4. Windows XP supports three authentication methods: _____, _____, and _____.

5. A _____ is either hardware or software that inspects traffic between an internal network and the outside world; its function is to block some traffic and allow other traffic through.

SESSION 9.5 SUMMARY

In this chapter you learned some of the security considerations dealing with having too much security versus too little. You also learned what security is and why it is important to any organization. You studied the importance of security planning and learned some strategies of how to prepare a plan. You learned what some of the potential security threats are and were given a profile of how an actual attack takes place. You learned about the Windows XP security model and the improvements that have been made over previous versions of Windows. You also studied passwords, what they accomplish, and what the best practices are to manage them.

Next, you learned what a user is and why this designation is so important to security in Windows. After that we discussed groups and the different types of groups. Next we studied permissions and how they interact with one another.

The final session presented the three major types of authentication used in Windows: key encryption, Kerberos, and certificates. Last, we learned what a firewall is and what the functions and features are.

task reference roundup

Task	Page #	Preferred Method
Changing your password	WINXP 9.8	• Press and hold the **Ctrl** and **Alt** keys as you press the **Delete** key
		• Click **Change Password**
		• Type your old password and your new password
		• Click **OK,** then **OK** again
Adding a new user	WINXP 9.10	• Navigate to the **Control Panel** and double-click **User Accounts**
		• Click the **Create a new account** link
		• Type a name for the new user and click **Next**
		• Choose an account type for the new user, then click **Create Account**
		• Click **Change an Account,** click the new user you just created, then click **Create Password**
		• Type a password twice, then click **Create Password**
Switching from the current user to another	WINXP 9.13	• Click **Start,** then **Log Off**
		• Click **Switch User**
		• Select the user name from the Welcome screen
Adding new groups	WINXP 9.15	• Navigate to the Computer Management window **(Start, Control Panel, Administrative Tools, Computer Management)**
		• Click the plus sign next to *Local Groups and Users,* then right-click **Groups**
		• Click **New Group . . .** from the context menu
		• Type a Group name and description, then click **Add**
		• Click the users to add, then click the **Add** button. Click **OK** when done
		• Click the **Create** button, then click **Close**
Deleting a user or group	WINXP 9.16	• Navigate to the Computer Management window **(Start, Control Panel, Administrative Tools, Computer Management)**
		• Click the plus sign next to *Local Groups and Users,* then click **Groups**
		• Right-click the group you want to delete
		• Click **Delete** from the context menu
Changing permissions for a shared folder	WINXP 9.19	• Click to select the folder you wish to change permissions for; then click **File,** then **Sharing and Security . . .**
		• Click the **Permissions** button
		• Click one of the listings under *Group or user names* to view their permissions and click in a check box to change the permission type to allow or deny
		• To add a user or group, click the **Add** button

task reference roundup

Task	Page #	Preferred Method
		• Click the name of the user or group you want to allow access to, then click **Add**
		• Click **OK**
Enabling the Internet Connection Firewall	WINXP 9.27	• Click **Start, Connect To, Show All Connections**
		• Right-click the icon for your Internet connection and click **Properties**
		• In the **Advanced** tab, click the check box in the ICF area
		• Click **OK**

CROSSWORD PUZZLE

Across

1. An entity that authenticates that a key is both valid and that it belongs to a particular individual or enterprise
7. A secret word or code used as a security measure against unauthorized access to data and resources
9. A process by which permissions assigned to a parent folder are all applied to the subfolders and files of that parent folder
12. A rule associated with an object that determines which users or groups have access and abilities to that object
13. A shared key that is secret and previously agreed on by two users

Down

1. A digital document that verifies that the public key contained in the certificate actually belongs to the entity names in the certificate
2. Hardware or software that filters all traffic between your network and the Internet
3. A collection of access control entries
4. What a user actually has access to, according to the rules that govern overlapping permissions
5. The user's personal preferences for his or her computer including such things as how the Desktop is displayed, network connections, printer settings
6. A collection of user accounts
8. The protection of data against unauthorized access
10. An Internet security protocol that authenticates users
11. A computer term meaning specifically or preciseness

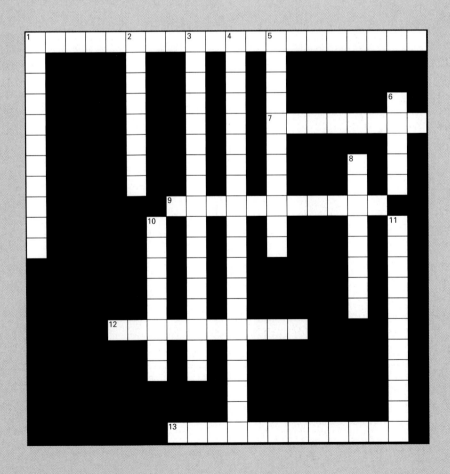

review of concepts

FILL-IN

1. A _____ is the user's personal preferences for his or her computer, including such things as how the Desktop is displayed, network connections, printer settings, and the like.

2. For someone new, it is wise to select the _____ option, as they will automatically be placed in the Users group.

3. Always _____ before leaving your computer unattended.

4. _____ permissions are stored in a central server and managed by the network administrator and provide greater protection than share level security, which is the security model for older versions of Windows.

5. _____ both authenticates a user and creates a session ticket.

CREATE THE QUESTION

For each of the following answers, create an appropriate, short question.

ANSWER

1. This profile is saved on a network server and is available on any computer within the network. The profile is particularly useful if you "roam" about a building and need to use whatever computer is at hand

2. A group for temporary or infrequent users with limited access and abilities, for instance, someone who connects via a computer outside your network to use shared folders

3. This permission allows overwriting of the file, changing attributes, viewing its ownership, and viewing the permissions

4. This security component is (ideally) easy for you to remember, but hard for others to guess

5. This security device analyzes traffic that passes between the Internet and your network and only allows approved protocols that you have designated to pass through

QUESTION

1. _____

2. _____

3. _____

4. _____

5. _____

TRUE OR FALSE

1. Removing a group or a user is permanent.

2. If the same user is a member of one group that is allowed access to a file and another group that is denied access to the same file, then this user would not gain access to the file.

3. When creating a new user account, you are asked to provide a user name and an authentication method.

4. Deny permission always overrides access permission.

5. If you want someone to be able to modify a file, but not delete it, assign the user Modify permission.

1. Adding Users, User Names, and Passwords

Crown, Cork and Bottle Corporation manufactures beverage packaging materials such as glass bottles, paper labels, as well as the caps and corks. Although this has been their core business for more than 50 years, recent trends have resulted in loss of market share. Many customers, especially juice customers, are packing more and more of their beverage lines in tetra-pack containers (the square aseptic drink packs used for children's lunch boxes). Since they don't have the expertise in tetra-packs, Crown, Cork and Bottle is hiring four new employees who have experience in this packaging area to develop the new lines of containers. These new employees will do the research and make recommendations as to new equipment to be bought, package designs, purchase of raw materials, all the way to the production marketing supplies such as brochures and product samples.

The new employees will need to work together much of the time and share resources. They will also need to be integrated into the existing network at Crown, Cork and Bottle. Since the plan is for this new division of the company to lead the sales growth for some time, eventually there will be additional new employees to accommodate.

You are brought in to set up User accounts for each of the four employees. Their names are:

1. Robert Stanton
2. Linda Ramirez
3. Leslie Warren
4. Arnold Lee

Using the methods discussed in this chapter for adding new users, create four new user accounts for each of these employees on your computer. Assign them user names and passwords (according to company policy, passwords must be 10 characters and include uppercase and lowercase letters, numbers, and symbols). Type a description for each user account indicating "Tetra-Pak Division." Designate each new user account as a Limited User.

1. Navigate to **Start, Control Panel, Users Accounts**
2. Click the **Create a new account** link
3. Using the list above, type a user name in the text box. Use the person's first initial and last name, for example, **rstanton** for the first name on the list. Click **Next** when done
4. Assign the user the **Limited** account type and click the **Create Account** button
5. Create a password for each new user that conforms to Crown, Cork and Bottle policy (at least eight characters long including uppercase and lowercase letters, numbers, and symbols; for example, use **!bObIeS159** for the first password). Type the password again in the *Confirm Password* text box, then click **Next**
6. Repeat this procedure for each of the additional names listed above

2. Switching Users

All Points Diving Inc. runs training classes for people who wish to be certified as scuba divers. All Points also offers advanced certification, sells diving equipment, and books travel packages for diving vacations. There are three locations for All Points Diving, and all the computers in each location are networked together using Windows XP.

Susan and Julie work different hours but share the same computer at one location. A couple of days a week their hours overlap and they both need to access the network. They need to be able to switch back and forth rapidly between each other on the computer. Susan comes to you asking for help. You explain that users can switch among themselves by logging off and on.

You will need to create two new user accounts on your computer named Susan and Julie before beginning this exercise.

1. Click **Start,** then **Log Off**
2. Click **Switch User**
3. Select the user name from the Welcome screen

When finished, assign Susan and Julie new passwords.

challenge!

1. Changing a Permission to Protect a Folder

Earl Mayo has just had two salespeople leave his company, Industrial Lubricants Unlimited (ILU), to work for a competitor. He plans to have two new sales hires shortly, but for now he is concerned about preventing the old employees from accessing the Industrial Lubricants sales database file, located in the ILU Sales Database Folder.

He asks you to help him. In his haste to prevent unauthorized access, Earl has denied access to the Everyone group. He asks you to get access back for himself without allowing anyone else. You know a best practice is to use share level permissions whenever possible, because file level permissions can get very complicated quickly and ILU does not have someone in-house with the skill or the time to manage file level permissions.

Using share level permissions, how do you get access to the ILU Sales Database File for Earl again? Create a folder named **ILU Sales Database Folder** and share it. Access the Properties dialog box and change the permissions so that only the Administrators group has permission to access that file in any way.

Another issue is that new hires are coming, and you are going to have to provide them with access to the same database. What's the best way to do that? Your first impulse is to just delete the old employees' user accounts. Why is that not such a good idea?

1. Creating Online Resources

www.foreign-trade.com is a B2B (business-to-business) Web site dedicated to providing information about all different types of trade-related topics. It also provides all types of tools such as metric and currency conversions.

Mandy Pappas is in charge of training new employees for Trading Specialists Corporation, a large multinational company. Mandy wants to provide information about resources online such as www.foreign-trade.com to her students to use after they graduate from her training sessions and have the skills. What she doesn't want is to let her students take a shortcut by having the Web page work out the metric and currency conversion problems she assigns.

You advise her to create a shared folder, which contains the links to this and other useful Web sites. By setting the permissions to the folder as Read only, the students will not be able to click the links to the sites, but will have a list of places they can use after they graduate.

1. Create a new folder called **Foreign Trade Sites**
2. Right-click on this folder and select **Sharing and security . . .** from the context menu
3. Click the *Share this folder on the network* check box
4. Click the **Permissions** button. The Permissions for Foreign Trade sites dialog box opens
5. Click the **Everyone** group to select it
6. Click the check boxes next to *Full Control* and *Change* to de-select these permissions and only allow the Read permission
7. Click **OK,** then **OK** again

FIGURE 9.15

The foreign-trade.com home Web page

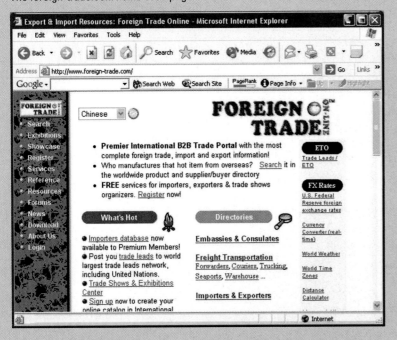

e-business

1. Securing Online Transactions

Weaver & Nelson Securities is a large stock brokerage firm that is making a big push to increase its Internet presence. Their market research has determined that one of the major reasons people do not buy and sell financial securities online is fear that the information will not be secure. Weaver & Nelson has spent a great deal of money preparing their Web site; they also plan on buying a lot of print and TV advertising. Consequently, they have a considerable investment in overcoming this security concern.

You were invited to a meeting with management where they declared that the new emphasis must be security. Management wants the hundreds of thousands of W&N customers to be able to connect to their Web site and buy and sell stocks privately without worry. It is also important to management to educate the salespeople so that they can push the security of the site to prospective customers with utmost confidence.

Using the concepts discussed in this chapter—including passwords, Virtual Private Networks, and authentication methods—write a short memo in WordPad to the management at W&N about how their goals can be met. Title it **W&N Security Proposals** with **by <your name>** underneath and print it out.

1. Creating Secure, Memorable Passwords

Rajiv Kumar manages Working-Wallah magazine, a humorous biweekly newsletter for Indians working in the United States who are nostalgic for home. Although his office is in Hicksville, New York, Rajiv gets article contributions from multiple authors based in different cities in India. Each of these authors prepares the article file on his or her local computer and then logs on to an ftp site on the Internet and posts the articles there. Rajiv wants to assign a unique and secure password to each of these contributors, but also wants the passwords to be easy to remember so that the users don't have to resort to writing them down because that would compromise security. He knows that if the contributors have to write the passwords down and keep the paper handy to the computer, it will defeat the purpose of creating the password.

Each of the authors writes from the following cities:

1. New Delhi
2. Bangalore
3. Bombay
4. Madras
5. Calcutta

Rajiv asks you for ideas about new passwords. You recommend that each password be eight-plus characters long and contain a mix of uppercase and lowercase letters, symbols, and numbers.

In order to do this exercise, you will need permission to change your password several times. At the end of the exercise, instead of entering your old password again, take this opportunity to create a new password for yourself.

1. Press and hold down the **Ctrl** and **Alt** keys, then press the **Delete** key
2. Click **Change Password**
3. Type your old password and then the new password for the first city, **1New?Delhi0**
4. Type the new password again to confirm it
5. Click **OK,** then **OK** again. Repeat steps 1 through 5 for each of the following passwords:

   2Bang!Lore9
   3Bom&Bay8
   4Ma*Dras7
   5Cal$Cutta6

did you

know?

a clothing company in Italy is marketing a coat called L.E.D., which tests the air quality around it. A microcomputer in the right breast pocket is connected to a filter and sensor that tests the air for methane, propane, Freon, and other gases. An illuminated scale gives the wearer an indication of whether the levels of these gases are above normal. Such purity comes at a price, however; the coat retails for $1,000.

about 75,000 Americans own businesses that operate only on eBay's Web site.

an exotic musical instrument, the glass harmonica, was invented by Benjamin Franklin in 1761 and had music written for it by Mozart and Beethoven. The instrument is made of hand-blown, tuned crystal bowls mounted sideways on a rotating spindle. Touching the turning edges of the bowls with wet fingers plays it. The otherworldly, flute-like tones it produces were used by Dr. Franz Mesmer to relax his patients during hypnosis. It fell out of favor because of claims that its otherworldly tones could shatter one's nerves, and it was banned in some German towns.

Chapter Objectives

- Learn what a compound document is
- Understand the difference between a server file and a container file
- Learn what ClipBook is and how to use it
- Practice copying objects from one application to another
- Understand the difference between an embedded object and a linked object
- Practice editing embedded objects
- Practice inserting a graphic into another application
- Learn what a scrap is and how it can improve your productivity
- Practice linking an object
- Practice editing a linked object
- Learn what .NET is
- Learn basic DOS commands

chapter case

Wiggins Wood Frames, Pine Bluff, Arkansas

Wiggins Wood Frames is a local manufacturer in Pine Bluff, Arkansas, and one of the leading producers of wood frames in the United States. Wiggins Frames, unlike other frame manufacturers, only makes wood frames and is known for its traditional country designs. Each product line uses different types of wood and is made from molds that were originally created in the 1950s. These designs are well regarded and distributed throughout much of the country.

Recently, under the impetus of the current president, Carl Wiggins, the company has developed some more modern lines with a Scandinavian look.

FIGURE 10.1

Wiggins Sales Report—1st version

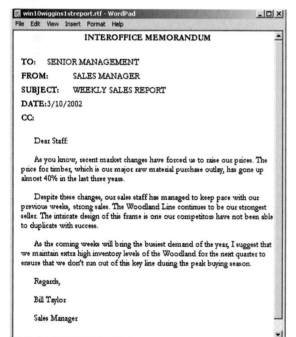

These new products have been very successful and in fact have revitalized demand for all types of wood frames. Over the last five years, Wiggins Frames has seen sales grow almost 60 percent. Because of this increase in business, new employees have been hired, the company has moved into larger quarters, and the need for greater sales coordination has arisen.

Carl Wiggins wants all senior management to keep in touch with sales developments. In order to do this, he institutes a weekly system of sales reporting. Every Friday at 5 p.m., the sales figures for the week will be sent to all senior management. The report will be in the form of a memo from the sales manager.

Ian Herold is one of the new additions at Wiggins Wood Frames. Among other tasks, he is responsible for the preparation and distribution of the sales report every Friday. He comes to you for help. The sales manager sends his report and comments to Ian in the form of a WordPad document. After going over what is needed, you show Ian how this information can be used for the body of the report by copying and pasting the sales manager's comments into a Memo template you have created. See Figure 10.1 to view the first report you help Ian put together.

SESSION 10.1 EMBEDDING OBJECTS

In chapter two, you learned that you can copy and paste data from one location in a document to another. The copied information gets stored in the Clipboard until it is pasted. This seemingly simple operation, however, becomes much more impressive and useful when implemented across different applications.

WORKING WITH CLIPBOOK

The Clipboard that's built into Windows XP allows you to take any material —document text, a video clip, or a digital image—and copy and paste it between the Desktop, the Internet, or any files and folders in your computer. The Clipboard serves as a temporary storage location for the last data that's been copied.

Although the Clipboard is useful, it has some drawbacks. For example, as soon as you copy new data, the data that were previously copied are written over, so you're limited to working with one item at a time. Additionally, sometimes you just forget what is copied into the Clipboard. **ClipBook** is a program bundled into Windows XP that allows you to handle and manage the items you've copied. ClipBook works together with Clipboard to provide added functionality. Let's take a look at how this works.

---

task reference

Viewing the Clipboard's Contents Using ClipBook

- Click **Start,** then **Run**

- In the Open dialog box, type **clipbrd.exe,** then press **Enter**

- Click **Window,** then **Clipboard** to display the contents of the Clipboard (Figure 10.2)

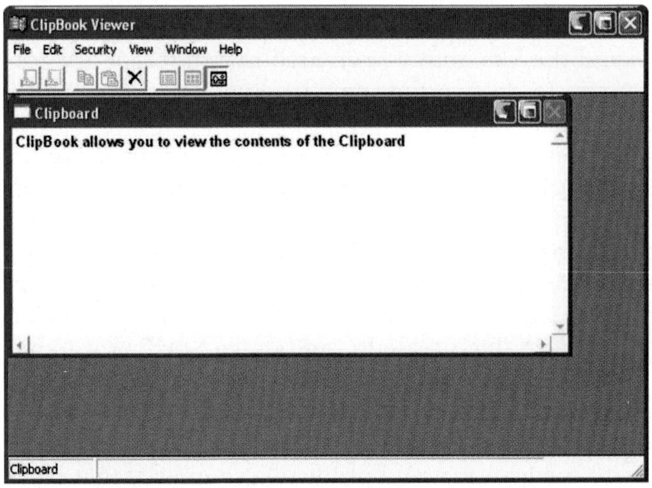

FIGURE 10.2

ClipBook allows you to view the contents of the Clipboard

In addition to viewing what's been copied in ClipBook, you can also paste an item into one of ClipBook's pages (up to 127) and give the page a name and description for future reference. You can also share the item for use by others on your network who have ClipBook installed on their computers, and they can share their ClipBook pages with you.

---

reference

Pasting Items into ClipBook

- Copy the desired data

- Open ClipBook

- Click **Window,** then **Local ClipBook**

- Click **Edit,** then **Paste**

- Type a name for the page in the Paste dialog box

- If you want to make the page available to others on your network, click the **Share Item Now** check box

- Click **OK**

In addition to creating a page in ClipBook, you can save what's been copied in a file format for later use. These files generally have the extension .clp and cannot be shared with others.

---

reference

Saving Contents Using ClipBook

- In ClipBook, click **File,** then **Save as . . .**

- Choose a location to save the file and type a name for it, leaving the filename extension as .clp

- Click the **Save** button

COPYING OBJECTS BETWEEN DIFFERENT APPLICATIONS

Often when working on a document it is useful to incorporate graphics, charts, spreadsheets, and the like, that you created in a different application. Windows allows you to do this the same way you would copy and paste within the same application.

This type of communication between different applications is known as OLE (pronounced oh-lay), which stands for *object linking and embedding.* OLE allows for the creation of a document that contains objects created in different applications than the one in which the document appears. For the purpose of this chapter, the term "object" means a piece of data, in the form of a graphic, spreadsheet, sound file, logo, and so forth, which you copy from an application that created it and embed or link it to another application.

For example, say you wanted to produce a birthday greeting for your mother. You compose a birthday message in Microsoft Word, create a graphic to go along with the greeting, and produce a sound file that plays "Happy Birthday." The graphic and sound objects can be placed, or embedded, in the Word document so that the finished document seamlessly contains all these disparate elements. Such a document is known as a *compound document,* because it contains objects from more than one application. The file that the objects are pasted into is known as the "client," "target," or "container" file, while the original file that produced the objects is known as the "source" or "server" file. The object that is placed in the container document is said to be "embedded" in that document, meaning that it is now a part of that compound document.

Windows puts whatever you have copied from one application into the Clipboard. This action is transparent to you as a user. When you execute either a cut or copy command in the original document, Windows copies the object into this area. When you select the new area in a different application and paste, the object is copied from the Clipboard in the location of the insertion point in the new file. Keep in mind that if you choose the cut command, the object is removed from the original location. If you choose copy, the object remains in its original document and a copy is made that is then put into the Clipboard.

---

task reference

Copying Objects between Different Applications

- Open the server document and select the desired object

- Click **Edit,** then **Copy**

- Open the container document and select the location where you want the information to be copied

- Click **Edit,** then **Paste**

Copying objects between different applications:

1. Open the Paint application **(Start, All Programs, Accessories, Paint)**

2. In Paint, click **File,** then **Open.** The Open dialog box appears

3. In the *Look in* drop-down list near the top of the box, navigate to **My Computer/Local Disk (C:)/Windows.** Inside the Windows folder, click the file named **Gone Fishing,** then click the **Open** button. A graphic object appears in Paint like the one shown in Figure 10.3

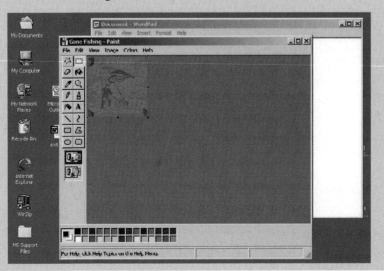

FIGURE 10.3

The Gone Fishing graphic displayed in Paint

4. From the **Edit** menu click **Select All**

5. From the **Edit** menu click **Copy.** The graphic object is copied to the Clipboard

6. Open the WordPad application **(Start, Programs, Accessories, WordPad)**

7. Click anywhere in the open WordPad Window; then from the **Edit** menu click **Paste.** The Gone Fishing graphic object now appears in the WordPad document

8. Save this document to your Desktop and name it **Gone Fishing**

Copying a bar graph from one application to another:

Ian comes to you and says that he showed the initial draft of the weekly sales memo to the sales manager and he approved of it. The sales manager did say, though, that he wants to include a bar graph of the week's sales as part of the memo. This would be more interesting visually and provide an additional level of information to management. Ian tells you a sales administrator in Excel generates the bar graph. He wonders how you will be able to include something like this from a different application into the report, which is in WordPad. You explain that you will be able to cut and paste the bar graph right into the memo, just like one does within the same application.

1. Open the file containing the information you wish to copy, located in your data files in the **Wiggins Wood Frames** folder and named **xp10wigginsgraph.rtf**

2. Select the Wiggins Wood Frames bar graph

tip: *It depends on what program you are in, but usually this is done by double-clicking the object or dragging the cursor around the object to select it.*

3. In the **Edit** menu click **Copy.** Windows copies the selected information into the Clipboard (you will not see the information copied into the Clipboard)

4. Open the file you want to copy the information into; this again is located in the **Wiggins Wood Frames** folder and named **xp10wiggins1streport.rtf**

5. Place the insertion point on the spot within the document where you want the information in the Clipboard to be placed, which in this case is in the blank space between the second and third paragraph

6. In the **Edit** menu click **Paste.** The information in the Clipboard is pasted into the document

7. The bar graph should appear inserted in the body of the memo like Figure 10.4. Save the document as **Wiggins Sales Report2**

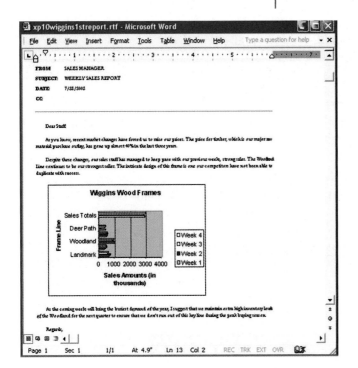

FIGURE 10.4
The Wiggins Sales Report with the bar graph inserted

EDITING EMBEDDED OBJECTS

The object that you have embedded in the container document is now a part of that document. It can be edited right there. There is no need to go back to the original application. In fact, Windows does an interesting thing to enable you to make your changes. When the object you have embedded is selected, Windows displays a unique interface that combines elements of both the server and client applications.

One thing to keep in mind when editing an embedded object is that the server application that originally created the object must be installed on your computer. If not, you will not be able to change the object. If you distribute an Excel spreadsheet, for example, the recipients must have the Excel application on their computer. It must also be the same version as the one that created the object. This limitation is discussed later in this chapter in relation to DCOM, which allows you to make changes even if you do not have the server application. For now, however, it is important to keep this limitation in mind.

anotherway

You can also choose to convert the object you have embedded in the container document to have it display as an icon, rather than as the object itself. This can be useful because your computer will use less memory and run faster this way. You can convert the object in the **Edit** menu by choosing **Convert . . .** In any case, regardless of how you decide to display the object, you can still edit it.

task reference

Editing an Embedded Object

- Open the document that contains the embedded object

- Double-click the embedded object

- Make the desired changes to the object

- When finished editing the object, click anywhere outside the object within the document

Changing an embedded object:

1. Open the Gone Fishing document you created earlier

tip: *Only one embedded object can be edited at a time.*

2. Move your mouse over the lower right-hand corner of the graphic until a double-pointed arrow appears; then click and, holding down your right mouse button, drag down and to the right to enlarge the image

3. Right-click the graphic object, highlight **Bitmap Image Object,** then click **Edit.** Note that the toolbars and menus of Paint appear while the Title bar still indicates that you are in WordPad

F I G U R E 10.5

The edit object interface, with the toolbars and menus of Paint while still inside WordPad

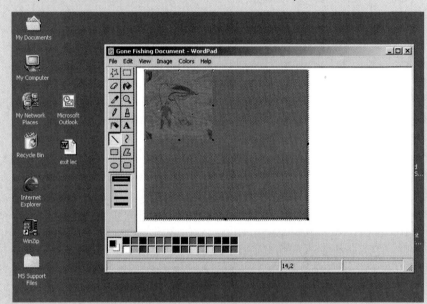

4. Use the Line tool from the Toolbox on the left to draw a border around the graphic object

5. When finished, click anywhere outside the object within the document. The original program interface returns

---

SESSION 10.1

making the grade

1. OLE stands for _____.

2. An _____ is a piece of data, in the form of a graphic, spreadsheet, sound file, logo, and the like, which you copy from an application that created it and embed or link it to another application.

3. A _____ is a document that contains objects from more than one application.

4. The object that is placed in the container document is said to be _____ in that document, meaning that it is now a part of that compound document.

5. Windows puts whatever you have copied into a temporary storage area called the _____.

SESSION 10.2 WORKING WITH OBJECTS

Now that some of the concepts of exchanging data between applications have been explored, we can look at other useful techniques of interapplication communication. As we will continue to see in this session, this entire topic is one that adds enormous amounts of functionality to your computer.

DRAGGING AND DROPPING DATA BETWEEN APPLICATIONS

As you have already learned, you can drag data from its current location within a document to another part of the same document or to another document within the same application. Many applications also allow you to drag and drop data between them. For instance, if both documents in different applications are displayed on your screen, simply highlighting the data in one document and then dragging it to where you want it in the new document will work.

Even if the target document is not displayed on your screen because it is minimized, you can still drag the selected data to its location on the taskbar. If you continue holding down your mouse button, in a couple of moments the document window opens on your screen and you can drag and drop as usual.

Certain programs will only act as servers in this exchange of data, not as clients. For example, you cannot drag an object you created in WordPad to Paint. You can do the opposite (as demonstrated earlier in this chapter). This issue of which applications can be servers and which can be clients (and which can be both) is something you need to be cognizant of, and it varies from application to application. Besides checking the manual, the quickest way to find out what a particular application supports is by experimenting with it. An icon appears as you drag the data across your screen and your cursor passes over the different files on it; if the icon changes to a circle with a slash through it, this means that you cannot drag and drop to that file.

---

task reference

Dragging and Dropping Data between Applications

- Open the server document and the container document
- Select the desired object
- Holding down the Ctrl key, drag the object to the target document

---

Dragging and dropping data between applications:

Because the report is put together quickly at the last minute on Friday afternoon, Ian wants to make sure that it is being done the quickest possible way. You show him that actually there is another way to move data in between different applications and that is by dragging and dropping. You explain that not all programs support it, but it is always a good idea to try as it makes the process of creating a compound document quicker. But it is better to have learned first to do it the way it works whenever data exchange is supported. This way, if dragging and dropping doesn't work, you can always go back to the tried and true method.

1. Open the file containing the information you wish to copy, the source document, located in your data files in the **Wiggins Wood Frames** folder and named **xp10wigginsgraph.rtf**

2. Open the file you want to paste into, the target document, named **xp10wiggins1streport.rtf**, located in the same folder

3. Position the two documents so that they are displayed side by side on your screen and so that you can see as much as possible of both windows regardless of which window is selected, similar to the position shown in Figure 10.6

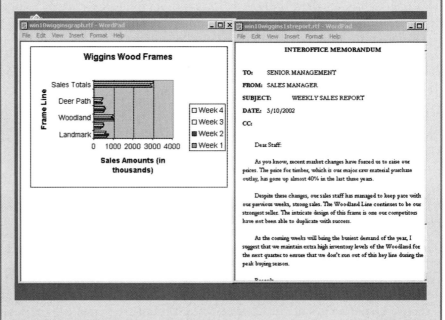

tip: *This fiddling with the position of the windows is for ease of demonstration; in reality all you really need is just enough room to get your mouse onto a sliver of each window.*

4. Select the Wiggins Wood Frames bar graph by double-clicking it

5. Place your mouse over the selected graph and, holding down the **Ctrl** key, drag the graph over to the **xp10wiggins1streport.rtf** window, to the location in between the second and third paragraphs. The graph should appear in the body of the sales memo as in Figure 10.7

another way

There is an easy way to go back and forth between open documents within the same application by clicking the **Window** menu and selecting the document you want.

task reference

Inserting a Graphic in Another Application

- Open the server document and select the desired object

- From the **Edit** menu click **Copy**

- Open the container document and select the location where you want the information to be copied

- From the **Edit** menu click **Paste**

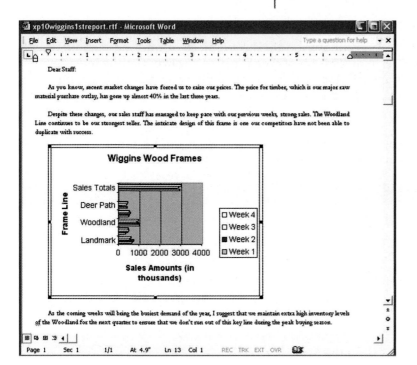

The Wiggins Sales Report with
the bar graph inserted

Inserting a graphic in another application:

One of the designers of the new Scandinavian lines is flying in from out of town
to attend a wood frame exhibition in Little Rock. Several competitors of Wiggins
will be there. To take advantage of this opportunity, some of the managers are
going to meet with the designer. In addition to letting the managers know the
time and date of the exhibit, the president wants to include a map of directions
to the conference center. He tells Ian that he has a graphic in Paint that he
wants to insert. He sends the graphic to Ian, who tries the method described
above to drag and drop the map into the Weekly Sales Report, but it doesn't
work. Ian realizes that Paint is one of the programs that this procedure doesn't
work with. He will have to use a standard method with cut and paste.

1. In the Wiggins Wood Frames folder of your data files, open the
   server file, **xp10exhibitmap,** which contains the map you
   want to place in the target document

2. In the **Edit** menu click **Select All.** The map is selected

3. In the **Edit** menu click **Copy.** The map is copied into the
   Clipboard

4. Open the target document, **xp10exhibit,** and click after the
   last paragraph of the memo where you want the map to be
   placed

5. In the **Edit** menu click **Paste.** The object is embedded in the
   target document in the specified location

6. Save the **xp10exhibit** document

WORKING WITH SCRAPS

Some applications allow you to select a piece of information and drag it onto your Desktop. This bit of data is called a *scrap.* Getting into the habit of using scraps will increase your productivity as having frequently used data on your Desktop provides you with quicker access than if the information is in a file. A scrap can be anything: a company logo, a sound file, or the standard ending you use for all your memos and letters.

If the application doesn't support dragging and dropping with scraps, then you will have to cut and paste, as shown earlier.

---

task **reference**

Dragging and Dropping a Document Scrap

- Select and drag the desired information from the server document onto your Desktop

- Drag and drop the scrap from the Desktop into the target document

---

Dragging and dropping a document scrap:

The president of Wiggins Wood Frames tells Ian that he wants to tag a little comment (in addition to the more lengthy comments the sales manager makes in the body of the memo) to the Weekly Sales Report before it gets passed around to the senior staff. Usually the comment is no more than a short phrase, such as "Wonderful job," if it's been a good week, or "Time for the tough to get going," if it's been a bad one. Occasionally, the president also likes to pass around an inspirational aphorism. He sends these weekly comments to Ian in an e-mail. Ian tries dragging and dropping from the e-mail program, Outlook Express, but finds he can't do it. He comes back to you to ask what's wrong. You propose asking the president's assistant if he could try sending the message as an attachment to the e-mail in a WordPad document by cutting and pasting. When Ian asks why you requested this, you say that you are trying to get the president's message in an application that supported scraps.

Since the president's comments are short, Ian usually just copies them by typing the comments right into the Weekly Sales Report. Ian realizes now, however, that there is a better solution to the problem. When he gets the comment from the president, he can select it and drag it as a scrap onto his Desktop. After the Weekly Sales Report is done, Ian can simply drag and drop this scrap with the president's comments right into the report.

1. Open the **xp10presmessage.rtf** document containing the scrap you want to put on your Desktop and select the president's message

2. Click and hold down the right mouse button over the selected information and drag it onto your Desktop. An icon that looks like a torn-off scrap of paper appears on your Desktop

3. Open the **xp10wiggins1streport.rtf** document

4. Click the scrap on your Desktop and, holding down the right mouse button, drag the scrap to the end of the body of the document where you want it to be inserted. The scrap appears in the document. Note that the scrap also remains on your Desktop so that you can use it again if you need to

OBJECT LINKING

OLE is more, however, than simple cutting and pasting between applications. The objects from the server file can be linked to the container file, meaning that any changes made in the server file will automatically be reflected in the compound document. This can be very useful if you have a compound document that includes information that is often updated, such as regular performance results.

The difference between embedding an object and linking an object is that when you embed an object, the object becomes a part of the compound document. On the other hand, when an object is linked, it remains a part of the original document and any changes made in that original document will be reflected in the container document. When an object is linked, you are creating a pointer in the container document that refers back to the server file. The object remains in the server document, but a link is established between the two documents. A compound document can have links from several different applications.

The advantage of linking is that you don't have to update the linked document when the server object changes. For example, a sales bar graph that has been linked to a separate document won't need to be updated in the compound document when the original bar graph is updated to reflect current information.

A potential difficulty, however, is that if you move, delete, or rename the server document, the link is broken. This is important to remember since it is usually the reason that links are accidentally broken.

---

reference

Linking an Object

- In the server document that contains the object you want to link, select the object

- In the **Edit** menu click **Copy**

- In the target document where you want to paste the object, click the location where you want the object to appear

- In the **Edit** menu click **Paste Special**

- Click the radio button next to Paste link

- Click **OK**

Linking an object:

Ian has been complaining that the pieces of information for the compound document he has to put together by 5 p.m. on Friday have been coming in very late. In particular, the Sales Department doesn't complete the bar graph until as late as possible because Sales is always expecting something to be coming in at the last minute that will make the sales figures for the week look much better. Additionally, once the bar graph is finally done, the sales manager has to take a few minutes to compose his comments.

Ian is concerned because it is getting more difficult to keep the president's directive to get the report out on time. He has spoken to the sales manager about the late arrival of the bar graph, but the sales manager says the final sales numbers have always been produced at the very end of the day on Friday. The bar graph is actually being done earlier than ever now, and Sales can't afford to trim away any more time. Many orders come in late Friday afternoon, and it is difficult as it is to get them processed and reflected in the bar graph for the week.

Ian comes to you asking about this situation. He says he doesn't want to do it, but he may have to go to the president and explain that he can't be responsible if the report to senior management comes out late.

You listen to his concerns and tell Ian you have an idea. By linking, rather than embedding, the sales graph to the Weekly Report, the graph in the report will automatically be updated along with the main sales graph. This will save a great deal of time.

1. Open the **xp10wigginsgraph,** which contains the graph you wish to link

2. In the **Edit** menu, click **Select All**

3. In the **Edit** menu, click **Copy.** The graph is copied to the Clipboard

4. Open the **xp10wiggins2ndreport.rtf** file and click between the second and third paragraph where you want the graph to appear

5. In the **Edit** menu, click **Paste Special.** The Paste Special dialog box opens (Figure 10.8)

F I G U R E   10.8

The Paste Special dialog box

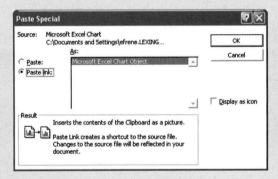

6. Click the *Paste link* radio button

tip: *If the Paste link option is not available, the document selected may not support OLE.*

7. Click **OK.** The object from the server document is now linked to the target document

It is when you need to make changes to the linked object that you really notice the time savings. When you make the change to the object in the server document, all the compound documents that are linked to the object will automatically be updated to reflect the change. This can be very handy if you need to distribute information that changes regularly to a group of users.

Remember that a compound document only contains a pointer to the original object. In order to edit the object, the source document must be open on your computer; in addition, you must have the server application installed on your machine.

To edit the object, you have the choice of making your changes either in the compound document or in the source document where the object was originally created. Since they are linked, both documents will be updated anyway, so the choice is up to you; however, the advantage of doing it in the compound document is that you can see how your changes are affecting the rest of the document. In either case, the user interface will reflect the server application that created the document originally, and you make your changes as you would with any object in that application.

It will usually take no more than a few seconds for the linked object to update itself in all the documents, but if you want to make sure you are dealing with an updated link, choose Links from the Edit menu and you will be able to view and update the links.

---

task reference

Editing a Linked Object

- Double-click the linked object you want to edit in the compound document

- Edit the object

- In the **File** menu, click **Save**

- In the **File** menu, click **Exit**

Editing a linked object:

1. Double-click the linked object you want to edit in the compound document. The server application, which originally created the object, opens with the linked object displayed

2. Edit the object, using the standard toolbars and menus of the program that created the object

3. In the **File** menu, click **Save.** The changes are saved

4. In the **File** menu, click **Exit.** The compound document is displayed with the edited object

---

making the grade   **SESSION 10.2**

1. Certain programs will only act as _____ in exchanging of data, not as clients.

2. Even if the target document is not displayed on your screen because it is minimized, you can still drag the selected data to its location on the _____.

3. An icon appears as you drag data across your screen; if the icon changes to a circle with a slash through it, this means that you cannot _____ to that file.

4. An easy way to go back and forth between open documents within the same application is by clicking the _____ menu and selecting the document you want.

5. A _____ is a bit of data that you can select and drag onto your Desktop.

SESSION 10.3 .NET AND OTHER CONCEPTS

Historically, interapplication communication is a relatively recent development, having only begun in the early 1990s. The booming popularity of the Internet in the mid-1990s led to an even greater emphasis on this topic and also pointed to some of the limitations of existing technology, among them the problem of having to have access on the local machine to the server application that created the object originally.

At one point not too long ago, the concept of having a computer be a "dumb terminal" to the Internet became a hot topic (a dumb terminal is a display terminal without any processing capability that is entirely dependent on a large main computer for processing). The idea was to simply have a local machine that was able to connect to the Internet. All the programs and data, so the thinking went, would be stored online and virtually nothing locally. Some commercial enterprises based their business models on this idea. They offered free computers if the buyers agreed to sign up with them as their exclusive Internet Service Provider for a period of time. While most of these early ventures failed, the concept continues to generate strong interest and development time, especially with the popularity of small handheld computers that don't have very much room for applications and instead rely on accessing the Internet where a server can do the brute processing work. This type of service is known by the acronym ASP, which stands for application service provider, where the user only sees the interface of a Web page while the actual application remains on the server in the provider's network. The provider makes the application available on the Web to users, thereby relieving the user of the trouble of having the hardware and software capabilities to run the program. Thus, the concept of interapplication communication is one that continues to push at the edges of computing.

COM, DCOM, AND ACTIVEX

The underlying technology that makes OLE work is called COM, which stands for Component Object Model. Parts of Windows and other Microsoft applications are built as COM objects. COM provides the interfaces between objects, and Distributed COM (DCOM) allows them to run remotely. COM includes COM+, Distributed Component Object Model (DCOM), and ActiveX.

One of the limitations of OLE is that it only works with documents that you access from your local machine. Additionally, your computer must perform any changes that need to be made in the linked object. In order to address these problems, the Distributed Component Object Model (DCOM) is used. DCOM used to be known as Network OLE, which gives you an idea of what it does. Many Internet and intranet applications use DCOM because it allows objects to be linked over a network. This is particularly useful because the server application can remotely handle all the processing required to edit an object. If you recall, one of the problems with OLE occurs when editing an embedded object. In this case, the server application must be available on your computer; otherwise, you will not be able to change the object. In addition, the version of the application that created the object must be the same. DCOM was designed to overcome these obstacles. DCOM is useful because it allows for different parts of applications to run on different machines while the user only sees one application at work on their interface.

ActiveX is a term primarily used to refer to controls. An ActiveX control was originally known as an "OLE control." These can be user interface functions such as a push button or a toolbar. These controls add functionality while blending in to appear as a normal part of a program. For example, a button in a dialog box is usually an ActiveX control. Sometimes the ActiveX control is hidden, but it still performs its function within an application. Like OLE, ActiveX is also based on COM.

.NET

The term *.NET* is used frequently, yet few people actually understand what it is. Part of the problem is (like many things with computers) that the term can mean different things in different contexts. First, .NET (pronounced "dot net") is a Microsoft initiative designed to replace COM and DCOM. .NET is Microsoft's software platform for the Internet (or an intranet) that allows for the exchange of data regardless of operating system or programming language. .NET is designed to allow for a customized, interactive session.

For example, a purchasing manager for a widget manufacturing company comes to work Monday morning and goes online. With .NET technology in place, he can set up a set of specifications for a particular kind of widget he is looking to buy. The purchasing manager indicates the quantity he is looking for, the price he is willing to pay, the delivery date he needs, and any other specifics. From this the .NET application will search throughout the Internet for potential suppliers and allow for negotiation to take place and an agreement on a price, specifications, delivery time frame, credit terms, and so forth. The .NET application will then allow the purchasing manager to track his order all the way from the plant or warehouse directly to his loading dock. If this sounds too good to be true, you're right in a way. There is software that can do this, but this technology is still in its infancy and is just being adopted in the marketplace. But that is the basic idea.

.NET is also the collective name given to various applications built upon the .NET platform. These are both products (like Windows.NET Server) and services (like .NET Passport). Windows .NET Server is the next upgrade from Windows 2000 Server. XP Professional is designed to be used on a workstation in a network that is managed by a Server operating system. Windows .NET Server manages a whole network of computers running XP Professional (and other operating systems). .NET Passport allows you to access multiple features and services across the Internet using only your e-mail address and password. XP Professional has a .NET Passport Wizard that guides you through the process of setting up a .NET Passport account.

---

task reference

Setting Up a .NET Passport User Account

- Click **Start, Control Panel, User Accounts**
- Click your user account
- Click the **Set up my account to use .NET Passport** link, then click **Next**
- Click the **Yes** radio button, then click **Next**
- Type your e-mail address, then click **Next**
- Type a password, then click **Next**
- Click **Finish**

Setting up a .NET Passport user account:

1. Click **Start,** then **Control Panel.** The Control Panel window opens
2. Click **User Accounts.** The User Accounts window opens
3. Click your user account. A list of tasks that can be performed appears (Figure 10.9)

FIGURE 10.9

The task list in the User Accounts window

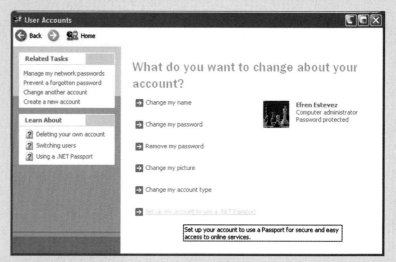

4. Click the **Set up my account to use .NET Passport** link, then click **Next**
5. The .NET Passport Wizard opens (Figure 10.10). Click **Next**

FIGURE 10.10

The .NET Passport Wizard

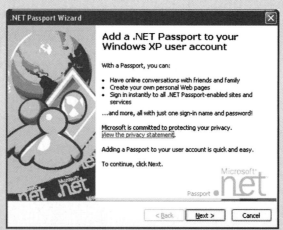

6. Click the **Yes** radio button to confirm that you have an e-mail address, then click **Next**
7. Type your e-mail address in the text box, then click **Next**

tip: *If the e-mail you entered is already associated with Passport, you will get a message to this effect.*

8. Type your password in the *Password* text box, then click **Next**
9. The Wizard displays a screen indicating that your .NET Passport account is set up. Click **Finish**

Once you have a Passport account, Windows enters your information at Web sites that use .NET Passport so you can quickly sign in. Windows retrieves the information stored in your Passport account and uses it to automatically enter it for you.

The Passport service has its critics. Some are concerned that by providing personal information to Microsoft, your privacy may be compromised, for instance, if Microsoft chooses to sell your e-mail address to vendors. These issues may prevent the widespread acceptance of the Passport service. Like the entire .NET initiative, time will tell how these issues play out.

> **another**word
>
> Go to www.passport.com/directory to view a list of Web sites that use .NET Passport.

---

making the grade   **SESSION 10.3**

1. The underlying technology that makes OLE work is called _____.

2. A company that provides an application service, where the user only sees the interface of a Web page while the actual application remains on the server in the provider's network, is called an _____.

3. One of the limitations of OLE is that it only works with documents that you access from your _____.

4. _____ controls add functionality while blending in to appear as a normal part of a program.

5. _____ allows for different parts of applications to run on different machines while the user only sees one application at work.

SESSION 10.4 USING MS-DOS

Going from .NET to DOS we move from the future of Microsoft computing to the past. MS-DOS established a Microsoft operating system as the standard for computing in the very early 1980s. MS-DOS, or DOS for short, precedes every version of Windows. At a basic level, every succeeding Windows operating system is based on DOS. Before there was a GUI (Graphic User Interface—popularized by the Apple Macintosh and later adopted by Microsoft into Windows), there was DOS performing text-based command line functions.

In a field where things go out of date constantly, you may wonder why it is worthwhile to study something as ancient as DOS. The world of DOS looks old-fashioned compared to the attractive GUI of XP. For one, several DOS programs are still in use. Certain games run on DOS. But the main reason is that many things can be done *more* easily and intuitively with DOS than with the latest version of Windows (which only goes to show that progress does not always move in a straight line), and as a power user, you always want to do things the fastest, most efficient way.

DOS is accessed through Command Prompt in the Accessories submenu of All Programs (Figure 10.11). Once opened, the Command Prompt window displays as a black screen and a prompt after the default drive and user name (Figure 10.12).

FIGURE 10.11

The path to the Command Prompt
in the Start menu

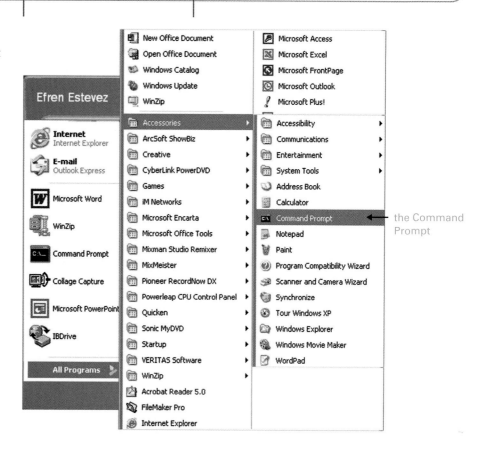

FIGURE 10.12

The Command Prompt window
displays as a black screen and a
prompt after the default drive
and username

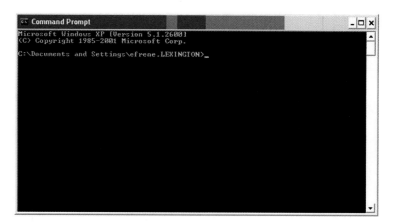

task reference

Opening the Command Prompt Window

- Click **Start, All Programs, Accessories, Command Prompt**

The first command you should learn to use is the HELP command.
The HELP command lists some of the various commands that are available to you. Once you find the command that does what you want, you
have to find out how to use it. To do this, type the name of the command
followed by a space and /? and then press Enter.

another way

. . . to Get Help in the Command Prompt

Type HELP <COMMAND> where <COMMAND> is the command you want help with.

task reference

Getting Help in the Command Prompt Window

- Type HELP, then press Enter to find out which commands you can use

- Type the command name followed by a space and /? to find out how to use the command

A useful skill when working with the Command Prompt is to make the Command Prompt window easier to read. This can be accomplished by enlarging the window to fill the entire screen.

task reference

Increasing the Screen Size of a Command Prompt Window to Full View

- Press and hold down the **Alt** key, then press **Enter**

Once you are in the full screen view, you can hold down the Windows key (Winkey) and press the Alt key to cycle through all your open files.

task reference

Cycling through All Open Windows from a Full View Command Prompt Window

- Press and hold down the **Windows** key, then press **Alt**

In full view, to return to the regular Windows view with the rest of the Desktop and open files displayed in addition to the Command Prompt window, repeat the keyboard sequence used to open a full view screen.

task reference

Returning to a Standard Windows View from a Full View Command Prompt Window

- Press and hold down the **Alt** key, then press **Enter**

Another step that can be taken to increase readability is to customize the colors in the Command Prompt window to something that's easier on the eyes than the default white on black. If you don't think this makes much of a difference, you probably haven't worked very much in the Command Prompt window. This step needs to be taken from a standard window, rather than full screen, as it involves right-clicking the Title bar of the window, which is not visible in full view. In the Properties window (Figure 10.13—reached by selecting Properties from the context menu), you can also change the font style and increase the text size for greater readability.

FIGURE 10.13

The Command Prompt Properties
dialog box

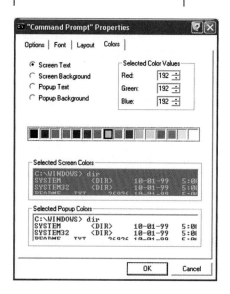

task**reference**

**Changing the Default Color, Font, and Text Size in a
Command Prompt Window**

- Right-click the Title bar of the Command Prompt window, then select
  Properties from the context menu

- In the **Colors** tab, click the **Screen text** radio button and choose a
  color from the color bar in the middle of the dialog box. Click the
  Screen background radio button and choose a color for it in the
  same way

- In the **Font** tab, choose a font from the *Font* list and a text size from the
  Size list

- Click **OK**

*another*word

You can have as many Command Prompt windows as you like, but you
should know that doing so may slow down your system speed.

Another useful command is the dir command, which is used in order
to list the contents of the current directory.

task**reference**

Listing the Contents of the Current Directory

- Type the **dir** command, then press **Enter** (Figure 10.14)

The text in the Command Prompt window can be copied into another
program. Again this is an operation that requires the standard windows
rather than full view, as it involves right-clicking the title bar of the window.

FIGURE 10.14

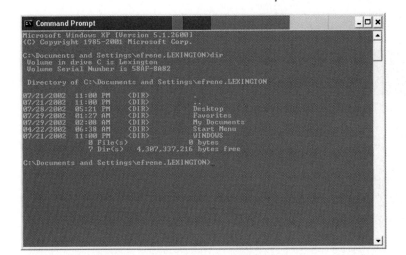

task reference

Copying Text from the Command Prompt Window

- Right-click the Title bar of the Command Prompt window; then click **Edit,** then **Mark** from the context menu

- Highlight the text you want to copy by dragging your mouse over it, then press **Enter**

- Open the target document and in the **Edit** menu, click **Paste**

Figure 10.15 presents the basic commands available for Windows XP in the Command Prompts window. There are others; in the next chapter we will look at some commands relating to troubleshooting networks.

FIGURE 10.15

Table of basic commands and their functions for XP

Command	Function	Command	Function
ASSOC	Displays or modifies file extension associations	CHCP	Displays or sets the active code page number
AT	Schedules commands and programs to run on a computer	CHDIR	Displays the name of or changes the current directory
ATTRIB	Displays or changes file attributes	CHKDSK	Checks a disk and displays a status report
BREAK	Sets or clears extended CTRL+C checking	CHKNTFS	Displays or modifies the checking of disk at boot time
CACLS	Displays or modifies access control lists (ACLs) of files	CLS	Clears the screen
CALL	Calls one batch program from another	CMD	Starts a new instance of the Windows command interpreter
CD	Displays the name of or changes the current directory	COLOR	Sets the default console foreground and background colors

FIGURE 10.15
continued

Command	Function	Command	Function
COMP	Compares the contents of two files or sets of files	GRAFTABL	Enables Windows to display an extended character set in graphics mode
COMPACT	Displays or alters the compression of files on NTFS partitions	HELP	Provides Help information for Windows commands
CONVERT	Converts FAT volumes to NTFS. You cannot convert the current drive	IF	Performs conditional processing in batch programs
COPY	Copies one or more files to another location	LABEL	Creates, changes, or deletes the volume label of a disk
DATE	Displays or sets the date	MD	Creates a directory
DEL	Deletes one or more files	MKDIR	Creates a directory
DIR	Displays a list of files and subdirectories in a directory	MODE	Configures a system device
DISKCOMP	Compares the contents of two floppy disks	MORE	Displays output one screen at a time
DISKCOPY	Copies the contents of one floppy disk to another	MOVE	Moves one or more files from one directory to another directory
DOSKEY	Edits command lines, recalls Windows commands, and creates macros	PATH	Displays or sets a search path for executable files
ECHO	Displays messages, or turns command echoing on or off	PAUSE	Suspends processing of a batch file and displays a message
ENDLOCAL	Ends localization of environment changes in a batch file	POPD	Restores the previous value of the current directory saved by PUSHD
ERASE	Deletes one or more files	PRINT	Prints a text file
EXIT	Quits the CMD.EXE program (command interpreter)	PROMPT	Changes the Windows command prompt
FC	Compares two files or sets of files, and displays the differences between them	PUSHD	Saves the current directory, then changes it
FIND	Searches for a text string in a file or files	RD	Removes a directory
FINDSTR	Searches for strings in files	RECOVER	Recovers readable information from a bad or defective disk
FOR	Runs a specified command for each file in a set of files	REM	Records comments (remarks) in batch files or CONFIG.SYS
FORMAT	Formats a disk for use with Windows	REN	Renames a file or files
FTYPE	Displays or modifies file types used in file extension associations	RENAME	Renames a file or files
		REPLACE	Replaces files
GOTO	Directs the Windows command interpreter to a labeled line in a batch program	RMDIR	Removes a directory
		SET	Displays, sets, or removes Windows environment variables
		SETLOCAL	Begins localization of environment changes in a batch file

FIGURE 10.15

continued

Command	Function	Command	Function
SHIFT	Shifts the position of replaceable parameters in batch files	TYPE	Displays the contents of a text file
		VER	Displays the Windows version
SORT	Sorts input	VERIFY	Tells Windows whether to verify that your files are written correctly to a disk
START	Starts a separate window to run a specified program or command		
SUBST	Associates a path with a drive letter	VOL	Displays a disk volume label and serial number
TIME	Displays or sets the system time		
TITLE	Sets the window title for a CMD.EXE session	XCOPY	Copies files and directory trees
TREE	Graphically displays the directory structure of a drive or path		

making the grade

SESSION 10.4

1. To get help in the Command Prompt window, type _____, then press Enter.

2. DOS is accessed through Command Prompt in the _____ submenu of All Programs.

3. To enlarge a Command Prompt window to fill the entire screen, press _____, then press Enter.

4. In order to copy text, right-click the Title bar of the Command Prompt window; then click **Edit,** then _____ from the context menu.

5. In order to list the contents of the current directory, type _____, then press Enter.

SESSION 10.5 SUMMARY

In this chapter you learned about communication between applications, specifically the capability built into Windows of being able to embed and link data into documents that are created with separate programs. In this context, several terms were introduced, some completely new, others that have been used in this book before but had a particular nuance of meaning that applied to the concepts in this chapter. The terms in this category included object, compound document, server file and server application, client file and container file, and Clipboard. All of these terms introduced the bigger idea of OLE, or object linking and embedding, the proper usage of which can make productivity soar.

Once some of these fundamental concepts were examined, you practiced copying objects from one application to another in various different ways and combinations. You copied and pasted using the menus to indicate the most basic way of embedding data, which can be used anytime data exchange is supported. You then practiced embedding objects in other applications by dragging and dropping.

The fact that not all applications allow you to drag and drop was examined. Further, the issue that certain programs can only act as servers and not as clients was brought up and discussed. The best way to find out whether this is the case with any application is simply to try to embed and link objects and see if it worked.

Additionally, you practiced inserting graphic objects of different types into different applications, which is a useful tool to liven up your documents and present additional layers of information to the recipients. You discovered that if you want to edit the information that you have embedded, a user interface appears that combines elements of both the server application and the container application.

You learned what scraps are and how they are produced. You practiced using scraps so that you could see how they can improve your productivity.

Next you examined the differences between linking and embedding. Although they have similarities, the results are quite different. Neither embedding nor linking is inherently better than the other; only by judging the purpose of the action can it be decided which is appropriate in what circumstance. You practiced linking objects to documents in different applications. Additionally, you learned that there are two different ways to edit a linked object, either in the container document itself or in the original application that created it. Just as with editing embedded objects, you learned that a hybrid type of user interface is what Windows provides to make your changes. You practiced editing a linked object, primarily by doing it in place, that is, in the document that holds the linked objects.

The concepts of COM, which underlies OLE, and the related topics of DCOM and ActiveX, which is also based on COM technology, were discussed in relation to the overall topic of interapplication communication. The Microsoft .NET initiative was explained.

Finally, you learned some basic commands in DOS and practiced executing them.

task reference roundup

Task	Page #	Preferred Method
Viewing the Clipboard's contents using ClipBook	WINXP 10.3	• Click **Start**, then **Run**
		• In the Open dialog box, type **clipbrd.exe**, then press **Enter**
		• Click **Window**, then **Clipboard** to display the contents of the Clipboard
Pasting items into ClipBook	WINXP 10.4	• Copy the desired data
		• Open ClipBook
		• Click **Window**, then **Local ClipBook**
		• Click **Edit**, then **Paste**
		• Type a name for the page in the Paste dialog box

task reference roundup

Task	Page #	Preferred Method
		• If you want to make the page available to others on your network, click the **Share Item Now** check box
		• Click **OK**
Saving contents using ClipBook	WINXP 10.4	• In ClipBook, click **File**, then **Save as** ...
		• Choose a location to save the file and type a name for it, leaving the filename extension as .clp
		• Click the **Save** button
Copying objects between different applications	WINXP 10.5	• Open the server document and select the desired object
		• Click **Edit**, then **Copy**
		• Open the container document and select the location where you want the information to be copied
		• Click **Edit**, then **Paste**
Editing an embedded object	WINXP 10.7	• Open the document that contains the embedded object
		• Double-click the embedded object
		• Make the desired changes to the object
		• When finished editing the object, click anywhere outside the object within the document
Dragging and dropping data between applications	WINXP 10.9	• Open the server document and the container document
		• Select the desired object
		• Holding down the Ctrl key, drag the object to the target document
Inserting a graphic in another application	WINXP 10.10	• Open the server document and select the desired object
		• From the **Edit** menu click **Copy**
		• Open the container document and select the location where you want the information to be copied
		• From the **Edit** menu click **Paste**
Dragging and dropping a document scrap	WINXP 10.12	• Select and drag the desired information from the server document onto your Desktop
		• Drag and drop the scrap from the Desktop into the target document
Linking an object	WINXP 10.13	• In the server document that contains the object you want to link, select the object
		• In the **Edit** menu click **Copy**
		• In the target document where you want to paste the object, click the location where you want the object to appear

task reference roundup

Task	Page #	Preferred Method
		• In the **Edit** menu click **Paste Special**
		• Click the radio button next to Paste link
		• Click **OK**
Editing a linked object	WINXP 10.15	• Double-click the linked object you want to edit in the compound document
		• Edit the object
		• In the **File** menu, click **Save**
		• In the **File** menu, click **Exit**
Setting up a .NET Passport user account	WINXP 10.17	• **Click Start, Control Panel, User Accounts**
		• Click your user account
		• Click the **Set up my account to use .NET Passport** link, then click **Next**
		• Click the **Yes** radio button, then click **Next**
		• Type your e-mail address, then click **Next**
		• Type a password, then click **Next**
		• Click **Finish**
Opening the Command Prompt window	WINXP 10.20	• **Click Start, All Programs, Accessories, Command Prompt**
Getting help in the Command Prompt window	WINXP 10.21	• Type HELP, then press Enter to find out which commands you can use
		• Type the command name followed by a space and /? to find out how to use the command
Increasing the screen size of a Command Prompt window to full view	WINXP 10.21	• Press and hold down the **Alt** key, then press **Enter**
Cycling through all open windows from a full view Command Prompt window	WINXP 10.21	• Press and hold down the **Windows** key, then press **Alt**
Returning to a standard Windows view from a full view Command Prompt window	WINXP 10.21	• Press and hold down the **Alt** key, then press **Enter**
Changing the default color, font, and text size in a Command Prompt window	WINXP 10.22	• Right-click the Title bar of the Command Prompt window, then select Properties from the context menu
		• In the **Colors** tab, click the **Screen text** radio button and choose a color from the color bar in the middle of the dialog box. Click the **Screen background** radio button and choose a color for it in the same way

task reference roundup

Task	Page #	Preferred Method
		• In the **Font** tab, choose a font from the *Font* list and a text size from the *Size* list
		• Click **OK**
Listing the contents of the current directory	WINXP 10.22	• Type the **dir** command, then press **Enter**
Copying text from the Command Prompt window	WINXP 10.23	• Right-click the Title bar of the Command Prompt window; then click **Edit**, then **Mark** from the context menu
		• Highlight the text you want to copy by dragging your mouse over it, then press **Enter**
		• Open the target document and in the **Edit** menu, click **Paste**

CROSSWORD PUZZLE

Across

2. An advanced form of OLE that permits applications to run on a remote computer
4. User interface functions such as a push button or toolbar
7. A document that contains objects from more than one application
10. Microsoft's software platform for the Internet that allows for the exchange of data
11. A bit of data that you can select and drag onto your Desktop

Down

1. A circle icon with a slash through it means you cannot do this
3. A temporary storage area for whatever has been copied from an application
5. An Internet Service Provider for applications
6. A program or file that acts as source for an object
7. A program or file that acts as container for an object
8. A piece of data that can be embedded in a different application
9. An operating system performing text-based command line functions
12. The technology that underlies OLE

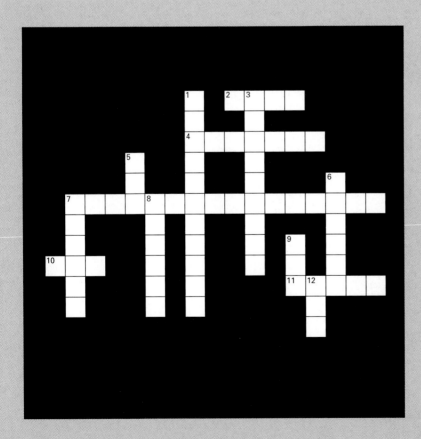

FILL-IN

1. DCOM stands for _____.

2. A _____ can be anything—a company logo, a sound file, or the standard ending you use for all your memos and letters that you keep on your Desktop.

3. When you _____ an object, the object becomes a part of the compound document, but when an object is_____, it remains a part of the original document.

4. The underlying technology that makes OLE work is called _____.

5. If you move, delete, or rename the server document, the _____ is broken.

CREATE THE QUESTION

For each of the following answers, create an appropriate, short question.

ANSWER	QUESTION
1. A compound document technology that allows an object to be embedded or linked to a document in a different application	_____
2. The "client," "target," or "container" file	_____
3. The "source" or "server" file	_____
4. This storage area only stores the last copied data, and if you cut or copy new data, the old data is overwritten	_____
5. Only one of these can be edited at a time	_____

TRUE OR FALSE

1. You can edit a linked object only in the target application's destination document.

2. Double-clicking an embedded object opens the application that created it.

3. Any changes made in the server file will automatically be reflected in the compound document.

4. Parts of Windows and other Microsoft applications are built as COM objects.

5. A compound document can have links from several different applications.

1. Creating a Compound Document

The Ridgewood School Chess Club meets weekly to compete against each other and take lessons from their coach, Dan Kennedy. Every two weeks during tournament season they play against other schools' teams in their local area. Dan has been teaching the members of the club how to keep track of their games by recording the moves.

Since the annual tournaments are coming up, Dan wants to go over some of the moves in recent games to demonstrate concepts of attack and defense. He tells everyone to keep track of their moves in a consistent way on a form he has created. He wants to distribute this form quickly to all the members of the club. Dan has the basic form in a WordPad document named **Chess Club**, which you will find in your data files for this chapter.

1. Launch the **Outlook Express** e-mail program on your computer and click the **New Mail** button
2. Open the **Chess Club** WordPad document
3. In the **Edit** menu click **Select All**
4. In the **Edit** menu click **Copy**
5. Click the blank text area of the New Message window in Outlook Express
6. In the **Edit** menu click **Paste**
7. Address the e-mail to yourself (or to a friend), adding any comments you wish, and send it

2. Object Embedding without Using Your Mouse

Louis Fine works for Tile Warehouse Liquidators and needs to send a picture of a surface tile along with the item description, size, and price. An actual sample tile fell out of his hands and on his mouse this morning, and the mouse is not working properly now. There is no other computer available. To get the mouse to do what he wants is excruciatingly slow, so he decides to use keyboard commands as much as possible.

Use the mouse only twice in the entire following exercise. All the rest of the actions are to be done only with the keyboard.

1. Open **Paint** by pressing the **Windows** key on your keyboard, then pressing **P** (for Programs)+ **Enter, A** (for Accessories) + **Enter,** and **P** (for Paint) + **Enter.** The Paint program opens
2. Press **Alt+F,** then **O** to open a new file in Paint
3. This is one of the steps where you can use the mouse; click the drop-down list next to *Look in* and select **LOCAL DISK (C:)**
4. Type **Windows** in the *File name* text box to select that folder and press **Enter**
5. Type **Santa Fe Stucco** to select that file and press **Enter.** The bitmap image that looks like Figure 10.16 appears in Paint
6. Press **Ctrl+A** to select the image, then **Ctrl+C** to copy the image to the Clipboard
7. Press the **Windows** key, **P, A,** then begin typing **WordPad** to open a new file in WordPad
8. Press **Ctrl+V** to paste the image into the WordPad document
9. Click below the image with your mouse (last time you are using the mouse!) and type the following information underneath the image:
   Santa Fe Stucco
   Size: 12" X 12"
   Price: $ 1.99 each
   Your final WordPad document should look like Figure 10.16
10. Save this document and name it **Santa Fe Stucco**

F I G U R E   10.16

Santa Fe Stucco bitmap image

challenge!

1. Reporting Monthly Gross Sales to Investors

Big Time Broadway Productions produces Broadway plays and musicals. Each show is sponsored by a group of investors who put up the front money necessary for all the expenses of the production: the costumes, the fees paid to the performers, the rental of the performance space, the marketing and publicity campaigns, and so forth. The investors recoup their money from the ticket sales. Accordingly, they are very interested in the monthly ticket sales figures.

You are responsible for faxing these figures to each investor on a monthly basis. The results for last month are as follows:

1. Noises Off—$ 546,784
2. Proof—$784,930
3. Contact—$821,865
4. Chicago—$517,376

Using a spreadsheet program such as Excel, enter the above figures on a spreadsheet. Prepare a pie chart that displays the total income for all the shows. Use Figure 10.17 as your guide.

Link this pie chart in a WordPad document that is addressed to All Investors from Big Time Productions, re: February's Ticket Sales.

After completing this section, you realize you made a mistake. Now change the sales figures for Chicago in the original Excel spreadsheet to $617,376. Have the link updated in your WordPad document. Print out the compound document.

2. Creating a Document That Displays All the Basic Commands in DOS

Carolyn Rodgers is customer service rep for Trade Winds Air, a carrier that flies out of Miami to the Caribbean. She spends most of her day in a DOS program that tracks flight information. She wants to post a list of the basic commands to use in the Command Prompt window next to her computer so she can be more efficient.

1. Open a Command Prompt window and type **HELP,** then press **Enter**
2. Right-click the Title bar of the Command Prompt window; then click **Edit,** then **Mark** from the context menu
3. Highlight the text you want to copy by dragging your mouse over it, then press **Enter**
4. Open a WordPad file and in the **Edit** menu, click **Paste**
5. Print out the final document, which should look like the one in Figure 10.18

FIGURE 10.18

The Dos command table

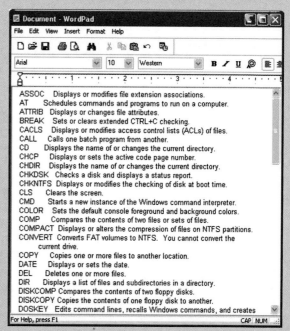

FIGURE 10.17

Big Time Excel pie chart

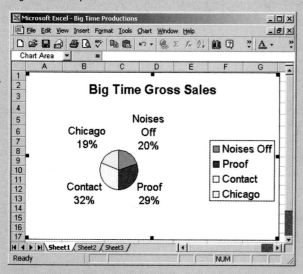

1. Embedding Information from a Web Site into a Document

Eric Gregory owns Better Business Books, an independent bookstore in downtown Minneapolis that specializes in all types of business titles. Eric has just completed renovations and wants to expand the number of titles in the computer section of his store since a computer training center is opening nearby. He wants to print out a list of some prospective titles to carry and give the list to the school so they can tell him which they will be using for their courses. He asks you to help him do this.

1. Go to the Web site http://shop.mcgraw-hill.com and navigate to a page that lists computer titles
2. Highlight (by clicking and holding down your right mouse button) the names and descriptions of three books that look interesting
3. Copy these names and descriptions by pressing **Ctrl+C**
4. Paste the book names and descriptions you copied from the Web site into a new WordPad document
5. Save the document and name it **BBB computer titles**

e-business

1. Using a Scrap to Edit a Web Page

Pay-it-plus.com is an online bill-paying service. Clients pay a monthly fee and provide pay-it-plus.com with access to a bank account. Pay-it-plus.com then contacts all the creditors that bill the client regularly and arranges to pay the client's bills. The creditors get paid on time, and the client doesn't have to worry about when a bill is due, writing a check, and mailing it.

Anita Hernandez works for pay-it-plus.com and is in the process of altering the Frequently Asked Questions (FAQ) Web page on the pay-it-plus.com Web site. She prepares a mock page to show to other staff members and get their feedback. The main response is that if the client cannot get the information they need from the FAQ page, they should be directed to call an 800 number for further assistance. Accordingly, Anita needs to insert the sentence "If your question was not answered, or you require further information, please call our Customer Service Department at 800-555-1111."

Anita realizes this will be a tedious and time-consuming task, as there will be multiple places where the phrase needs to be inserted. She explains the problem to you, and you mention that using a document scrap might be helpful.

1. Open a new WordPad document and type the sentence: **If your question was not answered, or you require further information, please call our Customer Service Department at 800-555-1111**
2. Select the typing in your WordPad document and drag it to your Desktop. A WordPad document scrap icon like the one in Figure 10.19 displays on your Desktop
3. Open the data file named **FAQ**
4. Drag the WordPad document scrap on your Desktop to the end of each of the sections titled How do I . . . ? Where can I find . . . ? and Why doesn't . . . ?
5. Save the document and print it out

FIGURE 10.19

The WordPad document scrap

1. Embedding a Map for a Meeting

Ryan White works as a sales manager for a trading company specializing in importing tungsten from Portugal. A technical representative from one of the tungsten factories in Portugal will be attending a symposium nearby next week. Ryan wants all the salespeople to attend as this will be a good opportunity to get some feedback on technical issues the salespeople have had questions about.

He asks you to prepare a memo to all the salespeople that will include a map he has obtained to provide directions to the Conference Center where the symposium is being held.

1. Using the **xp10exhibit** data file as a template, draft a memo from Ryan White addressed to the salespeople. Include the following information about the location:

   Delancey Conference Center at 222 5th Avenue in Morristown, New Jersey.

   The symposium will be held on October 11, 2003. Invite all the salespeople to attend

2. Open the data file named **xp10conferencemap**

3. Copy the map and embed it in the new memo you've created

4. Save it and rename it **Tungsten Conference**

5. Print the **Tungsten Conference** document

Chapter Objectives

- End programs that are not responding

- Produce a complete hardware report

- Learn to troubleshoot problems with devices

- Start your computer in Safe Mode

- Restore your computer after startup failure

- Learn how to generate reports on the current system status

- Practice network troubleshooting using command line prompts

- Back and restore the Registry

CHAPTER

11

eleven

Troubleshooting
and System
Management

Cold Spring Harbor Labs

Rob Stone is a research assistant working at Cold Spring Harbor Labs, one of the most prestigious research facilities in the country. His department recently received a federal grant to study the feasibility of developing new medicines from a rare fungus that grows deep in the Amazon rain forest.

Rob's familiarity with computers has made him the unofficial head of the research team's troubleshooting department. The researchers work with complex programs that use a great deal of memory and processing power. They also constantly use the Internet to connect with colleagues working on similar problems worldwide. Also, because researchers are curious types of people, they regularly try out new ways of doing things on their computers, sometimes without having much of a sense of how it all will work.

As a result, Rob spends a large part of his day trying to find solutions to computer problems. Since he knows that having a firm grasp of the settings and configurations on the machines is essential to keeping the systems operational, he also does quite a bit of fact-finding in advance on each machine.

SESSION 11.1 DEVICE AND PROGRAM TROUBLESHOOTING

INTRODUCTION

For all the impressive things computers can do, a basic fact of computing is that there are problems that require troubleshooting. Some types of systems are more reliable than others, but all require some degree of attention. The best way to avoid problems with your computer is to only do a few simple things with it, don't attempt to add anything new or upgrade it, and make sure it remains a stand-alone system without contact with any other networks or computers. Not very convenient, is it? It is similar to advising someone that the best way to avoid common colds is to never leave your hermetically sealed room. You would probably avoid colds, but your life would also be pretty unproductive and not very exciting.

Another important point to realize besides the fact that computer problems are inevitable is that computer problems are good for you. There is no denying that not being able to work because your system is down is aggravating (especially since computers have a strange intelligence about when you most need them and, therefore, when they are most likely to malfunction). However, it is by attempting to diagnose and repair problems that you learn the most about your system. Instead of despairing at having wasted hours trying to fix a problem, consider what you learned in the process. Troubleshooting is often the time that you will learn the most about your computer outside of a classroom or training seminar. Much more is accomplished by adopting a calm, methodical attitude rather than tearing your hair out and screaming.

Another thing about computer problems is that they make the people who have them feel very dumb. The opposite is usually true. The most advanced power users have plenty of computer problems. It's just that often their problems are much larger and more complicated than the beginner's. If you think of an IT professional, and what their typical day is like, you will see that most of what they do is problem solving.

All this is not to imply that you should go out looking for problems. Problems seem to do a very good job of finding you. One day using computers may be as easy and trouble-free as turning on a light switch. Until that time, it is worthwhile to learn some troubleshooting basics and hone your problem-solving skills.

WINDOWS TASK MANAGER

Windows Task Manager is one of the most effective tools you can use in your troubleshooting arsenal. The **Task Manager** is a tool for diagnosing and managing system problems. From within Task Manager, you can view the programs and processes running on your local computer. You can also monitor your computer's CPU and memory usage. There is also a screen that provides a graphical representation of your machine's performance.

The Task Manager contains at least three tabs:

- *Applications tab*. This tab provides information about each program that is currently running on your computer. The left side of the window displays the program name and program icon. The right side indicates the status of each program (Figure 11.1). You can change the way the programs are displayed by selecting the View menu and clicking Large Icons, Small Icons, or Details

FIGURE 11.1

The Applications tab of the Task Manager

• *Processes tab.* This tab provides information about the processes, services, and executable programs running on your computer (Figure 11.2). Task Manager displays a list that includes what process is running, who the user is, and the amount of CPU time and memory that a process uses. Each process is associated with and runs a particular program. You can see which process runs a particular program from the Applications tab by right-clicking the program and then clicking Go To Process from the submenu that appears. You are returned to the Processes tab with the associated process highlighted. You can end a process by selecting it from the displayed list and then clicking the End Process button. You should exercise caution when doing this, however, as ending a process that the operating system uses could cause your system to crash

FIGURE 11.2

The Processes tab of the Task Manager

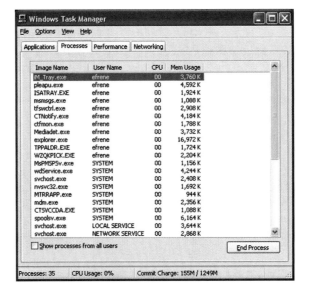

• *Performance tab.* This tab provides both numerical information and graphical representations of CPU usage and CPU usage history, page file usage, and page file usage history (Figure 11.3). This information is useful if you want to keep track of how installed devices use your computer's resources. The Performance tab also indicates the number of handles, threads, and processes; and the amount of physical memory, commit charge, and kernel memory in your computer. Handles and threads are used by Windows when running programs. Commit charge and kernel memory are part of the computer's memory used by the operating system

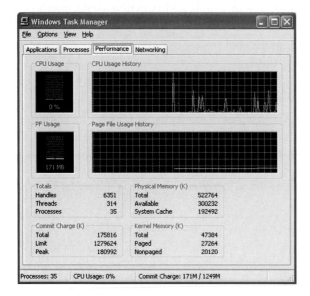

FIGURE 11.3

The Performance tab of the Task Manager

In addition, the Task Manager may display another two tabs if you are connected to a network and/or have other users running programs on your machine:

- *Networking tab.* This tab provides graphical information about the status and performance of your network (Figure 11.4)
- *Users tab.* This tab provides information about the users, either local or remote, on your computer, including the user name and ID

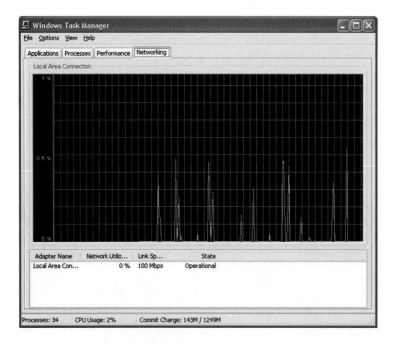

FIGURE 11.4

The Networking tab of the Task Manager

WINDOWS XP

*another*way

. . . to Display the Task Manager

Right-click an empty area of the taskbar and select Task Manager.

task reference

Displaying the Task Manager

- Press and hold down **Ctrl+Alt,** then press **Delete**

Using Task Manager

- In the Task Manager, click the Application tab to view the status of programs that are running

- In the Task Manager, click the Processes tab to view the status of the processes that are running

- In the Task Manager, click the Performance tab to check the status of your computer's performance

- In the Task Manager, click the Networking tab to view the status and performance of the network

Using Task Manager to Close a Program That Is Not Responding

The Task Manager is a very useful tool to employ when you are having problems with a program that is not responding. Unfortunately, this can occur often when working in Windows. It may happen because you ask a program to do something that it can't do, or simply because there is a conflict between the programs you are running. Whatever the reason, the Task Manager won't tell you what has gone wrong, but it will allow you to end the program task so that you are not left with a nonresponsive computer and can get back to work.

Note, however, that ending a program like this will result in losing any unsaved changes you've made. If there is any other way to get the program to respond, it will allow you to save your changes first before terminating the application. Because of this, ending the nonresponsive program in Task Manager should be a last resort after you've tried the conventional ways of closing a program.

Keep in mind that some tasks may take awhile to complete. What looks like an unresponsive program may simply be not responding because it is busy trying to complete the task you assigned it. If the loss of any unsaved changes is unacceptable, try giving your computer a few minutes without adding any input to see if the program just needs more time. If the program still is unresponsive, Windows may prompt you to end the task anyway. At this point you have little choice but to close the program and lose your changes. The motto of the story is to save your work regularly and often.

*another*word

...on Programs Not Responding

If a program is regularly not responding, you should determine exactly what type of task it is that causes this, make note of it, and attempt to get the problem fixed, by contacting either the manufacturer or someone within your organization. The Task Manager is designed to take care of occasional problems, not for regular use to perform a task. Program files can become corrupted if they are subjected to repeated forced closings. Corrupted programs can sometimes be fixed by uninstalling and then reinstalling them from the original source.

task reference

Using Task Manager to Close a Program That Is Not Responding

- Display the Task Manager and click the **Applications** tab
- Select the program that is not responding from the *Task* list
- Click the **End Task** button
- Click the **End Now** button to close the program

Using the Task Manager:

One of the utilities Rob uses most often is the Task Manager. Other researchers in his department frequently download large files from the Internet and it is not unusual for them to have their Web browser freeze. When they call Rob, the first thing he does is launch the Task Manager.

1. Press and hold down **Ctrl+Alt,** then press **Delete**

tip: *If the Windows Security dialog box appears, click the* **Task Manager** *button.*

2. Click the **Applications** tab
3. Select the program that is not responding from the *Task* list
4. Click the **End Task** button
5. Click the **End Now** button to close the program

DEVICE MANAGER

The Device Manager is particularly handy when you need to resolve hardware problems, or even for determining if the problem you are having is hardware related. As its name implies, the *Device Manager* is a utility that allows you to check the status of the various pieces of hardware connected to your computer. Besides peripheral devices such as printers and scanners, connected hardware includes things such as the hard disk, system hardware, and processors, which are not typically thought of as devices.

The Device Manager lists all the potential categories of hardware in a directory structure and then updates itself when new hardware is detected by creating an entry in the corresponding category for the new device. You navigate through the list of hardware categories just like a folder directory in Windows Explorer. Each category heading has a plus (+) sign next to it, and you view its contents by clicking the plus sign. Within the category folders, each listed device is represented by an icon. If Device Manager displays an exclamation point (!) over the icon, this means there is a problem with the device. If Device Manager displays a red X over the icon, this means the device has been disabled. Thus, just browsing through the directory can help you identify the possible source of a problem.

Another potential application for the Device Manager is if your computer is not starting properly. By restarting the computer in Safe Mode (see the section on Safe Mode later in this chapter), and then running the Device Manager, you can see if the startup problem has something to do with a hardware device.

The Device Manager can also be used as a management tool even if there are no problems with your system, for example, if you are installing a new piece of hardware and need to check which other hardware of the same type is already installed. New devices may need to be configured differently if there is a device of the same type that is already connected to your system.

---

task reference

Displaying the Device Manager

- Click **Start,** then **Control Panel**

- Double-click **System**

- In the **Hardware** tab of the System Properties dialog box, click the **Device Manager** button

---

FIGURE 11.5

The Hardware tab of System Properties

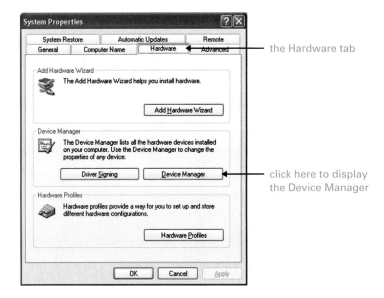

the Hardware tab

click here to display the Device Manager

---

anotherway

. . . to Display the Device Manager

In the Control Panel, click **Performance and Maintenance.** The Performance and Maintenance screen opens. Under the *Pick a task . . .* list, select **See Basic information about your computer.** This displays the System Properties dialog box. From there, proceed as shown by clicking the **Hardware** tab and then the **Device Manager** button.

You can change the way Device Manager displays its information by clicking the View menu. The options are to view the devices or resources organized by type or by connection. A bullet appears by the current view.

If a newly installed device does not appear in the Device Manager, it may be because the Device Manager screen needs to be refreshed. The Device Manager checks periodically for updates to your hardware, but this may not have occurred since the new device was installed. To prompt the Device Manager to update itself, select the Action menu and click Scan for hardware changes.

Printing Information about Hardware

From time to time, it may be necessary to print a hard copy of all the current devices attached to your computer. This can be accomplished from the Device Manager window.

FIGURE 11.6

The Device Manager

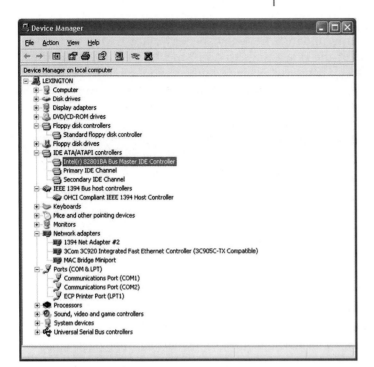

Printing Information about Hardware

- In the Device Manager screen, click the device or the category of device for which you want to print information

- In the **Action** menu, click **Print**

- In the Print dialog box, choose from one of the *Report types* by clicking the appropriate radio button: the *System summary* option prints a *summary* of the devices connected to your computer. The *Selected class or device* option prints a report for the individual device or the entire class of device types selected. *All devices and system summary* prints a report about every device installed on your computer along with a hardware summary

- Click the **Print** button

Using the Device Manager to Obtain Detailed Information about a Particular Device

The Device Manager tool is also useful for obtaining detailed information about a particular device installed on your computer; for example, the manufacturer of the device. It can also provide you with a status report indicating whether the device is working properly and, if not, launch a Troubleshooting Wizard that guides you through a series of methodical steps to determine what the problem is.

Another function in this same category is the ability to display information about the driver for a device. As you recall, a driver is software that enables a device to communicate with the computer. Drivers are also a common source of computer programs. Drivers can become corrupted or mix poorly with other drivers. New operating systems can have trouble with drivers that worked fine on legacy versions of Windows. Drivers are also constantly being updated. If you suspect you are having a problem with a driver, one of the first things to do is check to see if you have the most recent version. Using the Device Manager, you can access the individual device's Properties dialog box. In the Driver tab, the current version number is displayed.

---

task **reference**

Using the Device Manager to Obtain Details about a Device

- In the Device Manager, click the plus sign (+) next to the category folder that contains the device

- Double-click the particular device about which you want more information

- In the device's Properties dialog box, click the General tab to obtain the name of the manufacturer and the operating status of the device

- Click the Driver tab to obtain information about the version number or other information related to the driver provider, date, or digital signer

- Click the Resources tab to view the resources used by the device driver and a list of possible conflicting devices

- Click **OK** to close the Properties dialog box when done obtaining the information you need

---

F I G U R E   11.7

The General tab of the device Properties dialog box

F I G U R E   11.8

The Driver tab of the device Properties dialog box

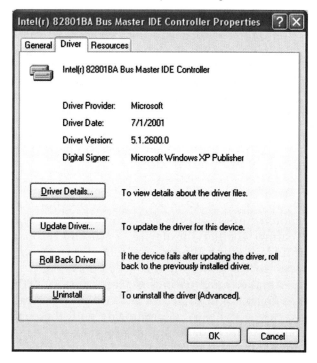

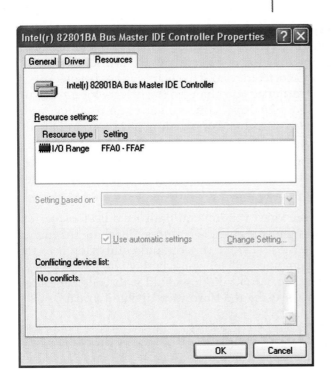

FIGURE 11.9

The Resources tab of the device
Properties dialog box

*another*way

. . . to Launch the
Device Properties
Dialog Box

Right-click the device
you are interested in and
select Properties from
the submenu that
appears. The Properties
dialog box opens.

Using the Device Manager to Update, Roll Back, or Uninstall a Driver

Not only can you obtain information about hardware drivers in Device Manager, but you can access the desired device's Properties dialog box from there also. This enables you to actively manage your hardware drivers.

Double-clicking the listed device in the Device Manager opens the Properties dialog box for that device. Depending on the particular type of device, there will be three or more tabs. In the Driver tab of the Properties dialog box, there are four buttons:

- *Driver Details.* Provides information about the driver as described above
- *Update Driver.* This button launches the Hardware Update Wizard, which guides you through the process of installing a new driver (Figure 11.10)

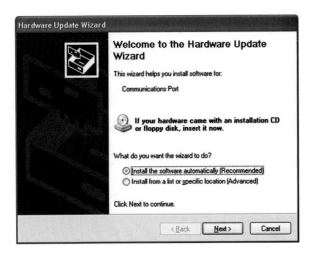

FIGURE 11.10

The Hardware Update Wizard

WINDOWS XP

- ***Roll Back Driver.*** Some consider this button one of the major improvements in Windows XP over previous Windows operating systems. It performs the function of reverting to the previous version of the driver for the selected device. This is important because often your problems start after you changed the drivers for a particular device. Troubleshooting drivers often involves uninstalling the last driver you updated. This handy procedure has been simplified to pressing this button
- *Uninstall.* This button uninstalls the driver completely. If you don't have another driver installed for the device, this will disable the device, so think before you do this

Updating a driver to the latest version can improve a device's performance by eliminating bugs and adding new features. Checking the manufacturer's Web site for the most current version and comparing it to the version installed on your computer will tell you whether you have the most recent driver version installed. After you download it to your computer, you can install the new driver using the Hardware Update Wizard.

---

*another*way

. . . to Launch the Hardware Update Wizard

From the Device Manager, select the device, then click the Update driver icon from the standard toolbar.

---

task *reference*

Updating a Driver

- In the Device Manager, double-click the device you want to update
- Click the **Drivers** tab of the Properties dialog box
- Click the **Update Driver** button
- Select the *Install from a list or specific location* radio button, then click **Next**
- Select the *Don't search, I will choose the driver to install* radio button, then click **Next**
- Click the **Have Disk** button
- Click **Browse,** then navigate to the file containing the driver update
- Click the **Open** button
- Click **OK**
- Click **Next**
- Click **Finish**

If the new driver you've installed causes problems, you can roll back the driver to the previously installed version. This process is referred to as rolling back the driver. Windows does not get rid of the old driver when a new driver replaces it; instead, it stores the information about the old driver so you can easily restore it.

task *reference*

Rolling Back a Driver

- In the Device Manager, double-click the device you want to roll back
- Click the **Drivers** tab of the Properties dialog box; click the **Roll Back Driver** button
- Click **Yes**
- Click **OK**

Rolling back a driver:

One of the researchers in Rob's department has installed a new driver for his monitor. In his haste, however, he didn't realize that the driver is for a different version of Windows and not for XP. Now his monitor is not working properly. When his colleague explains that the problem began when he installed the new driver, Rob knows he has to use the Device Manager tool to roll back the monitor driver to the previous version that performed correctly.

1. In the Device Manager, double-click the device you want to roll back

2. Click the **Drivers** tab of the Properties dialog box; click the **Roll Back Driver** button

3. Click **Yes**

4. Click **OK**

---

making the grade   SESSION 11.1

1. The _____ is a tool for diagnosing and managing system problems.

2. The _____ is a utility that allows you to check the status of the various pieces of hardware connected to your computer.

3. You can roll back the current driver in the _____ tab of the Device Manager.

4. The _____ is a very useful tool to employ when you are having problems with a program that is not responding

5. To display the Properties dialog box in Device Manager, _____ the particular device about which you want more information.

SESSION 11.2 SYSTEM TROUBLESHOOTING AND RECOVERY

Windows offers several tools in the event of system problems that are preventing you from booting your computer. Systemwide problems are those that affect your entire computer and may be due to a large variety of causes. These tools do not diagnose what the problem is, but they do make it easier to troubleshoot your system and get you back to at least a minimal operating capacity.

USING SAFE MODE

Running Windows in Safe Mode is an important troubleshooting technique when your computer is not starting properly. *Safe Mode* is a basic, minimal configuration of your operating system. Some functions, such as e-mail, and some hardware, such as printers or removable media drives, may not work in Safe Mode. This is because Safe Mode deliberately limits the complexity of the operation system to a bare-bones setup that may not support these devices and services. Starting in Safe Mode will enable you to get into your system and attempt to correct the problem without interference from nonessential devices and functions. For example, if you have just installed a program that is causing difficulties with normal startup, starting in Safe Mode enables you to get your computer started so that you can uninstall the program.

The other function of Safe Mode is as a diagnostic tool. If you are having problems starting the computer and can successfully start in Safe Mode, you eliminate the basic hardware and computer functions as the cause of your problem and can focus on other possibilities.

You can only enter Safe Mode if you have an Administrator account.

Safe Mode displays as a black screen with plain text on it. Each corner of the screen displays the words "Safe Mode." You use the up and down arrow keys in order to navigate through Safe Mode. For this reason, the NUM LOCK key should be turned off before entering Safe Mode so that the arrow keys on the numeric keypad will function.

When you are done in Safe Mode, simply restart your computer normally to return to the regular version of the XP interface.

---

task reference

Starting in Safe Mode

- If your computer is on, shut it off

- Turn on your computer and monitor, then immediately press and hold down the **F8** key

- The Windows Advanced Options menu appears. Use the up and down arrow keys to highlight the **Safe Mode** option, then press **Enter**

- Use arrow keys again to highlight the operating system you want to start, then press **Enter**

- At the Welcome screen, click the Administrator account to use

- Click the **Yes** button in the dialog box

- When finished using Safe Mode, restart your computer normally

---

Starting in Safe Mode:

A member of the Cold Spring Harbor Lab team is not able to use his computer for more than a couple of minutes before it crashes. He tells Rob he's not sure exactly when the problem started, but it's been becoming worse over the last week. Now it's at the point where he can't do anything at all with his machine. Rob decides as a first step to attempt to start the computer in Safe Mode.

1. Turn on your computer and monitor, then immediately press and hold down the **F8** key

2. The Windows Advanced Options menu appears. Use the up and down arrow keys to highlight the **Safe Mode** option, then press **Enter**

3. Use arrow keys again to highlight the operating system you want to start, then press **Enter**

4. At the Welcome screen, click the Administrator account to use

5. Click the **Yes** button in the dialog box

6. When finished using Safe Mode, restart your computer normally

The Advanced Options menu you access by pressing F8 during startup provides you with several options:

- *Safe Mode.* This option is the basic one described above, which uses the minimum capabilities necessary to start your computer
- *Safe Mode with Networking.* This option starts your computer in Safe Mode with some limited networking capabilities
- *Safe Mode with Command Prompt.* This option displays the Command Prompt screen upon startup, which is useful in case you have monitor problems that are preventing the standard Safe Mode options from working

In addition, there are other options available in the next section of the Advanced Options menu:

- *Enable Boot Logging.* This option records all the actions that take place during startup, which may help determine the source of your problem. If you enable this option, the records of the startup actions are placed in the ntbtlog.txt file located in the WINDOWS folder
- *Enable VGA Mode.* This option is related to problems with your monitor. It enables you to start Windows using a VGA driver if, for example, a newly installed video adapter is interfering with the normal startup process of your system
- *Last Known Good Configuration.* This option restores the last Registry settings that existed when you were able to start without difficulties. You can learn more about working with the Registry later in this chapter
- *Directory Services Restore Mode.* This option is used if your computer is a domain controller on a network. If this is the case, more than likely the person using the computer is a network administrator
- *Debugging Mode.* This option sends information about your system's problems to another computer that is attached to yours. This procedure is typically used by technicians or other qualified personnel to diagnose problems with a malfunctioning computer

RESTORING YOUR COMPUTER

If you are experiencing systemwide problems that started at a particular point, for example, when you changed your settings or installed new hardware, you can return your computer to an earlier time before the problems started happening.

WINDOWS XP

Restoring a computer involves taking the system back to a restore point. A ***restore point*** is an earlier time when the computer was not experiencing the current problems. There are different types of restore points. There are restore points called System Checkpoints, which are predefined instances when Windows will automatically create a restore point. When you first install your operating system, and when you upgrade it, are restore points. When an Automatic Update occurs is another restore point. Installation of certain types of programs will prompt the creation of a restore point. You can also manually create your own restore point.

FIGURE 11.11

The System Restore welcome window

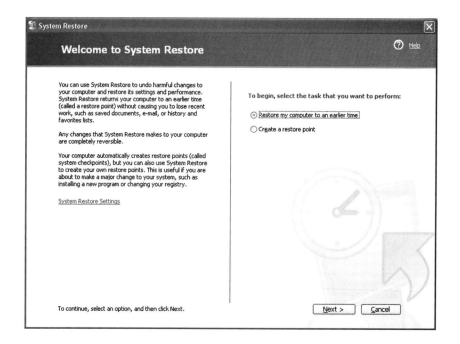

tasK reference

Restoring Your Computer

- Click **Start, All Programs, Accessories, System Tools, System Restore**

- Click the **Restore my computer to an earlier time** radio button, then click **Next**

- The Select a restore point screen opens showing a calendar with all the dates that have restore points in bold (Figure 11.12)

- Click the most recent day with a restore point before the problems started, then click **Next**

- The Confirm Restore Point Selection asks you to confirm the restore point you have selected and provides some information about the restore process; click **Next**

- A dialog box will detail the progress of the restoration, and the computer restarts when complete. Click **OK**

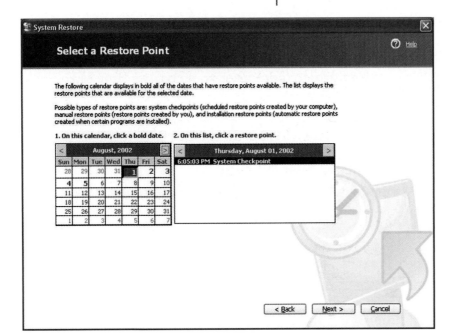

FIGURE 11.12

Select a Restore Point

task reference

Manually Creating a Restore Point

- Click **Start, All Programs, Accessories, System Tools, System Restore**

- Click the **Create a restore point** radio button, then click **Next**

- Type a description for the restore point and click **Create**

- Click **Close**

Restoring your computer will not affect e-mails, or Favorites, or History lists from after the restore points. Most files created after the restore point should also not be affected, but it is a good idea to put them in the My Documents folder as any documents there will not be affected. Programs installed after the restore point may be uninstalled; files created with these programs may not be, but you may need to reinstall the program to open them.

You can also reverse the changes made when your computer was restored by selecting the *Undo my last restoration* radio button at the Welcome window.

Restoring your computer:

Working on the computer that has trouble starting, Rob suspects that either a virus has crept into the system or one of the program files has become corrupted. He tries various strategies to diagnose the problem, but finds that he can't pinpoint it exactly. Since the user told him that the computer was working fine a short while ago, Rob decides to use the System Restore tool to return the system to a restore point from three weeks ago in the hope that this will revert the machine to functionality.

1. Click **Start, All Programs, Accessories, System Tools, System Restore**

2. Click the **Restore my computer to an earlier time** radio button, then click **Next**

3. The Select a restore point screen opens showing a calendar with all the dates that have restore points in bold (Figure 11.12)

4. Click the most recent day with a restore point before the problems started, then click **Next**

5. The Confirm Restore Point Selection asks you to confirm the restore point you have selected and provides some information about the restore process; click **Next**

6. A dialog box will detail the progress of the restoration, and the computer restarts when complete. Click **OK**

OBTAINING SYSTEM INFORMATION

A screen called System Information (located in the System Tools folder) lists a great deal of information, such as the version of Windows you are running, the system name and model number, the type of processor you are using, your total memory, and so forth. These data are useful as a reference or to troubleshoot a problem.

The System Information folder (Figure 11.13) is divided into four main categories:

- *System Summary.* This category provides general information about your computer
- *Hardware Resources.* This category provides information about the resources and hardware resource usage on your computer
- *Components.* This category provides information about the setup of the Windows components and the hardware devices and drivers on your computer
- *Software Environment.* This category provides information about the software installed on your computer

FIGURE 11.13

The System Information window

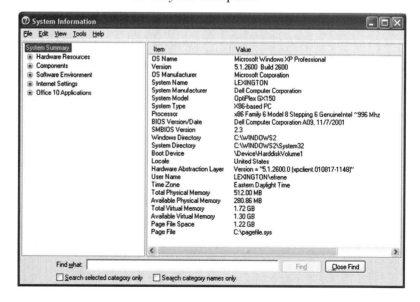

Other categories may also be displayed, depending on what you have installed on your machine, but these categories are the main ones.

---

task reference

Displaying System Information

- Click **Start, All Programs, Accessories, System Tools, System Information**
- Click the **System Summary** folder in the left pane to display general information
- Click the plus sign (+) next to a category name to expand the list, then click the specific item about which you wish to view more details

---

Displaying and printing System Information:

1. Navigate to the System Information window in the Control Panel **(Start, Control Panel, Accessories, System Tools, System Information)**

2. In the left pane, click **System Summary.** It takes Windows a few moments to refresh the current information

3. Click **File,** then **Print**

---

making the grade

1. _____ is a basic, minimal configuration of your operating system.

2. Returning your computer to an earlier time before the problems started happening is called _____ it.

3. You can only enter Safe Mode if you have an _____ account.

4. The System Information screen is located in the _____ folder.

SESSION 11.3 NETWORK TROUBLESHOOTING AND THE REGISTRY

TROUBLESHOOTING NETWORK PROBLEMS

Network configuration can be complex. Such things as the TCP/IP configurations—the address, subnet mask, and the default gateway—must be correct in order to have network access. Additionally, every machine in the network you are trying to communicate with must also be configured properly.

DOS offers three management and diagnostic tools to troubleshoot TCP/IP settings:

- IPCONFIG
- PING
- TRACERT

IPCONFIG

The ***IPCONFIG*** command identifies your current TCP/IP settings. IPCONFIG is short for IP address configuration, and it is a vital management tool. This is also used for troubleshooting because it tells you whether you have a TCP/IP setting at all. If your TCP/IP address is 0.0.0.0, you do not have an address.

---

task **reference**

Using the IPCONFIG Command to Check Your TCP/IP Settings

- Click **Start, All Programs, Accessories, Command Prompt**

- Type **ipconfig,** then press **Enter**

Note that in the example (Figure 11.14), the basic TCP/IP settings—IP address, the subnet mask, and the default gateway—are all configured. The IP address of 192.168.1.2 indicates a healthy connection. If your settings were not correct, you would receive an all zeros address (0.0.0.0) or an address like 169.254.x.x, which indicates that your network server (the DHCP server in this case) was not accessible.

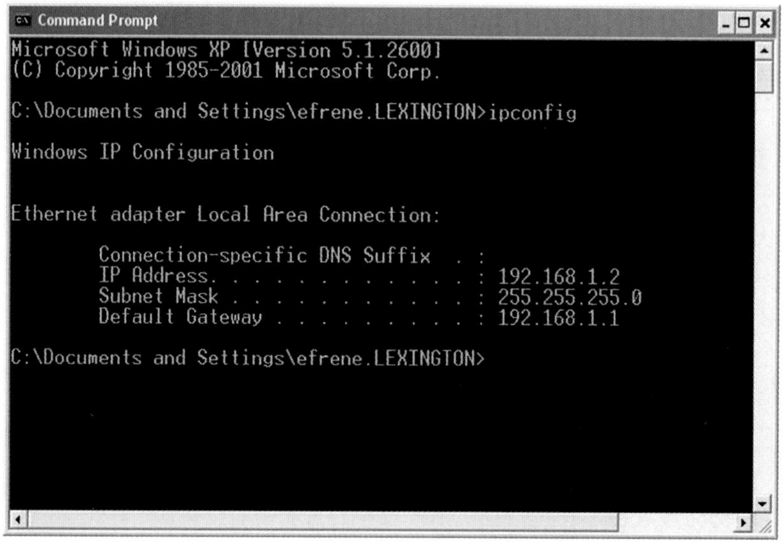

FIGURE 11.14

The IPCONFIG command provides information about your TCP/IP settings

```
Command Prompt                                             _ □ x
Microsoft Windows XP [Version 5.1.2600]
(C) Copyright 1985-2001 Microsoft Corp.

C:\Documents and Settings\efrene.LEXINGTON>ipconfig

Windows IP Configuration


Ethernet adapter Local Area Connection:

        Connection-specific DNS Suffix  . :
        IP Address. . . . . . . . . . . . : 192.168.1.2
        Subnet Mask . . . . . . . . . . . : 255.255.255.0
        Default Gateway . . . . . . . . . : 192.168.1.1

C:\Documents and Settings\efrene.LEXINGTON>
```

PING

Whereas the IPCONFIG command provides you with your current TCP/IP configuration, the ***PING*** command tests whether you can send a signal over the network and reach another computer. By typing PING x.x.x.x, where x.x.x.x is the address of the computer with which you want to test connectivity, you can determine if a connection exists between the two points. The standard PING command sends four requests, so if the connection is healthy, you should receive four responses, as shown in Figure 11.15.

FIGURE 11.15
A successful PING returns a response

If instead you receive a response like "host unknown" or "host unreachable," this means a problem exists in the connection. It could be a problem on your end, on the other end, or in between. You can narrow down the source of the problem by attempting to ping IP addresses that are progressively closer to your computer on the network, even down to pinging the network adapter card on your own machine. If you can't ping a computer on the Internet, try pinging the address of your default gateway of your local network. If you can get a response from your gateway, then that means the source of your problem is somewhere on the other side of your local network.

---

task reference

Using the PING Command to Test Connectivity

- Click **Start, All Programs, Accessories, Command Prompt**

- Type **ping x.x.x.x,** where x.x.x.x is the IP address of a remote computer, then press **Enter**

- If you receive a response, this means the connection between your computer and the remote one is good

---

Using the PING command to test connectivity:

One of Rob's colleagues is having difficulties accessing his e-mail. He can't connect to the Internet either. After making sure that the network cables are hooked up properly, and that the green light on the computer's network adapter is on, Rob runs the IPCONFIG command. The IP address shown begins with 169.254, which indicates that local network gateway is not being reached. His next step is to ping the computer's own address.

1. Navigate to the Command Prompt window in the Accessories menu

2. Type **ping 127.0.0.1,** then press **Enter**

tip: *IP address 127.0.0.1 is what's called a loopback address, and a response indicates TCP/IP is configured correctly on your machine.*

3. Type **ping x.x.x.x,** where x.x.x.x is the IP address of your network gateway, then press **Enter**

You can also ping a domain name, such as microsoft.com, by typing **ping www.microsoft.com.** However, if you are troubleshooting, you should try to ping an IP address first as an inability to ping a domain name could mean your domain name server is not working properly.

TRACERT

The ***TRACERT*** command is useful if you are having a problem reaching a particular remote IP address. What TRACERT does is tell you what links can be successfully established and which links are problematic. TRACERT can indicate whether the problem lies with your ISP's server, or the remote computer's ISP, or somewhere in between.

The TRACERT command is executed by typing TRACERT x.x.x.x, where x.x.x.x is a remote IP address, or by typing TRACERT name, where name is the domain name you're trying to reach.

Note the example in Figure 11.16. In this case, the TRACERT command traces a signal from a local server in New York to one in Japan. Each transmission from one router or server to another is called a "hop" and is indicated by a number, up to a maximum of 30. The example displays 20 hops; this means there are 20 servers between the local server and the server in Japan. The information also indicates that there is a problem with connectivity at the 10th hop, where I'm getting a "Request timed out" message. Unfortunately, there is little I can do about this connectivity problem on a remote server, but at least I know the problem does not lie with my local network, or even my local ISP's server.

F I G U R E   11.16

The TRACERT command outlines the route your signal takes between your computer and a remote one

```
 Command Prompt                                                          _ □ x

C:\Documents and Settings\efrene.LEXINGTON>Tracert typhoon.co.jp

Tracing route to typhoon.co.jp [202.33.21.38]
over a maximum of 30 hops:

  1    59 ms     9 ms     8 ms   10.11.64.1
  2     9 ms     7 ms     8 ms   dstswr2-vl2.rh.hcvlny.cv.net [167.206.32.34]
  3    13 ms    10 ms     9 ms   r2-ge9-1.mhe.hcvlny.cv.net [167.206.32.5]
  4     9 ms    10 ms     7 ms   r1-srp1-0.cr.hcvlny.cv.net [167.206.12.38]
  5     9 ms     7 ms    13 ms   r2-srp13-0.in.hcvlny.cv.net [167.206.12.130]
  6     8 ms     9 ms     9 ms   jfk3-core4-pos2-3.atlas.algx.net [198.180.44.101]
  7    19 ms    18 ms    17 ms   dca6-core4-pos3-0.atlas.algx.net [165.117.48.33]
  8    21 ms    16 ms    15 ms   dca6-att.peer.algx.net [165.117.69.10]
  9    29 ms    34 ms    18 ms   12.122.11.233
 10     *         *        *     Request timed out.
 11    77 ms    83 ms    78 ms   tbr1-p013302.sffca.ip.att.net [12.122.11.217]
 12    76 ms    75 ms    78 ms   gbr5-p100.sffca.ip.att.net [12.122.11.74]
 13    77 ms    75 ms    76 ms   gar2-p360.sffca.ip.att.net [12.123.13.149]
 14    80 ms    79 ms    75 ms   t1a5.us-sfo.concert.net [12.124.35.14]
 15    76 ms    75 ms    78 ms   t1a1-ge8-0-0.us-sfo.concert.net [166.49.228.39]
 16   231 ms   232 ms   231 ms   166-49-254-22.concert.net [166.49.254.22]
 17   200 ms   202 ms   200 ms   165.76.0.59
 18   202 ms   200 ms   200 ms   GE0-3-0.TKY01NJ8.TKY.SPIN.AD.JP [165.76.0.190]
 19   211 ms   216 ms   219 ms   att-r1.typhoon.co.jp [202.33.21.194]
 20   458 ms   466 ms   453 ms   storm.typhoon.co.jp [202.33.21.38]

Trace complete.

C:\Documents and Settings\efrene.LEXINGTON>_
```

task reference

Using the TRACERT Command

- Click **Start, All Programs, Accessories, Command Prompt**

- Type **TRACERT x.x.x.x,** where x.x.x.x is the IP address of a remote computer (or type **TRACERT name,** where name is the destination domain name), then press **Enter**

USING THE REGISTRY

The *Registry* is a database of configuration settings that Windows requires in order to run. The Registry contains information ranging from the Desktop's screen saver settings to the preference settings of applications. The Registry displays this information in the hierarchical directory tree structure similar to Windows Explorer (Figure 11.17). Although from the interface it appears that the Registry is all in one place, in fact it is stored in several files in different locations.

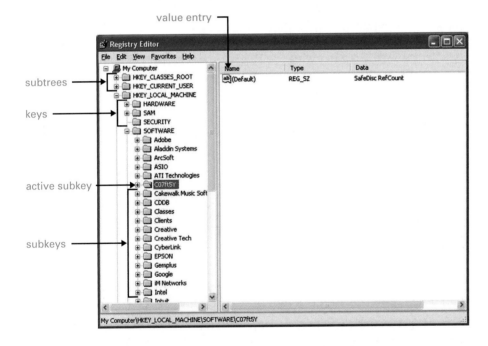

FIGURE 11.17

The Registry

The Registry can be edited with a program called the Registry Editor; however, this is an advanced tool, so any changes should be made with extreme caution. If you make a mistake when editing the Registry, you can damage your system and Windows may not be able to run. To avoid this, create a backup copy of the Registry before you make any changes and make sure you know how to restore it. If possible, try out your Registry changes first on a test computer before you implement them on a more vital machine.

Despite this warning, it is interesting to note that you *indirectly* edit the Registry all the time. Usually this is done through the multiple Properties dialog boxes one encounters in Windows. Each time you change the settings in a Properties dialog box, install or remove a program, change settings in the Control Panel, or configure a network connection, you are editing the Registry. Since these changes take place without too much difficulty, it may seem strange that you would bother with a tricky tool like the Registry Editor. This is generally true; in most cases, it is better not to have to use the Registry Editor. However, there are certain configurations that can only be accessed through the Registry.

Registry Interface Elements

The Registry Editor window displays two panes. The left pane holds the directory structure of the various subtrees, keys, and subkeys, while the right pane displays the values for the currently selected key.

As can be seen in Figure 11.17, the major components of the Registry are as follows:

- *Subtrees*. These are the top hierarchical levels just below My Computer, and they are divided into five main branches. Each of these five subtrees is further divided into keys, subkeys, and entries
- *Keys*. Analogous to folders in Windows Explorer, each of these keys contains additional divisions within them of subkeys and value entries
- *Subkeys*. One level down the hierarchy from a key, like a subfolder within a folder
- *Value Entries*. These pieces of information are what you actually edit when working with the Registry. Each entry is composed of a name, a data type, and a value

To begin with, let's take a look at the top level of the Registry—the five subtrees. Notice that subtree titles look like old-style filenames, spelled with all uppercase letters and with an underscore character (_) between the words instead of a blank space. The five subtrees are:

- HKEY_CLASSES_ROOT
- HKEY_CURRENT_USER
- HKEY_LOCAL_MACHINE
- HKEY_USERS
- HKEY_CURRENT_CONFIG

Each of these subtrees has a different purpose. All contain vital information for your computer to run smoothly, but some are more important than others in terms of the actual process of editing the Registry.

- HKEY_CLASSES_ROOT (HKCR). This subtree contains information about which file types are opened with which applications. As an example of the regular editing of the Registry that goes on behind the scenes all the time, when you open a file and Windows prompts you with a dialog box asking you to select a program to open the file, you are creating an entry in this subtree. The HKCR also contains definitions of every object that exists in Windows
- HKEY_CURRENT_USER (HKCU). This subtree contains the user profile for the currently logged on user. Included are all the personalized settings a user may have for their programs, Desktop image, the sounds that are played when certain Windows events occur, and so forth. One of these subtrees exists for each user, and the settings are stored in the user's Documents and Settings folder
- HKEY_LOCAL_MACHINE (HKLM). This subtree contains information about your current hardware and software settings, and as such, it is the most important subtree in the Registry. Although the

HKLM is a critical subtree, much of it is not very useful from a Registry editing standpoint, and changes to it are better made using the standard built-in Windows administrative and system tools you can access from the Control Panel or the Accessories Program folder. The exception to this is the Software key, which contains the settings for the system and applications and, as such, forms the bulk of the information you'll be interested in editing

- HKEY_USERS (HKU). This subtree contains separate keys for all the local users on your computer, including a default setting for a Guest account and a built-in profile for the Administrator. Every additional user who has an account set up on the local machine will have a separate key. Users' keys are identified by a string of numbers according to the users' security ID code. The HKCU, described above, is really just a link to the current user's key within this subtree. The reason for breaking out the current user's key as a separate subtree is that it resolves the problem of trying to determine who the current user is from several choices that are only named with a long string of numbers

- HKEY_CURRENT_CONFIG (HKCC). This subtree contains information about the hardware profile of your machine. This subtree is also just a link to the information contained in the HKLM, the local machine subtree

---

task reference

Displaying the Registry

- In the **Start** menu, click **Run**

- Type **regedit** in the **Open** text box, then click **OK**

- Click the plus sign (+) next to a key to expand it and display the contents

- Click an item to display its values

Backing Up and Restoring the Registry

Because it is easy to make mistakes when editing the Registry and because, unlike other Windows programs, changes take effect immediately after you make them (you don't get a dialog box summarizing the changes and asking you to confirm them), it is very important to back up the Registry *before* attempting to edit it. For this reason, the first thing to learn besides displaying the Registry is how to back it up. The easiest way to do this is to use the standard Windows Backup utility located in the System Tools.

task reference

Backing Up the Registry

- Click **Start, All Programs, Accessories, System Tools, Backup**

- In the Welcome to Backup or Restore Wizard screen (Figure 11.18), click the **Advanced Mode** link, then click **Next**

- Click the *Only back up the System State data* radio button, then click **Next**

---

*another*way

. . . to Back Up the Registry

Open the **Run** dialog box from the Start menu and type the following command: **ntbackup backup systemstate/j "backup name" /f "backup path."**

WINDOWS XP

FIGURE 11.18

The Backup or Restore Wizard

click the Advanced Mode link
when backing up the Registry

The backup file will have a .bkf filename extension. Copy this file to removable media, such as a rewritable CD (the file will be too large to fit on a floppy disk), and keep it in a safe place.

After creating a backup copy of the Registry, the next step is to make sure you understand how to restore from it. Remember that if Windows cannot open because of an error in the Registry, you may not have the luxury of using a Help menu to guide you through the Restore process.

*another*way

. . . to Restore the Registry

Restart the computer and hold down the **F8** key. In the Windows Advanced Options menu, click the **Last Known Good** Configuration, then press the **Enter** key twice. This will prompt Windows to start using a previous version of Registry

task reference

Restoring the Registry

- Click **Start, All Programs, Accessories, System Tools, Backup**

- In the Welcome to Backup or Restore Wizard screen click the **Advanced Mode** link, then click **Next**

- Click the **Restore Wizard** radio button, then click **Next** (Figure 11.19)

- Make sure the disk that contains your backup file is inserted in the drive

- Click the **Browse** button and navigate to the backup file on the disk

- Choose to restore the entire System state, not just the Registry, then click the **Start restore** button

- Answer the prompts in the dialog boxes, then click **Finish**

FIGURE 11.19

The Restore Wizard

Searching the Registry

You may come across suggestions or tips for editing the Registry on the Internet or in a computer magazine. Unfortunately, these tips are often poorly documented and can lead to much wasted time browsing through the various subtrees in order to find the value you're looking for.

anotherword

If you come across a tip in an article or on the Internet involving editing the Registry, make sure the article is talking about the Windows XP Registry. The Registry in different versions of Windows may work differently.

Fortunately, the Registry Editor provides a Find function. This Find function can help you locate specific information in the Registry very quickly. To use this function, go to the Edit menu and select Find. The Find dialog box (Figure 11.20) opens, allowing you to narrow down your search by specific parameters. You can search for a key name or the data contained in any key. By default, a search will look through all the keys, values, and data in the Registry. If you can specify whether you are searching for a key, value, or data, it will speed up your search significantly. An option called Match whole string only allows you to search for text that exactly matches the text you specify.

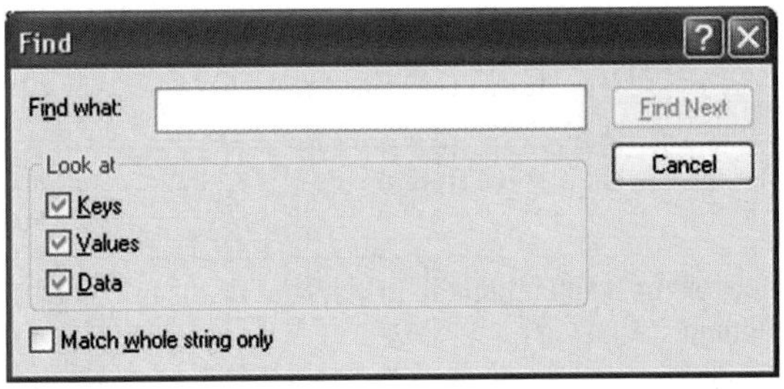

FIGURE 11.20

The Find dialog box

task reference

Searching the Registry

- In the Registry, click **Edit,** then **Find**

- In the Find dialog box, type the text you wish to find

- Narrow your search by clicking in the check boxes marked *Keys, Values, Data,* or *Match whole string only*

- Click **Find Next** to begin your search

making the grade | SESSION 11.3

1. The _____ command identifies your current TCP/IP settings.

2. The _____ command tests whether you can send a signal over the network and reach another computer.

3. The Registry backup file will have a _____ filename extension.

4. The Registry can be edited with a program called the _____.

WINDOWS XP

SECTION 11.4 SUMMARY

This chapter dealt with troubleshooting and began by reviewing two useful tools, the Task Manager and the Device Manager. You learned how to use these tools to end programs that are not responding, diagnose problems with devices, and produce a complete hardware report. You also practiced rolling back a driver that is malfunctioning.

Next you studied how to deal with problems involving your entire system. In this context, you learned and practiced how to restart your computer in Safe Mode, and how to restore your computer to a previous point in time when the current problems were not evident. You also were taught how to generate reports on the current system status.

Next, network troubleshooting was examined. You learned three commands: IPCONFIG, PING, and TRACERT to use in the event of network problems. You learned what the Registry is and the importance of making a complete backup and knowing how to restore the Registry in case something goes wrong. Finally, you learned how to edit the Registry.

task reference roundup

Task	Page #	Preferred Method
Displaying the Task Manager	WINXP 11.6	• Press and hold down **Ctrl+Alt**, then press **Delete**
Using Task Manager	WINXP 11.6	• In the Task Manager, click the Application tab to view the status of programs that are running
		• In the Task Manager, click the Processes tab to view the status of the processes that are running
		• In the Task Manager, click the Performance tab to check the status of your computer's performance
		• In the Task Manager, click the Networking tab to view the status and performance of the network
Using Task Manager to close a program that is not responding	WINXP 11.7	• Display the Task Manager and click the **Applications** tab
		• Select the program that is not responding from the *Task* list
		• Click the **End Task** button
		• Click the **End Now** button to close the program
Displaying the Device Manager	WINXP 11.8	• Click **Start**, then **Control Panel**
		• Double-click **System**
		• In the **Hardware** tab of the System Properties dialog box, click the **Device Manager** button
Printing information about hardware	WINXP 11.9	• In the Device Manager screen, click the device or the category of device for which you want to print information
		• In the **Action** menu, click **Print**

task reference roundup

Task	Page #	Preferred Method
		• In the Print dialog box, choose from one of the *Report types* by clicking the appropriate radio button: the *System summary* option prints a *summary* of the devices connected to your computer. The *Selected class or device* option prints a report for the individual device or the entire class of device types selected. *All devices and system summary* prints a report about every device installed on your computer along with a hardware summary
		• Click the **Print** button
Using the Device Manager to obtain details about a device	WINXP 11.10	• In the Device Manager, click the plus sign (+) next to the category folder that contains the device
		• Double-click the particular device about which you want more information
		• In the device's Properties dialog box, click the General tab to obtain the name of the manufacturer and the operating status of the device
		• Click the Driver tab to obtain information about the version number or other information related to the driver provider, date, or digital signer
		• Click the Resources tab to view the resources used by the device driver and a list of possible conflicting devices
		• Click **OK** to close the Properties dialog box when done obtaining the information you need
Updating a driver	WINXP 11.12	• In the Device Manager, double-click the device you want to update
		• Click the **Drivers** tab of the Properties dialog box
		• Click the **Update Driver** button
		• Select the *Install from a list or specific location* radio button, then click **Next**
		• Select the *Don't search, I will choose the driver to install* radio button, then click **Next**
		• Click the **Have Disk** button
		• Click **Browse**, then navigate to the file containing the driver update
		• Click the **Open** button
		• Click **OK**
		• Click **Next**
		• Click **Finish**
Rolling back a driver	WINXP 11.12	• In the Device Manager, double-click the device you want to roll back
		• Click the **Drivers** tab of the Properties dialog box; click the **Roll Back Driver** button
		• Click **Yes**
		• Click **OK**

task reference roundup

Task	Page #	Preferred Method
Starting in Safe Mode	WINXP 11.14	• If your computer is on, shut it off
		• Turn on your computer and monitor, then immediately press and hold down the **F8** key
		• The Windows Advanced Options menu appears. Use the up and down arrow keys to highlight the **Safe Mode** option, then press **Enter**
		• Use arrow keys again to highlight the operating system you want to start, then press **Enter**
		• At the Welcome screen, click the Administrator account to use
		• Click the **Yes** button in the dialog box
		• When finished using Safe Mode, restart your computer normally
Restoring your computer	WINXP 11.16	• Click **Start, All Programs, Accessories, System Tools, System Restore**
		• Click the **Restore my computer to an earlier time** radio button, then click **Next**
		• The Select a restore point screen opens showing a calendar with all the dates that have restore points in bold
		• Click the most recent day with a restore point before the problems started, then click **Next**
		• The Confirm Restore Point Selection asks you to confirm the restore point you have selected and provides some information about the restore process; click **Next**
		• A dialog box will detail the progress of the restoration, and the computer restarts when complete. Click **OK**
Manually creating a restore point	WINXP 11.17	• Click **Start, All Programs, Accessories, System Tools, System Restore**
		• Click the **Create a restore point** radio button, then click **Next**
		• Type a description for the restore point and click **Create**
		• Click **Close**
Displaying System Information	WINXP 11.19	• Click **Start, All Programs, Accessories, System Tools, System Information**
		• Click the **System Summary** folder in the left pane to display general information
		• Click the plus sign (+) next to a category name to expand the list, then click the specific item about which you wish to view more details
Using the IPCONFIG command to check your TCP/IP settings	WINXP 11.20	• Click **Start, All Programs, Accessories, Command Prompt**
		• Type **ipconfig,** then press **Enter**

task reference roundup

Task	Page #	Preferred Method
Using the PING command to test connectivity	WINXP 11.21	• Click **Start, All Programs, Accessories, Command Prompt**
		• Type **ping x.x.x.x,** where x.x.x.x is the IP address of a remote computer, then press **Enter**
		• If you receive a response, this means the connection between your computer and the remote one is good
Using the TRACERT command	WINXP 11.23	• Click **Start, All Programs, Accessories, Command Prompt**
		• Type **TRACERT x.x.x.x,** where x.x.x.x is the IP address of a remote computer (or type **TRACERT name,** where name is the destination domain name), then press **Enter**
Displaying the Registry	WINXP 11.25	• In the **Start** menu, click **Run**
		• Type **regedit** in the **Open** text box, then click **OK**
		• Click the plus sign (+) next to a key to expand it and display the contents
		• Click an item to display its values
Backing up the Registry	WINXP 11.25	• Click **Start, All Programs, Accessories, System Tools, Backup**
		• In the Welcome to Backup or Restore Wizard screen, click the **Advanced Mode** link, then click **Next**
		• Click the *Only back up the System State data* radio button, then click **Next**
Restoring the Registry	WINXP 11.26	• Click **Start, All Programs, Accessories, System Tools, Backup**
		• In the Welcome to Backup or Restore Wizard screen click the **Advanced Mode** link, then click **Next**
		• Click the **Restore Wizard** radio button, then click **Next**
		• Make sure the disk that contains your backup file is inserted in the drive
		• Click the **Browse** button and navigate to the backup file on the disk
		• Choose to restore the entire System state, not just the Registry, then click the **Start restore** button
		• Answer the prompts in the dialog boxes, then click **Finish**
Searching the Registry	WINXP 11.27	• In the Registry, click **Edit,** then **Find**
		• In the Find dialog box, type the text you wish to find
		• Narrow your search by clicking in the check boxes marked *Keys, Values, Data,* or *Match whole string only*
		• Click **Find Next** to begin your search

WINDOWS XP

CROSSWORD PUZZLE

Across

3. A basic, minimal configuration of your operating system used for troubleshooting
6. A recent working version of the Registry is the last _____
7. A manager for diagnosing and managing system problems
10. A command line prompt which identifies your current TCP/IP settings
11. Tells you what links can be successfully established and which links are problematic

Down

1. An earlier time when the computer was not experiencing the current problems
2. A database of configuration settings in Windows
4. The function of reverting back to the previous version of the driver
5. A program that allows the Registry to be edited
8. Manager utility to check hardware
9. Tests whether you can send a signal over the network and reach another computer

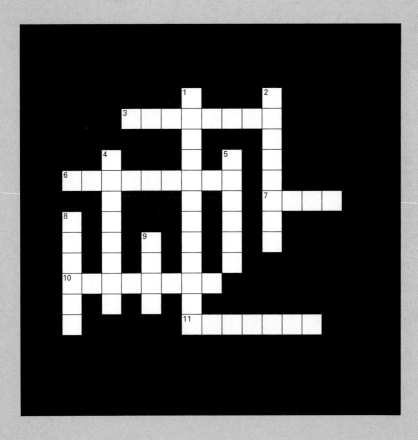

FILL-IN

1. The _____ command identifies your current TCP/IP settings.

2. The _____ command tests whether you can send a signal over the network and reach another computer.

3. _____ tells you what links can be successfully established and which links are problematic.

CREATE THE QUESTION

For each answer, create an appropriate, short question:

ANSWER	QUESTION
1. Hold down the Ctrl + Alt keys, then press Delete	_____
2. A basic, minimal configuration of your operating system	_____
3. This command will prompt Windows to start using a previous version of Registry	_____

SHORT ANSWER

1. Why it is very important to back up the Registry *before* attempting to edit it?

2. Returning your computer to an earlier time before the problems started happening is called what?

3. What tool do you employ when you are having problems with a program that is not responding?

4. What key do you hold down when restarting the computer to access the Windows Advanced Options menu?

1. Using Task Manager to End an Unresponsive Program

Curtis Palmer is employed in the Customer Service Department of the Super Clean Washing Machine Company. He has several customers anxiously awaiting a shipment of backordered parts so that their washing machines can be fixed. He tracks the status of the shipment on a company intranet Web site. This morning his first call was from one of these customers, asking for the latest ETA of the parts. When Curtis tries to log on, his Web browser seems to take forever to connect. Since the customer is holding on the line waiting for an answer, Curtis wants to forget about checking the company site and call the warehouse directly to get the latest information. The problem is that the warehouse telephone number is listed in a database program on his machine that he can't access because his computer is still attempting to log on. He wants to end the Web browser application so he can get back the use of his machine.

1. Press and hold down **Ctrl+Alt,** then press **Delete**
2. Click the **Applications** tab
3. Select the program that is not responding from the *Task* list (in this case, it would be Internet Explorer)
4. Click the **End Task** button
5. Click the **End Now** button to close the program

2. Printing Information about Hardware

Sal Mineo is a systems analyst for Titanic Brands. It is close to the end of his fiscal year and management has asked him to draw up a budget for the following year based on an assumption of a 10 to 15 percent growth rate. Sal wants to upgrade approximately 250 computers in the home office to accommodate the projected growth. He needs to provide recommendations and expected cost outlay for the upgrade. He needs to understand exactly what devices are connected to each of these machines. He asks you to give him a report summarizing all the devices by type and quantity.

1. In the Device Manager screen, click your computer's name
2. In the **Action** menu click **Print**
3. In the Print dialog box, choose the *Report type* by clicking the *All devices and system summary* radio button, which prints a report about every device installed on your computer along with a hardware summary
4. Click the **Print** button

challenge!

1. Checking the Status of Network Activity

Camilla Rhodes works at Lynch Consultants Worldwide, a business consulting organization. One of her clients is concerned that their employees are spending too much company time browsing the Internet. Besides wasting time, this also causes excessive loads on the company network. They want to make sure network activity is monitored and selectively limited on each machine. Camilla advises them that this can be done with the Task Manager tool.

1. Press and hold down **Ctrl+Alt,** then press **Delete**
2. Click the Networking tab of the Task Manager
3. Open Internet Explorer and visit three or four different sites
4. Open your e-mail program and send an e-mail to a friend or colleague
5. Check the graphic display in the Networking tab of the Task Manager for how each of these actions manifests itself as network activity on the displayed graph. Your graph should look something like the one in Figure 11.21

FIGURE 11.21

The Networking tab of the Task Manager displaying activity

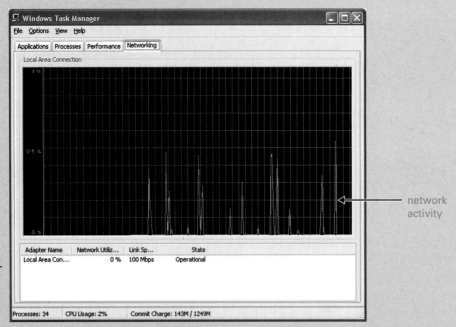

network activity

1. Testing Network Connectivity

Janet Conway works for D&M Career Training Seminars as a senior sales manager. She spends most of her day on the phone and at night attends company functions. She has no time to spare to troubleshoot problems receiving sales leads from the company Web site. One thing she has noticed is that there have been no requests for information from the Web site for the last two days, which is unusual. Typically she gets three to four requests per day.

Janet stops by the network administrator's office and advises him of the suspected problem. While Janet is still in his office, he does a quick check of the connection between the company server and the server that hosts the company Web site.

1. Navigate to the Command Prompt window in the Accessories menu
2. Type **ipconfig,** and then press **Enter**
3. Write down the IP address of your gateway
4. Type **ping x.x.x.x,** where x.x.x.x is the IP address of your network gateway, then press **Enter.** How many responses did you receive from your ping?
5. Now type **tracert microsoft.com,** and then press **Enter.** How many hops did it take to reach the Microsoft server?

e-business

1. Printing System Information

Bob Lovano is a network administrator for All Over It Inc., an e-broadcast company that provides access to bulk e-mail services. When Bob came in this morning, he received an e-mail indicating that a computer in the Legal Department is behaving strangely. One of the first things he wants to do is print a report, which will summarize the system information on the problematic computer.

1. Navigate to the System Information window in the Control Panel **(Start, Control Panel, Accessories, System Tools, System Information)**
2. In the left pane, click **System Summary.** It takes Windows a few moments to refresh the current information; then the summary is displayed, which should look like Figure 11.22
3. Click **File,** then **Print**

F I G U R E   11.22

The System Information report displayed in the Computer Management window

1. Starting in Safe Mode

Armando Reyes is a network administrator for Chilean Sea Lines, a commercial shipping enterprise out of Valparaiso, Chile. It is autumn in Chile when it is spring in North America. This means that the peak buying season in the United States and the fruit harvesting season in Chile coincide. It is the busiest time of year for Armando's company. Unfortunately, the computer systems also tend to go down during this time. One of the dispatchers has a problem getting his computer to boot up. Armando needs to get the machine up and running again so that the dispatcher can retrieve some vital information that's needed immediately.

1. If your computer is on, shut it off
2. Turn on your computer and monitor, then immediately press and hold down the **F8** key
3. The Windows Advanced Options menu appears. Use the up and down arrow keys to highlight the **Safe Mode** option, then press **Enter**
4. Use arrow keys again to highlight the operating system you want to start, then press **Enter**
5. At the Welcome screen, click the administrator account to use
6. Click the **Yes** button in the dialog box
7. When finished using Safe Mode, restart your computer normally

Chapter Objectives

- Determine whether your computer meets the system and installation requirements

- Produce reports to determine compatibility issues and to preserve information about your computer

- Learn the difference between an upgrade and a clean install

- Install Windows XP Professional from the CD-ROM, floppy drive, or a network folder

- Learn how to find out about and install updates to the operating system

CHAPTER

12

twelve

Installing and Updating Windows XP Professional

Associated Insurance Company, Duluth, Minnesota

Lisa Brendon just found out that the computers at her company would be upgraded from the Windows 98 operating system to Windows XP Professional. The company planned to allow all the employees to upgrade their machines from the setup program, which they would place on the network. The network administrators also provided information sheets to each employee listing the path to the setup program, the domain name, and the IP address of each computer.

Before performing the upgrade, Lisa wanted to make sure none of her data were accidentally lost. She made sure to back up her data onto one of the network servers. She also remembered to uncompress her hard drive, since the administrators let her know that Windows XP couldn't handle the DriveSpace program that ran on Windows 98.

Lisa also planned to start working at home part of the week. She had just bought a used computer system with Windows 95 on it and planned to install Windows XP Professional in order to have a consistent interface both at home and at work. She wanted to make sure that she was starting with a clean slate, so she decided to do a complete installation from scratch on her home computer. The company purchased a copy of Windows XP for Lisa to install at home and gave her the Windows XP Professional CD-ROM. Lisa wanted to make sure the new operating system would work with the equipment she had, so she took a look at the Hardware Compatibility List on the CD-ROM. She also produced a configuration report to have her previous settings on hand in case she needed them.

Lisa also wanted to make sure she kept her systems up to date with Microsoft's latest changes. She knew that the Microsoft Web site included a Windows Update program to automatically detect updates, and she planned to explore the Windows XP site regularly to find out about and download updates.

INTRODUCTION

Before you can begin to do anything using Windows XP Professional, it has to be installed on your computer. The installation process is fairly simple, and the Windows XP Setup Wizard guides you through the steps and prompts you for information as it's needed.

Before you install Windows XP Professional, you need to make sure your computer can accommodate the operating system. You also must decide whether you're going to upgrade from a previous version of Windows or do a clean install. Finally, you should back up previous data and determine whether any of your current hardware or software is incompatible with Windows XP Professional.

Once the operating system is installed, you can use Microsoft's Web site to find out about improvements and updates to the operating system.

SESSION 12.1 BEFORE YOU INSTALL

Installing Windows XP Professional is not a difficult process, but you do have to make sure your computer can handle the operating system, that you are able to install it, and that you won't have any compatibility issues with your current setup. You must also decide whether you're upgrading from a previous version of Windows or making a new installation.

BASIC SYSTEM AND INSTALLATION REQUIREMENTS

System requirements are the requirements for running the operating system once it's installed. ***Installation requirements*** are the requirements for performing the installation. Keep in mind that these are minimum requirements; depending on how the computer is used, your needs will probably necessitate increasing the minimum standards below.

You can check your current system's processor type, speed, and amount of RAM memory by right-clicking on My Computer in order to display the System Properties dialog box (Figure 12.1).

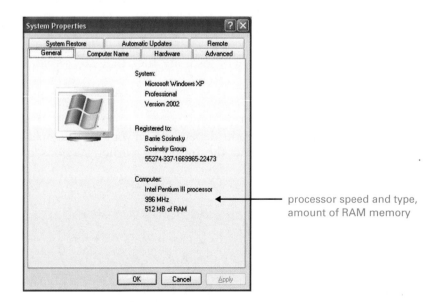

processor speed and type, amount of RAM memory

FIGURE 12.1

The System Properties dialog box

System Requirements

To run Windows XP Professional on your computer, it must have the following:

- A Pentium II or higher processor
- 233 MHz or faster processor speed; while less than this isn't a problem during installation, a slower processor speed will cause delays when you try to work
- 64 MB RAM, although at least 128 MB RAM is recommended
- An SVGA or higher resolution monitor
- A keyboard
- A Microsoft mouse or compatible pointing device
- 1.5 GB of free space on your hard disk

Installation Requirements

To install Windows XP Professional from the CD-ROM, you must have:

- A CD-ROM or DVD drive
- A 3.5", 1.44 MB floppy disk drive

To install Windows XP Professional from a shared network folder, you must have:

- A compatible network adapter card
- A working network connection
- Permission to get access to the shared folder

UPGRADE VERSUS CLEAN INSTALL

One early decision to make is whether you are upgrading from a previous version of Windows or doing a clean install of Windows XP Professional.

What's the Difference?

When you *upgrade,* you simply install the new Windows files onto your current machine. Your current Windows settings (colors, etc.) remain in place, and any programs you installed also remain.

A *clean install* wipes out all your previous files and installs Windows XP Professional from scratch. You will lose any files that are on your computer.

When Can You Upgrade?

You may not have the option to upgrade, depending on your current operating system. You can upgrade from the following earlier versions of Windows:

- Windows XP Home Edition
- Windows 2000
- Windows Me
- Windows 98
- Windows 95
- Windows NT Workstation 4.0
- Windows NT Workstation 3.5.1

If your current computer is running *any other* operating system, then you must do a clean install.

If you currently have either Windows NT 4.0 or Windows 2000 installed on your machine, then you cannot upgrade to XP Home Edition, only to XP Professional.

FIGURE 12.2

Upgrade versus new installation

You Should UPGRADE If All of the Following Are True:	You Should INSTALL a New Copy If Any of the Following Are True:
You're already using an earlier version of Windows that supports upgrading	Your hard disk is blank
—and—	—or—
You want to replace your Windows operating system with Windows XP	Your current operating system doesn't support an upgrade to Windows XP
—and—	—or—
You want to keep your existing files and preferences	You already use an operating system, but you don't want to keep your existing files and preferences, so that you can cleanly install

OBTAINING COMPATIBILITY AND CONFIGURATION INFORMATION

Before you install Windows XP Professional, especially if you're upgrading from a previous version of Windows, you should find out whether your current system has any compatibility issues with Windows XP Professional and generate a configuration report for your current system to have as a reference when doing the upgrade.

Hardware Compatibility List

The ***Hardware Compatibility List (HCL)*** is a list of equipment that is compatible with Windows XP Professional. The Windows XP Setup Wizard automatically checks your hardware and software and reports any potential conflicts. To ensure a successful installation, however, you should determine whether your computer hardware is compatible with Windows XP Professional before you start the Wizard.

> ### *another*word
>
> **. . . on Whether to Install Windows XP**
>
> A different issue is whether an organization should install Windows XP Professional at all: by mid-2002, only 17 percent of the marketplace had installed Windows XP. About 90 percent of the code base is the same as the previous Windows version, Windows 2000 Professional. Some people consider XP Professional to be Windows NT version 5.2 (Windows 2000 being version 5.1), since both Windows 2000 and XP are built on top of Windows NT. Additionally, many enterprises have invested a great deal of blood, sweat, and tears, not to mention time and money, into upgrading to Windows 2000 and getting the system stabilized. To upgrade again so soon, if there are no pressing needs, is not attractive.
>
> There are certainly improvements in XP over previous Windows versions, but the most definitive reason to upgrade may be that Microsoft is scheduled to end Windows 2000 extended support in spring 2003, while they have committed to supporting Windows XP until 2005.

You can view the Hardware Compatibility List at the Microsoft Web site: *www.microsoft.com/hcl/*

Windows XP Professional supports only those devices listed in the HCL. If your hardware isn't listed, contact the hardware manufacturer and request a Windows XP Professional driver for the component.

---

task reference

Viewing the Hardware Compatibility List (HCL)

- View the Hardware Compatibility List at www.microsoft.com/hcl/

Upgrade Report

The Windows XP Professional CD-ROM includes a tool for generating an *upgrade report,* if you're planning to upgrade. During installation, the Windows Setup Wizard creates an upgrade report that indicates any problems you may later have due to compatibility with installed programs and hardware on your computer. This upgrade can be printed.

Printing a Configuration Report

If you're upgrading from a previous version of Windows, a *configuration report* provides details about your current settings for the devices connected to your computer. You may need some of these settings in the unlikely event that the Windows XP installation program isn't able to detect and configure a device itself.

The process for printing the report is slightly different depending on the previous version of Windows from which you're upgrading.

---

task reference

Printing a Configuration Report from Windows 95 or Windows 98

- On the **Desktop,** right-click **My Computer**
- In the context menu, click **Properties**
- Click the **Device Manager** tab
- Click **Print**
- In the Print dialog box, select **System Summary**
- Click **OK**

Printing a Configuration Report from Windows NT

- In the **Start** menu, click **Programs**
- In the **Programs** menu, click **Administrative Tools (Common)**
- In the **Administrative Tools** submenu, click **Windows NT Diagnostics**
- Click **Print**
- Under **Scope,** click the **All tabs** radio button
- Under **Detail Level,** click the **Summary** radio button
- Under **Destination,** click the **Default Printer** radio button
- Click **OK**

OBTAINING NETWORK INFORMATION

If your computer is on a network, you need to obtain the following information from your network administrator:

- The name of your computer
- The name of your domain or workgroup
- The IP address of your computer

You will be prompted for this information during the installation process.

BACKING UP DATA AND UNCOMPRESSING YOUR HARD DISK

Backing Up Data

Before you upgrade from a previous version of Windows, it's a good idea to back up the files on your computer.

Windows 95, Windows 98, Windows 2000, and Windows NT all have a Backup program that allows you to back up files. For Windows NT, you can back up your files to a tape. For Windows 95, Windows 98, or Windows 2000, you can back up files to tape, to another hard drive, to a network drive, or to removable media such as a Zip disk or floppy disk.

---

task reference

Starting the Backup Program from Windows 95, Windows 98, or Windows 2000

- In the **Start** menu, click **Programs**
- In the **Programs** menu, click **Accessories**
- In the **Accessories** submenu, click **System Tools**
- In the **System Tools** submenu, click **Backup**

Starting the Backup Program from Windows NT

- In the **Start** menu, click **Programs**
- In the **Programs** menu, click **Administrative Tools (Common)**
- In the **Administrative Tools** submenu, click **Backup**

Uncompressing Your Hard Disk

Windows 95, Windows 98, and MS-DOS 6 come with DriveSpace or DoubleSpace, disk compression programs. There are also third-party programs you can use to compress your hard disk.

Windows XP Professional is incompatible with any disk compression program, so before you install Windows XP Professional on a hard disk, you must be sure to uncompress it.

WINDOWS XP

task reference

Uncompressing a Hard Disk from Windows 95 or Windows 98

- In the **Start** menu, click **Programs**
- In the **Programs** menu, click **Accessories**
- In the **Accessories** submenu, click **System Tools**
- In the **System Tools** submenu, click **DriveSpace**
- In the **DriveSpace** dialog box, select the compressed drive
- In the **Drive** menu, click **Uncompress**

Uncompressing a Hard Disk from MS-DOS

- If you're running MS-DOS 6.22 or higher, then at the Command Prompt, type **drvspace**
- If you have an earlier version, type **dblspace**
- Select the drive to uncompress
- In the **Tools** menu, click **Uncompress**

THE FILES AND SETTINGS TRANSFER WIZARD

New to XP is a Wizard that allows you to transfer your personal files and settings from one computer to another. Files such as My Documents and My Pictures, and settings such as your display settings, e-mail preferences, Address Book, and Favorites list from your Web browser—all your important data and personalized settings you have set up on an older version of Windows, such as Windows 95, 98, Me, NT, or 2000—can be automatically re-created when you convert to Windows XP. It doesn't matter which previous Windows operating system you have the files and settings in, but the computer to which you transfer the files must be running XP.

This is useful not only when upgrading operating systems but also when you want to set up the same files and settings on multiple computers or when you change computers.

You use the Windows XP CD-ROM disk to start the File and Transfer Wizard on a machine running an older version of Windows. Insert the disk, click Perform additional tasks, and then select Transfer files and settings.

You can transfer the information either through a network connection or by copying the data onto a removable media such as a CD or Zip disk. A direct cable connection can also be set up between two computers.

Once your files and settings have been imported to the destination computer, you must run the Files and Settings Transfer Wizard on this new computer in order to complete the transfer. Keep in mind that if you choose to transfer data using removable media, such as a recordable CD or Zip drive, you must connect that drive to the destination computer in order for the destination computer to access the collected data.

task reference

Using the Files and Settings Transfer Wizard

- In the source computer, click **Start, All Programs, Accessories, System Tools, Files and Settings Transfer Wizard**

- Click the **Old computer** radio button, then click **Next**

- Choose the transfer method, then click **Next**

- Choose the type of information to transfer, then click **Next**

- Click **Finish**

- In the destination computer, navigate to the **Files and Transfer Settings Wizard**

- Click the **New Computer** radio button, then click **Next**

- Click the radio button that indicates you have already collected your data, then click **Next**

- Specify the location of your data, then click **Next**

- Click **Finish**

Using the Files and Settings Transfer Wizard:

Lisa had spent some time setting up her old computer with all her preferences, so she wanted to keep these settings as much as possible on her new computer. She also had data on the machine that she would need to reference in the future, so she also wanted access to that. Given this scenario, and that she had plenty of room on her hard disk, she planned to use the Files and Settings Transfer Wizard.

1. In the source computer, click **Start, All Programs, Accessories, System Tools, Files and Settings Transfer Wizard.** The Files and Settings Transfer Wizard opens. Click **Next**

F I G U R E   12.3

The Files and Settings Wizard

2. Click **Old computer,** then click **Next**

FIGURE 12.4
The Select a transfer method screen of the Files and Settings Transfer Wizard

3. Click the radio button by the method you want to use to transfer, then click **Next**

tip: *If you select the* Floppy drive or other removable media *option, use the drop-down list to select the type of media.*

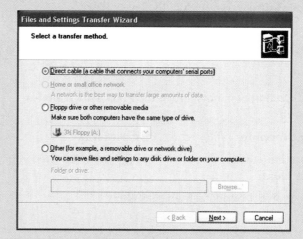

4. Click a radio button to indicate the type of information you want to transfer, then click **Next**

5. The Wizard indicates that you have completed the collection phase. Click **Finish**

6. In the destination computer, open the Files and Settings Transfer Wizard and click **Next**

7. Click **New computer,** then click **Next**

8. Click the radio button that indicates you have already collected your data, then click **Next**

9. Click an option to specify the location of the collected data, then click **Next**

tip: *If you can't remember where you put the collected data, click **Browse** to search.*

10. Click **Finish** to close the Wizard.

11. Click **Yes** to log off Windows at the dialog box that indicates you must do so for the transfer to be completed

---

SESSION 12.1   *making the grade*

1. A _____ clears all of your previous programs.

2. What is the minimum processor speed required to install Windows XP Professional?

3. Print a _____ to have your current device settings on hand before upgrading.

4. To detect possible compatibility issues, generate a/an _____.

5. Use the _____ Wizard to transfer your data from one computer to another.

SESSION 12.2 INSTALLING WINDOWS XP PROFESSIONAL

Once you know how you plan to install Windows XP Professional, and have gathered the information you need, the actual installation process is fairly simple. This session goes over the basics of starting the process and explains how to specify the information requested during the process.

INSTALLING FROM THE WINDOWS XP PROFESSIONAL CD-ROM

Installing on a Previous Version of Windows

If you're installing from a previous version of Windows, then just insert the Windows XP Professional CD-ROM into your CD-ROM or DVD drive. The Welcome screen displays (Figure 12.5).

FIGURE 12.5

The Welcome screen of the Windows XP Professional installation CD

In the Welcome screen, selecting to install the Windows XP Professional launches the Windows Setup Wizard.

---

task reference

Beginning Installation from the CD-ROM from a Previous Version of Windows

- Insert the Windows XP Professional CD-ROM into your CD-ROM or DVD drive
- Click **Install Windows XP**
- In the **Windows XP Setup Welcome** screen, click the appropriate radio button to indicate whether you're upgrading or doing a clean install
- Click **Next**

WINDOWS XP

Installing without a Previous Version of Windows

If you don't have a previous version of Windows installed, then you must first turn off your computer to allow Windows XP Professional to be installed as your machine boots up.

If you can boot from your CD-ROM drive, then when the machine is turned off, insert the Windows XP Professional CD-ROM into your CD-ROM drive.

If you cannot boot from your CD-ROM drive, you must use the Windows XP Setup Boot Disks. With the machine off, insert Windows XP Setup Boot Disk 1 into your floppy disk drive.

You then continue with the Windows XP setup.

---

task reference

Beginning Installation without a Previous Version of Windows

- Turn off your computer
- If you can boot from your CD-ROM drive, insert the Windows XP Professional CD-ROM into your CD-ROM drive
- If you cannot boot from your CD-ROM drive, insert the Windows XP Setup Boot Disk 1 into your floppy disk drive
- Power up your computer

INSTALLING FROM A SHARED NETWORK FOLDER

If you're installing Windows XP Professional from a shared network folder, you need to get the path to the setup program from your network administrator.

If you're installing Windows XP Professional from Windows 95, Windows 98, or Windows NT, then run the program *winnt32* in the setup folder.

If you're installing from Windows 3.1 or some other operating system, run the program *winnt*.

---

task reference

Beginning Installation from a Shared Network Folder

- Obtain the path to the setup folder
- If you're installing from Windows 95, Windows 98, or Windows NT, run the program **winnt32** from the setup folder
- If you're installing from Windows 3.1 or some other operating system, run the program **winnt** from the setup folder

---

COMPLETING THE INSTALLATION

License, Partition, and File System Information

Once you select whether to upgrade or to do a clean install, the License Agreement dialog box prompts you to accept Microsoft's licensing agreement. You cannot click Next to continue until you accept it.

The Your Product Key dialog box asks for the product key. Enter the key, and then click Next.

The Setup Wizard at this point gives you the option to generate an upgrade report that addresses compatibility issues with your existing system and XP. Select an option to set the report and click Next.

The next screen gives you the opportunity to download updated Setup files from Microsoft. Clicking Next allows the Setup Wizard to begin the process of installing Windows XP.

---

task *reference*

Setting License, Partition, and File System Information

- In the **License Agreement** dialog box, click **I accept this agreement,** then click **Next**

- In the **Your Product Key** dialog box, type the product key, then click **Next**

- In the **Special Options** dialog box, if you want to select a partition during installation, click **Advanced Options**

- In the **Advanced Options** dialog box, check **I want to choose the installation partition during setup,** then click **OK**

- In the **Special Options** dialog box, click **Next**

- After the computer restarts, if asked, select the partition on which to install Windows XP, then press **Enter**

- If prompted, indicate whether to convert the file system to NTFS, then press **Enter**

Regional Settings and Personalizing Your Computer

After the computer restarts, click Next from the Welcome screen. In the Regional Settings dialog box, click Next. In the Personalize Your Software dialog box, enter your name and an organization name, if appropriate, then click Next.

---

task *reference*

Regional Settings and Personalizing Your Computer

- When the computer restarts, in the **Welcome** dialog box, click **Next**

- In the **Regional Settings** dialog box, click **Next**

- In the **Personalize Your Software** dialog box, in the **Name** field, type your name

- If appropriate, in the **Organization** field, type the name of the organization

- Click **Next**

Computer Name, Date, and Network Information

After you specify your name and the organization, the next dialog box asks for the computer name and Administrator password.

If your network administrator has assigned a computer name, then type that name in the Computer Name field. Otherwise, you need to make up a name. Computer names should be 15 characters or less and be made up of letters and numbers only—no punctuation.

In the password fields, type and confirm the Administrator password. This is the password used to log onto your computer as Administrator, which allows the user to perform certain advanced tasks and to manage user accounts on your computer.

The Modem Dialog Information screen prompts you for information about dialing up using your modem. Fill in the information, and then click Next.

In the Date and Time Settings dialog box, make sure the information is correct, and then click Next.

In the Network Settings dialog box, stick with the Typical Settings unless your network administrator has indicated otherwise.

In the Workgroup or Computer Domain dialog box, if your computer is part of a network domain, click the appropriate radio button and type the name of the domain in the field. If your computer is not part of a network domain, click the other radio button and type the name of the workgroup in the field. If your computer is part of a domain, your network administrator needs to have set up a domain account for your computer before you start the installation.

After you click Next for the Workgroup or Computer Domain dialog box, the installation is almost complete. Click Finish in the Completing Windows XP Setup Wizard dialog box to complete the installation and restart the computer.

---

task reference

Computer Name, Date, and Network Information

- In the **Computer Name and Administrator Password** dialog box, in the **Computer name** field, type the name of your computer

- In the **Administrator password** field, type the password for your computer's Administrator account

- In the **Confirm password** field, type the password again

- Click **Next**

- In the **Modem Dialing Information** dialog box, specify the area code, outside line, and type of dialing, then click **Next**

- In the **Date and Time Settings** dialog box, make sure the date and time are correct, then click **Next**

- In the **Network Settings** dialog box, select **Typical Settings,** then click **Next**

- In the **Workgroup or Computer Domain** dialog box, if your computer is part of a network domain for which your computer has an account, click the **Yes** radio button and type the domain name in the **Workgroup or computer domain** field

- If your computer is not part of a network domain, then click the **No** radio button and type the workgroup name in the **Workgroup or computer domain** field

- Click **Next**

- In the **Completing Windows XP Setup Wizard** dialog box, click **Finish**

Configuring Logon Options

You're not completely finished when you click the Finish button on the Windows XP Setup Wizard. When the computer restarts, the Network Identification Wizard displays.

anotherword

. . . on Network Settings

If you're not sure about the settings or don't have all of the information, you can always change these settings after the installation.

You use this dialog box to determine how the logon will work on your computer. For security reasons, it's best to force users to log on whenever the computer starts. If you select this option, then after you finish the installation, log on as Administrator, and then create a user account for yourself.

If you're not concerned about security—for example, if you're working on a small network within your home—you can use the Network Identification Wizard to bypass the logon process.

To set up your computer to bypass the logon, click the radio button indicating that Windows assumes the same user is always logging on. Then select a user name and specify a password. If your computer is part of a domain, then you can select from any of the user accounts on the domain. Otherwise, you can only select your name or Administrator.

Click Next, then in the next dialog box, click Finish.

---

task reference

Configuring Logon Options

- In the **Users of this Computer** dialog box of the **Network Identification Wizard,** if users must log on to use this computer, click the **Users must enter a user name and password to use this computer** radio button

- To bypass the logon, click the **Windows always assumes the following user has logged on to this computer** radio button

- If you've selected the bypass option, then in the **User name** drop-down list, click the user

- In the **Password** field, type a password for the default user

- In the **Confirm password** field, type the password again

- Click **Next**

- In the **Completing the Network Identification Wizard** dialog box, click **Finish**

Activating Windows XP

When the installation is complete, the Welcome to Microsoft Windows screen appears. You will be prompted to activate your copy of Windows. In the attempt to curb software piracy, Microsoft has implemented this procedure to prevent unauthorized installations of Windows XP. XP must be activated within 30 days of installation or the system will not function. If you do not activate XP right away, every time you log on you will be asked to activate your installation. The prompts become more insistent as the deadline gets closer.

When you activate XP, your product key is entered into a database along with the hardware configuration of your system. Because of this, the activation policy has generated some concern in the marketplace about user privacy. Microsoft claims the information will be kept confidential and that the hardware configuration cannot be used to trace a particular computer. Like other things with XP, it remains to be seen whether in fact this is the case. Once you get around to it, the actual process of activation itself is fairly quick and painless and does not require any personal information from you.

---

*another*word

. . . on XP Activation

Since the point of the XP product activation is to prevent users from passing around an XP installation CD to be used by friends or colleagues to install XP on their machines, the process of activation takes a snapshot (so to speak) of your system's hardware profile. This being the case, if you are planning any major hardware changes, such as replacing the motherboard or CPU, it is wise to put off the XP activation until this is done and your system is running properly. You do not want to activate XP and then find that a new hardware configuration suddenly invalidates it. Adding peripheral devices, such as a scanner or DVD player, should not present a problem in this regard.

SESSION 12.2

making the grade

1. When should you not convert to the NTFS file system during installation?

2. For security reasons, you should force users to _____ whenever they use the computer.

3. Computer names should only be made up of _____.

4. If your computer is not part of a domain, it is part of a _____.

SESSION 12.3 FINDING SYSTEM UPDATES AND OTHER INFORMATION

The Microsoft Web site is a virtual treasure trove of information and resources. From the site, you can find and download updates to the system and get information about setting up different types of Windows XP environments.

While there isn't room here to go into the vast array of Windows XP material available from the Microsoft site, we will talk about three elements of that information:

- *Windows Update,* which examines your computer to determine which updates are available for it
- The Windows XP Downloads section, which provides access to downloadable updates and information
- The Technical Resources section, which provides access to tools, information, and kits for setting up and maintaining a Windows XP environment

USING WINDOWS UPDATE

Windows Update is the easiest way to find out the latest updates to install on your computer.

To display the Windows Update home page, in the Start menu, click Windows Update.

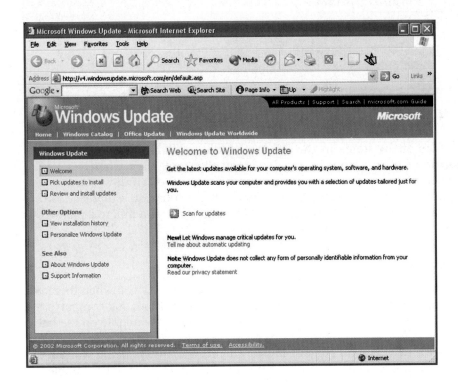

FIGURE 12.6
Windows Update home page

Click the Product Updates link. Windows Update prompts you to download the update program and then conducts an analysis of your computer to determine which updates are applicable to your computer.

When that's complete, Windows Update displays a page listing the available updates. Each update has a check box in front of it. For each update you want to download and install, check its check box. Uncheck boxes for updates you don't want to install.

When you're finished checking and unchecking boxes, click Download. Windows Update downloads and installs the updates.

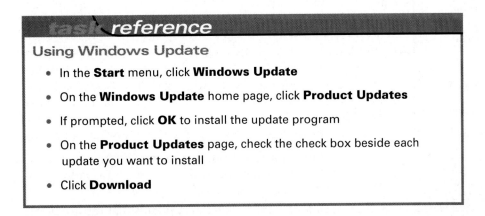

task reference

Using Windows Update

- In the **Start** menu, click **Windows Update**

- On the **Windows Update** home page, click **Product Updates**

- If prompted, click **OK** to install the update program

- On the **Product Updates** page, check the check box beside each update you want to install

- Click **Download**

WINDOWS XP

another**way**

... to Display the Windows Update Home Page

If Internet Explorer is already open, just use the Address bar to go to **www.windowsupdate .microsoft.com**

Using Windows Update:

1. Click the **Start** menu and then click **Windows Update**

2. After the **Windows Update** home page displays, click **Product Updates**

3. If prompted, click **OK** to install the update program

4. On the **Product Updates** page, check the check box beside each update you want to install

5. Click **Download.** The downloading process begins

One of the items in the Product Updates list is the *Critical Update Notification* function. If you download this tool, then whenever you're connected to the Internet, the program checks the Windows Update site for any new critical updates. If it finds any, it sends you a message letting you know that the updates are available and provides a link to a page from which you can download those updates.

Automatic Updates

XP can also be set up to automatically check and notify you when there is a new update available for downloading from the Internet. XP compares the information on your computer with the information available on the latest version of XP. Such things as fixes for security loopholes, compatibility updates for drivers, and general improvements are always being worked on, and you should take advantage of the updates as they become available.

FIGURE 12.7

The Automatic Updates tab of the System Properties dialog box

click this check box to enable Automatic Updates

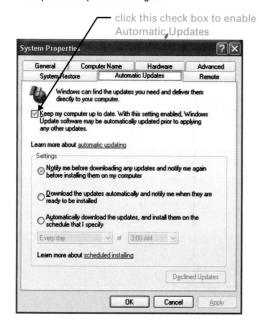

task reference

Setting Up Automatic Updates

- Click **Start, Control Panel, System**

- Click the **Automatic Updates** tab

- Click the *Keep my computer up to date* check box

- Click **OK**

WINDOWS XP DOWNLOADS

Windows XP also has its own Web site within the Microsoft Web site (Figure 12.8). One section of the Windows XP Web site is called Downloads (Figure 12.9). The Downloads section lists all the current updates and information available for Windows XP.

The downloads are divided into the following categories:

- *Critical updates.* Updates that resolve known problems with the operating system, especially issues dealing with security

- *Advanced security updates.* Updates that resolve more complex security issues

- *Recommended updates.* The latest noncritical updates to the operating system
- **Service packs.** A collection of updates grouped together. Service packs can become important later on, as newer software may require that you have a specific service pack installed
- *Tools and utilities.* Assorted tools that can help you perform certain functions. These are purely optional
- *Windows XP Help files.* You can download the Help files for Windows XP

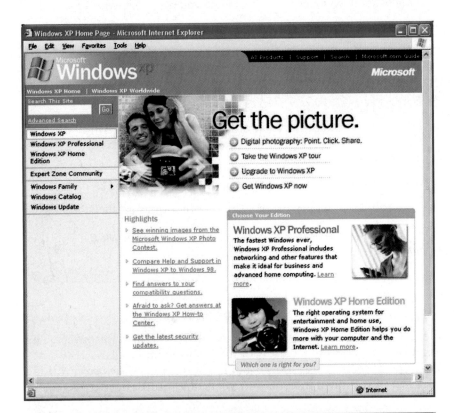

FIGURE 12.8

The Windows XP home page

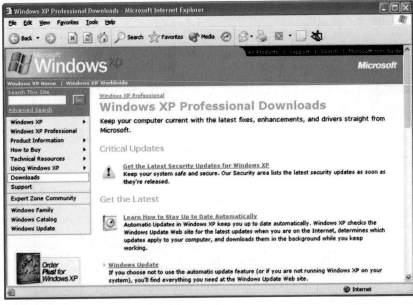

FIGURE 12.9

Downloads overview page

To download one of these items, first click the update in the list. A page displays providing additional information and specific instructions for that particular update.

---

task reference

Using the Downloads Page

- Select a type of download (Critical Update, Service Pack, etc.) to display the list of updates of that type

- In the list of downloads, click the update you want to download

- Follow the instructions provided for downloading the update

---

Using the Downloads page:

1. From the Products Update page, select a type of download (Critical Update, Service Pack, etc.) to display the list of updates of that type

2. Click the check box next to the update you want to download

3. Click the **Download** button. The downloading process begins

tip: *If you want to uninstall or reinstall updates, click **Show Installed Updates**.*

WINDOWS XP TECHNICAL RESOURCES

Another section of the Windows XP site is called Technical Resources. This section provides access to a variety of information and tools.

One type of technical resource is a Resource Kit. A ***Resource Kit*** is a complete set of technical information, tools, and utilities.

FIGURE 12.10

Technical Resources list

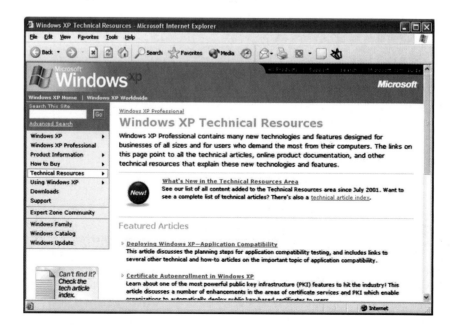

making the grade

1. _____ analyzes your computer to see which updates it needs.

2. _____ sends you an e-mail to let you know when there are important updates.

3. A _____ is a collection of updates packaged as a single unit.

4. A _____ provides complete information and tools for setting up and managing a Windows environment.

SECTION 12.4 SUMMARY

This chapter explained how to install Windows XP Professional. Before you install, you must first decide whether to upgrade or do a clean install. You can only upgrade from certain previous versions of Windows. Before upgrading, you must make sure your system is compatible with Windows XP, back up previous data, and uncompress the hard disk.

During the installation process, the Windows XP Setup Wizard prompts you for information about your computer and the network to which it's connected. When the installation is complete, you must also determine whether users must always log on to your computer before they can use it.

Once Windows XP is installed, the Microsoft Web site provides access to resources for updating your system. Windows Update examines your system and provides a list of available updates. You can also be notified automatically when there are critical updates. The Downloads section includes several types of system updates. The Technical Resources section provides access to more advanced information, including full Resource Kits for setting up and maintaining a Windows XP environment.

task reference roundup

Task	Page #	Preferred Method
Viewing the Hardware Compatibility List (HCL)	WINXP 12.6	• View the Hardware Compatibility List at www.microsoft.com/hcl/
Printing a configuration Report from Windows 95 or Windows 98	WINXP 12.6	• On the **Desktop**, right-click **My Computer**
		• In the context menu, click **Properties**
		• Click the **Device Manager** tab
		• Click **Print**
		• In the Print dialog box, select **System Summary**
		• Click **OK**

WINDOWS XP

task reference roundup

Task	Page #	Preferred Method
Printing a configuration report from Windows NT	WINXP 12.6	• In the **Start** menu, click **Programs**
		• In the **Programs** menu, click **Administrative Tools (Common)**
		• In the **Administrative Tools** submenu, click **Windows NT Diagnostics**
		• Click **Print**
		• Under **Scope,** click the **All tabs** radio button
		• Under **Detail Level,** click the **Summary** radio button
		• Under **Destination,** click the **Default Printer** radio button
		• Click **OK**
Starting the backup program from Windows 95 or Windows 98, or Windows 2000	WINXP 12.7	• In the **Start** menu, click **Programs**
		• In the **Programs** menu, click **Accessories**
		• In the **Accessories** submenu, click **System Tools**
		• In the **System Tools** submenu, click **Backup**
Starting the backup program from Windows NT	WINXP 12.7	• In the **Start** menu, click **Programs**
		• In the **Programs** menu, click **Administrative Tools (Common)**
		• In the **Administrative Tools** submenu, click **Backup**
Uncompressing a hard disk from Windows 95 or Windows 98	WINXP 12.8	• In the **Start** menu, click **Programs**
		• In the **Programs** menu, click **Accessories**
		• In the **Accessories** submenu, click **System Tools**
		• In the **System Tools** submenu, click **DriveSpace**
		• In the **DriveSpace** dialog box, select the compressed drive
		• In the **Drive** menu, click **Uncompress**
Uncompressing a hard disk from MS-DOS	WINXP 12.8	• If you're running MS-DOS 6.22 or higher, then at the Command Prompt, type **drvspace**
		• If you have an earlier version, type **dblspace**
		• Select the drive to uncompress
		• In the **Tools** menu, click **Uncompress**

task reference roundup

Task	Page #	Preferred Method
Using the Files and Settings Transfer Wizard	WINXP 12.9	• In the source computer, click **Start, All Programs, Accessories, System Tools, Files and Settings Transfer Wizard**
		• Click the **Old computer** radio button, then click **Next**
		• Choose the transfer method, then click **Next**
		• Choose the type of information to transfer, then click **Next**
		• Click **Finish**
		• In the destination computer, navigate to the **Files and Transfer Settings Wizard**
		• Click the **New Computer** radio button, then click **Next**
		• Click the radio button that indicates you have already collected your data, then click **Next**
		• Specify the location of your data, then click **Next**
		• Click **Finish**
Beginning installation from the CD-ROM from a previous version of Windows	WINXP 12.11	• Insert the Windows XP Professional CD-ROM into your CD-ROM or DVD drive
		• Click **Install Windows XP**
		• In the **Windows XP Setup Welcome** screen, click the appropriate radio button to indicate whether you're upgrading or doing a clean install
		• Click **Next**
Beginning installation without a previous version of Windows	WINXP 12.12	• Turn off your computer
		• If you can boot from your CD-ROM drive, insert the Windows XP Professional CD-ROM into your CD-ROM drive
		• If you cannot boot from your CD-ROM drive, insert the Windows XP Setup Boot Disk 1 into your floppy disk drive
		• Power up your computer
Beginning installation from a shared network folder	WINXP 12.12	• Obtain the path to the setup folder
		• If you're installing from Windows 95, Windows 98, or Windows NT, run the program **winnt32** from the setup folder
		• If you're installing from Windows 3.1 or some other operating system, run the program **winnt** from the setup folder
Setting license, partition, and file system information	WINXP 12.13	• In the **License Agreement** dialog box, click **I accept this agreement**, then click **Next**

task reference roundup

Task	Page #	Preferred Method
		• In the **Your Product Key** dialog box, type the product key, then click **Next**
		• In the **Special Options** dialog box, if you want to select a partition during installation, click **Advanced Options**
		• In the **Advanced Options** dialog box, check **I want to choose the installation partition during setup,** then click **OK**
		• In the **Special Options** dialog box, click **Next**
		• After the computer restarts, if asked, select the partition on which to install Windows XP, then press **Enter**
		• If prompted, indicate whether to convert the file system to NTFS, then press **Enter**
Regional settings and personalizing your computer	WINXP 12.13	• When the computer restarts, in the **Welcome** dialog box, click **Next**
		• In the **Regional Settings** dialog box, click **Next**
		• In the **Personalize Your Software** dialog box, in the **Name** field, type your name
		• If appropriate, in the **Organization** field, type the name of the organization
		• Click **Next**
Computer name, date, and network information	WINXP 12.14	• In the **Computer Name and Administrator Password** dialog box, in the **Computer name** field, type the name of your computer
		• In the **Administrator password** field, type the password for your computer's Administrator account
		• In the **Confirm password** field, type the password again
		• Click **Next**
		• In the **Modem Dialing Information** dialog box, specify the area code, outside line, and type of dialing, then click **Next**
		• In the **Date and Time Settings** dialog box, make sure the date and time are correct, then click **Next**
		• In the **Network Settings** dialog box, select **Typical Settings,** then click **Next**
		• In the **Workgroup or Computer Domain** dialog box, if your computer is part of a network domain for which your computer has an account, click the **Yes** radio button and type the domain name in the **Workgroup or computer domain** field
		• If your computer is not part of a network domain, then click the **No** radio button and type the workgroup name in the **Workgroup or computer domain** field
		• Click **Next**
		• In the **Completing Windows XP Setup Wizard** dialog box, click **Finish**

task reference roundup

Task	Page #	Preferred Method
Configuring logon options	WINXP 12.15	• In the **Users of this Computer** dialog box of the **Network Identification Wizard,** if users must log on to use this computer, click the **Users must enter a user name and password to use this computer** radio button
		• To bypass the logon, click the **Windows always assumes the following user has logged on to this computer** radio button
		• If you've selected the bypass option, then in the **User name** drop-down list, click the user
		• In the **Password** field, type a password for the default user
		• In the **Confirm password** field, type the password again
		• Click **Next**
		• In the **Completing the Network Identification Wizard** dialog box, click **Finish**
Using Windows Update	WINXP 12.17	• In the **Start** menu, click **Windows Update**
		• On the **Windows Update** home page, click **Product Updates**
		• If prompted, click **OK** to install the update program
		• On the **Product Updates** page, check the check box beside each update you want to install
		• Click **Download**
Setting up Automatic Updates	WINXP 12.18	• Click **Start, Control Panel, System**
		• Click the **Automatic Updates** tab
		• Click the *Keep my computer up to date* check box
		• Click **OK**
Using the Downloads page	WINXP 12.20	• Select a type of download (Critical Update, Service Pack, etc.) to display the list of updates of that type
		• In the list of downloads, click the update you want to download
		• Follow the instructions provided for downloading the update

WINDOWS XP

CROSSWORD PUZZLE

Across

4. Page listing all of the updates
6. The _____ report lists your current device settings
7. Analyzes your computer to determine available updates
9. To install Windows XP after clearing all previous data
11. A collection of information and tools for setting up an environment

Down

1. The area of a network to which your computer belongs
2. A change to fix a known problem, especially a security problem
3. Before upgrading, you must _____ your hard disk
5. A bundle of updates
8. Lists possible compatibility issues with your current system
10. To install Windows XP over a previous version

FILL-IN

1. The _____ represents a part of a network to which your computer belongs.

2. The _____ account allows a user to perform advanced functions such as setting up user accounts.

3. Before the installation can begin, you must accept Microsoft's _____.

CREATE THE QUESTION

For each answer, create an appropriate, short question:

ANSWER	QUESTION
1. A bundle of updates to the operating system	_____
2. Sends you an e-mail message if it finds vital updates while you're connected to the Internet	_____
3. Provides a complete package of information and tools for setting up and maintaining a Windows XP environment	_____

SHORT ANSWER

1. What is the minimum *required* RAM to install Windows XP Professional?

2. What is the minimum *recommended* RAM to install Windows XP Professional?

3. What *must* you do to a hard disk before upgrading to Windows XP Professional?

4. Can you upgrade to XP from Windows NT Server 4.0?

1. Printing a Configuration Report

Chris Liu works at Schumann Equities in the IT Department. He is in charge of migrating the computer system from Windows NT to Windows XP. Before upgrading to Windows XP, one task he knows has to be done is to have each user run the File and Settings Transfer Wizard in order to collect all the relevant data from each computer.

He wants to run several training sessions in order to show all company personnel how to carry out this task. Before he does this, he runs the Wizard on his own personal computer to familiarize himself with the process. The transfer will occur over the internal LAN.

1. In the source computer, open the Files and Settings Transfer Wizard in System Tools: **Start, All Programs, Accessories, System Tools, Files and Settings Transfer Wizard.** Click **Next** to begin
2. Click **Old computer,** then click **Next**
3. Click the **Other** radio button, then click **Next**
4. Click the **Settings only** radio button, then click **Next**
5. The Wizard indicates that you have completed the collection phase. Click **Finish**

2. Performing an Installation

John Madigan is installing Windows XP Professional on his computer. The machine he's working from currently runs Windows 3.5.1, as do most of the computers in his department at Allied Purchasing. His job is to facilitate the migration from the legacy Windows operating system by creating a short in-house training manual to teach the other members of his office how to do some basic things in Windows XP. That way, when Allied Purchasing begins to migrate all its machines to the newer operating system, the staff will have some idea of how to work with it.

In order to perform the following installation, you must have permission and access to a computer that you can perform an installation on for the purpose of this exercise. In addition, you must have access to the Windows XP Professional CD.

1. Insert the Windows XP Professional CD-ROM into your CD-ROM or DVD drive
2. In the dialog box that displays, click **Install Windows XP**
3. In the **Windows XP Setup Welcome** screen, click the radio button to indicate you're performing a clean install, and then click **Next**
4. In the **License Agreement** dialog box, click the radio button next to *I accept this agreement,* and then click **Next**
5. In the Your Product Key dialog box, type the product key listed on your CD, and then click **Next**
6. In the **Select Special Options** dialog box, click **Next**
7. Click the radio button next to *Yes, upgrade my drive* to convert the file system to NTFS, and then click **Next**
8. In the **Completing Windows XP Setup Wizard** dialog box, click **Finish**

challenge!

1. Using Windows Update

Serena Brown works at Central Valley Hospital as a billing administrator. There are 15 computers in her department that use Windows XP as their operating system. Through a newsgroup that she joined, Serena finds out that Microsoft has a new update to Windows XP that fixes some known bugs. Serena knows that Windows Update analyzes your computer to determine which updates are available to download.

1. Using the **Start** Menu, go to the Windows Update home page and find out which upgrades are available. Are there any critical updates? Recommended updates? Device drivers?
2. Select a type of download (Critical Update, Service Pack, etc.) to display the list of updates of that type
3. In the list of downloads, click the update you want to download
4. Follow the instructions provided for downloading the update. Download at least one of the updates not yet installed on your computer

2. Printing a Configuration Report

Bobby Goodwell is a network administrator for a Midwest-based enterprise. When he came in this morning, he received an e-mail indicating a large new account has been acquired. He immediately realizes that he will have to start updating some computers to Windows XP in order to handle the additional workload. One of the things he wants to do is print a configuration report that lists all of the device settings on each computer. He asks you to prepare these reports for him.

For the purpose of this exercise, print a configuration report from Windows XP Professional.

1. Navigate to the System Information window in the Control Panel **(Start, Control Panel, Accessories, System Tools, System Information)**

2. In the left pane, click **System Summary.** It takes Windows a few moments to refresh the current information, then the summary is displayed, which should look like Figure 12.12
3. Click **File,** then **Print**

FIGURE 12.11

A critical update displayed in the Windows Update Web site

FIGURE 12.12

The configuration report displayed in the System Information window

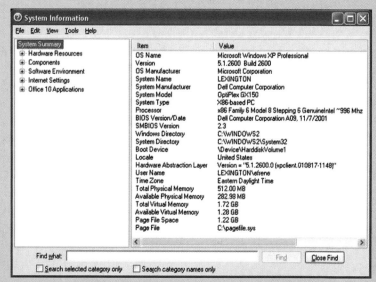

1. Finding Compatible Hardware

Marlene Wills works for Exhibitors Showcase Inc., which builds and designs materials for exhibitors at trade shows. Her department needs several new printers, and she is in charge of doing the research and making a recommendation on what models to purchase. Since all the computers in Marlene's department use Windows XP Professional, she wants to make sure that the model she's considering is compatible.

The Hardware Compatibility List indicates which hardware is compatible with the operating system. This information is available on Microsoft's Web site.

1. Use the Device Manager to see your current hardware. Right-clicking on **My Computer** and clicking **Properties** accesses the Device Manager. Click the **Hardware** tab and then the **Device Manager** button
2. Click the plus sign in front of *Printers* and write down on a piece of paper the name of the printer attached to your computer *Hint*: If *Printers* doesn't appear on your list, click **View** and **Show hidden devices**
3. Go to Microsoft's Web site to confirm that your current printer is compatible with Windows XP
4. Print the page that lists your current printer

e-business

1. Configuring Multiple Computers

Pens etc., a major office supply company, creates a Web site named pens.com. This new division will be run out of an office in St. Louis. Sam Rollins is assigned to go on-site and install Windows XP Professional on multiple computers in this new office. Once Sam finishes, he needs to configure the Logon Options. He asks you to help him with this.

1. Open the **System** Properties in **Control Panel** and click the **Computer Name** tab
2. Click the **Network ID** button
3. When the Network Identification Wizard opens, click **Next**

4. Select the radio button next to *This computer is part of a business network, and I use it to connect to other computers at work*, and then click **Next**
5. In the Connecting to the Network dialog box, select the radio button next to *My company uses a network without a domain*, and then click **Next**
6. In the Workgroup dialog box, leave the default workgroup name "WORKGROUP," and click **Next**
7. In the **Completing the Network Identification Wizard** dialog box, click **Finish**

FIGURE 12.13

The System Properties dialog box

1. Enabling Automatic Updates

Dieter Stroesser runs an all natural food coloring company in Aachen, Germany. The city of Aachen is very close to the border of Belgium and the Netherlands, where manufacturing costs are lower. Taking advantage of this economic difference, Dieter jobs out several manufacturing processes to affiliated factories in Belgium and the Netherlands. Since there is constant communication between the three locations via supply chain management software over the Internet, Dieter wants to make sure that all three locations of his company are using the exact same operating system with the latest updates. He institutes a policy that all locations must enable automatic updating on their computers.

1. Click **Start, Control Panel, System**
2. Click the **Automatic Updates** tab
3. Click the *Keep my computer up to date* check box
4. Click **OK**

WINDOWS XP

reference 1

Windows XP *file finder*

Location in Chapter	Data File to Use	Student Saves Data File as . . .
CHAPTER 1		
None for this chapter		
CHAPTER 2		
Moving and copying files	Bell Chapter Three_Brown.doc	
Moving and copying files	Jackson Article_Brown.doc	
Moving and copying files	Kelman White Paper_Brown.doc	
Moving and copying files	Bell Chapter Two_Dorman.doc	
Moving and copying files	Bell Chapter Four_Dorman.doc	
Moving and copying files	McDougal Proposal_Dorman.doc	
Moving and copying files	Bell Chapter One_Jones.doc	
Moving and copying files	Young Proposal_Jones.doc	
Deleting a file	Young Proposal_Jones.doc	
Typing your document text	xp02memo-data	JoeSmithMemo
E-Business project #1	B2B Marketplace.doc	My White Paper
Around the World project #1	China folder	
CHAPTER 3		
None for this chapter		
CHAPTER 4		
None for this chapter		
CHAPTER 5		
Practice Project #1	xp05robertson.rtf xp05arthouse.rtf xp05natinsurance.rtf	
E-Business Project #1	All Points article.rtf	
CHAPTER 6		
None for this chapter		
CHAPTER 7		
Setting Web Page Colors	xp07sample.html	
Printing a Web Page	xp07frames.html	
CHAPTER 8		
None for this chapter		

Location in Chapter	Data File to Use	Student Saves Data File as . . .
CHAPTER 9		
None for this chapter		
CHAPTER 10		
Copying a bar graph from one application to another	xp10wigginsgraph.rtf xp10wiggins1streport.rtf	Wiggins Sales Report2
Dragging and dropping data between applications	xp10wigginsgraph.rtf xp10wiggins1streport.rtf	
Inserting a graphic in another application	xp10exhibitmap xp10exhibit	xp10exhibit
Dragging and dropping a document scrap	xp10presmessage.rtf xp10wiggins1streport.rtf	
Linking an object	xp10wigginsgraph xp10wiggins2ndreport.rtf	
Embedding a map for a meeting	xp10conferencemap	Tungsten Conference
CHAPTER 11		
None for this chapter		
CHAPTER 12		
None for this chapter		

reference roundup

Task	Page #	Preferred Method
Starting Windows XP	WINXP 1.6	• Turn on the computer
		• Click your user name
		• Type your password and press **Enter**
Using the mouse	WINXP 1.9	• To select an object, move the mouse over the object, then click with the left mouse button
		• To display a context menu related to an object, move the mouse over the object, then click with the right mouse button
		• To open an object, move the mouse over the object, then double-click with the left mouse button
		• To move an item to another part of the screen, move the mouse over the object. Click the left mouse button and hold it down, then move the mouse in the direction you want to move the object. Release the mouse button when the object is in the correct place
Working with windows	WINXP 1.17	• To move a window, click and drag the Title bar
		• To resize a window, click and drag the Resize area at the bottom right
		• To minimize a window to the taskbar, click the Minimize button
		• To make a window full screen, click the Maximize button. Click the Restore Down button to restore the original size
		• To close a window and any program running in it, click **Close**
Working with dialog boxes	WINXP 1.17	• Fill in the fields in the dialog box
		• Click **OK** to close the dialog box and implement your changes
		• Click **Cancel** to close the dialog box without implementing your changes
Working with menus	WINXP 1.17	• On a menu bar, click a menu label to open the menu
		• To display a context menu, right-click an object
		• To select a menu option, move the mouse over the menu option, then click it
Working with toolbars	WINXP 1.17	• To display a ToolTip for a Toolbar button, move the mouse over the button
		• To select a Toolbar button, click it
Turning off Windows XP	WINXP 1.18	• Click the **Start** button
		• In the Start menu, click **Turn Off Computer**
		• In the Turn Off Computer dialog box, select the type of shutdown
Launching programs from the Start menu	WINXP 1.20	• Click the **Start** button
		• In the Start menu, click **All Programs**

task reference roundup

Task	Page #	Preferred Method
		• Navigate through the program groups until you get to the program you want
		• Click the program name to start the application
Creating and saving files	WINXP 1.22	• To create a new file using an application, click **New** in the application's File menu
		• To save the file to the computer, click **Save** in the File menu, then specify the file's name and location
		• To save a copy of the file with a new name or location, click **Save As** in the File menu, then specify a new name or location for the file
Printing a file	WINXP 1.24	• In the File menu, click **Print**
		• In the print dialog box, set any options for printing, such as printing multiple copies or printing only a portion of the file
		• Click **OK** to send the file to the printer
Closing and opening files	WINXP 1.26	• To close a file and the application, click the close button at the top right of the window
		• To close a file without closing the application, select **Close** from the File menu
		• To open a file from within the application, select **Open** from the **File** menu. Use the dialog box to find and open the file
		• To open a file directly from a Desktop window, double-click the icon representing the file
Installing a program	WINXP 1.27	• Click **Start,** then **Control Panel**
		• Click **Add or Remove Programs**
		• Click the **Add New Programs** button
		• Click the **CD or Floppy** button. Insert the CD or other disk if you have not already done so
		• Click the **Next** button
		• Click the **Finish** button
Removing a program	WINXP 1.28	• Click **Start,** then **Control Panel**
		• Click **Add or Remove Programs**
		• Click the **Change or Remove Programs** button
		• In the list under *currently installed programs*, click the name of the program you want to remove
		• Click **Remove**
		• Click **OK**
Displaying the Help and Support Center window	WINXP 1.31	• To display the Help and Support Center window, click the **Start** button, then click **Help and Support**

task reference roundup

Task	Page #	Preferred Method
Using the Help and Support Center search	WINXP 1.31	• In the *Search* text box of the Help and Support Center, type the keyword or words to search for, then press **Enter**
		• To display a topic, click the topic
Using the Set Search options	WINXP 1.33	• Click **Start**, then click **Help and Support**
		• Click the **Options** button on the navigation bar
		• In the Options list in the left pane, click the check box next to *Set Search Options*
		• Enter the desired options on the right pane and click the arrow next to the *Search* text box
Using Favorites in the Help and Support Center	WINXP 1.35	• Click the **Favorites** button on the toolbar to display the Favorites pane
		• To add the current topic to the list of favorites, click the **Add to Favorites** button
		• To rename a favorite topic, click the topic, then click **Rename**
		• To delete a favorite topic from the list, click the topic, then click **Remove**
Working with Remote Assistance	WINXP 1.36	• Display System Properties dialog box by clicking the System link of the Performance and Maintenance window of the Control Panel
		• Click the **Remote** tab
		• Click the **Advanced** button
		• Click **OK**, then **OK** again
Sending a Remote Assistance invitation using e-mail	WINXP 1.37	• Click **Start/All Programs/Remote Assistance**
		• Click **Invite someone to help you**
		• Type your assistant's e-mail address in the *Type an e-mail address* text box and click **Invite this person**
		• In the text box under *Message*, enter a description of the problem and click **Continue**
		• Specify a time limit for the response from the recipient and a password and click the **Send Invitation** button
Receiving Remote Assistance	WINXP 1.38	• Click the **Yes** button to begin the Remote Assistance session
		• To chat with your assistant type a message in the *Message Entry* text box and click the **Send** button
		• Give your assistant control of your computer in the Remote Assistance—Web Page Dialog dialog box by clicking the **Yes** button to accept
		• Click the **Disconnect** button to end the session

REFERENCE

task reference roundup

Task	Page #	Preferred Method
Navigating with My Computer	WINXP 2.4	• In the Start menu, click **My Computer** to display the drives on your computer
		• Double-click a drive to display the folders in that drive
		• Double-click a folder to display the contents of that folder
		• Double-click a file to open the file
Displaying and navigating with Windows Explorer	WINXP 2.5	• To display the Explorer, right-click **My Computer,** then click **Explore** in the context menu
		• Click a plus sign (+) to display in the tree the folders contained in the drive or folder
		• Click a minus sign (−) to hide the folders contained in the drive or folder
		• Click a drive or folder to display its contents in the right pane
Changing the folder view	WINXP 2.10	• On the menu bar, click the **View** button
		• In the list of views, click the view you want to use
Sorting files and folders	WINXP 2.11	• In the **View** menu, click **Arrange Icons,** or right-click the window, then click **Arrange Icons** in the context menu
		• In the Arrange Icons submenu, click the method to sort the objects
		• To reverse the sort order, sort the window again by the same method
Creating a folder	WINXP 2.11	• In the **File** menu, click **New,** or right-click the window, then click **New** in the context menu
		• In the New submenu, click **Folder**
		• Type the name of the new folder, then press **Enter**
Renaming a file or folder	WINXP 2.12	• Right-click the file or folder
		• In the context menu, click **Rename.** The Rename option is also in the File menu
		• Type the new name in the object label
		• Press **Enter**
Selecting files and folders to move or copy	WINXP 2.14	• To select a range of objects, click the first object, then press the **Shift** key as you click the last object
		• To select individual objects, click the first object, then hold down the **Ctrl** key as you click each additional object
		• To select all of the objects in a folder, click the **Edit** menu, then click **Select All**
Copying and moving objects by dragging	WINXP 2.15	• Select the objects to move or copy
		• Drag the objects until they are in the new location. Hold down the **Alt** key to make sure the files are copied, or the **Shift** key to make sure the files are moved
		• Release the mouse button to copy or move the files to the new location

task reference roundup

Task	Page #	Preferred Method
Copying and pasting objects	WINXP 2.15	• Select the objects to copy
		• In the **Edit** menu, click **Copy**
		• Open the location where you want to copy the objects
		• In the **Edit** menu, click **Paste**
Cutting and pasting objects	WINXP 2.15	• Select the objects you want to move
		• In the **Edit** menu, click **Cut**
		• Open the location where you want to move the objects
		• In the **Edit** menu, click **Paste**
Deleting files and folders	WINXP 2.16	• Select the objects to delete
		• In the **File** menu, click **Delete**
Retrieving deleted objects from the Recycle Bin	WINXP 2.16	• Double-click the **Recycle Bin**
		• Drag the object from the **Recycle Bin** to the Desktop or a folder on your computer
Emptying the Recycle Bin	WINXP 2.17	• Right-click the **Recycle Bin**
		• In the context menu, click **Empty Recycle Bin**
Opening recently used files	WINXP 2.18	• Click **Start,** then **My Recent Documents**
		• Click the file you want to open
Clearing the My Recent Documents list	WINXP 2.19	• Right-click the **Start** button, then click **Properties**
		• In the **Start Menu tab,** click **Customize . . .**
		• Click the **Advanced** tab
		• Click the **Clear List** button
Finding a file by name	WINXP 2.21	• In the Start menu, click **Search**
		• In the Search menu, click **All Files and Folders**
		• In the All or part of the filename field, type the name of the file you are looking for
		• In the Look in drop-down list, select the drive to search in
		• Click the **Search** button
Performing a text search	WINXP 2.22	• In the Start menu, click **Search**
		• In the Search menu, click **All Files and Folders**
		• In the *A word or a phrase in the file* field, type the word or phrase you are searching for

REFERENCE

task reference roundup

Task	Page #	Preferred Method
		• Click the **Search** button
Stopping a search	WINXP 2.23	• In the left pane of the Search window, click **Stop**
Clearing the Search fields	WINXP 2.23	• At the bottom of the left pane of the Search window, click **Start a new search**
Saving a search	WINXP 2.24	• In the Search window, run the search you want to save
		• In the File menu, click **Save Search**
		• Make any changes for the filename and location, then click **Save**
Using wildcard characters to search	WINXP 2.25	• To represent an individual character in a search field, type **?**
		• To represent an unknown number of characters in a search field, type *****
Starting the WordPad application	WINXP 2.26	• Click the **Start** button
		• In the Start menu, click **All Programs**
		• In the Programs menu, click **Accessories**
		• In the Accessories submenu, click **WordPad**
Removing and restoring window elements	WINXP 2.29	• In the **View** menu, click the element to remove or restore
		• The element, and the check mark next to the menu option, are removed or restored
Changing the unit of measurement	WINXP 2.30	• In the View menu, click **Options**
		• In the Options dialog box, click the **Options** tab
		• Click the radio button next to the unit of measurement you want to use
		• Click **OK**
Setting a document's margins	WINXP 2.31	• In the File menu, click **Page Setup**
		• In the Margins area, type the amount of space to use for each edge of the document
		• Click **OK**
Typing paragraphs	WINXP 2.32	• Click in the text area, then begin typing
		• Press the **Enter** key whenever you want to start a new paragraph
		• Use blank paragraphs to create additional space between paragraphs
Changing a paragraph's alignment	WINXP 2.33	• Move the insertion point to the paragraph
		• Click the toolbar icon representing the alignment you want
		or
		• In the Format menu, click **Paragraph,** *or* right-click the paragraph, then click **Paragraph** in the context menu

task reference roundup

Task	Page #	Preferred Method
		• In the Alignment drop-down list, click the alignment to use
		• Click **OK**
Adjusting indents using the Paragraph dialog box	WINXP 2.35	• Place the insertion point in the paragraph or select several paragraphs
		• In the Format menu, click **Paragraph,** or right-click the paragraph, then click **Paragraph** in the context menu
		• Type the indents you want
		• Click **OK**
Adjusting indents using the ruler	WINXP 2.35	• Place the insertion point in the paragraph you want to change or select several paragraphs whose setting you want to change
		• To adjust the left indent, click the **block** at the bottom of the left margin and drag it to the right
		• To adjust the right indent, click the **triangle** at the right margin and drag it to the right
		• To adjust the first line indent, click the **top triangle** at the right margin and drag it to the right or left
Adding bullets to a paragraph	WINXP 2.37	• Place the cursor in the paragraph to be bulleted or select a group of paragraphs
		• In the Format menu, click **Bullet Style,** or right-click the paragraph, then click **Bullet Style** in the context menu or click the bullet icon on the toolbar
Adjusting tab stops using the Tabs dialog box	WINXP 2.38	• Select the paragraph or paragraphs you want to use the tabs
		• In the Format menu, click **Tabs,** or right-click the paragraphs, then click **Tabs** in the context menu
		• To create a new tab, type the position in the box, then click **Set**
		• To remove a tab, click the tab in the list, then click **Clear**
		• When you're finished adjusting the tabs, click **OK**
Adjusting tabs using the ruler	WINXP 2.38	• Select the paragraph or paragraphs you want to use the tab settings
		• To create a new tab, click the ruler at the spot you want the new tab
		• To move a tab, click the marker and drag it to the new location on the ruler
		• To remove a tab, click the marker and drag it off the ruler
Changing the appearance of text using the Font dialog box	WINXP 2.40	• In the Format menu, click **Font**
		• In the Font list, click the typeface you want to use
		• In the Font style list, click the type style to indicate whether the text is bold or italic

REFERENCE

task reference roundup

Task	Page #	Preferred Method
		• In the Size list, click the size of the text
		• Under Effects, click the **Underlined** check box to add or remove underlining
		• In the Color drop-down list, click the color to use for the text
		• Click **OK**
Using the format bar to change text's appearance	WINXP 2.40	• Select the text
		• Select a typeface from the drop-down list
		• Select the type size from the drop-down list
		• Click the **B** button to make the text bold
		• Click the **I** button to make the text italicized
		• Click the **U** button to underline the text
		• Click the palette button to display a list of possible text colors, then click a color to select it
Starting the Notepad application	WINXP 2.43	• In the Start menu, click **Programs**
		• In the Programs menu, click **Accessories**
		• In the Accessories submenu, click **Notepad**
Wrapping text in Notepad	WINXP 2.44	• In the Format menu, click **Wrap**
Setting up Notepad headers and footers	WINXP 2.45	• In the File menu, click **Page Setup**
		• In the Header field, type the information to print at the top of every page
		• In the Footer field, type the information to print at the bottom of every page
		• Click **OK**
Adding an icon to the Quick Launch bar	WINXP 3.3	• Use My Computer or Windows Explorer to navigate to the object
		• Drag the object to the Quick Launch bar
Removing and restoring toolbars	WINXP 3.4	• Right-click a blank area of the toolbar
		• In the context menu, click **Toolbar**
		• In the Toolbar submenu, click the toolbar you wish to add or remove
Moving toolbars on the screen	WINXP 3.5	• Make sure the taskbar is unlocked by right-clicking it and selecting **Unlock the Taskbar**
		• Click the toolbar
		• Drag the toolbar onto the Desktop, then release the mouse button

task reference roundup

Task	Page #	Preferred Method
		• To attach the toolbar to an edge of the screen, drag it toward that edge until the toolbar snaps into place
Creating a taskbar toolbar	WINXP 3.6	• Right-click an empty area of the taskbar
		• In the context menu, click **Toolbars,** then **New Toolbar . . .**
		• Use the navigation tree to select a folder
		• Click **OK**
Adjusting the date and time	WINXP 3.7	• Double-click the time displayed on the taskbar
		• On the Date & Time tab, use the drop-down lists and calendar to select the month, year, and day
		• Use the up and down arrows to adjust the time
		• On the Time Zone tab, select a time zone
		• Click **OK**
Displaying the Display Properties dialog box	WINXP 3.7	• Right-click the Desktop
		• In the context menu, click **Properties**
Selecting a wallpaper	WINXP 3.8	• To select an existing wallpaper, click the wallpaper in the list
		• To select a picture from your computer, click **Browse,** then navigate to and select the file
		• In the *Display* drop-down list, click **Center** to center the picture on the screen, **Tile** to repeat the picture to fill up the screen, or **Stretch** to stretch the picture to fit the screen
		• Click **Apply** or **OK**
Selecting a scheme	WINXP 3.10	• Open the Appearance tab of the Display Properties dialog box
		• In the *Color Scheme* drop-down list, click the scheme to use
		• In the *Font size* and the *Windows and buttons* drop-down lists, click an option
		• Click **Apply** or **OK**
Setting up a screen saver	WINXP 3.12	• In the Screen Saver drop-down list, click the screen saver to use
		• Click the **Settings** button to view and set any settings for the screen saver
		• Click the **Preview** button to see a full screen preview of the screen saver
		• In the Wait field, adjust the number of minutes for the computer to be inactive before the screen saver activates
		• Click **Apply**
Adjusting monitor settings	WINXP 3.13	• In the *Colors quality* drop-down list, click the number of colors

REFERENCE

task reference roundup

Task	Page #	Preferred Method
		• Under *Screen resolution,* slide the bar to the left or right to increase or decrease the resolution
		• Click **OK**
Creating an Active Desktop	WINXP 3.14	• Right-click a blank area of the Desktop
		• In the context menu, click **Properties**
		• Click the **Desktop** tab and click the **Customize Desktop . . .** button
		• Click the **Web** tab, then click **New . . .**
		• On the New Active Desktop Item dialog box, in the Location field, select a Web page to make your Active Desktop
		• Click **Yes** and **OK** to confirm your selection
Switching to Windows Classic View	WINXP 3.16	• Click **Start**, then **Control Panel**
		• Double-click **Display**
		• In the Themes tab, under *Theme,* click **Windows Classic**
		• Click **OK**
Displaying the Control Panel	WINXP 3.18	• In the Start menu, click **Control Panel**
Opening the Mouse Properties dialog box	WINXP 3.18	• From the Control Panel, double-click the **Mouse** icon
Configuring your mouse buttons	WINXP 3.19	• In the Mouse Properties dialog box, click the **Buttons** tab
		• Under *Button Configuration,* click the **Switch primary and secondary** check box to switch the mouse buttons to the left-handed configuration
		• Under Double-click speed, use the slider bar to increase or decrease the space between clicks for a double-click
		• Under *ClickLock,* click the **Turn on ClickLock** check box to enable you to highlight or drag without having to hold down the mouse
		• Click **Apply** or **OK**
Changing mouse pointers	WINXP 3.20	• In the **Mouse Properties** dialog box, click the **Pointers** tab
		• In the *Scheme* drop-down list, click a scheme
		• To change an individual pointer within a scheme, click the pointer, then click **Browse** to begin searching for another pointer
		• To return a pointer to its default value, click the pointer, then click **Use Default**
		• Click **Apply** or **OK**
Customizing the mouse speed	WINXP 3.20	• In the Mouse Properties dialog box, click the **Pointer Options** tab
		• Use the Speed slide to adjust the mouse speed

task reference roundup

Task	Page #	Preferred Method
		• Select a mouse acceleration
		• Click **Apply** or **OK**
Displaying the Sounds and Audio Devices Properties dialog box	WINXP 3.21	• In the Control Panel, double-click the **Sounds and Audio Devices** icon
Displaying the Accessibility Options dialog box	WINXP 3.22	• In the Control Panel, double-click the **Accessibility Options** icon
Setting Keyboard Accessibility Options	WINXP 3.23	• Click the **Keyboard** tab on the Accessibility Options dialog box
		• Check **Use StickyKeys** to be able to press the Ctrl, Alt, Shift, and Windows logo keys separately instead of simultaneously
		• Check **Use FilterKeys** to be able to prevent unintended repeat characters
		• Check **Use ToggleKeys** to hear a sound every time you press the Num Lock, Caps Lock, and Scroll Lock keys
		• For each option, click the **Settings** button to customize the option
Replacing sounds with visual cues	WINXP 3.24	• Click the **Sound** tab on the Accessibility Options dialog box
		• Check **Use SoundSentry** to display a visual warning whenever a system sound plays
		• Click **Settings** to determine where the warning displays
		• Check **Use ShowSounds** to display a visual cue whenever a program plays a warning sound
Changing to a High Contrast display	WINXP 3.25	• Click the **Display** tab on the Accessibility Options dialog box
		• Check the **Use High Contrast** check box
		• Click the **Settings** button to display the list of available high contrast color schemes
		• Select a scheme, then click **OK**
Replacing the mouse with the keyboard	WINXP 3.26	• Click the **Mouse** tab on the Accessibility Options dialog box
		• Check the **Use MouseKeys** check box
		• Click the **Settings** button to display a dialog box for adjusting the mouse speed
		• Click **Apply** or **OK**
Using MouseKeys	WINXP 3.26	• To move the mouse pointer, press the **1, 2, 3, 4, 6, 7, 8,** or **9** key
		• To click with the left mouse button, press the **/** key, then the **5** key
		• To right-click, press the minus (−) key, then the **5** key
		• To double-click, press the plus (+) key

REFERENCE

task reference roundup

Task	Page #	Preferred Method
		• To drag, press the **0** key, then move the mouse to the target location. Press the **Del** key
Administering Accessibility Options	WINXP 3.27	• Click the **General** tab on the **Accessibility Options** dialog box
		• To turn off the options after a certain amount of time, check the **Automatic reset** check box, then click a time in the drop-down list
		• To display a warning when an accessibility feature is turned on, check the **Give warning message when turning a feature on** check box
		• To play a sound when an accessibility feature is turned on or off, check the **Make a sound when turning a feature on or off** check box
		• If you're an Administrator, to apply the current accessibility options at the log on screen, check the **Apply all settings to logon Desktop** check box
		• If you're an Administrator, to apply the current accessibility options as the default for all new users, check the **Apply all settings to defaults for new users** check box
Creating a shortcut	WINXP 3.28	• Right-click an object
		• Hold down the right mouse button as you drag the object to the Desktop
		• Release the mouse button
		• In the context menu, click **Create Shortcut(s) Here**
		or
		• Right-click the object
		• In the context menu, click **Copy**
		• Right-click the Desktop
		• In the context menu, click **Paste Shortcut**
		or
		• Right-click the Desktop
		• In the context menu, click **Create Shortcut**
		• In the field, type the path to the object, *or* click **Browse** to find the object
		• Click **Next**
		• Type a name for the shortcut
		• Click **Finish**
Renaming a shortcut	WINXP 3.30	• Right-click the shortcut
		• In the context menu, click **Rename**
		• Type the new name in the shortcut label
		• Press **Enter**

task reference roundup

Task	Page #	Preferred Method
Arranging Desktop icons	WINXP 3.31	• Right-click the Desktop
		• Click **Line Up Icons** to line up the icons in columns and rows
		• In the Arrange Icons submenu, click **Name** to sort the objects by name
		• In the Arrange Icons submenu, click **Type** to sort the objects by type
		• In the Arrange Icons submenu, click **Size** to sort the objects by size
		• In the Arrange Icons submenu, click **Modified** to sort the objects by the date they were created
		• In the Arrange Icons submenu, click **Auto Arrange** to turn on or off the Auto Arrange feature, which locks the objects in columns at the left of the Desktop
Deleting shortcuts	WINXP 3.32	• Click the shortcut to delete
		• Press the **Delete** key
Formatting a floppy disk	WINXP 4.4	• Insert the floppy disk and click **Start,** then click **My Computer**
		• Click the floppy drive icon
		• Click **File,** then click **Format**
		• Specify options, such as the size and name of the disk
		• Click **Start,** then click **OK**
Copying one floppy disk to another	WINXP 4.5	• Insert the disk you want to copy
		• In My Computer, click the floppy disk drive icon
		• In the File menu, click **Copy Disk**
		• Indicate the disk you want to copy from and the disk you want to copy to, then click **Start**
		• When prompted, remove the first disk and replace it with the disk you're copying to
Converting a drive to NTFS	WINXP 4.6	• Click **Start, All Programs, Accessories, Command Prompt**
		• Type **convert,** and then press the spacebar
		• Type the letter of the drive you wish to convert followed by a colon (:), and then press the spacebar
		• Type **/fs:ntfs,** and then press the **Enter** key
		• Type **Y** (for Yes)
		• Type **exit** and then press **Enter**
Using Disk Management to view drive information	WINXP 4.8	• Click **Start,** then click **Control Panel**
		• Double-click the **Administrative Tools** icon
		• Double-click the **Computer Management** icon

task reference roundup

Task	Page #	Preferred Method
		• Click **Disk Management**
Creating a new partition	WINXP 4.9	• Navigate to the Disk Management area of the Computer Management window (**Start, Control Panel, Administrative Tools, Computer Management, Disk Management**)
		• Right-click the unallocated space of a basic disk you wish to partition, then click **New Partition**
		• In the New Partition Wizard, click **Next,** click **Primary partition** or **Extended Partition,** and follow the instructions on your screen
Changing the default operating system	WINXP 4.10	• Click **Start,** then click **Control Panel**
		• Double-click **System**
		• Click the **Advanced** tab
		• In the *Startup and Recovery* area, click **Settings**
		• Select the desired operating system and then click **OK**
		• Click **OK**
Running Disk Cleanup	WINXP 4.12	• Click **Start, All Programs, Accessories, System Tools, Disk Cleanup**
		• Click **OK,** then click **Yes**
		• Click **OK**
Removing Windows components and installed programs	WINXP 4.13	• Click **Start, All Programs, Accessories, System Tools, Disk Cleanup**
		• Click the **More Options** tab
		• Click **Clean Up . . .,** then select the components you want to remove
Running Check Disk	WINXP 4.15	• Click **Start,** then click **My Computer**
		• Right-click the **Local Disk (C:)** drive
		• In the context menu, click **Properties**
		• Click the **Tools** tab
		• Click the **Check Now . . .** button
		• Click the two check boxes to accept both options
		• Click **OK,** then click **OK** again
Using the Disk Defragmenter	WINXP 4.17	• Click **Start, All Programs, Accessories, System Tools, Disk Defragmenter**
		• Click the drive you want to defragment and click the **Analyze** button
		• Click **Defragment**
		• Click **Close**
Using Scheduled Tasks	WINXP 4.18	• Click **Start, All Programs, Accessories, System Tools, Scheduled Tasks**
		• Double-click **Add Scheduled Task,** then click **Next**

task reference roundup

Task	Page #	Preferred Method
		• Click the program you want to schedule, then click **Next**
		• Click one of the radio buttons to select when to perform this task, then click **Next**
		• Click the appropriate box and type the Start time and frequency for the task, then click **Next**
		• Type your password, and then type it again in the **Confirm Password** field; then click **Next**
		• Click **Finish**
Using the Backup tool	WINXP 4.22	• Click **Start, All Programs, Accessories, System Tools, Backup**
		• Click the **Backup Wizard** button, then click **Next**
		• Click the appropriate radio button to select what you want to back up, then click **Next**
		• Click the check box beside each item you want to back up, and then click **Next**
		• Select the drive where you want to store your backup file and type a name for the backup file
		• Click **Open**, then click **Next**
		• Click **Finish**
Running the Restore Wizard	WINXP 4.26	• Click **Start, All Programs, Accessories, System Tools, Backup,** then click **Next**
		• Click the radio button next to *Restore files and settings* and click **Next**
		• Click the check box next to any drive, folder, or file that you want to restore and then click **Next**
		• Click **Finish**
		• Locate the file you want to use, then click **OK**
		• Click **Close,** then click the close button to close the Backup window
Printing a file from within an application	WINXP 5.3	• In the File menu, click **Print**
		• Click **OK**
Printing a file outside an application	WINXP 5.4	• Right-click the file to print
		• In the context menu, click **Print**
Creating a printer shortcut	WINXP 5.5	• In the Start menu, click **Printers and Faxes**
		• In the Printers window, right-click the printer
		• In the context menu, click **Create Shortcut**
		• Click **Yes** to allow Windows to create a shortcut on the Desktop

task reference roundup

Task	Page #	Preferred Method
Canceling a printing job	WINXP 5.6	• In the Start menu, click **Printers and Faxes**
		• In the Printers and Faxes window, double-click the printer you are using
		• Click the name of the file you want to cancel
		• In the Document menu, click **Cancel**
Using Pause Printing	WINXP 5.7	• In the Start menu, click **Printers and Faxes**
		• In the Printers and Faxes window, double-click the printer you want to pause
		• In the Printer menu, click **Pause Printing**
Opening the Add Printer Wizard	WINXP 5.8	• In the Start menu, click **Printers and Faxes**
		• In the left pane of the Printers and Faxes window, click the **Add a Printer** link
Using the Add Printer Wizard to install a local printer	WINXP 5.10	• From the Add Printer Wizard welcome window, click **Next**
		• Click **Local Printer**, then click **Next**
		• Click the port you want to use, then click **Next**
		• Select the manufacturer and model of the printer, then click **Next**
		• Select a name for the printer, then click **Next**
		• Decide if you want this printer to be your default printer, then click **Next**
		• Click that you don't want to share this printer, then click **Next**
Designating a default printer	WINXP 5.12	• In the Start menu, click **Printers and Faxes**
		• Right-click the printer you want to set as the default printer
		• In the context menu, click **Set as Default Printer**
Using the Add Printer Wizard to connect to a network printer	WINXP 5.13	• In the Start menu, click **Printers and Faxes**
		• In the left pane of the Printers and Faxes window, click the **Add a Printer** link
		• Click the radio button next to *Network Printer*
		• Type the name of the printer you wish to connect to, or Browse to find it
Sharing your printer	WINXP 5.14	• In the Start menu, click **Printers and Faxes**
		• Click the icon for the printer you wish to share
		• In the File menu, click **Sharing . . .**
		• In the Sharing tab, click the *Share this printer* radio button, then type a friendly name so that others can easily identify the printer. Click **OK** when done

task *reference roundup*

Task	Page #	Preferred Method
Changing the Printing Preferences	WINXP 5.16	• In the Start menu, click **Printers and Faxes**
		• Click the printer whose preferences you want to change
		• In the File menu, click **Printing Preferences**
		• Click the **Layout** or **Paper/Quality** tab
		• Click the appropriate button to change Orientation, Page Order, Pages Per Sheet, Paper Source, Media, Quality Settings, or Color
Changing the Printer Properties	WINXP 5.18	• In the Start menu, click **Printers and Faxes**
		• Click the printer whose properties you want to change
		• In the File menu, click **Properties**
		• In the Properties dialog box, click the **Advanced** tab
		• Click the appropriate button to change Availability times, Priority, Spooling, and to print a Separator Page between print jobs
Previewing a font	WINXP 5.23	• In the Start menu, click **Control Panel**
		• Double-click the **Fonts** folder
		• Double-click the font you wish to preview
Using the Character Map	WINXP 5.24	• Click **Start, All Programs, Accessories, System Tools, Character Map**
		• From the Fonts drop-down list, select a font
		• Double-click the desired character(s)
		• Click **Copy**
		• Open the document you want to copy into
		• In the Edit menu, click **Paste**
Installing New Fonts	WINXP 5.25	• In the Start menu, click **Control Panel**
		• Double-click the **Fonts** folder
		• In the File menu, click **Install New Font . . .**
		• Navigate to the folder with the fonts you wish to install
		• Click the font(s) you want to add
		• Click **OK**
Deleting fonts	WINXP 5.26	• In the Start menu, click **Control Panel**
		• Double-click the **Fonts** folder
		• Right-click the font you want to delete
		• Click **Delete**
		• Click **Yes** at the Alert message

REFERENCE

task reference roundup

Task	Page #	Preferred Method
Installing a Plug and Play device	WINXP 6.3	• Connect the device to the computer
		• If prompted, insert the disk containing the device driver
Installing a non-Plug and Play device	WINXP 6.4	• Connect the device to your computer
		• Click **Start**, then click **Control Panel**
		• Double-click **Add Hardware**
		• Click **Next** at the Welcome screen of the Add Hardware Wizard
		• Click the radio button next to *Yes, I have already connected the hardware,* then click **Next**
		• The Wizard displays a list of already installed hardware. Click **Add a new hardware device** at the very end of the list, then click **Next**
		• Click the radio button next to *Install the hardware that I manually select from a list (Advanced)*, then click **Next**
		• In the *Common hardware types* list box, select the type of hardware you're installing and click **Next**
		• If you allow Windows to detect the new device, click **Next.** If you select not to have Windows detect the device, click the check box next to *Don't detect my device; I will select it from a list*, then click **Next**
		• Select the brand name and model of the device, *or* click **Have Disk** if it isn't listed
		• Click **Next,** then follow the remaining instructions for installing the device
Displaying the Device Manager	WINXP 6.5	• In the Control Panel, double-click the **System** icon
		• On the System Properties dialog box, click the **Hardware** tab
		• Click the **Device Manager** button
Troubleshooting devices	WINXP 6.6	• If a device has a problem, a yellow exclamation point or red x is next to the device name
		• Double-click the device to display its Properties dialog box
		• If Windows has a possible solution, click the button below the problem description to begin that course of action
		• If Windows cannot determine the problem, click the **Troubleshooter** button to begin additional research on the problem
Starting the Paint application	WINXP 6.8	• In the Start menu, click **All Programs**
		• In the All Programs menu, click **Accessories**
		• In the Accessories submenu, click **Paint**
Removing and restoring Paint toolbars	WINXP 6.9	• In the View menu, click the element to remove or restore

task reference roundup

Task	Page #	Preferred Method
Using Undo and Repeat	WINXP 6.9	• To undo the last action, in the Edit menu, click **Undo** *or* press **Ctrl+Z**
		• To restore the action, click **Repeat** or press **Ctrl+Y**
Creating a screen capture	WINXP 6.10	• To capture the entire screen, press the **Print Screen** key
		• To capture only the active window, press **Alt+Print Screen**
		• Paste the capture into a word-processing or graphic file
Changing the System Sound Volume	WINXP 6.12	• Click **Start, Control Panel, Sounds, Speech, and Audio Devices**
		• Click the **Adjust the system volume** link
		• Click the **Volume** tab
		• Drag the slider to the *Low* or *High* volume marks to decrease or increase the sound volume
		• Click the **Mute** check box to turn off the sound
		• Click the **Mute** check box to turn the sound back on
		• Click the **Place volume icon in the taskbar** check box to display the speaker icon on your taskbar
		• Click **OK**
Changing the sound volume for individual devices	WINXP 6.12	• Click **Start, All Programs, Accessories, Entertainment, Volume Control**
		• Drag the volume slider for a device up or down to increase or decrease the volume
		• Drag the balance slider left or right to adjust the sound balance for a device
		• To turn off the sound, click the **Mute** check box
		• To turn on the sound, click the **Mute** check box again
		• Click **Options,** then **Properties** to specify which devices appear in the window
		• Click the **Playback** or **Recording** radio button to list the devices in either category
		• Click the check box next to the desired device to have it appear in the volume control window
Assigning sounds to events	WINXP 6.13	• Click **Start,** then click **Control Panel**
		• Double-click **Sounds and Audio Devices**
		• In the Sounds tab, use the drop-down list under *Sound Scheme* to select the desired scheme
		• In the list under *Program Events*, select the event for which to change the associated sound

REFERENCE

task reference roundup

Task	Page #	Preferred Method
		• Change the sound associated with the program event by selecting the desired sound from the *Sounds* drop-down list
Using Sound Recorder	WINXP 6.15	• Click **Start, All Programs, Accessories, Entertainment, Sound Recorder**
		• Click the **Start** button to start recording
		• Click the **Stop** button to stop recording
		• Click the **Play** button to play the recording
Inserting a sound file over an existing recording	WINXP 6.15	• Open Sound Recorder to an existing recording
		• Drag the slider to where you want to insert the new sound file
		• Click **Edit,** then click **Insert File . . .**
		• Click the sound file you want to insert, then click **Open** to add the sound to the existing recording
Starting CD Player	WINXP 6.16	• In the Start menu, click **All Programs**
		• In the All Programs menu, click **Accessories**
		• In the Accessories submenu, click **Entertainment**
		• In the Entertainment submenu, click **CD Player**
Changing to Tiny View	WINXP 6.17	• Click the button next to the **Close** button
Using the Taskbar icon	WINXP 6.17	• Click the **Options** button
		• In the Preferences dialog box, click the **Player Options** tab
		• Check the **Show Control on Taskbar** check box
		• Click **OK**
		• To run CD Player, click the icon
		• To display a context menu of options, right-click the icon
Changing CD Player's playback mode	WINXP 6.18	• Click the **Mode** button
		• In the drop-down list, click **Mode**
		• When in Preview mode, click the **Play** button to play the entire track
Displaying the Playlist tab	WINXP 6.18	• Click the **Options** button
		• In the Preferences dialog box, click the **Playlist** tab
Creating a Playlist	WINXP 6.19	• On the Playlist tab, click the CD that's in the CD drive
		• Click **Create Playlist**
		• In the Artist field, type the name of the artist
		• In the Title field, type the title of the CD

task reference roundup

Task	Page #	Preferred Method
		• For each track in the Playlist list, type the track's name
		• Click **OK**
Editing a Playlist	WINXP 6.20	• On the Playlist tab, click the CD for which you want to edit the Playlist
		• Click **Edit Playlist**
		• To move a track, click it and drag it up or down in the list
		• To remove a track, click it, then click **Remove**
		• To add another instance of the track, select the track from the **Available Tracks** drop-down list, then click **Add to Playlist**
		• Click **OK**
Starting Windows Media Player	WINXP 6.20	• In the Start menu, click **All Programs**
		• In the All Programs menu, click **Accessories**
		• In the Accessories submenu, click **Entertainment**
		• In the Entertainment submenu, click **Windows Media Player**
Playing and controlling a clip	WINXP 6.22	• Click the **Play** button to resume playing the clip
		• Use the control buttons to pause, stop, and jump to the beginning or end of the clip
		• Use the seek bar to go to a specific point in the clip
Repeating a clip	WINXP 6.22	• In the View menu, click **Options**
		• Click the **Playback** tab
		• To repeat the clip a specific number of times, type the number
		• To repeat the clip continuously, click **Repeat Forever**
		• Click **OK**
Starting DVD Player	WINXP 6.22	• In the Start menu, click **All Programs**
		• In the All Programs menu, click **Accessories**
		• In the Accessories submenu, click **Entertainment**
		• In the Entertainment submenu, click **DVD Player**
Starting the New Connection Wizard	WINXP 7.4	• In the Start menu, click **All Programs**
		• In the All Programs menu, click **Accessories**
		• In the Accessories submenu, click **Communications**
		• In the Communications submenu, click **New Connection Wizard**
Starting Internet Explorer	WINXP 7.5	• Click **Start,** then double-click the **Internet Explorer** icon
		• If prompted, click **Connect** to connect to the Internet

REFERENCE

task reference roundup

Task	Page #	Preferred Method
Displaying the Security tab	WINXP 7.6	• In the Tools menu of Internet Explorer, click **Internet Options**
		• In the Internet Options dialog box, click the **Security** tab
Adding sites to security zones	WINXP 7.7	• In the Security tab, click the zone to which you want to add a site
		• Click **Sites**
		• Click the **Advanced . . .** button
		• In the top field, type the address of the site
		• Click **Add**
		• Click **OK**
Setting a security level	WINXP 7.7	• In the Security tab, click the zone for which to set the level
		• Click the slider bar, then drag it to one of the four security levels
		• Click **Apply** or **OK**
Customizing a security level	WINXP 7.8	• In the Security tab, click the zone for which to customize the security level
		• Click the **Custom Level** button
		• In the Settings box, click the appropriate radio buttons to set the security options
		• To reset the values to one of the default levels, use the **Reset to** drop-down list to select the level, then click **Reset**
		• Click **OK**
Setting Web page colors	WINXP 7.9	• In the Internet Options dialog box, click the **General** tab
		• In the General tab, click the **Colors** button
		• To be able to select custom colors for the text and background, uncheck the **Use Windows colors** check box
		• To be able to select a color for when the mouse pointer is over a link, check the **Use hover color** check box
		• To change the color of an option, click the color button
		• In the Color dialog box, select the color to use, then click **OK**
		• When you've finished selecting colors, click **OK** in the Colors dialog box
		• In the Internet Options dialog box, click **OK** or **Apply**
Setting Web page typefaces	WINXP 7.11	• In the General tab, click **Fonts**
		• In the Fonts dialog box, in the Web page font list, click the typeface to use for regular text
		• In the Plain text font list, click the typeface to use for plain text
		• Click **OK**

task reference roundup

Task	Page #	Preferred Method
		• In the Internet Options dialog box, click **OK**
Customizing the size of text	WINXP 7.12	• In the View menu, click **Text Size**
		• In the Text Size submenu, click the size to use
Overriding Web page fonts and colors	WINXP 7.13	• In the General tab, click the **Accessibility** button
		• In the Accessibility dialog box, under Formatting, check and uncheck boxes to indicate which settings to override
		• Click **OK**
		• In the Internet Options dialog box, click **OK** or **Apply**
Using the Address bar to navigate	WINXP 7.15	• Double-click the Address bar to select the current address
		• Type the address you want to go to
		• Press **Enter,** or click the **Go** button next to the bar
Using the Back, Forward, and Home buttons	WINXP 7.18	• To return to the previous page, click the **Back** button. You can also select a page from the Back drop-down list
		• To return to the next page after using the **Back** button, click the **Forward** button. You can also select a page from the Forward drop-down list
		• To return to your home page, click the **Home** button
Using the Stop and Refresh buttons	WINXP 7.19	• To stop loading a page, click the **Stop** button
		• To reload the current page, click the **Refresh** button
Displaying Internet Explorer's Search tool	WINXP 7.19	• On the Standard Buttons toolbar, click the **Search** button
Using the Search tool	WINXP 7.20	• In the Standard Buttons toolbar, click the **Search** button
		• In the fields that display, type or select the information to use in the search
		• Click the **Search** button
Printing a Web page	WINXP 7.21	• Click the **Print** button
		or
		• In the File menu, click **Print**
		• Click the **Options** tab
		• Under *Print frames,* click a radio button to indicate how to print them
		• Check **Print all linked documents** to also print any pages that have links on this page
		• Check **Print table of links** to also print a list of links on this page
		• Click **Print**

REFERENCE

task reference roundup

Task	Page #	Preferred Method
Using the Links toolbar	WINXP 7.22	• To add a link from the Address bar, click the icon next to the address in the Address bar, then drag it to the **Links** toolbar
		• To add a link from a Web page, click a link, then drag it to the **Links** toolbar
		• To rearrange links on the toolbar, click a link, then drag it to its new spot on the toolbar
		• To remove a link, right click it, then click **Delete** in the context menu
Using the History tool	WINXP 7.23	• To display the History tool, click the **History** button
		• To change the view, click **View,** then click an option in the menu
		• To display a page from the History, click it
Customizing the History tool	WINXP 7.24	• In the Tools menu, click **Internet Options**
		• Click the **General** tab
		• Under History, in the *Days to keep pages in history* field, set the number of days to keep History information
		• Click **Clear History** to clear the History
		• Click **OK**
Adding the current page to Favorites	WINXP 7.26	• In the Favorites menu, click **Add to Favorites** *or* click **Add** on the Favorites tool *or* right-click the page, then click **Add to Favorites** in the context menu
		• In the *Add Favorite* dialog box, in the *Name* field, edit the Favorite's name as needed
		• If the Create in folder list is not displayed, click **Create in**
		• To create a new folder, click the folder in which to create the new folder, then click **New Folder.** Type the folder name, then click **OK**
		• To select a folder in which to place the new Favorite, click that folder
		• Click **OK**
Using the Organize Favorites dialog box	WINXP 7.27	• To display the dialog box, in the Favorites menu, click **Organize Favorites** *or* click **Organize** on the Favorites tool
		• To display the contents of a folder, click the folder
		• To move a page or folder, click and drag it to the new location
		• To create a new folder, click **Create Folder.** Type the name, then press **Enter**
		• To rename a folder or Favorite, click it, then click **Rename.** Type the new name, then press **Enter**
		• To move a Favorite or folder to another folder, click **Move To Folder.** In the tree of folders that displays, click the folder you want, then click **OK**
		• To delete a Favorite or folder, click it, then click **Delete**
		• Click **Close**

task reference roundup

Task	Page #	Preferred Method
Setting up an e-mail account	WINXP 7.29	• In the Tools menu, click **Accounts**
		• In the Mail tab of the Internet Accounts dialog box, click **Add**
		• In the pop-up list, click **Mail**
		• Use the Internet Connection Wizard to enter the information supplied by your ISP
Displaying or removing Outlook Express interface elements	WINXP 7.30	• In the View menu, click **Layout**
		• In the Window Layout Properties dialog box, click an element's check box to either remove or display the element
		• Click **OK**
Downloading messages	WINXP 7.31	• Click the **Send/Recv** button
Setting options for Check for Messages	WINXP 7.31	• In the Tools menu, click **Options**
		• In the General tab, under Send/Receive Messages, click the **Check for new messages** check box
		• In the field, type the number of minutes to indicate how often to check for new messages
		• To check for new messages when you start Outlook Express, check the **Send and receive messages at startup** check box
		• To play a sound when a new message arrives, check the **Play sound when new messages arrive** check box
		• Click **OK**
Managing a mail list	WINXP 7.33	• To change the width of a column, click a column border and drag it to the left or right
		• To change the order of the columns, click a column heading, then drag it to its new location
		• To hide or display columns, right-click the column headings, then click **Columns**. Check and uncheck columns, then click **OK**
		• To sort the mail list, click the column heading
Reading messages and attachments	WINXP 7.34	• To open a message window, double-click the message in the list
		• To open an attachment from the Preview pane, click the paperclip, then click the attachment
		• To open an attachment from the message window, double-click the attachment
Replying to and forwarding messages	WINXP 7.34	• To send a response only to the person who sent the message, click **Reply**

task reference roundup

Task	Page #	Preferred Method
		• To send your response to everyone who received the message, click **Reply All**
		• To send the message to someone else who didn't receive it, click **Forward**
Creating a mail folder	WINXP 7.35	• Right-click the **Folder List**
		• In the context menu, click **New Folder**
		• In the Create Folder dialog box, type the name of the new folder in the *Folder Name* field
		• In the folder tree, click the folder in which to place the new folder
		• Click **OK**
Moving, copying, and deleting messages	WINXP 7.35	• To move a message to another folder, click the message in the mail list, then drag it to the folder
		• To copy a message, hold down the **Ctrl** key as you drag it to another folder
		• To delete a message, click the **Delete** button or drag the message to the **Deleted Items** folder
Arranging to empty deleted items automatically	WINXP 7.36	• In the Tools menu, click **Options**
		• Click the **Maintenance** tab
		• Check the **Empty messages from 'Deleted Items' on exit** check box
		• Click **OK**
Creating and sending a message	WINXP 7.38	• Click **New** on the Outlook Express toolbar
		• In the To:, Cc:, and Bcc: fields, specify the e-mail addresses of the message's main recipients
		• In the Subject field, type the subject of the message
		• In the message text box, type the text of the message
		• To change the text format of the message, in the Format menu, click **Rich Text** or **Plain Text**
		• To attach a file to the message, click the **Attach** button, then navigate to the file and click **Attach,** *or* drag a file from a Desktop folder to the New Message window
		• To send the message, click the **Send** button
Displaying the Address Book	WINXP 7.39	• From Outlook Express, click the **Addresses** button on the toolbar
		or
		• In the Start menu, click **All Programs**
		• In the All Programs menu, click **Accessories**
		• In the Accessories submenu, click **Address Book**

task reference roundup

Task	Page #	Preferred Method
Creating an Address Book contact	WINXP 7.40	• Click the **New** button
		• In the pop-up list, click **New Contact**
		• In the Properties dialog box, type the information about the contact. You must at least specify a name
		• Click **OK**
Creating an Address Book group	WINXP 7.41	• Click the **New** button
		• In the pop-up menu, click **New Group**
		• In the Group Name field, type the name of the group
		• Click **Select Members**
		• In the Select Group Members dialog box, select the contacts for the group, then click **OK**
		• Click **OK** to create the new group
Editing a contact or group	WINXP 7.42	• Double-click the contact or group
		• In the Properties dialog box, edit the information
		• Click **OK**
Deleting a contact or group	WINXP 7.42	• Click the contact or group
		• Click the **Delete** button
Creating a News account	WINXP 7.42	• In the Tools menu, click **Accounts**
		• In the Accounts dialog box, click **News**
		• Click **Add**
		• In the pop-up list, click **News**
		• Use the Wizard to enter the information about the news server
Subscribing to a newsgroup	WINXP 7.43	• In the Folders List, click the news server
		• In the Tools menu, click **Newsgroups**
		• In the Newsgroup Subscriptions dialog box, click **All** to list the newsgroups on that server
		• To subscribe to a newsgroup, double-click it
Using the Network Setup Wizard	WINXP 8.8	• Click **Start, All Programs, Accessories, Communications, Network Setup Wizard**
		• At the Welcome window, click **Next**
		• In the Before You Continue window, review the checklist for creating a network, then click **Next**

REFERENCE

task reference roundup

Task	Page #	Preferred Method
		• Select the statement that best describes your network, then click **Next**
		• Follow the on-screen prompts
Making a new connection	WINXP 8.9	• Click **Start**, then click **Control Panel**
		• Double-click **Network Connections**
		• Click the **Create a new connection** link
		• Choose the type of connection, enter the phone number, and choose the availability you want for this connection, then click **Finish**
Changing the dial out settings	WINXP 8.10	• From the Network Connections window, click the connection whose settings you want to change, click **File**, then click **Properties**
		• Click the **General** tab to enter a new phone number or change an existing one
		• Click the **Alternates** button, then click the **Add** button to type an alternate phone number to dial in case the first number fails to connect
		• Click the **Options** tab to require a name and password, to change the number of redial attempts, to change the amount of time between redial attempts, to change the amount of idle time before automatically disconnecting, or to have Windows automatically redial if the line gets disconnected
Setting up an incoming connection	WINXP 8.13	• From the Network Connections window, double-click **Create a new connection**
		• Click the *Set up an advanced connection* radio button, then Click **Next**
		• Click the radio button next to *Accept incoming connections,* then click **Next**
		• Click the check box next to the connection device you want other computers to use to connect to your computer, then click **Next**
		• Click the radio button next to *Do not allow virtual private connections,* then click **Next**
		• Click the check box next to each user you want to allow to connect to your computer, then click **Next**
		• Click the check box next to each networking component you want to use for incoming connections, then click **Next**
		• Click **Finish**
Sharing a folder	WINXP 8.18	• Click the folder you wish to share. Click **File,** then click **Sharing and Security** . . . The Properties dialog box opens
		• In the Sharing tab, click the *Share this folder on the network* check box. If you wish to give the folder a Share name, do so in this dialog box
		• To allow others to modify data in the folder, click the *Allow network users to change my files* check box
		• Click **OK**
Sharing a printer	WINXP 8.19	• Click **Start**, then click **Printers and Faxes**

task reference roundup

Task	Page #	Preferred Method
		• In the Printers window, click the icon for the printer you wish to share
		• In the **File** menu, click **Sharing . . .**
		• Click the **Share this printer** radio button, then type a friendly name so that others can easily identify the printer
		• Click **OK**
Connecting to a shared printer	WINXP 8.20	• Click **Start**, then click **Printers and Faxes**
		• Click the **Add Printer** link
		• Click the **A network printer, or a printer attached to another computer** radio button
		• Type the name of the printer you wish to connect to, or browse to find it
Mapping a network drive	WINXP 8.22	• Right-click the folder on the network you want to map and click **Map Network Drive**
		• Select the drive letter you wish to use and click **Finish**
Browsing in My Network Places	WINXP 8.24	• Click **Start**, then click **My Network Places**
		• Double-click **Entire Network**
		• Click the hyperlink *entire contents*
		• Double-click the type of operating system, the domain, and the computer you want to access
		• Double-click the files or folders to open them
Adding a new network place	WINXP 8.25	• Click **Start**, then click **My Network Places**
		• Click the **Add a network place** link
		• Click **Choose another network location**
		• Type \\ followed by the name of the computer you want to access, then type \ (for example, **computer**)
		• Click **Next**, then click **Finish**
Searching for a computer	WINXP 8.26	• Open **My Network Places**
		• Click **Search**
		• Type the name of the computer you want to find
		• Click the **Search** button
		• Double-click the found computer name in the Search Results— Computers pane to view the folders and other resources available on the selected machine
Changing the identity of a computer on a network	WINXP 8.29	• Click **Start**, then click **Control Panel**

REFERENCE

task reference roundup

Task	Page #	Preferred Method
		• Double-click **System**, then click the **Computer Name** tab
		• Click the **Change** button
		• Indicate whether you want to join a domain or a workgroup, and indicate the name of the domain or workgroup you want to join
		• If you chose to join a domain, type the name and password of an account with permission to join the domain. Click **OK**
		• Click **OK** through the next four dialog boxes; then click **Yes** to reboot
Installing a network protocol	WINXP 8.32	• Click **Start**, then click **Control Panel**
		• Double-click **Network Connections**
		• Click the icon for the connection for which you want to add a protocol; click **File**, then click **Properties**
		• Click **Install**
		• Click **Protocol**, then the **Add** button
		• Click the protocol you want to install, then click **OK**
Determining your network interface settings	WINXP 8.35	• Click **Start**, then click **Control Panel**
		• Double-click **Network Connections**
		• Click **Local Area Connection**, and then click **File**, then **Properties**
		• Double-click **Internet Protocol** (TCP/IP)
		• Click the radio button next to *Obtain an IP address automatically* to have the IP address set by a DHCP server
		• Click the radio button next to *Use the following IP address* and enter an address in the text boxes below
		• Click the radio button next to *Obtain DNS Server address automatically* to get your network servers to provide the DNS server address
		• Alternately, click the radio button next to *Use the following DNS server address,* and enter the address in the text boxes below; then click **OK**
Changing your password	WINXP 9.8	• Press and hold the **Ctrl** and **Alt** keys as you press the **Delete** key
		• Click **Change Password**
		• Type your old password and your new password
		• Click **OK**, then **OK** again
Adding a new user	WINXP 9.10	• Navigate to the **Control Panel** and double-click **User Accounts**
		• Click the **Create a new account** link
		• Type a name for the new user and click **Next**
		• Choose an account type for the new user, then click **Create Account**

task reference roundup

Task	Page #	Preferred Method
		• Click **Change an Account,** click the new user you just created, then click **Create Password**
		• Type a password twice, then click **Create Password**
Switching from the current user to another	WINXP 9.13	• Click **Start,** then **Log Off**
		• Click **Switch User**
		• Select the user name from the Welcome screen
Adding new groups	WINXP 9.15	• Navigate to the Computer Management window **(Start, Control Panel, Administrative Tools, Computer Management)**
		• Click the plus sign next to *Local Groups and Users,* then right-click **Groups**
		• Click **New Group . . .** from the context menu
		• Type a Group name and description, then click **Add**
		• Click the users to add, then click the **Add** button. Click **OK** when done
		• Click the **Create** button, then click **Close**
Deleting a user or group	WINXP 9.16	• Navigate to the Computer Management window **(Start, Control Panel, Administrative Tools, Computer Management)**
		• Click the plus sign next to *Local Groups and Users,* then click **Groups**
		• Right-click the group you want to delete
		• Click **Delete** from the context menu
Changing permissions for a shared folder	WINXP 9.19	• Click to select the folder you wish to change permissions for; then click **File,** then **Sharing and Security . . .**
		• Click the **Permissions** button
		• Click one of the listings under *Group or user names* to view their permissions and click in a check box to change the permission type to allow or deny
		• To add a user or group, click the **Add** button
		• Click the name of the user or group you want to allow access to, then click **Add**
		• Click **OK**
Enabling the Internet Connection Firewall	WINXP 9.27	• Click **Start, Connect To, Show All Connections**
		• Right-click the icon for your Internet connection and click **Properties**
		• In the **Advanced** tab, click the check box in the ICF area
		• Click **OK**
Viewing the Clipboard's contents using ClipBook	WINXP 10.3	• Click **Start,** then **Run**
		• In the Open dialog box, type **clipbrd.exe,** then press **Enter**

REFERENCE

task reference roundup

Task	Page #	Preferred Method
		• Click **Window,** then **Clipboard** to display the contents of the Clipboard
Pasting items into ClipBook	WINXP 10.4	• Copy the desired data
		• Open ClipBook
		• Click **Window,** then **Local ClipBook**
		• Click **Edit,** then **Paste**
		• Type a name for the page in the Paste dialog box
		• If you want to make the page available to others on your network, click the **Share Item Now** check box
		• Click **OK**
Saving contents using ClipBook	WINXP 10.4	• In ClipBook, click **File,** then **Save as . . .**
		• Choose a location to save the file and type a name for it, leaving the filename extension as .clp
		• Click the **Save** button
Copying objects between different applications	WINXP 10.5	• Open the server document and select the desired object
		• Click **Edit,** then **Copy**
		• Open the container document and select the location where you want the information to be copied
		• Click **Edit,** then **Paste**
Editing an embedded object	WINXP 10.7	• Open the document that contains the embedded object
		• Double-click the embedded object
		• Make the desired changes to the object
		• When finished editing the object, click anywhere outside the object within the document
Dragging and dropping data between applications	WINXP 10.9	• Open the server document and the container document
		• Select the desired object
		• Holding down the Ctrl key, drag the object to the target document
Inserting a graphic in another application	WINXP 10.10	• Open the server document and select the desired object
		• From the **Edit** menu click **Copy**
		• Open the container document and select the location where you want the information to be copied
		• From the **Edit** menu click **Paste**

task reference roundup

Task	Page #	Preferred Method
Dragging and dropping a document scrap	WINXP 10.12	• Select and drag the desired information from the server document onto your Desktop
		• Drag and drop the scrap from the Desktop into the target document
Linking an object	WINXP 10.13	• In the server document that contains the object you want to link, select the object
		• In the **Edit** menu click **Copy**
		• In the target document where you want to paste the object, click the location where you want the object to appear
		• In the **Edit** menu click **Paste Special**
		• Click the radio button next to Paste link
		• Click **OK**
Editing a linked object	WINXP 10.15	• Double-click the linked object you want to edit in the compound document
		• Edit the object
		• In the **File** menu, click **Save**
		• In the **File** menu, click **Exit**
Setting up a .NET Passport user account	WINXP 10.17	• Click **Start, Control Panel, User Accounts**
		• Click your user account
		• Click the **Set up my account to use .NET Passport** link, then click **Next**
		• Click the **Yes** radio button, then click **Next**
		• Type your e-mail address, then click **Next**
		• Type a password, then click **Next**
		• Click **Finish**
Opening the Command Prompt window	WINXP 10.20	• Click **Start, All Programs, Accessories, Command Prompt**
Getting help in the Command Prompt window	WINXP 10.21	• Type HELP, then press Enter to find out which commands you can use
		• Type the command name followed by a space and /? to find out how to use the command
Increasing the screen size of a Command Prompt window to full view	WINXP 10.21	• Press and hold down the **Alt** key, then press **Enter**
Cycling through all open windows from a full view Command Prompt window	WINXP 10.21	• Press and hold down the **Windows** key, then press **Alt**

task reference roundup

Task	Page #	Preferred Method
Returning to a standard Windows view from a full view Command Prompt window	WINXP 10.21	• Press and hold down the **Alt** key, then press **Enter**
Changing the default color, font, and text size in a Command Prompt window	WINXP 10.22	• Right-click the Title bar of the Command Prompt window, then select Properties from the context menu
		• In the **Colors** tab, click the **Screen text** radio button and choose a color from the color bar in the middle of the dialog box. Click the **Screen background** radio button and choose a color for it in the same way
		• In the **Font** tab, choose a font from the *Font* list and a text size from the *Size* list
		• Click **OK**
Listing the contents of the current directory	WINXP 10.22	• Type the **dir** command, then press **Enter**
Copying text from the Command Prompt window	WINXP 10.23	• Right-click the Title bar of the Command Prompt window; then click **Edit**, then **Mark** from the context menu
		• Highlight the text you want to copy by dragging your mouse over it, then press **Enter**
		• Open the target document and in the **Edit** menu, click **Paste**
Displaying the Task Manager	WINXP 11.6	• Press and hold down **Ctrl+Alt**, then press **Delete**
Using Task Manager	WINXP 11.6	• In the Task Manager, click the Application tab to view the status of programs that are running
		• In the Task Manager, click the Processes tab to view the status of the processes that are running
		• In the Task Manager, click the Performance tab to check the status of your computer's performance
		• In the Task Manager, click the Networking tab to view the status and performance of the network
Using Task Manager to close a program that is not responding	WINXP 11.7	• Display the Task Manager and click the **Applications** tab
		• Select the program that is not responding from the *Task* list
		• Click the **End Task** button
		• Click the **End Now** button to close the program
Displaying the Device Manager	WINXP 11.8	• Click **Start**, then **Control Panel**
		• Double-click **System**
		• In the **Hardware** tab of the System Properties dialog box, click the **Device Manager** button

task reference roundup

Task	Page #	Preferred Method
Printing information about hardware	WINXP 11.9	• In the Device Manager screen, click the device or the category of device for which you want to print information
		• In the **Action** menu, click **Print**
		• In the Print dialog box, choose from one of the *Report types* by clicking the appropriate radio button: the *System summary* option prints a *summary* of the devices connected to your computer. The *Selected class or device* option prints a report for the individual device or the entire class of device types selected. *All devices and system summary* prints a report about every device installed on your computer along with a hardware summary
		• Click the **Print** button
Using the Device Manager to obtain details about a device	WINXP 11.10	• In the Device Manager, click the plus sign (+) next to the category folder that contains the device
		• Double-click the particular device about which you want more information
		• In the device's Properties dialog box, click the General tab to obtain the name of the manufacturer and the operating status of the device
		• Click the Driver tab to obtain information about the version number or other information related to the driver provider, date, or digital signer
		• Click the Resources tab to view the resources used by the device driver and a list of possible conflicting devices
		• Click **OK** to close the Properties dialog box when done obtaining the information you need
Updating a driver	WINXP 11.12	• In the Device Manager, double-click the device you want to update
		• Click the **Drivers** tab of the Properties dialog box
		• Click the **Update Driver** button
		• Select the *Install from a list or specific location* radio button, then click **Next**
		• Select the *Don't search, I will choose the driver to install* radio button, then click **Next**
		• Click the **Have Disk** button
		• Click **Browse,** then navigate to the file containing the driver update
		• Click the **Open** button
		• Click **OK**
		• Click **Next**
		• Click **Finish**
Rolling back a driver	WINXP 11.12	• In the Device Manager, double-click the device you want to roll back
		• Click the **Drivers** tab of the Properties dialog box; click the **Roll Back Driver** button
		• Click **Yes**

REFERENCE

task reference roundup

Task	Page #	Preferred Method
		• Click **OK**
Starting in Safe Mode	WINXP 11.14	• If your computer is on, shut it off
		• Turn on your computer and monitor, then immediately press and hold down the **F8** key
		• The Windows Advanced Options menu appears. Use the up and down arrow keys to highlight the **Safe Mode** option, then press **Enter**
		• Use arrow keys again to highlight the operating system you want to start, then press **Enter**
		• At the Welcome screen, click the Administrator account to use
		• Click the **Yes** button in the dialog box
		• When finished using Safe Mode, restart your computer normally
Restoring your computer	WINXP 11.16	• Click **Start, All Programs, Accessories, System Tools, System Restore**
		• Click the **Restore my computer to an earlier time** radio button, then click **Next**
		• The Select a restore point screen opens showing a calendar with all the dates that have restore points in bold
		• Click the most recent day with a restore point before the problems started, then click **Next**
		• The Confirm Restore Point Selection asks you to confirm the restore point you have selected and provides some information about the restore process; click **Next**
		• A dialog box will detail the progress of the restoration, and the computer restarts when complete. Click **OK**
Manually creating a restore point	WINXP 11.17	• Click **Start, All Programs, Accessories, System Tools, System Restore**
		• Click the **Create a restore point** radio button, then click **Next**
		• Type a description for the restore point and click **Create**
		• Click **Close**
Displaying System Information	WINXP 11.19	• Click **Start, All Programs, Accessories, System Tools, System Information**
		• Click the **System Summary** folder in the left pane to display general information
		• Click the plus sign (+) next to a category name to expand the list, then click the specific item about which you wish to view more details
Using the IPCONFIG command to check your TCP/IP settings	WINXP 11.20	• Click **Start, All Programs, Accessories, Command Prompt**
		• Type **ipconfig**, then press **Enter**

task reference roundup

Task	Page #	Preferred Method
Using the PING command to test connectivity	WINXP 11.21	• Click **Start, All Programs, Accessories, Command Prompt**
		• Type **ping x.x.x.x,** where x.x.x.x is the IP address of a remote computer, then press **Enter**
		• If you receive a response, this means the connection between your computer and the remote one is good
Using the TRACERT command	WINXP 11.23	• Click **Start, All Programs, Accessories, Command Prompt**
		• Type **TRACERT x.x.x.x,** where x.x.x.x is the IP address of a remote computer (or type **TRACERT name,** where name is the destination domain name), then press **Enter**
Displaying the Registry	WINXP 11.25	• In the **Start** menu, click **Run**
		• Type **regedit** in the **Open** text box, then click **OK**
		• Click the plus sign (+) next to a key to expand it and display the contents
		• Click an item to display its values
Backing up the Registry	WINXP 11.25	• Click **Start, All Programs, Accessories, System Tools, Backup**
		• In the Welcome to Backup or Restore Wizard screen, click the **Advanced Mode** link, then click **Next**
		• Click the *Only back up the System State data* radio button, then click **Next**
Restoring the Registry	WINXP 11.26	• Click **Start, All Programs, Accessories, System Tools, Backup**
		• In the Welcome to Backup or Restore Wizard screen click the **Advanced Mode** link, then click **Next**
		• Click the **Restore Wizard** radio button, then click **Next**
		• Make sure the disk that contains your backup file is inserted in the drive
		• Click the **Browse** button and navigate to the backup file on the disk
		• Choose to restore the entire System state, not just the Registry, then click the **Start restore** button
		• Answer the prompts in the dialog boxes, then click **Finish**
Searching the Registry	WINXP 11.27	• In the Registry, click **Edit,** then **Find**
		• In the Find dialog box, type the text you wish to find
		• Narrow your search by clicking in the check boxes marked *Keys, Values, Data,* or *Match whole string only*
		• Click **Find Next** to begin your search
Viewing the Hardware Compatibility List (HCL)	WINXP 12.6	• View the Hardware Compatibility List at www.microsoft.com/hcl/

task reference roundup

Task	Page #	Preferred Method
Printing a configuration Report from Windows 95 or Windows 98	WINXP 12.6	• On the **Desktop,** right-click **My Computer**
		• In the context menu, click **Properties**
		• Click the **Device Manager** tab
		• Click **Print**
		• In the Print dialog box, select **System Summary**
		• Click **OK**
Printing a configuration report from Windows NT	WINXP 12.6	• In the **Start** menu, click **Programs**
		• In the **Programs** menu, click **Administrative Tools (Common)**
		• In the **Administrative Tools** submenu, click **Windows NT Diagnostics**
		• Click **Print**
		• Under **Scope,** click the **All tabs** radio button
		• Under **Detail Level,** click the **Summary** radio button
		• Under **Destination,** click the **Default Printer** radio button
		• Click **OK**
Starting the backup program from Windows 95, Windows 98, or Windows 2000	WINXP 12.7	• In the **Start** menu, click **Programs**
		• In the **Programs** menu, click **Accessories**
		• In the **Accessories** submenu, click **System Tools**
		• In the **System Tools** submenu, click **Backup**
Starting the backup program from Windows NT	WINXP 12.7	• In the **Start** menu, click **Programs**
		• In the **Programs** menu, click **Administrative Tools (Common)**
		• In the **Administrative Tools** submenu, click **Backup**
Uncompressing a hard disk from Windows 95 or Windows 98	WINXP 12.8	• In the **Start** menu, click **Programs**
		• In the **Programs** menu, click **Accessories**
		• In the **Accessories** submenu, click **System Tools**
		• In the **System Tools** submenu, click **DriveSpace**
		• In the **DriveSpace** dialog box, select the compressed drive

task reference roundup

Task	Page #	Preferred Method
		• In the **Drive** menu, click **Uncompress**
Uncompressing a hard disk from MS-DOS	WINXP 12.8	• If you're running MS-DOS 6.22 or higher, then at the Command Prompt, type **drvspace**
		• If you have an earlier version, type **dblspace**
		• Select the drive to uncompress
		• In the **Tools** menu, click **Uncompress**
Using the Files and Settings Transfer Wizard	WINXP 12.9	• In the source computer, click **Start, All Programs, Accessories, System Tools, Files and Settings Transfer Wizard**
		• Click the **Old computer** radio button, then click **Next**
		• Choose the transfer method, then click **Next**
		• Choose the type of information to transfer, then click **Next**
		• Click **Finish**
		• In the destination computer, navigate to the **Files and Transfer Settings Wizard**
		• Click the **New Computer** radio button, then click **Next**
		• Click the radio button that indicates you have already collected your data, then click **Next**
		• Specify the location of your data, then click **Next**
		• Click **Finish**
Beginning installation from the CD-ROM from a previous version of Windows	WINXP 12.11	• Insert the Windows XP Professional CD-ROM into your CD-ROM or DVD drive
		• Click **Install Windows XP**
		• In the **Windows XP Setup Welcome** screen, click the appropriate radio button to indicate whether you're upgrading or doing a clean install
		• Click **Next**
Beginning installation without a previous version of Windows	WINXP 12.12	• Turn off your computer
		• If you can boot from your CD-ROM drive, insert the Windows XP Professional CD-ROM into your CD-ROM drive
		• If you cannot boot from your CD-ROM drive, insert the Windows XP Setup Boot Disk 1 into your floppy disk drive
		• Power up your computer
Beginning installation from a shared network folder	WINXP 12.12	• Obtain the path to the setup folder

REFERENCE

task reference roundup

Task	Page #	Preferred Method
		• If you're installing from Windows 95, Windows 98, or Windows NT, run the program **winnt32** from the setup folder
		• If you're installing from Windows 3.1 or some other operating system, run the program **winnt** from the setup folder
Setting license, partition, and file system information	WINXP 12.13	• In the **License Agreement** dialog box, click **I accept this agreement,** then click **Next**
		• In the **Your Product Key** dialog box, type the product key, then click **Next**
		• In the **Special Options** dialog box, if you want to select a partition during installation, click **Advanced Options**
		• In the **Advanced Options** dialog box, check **I want to choose the installation partition during setup,** then click **OK**
		• In the **Special Options** dialog box, click **Next**
		• After the computer restarts, if asked, select the partition on which to install Windows XP, then press **Enter**
		• If prompted, indicate whether to convert the file system to NTFS, then press **Enter**
Regional settings and personalizing your computer	WINXP 12.13	• When the computer restarts, in the **Welcome** dialog box, click **Next**
		• In the **Regional Settings** dialog box, click **Next**
		• In the **Personalize Your Software** dialog box, in the **Name** field, type your name
		• If appropriate, in the **Organization** field, type the name of the organization
		• Click **Next**
Computer name, date, and network information	WINXP 12.14	• In the **Computer Name and Administrator Password** dialog box, in the **Computer name** field, type the name of your computer
		• In the **Administrator password** field, type the password for your computer's Administrator account
		• In the **Confirm password** field, type the password again
		• Click **Next**
		• In the **Modem Dialing Information** dialog box, specify the area code, outside line, and type of dialing, then click **Next**
		• In the **Date and Time Settings** dialog box, make sure the date and time are correct, then click **Next**
		• In the **Network Settings** dialog box, select **Typical Settings,** then click **Next**

task reference roundup

Task	Page #	Preferred Method
		• In the **Workgroup or Computer Domain** dialog box, if your computer is part of a network domain for which your computer has an account, click the **Yes** radio button and type the domain name in the **Workgroup or computer domain** field
		• If your computer is not part of a network domain, then click the **No** radio button and type the workgroup name in the **Workgroup or computer domain** field
		• Click **Next**
		• In the **Completing Windows XP Setup Wizard** dialog box, click **Finish**
Configuring logon options	WINXP 12.15	• In the **Users of this Computer** dialog box of the **Network Identification Wizard,** if users must log on to use this computer, click the **Users must enter a user name and password to use this computer** radio button
		• To bypass the logon, click the **Windows always assumes the following user has logged on to this computer** radio button
		• If you've selected the bypass option, then in the **User name** drop-down list, click the user
		• In the **Password** field, type a password for the default user
		• In the **Confirm password** field, type the password again
		• Click **Next**
		• In the **Completing the Network Identification Wizard** dialog box, click **Finish**
Using Windows Update	WINXP 12.17	• In the **Start** menu, click **Windows Update**
		• On the **Windows Update** home page, click **Product Updates**
		• If prompted, click **OK** to install the update program
		• On the **Product Updates** page, check the check box beside each update you want to install
		• Click **Download**
Setting up Automatic Updates	WINXP 12.18	• Click **Start, Control Panel, System**
		• Click the **Automatic Updates** tab
		• Click the *Keep my computer up to date* check box
		• Click **OK**
Using the Downloads page	WINXP 12.20	• Select a type of download (Critical Update, Service Pack, etc.) to display the list of updates of that type
		• In the list of downloads, click the update you want to download
		• Follow the instructions provided for downloading the update

REFERENCE

reference 3

making *the grade*

CHAPTER 1

SESSION 1.1

1. user name, password
2. My Documents
3. right-click
4. Maximize
5. Restart

SESSION 1.2

1. application
2. Start menu
3. File
4. copy
5. Control Panel

SESSION 1.3

1. the Start menu, then Help and Support
2. Favorites
3. Search
4. Options
5. Start, Control Panel, Performance and Maintenance, System

CHAPTER 2

SESSION 2.1

1. tree structure
2. Alt
3. Thumbnails
4. Ctrl
5. emptying

SESSION 2.2

1. File naming conventions
2. text
3. size
4. an asterisk
5. save

SESSION 2.3

1. View
2. format
3. .5 inch
4. outdent
5. ruler

SESSION 2.4

1. current date
2. 256
3. text editor
4. word wrap

CHAPTER 3

SESSION 3.1

1. taskbar
2. folder
3. time
4. right-clicking

SESSION 3.2

1. scheme
2. screen saver
3. Desktop
4. wallpaper
5. resolution

SESSION 3.3

1. moving the mouse pointer over the object
2. Control Panel
3. StickeyKeys
4. 9
5. SoundSentry, ShowSounds

SESSION 3.4

1. Auto Arrange
2. link
3. Name
4. No

CHAPTER 4

SESSION 4.1

1. Yes
2. format
3. Copy Disk
4. removable

SESSION 4.2

1. NTFS
2. primary partition
3. volumes
4. Formatting

SESSION 4.3

1. Scheduled Task
2. Control Panel
3. defragmentation
4. Programs, Accessories, System Tools, Scheduled Tasks
5. Check Disk

SESSION 4.4

1. System Tools
2. week
3. restoring
4. Incremental or Differential

making the grade

CHAPTER 5

SESSION 5.1

1. Print queue
2. shortcut
3. Pause Printing
4. File
5. taskbar

SESSION 5.2

1. local printer
2. network printer
3. Add Printer
4. default
5. Plug and Play
6. printer driver

SESSION 5.3

1. Resolution
2. media
3. Printer Properties
4. Printing Preferences
5. Spooling

SESSION 5.4

1. font
2. Times New Roman
3. attributes
4. points
5. serif

CHAPTER 6

SESSION 6.1

1. driver
2. Device Manager
3. Add Hardware
4. Yes

SESSION 6.2

1. Line

2. press Alt+Print Screen
3. Print Screen
4. the Clipboard

SESSION 6.3

1. Playlist
2. seek bar
3. wave (.wav)
4. a DVD drive

CHAPTER 7

SESSION 7.1

1. Internet Service Provider (ISP)
2. Content
3. home page
4. Accessibility

SESSION 7.2

1. Back
2. domain name
3. .edu
4. Customize
5. frames
6. Links
7. Internet Options— General tab
8. Favorites
9. History
10. nonprofit

SESSION 7.3

1. Drafts
2. newsgroup
3. Address Book
4. Click the server, then select Newsgroups from the Tools menu
5. Rules

CHAPTER 8

SESSION 8.1

1. network
2. stand-alone
3. network interface card (NIC)
4. local area network (LAN)
5. bridge

SESSION 8.2

1. 56
2. New Connection
3. incoming connection
4. Peer-to-Peer
5. dial-up networking

SESSION 8.3

1. several, one
2. Mapping
3. file level permissions
4. Add Network Place

SESSION 8.4

1. domain controller
2. unique
3. member server
4. Active Directory
5. workgroup

CHAPTER 9

SESSION 9.1

1. seven, numbers
2. Windows 2000 Server
3. DNS
4. denial of service
5. user level security

making *the grade*

SESSION 9.2

1. user
2. user account
3. group
4. inherit
5. file, folder

SESSION 9.3

1. public, private
2. public key
3. Certificate Authority (CA)
4. Kerberos, certificates, and key encryption
5. firewall

CHAPTER 10
SESSION 10.1

1. object linking and embedding
2. object
3. compound document
4. embedded
5. Clipboard

SESSION 10.2

1. servers
2. taskbar
3. drag and drop
4. Window
5. scrap

SESSION 10.3

1. COM
2. ASP
3. local machine
4. ActiveX
5. DCOM

SESSION 10.4

1. HELP
2. Accessories
3. Alt
4. Mark
5. dir

CHAPTER 11
SESSION 11.1

1. Task Manager
2. Device Manager
3. Driver
4. Task Manager
5. double-click

SESSION 11.2

1. Safe Mode
2. restoring
3. Administrator
4. System Tools

SESSION 11.3

1. IPCONFIG
2. PING
3. .bkf
4. Registry Editor

CHAPTER 12
SESSION 12.1

1. clean install
2. 233 MHz
3. configuration report
4. upgrade report
5. Files and Settings Transfer

SESSION 12.2

1. If you plan to run multiple operating systems (multiple-boot configuration)
2. log on
3. letters and numbers
4. workgroup

SESSION 12.3

1. Windows Update
2. Critical Update Notification
3. Service pack
4. Resource Kit

REFERENCE

glossary

Active: Refers to the status of a window. The active window is the current window. All actions will affect that window.

Access Control Entry (ACE): A list of users allowed to access an object and what their rights and abilities are. The ACE also includes what group the user belongs to.

Access Control List (ACL): A collection of access control entries.

Active Desktop: A Web page turned into a Desktop background.

Active Directory: A hierarchical directory service whose primary purpose is the efficient management of users, groups, and network resources.

Address: A full path to a Web page. Also called a URL.

Alignment: How a paragraph is positioned within the margins. Can be left, center, right, or full justified.

Applet: Mini-programs of limited function that are bundled together as part of Windows.

Application: A computer program designed for a specific purpose, such as WordPad.

ASCII: The basic set of 256 characters (letters, numbers, punctuation). Used in plain text files.

Attachment: Other files included with a sent e-mail message.

Authentication: Verifying the identity of a user and the protection of a transmitted message from accidental or malicious modification.

Auto Arrange: Locks the Desktop icons in the columns at the left of the Desktop. When Auto Arrange is turned on, users cannot move the icons.

Bitmapped graphic: A graphic made up of a single image. Elements cannot be selected or moved once added.

Bridge: A device that connects two networks together.

Browser: Software that can process and display Web pages.

Bullet: A graphical marker used to set off a list item.

Cache: Temporary storage area on a computer where visited Web sites are stored.

Center justified: Text is aligned along the center of a text column.

Certificate: A digital document that verifies that the public key contained in the certificate actually belongs to the entity named in the certificate.

Certificate Authority (CA): An entity that authenticates that a key is valid and belongs to a particular individual or enterprise.

Clean install: To install Windows XP Professional from scratch; clears all installed programs and data.

Click: To press the left button of the mouse once while over an object. Selects the object.

Client: A machine that requests something from a server.

Client/Server network: A centralized form of networking where at least one computer is designated as a server, a central computer in the network. The other computers, called clients, come to this server for a variety of purposes, for example, to access information.

Clip: Term used by Windows Media Player to refer to a sound or video file.

Clipboard: A temporary holding area for cut or copied items.

ClipBook: A program that allows you to handle and manage the items you've copied.

Close button: Last button on the right of a window's Title bar. Also on dialog boxes. Closes the window or dialog box completely.

Compound document: A document that contains objects from more than one application.

Compressed: Reduced in file size by adjusting the colors.

Configuration report: A list of your current device settings.

Context menu: A menu that displays when users right-click an object. Contains options specific to that object.

Cookie: Small piece of information stored by a Web site onto a person's computer. Allows the Web site to personalize the person's next visit to the site.

Copy: To create a duplicate of an object.

Critical update: An update to the operating system that fixes a known problem, especially a problem with security.

Critical Update Notification: A program that checks for critical updates whenever you connect to the Internet. It sends an e-mail message to notify you of changes.

Desktop: The starting screen for Windows 2000. All activity begins at the Desktop.

Device Manager: A utility that allows you to check the status of the various pieces of hardware connected to your computer.

Device: Any piece of equipment attached to your computer.

DHCP (Dynamic Host Configuration Protocol): Automatically assigns IP addresses to client computers logging onto a network.

Dial-up: A method of connecting to the Internet using a telephone line.

Dial-up networking: Connecting to a network using a telephone line, rather than simply a cable.

Dialog box: Similar to a window, but contains fields and tools to allow users to specify information.

Directory: A simulated file folder on disk. This term is sometimes used interchangeably with folder.

Disk defragmentation: A process that reassembles file fragments on a disk so they are contiguous. This reduces the amount of time your computer will spend locating all the parts of a file.

Disk: A storage device.

DNS (Domain Name System): Software that converts descriptive host names to IP addresses.

DNS server: A server that manages the database of names mapped to IP addresses within an organization.

Domain: A logical grouping of computers that share network resources with one or more computers (called domain controllers) acting as administrators for the entire domain.

Domain name: The name of a Web location. Includes a three-character suffix to indicate the type of domain.

Double-click: To press the left button of the mouse twice quickly in succession over an object. Opens the object.

Download: To copy information from an Internet or e-mail server to one's computer.

Drag: To press and hold the left button of the mouse over an object, then move the mouse. Moves the selected object.

Driver: The software that controls a device.

Dual-boot configuration: Having more than one operating system installed and accessible on a computer.

Effective permissions: What a user actually has access to, according to the rules that govern overlapping permissions.

Enterprise network: A WAN owned and managed by one organization or company.

Extended partition: A division of a hard drive that can contain multiple drives, called logical drives.

File: An electronic document, picture, or other item created on the computer; a collection of bytes stored as an individual entity. All data on disk are stored as a file with an assigned filename that is unique within the folder it resides in.

File naming conventions: Naming rules for files.

File system: A method of organizing files on a computer.

FilterKeys: Option that prevents users from accidentally pressing the same key multiple times.

Firewall: Hardware or software that inspects traffic between an internal network and the outside world; its function is to block some traffic and allow other traffic through.

First line indent: How far from the left indent to position the first line of a paragraph.

Floppy disk drive: Allows users to save information to and retrieve information from 3.5-inch floppy disks.

Font: A style of type, a set of letter characters designed to look a specific way.

Footer: Text printed along the bottom of each page.

Format (disk): To set up a disk so that it can store information; the way information is structured on a disk.

Frame: A container for part of a Web page.

Full justified: Text is aligned so that the left and right edges are flush with the margins.

Group: A collection of user accounts.

Hard drive: The storage space that is built into the computer.

Hardware Compatibility List: List of hardware that is compatible with Windows XP Professional. Available from the CD-ROM and the Microsoft Web site.

Header: Text printed at the top of every page.

Help and Support Center: Displayed from the Start menu. Provides assistance to users and access to online data sources.

Home page: The first page that displays when users open Internet Explorer or navigate to a Web site.

Host: Any device connected via an IP address to a network.

HTML: Hypertext Markup Language. Tagging language used to create Web pages.

HTTP: Hypertext Transfer Protocol. The method used to transmit data over the Web.

Hub: A central connecting device in a network that joins all the computers and other devices together.

Icon: A small picture used to represent a file, program, or action on the screen. Users use the mouse to interact with icons.

Indents: Determine how far the edges of a paragraph are from the margins.

Inheritance: A process by which when NTFS permissions are assigned to a parent folder, all the same permissions are applied to the subfolders and files of that parent folder.

Installation requirements The required configuration of a computer to install software.

Internet: A network of many computers and networks spanning the globe.

Intranet: A network with Internet-like features intended to be used only within an organization to share information and not by the general public.

IP (Internet Protocol) address: Written as four sets of numbers separated by periods (for example, 192.171.64.2) that identify where a computer is located on the network.

IPCONFIG: A command line prompt that identifies your current TCP/IP settings.

ISP: Internet Service Provider. A company that provides an access point to the Internet.

Kerberos: An Internet security protocol that authenticates users.

Left indent: How far from the left margin to position a paragraph.

Left justified: Aligns text along the left margin, with the right edge left ragged.

Link: Text or a graphic used to display another Web page.

Local area network (LAN): A network that connects a group of users in the same physical location (such as in one building) so that they can share information and resources, like printers and files, with each other.

Local printer: A printer attached directly to your computer.

Mapping: A process that makes the folder or drive appear as an icon in My Computer just as if the drive itself was inside your computer.

Margin: The space around the edges of a page.

Maximize button: The second button at the right of a window's Title bar. Used to expand a window to fit the entire screen.

Member server: A server that provides network services without handling the security information.

Menu bar: A group of menus associated with a window.

Menu: A list of options.

Minimize button: The first button at the right of a window's Title bar. Used to make the window a button on the taskbar.

Modem: A device that allows computers to exchange information via telephone lines.

Modem: A piece of equipment that allows a computer to be connected to the Internet.

Mouse: A pointing device used to interact with objects on the Desktop.

MouseKeys: Option to replace the mouse with the keys on the keypad.

Move: To physically remove an object from one location and place it in another.

.NET: Microsoft's software platform for the Internet (or an intranet) that allows for the exchange of data regardless of operating system or programming language.

Network administrator: Someone in an organization who has the job of making sure the organization's network functions the way it is supposed to.

Network architecture: The method of transferring information on a network. All devices on a network must use the same network architecture to transmit and access information. The most common forms of network architecture are Ethernet and Token Ring.

Network interface card (NIC): A circuit board that controls the exchange of data between a computer and the network.

Network printer: A printer accessed through a network and typically shared by multiple users, often within one department or area of an office.

Network: A group of computers linked together for the purpose of sharing information and resources.

Newsgroup: An online discussion.

Object graphic: A graphic made up of individually selectable objects.

Object linking and embedding (OLE): A compound document technology that allows an object to be embedded or linked to a document in a different application.

Operating system: A computer program that controls all of the basic functions of a computer.

Outdent: When the first line of a paragraph is further left than the rest of the paragraph. Usually used for lists.

Packets: Blocks of data.

Partition: A section of a hard drive that acts like a separate disk or volume.

Password: A secret word or code used as a security measure against unauthorized access to data and resources.

Password: A secret word or code used to protect access to a computer.

Peer-to-Peer network: Two or more computers linked together, sharing resources such as a printer, scanner, or Internet connection, and storing files and programs on their own hard drives.

Permission: A rule associated with an object that determines which users or groups have access and abilities to that object.

PING: A command line prompt that tests whether you can send a signal over the network and reach another computer.

Playlist: The list of tracks on an audio CD. Includes the default order in which to play the tracks.

Plug and Play: A set of specifications that allows a computer to automatically detect and configure a device and install the appropriate drivers.

Points: The way font size is measured. There are 72 points to an inch; the higher the point number, the bigger the font.

Port: A number assigned to an application; packets can be blocked or allowed by a firewall based on the port number.

Primary domain controller; backup domain controller: A server that holds the security information for a domain.

Primary partition: The first division of a hard disk drive.

Print: To create a paper version of a file.

Print driver: Software that allows your computer to communicate with a printer.

Print queue: Disk space that forms a waiting line for output designated for a printer until the printer can receive it.

Program: A set of instructions to the computer.

Protocol: A language, or a set of rules, that determines how computers communicate with each other; a method for transmitting data over a network that allows different types of computers to communicate with each other.

Quick Launch bar: Next to the Start menu on the taskbar. Contains icons used to open commonly used programs.

Registry: A database of configuration settings in Windows.

Removable media: Any portable disks of various kinds—floppy disks, CDs, Zip disks, tape drives, DVDs, and the like.

Resize area: At the bottom right of a window. Users click and drag the Resize area to change the size of a window.

Resolution: The number of dots printed per inch on a page. Sharper, more detailed images have a higher resolution. Lower resolution prints quickly.

Resolution: The number of pixels per inch horizontally and vertically.

Resource: Any device that can be used by the members of the network.

Resource Kit: A collection of information and tools for setting up and maintaining a Windows XP environment.

Restore Down button: Replaces the Maximize button when a window is full screen. Restores a window to the size it was before it was maximized.

Restore point: An earlier time when the computer was not experiencing the current problems.

Restoring: The opposite of backing up; this process takes files on your backup and copies them back onto the hard drive.

Right indent: How far from the right margin to position a paragraph.

Right justified: Text aligned along the right margin, with the left edge left ragged.

Right-click: To press the right button of the mouse once over an object. Displays a context menu for that object.

Roll Back Driver: The function of reverting back to the previous version of the driver for the selected device.

Router: A device that forwards data from one network to another.

Safe Mode: A basic, minimal configuration of your operating system used for troubleshooting.

Sans serif: A font that lacks the embellishments of serif fonts. These fonts are best for headlines and titles because they are not as easy to read in text. Arial is an example of a sans serif font.

Save as: To create a copy of the current file under another name or in another location.

Save: To preserve the contents of a file in the computer.

Scheme: A collection of related properties to assign to the Desktop, mouse, or sounds.

Scrap: A bit of data that you can select and drag onto your Desktop.

Screen capture: An image of the current contents of the computer screen.

Screen saver: A picture or animation that displays on the screen after the computer has been inactive for a specified amount of time.

Security: The protection of data against unauthorized access.

Serif: Fonts that employ small lines to finish off a main stroke at the tops and bottoms of any straight lines in order to make reading easier. Times is an example of a serif font.

Server: A computer that responds to the request from a client with the desired data or service.

Service pack: A bundle of updates.

Shortcut key: Text to the right of a menu option, such as Ctrl+C. Indicates a key or combination of keys that will perform that option.

Shortcut: A link to a file, folder, program, or device. Usually placed on the Desktop for easy access.

Show Desktop: A button in the Quick Launch bar (displays on the taskbar) that minimizes all open windows.

ShowSounds: Option to replace sounds played by programs with visual cues.

SoundSentry: Option to replace system sounds with visual cues.

Spooling: The process your operating system performs of sending small bits of a print job at a time to the printer so that you can perform another task on your computer while the printer prints your documents.

Stand-alone computer: A computer that is not permanently connected a network.

Start menu: At the far left of the taskbar. Provides access to programs and files. Also provides access to the shut down function.

StickyKeys: Option that saves users from having to press certain keys simultaneously to perform functions.

Streaming media: Continuous sound or video on the Web, such as a live concert or sporting event, which can be heard or viewed using Windows Media Player.

Switch: Similar to a hub but provides more intelligent though limited routing capabilities.

System requirements: The required configuration of a computer to run software.

Tab stop: A stopping point in a line. Can be used to line up text columns.

Task Manager: A tool for diagnosing and managing system problems.

Taskbar: The bar across the bottom of the Windows Desktop. It contains the Start menu, Quick Launch bar, and buttons representing open windows.

TCP/IP: A protocol that allows computers with totally different architectures to talk to one another; it is also the common language of the Internet.

Text editor: Application used to edit plain text files. Does not allow formatting. Notepad is an example of a text editor.

Text search: Using the Search command to locate a file that contains a particular word or phrase.

Tile: To repeat an image over and over (like tiles on a floor) to fill the background.

Title bar: Runs across the top of a window or dialog box. Contains the name of the window or dialog box, plus buttons for resizing windows and closing both windows and dialog boxes.

ToggleKeys: Option to play a sound whenever the user presses the Caps Lock, Num Lock, or Scroll Lock keys.

Toolbar: A row of buttons near the top of a window and on the taskbar. Provides quick access to functions.

ToolTip: Displays when the mouse passes over a Toolbar button. Provides a hint to the button's function.

TRACERT: A command line prompt that tells you which links can be successfully established and which links are problematic.

Transmission medium: Something that allows computers and other devices to exchange information; cables are an example.

Undo: Command used to undo the last action.

Unicode: A larger character set than ASCII. Used in some text files.

Upgrade: To install a newer version of Windows XP Professional over an existing version without removing installed programs or changing settings.

Upgrade report: A report analyzing your current system and whether it is compatible with Windows XP Professional.

URL: Uniform Resource Locator. The full path to a Web page.

User: Any individual who interacts with the computer.

User level security: Access to a file, printer, or other network resource is based on the user name.

User name: Identifies a computer's user to the network.

User profile: The user's personal preferences for his or her computer including such things as how the Desktop is displayed, network connections, printer settings, and the like.

Volumes: Different logical sections into which a hard drive may be broken up. Also, this term is sometimes used interchangeably with disks.

Wallpaper: An image to display on the background of the Desktop.

Web page: A single file on the Web.

Web site: A collection of related Web pages.

Wide area network (WAN): A network that connects people in the same company or organization but in different physical locations.

Wild card characters The question mark (?) and/or the asterisk (*), used to replace unknown character(s) in a filename; the question mark replaces any single character, while the asterisk can represent several characters.

Window: The basic building block of Windows. Displays a file or program.

Windows Update: A program that analyzes your computer before displaying a list of available updates.

WINS (Windows Internet Name Service): Provides name-to-IP address resolution in a Windows-only network with clients using older operating systems such as Windows 95 or Windows NT; as such, it is the counterpart to DNS.

Word processor: An application used to create text documents. Allows formatting and layout.

Word wrap: Keeps the text of a text editor within the text editor's window.

Workgroup: A logical grouping of computers that share network resources without any one computer being given overall network administration responsibilities.

World Wide Web: A portion of the Internet. Uses Web sites and pages to display information.

GLOSSARY

index